Designing
San Francisco

Designing San Francisco

Art, Land, and Urban Renewal in the City by the Bay

Alison Isenberg

Princeton University Press Princeton and Oxford

Copyright © 2017 by Princeton University Press
Published by Princeton University Press,
41 William Street, Princeton, New Jersey 08540
In the United Kingdom: Princeton University Press,
99 Banbury Road, Oxford OX2 6JX
press.princeton.edu

Cover photograph courtesy of the Architectural
Archives, University of Pennsylvania, by the gift
of Lawrence Halprin

First Paperback Printing, 2024
Paper ISBN: 978-0-691-26454-7
Cloth ISBN: 978-0-691-17254-5

Library of Congress has cataloged the cloth edition
as follows:
Names: Isenberg, Alison, author.
Title: Designing San Francisco : art, land, and urban
    renewal in the City by the Bay / Alison Isenberg.
Description: Princeton : Princeton University Press,
    [2017] | Includes bibliographical references and index.
Identifiers: LCCN 2016034058 | ISBN 9780691172545
    (hardback : alk. paper)
Subjects: LCSH: City planning—California—San
    Francisco. | Land use—California—San Francisco.
Classification: LCC NA9127.S3 I84 2017 | DDC
    711/.40979461—dc23 LC record available at
    https://lccn.loc.gov/2016034058

This publication is made possible in part
by the Barr Ferree Foundation Fund
for Publications, Department of Art and
Archaeology, Princeton University

Cover Design by Amanda Weiss
Interior Design by Jena Sher Graphic Design

Printed in the United States of America

Contents

Introduction
Land and Landscape

In the years spent researching a book, there are always small stories that stick with you, disproportionate to their size. I found one such story in a mundane *San Francisco Examiner* clipping collected by banker David Rockefeller's New York staff. That 1970 article carried the headline "High Rises Favored by Mellon." It was filed among hundreds of other clippings documenting newspaper perspectives on Embarcadero Center, a large-scale urban renewal project of office towers and retail space under construction on San Francisco's waterfront. San Franciscans often called Embarcadero Center "Rockefeller Center West" because David Rockefeller was a lead investor and because of Embarcadero Center's design. This moniker sealed an association with the famous 1930s business complex in distant midtown Manhattan. On October 8, 1970, the city of San Francisco's chief administrative officer, Thomas Mellon, spoke to a Sierra Club audience about high-rise development at an event hosted by the San Francisco College for Women. Mellon was alone on the eight-person panel in his outright endorsement of skyscrapers. "Don't have hangups that just because a building is high, it might be ugly and can't be beautiful," he told the crowd. "Look at New York," he implored. The room erupted in "general, derisive laughter." New York had "the greatest examples of architecture in the world." Consider Rockefeller Center and the RCA building, he continued. "Look at the plazas and open spaces provided for people."[1]

Why the derisive laughter? San Franciscans valued architecture and urban design, supporting one of the nation's most active, extensive networks of design and redevelopment professionals. Certainly the laughter was not directed at architecture or public space ideals. But by 1970 many San Franciscans were responding skeptically to the presumed civic and economic benefits of skyscrapers. Open-space gifts by developers had been described by local critic Karl Kortum as "green hairpieces" covering up the city's irresponsible giveaway of public land. In 1970 the city of San Francisco was a defendant in several lawsuits challenging the city's policies of closing and selling public streets for large-scale private development. Sierra Clubbers and other urban-environmentalist allies were tired of being caricatured in the press as selfishly antidevelopment and obstructionist when in practice they had proactively influenced redevelopment by fighting for the responsible stewardship of public land. Tom Mellon signaled to his crowd that he anticipated aesthetic arguments from them against skyscrapers; he hoped that attractive plazas would satisfy the San Francisco public. He believed Manhattan would be an inspiring example. That was a miscalculation.[2]

Designing San Francisco explores the San Francisco Bay Area from the 1940s through the 1970s as a site for bringing fresh perspective to a national narrative of redevelopment and planning. I begin with the premise that during the 1960s—an era of civic and cultural expansion, protest, and participatory ferment—the principles and practices of urban planning and design in the United States in fact narrowed. Over the next several decades, they became rigid. In 1961, Jane Jacobs's book *The Death and Life of Great American Cities* helped galvanize a new framework that pitted neighborhood preservation against the symbolic bulldozer of urban renewal, itself a reference to legendary New York City planner and builder Robert Moses. The debate sparked by her critique was so sustained that more than fifty years later her frameworks still define the period's urban history: Jane Jacobs versus Robert Moses, preservation versus urban renewal, historic versus modern.[3]

This book retells the history of U.S. urban redevelopment by moving the focus west from New York to San Francisco's north waterfront. In the 1950s, large-scale redevelopment in San Francisco sparked the speedy evolution of numerous allied arts fields that became interwoven with the era's defining projects. The interactions of property managers, merchant-builders, publicists, graphic designers, architectural model makers and renderers, photographers, public artists, cartoonists, alternative press activists, public-interest lawyers, urban design critics, editors, and grassroots preservationists energized and structured the development contests and the ideas behind them. Such participants worked in partnership and in tension with the formal city-building professionals in the fields of planning, architecture, and landscape architecture. In the Bay Area, most of the urban-focused fields were strongly shaped by the same forces that nurtured (and resisted) the environmental movement so that the development issues of the urban built and natural environments often converged. Usually outsiders, the allied arts professionals generated critiques and conflicts that were not evident in the more intellectually homogeneous internal workings of the design and planning fields alone. The individuals at the heart of my chapters do not appear in existing urban and architectural histories except for a handful of leading architects, landscape architects, planners, and city administrators. This outside-in perspective takes some getting used to. People who are elsewhere peripheral and invisible in the history of urban design are here networked through the center.[4]

The allied design professionals knitted together the city's redevelopment history through their sustained, simultaneous, and sequential work on the same roster of projects between the 1940s and the 1970s. The chapters of this book follow the emergence and transformation of these professionals and their businesses as tied to the growing conflicts around large-scale redevelopment. From a focus in the early chapters on preservationist sites, the book turns to consider urban renewal assemblages, skyscrapers, and other modernist, clearance-based projects. Certain iconic north waterfront complexes stood out as testing grounds for redevelopment ideas, including Ghirardelli Square, Fontana Towers, Golden Gateway, Embarcadero Center, the proposed (but not built) San Francisco International Market Center, and the Transamerica Pyramid. I follow the networks that tied suburban and rural projects to the city, such as the 1950s Village Fair in

Sausalito and the 1960s Sea Ranch on the Sonoma Coast, asking what was specifically "urban" about a flow of ideas that traveled with consultants from rural to suburban to urban locations. Significant on their own terms, these sites also illuminated the full range of participants and distilled their ideas. Seeking out a story of "development-producing-antidevelopment" misses the proactive preservationists who in the 1940s advanced historical plans for the waterfront, rooted in public ownership, before the high-rises appeared. When the skyscrapers, renewal complexes, and plazas loomed large on the waterfront, citizens' groups organized, found lawyers, and worked with the alternative press to establish tougher standards of public interest in the city's land disposition policies.[5] By the 1970s, these urban-environmentalist community leaders, lawyers, preservationists, journalists, and disillusioned design professionals had formulated a now mostly forgotten critique of redevelopment. The final chapters follow the emergence in San Francisco's large-scale redevelopment, private and public, of a moral framework for understanding the competition for urban land as more consequential than urban design controversies and public-access easements to "open space."

As this book contributes to cleaving the preservation versus renewal binaries, along the way another binary unravels—the presumed male domination and female absence in urban design professions during the decades following World War II. At the beginning of 1971, out of 725 licensed architects in the Bay Area, 9 were women, according to the American Institute of Architects.[6] The social revolutions of the era—civil rights protests, urban unrest, feminism, and the youth, counter-culture, and peace movements—transformed professional practice with particular intensity in the Bay Area, including in architecture and planning. Yet the second-wave feminism of the late 1960s and early 1970s layered over a potentially even more significant period of gender collaborations that had begun in the 1940s. These earlier collaborations were prevalent—sometimes dominant—in the allied urban arts and design fields. In 1952, for example, partners Virginia Green and Leila Johnston founded the "Cadillac" of architectural model-making companies in the Bay Area and the nation. Their business thrived on the large-scale commissions of urban renewal, and they built the presentation scale models for most of the city's big projects. Marion Conrad's public relations firm specialized in launching careers in the interrelated worlds of architecture, real estate, and politics. Conrad moved complicated projects from the stage of land acquisition and brainstorming through Board of Supervisors hearings and, over any obstacles, to completion. Beginning in the 1940s and 1950s, property managers and merchant-builders Stuart and Caree Rose carved an influential niche in redeveloping unusual, historical real estate into commercial destinations. According to this broad definition of urban design, the very nature of postwar large-scale redevelopment and urban experimentation transformed the gender composition of these allied fields before the impact of women's liberation was felt in the 1970s. The 1968 controversy over Ruth Asawa's mermaid sculpture and the plaza in Ghirardelli Square offers a potent example of the ways feminist concerns permeated "urban design" conflicts between modernism and historicism. Examining how women's liberation later intersected with the earlier work of Green, Johnston, Conrad, Asawa, and the Roses will be as generative of new insights into the city's gender and power dynamics as probing the seemingly failed long-term impact of 1970s feminism on a field like architecture.[7]

Ultimately, this book shifts the approaches to constructing a national redevelopment narrative in several interrelated ways. It identifies the 1950s as a formative decade for retrieving alternative frameworks before the narrowing of the 1960s. It shifts perspective from the East Coast to the West Coast. It refocuses the center of urban planning and design to include core contributions by allied urban-focused fields usually relegated to the edges. And *Designing San Francisco* follows construction cranes and what might be *built* rather than bulldozers and demolition. By centering on the sustained, networked participation of allied professionals in the novel projects of the day, this account raises them to a level of interest usually reserved for architects, landscape architects, and planners. I hope to inspire the question of how gender figured in urban redevelopment work elsewhere in the United States and abroad during the 1950s and 1960s. Finally, this book traces concretely how the juggernaut critiques of urban renewal in the 1960s and 1970s—especially Jacobs's *Death and Life* and Robert Caro's monumental study of Robert Moses, *The Power Broker*—shouldered other influential publications and perspectives off the shelf. In so doing, *Designing San Francisco* leaves readers with a freshly dusted-off set of land-centered frameworks through which to evaluate current urban debates and policies. But before settling in to the San Francisco waterfront in chapter 1, there is more meaning to be gleaned from shifting the redevelopment story from New York to the Bay Area.

THE LONG VIEW OF SAN FRANCISCO'S ANTI-MANHATTANIZATION

More than most U.S. cities, San Francisco has had an ambivalent relationship with New York in the postwar era, when the desire to be the "Wall Street of the West" coexisted with a fierce anti-Manhattanization sentiment.[8] Louis Dunn's drawing "Plop!" (fig. 1) captured San Francisco's resentful 1960s resistance to New York's model.[9] The illustration propels our perspective westward. Manhattan Island, sinking under the weight of its own towers, lobs another skyscraper across the continent to stick it to the city of San Francisco. The slabs are identical, having no distracting variations in architectural form. San Franciscans disagreed often over the impact of Manhattan on their city's aspirations during these decades. Looking back from the 1970s, one Bay Area critic recalled (with some regret): "When we were all young and dumb, it was an article of faith that there were only two Real Cities in the land—New York and San Francisco."[10] Closer to home, San Francisco warily watched the threat posed by Los Angeles during these years in almost every realm, including population growth, arts and culture, banking, tourism, the port, property values, and economic health. In the 1960s, developers in San Francisco often invoked business competition from Los Angeles in order to get projects approved.[11] San Francisco's preoccupation with New York was different. It grew more from the decades-old "Wall Street of the West" motif and the two cities' shared goals of attracting national corporate headquarters, especially those of finance and banking. Manhattan was, and San Francisco was becoming, what Lewis Mumford and others called "topless" cities, with skylines dominated by high-rises.[12] Less spectacular but equally important were the planned plazas and open spaces that proliferated alongside the skyscrapers.[13] Both cities were expensive, with valuable real estate—a distinguishing characteristic in an era of lamented urban blight and crisis. They were tourism and convention cities, with nightlife, bohemian neighborhoods, cutting-edge culture, and good food. They brought together diverse populations and had done so since their respective origins. In the decades after Dunn sketched the drawing, these two cities also became the United States' most gentrified metropolitan areas.

Yet New York had Manhattanized, so to speak, much earlier. In 1907 Henry James had famously bemoaned the pincushion of towers dominating his city when he returned to New York after a twenty-five-year absence.[14] During the Depression, Lewis Mumford's *New Yorker* series "The Sky Line" cautioned that the skyscraper trend should be abandoned as "a blind alley and an insupportable luxury."[15] Such critics represented a minority opinion in Manhattan, however. Skyscrapers did not provoke Jane Jacobs. Quite the opposite. In *Death and Life* she described Manhattan's "dramatic" and "romantic" towers "rising suddenly to the clouds like a magic castle girded by water."[16] Jacobs protested the "tower-in-the-park" prototype popularized in planning circles by Le Corbusier, but she romanticized lower Manhattan's skyline (fig. 2).

In San Francisco the new problems of skyscrapers and urban renewal combined in a manner that was inherently different from what New York experienced in the 1950s and 1960s. Outside of New York City and Chicago, the skyscrapers going up during these years were novel and sometimes unnerving. When San Francisco's first steel-frame, curtain-wall skyscraper—the Crown Zellerbach office tower—topped out at 20 stories in 1960, the city's two tallest buildings were 30 and 31 stories. Thirty years earlier, in midtown Manhattan, the Empire State Building had already reached 103 stories. In the 1960s, outside of Manhattan Island, the large-scale redevelopment mix included taking a position on Manhattanization, particularly the proliferation of skyscrapers but also the triumph of business values they represented. In San Francisco that position was hotly contested.[17]

Of course, 1960s readers knew that New York City and Greenwich Village, Jane Jacobs's inspirations for *Death and Life,* were hardly typical America. Yet Jacobs succeeded in rising above the particularities of her case to formulate a definitive national critique of

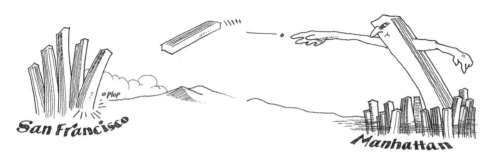

1 Shifting the focus from Manhattan to San Francisco, postwar urban redevelopment tells a different story, in a different frame. Louis Dunn, 1971.

2 In her 1961 book *Death and Life,* Jane Jacobs described Manhattan's "dramatic" and "romantic" towers "rising suddenly to the clouds like a magic castle girded by water." Louis Dunn's 1971 drawing "Up for Grabs" evoked that romantic view of lower Manhattan's financial district but critiqued the high-rise city as overdeveloped and emblematic of corporate exploitation and public giveaways. Chester Hartman called this the "City for Sale" or "land grab" in his books about San Francisco redevelopment by those names.

urban renewal and advance the search for better models. At that time, San Francisco had several neighborhoods on the cusp of gaining international prominence through tourism and new investment. One piece of San Francisco geography triggered especially intense debates about the urban future. San Francisco's north waterfront (fig. 3) stood out as a touchstone for that city in a manner similar to Greenwich Village in Manhattan. With spectacular views of the San Francisco Bay, the waterfront concentrated pressing redevelopment questions. This was particularly true of the stretch curving around the city's northeastern edge, between Fort Mason and the Ferry Building at the end of Market Street. Where planners saw a long strip of transitioning waterfront property, most San Franciscans in the 1960s would have imagined a sequence of distinct neighborhoods and destinations, each with different personal associations. Developers saw remarkable opportunities to buy land. Dozens of acres of Title I urban renewal land were for sale, interspersed with hundreds of public acres administered by the port and, of course, the parcels available through the private real estate market (fig. 4).[18]

In the late 1950s, as the rest of the United States took notice of the population migration to California, the design professions oriented toward New York and Chicago began to take the West Coast more seriously. In 1960, several thousand architects descended on the Bay Area for the annual American Institute of Architects (AIA) meeting. Such conventions, especially for redevelopment-related professionals like planners, builders, property managers, city officials, and landscape architects, served as efficient pipelines for national publicity. Air travel had turned the convention business into a major tourism engine, including demand for conference hotels and convention centers. The 1960 AIA convention offered snapshots of how San Francisco redevelopment was interpreted on the national scene.[19]

New York Times architecture critic Ada Louise Huxtable was one of the visitors who returned home impressed. Despite its "generally undistinguished commercial structures," San Francisco retained "a personal scale, a direct and pleasurable relationship to people, that is the city's greatest asset." The city had few skyscrapers, Huxtable noted. She quickly concluded that, whatever the reason for this, the outcome was positive. The "lesson is potent," she wrote. The gift of light, air, and human scale was precisely what she feared New York had lost. San Francisco in 1960 proved that a city could thrive "even with bad or anonymous" architecture. Yet San Franciscans took an unusual interest in "the community's architectural future." The architectural models for the Golden Gateway urban renewal competition had been displayed during the AIA convention, Huxtable pointed out, providing local and national exposure for these high-quality designs. She approved of the city's "unique record of fighting the hideous, encroaching freeways that threaten the visual and physical dismemberment of every American city." In 1960, Huxtable believed that San Francisco offered stimulating alternatives, especially to New York City. "To today's architect, concerned almost exclusively with abstract design standards and sociologically approved planning, San Francisco is a city that breaks all the rules," she wrote.[20]

3 Aerial view of San Francisco's north waterfront ca. 1960, from the files of landscape architects Lawrence Halprin & Associates. The perspective flattens the topography, allowing the unusual location of the residential hills pressed close to the working waterfront to emerge, as well as the "man-made" hill of the financial district and the generally low-rise character of the city. Immediately above the Ferry Terminal building is the low-rise produce market district soon to be cleared for Golden Gateway and Embarcadero Center urban renewal. Just north (to the right) of the produce district is the dark-brick warehouse neighborhood at the base of Telegraph Hill. Inspired by the adjacent government-supported projects, a private developer quietly purchased this warehouse district in the early 1960s and announced clearance plans a few years later. The Bay Bridge is in the foreground, and the Golden Gate Bridge and part of Marin County and Sausalito appear in the upper-right background of the photograph.

When the Republican National Convention met in San Francisco four years later, the national press zeroed in on a very different sort of neighborhood development. At the time the convention opened in July 1964, Ghirardelli Square—soon to introduce urban designers to large-scale adaptive reuse—was still under construction. Topless dancing at the Condor Club in adjacent North Beach, on the other hand, had been on stage for a month. Republicans scrutinized the phenomenon closely. Within weeks, Barry Goldwater's campaign featured Condor Club performer Carol Doda in a thirty-minute film set for national distribution. Campaign strategists made North Beach symbolize the supposed moral decline of U.S. cities, which they attributed to Democratic Party leadership.[21]

One San Franciscan, Herb Caen, made it his job to write daily about the city and its transformation, always attentive to both obscure local detail and the larger world's curiosity. His thousand-word *San Francisco Chronicle* column ran from 1938 until his death in 1997.[22] Caen's columns unhappily followed the honky-tonk influx to North Beach, but he had seen too much to make an example out of the lamentable topless fad. Caen found topless buildings more disturbing than topless dancers. The clean, well-managed Golden Gateway competition and the dirty-dancing Condor Club might seem diametrically opposed, but topless buildings and topless dancers were part of the same waterfront redevelopment story in the Bay Area. Both tapped into sentiments about the end of the city.[23]

Overall, in the early 1960s East Coast cultural institutions regarded San Francisco as lagging behind New York. Typical were the comments of a philanthropic foundation officer returning from an otherwise impressive talk by San Francisco's director of city

4 The San Francisco *Bay Guardian* critiqued developers rather than architects. The "Empire Building Kit" referred to assembling the Manhattan model on San Francisco's waterfront. The drawing suggests that the developer's power was unchecked. The *Bay Guardian* dismissed architects collectively for their complicity in imposing endless high-rises on the city.

Sketch by Mick Stevens
©1970, The San Francisco Bay Guardian Co.

planning, James McCarthy. McCarthy had not touched on "causes of the increasing middle-classness and commercialization of S.F. and why it ranks so amazingly behind NYC in the use of economic and cultural power to make it a great city in its institutions of art, publishing, and ideas."[24] In the eyes of national culture brokers, the West Coast was magnetic and booming with postwar growth, but simultaneously quirky and exceptional, and thus somewhat irrelevant. Local writers, like Caen, felt compelled to defend the state of "culture" in San Francisco. "Our museums are not as bad as indicated by the nasty crack of an Eastern museum director," Caen wrote in 1964, quoting the unnamed administrator: "San Francisco should amalgamate its three bad museums; then it would have only one bad museum." Caen conceded, "It is principally the San Francisco Opera Company we can boast of without qualification."[25] For Caen, the coexistence of the city's conservative elite with longshoremen, beatniks, hippies, tourists, artists, and gays was transformative and liberating. He had an eye toward explaining the city's distinctive character for the national press, which dwelled on the Bay Area's "freaks" and "kooks," terms (like "beatnik" and "hippie") that he himself coined or popularized.[26] Boiling San Francisco down to its essence, Caen saw the strengths and peculiarities of a beautiful, pleasure-loving, diverse, humane, small Western city.

A LOST 1962 MANUSCRIPT

Near the end of my research for this book, another incidental reference buried in the immaculately kept archives of the Rockefeller Foundation led to an unexpected discovery. Chadbourne (Chad) Gilpatric, the foundation officer working in the field of urban design criticism (and with Jane Jacobs), jotted down in 1960 that Grady Clay was writing a book about redevelopment in San Francisco. Clay—a real estate editor with the *Louisville Courier-Journal*—also had a new editorial position at *Landscape Architecture* magazine. What Grady Clay book was this? I wondered. This stray comment sent me on a detour to locate the book, still an unpublished manuscript in Clay's possession. "The Competitors: A Study of Competition for Urban Land" focused on San Francisco's Golden Gateway redevelopment competition. Clay, a leading figure in landscape studies, had written an unknown first book about land. The manuscript featured the allied design fields of architectural model-making and urban journalism. Clay's records from the late 1950s and early 1960s disclosed the circumstances under which he had written the manuscript, and the story's logic began to fall into place.

Little touched since 1962, the manuscript on San Francisco proved a unique introduction to the genre of urban renewal critiques that vied for attention with but were eclipsed by *Death and Life*. Clay's San Francisco study, with comparisons to London and Brookline, Massachusetts, confirmed that unlikely places could enter and frame the central accounts of U.S. urban renewal if New York City were decentered. Encouraged by the same foundations and publishers, Grady Clay and Jane Jacobs had begun in the 1950s from a similar position within urban criticism. Then they had diverged. This makes Clay's unpublished manuscript on San Francisco an ideal starting point for excavating alternative redevelopment narratives rooted in places besides New York.

If Greenwich Village inspired Jane Jacobs in the late 1950s, Grady Clay's muse was San Francisco. By 1960, Jacobs and Clay were at the cutting edge of research and writing on urban renewal in the United States. Their names were among the first to come up in 1958 when Gilpatric began the Rockefeller Foundation's "talent search" in what the program manager called "civic design criticism" or, officially, "Studies in Urban Design." Rockefeller's Humanities Division, where Gilpatric worked as associate director, had supported disparate projects in this field since the early 1950s. The most successful publication he had backed before Jane Jacobs's would have been Kevin Lynch and György Kepes's path-breaking research at MIT, which resulted in the admired 1960 book *The Image of the City.*[27]

Gilpatric's inquiries in 1958 tapped into a pervasive frustration among editors and academics over the scarcity of original, research-based analysis in universities on the topic of cities and the inadequate press coverage of the work that did exist. This mirrored an absence of creative thinking in civic design itself. Large-scale, monolithic redevelopment projects had made significant inroads into American cities, pushing total clearance and the construction of sterile towers. Urban design and urban renewal had interlocked, and few critics seemed qualified or even driven to interpret this trend. These problems in planning practice and criticism merged into what Gilpatric called "the inchoate field of how to make our cities better."[28]

In March 1960 Gilpatric sought advice from William "Holly" Whyte, retired *Fortune* editor and author of penetrating social commentary. Gilpatric noted that Whyte "has been astonished to find how few people have interesting and sustained ideas" on these subjects. Whyte told Gilpatric that Jane Jacobs and Grady Clay were the only informed writers Whyte could track down when he assembled the 1958 collection *The Exploding Metropolis.* Symbolic of Clay's proximity to Jacobs in 1958 is the fact that Whyte inserted Clay's essay "What Makes a Good Square Good?" into Jacobs's *Exploding Metropolis* chapter, "Downtown Is for People." Three years after scoping out writers for *Exploding Metropolis,* Whyte thought the scarcity of writers had little improved. He anticipated that Jacobs's book, still a year and a half from publication, would be a "major contribution."[29]

Jane Jacobs's 1961 *The Death and Life of Great American Cities,* of course, succeeded beyond her supporters' wildest dreams. Her publication crystallized frameworks that would define city planning for the next half-century. She identified the destructive habits of monolithic urban renewal, and argued that planners and designers were "copying failure." Her book distilled a cohesive critique, offered reflection and intervention, and assessed current projects on the ground.[30] Because of her unprecedented impact, Jacobs's ascension is one of the best-known personal narratives in mid-twentieth-century urban history. Her *Exploding Metropolis* essay attracted attention from Jason Epstein at Doubleday, who then moved to Random House. In February 1958, Chad Gilpatric wrote in his notes that Jacobs "might be a person worth talking to soon," after he spoke with her boss at *Architectural Forum,* Douglas Haskell. By September, Jacobs had secured her first Rockefeller Foundation grant, shepherded through The New School. This gave her the opportunity to take the leave of absence from *Forum* she needed in order to write. Several letters to Gilpatric in the summer of 1959 detailed her progress, as well as the turmoil and disarray in her thinking. Holly Whyte, she assured Gilpatric, had similarly "got himself and the work bolluxed up at one point" when writing *The Organization Man*. It would be a waste to revise her drafts, she calmly elaborated, before she rethought the entire book. She attributed her frustrations to the fact that "this book is neither a retelling in new form of things already said, nor an expansion and enlargement of previously worked out basic ground, but it is an attempt to make what amounts to a different system of thought about the great city." Gilpatric would have to be patient. By the spring of 1960 she was back on track and circulating chapters. In March of 1961 she was "elated" by her progress on the completed manuscript.[31]

Grady Clay never published his urban renewal book, the one on San Francisco. Like Jacobs, Clay cleared the hurdle of winning foundation and institutional support for his book proposal. Whereas the Rockefeller Foundation and The New School sponsored Jacobs's time off from *Architectural Forum,* the Ford Foundation paid for Clay's year away from the *Louisville Courier-Journal*. Paul Ylvisaker, director of the Ford Foundation's division of public affairs, arranged for Clay to spend the year at MIT through the new Joint Center for Urban Studies of MIT and Harvard University. The Joint Center, funded by the Ford Foundation, was a beneficiary of the same foundation initiatives to seed meaningful research and fresh perspectives to improve urban life in an era of large-scale rebuilding.

Grady Clay's focus on San Francisco did not derive from residing there or from closely observing the streets as a visitor. It would be an oversimplification to say that Jacobs found her topic from her apartment window in Greenwich Village while Clay settled on San Francisco through research and an abstract interest in urban renewal land. Yet there is some truth in this. Instead of the "ballet" of densely populated urban spaces famously documented by Jacobs, Clay described the "brilliantly conducted performance" of San Francisco's Golden Gateway competition.[32] Jacobs's inspiration may have been more poetic, but Clay was smitten by the administration of San Francisco's urban renewal program. He reserved particular admiration for the city's redevelopment chief, Justin Herman. Clay pored patiently over meeting minutes, transcripts, articles, and scrapbooks and conducted interviews. Then he wrote quickly as his fellowship year drew to a close.

Clay's manuscript then entered its own period of disarray. He circulated chapter drafts for feedback during the fall and winter of 1961, and by 1962 he had completed "The Competitors." After Clay's attempts to publish the book failed, in 1964 he excerpted an article-length working paper for the Joint Center. His revised title read simply "Competition for Urban Renewal Land." Pieces derived from his San Francisco research appeared in a few articles and speeches given at professional meetings. Other traces of Clay's San Francisco book are buried in Ford and Rockefeller Foundation correspondence; a few copies of the Joint Center working paper filed in libraries; and the extant version of the 225-page manuscript shelved with Clay's professional records.[33]

Why did Grady Clay's book disappear, while Jane Jacobs's *Death and Life* thrived? Solving this mystery, one retrieves a potent critique of renewal that assumed a different starting point from that of Jacobs. For Clay, the disposition of land was the moral core of the redevelopment problem. Clay's argument was important: Title I of the federal Housing Acts of 1949 and 1954 was first and foremost a land redistribution program whereby cities assembled and sold huge parcels of discounted land to private investors. What separated one city from another was how it sold that land, to whom, and with what kinds of strings attached. San Francisco led the new trend of incorporating design competitions into the city's choice of developer. Design competitions—an experimental means of distributing redevelopment land and shaping a city's future—had not hardened into set practices. The city's redevelopment chief, Justin Herman, questioned during the Golden Gateway competition whether the city should sell renewal land or try to retain more control over that public domain.[34] Clay's book captured a forgotten, fluid moment in late 1950s and early 1960s redevelopment when the rules were shifting rapidly, and the devastating consequences of urban renewal's first-generation clearance projects were widely protested, especially "Negro removal."

Grady Clay's 1962 manuscript, long predating Caro's *Power Broker,* pulled San Francisco's redevelopment director—Justin Herman—out from under Robert Moses's shadow. Clay's focus on land helped tie together what in the 1960s looked like two contrasting types of Title I federal urban renewal—building extravaganzas such as downtown's Golden Gateway and Embarcadero Center that were rising in sparsely populated districts and extreme removal projects like the Western Addition and Yerba Buena that devastated existing mixed residential and commercial neighborhoods.[35] Whereas City Hall anointed "Saint Justin" for speeding up both kinds of redevelopment, Thomas Fleming, editor of San Francisco's leading African American newspaper, the *Sun-Reporter,* summed up the neighborhood view in 1965: "Negroes and the other victims of a low income generally regard him [Herman] as the arch villain in the black depopulation of the city."[36] Clay's story, however, began after the bulldozers, at the time when cities were making decisions about how to sell the land. Land giveaways characterized both types of renewal, and the equity challenge of safeguarding the public's interest in renewal land applied equally.

In 1971, the *Sun-Reporter* was ready to back up Grady Clay's view of Justin Herman, describing Herman as a fair-minded redevelopment administrator capable of reaching across racial divides to openly address the land-grab critique of urban renewal. Responding to Herman's sudden demise, a *Sun-Reporter* editorial described how "in the last few years he showed profound dedication to racial minority participation in redevelopment." Although Herman still deeply angered many people, "approximately three years ago he [had] changed his approach from doing things—for—to doing things—with—racial minorities, and let community-based controversy find its common level before initiating the final decision-making process." Herman had responded constructively to "severe community criticism by Blacks" regarding "Black removal" and had become "interested and informed concerning the bases of racial minority protest." Columnist Emory Curtis also noted that Herman "utilized Black men in positions of responsibility in his organization" and ensured that minorities gained a "share" of Redevelopment Agency contracts. Herman, Curtis wrote, had a "sharp mind and an incorruptible ethic which kept him fighting for what he believed was best for the public good—with ability and honesty."[37] Justin Herman could negotiate land-grab debates openly because he acknowledged the competition for urban land at the heart of redevelopment. This measurement of the public good was legible (if high-stakes and painful to debate) on different sides of the building battles.

Clay's lost manuscript on San Francisco helps explain why, although many groups competed openly for redevelopment land, only the "community" perspectives (whether those of black leadership or the organized urban-environmentalists) became identified with angry "protest." The surge of land-centered initiatives during this period, especially large-scale renewal, pushed such discussions into the daily news. Clay recognized design competitions as new mechanisms for distributing urban renewal land, but the growing popular interest in urban design soon outpaced the public's interest in urban land ownership. Clay's 1962 account dramatizes the tension between landscape and land viewpoints in urban analysis. Centering the competition for urban land makes it easier to imagine how "arch villain" redevelopment chief Justin Herman and black community leadership might possibly have hammered out some mutual dialogue and respect despite their bitter disagreements.

The postwar high-rise office complexes represented, of course, more than design controversies. For one thing, they were metaphors for the economic displacement of industrial work, and many writers have tried to bridge the racially constructed divides between central city office districts and majority-minority neighborhoods. Herb Caen saw that disjuncture in 1964 when he wrote: "The Negro marching in a picket line couldn't care less about the Fontana [Towers], and the worker who lives in Deep Mission isn't likely to shed any tears over a freeway that nips off a corner of a Park he never visits."[38] True, the *Sun-Reporter* did not usually weigh in on skyscraper controversies; regarding high-rises it focused instead on increasing the hiring of people of color for the promised construction jobs.

Like Grady Clay, the black press (in San Francisco and nationally) framed urban renewal as a program of land control. *Sun-Reporter* editor Thomas Fleming stood just behind Herb Caen as the second-longest-running journalist covering San Francisco. On the topic of urban renewal, Fleming wrote regularly about the city's giveaways of redevelopment land to private developers.[39] The *Sun-Reporter*'s vigilance over public land stewardship also meant that the paper protested redevelopment decisions to build office complexes and expensive residences rather than affordable housing. The displacement of what might have been new affordable housing by new office and commercial construction "will do more to 'Manhattanize' San Francisco than all the Transamerica buildings, Alcatraz-based Space Needles, and Fisherman's Wharf wax museums put together," said the lead litigator in the citizens' lawsuits over the city's clearance and rehousing policies.[40] The *Sun-Reporter* pointed out that the litany of design controversies over downtown buildings distracted San Franciscans from the true Manhattanization threat—namely displacement and what would soon be called gentrification. The core decisions after the bulldozers had done their job addressed what should be built on urban renewal land and where the former residents would go next.

Why were Golden Gateway urban renewal and the Transamerica Pyramid seen as design controversies while the land stewardship controversies they provoked were forgotten? Why did the land-grab debate raised effectively by the black press in protesting the removal of majority-minority neighborhoods fail to adhere to the downtown towers? *Designing San Francisco*'s focus on construction cranes rather than bulldozers helps bring answers into view, and the frame of land stewardship promises to reunite the two "different types" of renewal. The San Francisco case helps explain how, historically, the land-centered traditions of urban critique that had receptive audiences and mainstream advocates in the 1950s through the 1970s were diverted, like Grady Clay's manuscript, to the margins of civic dialogues about the urban public domain in the United States.

Finally, Clay's perspective leveraged recognition that the 1960s land-based critiques of urban renewal originated in measured professional analyses from allied design fields and from mainstream administrators like Justin Herman, not from angry antidevelopment positions. Emory Curtis of the *Sun-Reporter,* for example, was an engineer who founded his own planning and consulting firm, Curtis Associates.[41] Urban-environmentalists and preservationists such as Jean Kortum and Karl Kortum or the young disillusioned designers of the Environment Workshop offered proactive urban visions based in expertise, although the press all too easily painted them as "obstructionists and cranks."[42] When the Black Land movement energized by Black Power found momentum in the late 1960s, it, too (like so many other planners and developers), eyed the techniques of urban renewal and saw some possibilities to compete better for urban land. The large scale of 1960s projects intensified and multiplied the debates over land and engaged many more journalists, artists, property managers, publicists, investors, editors, and activists who brought their ideas and models into the redevelopment dynamic alongside the architects, landscape architects, and planners.

How provocative that Grady Clay, a future founder of cultural landscape studies, wrote a first, unpublished book that took land—not landscape—as its starting point. In the early 1960s, Clay chose not to critique redevelopment by studying San Francisco's urban form and space. Ironically, perhaps, Clay left reading the landscape to Jane Jacobs. His fascination with the competition stage of planning, when decisions about land ownership and urban design were still unresolved, led him to study architectural models and renderings instead of finished buildings, plazas, and streets. Clay was a real estate editor, not an architecture critic. He had a newsroom view of urban renewal, and he thought constantly about land value.

Grady Clay's lost book presented a lost opportunity for galvanizing public dialogue around the question of whether cities undergoing Title I urban renewal should sell their land to private investors. The dead-filing of Clay's first book manuscript had no discernible impact on his career. That the book's arguments about land faded from public debate and published discussions, however, was a different matter.

"WHO HAVE GOT OUR LANDS?"

The task of shifting the barometer of place for urban redevelopment from New York City to San Francisco might be considered a "touchstone." The term entered general

English language usage describing a testing point, criterion, and sometimes inspiration for establishing the fundamental meaning of a thing. The word's origins in the late fifteenth century, however, lie in the hard, black stone that measured the quality of gold or silver by the streaks left when precious metal rubbed against siliceous stone.[43] San Francisco in the mid-twentieth century was the Western city of the Golden Gateway urban renewal project and the Golden Gate Bridge, a place where investors saw "dollars in them thar skyscrapers," Herb Caen wrote.[44] Excavations for the Embarcadero Center towers and the Transamerica Pyramid literally struck gold, or at least artifacts from the Gold Rush era. Reports of construction workers' finding gold slugs and buried ships in an 1850s landfill gratified treasure-hunters.[45] Accordingly, the 1960s skyscraper boom reignited interest in the Gold Rush frontier and the generations who had first built San Francisco.[46]

Understanding why *Designing San Francisco* is a Western story, not just a West Coast story, requires returning to the San Francisco Bay of the 1860s. An 1871 booklet by political economist Henry George, *Our Land and Land Policy, National and State*, has the perhaps surprising effect of extending the themes of anti-Manhattanization over the longer historical frame. The 1871 essay became the basis for George's 1879 book *Progress and Poverty*, which ranked as one of the most popular nonfiction works of its day, selling millions of copies.[47] George's travels between San Francisco and New York City, juxtaposing these two cities in the late 1860s, sparked his critique of undemocratic land policies and inspired his remedy—the "single tax" on land. Primarily, his ideas were conditioned by disappointment in California's trends toward private monopolization of the public domain and his close observation of San Francisco's growth. For New York, it was too late. But young San Francisco was early in its development. San Francisco could still remember its ideals of egalitarian land allocation, and in this fact George found hope. In *Progress and Poverty* Henry George made California the foundation for a path-breaking national critique.[48]

The most influential analysis in American history of "the land question" originated in the hills overlooking San Francisco Bay. Henry George's theory of land value creation came to him "like a flash," he later wrote, one day in 1870 while riding in those hills. George made small talk with a passing teamster by asking about the price of land in the vicinity. George was preoccupied with the recent arrival of the transcontinental railroad in Oakland and the ensuing frenzy of land sales. The teamster's answer provoked George's revolutionary understanding of the relationship between land and labor. George used San Francisco to illustrate how land at the city center gained value from people settling nearby, not from improvements the owners made. George proposed a land tax to recapture this increased value, which had been created by ordinary laborers' hard work. Without such a tax, landowners would unfairly collect and concentrate the economic benefits of urbanization.[49]

For George, this new way of looking at land value helped to explain why poverty persisted amid the abundance of a productive manufacturing and agricultural society. George himself came from a modest background. His formal education had ended at age thirteen. At eighteen, in 1858, he traveled from Philadelphia to San Francisco, where he struggled to make ends meet working as a printer and newspaper editor.

A decade later, George shaped the ideas from his ride in the hills into the dense booklet *Our Land and Land Policy, National and State*. As a printer, George did not have difficulty publishing a thousand copies of the essay. He sold twenty-one booklets and gave the rest away.[50]

"Who have got our lands?" Henry George asked in 1871. He turned to the topic of how land had been distributed in the first place to create the inequities he observed in San Francisco. The nation was "giving away land" while simultaneously making it "dear" and beyond the reach of the ordinary citizen.[51] In a poignant passage, George wrote: "A generation hence our children will look with astonishment at the reckless-ness with which the public domain has been squandered. It will seem to them that we must have been mad. For certainly our whole land policy, with here and there a gleam of common sense shooting through it, seems to have been dictated by the desire to get rid of our lands as fast as possible." These developments were ubiquitous but most evident in young, Western states: "In all the new States of the Union land monopolization has gone on at an alarming rate, but in none of them so fast as in California, and in none of them, perhaps, its evil effects so manifest." George included a map of California land grants (fig. 5) as "absolutely startling" visual testimony to the squandering of public lands, primarily the millions of acres given to the railroads.[52]

Visiting New York in 1869 gave George the foil for understanding San Francisco. New York was the "greatest of our American cities," he thought. Yet there one had to accept palaces and stocked warehouses alongside tenements and poverty. To borrow 1960s language, George's "anti-Manhattanization" views conditioned his protective stance toward San Francisco. In 1869, Manhattan offered a glimpse of San Francisco's future—the wealth disparities George hoped political action could mitigate.[53] He drew upon the egalitarian inheritance of his adopted city. Recently a pueblo, San Francisco was now a new city of the U.S. West. George wrote:

The American city of San Francisco, as the successor of the Mexican pueblo, came into a heritage such as no great city of modern times has enjoyed—land enough for a city as large as London, dedicated to the purpose of providing every family with a free homestead. Here was an opportunity to build up a great city, in which tenement houses and blind alleys would be unknown; in which there would be less poverty, suffering, crime and social and political corruption than in any city of our time, of equal numbers.

San Francisco's heritage of Spanish colonial settlement modeled a mid-nineteenth century vision of equitable, family-based land distribution. But, George wrote, "This magnificent opportunity has been thrown away." In fact, California was home to the nation's worst "land grabbers" and "land sharks." Much had been lost, but it was not too late for California.[54]

This motivation to change national and state land policy fueled George during the difficult writing of *Progress and Poverty*. In 1880 he moved his family to New York City, ultimately running in 1897 for the first mayoralty of the consolidated city. Although George died before the elections, his message was taken up and debated around the world. George's moral critique of capitalist economic development became one of the most influential in U.S. history. Based on what he saw in San Francisco's hills and Manhattan's streets in 1869, his ideas found popularity in part because they resonated with mainstream land policies such as the 1862 Homestead Act, under which Western settlers could claim 160 acres of "free" government land. As Grady Clay and others would argue about urban renewal nearly a hundred years later, there were good reasons to distinguish between land and buildings and to reconsider before selling the public domain. Henry George's San Francisco–New York land theories enfold twentieth-century urban redevelopment in a fresh narrative arc; they illuminate why urban renewal was the land grab of the twentieth century and why *Designing San Francisco* is a Western story.[55]

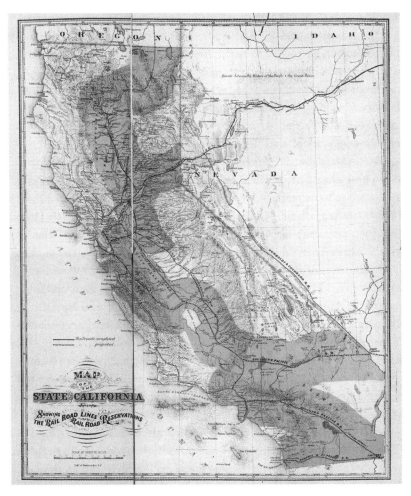

5 Henry George included this map in his 1871 booklet *Our Land and Land Policy, National and State* to illustrate Congress's granting of the "public domain" to railroad corporations in the state of California. George compared San Francisco and Manhattan; in California the railroad giveaways were a live political issue at the time.

The 1950s and 1960s revolts against urban renewal in the United States opened the door to a mainstream critique of land stewardship decisions regarding the public domain. This trend was most perceptible in San Francisco, but it also seeped into contestations elsewhere in the United States. The large parcels changing hands in city centers, the drama of political machinations, public-interest lawsuits, famous corporate investors, demolition, and big-ticket construction—these conditions edged urban land ownership patterns into daily conversations. The value of land vied with the meaning of landscape in redevelopment. Yet landscape-oriented battles over urban form— especially Jane Jacobs's small-scale neighborhood pitted against monolithic, top-down renewal—came to dominate critiques of renewal. The democratic values seemingly inherent in "open space" and good urban design—in the street, sidewalk, plaza, park, building, or skyline—became more significant to evaluating redevelopment than who owned and sold land and what those ownership trends meant. In other words, space, design, and "landscape" became the dominant tools for assessing the moral imperatives of rebuilding in the twentieth century. The 1960s, a period of expanding participatory possibilities, also enacted a narrowing of vision. After the mid-1970s, the momentum behind mainstream urban critiques based on equitable public land stewardship slowed. *Designing San Francisco,* by tapping into the networks of allied urban redevelopment fields—people embedded in the redevelopment process, usually with an outsider's perspective, at times deeply disillusioned—provides perspective on how that happened.

Louis Dunn's drawings "Plop!" and "Up for Grabs" (see figs. 1 and 2) illustrated the 1971 book *The Ultimate Highrise: San Francisco's Mad Rush Toward the Sky* (fig. 6).[56] Odds are that you have never heard of this book. Most people who write about redevelopment in San Francisco have not heard of it. Yet one 1972 review in a national newsletter said of *The Ultimate Highrise:* "There has probably been no more important book on the urban question since Jane Jacobs' *The Death and Life of Great American Cities.*"[57] San Francisco redevelopment in the 1950s, 1960s, and 1970s generated an unusually high number of significant written and visual works that have been forgotten. When these individual works dropped from sight, so did the relationships among them and their cumulative narratives. These include but are not limited to *The Ultimate Highrise,* Grady Clay's 1962 manuscript on the competition for urban land, Barbara (Bobbie) Stauffacher's memoir "Duped by Design," the street vacation lawsuits, the San Francisco International Market Center plans, and so forth. Aligning these intellectual artifacts has the effect of suggesting different historical patterns. It becomes easier to see why some perspectives have emerged to set popular and scholarly frameworks while others remained at the margins. Historically, where have new ideas, forms, and insights originated? At its broadest and most abstract scale, this is the question I investigate regarding the small stretch of San Francisco's north waterfront in the boom decades of downtown and suburban construction following World War II. By the end of the book, it will be clear how *The Ultimate Highrise* could *possibly* have earned a spot next to Jane Jacobs's *The Death and Life of Great American Cities.*

The story begins with the north waterfront in the 1940s and Karl Kortum's inspiration for a historic maritime district. This was long before the first of the twin seventeen-story

Fontana apartment buildings seemed to spring up overnight among the old factories and warehouses, jolting San Francisco's Board of Supervisors to pass a 40-foot height limit. It was also long before Disneyland might have made Kortum's plans for a Gold Rush Plaza near the Ghirardelli chocolate factory seem derivative. These were Kortum's ideas, and it is possible to trace their origins and impact.

6 "There has probably been no more important book on the urban question since Jane Jacobs' *The Death and Life of Great American Cities*." That is what the "National Transportation Newsletter" said in 1972 of the *Bay Guardian* publication *The Ultimate Highrise*. Book cover, Louis Dunn, 1971.

The Illustrated Pitch

"Guys with Ideas" and a 1940s Vision
for a Historic Waterfront District

By 1981, when historian Randy Delehanty interviewed ten original participants in the development of Ghirardelli Square two decades earlier, the converted factory complex had established its legacy as a historic preservation landmark. Private benefactor William Roth, heir to Matson Navigation Company's shipping empire, had purchased the factory to save it from demolition and a high-rise fate. A far-sighted team of modernist architects had finessed a pathbreaking redesign combining old and new elements, producing a vibrant commercial destination. In seeking to document innovative preservationist design, however, Delehanty inevitably captured other significant stories. His interview with Karl Kortum, director of the San Francisco Maritime Museum (SFMM), opened up an older, more sweeping account of the north waterfront's transformation. Delehanty spoke with Kortum in the museum, which since 1951 had occupied the former Aquatic Park Bathhouse, a ship-shaped building sandwiched onto the thin bank of land between Ghirardelli Square and San Francisco Bay. In 1981, the museum stood at the heart of a fifty-acre national maritime park that owed its existence to Kortum (fig. 7).[1]

7 Aerial view (ca. 1961) focusing on what would become the maritime historic district, framed by the curved municipal pier and Hyde Street Pier (on the right). On the far left are the horizontal Presidio buildings. The first Fontana apartment tower is closest to the water, on the left. A block to the Fontana's right stands the Ghirardelli factory complex, with the rounded, white form of the San Francisco Maritime Museum looking like a ship sandwiched between Ghirardelli and the waterfront. Flat-roofed, low warehouses (including the large Haslett complex Kortum hoped would become the railway and transportation museum) and working waterfront buildings are just inland from Hyde Street Pier.

In truth, the interview was a monologue. Kortum answered Delehanty's narrow queries about Ghirardelli Square with a virtually uninterrupted narrative recalling the Maritime Museum's municipal origins, its expansion into San Francisco's first state park in 1957, and its 1978 transfer to the National Park Service. In the complex, colorful account that followed, Kortum told how in the 1940s he had sold the relevant city and state landowners his vision to develop the waterfront as a historical maritime destination; how he had lined up supporters including the newspapers, the head of the sailors' union, and city commissioners and supervisors; and how he had reached the right state legislators to ensure transfer of waterfront property into hands that would assemble and showcase historical resources. Karl Kortum had been the most vocal and tireless advocate behind saving the Ghirardelli block. Yet he saw preserving the factory as only one brief phase in a long-term campaign for a public maritime district. At some point in the interview, Delehanty gave up trying to reel Kortum in to focus on Ghirardelli and allowed the broader story to unfold.[2]

The dynamic postwar possibilities playing out among the north waterfront's old warehouses, factories, piers, and parks narrowed during the 1960s into a preservationist script that pitted modern high-rises against old brick buildings. There is much truth to this rescue narrative, in which demolitions fired up preservationists. Most memorably, in 1961 the construction of the first of the twin seventeen-story Fontana Towers on the former site of a factory adjacent to Ghirardelli violated the city's "unwritten" rules dictating a low-rise waterfront.[3]

Yet Karl Kortum's 1949 civic vision of creating a historical maritime district significantly preceded the skyscraper panic of the 1960s. Kortum prioritized public ownership as a means to plan the waterfront neighborhood. He built upon the city's parks initiatives, including a troubled municipal–federal partnership that gave San Francisco the Works Progress Administration's Aquatic Park in 1939. Kortum endorsed the parallel private planning initiatives, such as the Jackson Square wholesale home furnishings district where entrepreneurs began revamping nineteenth-century buildings in the early 1950s. But he did not wait for the private sector to "save" old buildings. In the mid-1950s, for example, Kortum laid the groundwork for the state to purchase the Ghirardelli factory and the Haslett Warehouse and incorporate them into the public domain.

Later, Karl Kortum would fight high-rises, adopting new tactics in the late 1960s and 1970s as the buildings got taller and the threatened loss of public land took new forms. But he had formulated the core land stewardship critiques of his career in the 1940s and 1950s. During that time he had learned how to "pitch" ideas, as he said, so that they were seen and heard by those with influence over public purse-strings. In addition to having a talent for drafting hard-hitting prose, Kortum was a photographer and a visual thinker who enlisted the power of renderings to promote planning concepts. He left behind not only voluminous business correspondence and diaries but also a closely curated archive of watercolors, drawings, and models tracking the evolution of his historic maritime district proposals since the 1940s. In these earlier plans, the roles of the city's museum and parks advocates, maritime buffs, newspaper editors, and politicians in drafting blueprints for a historical waterfront emerge from the long shadows later cast by the high-rises.

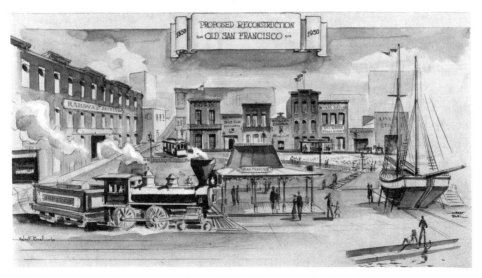

8 Karl Kortum's 1950 vision of a reconstructed Gold Rush Plaza, also called Argonaut Square, depicted by Hubert Buel. The Haslett warehouse, on the left, would house a railway museum, and modern retail would occupy the new nineteenth-century-styled buildings at the back of the square. The Ghirardelli factory faced the square to the right, out of the frame. This perspective from the water included a shipyard and the effect of bringing the Hyde Street cable car line down to the bay. Kortum's inspiration for this unused eastern end of Aquatic Park came more from the Gold Rush centennial celebration than from threatening high-rises. The reconstructed businesses included Wells Fargo Express, Ship Chandler, Niantic Hotel, Golden Eagle Saloon, Miners Supplies, a blacksmith, and a livery stable.

One 1950 rendering opens up a vista that places the singular preservation of the Ghirardelli factory within Kortum's wider view of the waterfront district (fig. 8). "Proposed Reconstruction of Old San Francisco, 1850–1950," by artist Hubert Buel, projects a cohesive historic waterfront plaza onto the unused, undefined eastern edge of Aquatic Park.[4] An invented row of nineteenth-century retail buildings completes the enclosure of "Argonaut Square," framed on two other sides by the extant Haslett Warehouse to the left and the Ghirardelli factory to the right (but out of the frame). Kortum's vision of an integrated historical district—incorporating two proposed museums, piers, ships, cable-car tourist transit, and modern retail—was inspired by the occasion of the Gold Rush centennial rather than by high-rises. The story of Argonaut Square shifts the preservation drama from benevolent private rescue by a wealthy, civic-minded San Francisco family to an independent activist vision paired with public ownership of the waterfront. Taking its cue from Kortum's interview with Randy Delehanty, this chapter begins with competing visions for the same narrow stretch of land and then reveals an older, deeper, and more sweeping story.

"A MAGNIFICENT ACT OF CIVIC RESCUE"

A 1961 rendering of a gleaming residential high-rise, "Ghirardelli Center," launched the preservationist script for the Ghirardelli block (fig. 9).[5] The rendering, in which San Francisco's brick waterfront factories and warehouses had disappeared, substantiated newspaper reports that investors intended to tear down the factory. Early in 1962, the *San Francisco Examiner* confirmed the Ghirardelli family's "tentative negotiations" with a suburban developer to "sell the property as a site for an apartment house."[6] Karl Kortum bumped into Harvey Ghirardelli in the neighborhood. Ghirardelli told Kortum that he hoped to sell the property for $5 million but that he would accept $3 million from the state in condemnation proceedings. Kortum and others approached private citizen Bill Roth about "saving" the buildings. The prospect of Ghirardelli Center appalled Roth. Kortum described the 8-by-10-inch glossy as "pure horror." He warned Roth of the Fontana's symbolism: "Like a pair of enormous tombstones, side by side, these structures will signalize a dead chance that the city once had." With his mother Lurline Roth's financial backing, Roth preemptively purchased the factory. Kortum suggested using the distinctive buildings for an extension campus of the University of California, where Bill Roth served on the Board of Regents. Roth had another experiment in mind (fig. 10).[7]

And so the wrecking ball was stopped, and Maritime Museum archivists would one day label the image "Scuttled High Rise Plan for Ghirardelli Center."[8] Responsible private ownership promised to secure the old factory buildings, and the newspapers lauded Roth's "magnificent act of civic rescue."[9] The real estate brokers assured the public that even if the current 40-foot height restriction was overturned, the new owners had "no intention of building high-rise structures on the land." They valued historic character "rather than just investment for profit" (fig. 11). Roth explained, "Our plan is not for the highest economic use of the property . . . but what would be of most value to the people of San Francisco." No ordinary piece of real estate, the bay-front parcel counted as "one of the most magnificent properties in San Francisco," architect Robert Anshen advised Roth. Kortum agreed: "The view—always a subject of discussion and an intrinsic value on this face of San Francisco—is incomparable." It took in "the bay, passing ships, purple [Mount] Tamalpais and the lights of Sausalito."[10]

Bill Roth's investment was hailed as "intelligent and thoughtful" private planning of the type encouraged in 1950s urban renewal circles. His ties to Matson Navigation Company steeped Roth in the maritime industries and made him a leader of one of the city's most influential families. The Roths enjoyed the gratitude of San Franciscans for the "gift" of saving the bay view and factory buildings. Instead of cashing in, Roth's "public spirited" development of Ghirardelli Square energized a new urban design model that blended historical and modern, local and tourist (fig. 12).[11]

Another recently vanished city landmark haunted Roth and deepened the public's appetite for Ghirardelli as a civic rescue story. Roth regretted his failure in 1959 to stop the demolition of the 1853 Montgomery Block. Known locally as the Monkey Block, by the late nineteenth century the building was associated with writers, artists, actors— what one reporter called San Francisco's first bohemians. By the 1950s, the building occupied the border between the financial district and low-rise Jackson Square, which included the faded Barbary Coast red-light district. Once cleared, the Monkey Block site moldered and rankled as a parking lot for ten years. In 1969, Transamerica Corporation announced plans to build the city's tallest skyscraper at this prominent

9 A rendering of the proposed yet unbuilt "Ghirardelli Center" that would have replaced the factory complex, ca. 1961. Ghirardelli Center aligned with the vertical hillside towers behind it and with the horizontal bands of the Maritime Museum Aquatic Park building below. Coit Tower appeared as a remote floating island on the left. The Mooser architectural firm behind this high-rise also designed the Ghirardelli factory's signature buildings, as well as the modern Aquatic Park Bathhouse. Karl Kortum and others circulated this rendering to galvanize interest in buying the factory to prevent this fate.

10 Not the Ghirardelli Center design by the Mooser firm but a composite portraying the threat to the historic waterfront posed by new glass boxes. The Maritime Museum is on the right. Published on March 7, 1962, the news copy read: "How apartment group in Aquatic Park area would appear from the bayside." At this time, Bill Roth was collecting development ideas from Bay Area architects.

intersection, which aggravated critics even more. Later, Roth lamented what he called the "planning effects" of losing the Montgomery Block. Not only had the city missed an opportunity to extend the impact of a unique Gold Rush–era structure but the subsequent void also allowed Transamerica to build its Pyramid and set a precedent for further encroachments into Montgomery Street. In 1959, however, one could pardon San Franciscans for thinking that threats to the Monkey Block lacked teeth. The city's papers had regularly proclaimed the building "doomed" since the late 1940s. Roth actually hired an architect to review the structure's potential in 1959 and declined the purchase because of the architect's ambivalence.[12]

Even a cursory consideration of Bill Roth's role, however, suggests a more complex picture than a one-man stand against high-rises that obliterated history. Roth stood on both sides of the preservation/tear-down divide. Roth was an insider intimately familiar with city planning and the waterfront. He led the San Francisco Planning and Urban Renewal Association (SPUR), a business-backed citizen's advocacy organization behind

11 Undated photograph of the waterfront Ghirardelli factory complex, circa 1961, before demolition of the large box factory filling the lower left of the photo. Encroaching residential high-rises dominate this view from the municipal pier.

opposite
12 Groundbreaking for Ghirardelli Square, November 1963. Lurline Roth, Bill Roth's mother, was a major backer of the project and was featured in this news photograph as "a principal stockholder."

judicious redevelopment. Roth did not want a wall of Fontana high-rises to replace brick factories and cut off the waterfront, but he did not object to skyscrapers or clearance on principle. At Ghirardelli, he quietly reserved the right to decide whether the income from a few towers might profitably preserve the rest of the site. As an executive in his family's shipping business, Roth helped introduce revolutionary container technology in the late 1950s at the Port of Oakland. In the longer historical view, Bill Roth ultimately contributed more to rendering San Francisco's port facilities obsolete and modernizing the regional port economy than he did to preserving its seafaring past.[13]

In the years after Ghirardelli Square opened, the site's property managers kept the rescue story alive. Whenever hillside neighbors complained about intrusive bright lights or loud noise, the managers pulled out the rendering of the high-rise Ghirardelli Center "as a weapon." The rescue narrative—by starkly pitting modernist high-rise against historic factory as competing rebuilding models—elevated themes of architecture, urban design, and private benevolence in the waterfront's renewal. Architecture was

Mrs. William P. (Lurline) Roth, (dark coat) participated yesterday in the ground breaking ceremony of the Ghirardelli Square Co., of which she is a principal stockholder. Shown, left to right, are: Stuart Rose, project developer; Warren Lemmon, president of Ghirardelli Square Co.; Mrs. Rose, Architect William Wooster; Bill Coleman, general manager, Trader Vic's, Inc., and William Swinerton, president of Swinerton and Walberg, contractors for the new garage and building.

indispensable to the debates clouding the city's future, to be sure, but ultimately it provides a narrow and incomplete accounting of the wide-ranging experiments unfolding during these decades. If we step back from the factory versus high-rise binary, the vision and broader context of Karl Kortum's historic maritime district comes into focus, a vision founded on an argument for responsible public ownership of the waterfront domain—in the public's trust, as dictated by state law.

Neither Ghirardelli Center nor Argonaut Square was actually built, but both had a discernible impact on what came next. Their ripple effects traced the flow of ideas that remade San Francisco's waterfront during these decades. Following the renderings and their travels illustrates how some ideas took hold and became visions, while others did not.[14]

PRIVATE PLANNING AND THE PUBLIC EYE

Although it became popular in the 1950s and 1960s to uphold examples of enlightened private investment as distinguished from government-funded, expensive "urban renewal," Ghirardelli Square and the Maritime Museum fit into a larger, complex redevelopment of the city's northern waterfront that sprawled over private and public realms (fig. 13). A brief tour of how private rebuilding interacted with public-sector forces on the waterfront—particularly the San Francisco Port Authority, the city Planning Department and Commission, and the San Francisco Redevelopment Agency—also introduces many of the most relevant neighborhood sites. Placing two private preser- vationist cases, Jackson Square and The Cannery, next to the Crown Zellerbach tower and plaza marks the 1950–65 period as modeling how private investment could oversee the public good. By the late 1960s, relying on public-spirited private stewardship, as had been done for Ghirardelli, The Cannery, Jackson Square, and Crown Zellerbach, would be stunningly inadequate in the face of a new generation of large-scale private clearance and high-rises. And as San Francisco's public and private revitalization projects multiplied and grew more complex, they increasingly intersected in terms of the people involved, especially the consulting designers and architects, as well as others in allied fields such as public relations, model-making, architectural rendering, property and retail management, and graphic design.

Through most of the 1960s, the public sector had surprisingly little direct leverage over the shape and design of private development in San Francisco as long as proposals conformed to land-use, zoning, safety, and planning regulations such as height limits, parking requirements, and emergency access. Historically themed revitalization emerged on a private, grassroots basis, without active preservation mandates. Skyscraper developers faced few constraints as long as they did not ask the city to exempt them from existing height limits or close a street. Nonetheless, many trends in the public domain directly shaped private redevelopment agendas and policy contexts within the city. Particularly important to the waterfront were the San Francisco Port Commission, Planning Department, Redevelopment Agency, and Board of Supervisors. In San Francisco, as in many U.S. cities, public parks and open-space planning would prove to be an instrumental lever directing government resources to the historical waterfront. This was especially true for the Maritime Museum, as this chapter shows. Because in the mid-1960s and

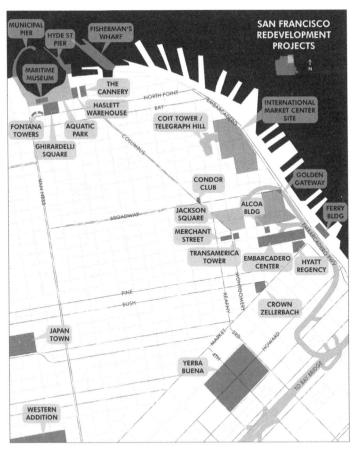

13 Locator maps.

SAN FRANCISCO
REDEVELOPMENT
PROJECTS

MUNICIPAL PIER

HYDE ST PIER

FISHERMAN'S WHARF

MARITIME MUSEUM

THE CANNERY

HASLETT WAREHOUSE

FONTANA TOWERS

AQUATIC PARK

COIT TOWER / TELEGRAPH HILL

INTERNATIONAL MARKET CENTER SITE

GHIRARDELLI SQUARE

CONDOR CLUB

GOLDEN GATEWAY

JACKSON SQUARE

ALCOA BLDG

FERRY BLDG

MERCHANT STREET

TRANSAMERICA TOWER

EMBARCADERO CENTER

HYATT REGENCY

CROWN ZELLERBACH

JAPAN TOWN

YERBA BUENA

WESTERN ADDITION

NORTH POINT · BAY · COLUMBUS · VAN NESS · BROADWAY · PINE · BUSH · MARKET · KEARNY · MONTGOMERY · 3RD · 4TH · HOWARD · EMBARCADERO · TO BAY BRIDGE

EUREKA

REDDING

MENDOCINO

THE SEA RANCH

MARIN COUNTY

SONOMA

SACRAMENTO

MILL VALLEY

MOKELUMNE HILL

SAUSALITO

BERKELEY / OAKLAND

SAN FRANCISCO

PALO ALTO

MONTEREY

FRESNO

BAKERSFIELD

LOS ANGELES

SAN DIEGO

1970s the Board of Supervisors meetings became a critical forum for public debate concerning the exercise of municipal power over development (as private rebuilding controversies arose), those meetings are examined in greater detail in the later chapters of this book.

On the San Francisco waterfront, the port's domain was distinctly interwoven with those of smaller private projects like Ghirardelli Square, the parcels assembled for the massive unrealized San Francisco International Market Center, and public urban renewal sites like Golden Gateway and Embarcadero Center (fig. 14). In 1863 the state of California had seized the port's property from the city to protect it from exploitation by municipal leadership. Nearly a hundred years later, this state jurisdiction had many direct implications for the hundreds of acres of port holdings as well as indirect implications for adjacent private and public development. Constitutionally protected by California's Doctrine of Public Trust, port land could not be sold—only leased. This fact set the stakes for San Francisco's downtown real estate market, exerting particular influence over the inland blocks along the entire waterfront edge.[15]

By the 1950s, the shipping executives, port administrators, labor leaders, and city and state entities agreed that the port was struggling economically and required a concerted planning vision. In 1959, the state passed legislation allowing the port to issue ninety-nine-year leases, more than double the current forty-year maximum. Advocates behind this change hoped to stimulate nonmaritime commerce and attract large-scale developers. That same year, a modernist conceptual planning study for the port by consultants John S. Bolles and Ernest Born proposed a radical break with the maritime economy via a massive mixed-use project they called Embarcadero City. The Bolles and Born study bolstered the demands to ease port lease terms and drew city leaders' attention to the challenge of coordinating nascent port planning with San Francisco's growing commitment to master planning.[16]

A decade later, in 1969, the uncertainty surrounding the port's land-use and leasing arrangements intensified when the state passed stewardship of the port back to the city. Developers saw a door opening to incorporating port property into their investments in nonmaritime projects such as office towers, apartment buildings, and wholesale trade marts. The 1968 Burton Act authorizing the transfer lowered the maximum lease from ninety-nine to sixty-six years but left almost everything else up for grabs. Developers tested the boundaries of what the new regime would allow and took advantage of the transitional disarray. The port's 730 acres encompassed a motley yet supremely valuable patchwork of seawall lots, roads, piers, wharves, and bulkhead buildings. The port administrators agreed at this time to concentrate shipping and related industrial activities along the southern portion of the waterfront, opening the north waterfront to newly permitted nonmaritime real estate development and urban planning.[17]

The somewhat belated efforts to plan the port's open future crossed paths with the increasingly influential San Francisco Planning Department (SFPD). On the port side, the 1959 Embarcadero City plan was followed by a trail of primarily modernist waterfront studies, with John Bolles, Esther Born, and Ernest Born's *A Plan for Fisherman's Wharf* (1961), Arthur D. Little's *Port of San Francisco* (1966), and John Bolles's *Northern*

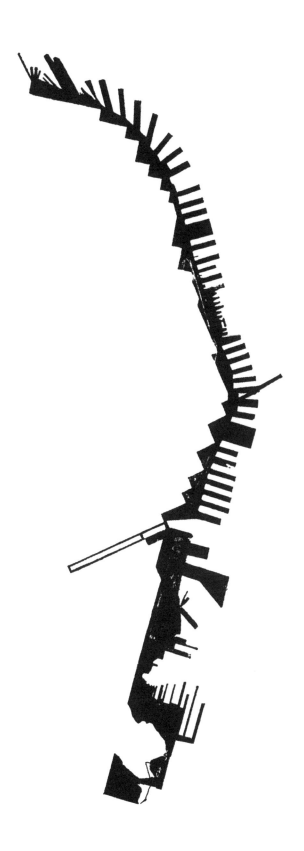

14 This promotion for the San Francisco Port announced: "You own this property. Size: more than 200 acres. Value: over $120 million. It has its own railroad, police force, and fire department. And it has never cost you a cent." Waterfront private developments like Ghirardelli Square, The Cannery, or the proposed but unrealized San Francisco International Market Center, as well as public urban renewal sites like Golden Gateway and Embarcadero Center, were physically interwoven with the public domain of the Port of San Francisco. The struggling port's future and its state jurisdiction were under constant review during the 1950s and 1960s. Investors vied for advantage over the port's "public trust" lands, anticipating the switch to city administration in 1968.

Waterfront Plan (1968) receiving broad circulation. On the city side, San Francisco hired its first full-time professional director of planning in 1942 and issued its first master plan in 1945. The relatively undetailed 1945 plan (addressing only land use, transportation, and public facilities) offered sketchy guidance when development pressures escalated in the 1960s. San Francisco planning matured quickly in these decades, evolving hand in hand with the rise of organized citizen movements protesting freeway locations, environmental degradation, and high-rises.[18] Beginning in 1966 the new city planning director, Allan Jacobs, led the department through major controversies involving the San Francisco International Market Center proposal, Embarcadero Center, and the Transamerica Pyramid. With each local development fight the SFPD had to redefine the relationship of municipal planning power to private property.

The experience of lurching from one developer-driven controversy to another fundamentally set Allan Jacobs's course toward proactive policies, culminating in the city's 1971 *General Plan* and its pathbreaking *Urban Design* guidelines. Beginning in the 1950s, district height and bulk restrictions offered some protection to low-rise neighborhoods, although these districts' historical qualities were only indirectly protected. Each fight exposed how the city's historical character depended on private-sector benevolence. Through the 1960s, none of the city's planning reports advocated for cohesive historical redevelopment. Tellingly, San Francisco's first historic district was Jackson Square, designated in 1972; its National Register of Historic Places nomination included the SFPD's first-ever study of historical resources, conducted in 1971.[19] In the mid-1950s, the San Francisco Redevelopment Agency (SFRA) announced plans to clear the city's bustling 8.5-acre wholesale food and produce market sited on the Embarcadero just north of the financial district. The city demolished the market in 1960. The site became anchor to a 50-acre staged redevelopment project called Urban Renewal Project Area E-1, or the Embarcadero–Lower Market urban renewal area—known colloquially as Golden Gateway. In the 1950s, the city's business leadership, through the Blythe-Zellerbach Committee, pushed to professionalize the SFRA and SFPD and to revive the city's stalled federally supported urban renewal projects, including Area E-1. These pressures resulted in the city's hiring Justin Herman in 1959 to direct the SFRA.[20]

Justin Herman's acceleration of Area E-1's redevelopment had an immediate impact on neighboring historical initiatives on the north waterfront. Herman organized the 1960 national competition to develop the project's first phase, a 19.7-acre primarily residential project that would carry the Golden Gateway name (see fig. 124). A smaller second phase encompassed the Maritime Plaza project, which included the Alcoa tower and underground parking. Maritime Plaza connected Golden Gateway to Area E-1's third phase. When the SFRA unveiled the developer's designs for this third stage in 1967, the 8.5-acre office and commercial complex became known as Embarcadero Center (although the colloquial "Rockefeller Center West" proved hard to shake). Not only did urban renewal obliterate Embarcadero neighborhoods and a vast array of waterfront businesses, it tossed aside height-limit ordinances, reset downtown real estate values, raised the stakes for planned open-space amenities, and altered San Franciscans' sentiments about the remaining, adjacent historical landscape. While the ramifications of these events are described in the book's later chapters, here they help set the stage for understanding how private and public properties influenced one another and defied simple boundaries on the waterfront.[21]

The city's new and proposed skyscrapers and plazas became lightning rods for conflicts over responsible stewardship of the public domain, generating sparks that touched city, state, and federal jurisdictions, the port, the SFPD, the SFRA, the courts, and of course private investors and organized citizen groups. Across from the Embarcadero Center site, the long, horizontal 1898 Ferry Building with its signature tower offered an example of embattled waterfront public property. During these years Ferry Building advocates lost a close fight with the Maritime Museum in 1958 over which would become San Francisco's first state park, but the building was simultaneously coveted by developers who hoped to lease the site from the port and build a skyscraper office complex. Although the Ferry Building anchored Market Street, in 1958 the construction of the double-decked Embarcadero Freeway blocked the landside view of the terminal and isolated the building from the city streets. This "design" provocation culminated in San Francisco's freeway revolt led by Jean Kortum, Karl Kortum's wife, which stopped the Embarcadero Freeway in its tracks. The Freeway defacement hurt the city's case for putting the Ferry Building at the center of a state historic park. A short distance up Market Street stood the Crown Zellerbach building, the city's first glass-walled skyscraper, which had been announced in 1956. A modest 20 stories, Crown Zellerbach nevertheless led San Francisco's postwar downtown high-rise boom. Its peaceful cobblestone plaza retreat for the public became a touted example of voluntary corporate benevolence.[22]

Within this complex context of overlapping public domains and the port's decline, the Maritime Museum and Ghirardelli Square joined other independent private initiatives converging in the 1950s and 1960s to imprint history-themed redevelopment on the north waterfront. Two in particular—Jackson Square and The Cannery—illuminated different approaches to grassroots historical revitalization.[23]

Jackson Square, relying on cooperative private ownership, represented the earliest concerted effort in San Francisco to rehabilitate historic properties for commerce. In 1951 a handful of the city's interior decorators, furniture manufacturers, and home furnishings experts "reclaimed" several old buildings from "relative obscurity" to consolidate a wholesale design district. Several decorator-proprietors formed the Jackson Square Land Company, and together they purchased the original row of six buildings (fig. 15). They planned for growth, envisioning seventy-five exhibitors and a trajectory taking them from West Coast dominance to national stature. Despite the name, Jackson Square did not have a central open space. It did, however, have the city's largest concentration of extant nineteenth-century commercial buildings. It offered a rare glimpse of Gold Rush San Francisco in a downtown neighborhood that had survived the 1906 earthquake and fire. These streets included, for example, the Ghirardelli Company's first building, constructed in 1856, along with an array of vernacular commercial architecture.[24] In the mid-nineteenth century this neighborhood delineated the city's shoreline at roughly Montgomery Street. Subsequent landfill moved the waterfront to the east, but this meant that high-rise excavations at the edge of Jackson Square regularly unearthed historical maritime artifacts. In one vivid case, construction workers in 1978 struck a forty-five-ton piece of a Gold Rush whaling ship, the *Niantic,* lying partly underneath the Transamerica Pyramid's small Redwood Park.[25]

The 1971 National Historic Register nomination for Jackson Square explained that private-sector initiative had revitalized the neighborhood with little government help. Although one photograph included in the nomination showed the steel frame of Transamerica's base under construction, the inspiration behind Jackson Square had originated twenty years earlier, long before the Montgomery Block was demolished. The nomination documents asserted that the public sector now needed to actively protect the district. The neighborhood's historic character already relied on atmospheric, smaller-scale public properties such as alleys and streets, courtyards and sidewalks, and on benches and other street furnishings (fig. 16). The city had played a supporting role in 1960 when it approved the Jackson Square merchants' proposal to convert the narrow block-long Hotaling Place, connecting Jackson and Washington Streets, into a pedestrian mall. The city agreed to split the $16,000 expense with the merchants for removing the sidewalks and installing decorative pavers, potted trees, and streetlamps.

15 This January 1952 photograph looks east along Jackson Street, capturing the original block that was on the verge of initiating renovations of nineteenth-century buildings into a wholesale home furnishings district that would become known as Jackson Square. This view peers down the one-block alley Hotaling Place, which connected south to Washington Street. Despite its name, Jackson Square lacked a central plaza and relied instead on the alleys, sidewalks, façades, and street furniture for its historical atmosphere.

16 A circa 1970 view down Hotaling Place from Jackson Street, taken from roughly the same location as the previous photo (fig. 15). In 1960 the City of San Francisco supported Jackson Square's private renovations by redesigning narrow Hotaling Place with new, wavy-curbed pavers, potted trees, and "Victorian" streetlamps. Although Jackson Square served the wholesale trade, this photograph captured the one day annually when the shops opened to the public. This photograph was used in the City's 1971 application to the National Register of Historic Places, which, once approved, made Jackson Square the first official historic district in San Francisco. In 1972, this view would dead-end in the Transamerica Pyramid; the upgrading of this alley countered developers' arguments that small streets were useless and should be sold to private investors.

Whereas planning director John McCarthy praised this "kind of urban renewal" based on private initiative in 1960, ten years later the Transamerica Pyramid's rising profile drove home the fact that Jackson Square needed proactive government protections.[26]

Jackson Square's success testified to the size and influence of San Francisco's design community and its power to transform a neighborhood, even without direct public patronage. In fact, the wholesalers excluded the public, except for an annual one-day open house. The district's home furnishings entrepreneurs solidified ties between contemporary interior design trends and the historic architectural context of the Gold Rush–era built environment. Design networks expanded as businesses unable to find space in Jackson Square reenergized other streets. Union Street's retail renaissance, for example, benefited from Jackson Square's overflow.[27] Primarily, however, Jackson Square modeled its brand of urban rebuilding by reaching its clients: the members of the Bay Area's professional design community, who at one point or another entered Jackson Square's businesses. By 1960, architects and other designers eyed the waterfront's underused warehouses as potential office spaces in which to replicate the success of Jackson Square. Jackson Square's rising real estate values, moreover, affirmed the viability of reusing old commercial structures. What seemed risky in the 1950s became a local formula by the 1960s.[28]

Soon after the Roths' purchase of the Ghirardelli block in the spring of 1962, another high-profile rescue strengthened the private-public patchwork of the historic waterfront. The Cannery was Ghirardelli's slower-moving twin. Together, these two projects stimulated business for one another, competed, and generally set expensive standards for historic revitalization. Whereas Ghirardelli's Bill and Lurline Roth were leading citizens enmeshed in the city's history, industries, and civic organizations, The Cannery's Leonard Martin was an immigrant from East Asia who made the transformation of the Del Monte Fruit Canning Plant his life's work (fig. 17). In 1963 Martin bought the plant (defunct since 1937) "before the wrecker's ball could destroy it." He outbid an unnamed competitor who "intended to put a Fontana-like highrise apartment on the site." Martin said he had "trouble getting a loan until Bill Roth bought Ghirardelli Square. Then the banks knew I had a good idea."[29]

In these ways and others, The Cannery provided an illuminating mirror for Ghirardelli Square and the larger waterfront redevelopment. Martin, like Roth, cited old-world European models of layered historical cities, but when it came to hiring designers, Martin also employed modernists. Martin's choices in architects, landscape

17 Leonard Martin announcing his plans in June 1965 to redevelop the Del Monte factory building (next to the Haslett Warehouse) into The Cannery on the north waterfront, with many similarities to Ghirardelli Square. Although Martin cultivated a public image as a lone operator, he collaborated closely with Ghirardelli Square and the Maritime Museum on projects supporting the neighborhood's historical maritime themes.

architect, graphic designer, and manager shadowed Roth's.[30] The AIA recognized The Cannery with an award in 1970, as it had Ghirardelli Square in 1966. The planning for both initially unfolded in tandem, with The Cannery finally opening officially in May 1967 between Ghirardelli's two phased openings. Martin's upbringing in Manchuria (he had arrived in the United States in 1940), his fluent Mandarin and Russian, his love of good food and wine—all reinforced The Cannery's promotion of international artifacts, international food, and antiques.

The force of Leonard Martin's personality and the depth of his pockets, together with forgiving press coverage, carried The Cannery through a rough first decade and added to the foundations for historical redevelopment laid by Kortum, Roth, and others. The complex opened in a recession. As Martin struggled to find and keep tenants, Bank of America looked the other way and decided to not foreclose on its substantial loan to Martin. In the face of his debts and struggles, Martin told Herb Caen: "Stop worrying about the Cannery. . . . I'm a loner, you know. I don't have any friends, really. But I have the Cannery and it's a one-man show."[31] Ghirardelli Square's second phase, which opened in 1968, faced the same economic slump. The vulnerability of the experiment— privately developed, historically themed urban shopping centers in old factories and warehouses—became evident to tenants and owners alike.

Although he called himself a loner, Martin tallied the collective benefits for the city of his investment, along with Bill Roth's: "What we've accomplished in this neighborhood is a privately-supported urban renewal project." The local press admired Martin's gumption, but he never won the mantle of civic benevolence granted to Bill Roth and to homegrown corporate powerhouses such as Levi Strauss or Bank of America. Instead, Martin was described as eccentric and "aristocratic." The *Chronicle* noted that Martin, "who conceived the reconstruction and performed it single-handedly, wonders if he really did build a monument to himself." Meanwhile, Martin quietly backed with his own money virtually all of the historical maritime collaborations proposed by Karl Kortum and Roth for the neighborhood.[32]

In 1967 *Sunset* magazine proclaimed San Francisco's north waterfront transformed: "Today this small 22-block district fronts on two small parks, contains two unusual museums and two art galleries, five old ships on public display, 43 places to eat (some of them very good), much excellent shopping (imports, fashions, antiques), three small live theaters, and good parking—and then good walking." Crowds thronged structures that a decade earlier were "run-down and neglected." *Sunset* attributed this dynamic revitalization to an obscure museum. In 1950, the magazine explained, "the old city building at Aquatic Park was turned over to the Maritime Museum, an organization that advocates setting aside land, buildings, and piers in the district to commemorate the city's rich transportation history."[33]

Behind the Maritime Museum and its advocacy for setting aside public land was preservationist Karl Kortum. It is time to let his lesser-known story unfold, tracing how his outsider's vision in 1949 gave focus to city, state, and federal decisions about public land stewardship that supported his historical waterfront plan. Kortum's initiative not only expanded to ultimately found the city's national historic maritime park but also set the stage for the thriving commercial historic district described in *Sunset* in 1967. The redevelopment models offered by Jackson Square, Ghirardelli Square, and The Cannery credited entrepreneurial private investment and modernist designers. That was the story Randy Delehanty sought to embellish in his Ghirardelli Square interviews. Kortum and the Maritime Museum put that Ghirardelli rescue in a much wider context.

THE MARITIME MUSEUM AND THE "ILLUSTRATED PITCH"

The 1950 rendering of Argonaut Square committed to paper the vision Karl Kortum hoped to sell to newspaper editors, the mayor, commissioners, and other influential citizens (see fig. 8). The 1940s plan began small and ephemeral, based on Kortum's personal love for old ships and San Francisco's maritime past. He lived at the time with his family in Petaluma, a Sonoma town known for its chicken ranches and egg production. An outsider with few city contacts, Kortum initially proposed converting the underused bathhouse building in Aquatic Park into a maritime museum. A visit to the north waterfront in April 1949 inspired him to expand his museum concept into an entire district encompassing a historic park that integrated ships, piers, factories and warehouses, two museums, a "Victorian" park, and a reconstructed mid-nineteenth-century business street with modern commerce. Scott Newhall, an editor at the *San Francisco Chronicle*, endorsed the plan and lent artist Hubert (Hugh) Buel to Kortum's cause. Buel's renderings clinched the support of San Francisco's mayor, Elmer Robinson, for Kortum's plan, although not for the reasons Kortum anticipated.

The forgotten watercolors archived in the Maritime Museum capture Kortum's proposal for a public maritime historic district that predated the Roths' private rescue of Ghirardelli by more than a dozen years. Saving the factory fit into Kortum's long-range vision as much as it sprang from Bill Roth's civic initiative or from architects' drawing boards. Buel depicted the factories and warehouses as unadorned boxes—simultaneously useful containers for displaying museum collections and atmospheric red-brick backdrops for the storied ships. Although today the watercolors of factories and nautical artifacts seem hopelessly old-fashioned, they more accurately predicted the waterfront's future than the rendering of the Ghirardelli Center high-rise from 1961.[34]

Kortum's 1940s historical concept for the neighborhood offered a private vision that differed from Bill Roth's. Whereas Roth based his preservation model on private ownership and private planning, Kortum tendered a civic vision without staking out personal ownership. Instead, Kortum pursued responsible stewardship rooted in *public* ownership. He contributed to private "rescues" such as Ghirardelli but above all pursued orchestrating the assignment and transfer of public land. Kortum's advocacy and his illustrated pitch for Argonaut Square focused on what the district offered the city and why reusing the port's factories and warehouses was a worthwhile mission.

Karl Kortum's lifelong relationship with the city's north waterfront had begun in the 1930s. During that decade he sometimes hitchhiked the fifty miles south from Petaluma to San Francisco to attend Marine Research Society dinners at which the city's maritime experts shared their independent research and discussed relevant exhibitions. This connection deepened in the 1940s with Kortum's growing conviction that the padlocked bathhouse building in Aquatic Park would make a logical place for a maritime museum. The structure earned its "white elephant" moniker from underuse, not age. It was a gleaming New Deal addition to the waterfront in 1939, one of the largest WPA projects in California. Between 1936 and 1939, the city's new Aquatic Park converted the water's edge from an uneven mix of docks, sand, and trees into a graded beach rimmed with neatly aligned concrete viewing stands and speaker towers for public events. Earlier known as Black Point Cove, this waterfront stretch had uneasily accommodated nineteenth-century factory development like Ghirardelli alongside recreational swimming and boating. Aquatic Park's development followed decades of agitation to reclaim the shore from industrial use by buying (back) the land from private owners and establishing public recreation. These efforts included moving a railroad trestle that cut across the lagoon further inland and constructing a curved concrete Municipal Pier. Kortum remembered attending a jazz session at the bathhouse in 1940, when briefly it was known as the Casino. The city shuttered the Casino enterprise later that year because the concessionaire had privatized the public facility. During World War II, the military used the site for maneuvers, returning the structure to the city in 1948. The building's future was uncertain.[35]

Early the next year, from his family's poultry farm in Petaluma, Kortum began to write to leading San Franciscans regarding his proposal to convert the bathhouse, which he called a wasted public investment, into a maritime museum. He struck out in his first two attempts. Neither Mayor Robinson nor maritime patron Alma Spreckels could see a way forward. Mayor Robinson politely declined the proposal citing budget challenges, and Spreckels had her own maritime history agenda.[36] Kortum found his first toehold with Scott Newhall, influential editor at the *San Francisco Chronicle* (and brother of one of Kortum's Navy shipmates). Kortum had recently initiated a conversation with Newhall over a different land-use matter. In Petaluma, the State Highway Department's proposed routing of Highway 101, one of the region's principal north-south arteries, threatened to bisect his family's farm. On a trip to the city Kortum managed to get a last-minute appointment with Newhall, who overlooked Kortum's innocence in trying to meet with him on the day of the 1948 presidential election. Kortum explained to Newhall that he and his father "had just organized 140 small ranchers . . . into an anti-freeway organization." Newhall sent a reporter the following week to cover the hearing, which Kortum said was "of inestimable help in bringing the fight out into the open." Kortum later described their eventual victory as California's first successful "freeway revolt," halting bureaucracy in its tracks.[37] This was Kortum's most relevant civics lesson prior to entering the San Francisco fray.

Soon thereafter, Kortum happened upon a review Newhall had written of the sailing memoir *The Set of the Sails,* by Alan Villiers. Kortum penned a letter in March 1949 to his "newfound acquaintance" detailing his rationale for a permanent maritime museum in Aquatic Park. Waking the city up to its "sailing ship tradition," he wrote, "has haunted me for some ten years." The museum project, he believed, "is the stuff whereof a good newspaper campaign is made, and which, conversely, needs a newspaper campaign to put it over." Despite the millions invested in it, Aquatic Park reminded Kortum of "an empty stage." Kortum proposed that the "star" of that stage be a fully outfitted square-rigger—a ship straight out of the city's past—moored at the curved municipal pier. The former bathhouse, shaped like an ocean liner, could house a maritime museum based on a collection already assembled by shipping executive Edward Strong Clark. San Francisco had devolved into the nation's "dullest" waterfront, Kortum said. As for Aquatic Park's future, "the imagination of the Park Commissioners does not extend much further than converting it into a fish food grotto." They knew "nothing about ships." For Kortum, maritime tourism held the key to the waterfront's success; this was "just what the middle-western visitor expects of San Francisco." He enclosed an article about Mystic Seaport in Connecticut and added an illustration by his Petaluma friend and amateur artist, Frank Eatherton, of what "could be done" at Aquatic Park (fig. 18). Eatherton's watercolor of Kortum's original proposal appears in striking contrast to Buel's later illustrations. Eatherton depicted a peaceful setting for the square-rigger, emphasizing the lagoon's natural surroundings rather than the city's edge. The picture, Kortum told Newhall with a flash of humor about his own intensity, "adds another ten thousand words, but at least they will not be single spaced."[38]

Scott Newhall saw promise in Karl Kortum's ideas for a permanent maritime museum. Newhall was an activist editor who believed in putting the power of city newspapers behind initiatives judged worthy. Like Kortum, he was a sailor, photographer, and writer. Newhall took Kortum's concept to the *Chronicle's* editor-in-chief, Paul Smith, packaging it as a reader's suggestion worth backing. With Smith's support, Newhall invited Kortum to go down to San Francisco to investigate the prospects in more depth.[39]

Kortum's April 1949 follow-up visit to San Francisco expanded his preoccupation with the ships, pier, and bathhouse into a vision for a larger historic maritime district. After meeting with Newhall, Kortum made a pilgrimage to the north waterfront, which he approached from the Hyde Street trolley's last stop in front of the Buena Vista Café. He walked downhill toward the bay. A brilliant light illuminated the old industrial waterfront of warehouses and factories, opening up a startling view. As a photographer, Kortum told Delehanty, his "eye responded to the scene," and he stopped in his tracks. "Right bang then and there I realized that there was a wall of superb big brick structures that cut the place off from the rest of the city." Preoccupied with the bathhouse, he had not noticed the surrounding buildings. That April day in 1949, however, "the cross-lighting picked out the handsome architectural details of the Haslett Warehouse." The cohesive wall of brick structures defined the district, a "picturesque and anti-quated island" at the edge of the city. Kortum inverted what would soon become the standard critique of high-rise construction; instead of skyscrapers cutting the city off from its waterfront, the old factories and warehouses "walled off modern San Francisco." He "expanded the plan then and there" (fig. 19).[40]

The next day, Kortum explained to Newhall that recognizing this "kind of square or plaza—the undeveloped eastern end of Aquatic Park"—had caused him to recast the Maritime Museum concept into a maritime historic district (fig. 20). This unused land, a field strewn with discarded cans, had just been acquired by the city. The old factories and warehouses mostly enclosed the area, and "only one short block of businesses . . .

18 Frank Eatherton's ca. 1949 watercolor of Karl Kortum's original Maritime Museum concept, including a historical ship. This peaceful setting evoked natural surroundings and a simpler vision rather than the edge of a busy city, factories, and tourism. This painting contrasted with the illustrations commissioned from Hubert Buel soon thereafter. Eatherton was a friend of Karl Kortum from Petaluma. A square-rigger similar to the one moored here became the museum's first restored ship in the mid-1950s. *The Balclutha*'s impressive income from visitors proved the public appeal Kortum had predicted.

on the upper side of the square would have to be revamped to complete the illusion." Regarding those businesses, Kortum wrote, "In time the city could take over these locations, or else the proprietors might consent to a face lifting." For Kortum, the reconstructed square anchored an array of exciting ideas: paving with salvaged cobblestones, extending the cable car into the district to bring tourists, recreating an "old time shipyard" in one corner (fig. 21). The Haslett Warehouse could be "taken over" to display railroad cars and artifacts in a second museum. As "the late afternoon sunlight was mellowing these old buildings," Kortum believed these changes would "bring to life some of the atmosphere of one of the city's old squares." Kortum's civic vision expanded to maximize the potential of a longer list of languishing public facilities, and he aspired to incorporate private structures into the public realm as needed. In the name of recovering the city's maritime past, Kortum laid out two museums, two parks, ships, trains, and a public transit lifeline (the trolley) to the city's tourist trade. In April 1949 he wrote, "The whole thing wants the services of an able landscape architect, and I am sure it could be integrated." Kortum wrote, "The place is alive with possibilities." He presciently anticipated that this was "only a beginning for a program of development to take place over the years." He signed off, "Ideas are cheap, accomplishment comes much harder." Kortum had set his life's work (see figs. 8, 20, and 21).[41]

Scott Newhall assigned sharp young staff reporter Dave Nelson to assist Kortum full time in preparing a strategy. Kortum and Nelson devoted the summer to meeting with community leaders from the shipping industry, labor unions, and politics. Labor conflict had jeopardized the Port of San Francisco's national reputation, and both Newhall and

Kortum saw the potential for maritime history to bring together shipping magnates, shipyard workers, and regular seamen on common ground. Newhall took charge of the newspaper endorsements, working to align powerful rivals behind Kortum's plan to leverage underused public resources and build "a bit of civic unity." In September 1949 Newhall approached his skeptical rival at the *Examiner*, Charles Lindner: "The plan at first sight might seem to be visionary, yet Nelson and Kortum met with astonishing success." For practical politicians and editors, the term "visionary" was not necessarily a compliment. But Kortum's ideas had traction with the city's leadership. He argued that Mystic Seaport's " enormous monetary success" suggested that the San Francisco project would not drain the public treasury. Gilbert Kneiss of Western Pacific Railroad and the Historical Railroad and Locomotive Society had already "offered to turn over that organization's magnificent collection of western locomotives and cable cars to be displayed," endorsing the use of the Haslett Warehouse as a transportation museum. "Guys with ideas come into any newspaper office every hour on the hour," Newhall told Lindner, but Kortum, the "lad . . . from Petaluma," was different.[42]

The historic maritime district moved from vision to political endorsement and then reality with unlikely speed. During several "tense" weeks in September 1949, Kortum set himself up in the *Chronicle*'s offices to prepare for meetings with the mayor and

19 This undated Buel painting is close to the vantage point from which Karl Kortum described experiencing his first inspirational view of the historic harbor as a wall of warehouses holding the modern city at bay. At the time he was walking down Hyde Street toward the waterfront, past the Buena Vista Café (visible on the left). The brick Haslett Warehouse and a cable car are prominent in the right foreground, while Alcatraz and Angel Island are in the background. Hyde Street Pier and the Sausalito Ferry embarkation point lie at the bottom of the street.

editors of the city's major papers. Kortum, Nelson, Buel, and Newhall prepared a "plastic-bound" prospectus. Kortum described how Buel "made splendid big watercolors of all of these concepts of mine" for the campaign (fig. 22; see also figs. 8, 20, and 21). For Mayor Robinson, "Dave got up and made his illustrated pitch." The mayor reviewed their binder. Kortum remembered, "We were feeling that we had been moderately successful when I suggested to Dave that he show the railway train pictures. Nelson put up the "'Argonaut Square' scene." And "that did it," said Kortum. "Apparently the Mayor is only mildly interested in ships but keenly interested in old trains." The railway museum won the mayor's backing for the historical district. Mayor Robinson offered the assistance of the city comptroller to develop the budget and financing. Shortly thereafter, Newhall secured the editors' support.[43]

Kortum, ever the sailor, hoped they could now turn from "fancy booklets" to "figure out how to get old ships off mud banks."[44] The mayor designated a thirty-seven member Citizens' Committee in January 1950, chaired by Edward Harms, a shipping executive at Pope and Talbot Lines and president of the San Francisco Propeller Club. The non-profit San Francisco Maritime Museum Association took offices in City Hall that spring. Harms's committee reported in April that consultations with the Board of Supervisors, Park Commission, Chamber of Commerce, hotel industry, and Planning Commission had

20 An early view of Kortum's Maritime Museum concept published in the newspapers in May 1950 as a companion to the close-up "Proposed Reconstruction of Old San Francisco" (see fig. 8), here visible to the right. The Haslett Warehouse at far right is used as a Railway Museum, and an antique steam locomotive moves on the Jefferson Street tracks. The reconstructed stores face both Beach Street and Gold Rush Plaza. Hyde Street pier, to the right, displays a ship but otherwise lies empty. Maritime Museum records say that moored in the lagoon are a three-masted bark, a three-masted schooner, a stern-wheel riverboat, and a steam schooner. Vessels resembling *Gjoa* and *Alma*, two of the actual ships moored in the bay later, are displayed on shore. The partial prow seen in the next image (fig. 21) is visible here, in the left foreground. This view ignores the Ghirardelli factory buildings and focuses on the historical district concept, which had expanded from simply converting the Aquatic Park Bathhouse into a maritime museum with one ship, to this well-defined district enclosed by the piers.

21 Hubert Buel's 1949 conceptual rendering of Karl Kortum's Maritime Museum, depicting a sternwheeler and sailing ship. This perspective from Van Ness Street foregrounds a prow displayed on uphill dry land. The view of the bay, the Marin headlands, Angel Island, and planted trees extends Eatherton's emphasis on the peaceful natural surroundings but adds in the visitor parking and more outdoor maritime displays. This painting is a bridge to the more commercial view of Argonaut Square seen in figure 8.

22 This late 1953 Buel rendering was "an artist's conception of the development of 'Argonaut Bay'" mounted on a carrying board for use in presentations. This painting resembles the 1950 renderings of a reconstructed Old San Francisco plaza and railroad museum, adding a roundhouse and a more elaborate shipyard. The Ghirardelli factories completed the ring of old factories and warehouses connected by the reconstructed business street.

generated "uniformly" positive reviews of the concept. This "living museum" would occupy Aquatic Park's 34.5 acres, including the lagoon, and coexist with recreational activities. The Committee proposed fund-raising toward an initial goal of $200,000. The museum leased the Aquatic Park Center from the city for a dollar in September 1950. Eight months later, it opened its doors with Kortum as curator and sole employee.[45]

In two years Kortum had made the SFMM one of the city's top tourist destinations, all while building the interior displays, securing collections, and raising funds. In 1954 the Museum Association purchased and renovated the square-rigger *Balclutha* (then named *Pacific Queen*) with contributions and volunteer labor from the steamship company presidents and the sailors' union. *Balclutha* opened to the public in 1955 at Pier 43 ½, just to the east of Fisherman's Wharf. School groups, alongside tourists and maritime buffs, boosted attendance to 4,500 a week by 1953.[46] When a woman named Jean Edmonds applied to the *Chronicle* for a newspaper job in 1951, Scott Newhall sent her to the Maritime Museum, where she began as a volunteer and then spent several years as executive secretary. Edmonds had studied journalism in college; her first job, with the *Oakland Post-Enquirer,* had evaporated when that paper folded. Karl Kortum and Jean Edmonds got along unusually well at the SFMM and were married later that same year. The museum was a "shoestring" operation, the *Chronicle* noted in early 1953, where "the busy Kortums have managed to hold the museum's body and soul together." Jean's pay was an irregular $200 per month, in addition to Karl's monthly salary of $450 from the city. Jean Kortum left the museum in 1955 to make a name for herself in the region's major environmental and urban preservation fights of the 1950s, 1960s, and 1970s. She began working with the new Telegraph Hill Dwellers neighborhood organization in 1954 and became a force in the city's antifreeway campaigns. As her strategies against development policies expanded to include lawsuits against the city and developers in the large-scale rebuilding battles of the 1960s, Jean Kortum kept her distance from the Maritime Museum to protect her husband's career in first the city, then the state, and later the federal government (fig. 23). In these early years, however, the museum operated as a family affair. Soon the Kortums' infant daughter, Jeanie, came to work most days, crawling about the premises.[47]

Several years into this successful but shoestring museum operation, Karl Kortum seized an unparalleled opportunity for state funding—from the Tidelands Oil Royalty Funds. This windfall arrived through a federal settlement of tidelands jurisdiction in March 1954 that yielded California $62 million to support historical resources, to be administered through the Division of Beaches and Parks in the State Parks office. The funds represented seven years of impounded royalties on oil leases permitting private interests to extract oil in the tidelands zone extending three miles off the California coast; the royalties covered the period since 1947, when the federal government had taken over tidelands from the coastal states. The 1954 settlement returned the tidelands to the states, along with the accumulated royalties. Initially, the City of San Francisco backed a proposal to use the city's prospective allocation to create a Ferry Building Park at the foot of Market Street. Kortum rallied support behind his master plan for a state historic maritime district that, when it was unveiled in late 1956, included state purchase of the Ghirardelli chocolate factory. Working through Assemblyman Tom Maloney and Harry Lundberg, head of the sailors' union, the SFMM managed to trump the establishment proposal. A preliminary $200,000 allocation from the state in 1955 enabled the SFMM the following year to seek $2 million, which it won after hard battles in Sacramento and San Francisco. Kortum moved his project to the next level, "talking the state into a historical monument consisting of ships instead of buildings."[48] After the state agreed to fund the San Francisco Maritime State Historical Monument in 1958, Kortum would be able to realize the "living, floating museum" concept of Argonaut Bay (fig. 24).[49] By 1969 the state of California had invested at least $2.273 million in the project, allowing the museum to acquire and restore four historic ships (the *Thayer, Wapama, Eureka,* and *Alma*), buy the Haslett Warehouse, develop Victorian Park and Hyde Street Pier, and undertake miscellaneous land acquisitions and investments on site.[50]

State park designation did not unify the public domain for the acreage under the Maritime Museum's influence. If anything, it introduced a more complicated terrain of jurisdictions. Each of Kortum's initiatives took the museum into a different patchwork of public and private authority. In 1968, for example, the SFMM had a forty-year lease from the port for Hyde Street Pier and operated Victorian Park under a nonmonetary fifty-year lease from the city and the county. Although the state had bought the Haslett Warehouse in 1962, the SFMM had been unable to claim it for the promised railroad museum. Complicating matters further, the question of whether the city should take

23 Jean Kortum on Third Street near the *Examiner* building on January 15, 1963, after "delivering a press release in the (successful) campaign to stop PG&E [Pacific Gas and Electric] from building a nuclear plant on Bodega Head." Karl Kortum took this photograph of his wife. They had parallel but separate careers in preservation activism. The Bodega Head campaign solidified Jean Kortum's arrival as an effective urban-environmentalist leader who influenced the region's development decisions.

24 In 1963 Karl Kortum could point to the realization of San Francisco's first state park. This model documented the "growing" San Francisco Maritime State Historical Monument at Aquatic Park. Kortum had won $2 million in state funds in 1956 from California's Tidelands Oil Royalty Funds to expand the municipal maritime park. Additional historic ships (the *Thayer* and ferry boat *Eureka*) purchased through the state were on their way at the time of the press release accompanying this fall 1963 photograph. Demolition had just begun at the neighboring Ghirardelli factory to make way for redevelopment. This architectural model merged uniquely with ship model-building traditions.

over the San Francisco Maritime State Historical Monument was opened for discussion in 1969, at the same time the port passed from state to city authority.[51]

Several examples from the SFMM's planning initiatives show that what public ownership meant on the ground could be very complicated. For good reasons that kept multiplying, Karl Kortum believed in the galvanizing force of public investment. His leveraging of municipal and then state support for the historic district offered successful examples of harnessing a private civic vision to the power of public ownership. At the same time, the mixed public jurisdictions structured the outcomes of north waterfront development into the 1960s. Three examples illuminate the conflicts over such boundaries: the collision of the port's 1961 *Plan for Fisherman's Wharf* with the SFMM, Kortum's ill-conceived attempt to build underground parking beneath Victorian Park in 1966, and the fate of Kortum's development ideas for Hyde Street Pier and Fisherman's Wharf, including his efforts to reconstruct the Gold Rush Plaza that had inspired him in 1949.

In April 1961, with apologies, the president of the San Francisco port authority, Cyril Magnin, sent Karl Kortum a copy of the Bolles and Born *Plan for Fisherman's Wharf*. Magnin, a civic leader and chair of the Joseph Magnin department store chain, did this as a courtesy; parts of the plan had leaked prematurely to the newspapers. Upon reading the study, Kortum was stunned to realize that its provisions "would eliminate completely" the San Francisco Maritime State Historical Monument, which California had already agreed to fund at more than $2 million. Kortum and the SFMM trustees had participated in two years of meetings to coordinate the state park with the port's plans. Yet the Bolles and Born proposal would "crush" the state's plans, which now included converting Aquatic Park's eastern end into a gaslit Victorian Park, the Haslett Warehouse into a Western rail museum, and Hyde Street Pier into a replica of a famous old San Francisco wharf with a floating schooner display. The museum trustees reminded the port director that all of these initiatives were demonstrably under way and deplored the "high-handed manner" in which the *Plan for Fisherman's Wharf* appropriated the museum, its administration, and the "State's $2,000,000 historical monument."[52] In this case of the port authority's engaging State Parks authority, the port's consulting architects had overstepped their client's geographical and administrative boundaries, as well as their own design jurisdiction.

Another episode, Kortum's failed effort to develop an underground parking garage in Victorian Park, seems insignificant when measured against Kortum's overall impact on the maritime district, but it reveals the consequences he faced when he overstepped his authority as a State Parks employee. It also underscores the energy Kortum devoted to the numerous small squares, parks, and miscellaneous corners of the waterfront. Kortum forged ahead with his garage proposal, despite the misgivings of several of his usual collaborators, including Bill Roth, about the garage's expense and the impact of access ramps and ventilation shafts on Victorian Park. Kortum hired Osborne and Stewart Architects to work out the designs in 1966 and 1967. He anticipated guiding the firm's "pencil," although he trusted Zach Stewart and Daniel Osborne. Ultimately, Kortum's exaggerated sense of personal jurisdiction over the maritime district combined with his disregard for the state's authority to undermine his negotiating position. This killed the project. His presentations of the garage proposal excluded state leadership, whom he brought in much too late in the process. Making matters worse, Dave Nelson tried to "fix" the problem with an end run around the State Parks bureaucracy in December 1967 that failed miserably. Kortum intended for the city to lease the land to the garage developer, Queen Victoria Parking Garage Corporation, with the state's approval but had not taken steps to make this happen. Both the State Parks department and San Francisco's City Planning Commission rejected the proposal.[53] That Kortum pushed the garage proposal so far, running on the steam of his own convictions, speaks to his method and its limits.

Within State Parks authority and the state's complex and overlapping public domains, examples of this arrogance over presumed jurisdiction cut several ways. The same year that Kortum failed to include the state in his garage plans, the head of the State Parks planning office, Harry Dean, wrote a key memo that left out the role of the Maritime Museum Association in designing and developing the park. Dean then recommended razing the existing Maritime Museum building and bleachers (which would soon have National Landmark status). Dean's plans, like Kortum's, "proposed sweeping changes to resources over which his agency had no control." Such incidents belied any straight-forward power attributed to public ownership.[54]

The third example, a sampling of plans for Hyde Street Pier and Fisherman's Wharf, illuminates how state bureaucracy could both empower and constrain. Both the pier and the wharf were under the port's authority, but each offered different challenges to the waterfront's future as a historic district. Late in 1964, port president Magnin invited designer Marget Larsen to review the current plans for Fisherman's Wharf and offer suggestions for their improvement. As art director for Joseph Magnin stores since the 1950s, Larsen had displayed striking creativity with marketing and packaging and made singular contributions to the chain's success that had attracted the attention of architects, planners, and developers active in urban design. In 1964 she had just branched out into freelance consulting, soon picking up Leonard Martin and The Cannery as a client, along with the Stanford Shopping Center, the Sierra Club, and Alvin Duskin, who would lead one of the city's anti-high-rise campaigns at the end of the decade. She also had the reputation for identifying immediately the weaknesses in others' designs when asked for her critique.[55] Karl Kortum teamed up with Larsen to consult on the wharf venture. After several months of work, they presented their critique to Magnin and an assemblage of port commissioners and engineers.

The consultation, merging urban design input from businessmen, artists, and a museum director, did not go well. Although Magnin appeared receptive to Larsen's analysis of the current landscape plans, the port representatives dismissed her own planning recommendations and Kortum's as old-timey, impractical, and too "visionary." Larsen and Kortum had anticipated that they might be viewed as "fuzzy-headed artists," but Kortum primarily blamed their own lack of renderings for hurting their case. Kortum wrote Larsen a long debriefing letter. He resented the "dabbling in design by amateurs," which had perpetuated the wharf's disappointing mediocrity. "I do not believe in potato merchants, and stove manufacturers, and stock brokers, and port engineers doing design," he added. The commissioners lacked "taste" and were not qualified to make such decisions. At least Magnin knew to bring in Larsen as an expert. "As far as the old-fashioned versus the modern controversy goes (a controversy of their devising), that is a ploy," Kortum reminded Larsen. An "amateur" designer himself, Kortum critiqued where others drew the lines of expertise.[56]

The Fisherman's Wharf episode pointed to the frustrations of endlessly pitching ideas to multiple bosses in evolving planning scenarios. Although Kortum owed "his" park to public-sector leadership, he remained ambivalent toward government. Kortum told Larsen that they had encountered "the little foxes of government," explaining: "Try to make the city a little better and they don't hurl themselves in your path; they kind of sidle in." Like the port engineer who had rejected their recommendations outright, bureaucrats resisted "anything a little different—anything a little imaginative." Kortum's own career showed that the opposite was also true; if someone within the power structure, such as Mayor Robinson or Cyril Magnin, backed imaginative ideas, they did have a chance at realization.[57]

Hyde Street Pier did its own unique dance among public and private jurisdictions over the decades, beginning with its key role in the first 1950s State Park proposal. In the early 1960s Kortum salvaged structures from urban renewal demolitions to furnish the pier with "authentic" artifacts, and ten years later the SFMM sought a private investor to develop the pier and the Haslett building into a major commercial attraction. When the State Park plan took off in 1954, Kortum relocated his concept for a reconstructed Gold Rush commercial street from the eastern end of Aquatic Park to focus on Hyde Street Pier (fig. 25). Although the invented row of sail lofts and ship chandleries on the pier soon would be critiqued as Disneyesque, in fact Buel's rendering of the Argonaut Square reconstruction was dated 1950 and his first drawing of the pier was from 1954, both before Disneyland opened in 1955. The 1954 ink-and-pastel illustration of the pier unleashed the energetic potential of an expanded budget for historic ships underwritten by the Tidelands Oil Funds. The 1954 scene, which included a carousel, an aerial tram, and a bustling shopping district, affirmed frenetic tourism in its rendering. A relatively sedate 1957 painting depicted a more settled State Park vision, where the enfolding arms of the piers encircled docked historic ships and traditional parklike greenery lent cohesiveness (fig. 26).

By 1960, the accelerated pace of urban renewal demolitions in the Bay Area provoked Kortum to replan Hyde Street Pier as a reserve for historical artifacts. He began to collect façades, entire buildings, and furnishings, all of which he hoped to relocate to the pier. He relished the "historical save" represented by each salvage and thought that authentic artifacts would quiet critics who objected to the reconstruction as kitsch. Early in 1962, Kortum struck up a cooperative relationship with the SFRA's property manager "in the matter of saving various relics, large and small, from old time waterfront and commercial San Francisco." He reached a similar agreement with the Acorn Redevelopment Agency in Oakland to obtain the façade of Benny's Bar in 1963. In 1962 he salvaged the Jackson Street Barber Shop interior from the Golden Gateway urban renewal site and shared negatives with the pleased historian of the state beaches office. He approached downsizing maritime businesses, such as Tubbs Cordage Works, which gave the museum a small wooden "gingerbread" office structure.[58]

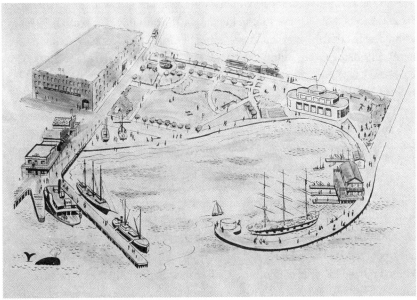

25 A 1954 Hubert Buel ink and pastel drawing of Hyde Street Pier from Jefferson Street and the roof of the Haslett Warehouse. Karl Kortum's historic reconstruction concept had been extended from Gold Rush Plaza to the pier. These pre-Disneyland recreations remained part of Kortum's vision, although in different locations on the waterfront. Kortum pursued this idea with various partners into the early 1970s, but this type of reconstruction was never built for the museum. The sky tram and carousel indicate the growing tourism and entertainment components in Kortum's plans.

26 This ca. 1957 illustration shows that the historic reconstruction had shifted from the Gold Rush Plaza plan to the Hyde Street Pier. The more verdant state park concept was evident, emphasizing the museums, ships, trains, and factories situated amid green lawns and the blue lagoon. Kortum's planning experience in creating the state maritime park prepared him well for his critiques in the late 1960s of what he said were developers' duplicitous park designs in several rebuilding controversies.

In 1970 Karl Kortum's role brokering among shifting public and private jurisdictions on behalf of the maritime historical park took yet another turn. The city told the state that it would be willing to take over the park in 1971 if the SFMM located a developer who could guarantee that there would be no burden to taxpayers. Kortum took up the challenge of finding a private investor capable of remaking the Haslett building and Hyde Street Pier into a profitable commercial destination while respecting the educational value of historical sites. Jack Hayward, president of the Wrather Corporation, a Southern California–based entertainment company, quickly became Kortum's best prospect. In July, Kortum tested Hayward's interest in developing "a kind of compact Williamsburg of the Sea, a much punchier shown [sic] than Mystic Seaport." Ghirardelli Square logged 3.75 million annual visitors; imagine the market if the historical park provided visitors with educational entertainment in addition to eating and shopping, Kortum wrote. This could be "Northern California's answer to Disneyland." In the fall, Kortum suggested to Piero Patri, the other architect he trusted besides Osborne and Stewart, that "Hyde Street Pier be made into an old time San Francisco waterfront street scene," evoking the world's "lusty crossroads" on the waterfront "before the coming of the high rise." Kortum endorsed Dave Nelson's suggestion of a "Disneyland type 'ride' experience" in the Haslett Warehouse, which would whisk visitors "amongst the big and palpable exhibits that we have long collected for the building." This might get him "stricken from the list of the American Association of Museums." Yet why shouldn't the museum sell history to the public, he said, since "precariously, painstakingly, expensively—we have saved the real thing." He hoped that about half of the pier's buildings would be authentic structures.[59]

Ultimately Kortum's 1970 courting among city, state, and private developers floundered, and it was the National Park Service that "took over" the San Francisco Maritime State Historic Park in 1978. From the first glimmer of the expanded waterfront project in 1949, Kortum had incorporated the idea of a reconstructed maritime street with a bustling tourist economy. He approached his first visit to Disneyland, hosted by Hayward in 1970, with an open mind. Kortum refused to juxtapose a purist "historical" construct against a purist "modern" one, just as he refused to exclude commerce and profit from a historical vision. Throughout the negotiations with the Wrather Corporation over Hyde Street Pier and the Haslett building, Kortum admired Hayward's "showman-ship." Kortum enjoyed his tour of Southern California's historically themed tourist attractions. Disneyland entertained him enormously, especially its Pirates of the Caribbean ride. At the same time, it convinced him that the SFMM should not go in the Disney direction advocated by Hayward. Kortum worried about "cute," "camp," and "clichés" and thought it "not necessary to transmogrify historical artifacts into some-thing else." Southern California lacked "the real thing," and so developers there had to "paraphrase," Kortum believed. This approach would not work in San Francisco, "a sophisticated city." Where Southern California's attractions had to create artificial boundaries, the SFMM benefited from two authentic "perimeters"—the "circle of historic ships" and the bay. Kortum's misgivings had nothing to do with commercialism: "I like to see historic projects make money; they are safer that way than in the hands of government." Although the city was ready to put the state park's pier and warehouse out for developer bids, the initiative ultimately failed.[60]

Despite the State Park designation and Kortum's surveillance, the historic waterfront district remained vulnerable to destructive development. A 1968 modernist plan for Hyde Street Pier by the lead architects for Ghirardelli Square (fig. 27) fortified Kortum's determination to work with developers and architects of his own choosing, such as the Wrather Corporation and Patri in 1970. Over the long term, only the transfer of the state historical park to the National Park Service in 1978 made the historic district's boundaries seem more secure.[61]

Karl Kortum's 1940s civic vision of a commercially viable, historically themed maritime district rimmed by "a wall of superb big brick structures" would come to pass—though not in the forms captured by Hubert Buel's original watercolors of Argonaut Square. Kortum navigated the maritime district through municipal, state, and national jurisdictions and through negotiations with private investors like Bill Roth, Leonard Martin, and Jack Hayward, as well as with the city newspapers and Scott Newhall. The prospects for this historical concept varied along with the shifting sands of overlapping public and private waterfront domains—whether the state's Tidelands Oil Royalty windfall, Golden Gateway's urban renewal site clearance, or the port's transfer from state to city.

Without diminishing Bill Roth's "magnificent act of civic rescue," this north waterfront context puts the private sector's uncomplicated "save" of the Ghirardelli factory in perspective. It is true that the private purchase of individual endangered buildings

27 The historical waterfront vision remained vulnerable despite the creation of the state park. This ca. 1968 Donn Emmons design for the Hyde Street Pier obliterated the site's historical elements. Kortum told Scott Newhall that "Emmons doesn't know what to do with a pier" (Kortum to Newhall, August 9, 1968).

HYDE STREET PIER 6

DILLINGHAM CORPORATION DEVELOPERS
WURSTER, BERNARDI, & EMMONS, INC. ARCHITECTS

was symbolically and economically significant. It documented the confidence of investors and showcased the city's range of emerging grassroots historical models, such as Jackson Square in the early 1950s or The Cannery. Kortum hoped Roth's purchase would "prove a turning point in modern day San Francisco history in that it would blunt, divert, and edify the 'high rise' mystique that threatens this part of the city."[62] Height limits and zoning laws set development parameters but were heavily contested and in constant flux. Private investors voluntarily choosing low-rise development and preservation strengthened the historical elements of this larger, living urban puzzle.

What the story of the north waterfront in the late 1940s and 1950s shows, however, is that Roth's purchase of the Ghirardelli complex built on Kortum's previous momentum in establishing the neighborhood's historic character and in fact realized Kortum's plans to mobilize across public domains and private investment. Yes, Kortum said as he dispensed with another Delehanty question about Ghirardelli, the factory "was a marvelous live chocolate plant in the 1950s as we worked on the state park." The factory's real contribution lay more in framing the larger north waterfront district than in its reinvention as a stand-alone historical artifact.[63]

Whatever Karl Kortum's frustrations over government, he placed his faith in the levers of public ownership. Kortum described for Bill Roth in 1962 the qualities of the protective mantle he saw in the public domain. The Ghirardelli redevelopment would benefit, Kortum thought, from its adjacency to the new Victorian Park, which had recently supplemented the protected acreage of Aquatic Park. Writing of Ghirardelli's location, Kortum said: "By reason of being fronted by a park which is increasingly coming into the public eye (and is therefore not liable to be vitiated) this view will never be obscured."[64] Victorian Park preserved the factory's bay view, just as the low Ghirardelli skyline protected the view for others. The public eye, and the public park, helped preserve the waterfront and view as true public resources. The factory, on the other hand, may have been beloved by San Franciscans, but of course, as a factory, it had been closed to the public. A 1963 promotional booklet for the redevelopment announced: "For the first time in a century San Franciscans will be invited to visit historic Ghirardelli Square."[65] Converted to a private retail, dining, and entertainment center, the factory buildings would open to the public at last.

Thus San Francisco's historic maritime park grew through its mutually beneficial relationship with private enterprises such as Jackson Square, Ghirardelli Square, and The Cannery, but it expanded more directly through the SFMM's ability to harness the era's public parks imperatives and navigate the simultaneous growth of port planning, city planning, and federally supported urban renewal clearance. The disparate levers of government jurisdiction ultimately shaped the historically themed outcome for the north waterfront and exercised expansive powers over redevelopment. As a young out-sider in the late 1940s, Kortum successfully manipulated these levers of public ownership, while working closely with private investors like Roth and Martin. He devoted his primary energies to moving waterfront property into the hands of what he judged to be the right city, state, and ultimately federal agencies. His 1956 effort to get the state to buy the Ghirardelli factory might seem far-fetched, but it failed only because the SFMM had to scale back to a smaller budget (that nonetheless included the Haslett Warehouse). Roth's purchase was thus the next strategy, and it worked. Kortum channeled the persuasive powers of ideas and deployed visual renderings to convey them. He used the press to translate his ideas for a historic waterfront district from plastic portfolios to implementation. Kortum made many missteps and harbored misgivings but he stuck to his long-term vision.

Five years after Bill Roth bought the Ghirardelli factory, private developers seeking the protective mantle of civic benevolence for their large-scale, mixed-use waterfront projects met with skepticism, protest, and ultimately lawsuits over the sale of city land. As proposals for new plazas, squares, parks, and high-rises increasingly overlay the waterfront in the 1960s, the private sector's civic activism in providing "open space" amenities as a substitute for public land ownership particularly came under fire. In 1967 one development team of influential San Franciscans proposed a wholesale furniture mart called the San Francisco International Market Center (SFIMC) for the base of Telegraph Hill, offering the public access to rooftop parks in exchange for permission to buy city streets. Their proposal brought the forces of private land assemblage and public exclusion onto a collision course and provoked a citywide reevaluation of how the public's interest was safeguarded in supposedly benevolent, large-scale private investment. At a showing of the model, a woman with tears in her eyes confronted lead developer Roger D. Lapham Jr. (whose businessman father had served as mayor in the 1940s), telling him: "Your father wouldn't do a thing like that to San Francisco."[66] The SFIMC case, which enters this story at the end of the book, in chapter 10, helps mark what had changed in San Francisco development between the 1940s and the 1970s. Karl Kortum took up the 1960s fights with different tools from those he crafted in 1949, but his orientations toward defending and expanding the public domain remained constant and found more allies. His preoccupation with the power of architectural and planning visualization increased to match the acceleration of large-scale redevelopment. Because of his own waterfront planning vision of the 1940s and his background as a photographer, Kortum particularly understood how the growth of visualization professions such as graphic design, rendering, architectural model-making, and photography enabled the increased scope and reach of urban redevelopment and design.

The watercolor plans of Ghirardelli Center and Gold Rush Plaza were two manifestations of the ferment of ideas and experimentation percolating through the Bay Area in the 1940s and 1950s. Each rendering became a force in the history of the waterfront's development; they were motivating documents remembered vividly by many participants. Both represented private visions, but Kortum's stood out for its reliance on the complicated stewardship of public lands, integrated with civic-minded private commercial development. In the twenty-first century, we know that San Francisco ended up with neither a reconstructed Gold Rush Plaza nor a solid cascade of modern towers from the hills to the bay. Karl Kortum's proactive historic waterfront plan illuminates how new hybrid urban renewal models emerged and which actors made them concrete.

"Not Bound by an Instinct to Preserve"
The Modernist Turn toward History

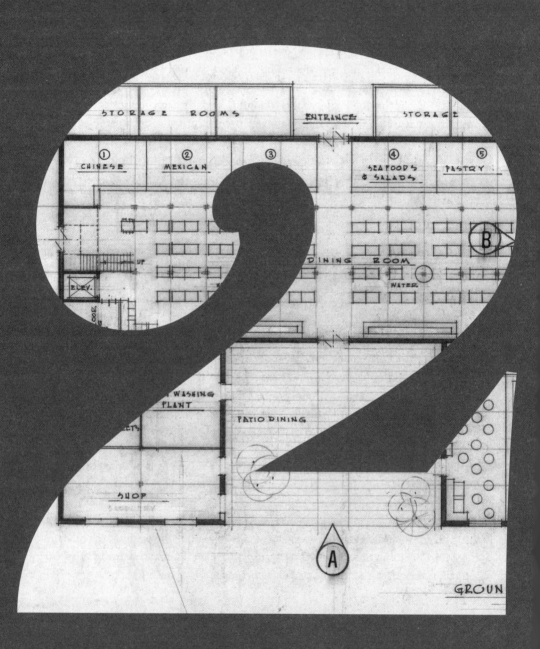

In late September 1958, a crane settled the six-story, two-ton abstract sculpture *Polyvescence* into its temporary site on bustling Fisherman's Wharf. The sculpture was destined for a very different, seemingly distant rural environment—the Paul Masson champagne cellars in Saratoga, California. *Polyvescence* had been commissioned for the fountain of this new modernist winery designed by architect John Bolles and landscape architect Doug Baylis. Once in wine country, the sculpture would preside over a quiet agricultural domain. It would be measured against rustling trees rather than tall buildings. In the meantime, however, *Polyvescence* was the centerpiece of the 1958 San Francisco Art Festival taking place at the wharf.[1] Uncannily, the sculpture's form echoed the masts and sail rigging of nearby ships (fig. 28).

The sculpture's route hinted at the sometimes unlikely paths followed by the ideas and experts remaking the deindustrializing city and its agricultural hinterlands in these decades. As they experimented with new models for urban life, designers like Bolles and Baylis moved from the San Francisco waterfront to Saratoga wineries and Palo Alto shopping malls, while preservationist-historian Karl Kortum moved from a Petaluma chicken farm, around the maritime world in the Navy, to planning San Francisco's waterfront. Such mobility and the connections it generated help explain why a sculpture destined

28 In September 1958, the six-story abstract aluminum sculpture *Polyvescence,* by Gurdon Woods, was settled by crane into its temporary berth at Fisherman's Wharf. After the 12th Annual San Francisco Art Festival the fountain sculpture moved to its permanent home at the Paul Masson Vineyards winery in Saratoga, California. Asking why the sculpture destined for a landlocked modernist winery seemed so much at home amid the old ship masts evoked the mobility of new "urban" design ideas among city, rural, and suburban settings.

for a landlocked modernist winery could be so much at home amid the old ship masts of Fisherman's Wharf in 1958. Little-known regional projects, as much as the international exposure of globetrotting design professionals, fed the experimentation merging old and new on the city's north waterfront. Backstage real estate managers, publicists, sculptors and other consultants—alongside well-known architects—tied together these places regardless of context, borrowing ideas from wineries, ranches, suburban shopping malls, or downtown office towers and plazas. One has to ask what was specifically "urban" about this flow of "urban design" ideas that traveled among farm, suburb, and city.

At the time of *Polyvescence*'s brief sojourn at Fisherman's Wharf, the Ghirardelli factory still filled the neighborhood with the aroma of chocolate. The Maritime Museum had worked to repopulate the wharves with historic ships and attract tourists since 1951, but the north waterfront had not yet gained momentum as an internationally recognized example of urban revitalization. During these years modernists such as Bolles, Baylis, Beverly Willis, Lawrence Halprin, Bill Wurster, John Matthias, and Joseph Esherick undertook architectural projects reworking the city's historic waterfront neighborhoods. These architects garnered the credit for preservation-oriented urban design models such as Ghirardelli Square and The Cannery. By the mid-1960s, San Francisco would inspire other cities juggling aging industrial and warehouse districts with the potential for the same waterfront property to attract skyscrapers and exploit dramatic views. From its inception, the emerging preservation design field centrally featured hybrids of historic and modern.

Yet many other factors and professions besides architecture—outdoor dining, art festivals, fountains, plazas, crafts, wine, international food, retail, interior design, tourism, views, and sculpture—leavened the mix of historical and modern across urban, rural, and suburban contexts. As redevelopment transformed downtown streets, suburban fields, and coastal meadows, the projects and resulting debates multiplied employment for aspiring visual artists, writers, editors, restauranteurs, and designers. These proliferating arts fields gained influence in the Bay Area. By the mid-1960s the region became known as "the designer's city," with architects and allied artists dispersing widely, living and working throughout San Francisco's neighborhoods and suburbs, including this small sampling of addresses: the old waterfront, Noe Valley, Telegraph Hill, North Beach, Berkeley, and Sausalito. San Francisco's north waterfront battles concentrated and publicized these emerging trends.[2]

Hiring modernists to design the 1960s preservation experiments had consequences. Architects such as Halprin and Wurster revealed ambivalence toward the historic city even as the hybrid preservationist projects advanced their careers. The modernist turn toward history also broke open blunt critiques of the capacity of architecture and real estate professionals (for different reasons) to take the lead in redesigning old buildings and neighborhoods. The crossing of so many professional and geographical borders in urban design projects sparked tensions over ideas generated by architects, real estate brokers, historians, and others. The critiques sparked between fields (such as real estate and architecture) were often more articulate and accessible than those sparked within fields. Within professions like architecture and landscape architecture, shared assumptions and stakes allowed much to be taken for granted. Given the common ground of architecture, landscape architecture, and planning, even pointed internal critiques were fundamentally respectful of the professions. Not true for pointed critiques from allied design experts outside of architecture.

Moving closer to the edges of the architecture profession, we see its permeability to real estate perspectives and other "lay" participation in a city on the cusp of a contested high-rise construction boom. The very concept of "laymen" embodied the insider professional architects' perspective that nonarchitects' contributions lacked expertise. An anchor to these waterfront trends integrating historical and modern, Ghirardelli Square's unusually thorough redevelopment process offers a window into urban design experimentation in the early 1960s. The ferment in the portfolios of development advice collected for owner Bill Roth takes us back to 1962, before blueprints were drawn. In the early 1960s, the fluid planning for the city's north waterfront invited many participants with "good ideas" from allied fields. Ghirardelli's research phase equalized the prospects of laypersons' and professional designers' ideas, mingled modest local models with celebrated international ones, and mixed historical and modernist inspirations. Alongside Karl Kortum's 1950s activism on behalf of the historic waterfront, Ghirardelli's redevelopment captured the strategies evident in the Bay Area for rethinking the past and future of cities. The architects Roth hired and others who walked the factory site in 1962 understood the factory's potential as an international example for urban designers. Thanks in part to good publicity, Lawrence Halprin, Bill Wurster, and John Matthias could feel the eyes of their professional colleagues on them.

"LAYMEN AREN'T SUPPOSED TO HAVE SUCH GOOD IDEAS"

At the Ghirardelli factory, different machinery from that used for chocolate production would soon kick in. The Roths' purchase of the Ghirardelli block in the spring of 1962 set in motion systematic consultations with dozens of real estate experts, property managers, and architects to generate concepts for the property. The developer's thick portfolio of proposals and advice letters boosted the chances for ideas to be anointed regardless of their source, and experts from numerous urban arts and renewal fields weighed in on the intriguing rebuilding project. Architect Henrik Bull offered the back-handed compliment to this open process that "laymen aren't supposed to have such good ideas." Some architects might call preservationists, property managers, and other allied renewal professionals "laymen" and downgrade their expertise, but they could still admire the nonarchitects' good ideas for the site's redevelopment.[3]

Roth's business and civic obligations did not diminish his commitment to controlling the Ghirardelli planning, but he required strong on-site management to solicit advice and broker decisions amid contradictory recommendations. Roth brought Warren Lemmon on board from Matson Realties, the company that had handled real estate for the Matson family. Roth charged Lemmon with daily oversight and soon appointed him president of Ghirardelli Square Inc. Roth remained deeply involved in all Ghirardelli decisions even after leaving San Francisco in August 1963 to begin a position in Washington, D.C., as a trade negotiator for the Kennedy (and then Johnson) administration. His confidence in Lemmon's administrative leadership proved well placed. Lemmon, a pragmatic real estate professional, remained unflappable, steady, and loyal to Roth's priorities. While his job immersed him in construction matters, Lemmon approached design-related questions from a nonarchitect's perspective.[4]

When the factory purchase became a possibility in February 1962, Roth consulted with an inner circle of colleagues. He soon took the unusual step of appointing an advisory board, a relatively untested mechanism in private real estate development. For preliminary ideas of what to actually do with the factory, Roth enlisted *Sunset* magazine's Proctor Mellquist and architect John Matthias. The three men had collaborated on past projects. In the late 1950s they had invented a glass-box prototype for inexpensive, lightweight construction that they proposed for manufacture by the Aluminum Corporation (Alcoa). They shared this entrepreneurial history of "kicking around ideas" and finding design "talent to carry on pursuit."[5] Mellquist's editorship of *Sunset* made him a key player in shaping regional design trends as part of the rising tide of popular shelter magazines. Outdoor entertainment, retail, food and restaurants, leisure, interior design, and architecture—Mellquist drew upon vast experience in all of them.

Architect Matthias sketched. He began with photographs of the factory buildings and garden and drew color overlays with ephemeral new forms and accents. These he compiled into a booklet, "Exterior Treatment of Ghirardelli Buildings." Matthias's light touch in these early drawings, working with existing exteriors, would persist when Roth later hired him to design a few signature structures for Ghirardelli Square.[6] Landscape architect Lawrence Halprin later published his own Ghirardelli drawings to document his authorship of core design concepts. But in this brainstorming phase everyone sketched. Editor Mellquist and developer Roth accompanied their memos with illustrations. The exchange of quickly made drawings on loose paper informed their conversations. Professional architects had no monopoly on drawing.[7]

Warren Lemmon recalled, "The first thing Bill Roth desired me to do was contact leading real estate brokers to develop ideas." San Francisco's real estate community was not enthusiastic about Roth's plans. Lemmon sat down "with the top man of each firm," but when realtors heard the proposal to remake factory buildings into a modern retail complex, they expressed "disbelief in the future of the property."[8] Several suggested a major hotel or motel but questioned the viability of a shopping center removed from the downtown core. No broker was willing to handle retail leasing. Roth's disinterest in chain-store tenants further hurt his case with brokers. Roth brushed off disappointment, concluding, "You certainly don't go to real estate people for ideas," at least not new ones.[9] Similarly, lenders were reluctant to finance the project, forcing Roth to rely on family funds longer than he intended.[10]

If soliciting ideas from real estate brokers proved discouraging, Lemmon's subsequent consultations with professional designers opened the door to a stampede of suggestions. Several dozen architects, landscape architects, and planners toured the site with Lemmon and Roth during the spring and summer of 1962.[11] These personal visits and the subsequent advisory memos gave the architects a modest investment in the outcome and some sympathy to the challenges facing the owner—or at least curiosity about how it would all work out. Lemmon hoped for imagination.[12] His open invitation sparked recommendations that ranged from clearing the site to selective demolition to painting the buildings yellow. Most of the options in 1962 involved new construction. Many consultants incorporated partial demolition and kept the high-rise option alive, despite the post-Fontana crusade for a 40-foot height limit. Roth put off that decision, writing that the "question of motel or high-rise apartment, hotel, etc., comes later," after the district's zoning plans were resolved.[13] On the fundamental question of land use, the consultants offered a wide mix of apartments, hotels, offices, retail, entertainment, and open space. There were convergences amid a cacophony of suggestions about specific businesses and design concepts. For example, the restaurant propositions leaned toward the international. Some designers proffered ideas but disavowed interest in handling the risky project. Others made a preliminary bid for the work.

The professional designers generously shared advice even as they relinquished control of credit for those ideas. Strictly speaking, the architects said relatively little about architecture. Instead they offered their views about the site's master plan, potential land use, tenanting, retail possibilities, investment prospects, and event programming. In an application for the project's property manager position, David Pesonen wrote, "You've drawn on the talents of a real galaxy of the Bay Area's architectural lights."[14] This particular constellation of architects did not seem to expect stardom. The absence of commentary about architecture, in favor of development and real estate advice, helps delineate the emergence of new professional design roles in planning these often collaborative, postwar redevelopment complexes. As architects stepped into preservation experiments like Ghirardelli Square, architecture was not always their primary concern.

Few of the architects advising Roth had direct experience in adapting old buildings to modern uses. Campbell & Wong was an exception. They listed among their projects older private homes and restaurants that they had "remodeled," as well as North Harbor in Alameda, which they called "a major planning project" reusing warehouses.[15] Although San Francisco design firms recently had begun moving their offices into former warehouses and factories, they rarely branched out to adaptive reuse for clients outside Jackson Square. Most modernist firms Lemmon spoke with at least understood the pressures to retain the old Ghirardelli buildings, even if they didn't agree. Their advisory letters cited regional examples of renovations carried out by others. Warren Lemmon even consulted with clearance-oriented developers to better understand the preservation options. Fontana Towers, as the neighborhood's embodiment of destructive high-rises, was the foil against which preservation success would be measured. But Fontana's developer, Paul Hammarberg of the Albert-Lovett Corporation, possessed useful studies of the Ghirardelli block because of his company's prior interest in buying and developing it. Lemmon tapped into that expertise.[16]

Following these consultations with numerous designers, Bill Roth hired Wurster, Bernardi & Emmons (WB&E) as the lead architects but prioritized "diversity of architecture" so "Ghirardelli Square did not end up as simply a project which was the hallmark of one talented person."[17] And Roth did, in fact, diversify. Once he judged that WB&E's plans "architecturally needed a little more jazz," he invited his longtime collaborator John Matthias to design several of the plaza buildings.[18] Architect Rex Goode was given charge of the kiosk to enhance the square's lighter, more playful aspects. Matthias, grateful for Bill Wurster's accommodation of this potentially awkward arrangement, emphasized that "The situation would have been unpleasant if he had not been so gracious about it." This confirmed Roth's expectation that Wurster "would not wish to erect a monument to himself."[19] The choice of architecture firm streamlined the selection of a landscape architect, since two equally respected landscape architects worked often with Bill Wurster. Both Lawrence Halprin and Thomas Church walked the factory site in 1962. Church's small office produced more formal plans; Halprin's larger firm emphasized the power of design to generate interaction and social vitality. Ultimately, the fact that Lawrence Halprin & Associates shared a renovated warehouse at 1620 Montgomery Street with WB&E gave Halprin the edge. Lemmon believed physical proximity would allow for a dynamic "working out" of the Ghirardelli concepts.[20]

Roth's Ghirardelli Square Advisory Board formalized the mixed input of associated professional fields alongside architects; the participation of Justin Herman, director of the SFRA, particularly marked the permeability of the preservationist model to advice from urban renewal and high-rise advocates. Herman played a role in narrowing the land-use options for the Ghirardelli site. Retail and entertainment, infused with arts and culture themes, took an early lead. When Herman proposed an Italian cultural center motif, Lemmon broke with his usually neutral tone to write Roth:

Justin Herman has come up with what I believe is the best idea yet for utilization of the property. He suggests that we develop the block as an Italian cultural center. He sees it as a natural extension of the North Beach area and feels that much of the Italian character of this area has been lost within recent years and could be recaptured in the Ghirardelli block. The block could be developed as a center for all types of Italian merchandise, such as automobiles, clothing, furniture, gifts, food, liquor, etc. The center could also feature Italian restaurants and bars, art galleries, and an opera nightspot.

Lemmon tested the Italian concept on others. Independently, Proctor Mellquist, architects John Wiese, Charles (Chuck) Bassett, and John Woodbridge of Skidmore, Owings & Merrill (SOM), art appraiser George Frizzell, and two Bank of America executives all counseled that the theme seemed narrow. Of this group only Herman and Mellquist would join the advisory board. All saw wisdom in building on Italian connections through the Ghirardelli company name, its employees, and the North Beach neighborhood. Several suggested expanding from Italian to Mediterranean.[21] Herman, fresh from including a Japanese Cultural Center in the bulldozed Western Addition urban renewal district, saw no need for feasibility studies.[22]

Although interest in an Italian theme for Ghirardelli quickly atrophied, the support for an international, commercial approach to arts and culture took off. Programming ideas that won favor included the "neglected art—dining" (especially at the international restaurants still relatively unfamiliar to American consumers), art galleries, outdoor performances of music and dance, design-oriented retail tenants, a radio station, a theater, a historical museum, and international shops emphasizing crafts.[23] Architects contributed as much to elaborating these development concepts as did the bankers, retail experts, property managers, and arts executives.

THE SUBURBAN, RURAL, AND REGIONAL ROOTS OF URBAN DESIGN

When modernists such as Lawrence Halprin and William Wurster reworked the historic city, they attracted design journal coverage of experimental renovations like Ghirardelli Square. In press interviews, architects mostly credited internationally significant examples for inspiration, particularly the 1962 Seattle World's Fair and Expo58 (the Brussels World's Fair).[24] For this generation, Copenhagen's Tivoli Gardens served as another resource for festive urban entertainment integrating arts, dining, open space, and commerce. Tivoli often slipped into Halprin's suggestions for Ghirardelli and elsewhere. To achieve outdoor lighting that was "gay and jolly and full of liveliness," he recommended "pinpoint lights of the type which have been used in the Tivoli Gardens in Copenhagen."[25] Roth and Leonard Martin each cited European cities for layering contemporary structures into the historic urban fabric.[26]

However, the era's new urban design ideas crossed rural, suburban, and urban borders in provocative ways and with more impact than international crossings. The binder of advisory letters regarding Ghirardelli Square found inspiration close to home in local models like Jackson Square, the Union Street stores, and Sausalito's Village Fair. Regional California cases far outnumbered the international ones. In 1962 the Old Barn at Stanford University in Palo Alto and Mokolumne Hill in gold country provided the most up-to-date lessons for modernists experimenting with remaking local landmark buildings for dining, shopping, and tourism. More surprising was the inclusion of local suburban shopping centers, few of which had evident cultural or historical themes. They primarily offered management and ownership strategies.

Warren Lemmon's investigation of property management models tipped increasingly toward shopping malls. Lemmon scrutinized property managers more closely than architects. He visited recommended sites to assess the management capabilities of his correspondents. Ghirardelli's advisors praised the Town & Country Shopping Center in Palo Alto for its small shops, quality control, and individuality. The center's manager, Al Waller, kept the door open to consulting for Ghirardelli "on an after-hour basis." In early 1963, Lemmon spoke at length with Paul Hulderman, president of the merchants' association for the Fifth Avenue Shopping Center in Scottsdale, Arizona. Hulderman explained that after the shopping center launched in 1952 he had opened an "Indian" arts store there in 1958. The center sought to add small "shops with individual character in both architecture and merchandise" to the existing street. Hulderman described the center's leasing and publicity and its decision to coordinate rather than control tenants. He saw promise in having "working artists and craftsmen on the premises where they could be seen in productive work." Hulderman also recommended owner-operated businesses so tenants could "talk on equal terms with customers." This meant that "friendships were easily developed between the merchandiser and customer, an important factor in building business by word of mouth and in developing repeat business."[27]

Lemmon also met with Robert Powers of the Nut Tree in Vacaville, on Highway 40 between the Bay Area and Sacramento. The Nut Tree offered Ghirardelli an example of what Proctor Mellquist called "absolute quality control."[28] By owning all of the businesses, the developer dictated merchandise and design quality, along with everything else.

As usual, Lemmon both asked for advice and inquired whether the Powers family might consider renting space in the Ghirardelli block. Robert Powers declined the latter but offered plenty of the former. The Nut Tree was a popular luncheon destination for businessmen and shoppers. Its facilities included the well-regarded restaurant, an imports shop, a toy store, a train ride, and other activities. Business was good; Powers planned a renovation, more Tivoli-type elements, and a motel. Lemmon and Roth sought assurance that the skepticism of San Francisco's real estate community was misplaced. Powers thought that the north waterfront could draw enough foot traffic to sustain retail. After all, Fisherman's Wharf "had become a great success despite unattractive and poorly built structures, generally mediocre restaurants and services and a less than out-standing water view." Provided Ghirardelli had "high quality, interesting shops," parking, and "outstanding management" and made an "effective promotional effort," Powers believed it could succeed. Ghirardelli, he predicted, could "commercialize on the historical background of California and the West." Powers (and others) criticized the loose management at the popular Los Angeles Farmer's Market, where diverse concession-based rentals resulted in uneven quality.[29] "Big modern" shopping centers such as Portland's Lloyd's Center and Fashion Square in Orange County received endorsement in the Ghirardelli research binders for their "variety of activities."[30]

Ghirardelli's developer investigated adding popular entertainment alongside more elevated cultural offerings. Lemmon visited the American Heritage Wax Museum in Scottsdale with great interest. Scottsdale merchant Hulderman, however, cautioned Lemmon that wax works eroded any "snob appeal" and "draws large numbers of youngsters and 'tourist gawkers.'" These customers did not spend much money in nearby shops and discouraged "discriminating buyers." Lemmon also tried to locate an old or new carousel for the Ghirardelli property. Roth and his advisors attempted to galvanize a fresh model and not merely lure tenants from other commercial centers. They tested out the concept of a Museum of the City of San Francisco. None of these particular tenants materialized, but the discussions included popular as well as refined institutions.[31]

Roth and the advisory board believed restaurants and entertainment would replace department stores as the main draws to this renovated factory at the downtown's northern waterfront edge. The emerging role of food, ethnic and international dining, outdoor eating, and entertainment pinpoints one of Ghirardelli's contributions to urban revitalization trends of the 1960s, one that straddles the historical and modern divide. The future outlines of urban America can be seen in the advisory board's careful discussions, of, say, Japanese restaurants and intimate bars. A few decades later, the restaurant phenomenon became such a prevalent redevelopment strategy that it was taken for granted, but in 1963 it was still novel.

The largely forgotten local and suburban contexts for understanding this particular "urban" planning innovation are worth excavating. Food and drink had a longer, organic history on the north waterfront. Before neighboring Fisherman's Wharf became what critics called overcommercialized and inauthentic, it supplied carry-out fried fish, crab in season, and Italian-style fish stew (cioppino) to hungry cannery workers, visitors, and fishermen. In the 1930s a few restaurants began to move into the wharf area, including Exposition Fish Grotto, built in 1937. Other restaurant entrepreneurs remodeled existing structures, such as the tile-roofed Booth Fish Packing House and Market and the Crab Boat Owners Association building. The fish stalls on Taylor Street, a few blocks from the Ghirardelli factory, were slowly taken over by restaurants until the older street scene was obliterated. Saloons crowded the district as well. The Buena Vista Café at the corner of Hyde and Beach Streets was another "old-time" dining destination, serving meals and a late-night atmosphere. By 1967 there would be too many restaurants to mention by name in reviews of the transformed north waterfront district. In contrast, there was little retail tradition to build on.[32]

By U.S. standards, San Francisco claimed an unusually complex history of ethnic restaurants, whether Mexican, Italian, Chinese, or other Pacific Rim. The orientation of leading figures Mellquist, Roth, and Leonard Martin toward food culture also relied on the agricultural history of the state, including the growth of the Napa and Sonoma wine regions, the availability and popularity of fresh produce, and the growing food and wine tourism. California's climate favored outdoor living, and contemporary residential designs emphasized the close relationship between indoors and outdoors.

Ghirardelli Square propelled these ingredients into an urban revitalization model. Mellquist explained to Roth that eating outdoors could be one of the great draws of the Ghirardelli complex either through restaurant seating (sheltered from the San Francisco wind) or through a new collective seating concept that would soon become popularized as the food court. Mellquist assumed that food-court dining was unfamiliar in 1962, even to a restaurant aficionado like Roth. "There might be a variety of small places for inexpensive eating, including eating out-of-hand," Mellquist carefully explained. "You walk your meal to a bench or table."[33]

For dining inspiration in 1962, the Ghirardelli advisory letters added the obscure, remodeled "Old" Stanford Winery to the architects' internationally known touchstones of Tivoli, Brussels, and the Seattle Fair's Food Circus. This Palo Alto example of an early food court featured restaurants of "various nationalities" in a reinvented historic building. Both Mellquist and mall manager Al Waller worked within a few miles of Stanford University; each invoked the winery, also known as the Stanford Barn, as a model.[34] In December 1960, Stanford University and the San Francisco architectural firm of John S. Bolles announced an agreement to redevelop the 1880s campus winery into a business complex that would "preserve the old building's charm." They planned to restore the landmark's exterior and rebuild the interior for a business and arts center accommodating a bank branch, a brokerage firm, specialty retail boutiques, an art gallery, and a shared dining courtyard with hundreds of seats serving ten restaurants (fig. 29). Food led the way; the Bolles office labeled this project file "International Cuisine—Stanford Barn." When the complex opened in December 1961, the restaurants included Mexican, Chinese, Italian, seafood, and two barbecue restaurants, as well as a salad bar, rotisserie, donut shop, and soda fountain. One editorial connected the international restaurants to the university's educational mission to foster "understanding among peoples and their ways."[35]

The architect served as the developer in this commercial preservation venture, leasing the property for thirty-five years and investing a half-million dollars in the site. Stanford had long hoped to save the building, but "previously the cost [had] been deemed excessive." Now, however, barns and wineries had recently acquired cosmopolitan marketing appeal through their historical associations with rural, agricultural life.[36] The Stanford building exploited that niche through contrast with its neighbors. It stood between the Stanford Shopping Center and the Stanford Medical Center—two new landmarks in a booming suburb. The confusion over whether this structure should be called a winery or a barn was due to the fact that it had spent time as both.

The Ghirardelli Square Advisory Board understood that the suburban Stanford Winery shared design elements with their project that went beyond the business model emphasizing dining and the arts. Both sites were known locally as rare relics of the pre-earthquake, nineteenth-century built environment. Although dwarfed by the Ghirardelli factory, in Palo Alto the winery was described relative to its low-rise, suburban setting as "massive" (fig. 30).[37] Like The Cannery, it had walls that were two feet thick. The Barn sat at an angle to the grid layout that was imposed later, as did the Woolen Mill at the Ghirardelli complex. Bolles left little of the interior; Roth's designers similarly erased Ghirardelli's interiors. The suburban barn emphasized landscaping and sculpture, which Ghirardelli would, too. The Palo Alto building's atmosphere and "charm" in

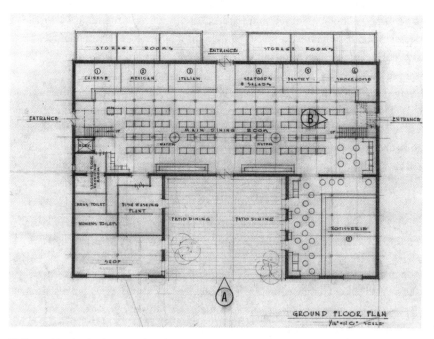

29 The multiuse redevelopment plans for Stanford University's Old Barn were labeled "International Cuisine." The October 1959 Bolles plans showed the early "international" food court design. Food vendors were aligned along the top of the plan and on the bottom right, while they shared seating in an indoor dining room and outdoor patio. This obscure suburban project was typical of the local experiments Ghirardelli Square's developers investigated.

STANFORD LANDMARK TO BE DEVELOPED
This is the Stanford winery at Quarry and Welch roads.

BANK ENTRANCE
This will be the main entrance to the proposed Wells Fargo Bank American Trust Company branch. Developers plan to preserve most of the winery's original exterior.

COURTYARD DINING PLANNED
Diners at the international restaurant may eat in the winery courtyard on the west side of the building.

30 By suburban scale, the Old Stanford Barn was seen as "massive"—a pre-earthquake structure that sat at an irregular angle to the later street grid, like Ghirardelli's Woolen Mill building. The barn's sophisticated suburban redesign betrayed its rural roots. Architect John S. Bolles's firm conducted influential waterfront planning studies for the San Francisco Port Commission at the same time that it was designing the Old Stanford Barn, modern suburban shopping malls, and the Paul Masson winery in rural Saratoga.

31 Renderings of the Stanford Barn's refurbished "old structure" released to the newspapers in December 1960 emphasized the courtyard atmosphere and outdoor international dining. Adjacent to the new Stanford Shopping Center, the suburban redevelopment was also minutes from *Sunset* magazine's offices.

publicity materials rested heavily on the appealing interior courtyard, together with exterior views of the irregular, multibuilding complex, brick walls, and gas lamp replicas—much as would be the case for Ghirardelli Square (fig. 31).[38] The Barn's local status as "an attractive addition to the Stanford Shopping Center" also enhanced its relevance for Ghirardelli's advisory board.[39]

The movements of Halprin and Bolles between Palo Alto and San Francisco deepened the connections among the new suburban Stanford Shopping Center, the Barn, and the urban Ghirardelli site. Before working on Ghirardelli, Halprin had been the landscape architect for the 1955 Stanford Shopping Center. Halprin pioneered in suburban mall design throughout the United States. He was recognized for the novel, "integrated landscaping" of the Old Orchard regional shopping center, which opened on Chicago's north side in October 1956.[40] Just prior to the Stanford Barn commission, Bolles designed the Macy's department store in the adjacent Stanford center. The Stanford Macy's was one in a string of modernist retail commissions and shopping-mall designs in northern California that Bolles worked on in the 1950s.[41] Bolles also had experience in California's burgeoning wine tourism industry, having designed the modernist, rural Paul Masson winery at Saratoga.

But of all the regional interests tying modernist designers to historical projects around 1962, John Bolles's deep involvement in San Francisco's waterfront planning mattered most to understanding the context of the Ghirardelli factory. During these years Bolles rapidly became the "go-to man for the planning department and the port" as San Francisco's leadership attempted to get ahead of the port's economic difficulties and channel the growing investor interest in building on waterfront land. For the San Francisco Port Authority, Bolles authored a series of ambitious waterfront plans in the "modernist mold." He joined with Ernest Born and Esther Born to write the sweeping "Embarcadero City" plan (1959) and *A Plan for Fisherman's Wharf* (1961)—the study that angered the San Francisco Maritime Museum with its disturbing erasure of the museum's historic state maritime park. These studies culminated in Bolles's most wide-ranging and widely read report, *Northern Waterfront Plan: San Francisco* (1968). Although never implemented, these proposals fundamentally shaped public debate.[42] Bolles's waterfront planning role looped his modernist-historical experiments from wineries to suburb to urban waterfront. *Polyvescence* settled in a little more deeply on the wharf, among the ship masts.

In the 1961 Fisherman's Wharf study, Bolles and the Borns eschewed sentimental treatment of old commercial structures to focus on open space, restaurants, and sidewalk cafés. They sketched concepts that would soon emerge in Ghirardelli Square and, twenty years later, in renewal projects like Baltimore's Inner Harbor. Their description of a little plaza in front of the Taylor Wharf restaurants forecast the mix that would become hallmarks of urban waterfront revitalization: "Many festivals are staged and traditions are celebrated with merry and appreciative audiences. Every day is a festival at the Wharf, so much to see, so much to do." Although the restaurant buildings had once been "simple unaffected structures," they had become "self-acclaiming and bristling with brash signs of every color and description jutting from walls and roofs." Several restaurants, though "well designed," were "engulfed in the morass of mediocrity." Although maritime history had significance to Bolles and the Borns in 1961, it barely touched their design concepts. They did not propose stripping off the commercial curio excess to reveal the "simpler" structures beneath. Nor did they suggest historical re-creations, as had Karl Kortum with regard to Gold Rush Plaza. Instead they recommended a modular, organized waterfront structure to replace the haphazard restaurants. Restaurants would be located on the upper floors, leaving the ground level open for views and direct connection with the water. Karl Kortum's "historic ship Balclutha" earned their sole "historical" reference.[43]

As modernists worked more frequently with historical neighborhoods and buildings, preservation-oriented redevelopment would soon have a track record, but at this early stage practitioners were still testing language for measuring success and even just describing it. *Architectural Forum*'s correspondent Allan Temko scoured the West Coast for stories of national interest. He admired Bolles's "scheme for refurbishing the old Winery on the campus, whose interior will be transformed into a bank and restaurant while the lovely exterior remains the same: this is another excellent candidate, I think, for the rebuilding section." By contrast, Temko thought Bolles's effort to relate Stanford Shopping Center's modern Macy's building to the historic campus failed, except for its "big entrance arch which attempts to establish 'continuity' with the old Romanesque structures on the campus."[44] Architect John Campbell was a principal in Campbell & Wong—the only firm in the Ghirardelli development binder with experience in rehabilitation work. Campbell thought the Barn lacked "sensitivity to the nature of the building in the ultimate use." The modernists' focus remained on enhancing interior courtyards and "charming" exteriors, without reservations over gutting interiors.[45] Other items from the new preservation vocabulary of these years dotted correspondence and reviews. Campbell sent a glowing report to *Forum* about the "refurbished" Gold Rush town Mokelumne Hill but received an unenthusiastic reply. Temko wrote to his *Forum* editors: "I happen to consider Campbell more decorator than architect. But we would be wise to cover this project. Make a dead town into a going venture, rather than museum."[46] In 1960, modernist architects experimenting with historical material were potentially diminished as "decorators" or refurbishers.

Bill Roth was already familiar with Mokelumne Hill, being one of its investors. The concept for turning the Gold Rush town into a tourist destination embodied the range of historical inventions that appealed to modernist designers at the time. In 1961, Warren Lemmon became president of the company behind the restoration (Leger Limited) in an effort to put the project on sound financial footing. The core property, Hotel Leger, had a strong run when it opened in the summer of 1960. It filled its thirteen air-conditioned rooms with customers who appreciated "the lavish clutter of Victorian memorabilia" (figs. 32 and 33). Only two and a half hours from San Francisco, the town offered "a treasure of virtually untouched 100-year-old buildings." The investors anticipated "a new and stronger interest in our past history; a trend even now gaining momentum." Leger Limited owned several other buildings, including the 1854 Odd Fellows Hall, which Campbell had purchased "just in case any one pulled it down."

Campbell had visited Mokelumne Hill for twenty-five years before buying a house there. When the hotel was offered for sale, the concept of a resort crossed his mind, and Campbell consulted with friends Irmine Droeger, who worked in the city as a civil engineer, and interior designer/art director Peter Rocchia. They founded Leger Limited in August 1959 with twenty-five friends as stockholders. Many of the investors, also designers, stayed at the hotel. Droeger became the hotel manager.

Campbell incorporated his affection for the "untouched" buildings into a modern sensibility. One local resident challenged the accuracy of the restoration, asking, "Who ever heard of a bright blue house in the Gold Rush?" Campbell replied, "We don't want to restore the town exactly as it was. We could, for instance, put our barman into a striped vest and string tie, but it would be awfully corny. We want to preserve the historical features of the place, but also bring it back to life. The blue house looks wonderful next

32 The 1959 development of historic Hotel Leger and related "ruins" in Gold Rush–era Mokelumne Hill marked another project in the regional network of connections with San Francisco architects, planners, interior designers, and Jackson Square. Here architect John Campbell's two original collaborators sit outside the hotel in 1960. Peter Rocchia, left, was an interior designer, Irmine Droeger a "draftsman" in 1959, when they founded Leger Limited. Bill Roth and Warren Lemmon became involved in the venture to renovate the town's historic properties into a modern tourist resort. The Leger project failed in late 1963, just as Roth and Lemmon began demolition at the Ghirardelli complex.

33 The Hotel Leger's interior rooms and exterior re-created a Gold Rush "period" effect, evidencing little melding of old and new by the modernists in charge. The thirteen bedrooms were "redecorated in a Victorian style" but with modern bathrooms. This photo could have appeared in an antiques magazine of the day. Outside (see fig. 32), the porch's simple spherical lighting fixtures were the only modern design elements. By March 1960 the project generated interest in design magazines. Working on Ghirardelli Square, Lemmon and Roth never mentioned this failed investment in Gold Country tourism.

to the yellow hotel." They planned a unique motel property, The Ruins, which would be sited amid derelict structures without disturbing them. With Lemmon in charge, they considered opening a museum in town, adding historical attractions, and expanding the hotel property with new construction.[47]

Whereas revitalizing a historic town with untouched Gold Rush buildings appealed to architects and their friends, Mokelumne Hill did not mature as a viable tourist attraction. The hotel could not sustain occupancy. In 1962, midway through the third summer, the board of directors decided to close the hotel that fall and liquidate the company's assets. When Lemmon failed to find buyers for the buildings (although he did sell the liquor license), he told the investors to write off their losses. There was "currently not a market" for such a property, he concluded.

Lemmon speculated about the limitations to what had seemed such a promising tourism and design concept. Although central to the network of Gold Rush towns, Mokelumne Hill was poorly located in relation to modern highways. He added other observations that served as lessons: "insufficient activity and historic points of interest in the immediate vicinity of the town; too small an operation to attract skilled professional management and talented hotel personnel and insufficient corporate capitalization."[48] San Francisco designers continued to purchase homes in the area over the following years for their private retreats from the city; architect Beverly Willis snapped up an 1855 schoolhouse in Volcano in 1964. Jack Johannsen, a department store display designer, bought a former commercial property on Mokelumne Hill's main street and decorated it with a "camp" hodgepodge of memorabilia (including a sign on the ceiling that read "Julia Child Cooked Here"). But for Roth and Lemmon in 1962, the bottom line was that Mokelumne Hill was failing just as Ghirardelli Square was getting off the ground. For Ghirardelli they considered, but rejected, a hotel or motel.[49]

The general public may not have been ready to "wine & dine with the Argonauts," but Bay Area investors and modernist designers gained relevant experience with these hybrid historic projects in places like Mokelumne Hill, Palo Alto's Old Barn, and the San Francisco waterfront. The Ghirardelli advisors drew upon these local models in making what became a waterfront revitalization template. Roth and Lemmon were particularly optimistic about the prospects for an urban center focused on unique retail, restaurants, bars, specialty foods, and dining-related enterprises. Roth proposed attracting "interesting small shops from various areas of the City." Typical of his close involvement, he explicitly envisioned an ice cream parlor, coffee store, wine shop, bakery, delicatessen and sandwich shop, gourmet shop, liquor shop, and several bars— "small, intimate. Perhaps one with early San Francisco atmosphere." Roth specified businesses and described the food "(Danish open sandwiches—select own makings)." He favored "international" restaurants, proposing French provincial, Japanese, and Mexican ("with guitar"). A fish store was an obvious choice on the waterfront. And he liked the food court concept. "Would it be possible to have a common indoor-outdoor courtyard with tables where food from specialty stores around could jointly serve their specialties? Coffee and rolls; wine and cheese; sandwiches; drinks; etc." Roth included his sketch of a "cooking utensil store" built around a functioning kitchen where cooking lessons could be offered. This unit would be tied to a restaurant. He floated hosting an annual San Francisco Food Fair modeled on the Dijon Food Fair and housing a California Wine Institute Museum. Roth devoted similarly exhaustive attention to the other tenant categories, whether retail, garden-oriented, or services.[50]

In the early 1960s, when developers applied the term "international" to dining or retail, they intended to evoke a rich diversity of world cultures. Usually that diversity exerted an appealing and specifically urban counterforce against the supposedly homogenizing impact of consumer options in U.S. suburbs. International crafts and food signaled a cutting-edge revitalization strategy, one newly emerging in large-scale projects and urban districts like San Francisco's north waterfront.[51]

When critics used the term "international" to describe *architecture* during the same years, however, it carried the opposite meaning. Applied to architecture in the 1950s or 1960s, "international" suggested a homogenizing force. For advocates of the International Style in architecture, the term did not suggest diversity, history, or culture but in fact denied the same.[53] For critics such as Roth's Ghirardelli advisor Karl Kortum, the International Style of architecture pointed to an insidiously universalizing design influence perpetrated by modernists like Larry Halprin and Bill Wurster. When Kortum described architecture as "international," he invoked the homogenizing threat modernists posed to cities; he had no interest in accurately describing design genres. This fact that the international style in dining and the international style of architecture had opposite meanings within the language of urban revitalization is suggestive. It signals that the modernist architects who engaged with the historic urban context, working collaboratively on larger projects and increasingly with "laypersons," did so from a markedly different professional vantage point than when they built isolated new structures from the ground up.

ARCHITECTS "'BEING CREATIVE' AT YOUR EXPENSE"

Because the Ghirardelli redevelopment process invited multiple perspectives from professional designers and allied fields, the portfolio of revitalization ideas was laced with strong opinions. Particularly electric were the blunt attacks by museum director Karl Kortum and others on the creative capacity of architects. These critiques implicitly drew attention to an unspoken but obvious fact of design practice in 1962: there was not yet a consulting niche for preservationist design rooted in a different discipline from architecture or in its own, new discipline. When modernist architects were hired to design the early "historic" renewal projects, they often took charge of the overlapping architectural, planning, and urban design dimensions. In the case of Ghirardelli Square, Karl Kortum and David Pesonen's advice to Bill Roth laid the foundation for a preservationist critique of how modernist architectural practice related to urban form.

Kortum and Pesonen approached the professional design fields based on their leadership of development fights and civic environmentalist crusades. A graduate of the Berkeley forestry program, Pesonen had edited Sierra Club publications, worked for an assemblywoman, and was spearheading (with Jean Kortum, Karl Kortum's wife) the ultimately successful early 1960s campaign against a proposed Pacific Gas and Electric nuclear power plant at Bodega Bay in Sonoma County. Kortum's planning education came from founding the Maritime Museum and state park and from his earlier Petaluma battle (also successful) to reroute Highway 101. Karl Kortum, David Pesonen, and Jean Kortum represented the direct, dynamic connections in the Bay Area between campaigns to preserve the natural and urban built environments.[53] Karl Kortum and Pesonen offered the engaged "laymen's" advice Roth invited during this fluid phase when the Ghirardelli development process was the most susceptible to their recommendations. They took up the same rebuilding agenda as the architects (Pesonen by throwing his name into the hat for property manager) and articulated why the modernists were failing in this job.

Kortum's antagonism toward architects was provoked by the cross-over of modernists like Halprin and Wurster to revitalize historic sites rather than by inherent opposition between the two sides of renewal and preservation. Kortum and Pesonen separately counseled Bill Roth that architects and landscape architects simply should not be entrusted with historical projects. They did so in private letters, and neither man minced words. Pesonen, hoping to be hired to work on Ghirardelli, remained more measured. Kortum rarely held back, but in these memos he was especially unrestrained. In August 1963, having reviewed Halprin's preliminary designs, Kortum wrote to Roth immediately:

I commented on another aspect of this phenomenon in a letter to you last year—on the curse of the architect's (landscape architect's) "being creative" at your expense. Well, these fellows are so seldom creative that it is pitiful. But they have this ego-involvement in the word, and they have to strain away at it, rejecting everything that is good in the past in the process. Their almost uniform failure—because so damned few are really talented—moves me to contempt and to a kind of rage when they start to spoil something as fine as the Ghirardelli property.[54]

For Kortum, it was precisely because architects held pretentions about their singular artistic originality that he judged their lack of creativity to be contemptuous. In an earlier memo, he had written to Roth, "Most architects that I've encountered have this idea that they are on center stage and it all has to come out of their own noggin."[55]

David Pesonen, for his part, diplomatically conceded that architects possessed artistry and originality in new construction, which he argued was their natural turf. As part of his application for the Ghirardelli manager position, Pesonen reviewed Lemmon's development portfolio. "Ordinarily architects take on jobs to build new buildings," he wrote. Regarding the factory site, most of the designers had advised tearing out chunks and filling in the holes with contemporary buildings. In doing so, architects missed the point of remaking a historical place. "If we grant that the Ghirardelli property poses a very tough and subtle problem of restoration—respectful restoration—then we are presented with a problem that architects are little better equipped to cope with than anyone else who has a sense of the future and the past." Pesonen allowed architects capacity for talent, but he reached the same conclusion as Kortum. Ghirardelli "must be approached from a direction which is just exactly the opposite from the route an architect would normally take—no matter how splendid—and isolated—an achievement his arrival might be. It has to be approached backwards, hat, not scalpel, in hand."[56] Architects' training made them incapable of effectively reimagining a historical site such as the Ghirardelli property, or the north waterfront.

Halprin's first plan for Ghirardelli confirmed Kortum's worst fears. "I have long thought that Larry was out to prove something in this project." Halprin had succeeded in proving that he was "in rebellion against everything that the Ghirardelli buildings stand for. With determination, almost brutality, he has used the style of architecture I call 'world's-fair-hasty' throughout. He has *forced* the site to accept it." Kortum added that "it is not even particularly good modern-world's-fair architecture."[57] Kortum claimed that Halprin applied the generic trends of landscape architecture to this unique historical site and turned architects' supposed world's fair sophistication against them. Ghirardelli Square would look like an international airport or the top of a garage anywhere in the world. He detected similarly forced themes in Proctor Mellquist's draft of the brochure. "I'll be damned if I can see any reason to pursue the insipid, trees-planted-in-big-tubs, let-us work-at-being-gay theme," given the site's rich historical qualities.[58]

Pesonen believed that the rendering submitted by Wurster, Bernardi & Emmons with their proposal encapsulated the risks of hiring a modernist architectural firm.

The clue to this wrong conception of the Ghirardelli character is not only in the building proposed but in its situation. The motel is bounded by what appear to be expressways. No beach, no maritime museum, no sense of the shape of a living page in San Francisco's character that is rapidly developing in this micro-region. The Balclutha, Thayer and Palmer—the Hazlett Railroad Museum—the Victorian Park—all appear to be dim and vaguely troubling sattelites [sic] to the property, not integral parts of the area. And the unduplicated relation to the bay is utterly ignored. . . . I know this was not their intention (which is why the rendering is so revealing), but one might conclude that the place shown is any other block, from the corfields [sic] of Kansas to the South of Market—not one of the most remarkable urban settings anywhere in the world.[59]

Pesonen's critique paid tribute to the realization of Kortum's 1949 vision of a maritime cultural district. The architects' rendering missed the interrelated factory, museum, and park sites and their rootedness in the historic waterfront. The bay provided the district's underlying logic. Without the context of the bay or the historic district, Ghirardelli could be "any other block." The architects had not grasped that Ghirardelli "is the focus of an urban region, and it should be handled carefully to respect the place it occupies in that region. . . . Development of the Ghirardelli property is not simply a problem of architecture; it is a problem in city planning." Architects regularly engaged in master planning for clients. Yet, Pesonen noted, "even the brightest stars can have their blind spots."[60]

Kortum and Pesonen staked out this contentious dialogue with the modernists like Halprin and Wurster who were gaining professional recognition for historical projects. Understanding the need for commercial redevelopment, Kortum and Pesonen prioritized the site's long-term profitability. Pesonen predicted that "whoever finally threads his ideas through the property will have to tie them to the building code and the accounts ledger." Of Ghirardelli, Pesonen concluded, "A person would have to get the feel of every brick, pillar and cornice in his bones to be ready to begin changing it." Change was desirable. Could modernists offer solutions sensitive to the planning impact on the historic city? As far as Kortum and Pesonen were concerned, the answer was a blunt no. Allied preservationists, environmentalists, and historians such as themselves offered the closest match for the job.[61]

The historical view implied a rootedness and "character" that would not just survive changes but dictate them. Like Roth's architecture and real estate consultants, Pesonen and Kortum appreciated the need for altered buildings, new uses, and secure finances. But their preoccupation with historical values gave them a different starting point. Architects and real estate consultants saw development decisions as arising from transient neighborhood factors and external laws governing height limits and zoning, or from a reservoir of personal design talent. For example, Lemmon reported that "Mr. Waller believes that the property should not be tied up for a period of more than ten years on the use initially given to it—that the ultimate use for the property as values continue to rise and the character and development of the area changes, may be substantially different from what would appear to be a desirable use today."[62] In contrast, when Pesonen and Kortum calculated the bottom line, they argued for the site's land use based not on property values or municipal ordinances but rather on its relationship to local history and the public interest.

Karl Kortum loved towing decrepit, obsolete ships to a San Francisco waterfront in the throes of modernization. Kortum decried the destructive Fontana Towers and the city's "high rise mystique" and proposed building a new Gold Rush Plaza. Yet the most vocal preservationist voice in the Ghirardelli project—that of Kortum—was effective because Kortum understood the power of modernist transformation. Karl Kortum and David Pesonen accepted the fact that modernism, and even skyscrapers, had much to offer their efforts. During the phase of brainstorming for the factory, they were the two advisors who grasped a dynamic, generative relationship with the city's recent sky-scraper designs. Cross-fertilization between modernist high-rises and the old factory, for example, included a shared respect for open space. Kortum called Ghirardelli "the original Zellerbach building as far as leaving much of the city block open is concerned." Pesonen praised Crown Zellerbach's "dazzling creativity" and "halo effect" on the financial district and the "exquisite sensitivity" of the John Hancock skyscraper. Kortum used Crown Zellerbach again when explaining why Roth needed "more than a single architect for Ghirardelli." Differentiating the factory buildings would "stretch" the "inventiveness" of one architect: "one Zellerbach building is fine, but if we had four there would be too many." Repeating homogenized brick factories was no better than a row of modernist skyscrapers. At the scale of infusing "an overtone of modernity" into the square through architectural detail, Kortum counseled Lemmon, "Some of the detailing in the Hancock building and a little of the detailing in the Zellerbach plaza is sophisticated enough to go with Ghirardelli."[63] Kortum and Pesonen described a mutual attraction between renewal and preservation, not a repelling force between static and opposed sides.

Within a few years, the enthusiastic response to Ghirardelli Square's design and novel commercial concept exceeded the developer and designers' hopes. But privately, the redevelopment consultations for the project produced pointed critiques of architects' abilities to succeed in historical work. Kortum and Pesonen lobbied the developer to minimize the architects' influence. Reviewing the portfolio of architects' recommendations, Kortum and Pesonen bemoaned the homogenizing impact of trends in the design professions. Kortum felt the architects were interchangeable. When asked to suggest a firm, he had "nobody particularly in mind."[64] For him, the principle of assigning more than one designer to the project held out possibilities for a better outcome. A mix of architects could mitigate generic designs and simultaneously avoid catering to what he saw as the destructive self-importance of individual designers.

As modernists plunged into remaking the historic waterfront in the early 1960s, some openly expressed ambivalence even while offering compelling explanations of how they blended old and new. Beverly Willis was one of the first architects hired by interior design firms in Jackson Square to modernize their mid-nineteenth-century facilities, and she also conducted a historical resources planning study for that neighborhood. She led the way in revitalizing old buildings on Union Street in Cow Hollow, where she owned the kitchenware store Capricorn, and designed a master plan for the Union Street Merchants' Association. Her redesign of 1980 Union Street won a top honor in 1966 from the Governor's Design Awards program, alongside Ghirardelli Square.[65] A 1968 cover story for *San Francisco* magazine on restoring commercial buildings probed how Willis balanced historical renovation with her views on the modern city. "While Miss Willis is involved in preservation she is not bound by an instinct to preserve. 'I will not hesitate to demolish any old structure if I feel through new construction I can improve on its charm and beauty.' This attitude is shared by many architects involved in restoration." Surely Willis wished to avoid being associated with an earlier generation of twentieth-century preservationists, often women, who were caricatured as clinging blindly to old buildings and resisting the modern world. Her firm's commissions for high-rises and new towns expanded during this growth decade, and Willis continued to design old and new, achieving a high-volume business.[66]

Some architects interpreted the rise of preservation-oriented redevelopment in the 1960s as a slap in the face. John Hirten, who replaced Bill Roth as the director of SPUR, sat on the square's advisory board. He told *San Francisco* magazine, "If we were doing really good things in our contemporary architecture we wouldn't have to rely on our history so heavily." The reporter observed: "This was reinforced by architect Beverly Willis, who considers restoration not so much a threat as an insult to modern architects— 'as if today's architect is not capable of creating anything as beautiful as they did in the good old days.'" Others implied that preservation merely copied the creativity of the original work: "Some feel that it is a crutch, fostering a feeling that you cannot get charm without preserving it." Willis, however, acknowledged that working with old buildings was more challenging than designing a cleared site. The existing structural elements and their physical deterioration constrained architects. The building codes guiding reuse were more complicated. "From a sense of design," Willis explained, "restoration requires far more skill than new construction."[67]

Other collaborating modernists questioned whether "charm" was an appropriate goal for a city like San Francisco. Bobbie Stauffacher handled graphic design at Ghirardelli Square, including way-finding signs, directories, garage markers, an exterior mural, and several store interiors. Like Willis, Stauffacher earned architectural honors for her contributions to urban design and recognition for boosting economic viability. In 1970, as the anti-high-rise movement was taking off, Stauffacher supported the "Manhattanization" of San Francisco and the "influx of big money and big business." She worked simultaneously for Ghirardelli Square and the Bank of America headquarters, which at 52 stories was the West Coast's tallest building when it opened in 1969. "I like the tall new buildings," Stauffacher said. "I think they are good. San Francisco should be more than Union Street and all that goochy goochy stuff. It's time we grew up and behaved like a big city."[68] Indeed, modernist designers working on historic-themed projects were "not bound by an instinct to preserve."

The view from San Francisco's north waterfront in the early 1960s galvanized a kind of grassroots "regional" planning, a novel urban renewal model that depended on the circulation of ideas and consultants across suburbs, wineries, ranches, and cities in the Bay Area. Unknown regional examples mingled with celebrated international cases. The research behind the design and management options for the Ghirardelli factory site in 1962 blended modernist architects, historian activists, editors, urban renewal administrators, and pragmatic real estate managers. Ghirardelli's thick binder of advice letters equalized the prospects for "laypersons'" and professional designers' ideas, and appealing concepts were plucked without attribution. At this stage, the land-use question of what to do with the property fused urban design with real estate advice, even as the two were kept separate in Roth's hiring of architects and property managers. Well-known architects weighed in on investment decisions, management practices, and retailing; historians, investors, and managers critiqued architecture and design.

This mingling was pervasive but not muddled. Fundamentally, in 1960 modernist architects were stepping into preservation work and establishing a niche for themselves. Whatever the sources of ideas, professional architects usually earned the credit. San Francisco's urban revitalization model merging historic and modern gained momentum and created more design and management jobs as the scale and pace of redevelopment accelerated. Over the next decade, these allied urbanist design fields thrived on the work generated by the competition and the battles that ensued. While the participants agreed on the significance of the experiment, their combined efforts also provoked disagreements along the fault lines of fields. As modernist architects moved their practices into the city's historic neighborhoods around 1960, they gained public credit for preservationist innovation, while preservationists like Karl Kortum and David Pesonen honed an articulate critique of architectural creativity. When the buildings, the property stakes, and the public's interest in redevelopment grew during the decade, that critique of professional design and architects would break out into the public domain.

When the Roths bought the Ghirardelli property, it seemed that the bulldozers had been stopped. Construction, however, had just begun. By the time the second half of the square opened in 1968, the waterfront had become a vibrant maritime district with a national reputation for fusing historical and modern in ways that had been suggested presciently by *Polyvescence* ten years earlier. The extensive research behind the square's creation—and its intense snapshot of revitalization ideas in 1962—gave way to the churning realities of rapidly changing neighborhoods across the city and the region. Skyscrapers and large-scale urban renewal were key to these transformations, of course. But this was San Francisco in the 1960s. Anti–Vietnam War demonstrations, the Summer of Love, Black Power, gay political organizing, the free speech movement, topless dancing—all redefined the region and made it the center of national media attention. For columnist Herb Caen, the Transamerica Pyramid and the North Beach nude dancing clubs were equally bellwethers of San Francisco, marking an end to the "old" city. More so than in most U.S. cities, it was difficult to isolate the story of urban redevelopment from the larger societal transformations under way. Streets, plazas, and civic-commercial spaces like the one built into the heart of Ghirardelli Square and so many of the planned 1960s complexes took on lives of their own, beyond what their planners, architects, and owners ever imagined.

"Culture-a-Go-Go"
The Mermaid Sculpture Controversy
and the Liberation of Civic Design

Most of the openings and gala events at Ghirardelli Square and The Cannery in the 1960s were boisterous celebrations. The evening that noted chef Julia Child fell into the men's room at a new restaurant in the square, a number of realms converged—in urban design, the arts, civic life, and commerce—and boundaries were suggestively crossed. The party was the culmination of the opening night of the 1965 Tour de Dining Décor, a fund-raiser organized by the Women's Board of the San Francisco Museum of Art. The evening began inside the museum. There socialites and various city elites acted as "salesgirls" and "models" in a staged market where patrons could buy fancy kitchen-wares. *San Francisco Chronicle* columnist Herb Caen described the scene: "At the Museum," he quipped, "mink stoles were a dime a dozen, and some of them looked it. Most of the men wore vests, as befits the Culture Capital of the Vest, and stood around in the main salon, belting the free wine and eating the free cheese. The ladies wandered through the various displays of interior décor."[1]

When staid patrons in minks and vests moved over to Ghirardelli's outdoor plazas, the mood changed. "There, fountains and musicians were playing as the happy hordes attempted to squeeze into a delightful new Italian restaurant" named Giovanni's. The crowd now jostled excitedly for seats, and half were "thrown out." Julia Child, a television star and master chef who brought French cuisine to the American kitchen, was the featured guest. Child provided the event's "high point," although not in the manner intended. While waiting for a table, she leaned against the door of Giovanni's men's restroom. The door opened unexpectedly, and Julia Child "fell right into enemy territory." A woman in the men's room. "For just plain Culture-a-Go-Go, you can't beat that," Caen wrote.[2]

Ghirardelli Square shared a pedigree with the city's old families and white-glove shopping era, but it also shared ground with the Italian businesses, go-go bars, and tourist trade of neighboring North Beach.[3] Its glittering fountain, terraces, ethnic restaurants, unique stores, crowds, warmly lit building exteriors, and spectacular views all added up to a fresh and captivating open-air hospitality. That March 1965 evening, the heady and urbane mix of commerce, culture, and nature overshadowed the sculptures and paintings that had been hauled out to the former factory for display against its bare brick walls.[4] The square had flourished since opening as a daring experiment in November 1964. Caen admired Ghirardelli's historic architecture, especially the early twentieth-century clock tower that became the square's publicity motif: "That's culture, man, right out there for everybody to see, and if the critics can't see it, they're looking in the wrong places. Museums, for instance" (fig. 34).[5]

Ghirardelli Square in the 1960s interwove the local social, sexual, and generational revolutions in San Francisco with the national experiment in urban revitalization. These two stories of arts and place—the local and the national—were entwined as San Francisco's rebuilding crossed boundaries and redrew distinctions between historical and modern, men's and women's realms, art and urban design, benign form and radical content, and civic and commercial sites. American cities faced obvious, accelerating challenges: the "blight" that justified urban renewal, race rebellion, the bulldozers of redevelopment clearance, the moral degradation posed by the spread of go-go bars and commercialized sex industries, and population dispersal to the suburban fringes. More than in most cities, San Francisco's parks, streets, and commercial establishments filled with daily expressions and demonstrations of sexual revolution and liberation.[6] In this decade San Francisco inspired other cities with new models of civic-commercial vitality, one of which Caen glimpsed on that crowded 1965 evening at the square.

Against the background of Ghirardelli's early success, in 1968 a public controversy over a new sculpture by Ruth Asawa stirred up latent attitudes among San Franciscans toward the square as a civic place and as an artifact of urban design. What began as a formulaic, familiar battle over the appropriateness of abstract or representational art soon became engulfed by unscripted opinions about gender and sexuality in civic design. The heated confrontation exposed how the far-reaching 1960s experimentation in urban design and civic arts was energized and defined by the era's gender and sexual revolutions. Focusing on the plaza and Ghirardelli's mermaid sculpture controversy, this chapter explores how such civic-commercial sites brokered as well as distilled urban transformation.

The open-air plazas of Ghirardelli Square imbued this entirely private development with independent civic meaning (fig. 35). The vibrant plaza packed with guests during the Tour de Dining Décor fulfilled the aspirations of the square's many designers. Early on, Proctor Mellquist had advised owner Bill Roth to exploit the factory's open spaces:

34 Ghirardelli Square from San Francisco Bay, ca. 1966. A landmark in the turn toward reusing old buildings for modern retail, dining, and entertainment, the square also helped broker a new model of urban civic-commercial life that extended beyond preservationist sensibilities. Note the darkened western portion of the complex (to the right); at the time of this photo only the factory's redeveloped eastern section had opened. The factory clock tower (left) stands next to the old Mustard building (center). In the foreground the concrete stands fill the waterfront sliver of Aquatic Park and the edge of the Maritime Museum is visible on the right.

35 This ca. 1965 view was taken from a lower terrace in Ghirardelli Square, near the entrance to Señor Pico's restaurant in the Wurster building (on the right). One of the complex's many modern buildings is the bookstore (at center), designed by John Matthias. Beniamino Bufano's bear was the square's only other significant sculpture besides the one by Ruth Asawa that is the focal point of this chapter. The Fontana apartment towers, named after a demolished factory on an adjacent block, loom in the background near the center of the photo. The first of these twin 17-story towers galvanized anti-high-rise sentiment on the north waterfront.

"There are certain simple things which most people consider luxuries. I think all or most of them could be supplied within the block. If they were, then the attractive power of the block would rise." Mellquist proposed live music ("people seem to consider this a luxury no matter what the quality of music"), outdoor dining, views of water, "flags flying on a row of poles," and the sight and sound of a fountain splashing. He listed "trees and planting, somehow never quite expected in an urban place. Also masses of bulbs in bloom; hanging baskets of annual flowers." Pedestrians would be drawn by benches, interesting pavement, "tubbed trees, gay umbrellas, outdoor tables." Strong management "could stage a succession of events to attract people to the shops."[7] The appeal of the outdoor spaces depended little upon architecture, or at least upon its historical or modern qualities.

In the 1960s, planned plazas carried a heavy public relations burden for urban designers and downtown developers. Both were anxious to offer meaningful amenities for the public, yet they faced mounting accusations that plazas were merely windswept, empty, sterile hardscapes; this helps explain the seemingly overblown hopes for Ghirardelli's terraces. Lawrence Halprin, the square's landscape architect, believed that Ghirardelli's plaza was "the best piece of urban space in the country."[8] Ghirardelli was not just the

36 By 1968 the terraces, outdoor dining, entertainment, night lighting, international cuisine, and merchandise, had achieved a vibrant cosmopolitan culture blending modern and historical. Until Asawa's mermaid sculpture's installation in 1968, the main plaza fountain (designed by landscape architect Lawrence Halprin) was composed of this simple bowl, with stepped seating at the rim and a single vertical jet of water. Halprin's firm had designed unique "street furniture" such as the planters, lampposts, benches, and paving, and Halprin was deeply invested in what sculpture would complete "his" fountain. On the left is the Wurster building's roof; to the right is the edge of the old apartment building (the location of Giovanni's Restaurant).

best-revitalized historical urban space. For Halprin, it was the best urban space, period, based largely on the scale, orchestration, and richness of the pedestrian experience (fig. 36). The square provided "a prototype of what a city could be like."[9] Many others recognized the plaza's significance to the national urban design community. *Interiors* magazine drew "lessons of great importance to those who control the development of our cities," especially from the square's "use of open space to enhance, even to make possible a commercial development." *Interiors* described the revelation of the open middle of the urban block, the pedestrian flow, the terraces, and the education of Americans to use such outdoor spaces: "Ghirardelli Square is a superb example of what can be done by building upon values already in existence." Hopefully "its influence will extend far beyond a local, single city block in San Francisco."[10]

As local populations and commerce shifted, urban sites such as Ghirardelli accumulated new significance and shed old associations. The physical remaking of San Francisco, its culture and countercultures, was inseparable from the flux of people and neighborhoods—some of it instigated by urban renewal dislocation. During the preceding decade, the beat character of North Beach rose and waned, gay businesses were forced out of the Embarcadero, Haight-Ashbury emerged as a hippie mecca, the Italian women working at the Ghirardelli chocolate factory moved on, and the old produce market was replaced by a mixed-use urban renewal district (Golden Gateway and, soon, Embarcadero Center). Within this changing climate, one trend involved the proliferation of openly promiscuous commercial sex businesses in U.S. cities. The go-go incursion manifested itself differently in every city, shaped by distinctive themes, dances, dress codes and costume traditions, union contracts, local ordinances, live or jukebox music, and performance props such as cages, bars, or pianos. In North Beach, go-go was topless. A *New York Times* reporter made his way through "knots" of conventioneers ogling the North Beach girlie joints in 1969. When a well-known topless dancing promoter was asked whether he remembered recently deceased local writer Jack Kerouac, he replied, "Who?"[11]

For how long would anyone recall the Italian factory "ladies" enjoying their lunches in the garden destroyed by Ghirardelli's new plaza and ten-level underground parking garage? U.S. cities always experience fluctuations in form and population, but in the 1960s the dual pressures of accelerating skyscraper construction and urban renewal clearance intensified these trends. In San Francisco, such rebuilding intersected with the social revolutions underway, sometimes with explosive outcomes (as in urban renewal) and sometimes with more indirect contests over urban terrain—as revealed by the Ghirardelli Square sculpture controversy.

THE "GHIRARDELLI GHIRLS"

In 1968 an unlikely event unsettled and transformed the square's familiar, comfortable identity for San Franciscans and design professionals alike. At the heart of the main plaza stood a fountain designed by Lawrence Halprin (see fig. 36), which had remained incomplete for nearly four years. After dark on March 18, artist Ruth Asawa, along with her friends, family, and several foundry workers, installed the mermaid sculpture

Andrea in Halprin's fountain (fig. 37). This was not a rogue action; Asawa's helpers were merely wrestling into place a bronze artwork commissioned by Roth. The controversy that nevertheless erupted tapped hidden societal fault lines that otherwise silently shaped the square's significance. Many arts—in the forms of outdoor and international dining, spectacular views, retail design, gardens, history, architecture, and even Disney-like features—had converged in the Bay Area to create this carefully crafted redevelopment. Compared to these arts, sculpture was a very conventional form.

Like the square itself, the mermaid sculpture's apparently benign, charming character both belied its expansion of the urban public realm in the 1960s and provides a lever for prying open a view into that realm. The effect of this sculpture of mermaids, turtles, and frogs proved to be a bit like Julia Child's falling into the "enemy territory" of the men's room. The naked mermaids were simultaneously comforting and transgressive; they betrayed more than a little go-go. On one hand, Ghirardelli Square was the delightful commercial-civic destination described by Caen and Mellquist. But the square also mediated accommodation among generational, social, and sexual forces in a decade of restless urban rebuilding. By installing the sculpture at night, Asawa hoped to create the impression that it had always been there.[12] Now two cast bronze mermaids, one cradling a merbaby, would splash in the fountain with large sea turtles and numerous frogs (fig. 38). Upon finishing the installation, Asawa popped the cork from a champagne bottle. Countering the modernist architects' views of the historic square, Asawa seized the platform offered by the plaza fountain and surreptitiously launched an entirely different debate.

Most of San Francisco learned of the mermaids a few days later in the newspapers. On March 26, the *Chronicle* reported that "a seemingly innocent and conventional piece of sculpture" had been "bitterly attacked" in the press. Halprin had mailed a two-page diatribe against Asawa and her sculpture to the press and to design professionals, in the Bay Area and nationally. He demanded the artwork's removal. His main objection was that "this sculpture is out of character with the space it is in; it is at the wrong scale for the plaza; and in my view completely out of character with the design intent of Ghirardelli Square." He claimed that the mermaids destroyed the square's balance between modernism and "Victoriana." Instead of representational art, Halprin had envisioned "an abstraction for the fountain, a shaft of metal about 15 feet high." In his conception, the "interplay of water and metal would give free play to the essential qualities of water—not formalized and constrained but organically evolved."[13] With four years to anticipate how a sculpture would complete the square, every drawing of the plaza fountain from Halprin's office included a different, hypothetical abstract sculpture. In 1963 Halprin had suggested that Roth look for something like James Fitzgerald's *Fountain of the Northwest,* recently installed at the Seattle World's Fair (figs. 39 and 40).[14]

In his statement against Asawa's sculpture, Halprin invoked the "principle of the second man," a concept recently given prominence by Philadelphia planner Edmund Bacon. Later designers reworking "groups of buildings, of plazas and squares," Halprin explained, had an obligation to honor the "seminal concept" of the first designer. These ties of responsibility and inspiration, originally hammered out in the Renaissance, applied especially to larger civic complexes as they evolved over time. Halprin described

37 Foundry workers, together with Ruth Asawa and her family and friends, installed the heavy bronze sculpture in Halprin's fountain after dark on March 18, 1968. From plaster casting to installation, Warner Jepson photographed the long artistic process behind the sculpture. His wife, Andrea Jepson, was the model for the mermaid.

38 Lawrence Halprin demanded removal of this seemingly innocuous, charming artwork depicting mermaids, a merbaby, sea turtles, and frogs. What began as a formulaic battle over the appropriateness of abstract or representational art evolved into an unscripted public conversation about the boundaries of gender and sexuality in civic design and urban space. In the days after Halprin's attack, as in this 1968 slide, the water feature had not been activated yet. The police officers appear to be scrutinizing the largest pile of frogs on a lily pad. The merbaby is held by the mermaid to the right.

Asawa as "the second man." Here, "The second man has given no thought to the idea or concept or the purpose. He has done only what has pleased him and his own ego. He has not been able to work within the overall concept and its basic intention. He has violated the Square."[15] Halprin's critique elevated his own role relative to the other design professionals who contributed to the modern square, and, for that matter, relative to the factory's original architects. His statement obscured Asawa's gender and her agenda, but his pique—along with the "principle of the second man"—confirmed her influence over the site.[16] One letter to the editor responded that Halprin's "statement, unfortunately, sounds like the whimperings of a petulant child who has discovered someone else playing in his sandbox."[17] The outpouring of public support for the mermaids indicated that most San Franciscans thought Lawrence Halprin had behaved inappropriately.

Some attributed Halprin's imperious behavior toward the mermaids to his increasing professional status. One note read: "You're way out of line, Halpie! Yer gitten a lil tu big fer yer britches, huh."[18] By 1968, largely through Ghirardelli, Halprin had achieved national stature as an expert in melding modernist landscape principles with older structures in this new redevelopment genre. He had just agreed to speak about "his" Ghirardelli project at a June AIA workshop titled Design for Preservation. In turn, as a "famous

39 *Fountain of the Northwest.* Lawrence Halprin admired James Fitzgerald's "brilliant bronze sculpture" installed for the 1962 Seattle World's Fair as an ideal model for the Ghirardelli Square fountain. This slide was in Halprin's collection.

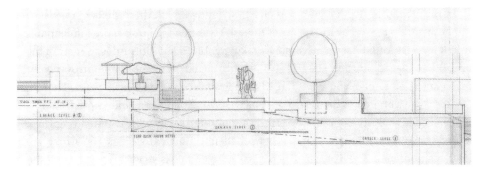

40 Sketches and plans from Halprin & Associates' archive show that the firm imagined different types of abstract sculptures for the plaza fountain setting; this particular drawing evoked James Fitzgerald's *Fountain of the Northwest*. This drawing also revealed how Halprin's fountain and tree plantings had to relate to the underground garage structure.

professional ally," Halprin helped the preservation session move from its usual "pre-dawn" time to a central spot on the AIA program—aiding the preservationists' "long and hard drive for respectability."[19] Through Halprin and Ghirardelli, preservation could be included within design.

There were other signs of Halprin's new national profile. Until recently, like most landscape architects, he had made his living primarily by designing gardens for private homes. Now, East Coast architects and developers such as James Rouse and Ben Thompson had begun inviting him to join in partnerships to compete for large-scale projects around the country. Halprin was the sole West Coast member of the first President's Advisory Council on Historic Preservation, appointed in 1967, and he was tapped for the first National Council on the Arts in 1966. He had launched his book-publishing career with *Cities* (1963) and *Freeways* (1966). He enjoyed a friendship with Lady Bird Johnson, who had introduced a national conversation about urban beautification and improving roadside landscapes. She visited Ghirardelli Square and proclaimed that it exemplified her ideal for urban revitalization.[20]

When Halprin demanded the mermaids' ouster and deflected blame for the fountain, he was also aggressively claiming credit for the highly regarded plaza. Although landscape architecture's proponents argued that it had the potential to knit architecture and urban planning together into meaningful spaces, the design fields jostled for credit for so-called open space. One critic noted: "It doesn't detract from the architects' achievement to state that the sparkling, crystallizing agent that accounts for this unity is Halprin's design of the out-of-door spaces. . . . At their best—and Halprin's work is of the best—[landscape architects] now supply the indispensable yeast that molds the work of the city planner and the architect into a creative environment."[21] Another reviewer said Halprin "was responsible for the plazas, plantings, and total concept— Wurster, Bernardi and Emmons did the buildings."[22] Especially relevant to Halprin's outburst and demand for credit were the collaborative pressures inherent in large-scale projects, which are explored further in chapter 5. This crowded terrain, along with the design-world spotlight on the square and plaza, set the stage for Halprin's diatribe.

In the meantime, Ruth Asawa was charting her own path through San Francisco's public arts culture, and by the spring of 1968 she was moving into a more influential role. That year found Asawa increasingly taking public stands in battles over art in the city's civic spaces. She and Halprin had recently faced off in another controversy involving a redesigned landscape plan for San Francisco's Civic Center plaza. The Civic Center, Asawa argued to the Board of Supervisors, "didn't need landscaping, but it really needed sculpture or mosaic or really a sculptural focus." She counted Halprin as a friend and "wasn't interested in trying to challenge him or anything." Her strongly held positions on the role of artists in the city marked her as an effective player. When newly elected mayor Joseph Alioto needed a replacement appointment for the Art Commission some months later, Asawa topped the list.[23]

The mermaids were experimental for Asawa and at several levels signaled a turning point in her career. In 1968 she was internationally recognized for her abstract work (fig. 41). For nearly two decades Asawa's hanging and tied-wire sculptures had attracted critical acclaim.[24] Her wire forms aligned with the natural world; the rounded and spiky shapes evoked variously blossoms, gourds, plants, and trees.[25] Halprin admired Asawa's abstract work and had initially supported giving her the commission. But the Ghirardelli assignment inspired her to design her first representational sculptures and to begin working in cast bronze. Most significantly, the mermaid sculpture was the first of Asawa's many commissions for resonant civic and commercial plazas. Asawa soon translated her experiments with life-casting and masks, paper folding, and dough sculpture into bronze sculptures for civic sites. The week the mermaid controversy broke, she was preparing for her first San Francisco Art Commission meeting. She was also planning a grassroots community arts project that would engage her energies for the rest of her professional life. That summer Asawa launched a program to bring art and artists into the public schools, working with Sally Woodbridge (an architectural writer and historian), Andrea Jepson (the mermaids' model), and other neighbors and friends. The Alvarado Art Workshop, begun in their neighborhood elementary school, eventually expanded to nearly fifty schools. The experience of founding the program in 1968 inspired Jepson and many of the women who worked with Asawa and Woodbridge to begin community-based careers that spanned politics, the arts, business, city planning, gay rights, civil rights, the environment, and the anti-war movement, but they shared a belief in combining the creative power of the individual with community mobilization.[26]

For San Franciscans generally and design professionals specifically, Halprin's attack raised worthy issues concerning the place of modernism in remaking their historic city. What could professional architects, planners, and landscape architects—the same individuals who had endorsed clearance-based urban rebuilding and delivered forests of high-rises—offer the nation that was better? Halprin made accessible to the public otherwise hidden skirmishes over who contributed to the outcome of redevelopment. In larger-scale projects with public relevance, how were collaboration, credit, and blame to be negotiated? Even when participants agreed over fundamentals—for example, the importance of context and environment in shaping urban sites—they clashed in defining which contexts and environments mattered.

41 In 1968 Ruth Asawa was known for her abstract hanging and tied-wire sculptures, and her professional identity overlapped with her role as "mother of six." This 1957 photograph by her friend Imogen Cunningham was one of Asawa's favorites; it captured how work and family were unified in her life. In this image, hanging sculptures partly obscure Asawa, who is weaving wire on the right, working from the spool at center.

A "PLEASANT PIECE OF CONVENTIONAL SCULPTURE"
OR A FEMINIST STATEMENT?

Because he initiated the heated public conversation, Halprin began with an advantage— but he quickly found the debate diverging into unexpected terrain. Asawa explained her concept of offering "something for the old to remember the fantasy of their childhood and something for the young to remember when they are old." She underscored the square's role in preserving views of the bay (itself a natural and historical environment) and in slowing the high-rises. In a statement answering the public's curiosity, she wrote: "As you look at the sculpture you include rather than block out the ocean view which was saved for all of us, and you wonder what lies below that surface." She intended "to make a sculpture that would relate to more than just the Plaza" and acknowledged the site's "rich San Francisco environment," especially the waterfront and ocean.[27] Asawa selected the model, her friend Jepson, because she "happens to be appropriately Italian, and her figure was just perfect for the mermaid." The Italian "tie" worked "because of the Ghirardelli name" and "the location adjacent to the North Beach area with its Italian character."[28]

The public heard different priorities for Ghirardelli Square from Asawa than from Halprin. She named her collaborators, from artistic partner Mae Lee to the San Francisco Art Foundry workers who had cast the sculpture. In contrast, Halprin, when working through the drafts of his own statement, resisted sharing credit for the plaza and the square design. He did eventually acknowledge the associates in his firm and the architects of Wurster, Bernardi & Emmons. Asawa had a more expansive view not only of the plaza's design origins but also of its audience. Her hope that the sculpture "could be enjoyed by everyone" defied modernist artistic conventions that gave low priority to the viewer's pleasure compared with designers' adherence to powerful ideals.[29]

Juxtaposing Halprin's attack with Asawa's artistic vision still did not fully encompass the issues of public art and civic design provoked by this 1968 episode. Clearly, "prestigious" landscape architect Halprin had "let fly a two-page howitzer bombardment against a pleasant piece of conventional sculpture."[30] But was the fountain indeed "a pleasant piece of conventional sculpture"? Halprin dismissed representational sculpture because he believed that it constrained the imagination. The mermaids, he argued, would "fix the design into an immutable, established shape which would inevitably have specific meaning."[31] Asawa disagreed: "I feel that by making a literal sculpture I do not water down my integrity as an artist, or limit the imagination of those who see it."[32] On this matter, at least, Asawa was right. The mermaids, turtles, and frogs have had anything but immutable or inevitable meanings.

The sculpture's supporters rejected Halprin's claim that the mermaids upset the square's balance between modern and historical and asserted that a very different modernism was at stake: namely, the boundaries of feminism and the presence of women and female sexuality in public. Many locals saw the Ghirardelli mermaids in the context of the city's topless go-go bar phenomenon, which was centered in the neighboring North Beach district. This case played out a drama that cities were reluctantly facing during the 1960s—just how central to their culture and economy were the go-go businesses and other marginal industries showcasing female nudity. In that context, the mermaids offered either a wholesome, maternal alternative to the topless club scene or confirmed fears of an encroaching, corrupting public sexuality. Others were unconcerned by the sculpture's nakedness but still saw gender issues. For example, some followers of the urban design scene saw Asawa's sculpture as defying the male domination of architectural fields. Of the far-reaching matters of civic space, modernism, historicism, and design raised in the mermaid sculpture controversy, the pervasiveness of gender and sexuality in underpinning these debates is the most instructive.

If the mermaids, turtles, and frogs were "representational," what did they represent? The artist's supporters described the sculpture as "charming" and "delightful" in letters and calls to Asawa, Halprin, the square's management, the Art Commission, and the newspapers. There were enough abstractions in San Francisco, they declared. One couple wrote: "Too often we find ourselves surrounded by modern abstract—sometimes meaningless modern." A modern fountain would be especially inappropriate at Ghirardelli. In contrast, the mermaids were "enchanting" and the square was "charming."[33] Mrs. Dandee Douglas also voted to retain the "charming" fountain, explaining that abstractions "confuse those of us who like to recognize what we see." Another letter-writer, "not unschooled in art," had stopped going to museums. Tired of the "avant-garde," she was "sick of looking at circles, squares, hunks and spots deliriously designed to hood wink the American taste in arts." Asawa's design "gives you something to enjoy, to dream on, to smile, to revel in." Mrs. Gordon Grannis conceded that "Abstract Art has a place in Society, but not to the extent to which it is being permeated throughout our area."[34]

For San Franciscans eager to contain the proliferation of abstract art to museums, the mermaids encouraged imagination, play, and an ageless "emotional appeal." Supporters responded to the sculpture's magnetism for children—the splashing water, tails, frogs, baby, and turtles.[35] From the earliest meetings in 1963, the square's advisory board had favored including child-centered objects such as a carousel. Halprin's preliminary plans incorporated a children's area into the main plaza. Some worried that children might "run around and break things," and the property manager anticipated that carousel music would annoy tenants. But most board members hoped that this could be "a lure for children to let ma shop."[36] One of the square's first sculptures was a large, stylized bear (with an abstract conical head) by irreverent Bay Area artist Beniamino Bufano (see fig. 35). Although Ghirardelli as built did not include a children's area or carousel, observers' descriptions of the mermaids as "pleasing to children" were consistent with the original goals for the plaza.[37]

Critics of the mermaid sculpture sneered that it had limited itself and its impact on the surrounding plaza through a singular focus on children.[38] Halprin suggested that the sculpture belonged in a suburban America where the imagination revolved around Disney vacations and the needs of children. He compared the bronze mermaids to lawn ornaments: "The cast iron deer, the little duck waddling on the lawn, now this sculpture are for other times, other places. The cuteness of Disneyland is appropriate for children— this is not meant to be only a playground for children."[39] Asawa's insistence on adding the recorded sound of croaking frogs infuriated Halprin and gave credibility to his comparisons with Disney (Asawa ultimately abandoned the sound effects). Indeed, some of Asawa's earliest art instruction had come from Walt Disney studio artists during the six months her family spent at the Santa Anita racetrack, a detention center for Japanese Americans during World War II.[40] In condemning the sculpture and the plaza as child-centered, Halprin also alluded to Asawa's public image. Her professional identity embraced her role as "mother of six." Typical was the *Chronicle*'s introduction after Halprin's attack: "Ruth Asawa, wife of architect Albert Lanier, is the mother of six children and a new appointee to the San Francisco Art Commission." A favorite photograph of herself, taken by her friend Imogen Cunningham, shows Asawa weaving a sculpture at home, surrounded by her young children (see fig. 41). Wire sculpture could be picked up or put down depending on family needs.[41] Asawa rejected employment offers from commercial design firms that hoped to entice her to work outside her home by offering child care and housekeeping services.[42]

Halprin had been dogged by insinuations that his own designs were standardized, cute, and tainted by an aura of the commercial amusement park; such critiques help explain his sensitivity on this point. In 1967 the *Wall Street Journal* had reported: "A member of one of the nation's largest firm of architects says Mr. Halprin's projects are 'often too cute.' He adds: 'Everything seems to come out like Tivoli Gardens (Copenhagen's famous amusement park).'"[43] Long before Asawa became involved, reviewers had sniffed out a Disney sensibility in the square. *House & Garden* had likened Ghirardelli to "a Disney fantasy plumped down in a sober commercial setting."[44] Five months before the sculpture installation, another magazine called the square a "sophisticated and beautiful kind of Disneyland for adults."[45] In the mermaids, turtles, and frogs, Halprin saw representational figures that simultaneously invoked the cartoonish, animated figurines of Disney amusements and a sentimental, corny, Victorian scene. Halprin could not imagine two worse reference points for his designs. He worried that critics would regard the sculpture as the culmination of his vision for the plaza rather than as Asawa's addition.

Although the mermaids' defenders described a delightful, family-oriented fountain, the story of what the sculpture represented to the public only began there. After all, the mermaids were naked, more "maid" than "mer."[46] In private, the people closest to the sculpture brought up the mermaids' shapely figures freely. Warren Lemmon told Roth: "Ruth commented that she thought you were quite pleased, incidentally, with the rather voluptuous, bosomy mermaid she has designed!" Roth said that "if it didn't end up in the fountain, it might end up in my bathtub."[47] In November 1967, when Halprin's "intense" distaste for the sculpture weighed on Roth's mind, *Sunset* editor Proctor Mellquist gave Roth his candid opinion: "I like Ruth's mermaid very much, and I do not think it is in any sense corny. Rather, I think it is a quite beautiful and astonishingly realistic portrait of a young woman's body."[48] Halprin never mentioned the mermaids' bodies. He focused on the sculpture's style and scale, variously describing Asawa's efforts as corny, camp, Pop Art, Victorian, and Disneylandish.[49]

Asawa's defenders dismissed Halprin's diatribe about the sculpture's style and argued that he, possibly unconsciously, had viewed the bronzes as a female intrusion— a threat to the accustomed male domination of the public realm. Quite a few had ideas for what Halprin could do with the abstract "shaft" he would have preferred. One woman called his office and wished "you would take your 15' shaft of metal and go sit on it somewhere." On television another proposed that Halprin wear the shaft on his head. One woman raised this issue with Asawa: "May I suggest that Mr. Halprin is offended more by the fact that a phallic symbol has been changed into a maternal one than by his logical objections to the mermaid piece in the Square? . . . I interpret your fantasy just as I please, but I still suspect Mr. Halprin's anger is based upon quite other motives than he is consciously aware of!"[50] The most explicit visual rendering making the same point was delivered to Halprin's office from a pseudonymous critic calling himself "Art Kutecture" (fig. 42). "Art" altered the photograph of the fountain that had appeared with the *Chronicle*'s original story. Over the mermaids Art drew a detailed image of a male sexual organ, measured vertically with the notation "About 15'."[51]

The sexual and gender overtones permeating Halprin's language for the plaza, sculpture, and designers reinforced his seeming inability to make space for female representation or participation in design. Asawa had stepped into the "men's room." Men wrote to support Asawa, but she singled out women's concerns for "saving" the sculpture: "A lot of women wrote to me. Some wrote me long letters on the meaning of the circle, and about mythology and about motherhood and the significance or the symbolism of the mermaid and the frogs and the turtles."[52]

Through public art, without the explicit acknowledgment of Halprin, Asawa explored and expanded the boundaries of acceptable female behavior in public. Private correspondence specified that the sculpture was not merely maternal; it portrayed a mermaid nursing a merbaby (figs. 43 and 44). Today the fountain's interpretive marker describes the "nursing mermaid," but news reporters in 1968 did not discuss this.[53] Mrs. Samuel H. Coxe III privately wrote to Bill Roth, "With so many irresponsible abstractions claiming our time and attention today, it is refreshing to see a mermaid in the very real situation of nursing her young one." She sent a copy of her letter to La Leche League International,

42 After Lawrence Halprin's public demand for the mermaids' removal, a pseudonymous critic, "Art Kutecture," sent Halprin this drawing. "Art" altered the photograph (by Joe Rosenthal) that had appeared in the *San Francisco Chronicle*'s March 26, 1968, story about the landscape architect's "scorn" for the sculpture. The notation "about 15'" mocked Halprin's stated preference for "a shaft of metal about 15 feet high." The drawing made graphic what letter-writers alleged, namely that Halprin wished to convert a maternal symbol into a phallic one.

an advocacy organization that encouraged women to breast-feed. Herb Caen wrote of the new sculpture: "Among its features is a mermaid holding a baby, and the question, Professor is—????" Caen indirectly asked whether mermotherhood was possible. A poem mailed to Asawa in January 1969 raised yet another possibility that was not openly discussed at the time. The sculpture included not one, but two mermaids with a baby. Was this a lesbian family? The poem began: "soft bellied/mermaid a-/lone lesbian/ created, knocked up/in a foundry/left pregnant/one day/in a fountain/to bathe awhile/ among the frogs." In the fountain, straight and queer mingled, as did the erotic and the maternal.[54]

Those who responded to the serene provocation of a nursing mother and child in a public plaza followed the artist's intentions. Ruth Asawa had selected her neighbor Andrea Jepson as the model for the mermaids partly because Jepson's body reflected the recent birth of her second child.[55] The two women had become friendly when Jepson was pregnant with her first child, and Asawa would sketch her. Jepson recalled that soon "I was pregnant again and right after I had Matty, Ruth, who had really gotten into plaster during her mask period, asked me if she could do a plaster cast of my body because she wanted to make a statement about nursing mothers. The statement, after months of plaster, then wax and finally bronze, turned into the mermaid fountain at Ghirardelli Square."[56] The sculpture's title *Andrea* solidified the link to Asawa's friend's

43 Ruth Asawa's intent was to place a sculpture of a mother nursing a baby in the midst of a crowded urban plaza, thus integrating the pair into mundane city life. In 1968, public breast-feeding was stigmatized. Many photos of the fountain, like this one, show eye-level perspectives that blend the mermaids with the visitors. The mermaids' postures resembled those of seated visitors leaning forward over their books, games, or lunch.

44 The merbaby cradled in a mermaid's arm. The merbaby is not literally nursing. Viewers infer this relationship from the posture, positioning, and intimacy of the figures.

45 The wax casting phase of the mermaid sculpture bore a close resemblance to model Andrea Jepson's body. Here the wax form reclined in a chair, cushioned by a piece of foam. The sun brought out the warmth and soft texture of the oxblood-red wax. One of Asawa's abstract sculptures hung from the ceiling in the background on the left.

real body and circumstances of motherhood. Andrea Jepson's husband, Warner Jepson, documented Asawa's sculpting process, including the plaster casting of Jepson's body, the wire "crocheting" techniques used to form the tails, and the foundry work. His photographs of the wax model phase, in a warm oxblood red, made the figure's connection to a living human body better than any other perspective (fig. 45). In the next production stage, the wax sculpture melted out as an encasing mold created a negative impression into which the molten metal was later poured.

If Asawa "wanted to make a statement about nursing mothers," part of the sculpture's "fantasy" included nursing mothers in the center of a crowded, intimate urban plaza drawing ten thousand visitors a day.[57] In the late 1960s, proponents of breast-feeding hoped to break down what one physician called the "public taboo against public nursing," and what *Our Bodies, Ourselves*, a best-seller on women's health and sexuality first published in 1971, described as "puritanical prejudices against public breast-feeding." The latter called it "ridiculous that a woman cannot feed her child in public without breaking a law or being accused of exhibitionism."[58] But as the proportion of breast-fed babies plunged in the United States after World War II, nursing was embattled in private as well as in public. Most Americans had never seen a mother nursing, and most babies only saw a breast by accident.[59] The baby bottle had provided "tangible evidence of woman's liberation from drudgery."[60] One author explained that "ambitious" girls "felt that breast-feeding was a symbol of women's past servitude to home and husband whereas bottle-feeding was modern and gave them more freedom to be away from home."[61] Breast-feeding may have been "nonconformist" in 1968, but it was not uniquely promoted as modern or inherently feminist.[62] Nevertheless, rare public reminders of nursing as portrayed by the mermaids indirectly addressed women's freedom to choose their paths.

For most observers, the ambiguous sexuality of the fountain scene entertained more than it offended. In the first heat of controversy, publicist Marion Conrad (see chapter 6) parodied the response of an offended matron. Conrad expressed her "shock at seeing in a family-frequented public place . . . one pair of frogs fornicating on a lily pad," and "another pair of frogs fornicating on another lily pad." She added, "As if the above weren't enough, each mermaid had clearly visible, at the end of her tail, a large open orifice completely unobstructed to the public's view" (figs. 46 and 47). This was no charming family fountain. Conrad declared, "My children, for three, will certainly not be encouraged to visit this 'public place' until something is done."[63] Decades later the *Bay Guardian* endorsed the fountain as the city's "Best Public Orgy." The reporter wrongly attributed the original controversy to the nursing merbaby: "You see, the figures in her [Asawa's] mermaid fountain were breast-feeding, and that's still a touchy subject in public spaces in this country. But the lactating ladies are just a front for the fountain's truly scandalous feature. Bend down and take a good look at the lily pads—what the hell are those frogs doing together?" This was "subliminal amphibian sex."[64]

Over time, Larry Halprin's urgent issue—the need for abstract rather than representational art to preserve the square's balance between modern and historical—vanished from memory. The concerns Asawa raised—motherhood, nursing, and sexuality in public space—persisted and became increasingly newsworthy. The fountain's current plaque describing the "nursing mermaid" makes Asawa's agenda more explicit today than it was in 1968.

In the late sixties, sexual stigma surrounded women nursing, in public or private. The law framed both public breast-feeding and topless dancing as indecent exposure. A writer to advice columnist Ann Landers in 1969 was repulsed by the sight of a young mother nursing her child in an airport. "If you say there's nothing wrong with this sort of thing I'll take your word for it, but to my way of thinking, breast-feeding a baby in public is the same as being a topless waitress." Landers rejected the comparison: the "poor woman is ignorant, not lewd. In our culture it is not considered good taste to breast-feed a baby in public, but she didn't know better." Landers went further: "There's no more similarity between breast-feeding a baby in public and being a topless waitress than there is in undressing to take a shower and posing for the center spread of a girlie magazine."[65] In the topless clubs of the North Beach neighborhood close to Ghirardelli, the "standard joke" involved "a customer asking a topless waitress for some cream in his coffee."[66] For the mermaid sculpture, the North Beach clubs provided the local context for San Franciscans uncomfortably trying to isolate sexual dimensions in nursing.

46 Lawrence Halprin insisted that the sculpture's representational subject matter—mermaids, sea turtles, and frogs—limited the viewer's imagination and skewed the square's character toward Victoriana and children's concerns. Most letter-writers found the sculpture "delightful," while others wondered whether the frogs on the lily pads were "fornicating."

47 One observer noted the sexual connotations of an "orifice" at the end of each mermaid tail. An inquisitive frog sits at this tail opening.

THE BOUNDARIES OF "SEXLAND"

North Beach was not just any topless strip—it was where "the topless" was born. North Beach had a long history as one of the city's commercial sex districts.[67] By the 1940s and 1950s, the neighborhood had added a reputation for its lesbian bars and nightspots. In 1964, it began a new phase.[68] In June of that year, Carol Doda invented the performance of topless dancing at the Condor Club on Broadway in North Beach (fig. 48). Donning a designer-made topless bathing suit, Doda inspired the speedy reincarnation of Broadway into a gauntlet of topless joints.[69] For many cities, the appearance of go-go bars in the 1960s signaled the beginning of the end of respectable entertainment. The girlie clubs were economically vibrant, to be sure, but also exploitative and inattentive to neighborhood needs. They attracted a loitering clientele that intimidated more upscale visitors. The topless bathing suit, the "marquees of 'nudie theaters,'" and "pornographic magazines" were inflammatory symbols in national politics—easy targets for those hoping to rally Americans, especially women, against supposed urban-rooted moral decay.

Even before the Condor Club unveiled a 40-foot sign featuring a nude likeness of Carol Doda, Doda and her breasts were San Francisco landmarks. She may have offended self-appointed guardians of American morals, but in San Francisco Doda's exploits were followed in the city's reputable papers. When she had breast implant surgery, the newspapers invited doctors to comment on the procedure's safety. She rallied U.S. servicemen headed to Vietnam.[70] Although she offered not exactly wholesome family entertainment, she had legitimacy among respectable, if mature, San Franciscans. Doda's North Beach was also known for its thriving nightclub scene of avant-garde music, comedy, and theater. The city's first sidewalk cafés had opened there in the 1950s. A few blocks from the Condor Club was City Lights Bookstore, an epicenter for the beat literary counterculture emulated by rebels everywhere in the 1950s and consumed vicariously by a generation of suburbanites.

The international world of design professionals took note of San Francisco's topless clubs. Cambridge-based architect Ben Thompson, who had been chair of the Department of Architecture at Harvard's Graduate School of Design since 1963, was the founding owner of the innovative home furnishings and "good design" chain Design Research (D/R). In July of 1965 he described the West as "a big rough topless place these days" as he oriented the managers of his new store in Ghirardelli Square's clock tower building. A month later, for his Finnish business partners from Marimekko, he wrote: "San Francisco is a big overgrown frontier of people-gone-west, and grisly [sic] bears still run up and down Market Street. The place is a kind of open nightclub and the air so healthy or at least air conditioned at about 65 degrees that you can play all night and still feel reasonably unmuddled in the morning. Our public relations man, Jerry Mander, told Lorna and me that San Francisco was the great city of whores because of the pleasant temperature."[71] Here the growing preoccupation with outdoor living—found in civic-commercial plazas like Ghirardelli Square and in *Sunset* magazine—was sexualized. Outside of San Francisco the aura of respect protecting Carol Doda faded—in this case, next to a Wild West version of San Francisco, where loose women inhabited a night-club scene so expansive it seemed to define the entire city. Thompson's comments

48 The Condor Club and topless dancing of nearby North Beach provided one backdrop against which the mermaids were understood. Although the neighborhood had long enjoyed its share of clubs, the topless craze remade this commercial strip in 1964, just in time for the Republican National Convention. Photo ca. 1978.

exemplified the capacity for "the topless" to overflow distinct neighborhoods and infiltrate the city's identity.

Nationally, by the late 1960s go-go clubs were associated not only with marginalized neighborhoods and generically deteriorating urban conditions but also specifically with the burgeoning "historic-preservation-for-profit" ventures like New Orleans's French Quarter, St. Louis's Gaslight Square, and Denver's Larimer Square. In 1970 the developers of Underground Atlanta looked warily to the lessons of these other entertainment districts as they sought to emulate the model. Gaslight Square "had a few good years before going into an abrupt decline, due in part to an increasing reputation for having clip joints." Underground's board of directors learned that New Orleans had "strict architectural zoning there, but they have no control over what happens inside"—in other words, an architecturally historical ambiance on the outside, commercialized sex within. Underground's president curbed the incursion of undesirable businesses through "iron fist" tenant controls. A typical letter to potential tenants dictated: "In no event shall tenant allow entertainment such as 'go-go girls,' dancing girls, striptease artists, employes [sic] sparsely clad (topless, g-strings, negligees, etc.), 'acid rock' bands, psychedelic lights, or entertainment which will cater to, or attract persons of any particular clique, such as homosexuals or 'hippies.'"[72]

San Francisco's history already saturated the waterfront with sex tales, including its storied frontier past, the Barbary Coast and the port's "lusty" world crossroads, and, more recently, gay cruising at Aquatic Park, lesbian nightspots, and topless clubs.[73] Yet the themes favored by the preservation-for-profit districts—1890s (saloons), 1920s (speakeasies), the West (saloons again)—also legitimized more bars and alcohol in the districts' commercial mix and linked them with sex appeal and prostitution. The mermaid controversy amplified the fact that go-go and other marginalized and politicized combinations of sexuality and gender had charged Ghirardelli Square's genteel civic setting within the historical maritime neighborhood.

Part of Ghirardelli Square's success was that it invited in, on specific terms, elements of a neighboring risqué world of art, sex, culture, entertainment, and the avant-garde. The square lured North Beach nightclub impresarios. In the 1950s, Keith Rockwell helped found in North Beach the Purple Onion—a cornerstone of the alternative beat/folk/comedy scene and the club that launched Phyllis Diller. Rockwell opened a theater in Ghirardelli Square to house a production of *The Fantasticks*. A 1966 article described how Rockwell danced on the edge: "Rockwell is one of the few San Francisco nightclub owners to have successfully avoided the Topless. 'I'm not against it,' he says. 'I just don't find it very entertaining. Sure, it's brought a lot of business to the area. But personally, I'll take a good, artistic stripshow any day.'" He might look like "an insurance man," and he kept the topless at bay, but people like Rockwell who defined the line inevitably knew both sides. One of Rockwell's ventures, El Cid, began as a sidewalk café but had "long since passed into the arms of the Topless."[74]

This Ghirardelli formula negotiated encroachments from commercialized sex, balancing the volatile combination of economic vitality with anxiety about immorality. The club hungry i was more famous than the Purple Onion. Enrico Banducci built this

North Beach basement club into a legendary institution in the 1950s and early 1960s. Famed for nurturing independent talent and taking chances in a conformist time, Banducci cultivated comedians Mort Sahl and Woody Allen and gave a boost to the Kingston Trio and Barbra Streisand. In 1968 he opened a theater in the square's power-house building, but the expensive renovation forced the venture into bankruptcy two years later. Banducci sold the hungry i name to an investor who used it for a strip club near the Condor. Shortly afterward, the newspapers announced that "fans of sexy art movies will soon be able to see them in Ghirardelli Square," in the former hungry i theater. Warren Lemmon distinguished art films from "the ones that run in the honky tonks." In the square there would be "plenty of sex in the movies," but they wouldn't be "vulgar." A reporter winked at Lemmon's discomfort, relishing the prospect of sexy "dames" in the square.[75] In Ghirardelli, society ladies donned Pucci bikinis behind screens for charity, and the upscale mod shop Paraphernalia sold "Flash panties for a new freedom" (that is, underthings designed to be seen). These smacked of the peep show.[76] Sexy "dames" in art and high-society culture meant sex without vulgarity, or so Ghirardelli's management hoped.

Author Naomi Wolf, who grew up near San Francisco, recalled in her 1997 book *Promiscuities* her fascination with Carol Doda and the Broadway strip. Wolf was too young to remember the 1968 mermaid controversy, but the Ghirardelli fountain, Doda, the Condor Club and its girlie sign—all had been reference points during her adolescent years. These city landmarks offered alternative visions of "female sexuality." The absurd yet mesmerizing Doda and the off-limits clubs Doda inhabited ("Sexland") contrasted with the "maternal" yet "sexy" mermaids.

My favorite was the scene in the bronze fountain at Ghirardelli Square, where two young mermaids played. They were surrounded by pond lilies, and on each lily pad was a welter of jolly toads. The scene was lewd: toads were kissing, small toads jumped on the backs of big toads, and water spouted over it all. One mermaid held out her arms and toads leapt from her outstretched fingers. The mermaid bodies, though cast in metal, looked at once soft and strong. Each was a little pouchy in the belly and a little slack in the full breast. One mermaid cradled a merbaby in her arms. The baby was laughing. The grown mermaids were naked in the most public of spaces— yet merry, confident, young, and maternal. This also seemed to me to be part of Sexland but of a different kind. The fountain was reassuring to me. These mermaids were happy and playful as well as "sexy." The bronze mermaids were imaginary, of course, and Carol Doda was real; but to me they seemed more real than she did. As I grew older, the Carol Doda images proliferated and became active and three-dimensional, and the glimpses of what the mermaids represented grew rarer and quainter.[77]

Naomi Wolf's memoir validated Asawa's expectation that the mermaids would expand the boundaries of women's presence, particularly their maternal and sexual presence, in public. Wolf described all the intentional details of the artist's casting—pouchy here, slack there, "at once soft and strong"—that had led Asawa to choose Andrea Jepson as her model in the first place. Decades later, Wolf saw the mermaids as a touchstone for remembering her youth. While young, Wolf recognized the plaza's juxtaposition with Carol Doda and the neighboring topless district, as well as the larger questions posed about the place of sexuality, ambiguously wholesome and degraded, in urban commerce and the civic domain.

THE LIBERATION OF CIVIC DESIGN

As a political statement, Ruth Asawa's sculpture marked an early skirmish in the emergence of second-wave feminism. Women's liberation had not yet found the national stage of the Miss America protest in Atlantic City, feminist art theory had yet to be launched, and public art had not yet explicitly taken up subjects of female sexuality from feminist perspectives.[78] Nursing in public was a radical position, as were public representations of lesbian couples or sexual organs. The plaza's feminist statements were effective precisely because they were clothed in the guise of a charming sculpture for families. Their distinctive quaintness, as Naomi Wolf wrote, would become more obvious only over time, but that did not detract from their power to expand the boundaries for women.

Lawrence Halprin's diatribe against Asawa galvanized feminist responses about men's domination of the symbols and design of urban civic spaces. Such responses would likely have remained dormant, or at least private, if Halprin had not spoken out. Halprin's language ("the second man" and the "shaft") irked others into claiming that gender defined the battle over the plaza even if Halprin did not realize it. San Franciscans' strongly expressed reactions to Halprin's strongly stated views draw attention to the fact that Asawa's public comments at the time were noticeably restrained on the topics of gender and sexuality, in contrast with the sculpture's boldness. In 1968 San Franciscans saw relatively unprecedented scenes in Ghirardelli Square—breast-feeding, a lesbian family, an amphibian orgy, possibly mermaid vaginas. In trying to raise a controversy over abstraction versus representation, modern versus historical, and the sculpture's artistic style, Halprin precipitated a public conversation about gender, sexuality, and power and their location and role in urban space, neighborhood revitalization, tourism, and the city's future.

On the ground at the Ghirardelli redevelopment experiment, the design professions' attention to historicism and modernism in the 1960s was overlaid with issues of gender and sexuality in ways that only slowly became visible. The urban design issues integrating modernism, gender, and sexuality differed from those provoked by Carol Doda and the Broadway strip, but the mermaids revealed how they shared the same terrain. The tourist attractions concentrated in these neighborhoods—North Beach, waterfront redevelopment, Ghirardelli, The Cannery, the Maritime Museum, Fisherman's Wharf, the wholesale design district in Jackson Square—introduced a successful mix of historical themes, commercial development, sex industries, ethnic restaurants, and outdoor living that inspired developers and city administrators across the nation for decades. Determining what exactly the representational mermaids represented proved to be complicated.

Between Ghirardelli Square's opening in 1964 and the 1968 sculpture controversy, a great deal had changed in San Francisco and the nation's cities. The square was steeped in the era's transformative currents—in feminism, environmentalism, countercultures, urban renewal, race rebellions, suburbanization, and political protest. Like the society women of the Tour de Dining Décor and the professional designers of Ghirardelli Square, Ruth Asawa also worked within a benign, familiar artistic form (in her case, a charming fantasy sculpture of splashing mermaids) to reflect and articulate but, more importantly, to provoke change.

Ghirardelli Square built bridges between the old and the new San Francisco. New arts emerged in new places, due in part to the alternative cultural scenes and outdoor living cultivated in the Bay Area, fueling tourism and an urbane vitality that diverged from the existing city historic preservation models offered by Boston, New Orleans, or Charleston.[79] For one, in San Francisco modernists (Lawrence Halprin and Bill Wurster among them) and urban renewal leaders (including Bill Roth) shepherded the efforts to reuse historic buildings. Ghirardelli Square was a key piece in a chain of new plazas woven through the city fabric, merging civic, commercial, and natural assets. Like Ghirardelli, most obscured the underlying realities of public or private ownership, and many blurred the lines between historic and modern, wholesome and morally disruptive, staid and countercultural. Cropping up in diverse neighborhoods—from the financial district to retail centers, red-light strips, parks, and the waterfront—these plazas and strips distilled and propelled the transformations under way. Most of these planned commercial plazas, as built, were neither public parks nor official civic institutions.

Ghirardelli Square melded two "old" San Francisco families (Matson and Ghirardelli) while also fashioning an emerging model of the built environment that reworked the old into an essential part of the new.[80] Just before the square's official opening in 1964, the city's cultural arts leadership came under fire from developer and later arts commissioner Jeremy Ets-Hokin. Ets-Hokin "declared that San Francisco hasn't advanced culturally since the 1930s and that the 'moneyed elite' is stifling progress in artistic fields. . . . Descendants of the old families have become 'docile.'" Society columnist Frances Moffat held up Bill Roth as a counterargument: "All hands will come here for Sunday's opening of Ghirardelli Square, a project of Bill Roth—another non-docile descendant of an old family."[81] Roth backed urban renewal and Ghirardelli Square, Halprin and Asawa.

San Francisco's network of planned public and private plazas and gathering spaces emerged from the broken ground of the city's large-scale downtown clearance projects (Golden Gateway and Embarcadero Center), from single-tower skyscrapers (Crown Zellerbach), and from historically inspired commercial revitalizations like Ghirardelli Square.[82] Ultimately, these civic-commercial open spaces eroded rather than exacerbated the distinctions between historical and modern. Ghirardelli Square and Crown Zellerbach were landmark firsts in San Francisco for opposing reasons—preservationist rescue of a historic site from the march of high-rises versus sleek tower clearing away "rapidly declining waste." Yet through the plazas integrated into their cores, historic Ghirardelli Square and modern Crown Zellerbach were both part of the new San Francisco. The square's terrace and the Zellerbach plaza shared many motifs emphasized in promotional views capturing natural cobblestone and brick pavers glimpsed through olive trees, creating oases for casual outdoor dining (figs. 49 and 50). In 1966 SPUR honored both

49 The novelty of the preservationist Ghirardelli plaza was enhanced by atmospheric olive trees, cobblestones, and bricks. The designers integrated retail and entertainment venues with the outdoors, where dining and people-watching were major attractions. A similar slide [CC308] in Halprin's collection was labeled "paving thru olives," hinting at the sought-after effects of viewing textured stones through a halo of olive branches—irrespective of historical or modern design context.

sites as San Francisco "Bright Spots," places "where nature and structure gracefully supplement each other." Forty-four huge yellow balloons were anchored around the city for ten days to recognize old and new designs that left "ground space" for the public.[83] For their respective contributions to the new civic-commercial urban environmental models emerging in the Bay Area, Lawrence Halprin and Ruth Asawa had far more in common than the mermaid controversy suggested.

With one corner in the North Beach topless clubs and another corner in the city's "old families," with input from unrecognized property managers as well as from prestigious architects melding historical and modern, Ghirardelli Square proved a rich experimental domain. Ghirardelli provoked debates about gender, sexuality, and the role of urban open space in San Francisco that Crown Zellerbach and other modernist icons could not generate or sustain alone. The public claimed authority over the fountain sculpture and its resonant meaning, made the private plaza a civic forum for public debate, and rejected the modernist landscape frameworks imposed by Halprin. Ghirardelli Square, Herb Caen knew, achieved something "swinging" and transgressive. The dynamic relationship between the "preserved" commercial plaza and the "modern" museum or high-rise—the distance traveled between old and new, representational and abstract— would continue to matter.

The same month that the sculpture controversy broke, Larry Halprin spoke to *San Francisco* magazine about his aspirations: 'We are terribly hung-up on developing schemes for a generation that doesn't realize how outmoded it is. It has a certain set of values—making a nice place, making the world beautiful, making the family happy. And these values are being challenged right now to a degree most middle-aged people simply don't realize. As for me, I'd like to explore with young people what they want in the environment of the future.'" The story of San Francisco's transformation was in part the story of a middle-aged generation coming to terms with its own labors of urban renewal and suburban homemaking in the midst of social upheaval, sexual revolution, and unrest. From the waterfront in 1968 you could see the subversively transformative power of the old, quaint values Halprin tended to dismiss, and also catch a glimpse of the new.[84]

50 A ground-level view of the plaza in the new Crown Zellerbach high-rise office complex. The elevated base of the skyscraper is visible on the left. This plaza and Ghirardelli Square were both recognized by the San Francisco Planning and Urban Renewal Association as integrating nature into the city in fresh ways. Like Ghirardelli Square, this high-rise plaza had olive trees, outdoor dining, and many more cobblestones. Such 1960s civic-commercial plazas eroded rather than exacerbated the distinctions between historical and modern.

Married Merchant-Builders

From Home-Making to City Planning
in the Postwar Suburban Boom

A construction photograph of Ghirardelli Square's main plaza sidesteps the polarity of modernism versus preservation and reorients the north waterfront renewal story to the role of builders and the ideas and expertise they brought to revitalization (fig. 51). For viewers with purist assumptions about what constitutes historic preservation, the photograph exposes the excavation, engineering feats, and new structures that made the end result possible. This 1963 excavation carved out space for the ten-level underground garage at the heart of the square. Construction photographs for projects were usually not taken by professional photographers. More documentary than publicity shots, they became part of planning, problem-solving, and meeting insurance needs. They document cranes, building foundations, temporary timber bracing, scaffolding, concrete pouring, steel beams, work benches, and demolition. Construction photographs also provide rare glimpses of the workers who built sites.

Consider two additional contrasting 1960s photographs of the same plaza that, together, establish the distinctiveness of the construction perspective (figs. 52 and 53). The first photograph (see fig. 52) emphasizes the bay view preserved first by the Roth family's purchase of the factory and then by redevelopment. Taking in the old and new buildings, the photographer's lens connects the plaza with the historic ships anchored

51 View of the terraced east plaza and new shop buildings being constructed on top of an underground parking garage in the spring of 1964. The ten-level garage was the most dramatic, and invisible, alteration to the Ghirardelli site.

52 This perspective from Ghirardelli Square's upper levels underscored the east plaza's intimacy and its connection with the bay, history, Alcatraz, and the views—all qualities that Ruth Asawa emphasized.

53 A "modernist" view of the same plaza before the sculpture was installed, emphasizing hard surfaces and the new structures by John Matthias and William Wurster. Straining the eye to locate the tubbed plants at the far edge of the plaza, one understands why Halprin's critics on the advisory board pressed the landscape architect to include more greenery and flowers. Halprin sought a powerful, stark impact.

at water's edge, courtesy of the neighboring Maritime Museum and its director, Karl Kortum. In the enclosed and intimate plaza, people linger and find spots for their varied activities. Ruth Asawa's mermaids blend in, sitting as comfortably on sea turtles as the visitors are perched on benches and steps. Olive trees shade and soften the plaza. The connection to the bay, to history, to Alcatraz and Marin County, was secure in this appealing modern dining and retail destination.

Dated a few years earlier, before the installation of the fountain sculpture, the second photograph (see fig. 53) shows the historic square as a modernist urban design prototype in delicate balance with the factory's past, just as Halprin imagined it.[1] The photograph gives no evidence of the neighborhood or its relationship to the bay. Indeed, this plaza could be anywhere. The photographer's framing includes only the square's new structures—the long, low line of the Wurster building on the right and, at center and left, John Matthias's stores. Hard surfaces dominate, especially in the foreground. Here the same olive trees are impotent against the bright sun and the plaza's stark demeanor. The pedestrians look isolated and static.

In a tall stack of his own construction photos was a single snapshot that Stuart Rose took of his wife, Caree, seated behind her desk in their Ghirardelli Square office (fig. 54). If Ruth Asawa's sensibility could be said to animate the preservationist view (see fig. 52) and Lawrence Halprin's imagination to anoint the modernist view (see fig. 53), the key personalities behind the construction photographs were Stuart and Caree Rose, the square's first property managers. Together on site every day, the husband-and-wife management team oversaw the complex from its planning stages through phased construction, tenanting, publicity, and programming.

54 In a stack of construction photos from October 1963 that project comanager Stuart Rose took of Ghirardelli Square there is a single snapshot of his wife, comanager Caree Rose. She is seated behind her desk in their office at the site.

Like the hidden work of the underground garage, the contributions of Stuart and Caree Rose to the Ghirardelli Square redevelopment were submerged but are essential to grasping the project's significance. Underground parking lacked the design glamor of other commercial construction, but Stuart Rose was pleased to take credit for the garage. The garage was simultaneously the square's most dramatic and most invisible alteration. By far the most expensive aspect of the redevelopment, the garage not only physically supported the terraced plaza but also set the design terms for the plaza and its surrounding new retail buildings. Stuart Rose prepared thirteen alternate underground parking plans for the square's advisory group in May 1963. Roth anticipated that the Roses would help the architects achieve better economic returns. The garage proved to be the square's leading revenue producer.[2]

As much as the architects and landscape architects, merchant-builders Caree and Stuart Rose developed the principles of what city planners would soon call "adaptive reuse" in the United States. During Ghirardelli Square's construction phase, the Roses had the job of bringing the future to life when the project remained an unnamed cluster of defunct factory buildings in an eddy of a waterfront neighborhood at the margins of downtown. Described by the press as "the charming couple in charge of the Square," the middle-aged Roses brought "youthful vitality" and convincing energy that dispelled the unappealing present conditions. At that moment, wrote journalist Richard Reinhardt, "seen in the midst of reconstruction, with the old box factory torn away and the pit of the underground parking garage gaping among the dark red walls, the chocolate plant is less romantic than a South of Market loft."[3]

Viewed from the gaping pit of the garage excavation, the stature of urban design comes down a few pegs (fig. 55). From the earthen floor, architecture and landscape architecture appeared distant concerns. Design was only one element of the machinery that converted land into the "urban space" prized by architects and critics (and also historians) and the real estate prized by investors. Construction cranes, reinforced foundation walls, and construction workers brought into focus the challenges facing builders and engineers. The dichotomous frameworks of modern versus historical, abstract versus representational, had purpose but were inadequate for capturing the transformations under way on San Francisco's north waterfront in the 1960s. Even as the innovations on the ground at Ghirardelli Square contributed to the emerging framework of renewal versus preservation, they provoked critiques and rethinking of that frame and evoked alternatives.

Centering the role of the Roses in the redevelopment story, an unlikely perspective in architectural or urban history, reveals a longer account of how merchant-builders became entangled with and disentangled from the architectural design professions in the postwar period. Caree and Stuart Rose brought two decades of design credentials to the Ghirardelli collaboration that put them in tension with the professionally trained architects involved with that project. They had experience in residential and commercial construction and in redeveloping historic structures. If there is a constant in their construction photographs, it is the presence of cranes. Construction cranes represented building, rebuilding, engineering, and management, whereas bulldozers were closely

55 Ghirardelli Square garage excavation, ca. January 1963, revealing the extent of the hidden underground work necessary to remake the factory.

associated with demolition and urban renewal (fig. 56).[4] The Roses' redevelopment work underscores the novel blends of expertise required by building a new generation of large-scale mixed-use complexes.[5]

The Roses had accrued these credentials in the same postwar suburban Bay Area boomtowns where the architects and landscape architects found their commissions. The Roses' success buying and developing properties in a community like Sausalito was simultaneously ultralocal and nationally relevant, given Marin County's concentration of resident architects. Although the region's postwar growth meant that there were enough homebuyers to go around, the Roses nonetheless pitched for space in the same shelter magazines and courted the same writers and editors, hired the same photographers, and engaged the same suppliers as the professional architects (and also labored next door to them). The stature of Bay Area merchant-builders and architects alike during these formative decades of the 1940s and 1950s grew through activating similar networks of allied design fields such as trade magazine writing and architectural photography.

Within the familiar story of the 1940s and 1950s suburban residential construction boom are surprising glimpses into the defining 1960s urban redevelopment conflicts over skyscrapers and plazas. The key professional distance traveled by both builders and architects from the 1940s to the 1960s was from the suburban residential to the urban commercial context, and also from private domestic spaces to broadly symbolic urban sites. The Roses' 1950s retail adaptive reuse project in Sausalito, The Village Fair, proved to be one of the pivots for this move from suburban edge to urban design prototype.

GHIRARDELLI SQUARE IS A FAMILY PROJECT FOR THEM
Mr. and Mrs. Stuart Rose are codirectors of the historic complex

56 Stuart and Caree Rose secured good press for their work at Ghirardelli Square. The construction crane and blueprints underscored their roles as builders. As in this article, reporters usually described them as directors or developers.

The fact that the married Roses merged their personal and professional futures to forge new careers together in real estate and urban development was equally emblematic of Bay Area design during these decades. Similar partnerships were behind all three plazas whose photographs open this chapter. Behind the historicist view of Ghirardelli, for example, were Ruth Asawa, joined by her husband, architect Albert Lanier, as well as maritime historian and museum director Karl Kortum and his wife, the urban and environmental preservationist Jean Kortum. Behind the modernist view was architect Bill Wurster and his spouse, the pathbreaking urban planner and housing expert Catherine Bauer Wurster, and landscape architect Larry Halprin, with his collaborator and spouse, the equally influential dancer Ann Halprin. At the edges of the stories behind the three photographs were many others who touch down in these chapters, such as writer Sally Woodbridge and her husband, architect John Woodbridge, and landscape author Maggie Baylis and her spouse, the landscape architect Douglas Baylis.[6] Caree and Stuart Rose illustrate how this pervasive dynamic melding personal collaboration and business partnership structured planning and design in the postwar period, which raises significant historical questions. The career transformations that were achieved between the 1940s and the 1960s, especially for women in the years just prior to feminist liberation, helped define what was possible in the move from home-making to city planning in urban design. Without spending a day in college, Caree Rose leveraged a lucrative career in real estate development with her husband and played a lead role in widely emulated urban design innovations of the 1960s.

THE ROSES: "THEY HAD *NOTHING* TO DO WITH DESIGN"

When Bill Roth struggled to recall the person he had charged with "design control" of Ghirardelli Square, interviewer Randy Delehanty interjected: "Overseeing it would be Stuart Rose I suppose." Instantly switching from hesitant to firm, Roth interrupted to correct Delehanty. "Oh my goodness," Roth said. "Oh no no no no no. He was—he and Caree—were managers. . . . They had *nothing* to do with design."[7]

In responding "Oh no no no no no," Bill Roth did not intend to belittle Stuart and Caree Rose's contributions, which he knew to have been significant. From 1963 to 1970 the Roses had guided the square from original concepts through construction, tenanting, and marketing. Roth consistently credited them for their indispensable work. When asked whether he had ever seen a similar project prior to purchasing the chocolate factory, Roth replied: "The Village Fair in Sausalito, and that's why as a matter of fact I got Stuart and Caree to be our first managers. . . . *That* was a kind of a prototype."[8] Roth lived in Sausalito and had witnessed firsthand the Village Fair's role in heating up the sleepy town's tourist economy. Postwar, the bohemian waterfront community at the southern tip of Marin County had been rapidly transformed, in part because of the opening of the Golden Gate Bridge in 1937.[9] In the mid-1950s the Roses had converted an obscure former garage for ferry travelers into an interior "village" of unique shops. By early 1957, they had remade Sausalito's "traditional 'white elephant'" building, at four stories the town's tallest, into a novel shopping center near the water. The Roses accomplished this in a place where, as Caree Rose recalled, "there was nothing to do" and "no place to shop."[10]

Nevertheless, Roth's insistence that the Roses "had *nothing* to do with design" hinted at the disdain the couple experienced in the world of architecture. The sharp distinctions Roth drew between designers and property managers proved telling, as he expressed a profession-based definition of design that was narrow and proprietary. The Roses daily negotiated the design disdain of architects; they lived the distinction Roth drew between management and design and sometimes drew it themselves. At least the condescension was mutual. The Roses, having undertaken in their own careers most of the work of architects, felt qualified to critique the architects. They gave as good as they got.

As a hands-on owner, Bill Roth must have noted that the press described the Roses as developers as often as it referred to them as managers. After Caree's death in 1989, Stuart made sure the papers characterized her career and legacy correctly. Her obituary ("Caree N. Rose, Developer") opened with this: "Caree Norma Rose, who developed Ghirardelli Square and other shopping complexes throughout the world with her husband," had passed away. The Roses were called "development managers." Stuart Rose's brother Robert, also a Marin County–based real estate developer, guarded Stuart's profile when Stuart died ten years later. Stuart Rose's obituary remembered him as the "guiding force behind the Ghirardelli Square project in San Francisco." Robert Rose said, "The whole Ghirardelli Square concept from start to finish was his idea."[11] Developer Roth, and not just landscape architect Lawrence Halprin or architect William Wurster, had reason to feel crowded by the couple.

The Roses' experience as builders in Marin County gave them the qualifications, skills, and development concepts they would deploy in San Francisco. They tended to the bottom line and offered engineering solutions, building code expertise, construction supervision, landscape and interior design knowledge, events programming, marketing, and tenant selection. The Roses created the prototype that would be modified for Ghirardelli Square, and, in turn, Ghirardelli Square became one of the most widely emulated urban design innovations in 1960s and 1970s commercial revitalization. Among the fields allied to the design professions, property development and management came close to covering the range of work assumed by architects, landscape architects, and planners. Yet property, not design, lay explicitly at the field's core.

THE 1940S SUBURBAN BOOM:
HOME-MAKING "DONE WITHOUT PROFESSIONAL AID"

The tensions between Ghirardelli Square's property managers and prestigious architects began decades before Bill Roth bought the block in 1962. The key encounter occurred in September 1940. Stuart Rose and Carissima Norma D'Orso met on a Monday, and they married two days later. She was twenty-eight years old and single, working as a secretary at Shell Oil in the legal-chemical department. He was two years older and divorced, with a five-year-old daughter. Trained in aeronautical engineering, in 1940 Stuart Rose had his hands full as a purchasing agent at Western Pipe and Steel Company. Western Pipe was one of the West Coast's most productive shipbuilders. From the 1930s, the company had government contracts supplying ships, first to the Roosevelt administration's Maritime Commission and then, with the war, to the U.S. Navy. The Roses' marriage and partnership would merge and transform both of their careers. For them the operative unit of collaboration in urban design would be at the family level.

Caree Rose gave notice at Shell Oil, where she earned $120 a month (a helpful baseline for following her career), and moved to Sausalito with her new husband. She had worked as a stenographer since graduating from high school in 1929, having spent most of her career as a private secretary in foreign banking for Bank of America.[12] Growing up, Caree had seen secretarial work provide the young women in her family with some financial security, and her older sister Iris had also chosen to work as a bank stenographer. Caree Rose's mother, Norma, had followed the calling of clairvoyancy and gave her primary occupation as a medium. Her father, Gennaro, was a ceramic artist. The stability of secretarial employment proved to be a good anchor for Caree during the Depression, and it became clear that she had a knack for the business world. Caree Rose did not attend college, and never regretted that fact. Her polish was such that her first employer "didn't know I had never gone to business school."[13]

Thanks to Carissima Norma D'Orso Rose's participation in an early longitudinal social-scientific study, she left behind an unusually thorough record of how her upbringing and her marriage intertwined with her professional career in urban redevelopment. The Genetic Studies of Genius study, organized by psychologist Lewis M. Terman, followed 1,470 California children identified in 1921–22 as "gifted." From age ten in 1922 until her death in 1989, Caree Rose's life was probed by the Stanford University–based Terman team. In the beginning, she was evaluated by her teachers and parents and by Terman's field representatives. Soon she began filling out detailed questionnaires herself. The study collected information about most aspects of her schooling, hobbies, family, and work. When the survey did not ask the right questions, she appended personal letters and enclosed newspaper clippings about her achievements. Inasmuch as the study continuously inquired about her work, goals, and life satisfaction over many decades, it offers a nuanced record of her career transformation. The Terman surveys did not add questions targeted to women participants until 1972, but it still collected an unmatched qualitative record of gender-sorted material pertaining to this generation of women and men born about 1910. Since this record documents Caree Rose's point of view, it inevitably subsumes Stuart Rose's experience of their collaboration. Her perspective illuminates the experience of a generation of professional women whose careers peaked before women's liberation made its mark, although it is difficult to say how typical her commentary is of the women and men whose careers came together in economic depression and wartime. Caree Rose's career in real estate development certainly offers pointed questions to bring to the study of other married partnerships in urban design at the time, in the Bay Area and nationally.[14]

Because of the Terman study, it is possible to trace the transformative spark of professional inspiration that flamed when Carissima D'Orso and Stuart Rose met in September 1940. Stuart soon abandoned his secure but uninspiring corporate job, while Caree used her business skills from secretarial work to join forces with her husband in a new venture—postwar home design and construction. Together they then saw the promise of the bay views from their rented downtown Sausalito studio in the 1940s.

Arising from their combined skills, the Village Fair took shape, and the foundations for their careers in master planning and urban commercial development were laid. A few months before she met Stuart Rose, Caree D'Orso had told the Terman researchers that she suffered from an overall lack of direction. A matter-of-fact person, she was frank about her attitude toward her future: "Drift entirely, no definite life plans; leave everything to chance." The timing of this response was important. It documents how the dynamic of the Roses together galvanized something new and original that they had not possessed separately. Their marriage helped their careers, and their careers helped their marriage. In property development and later real estate consulting, Caree Rose and Stuart Rose "worked as a team," they always said.[15] Their business partnership and their marriage inseparably shaped their work in real estate.

After leaving her secretarial job and moving out of the city, Caree Rose described herself as being "completely absorbed in being a housewife." However, during the first year of their marriage, "homemaking" took on an unusual meaning—that of home-making. Building their newlywed home in 1940 and 1941, Caree and Stuart sowed the seeds for their postwar business: designing and constructing residences in Sausalito. In 1941, she reported to the Terman team on the recent turn of events: "Since my marriage I have not worked. I am now living in Sausalito where we have just finished building a house which we designed and decorated without benefit of [an] architect or decorator. Consequently we think it quite outstanding. Aside from that my other activities consist of flying, gardening, traveling, Red Cross, National Defense and Baby Welfare Work, as well as a fair amount of entertaining and being entertained." For Stuart Rose in 1940, building the house with his new wife was one of many "avocational interests," which included "flying, hunting, fishing, designing houses, electrical work, ships." When asked in 1940 about her husband's future plans, Caree Rose expected that he would "continue in his present line of work" at Western Pipe and Steel. She did not know that building their home would prove to be more rewarding than their regular jobs (Caree returned to secretarial work during the war, while Stuart enlisted in the Air Force). Yet five years before the Roses turned their own home into their first joint business venture, and nearly a quarter century before tensions broke open with the architects at Ghirardelli Square, the Roses relished the underdog satisfaction of designing and building a home "without benefit of [an] architect."[16]

By the end of the war, Stuart and Caree Rose had a foundation that propelled them to take career risks. Pried loose from routine by wartime service, the Roses "decided to chuck corporate image and go into business for ourselves," Caree noted. They gave up "fat, cozy" corporate security and became residential real estate developers. In 1945 they hired a professional architectural photographer, Philip Fein, to take pictures of their home. With Fein's photos in hand, the Roses persuaded *Sunset* magazine to run a feature story; Caree had always expressed more professional than domestic pride in that first home.[17]

They also began to buy up what they saw as undervalued, "undeveloped land" in Sausalito, including a 7-acre parcel that they purchased for $15,000 and subdivided into twenty-one lots. After opening their workshop in 1946 in the old Mason garage, they designed and built speculative homes one at a time, working up to a pace of three or more annually. By 1952 they had completed forty-two homes. During these years, their practice was to live in one of their homes until they were ready to sell and move into the next house under way. Sausalito and other Marin County communities were rapidly emerging as hotbeds of high-end residential modernism engaged in by elite Bay Area architects. Later the Roses liked to say that they built the last home in Sausalito before the war and the first homes afterward (fig. 57).[18]

Working together, the Roses accomplished more—in terms of fulfilling creative, professional, and personal milestones—than they likely would have had they remained apart. Their gamble in real estate development paid off financially. Caree's wages had been $250 a month in 1946, but ten years later she and Stuart netted $10,000 a year together.[19] Marriage energized their leisure pursuits as well. Caree leapt into a more active lifestyle of flying, hunting, fishing, playing tennis, and gardening. She got a pilot's license in order to keep up with Stuart, who had been flying since 1927. They both flew for the Southern Land Frontier during the war.[20] Together, they transformed from secretary and purchasing officer/aeronautical engineer into entrepreneurial real estate developers. Stuart's initiative might have animated their hobbies, but it was Caree who had the most drive for commercial real estate development.[21]

"My marriage," Caree Rose wrote in 1941, "has completely changed my life." But within this potentially clichéd story of 1940s suburban housewifery and homemaking

57 View of downtown San Francisco's north waterfront from Sausalito in Marin County. Many leading participants in the city's redevelopment, from artists and architects to large-scale developers, lived in Marin and commuted to San Francisco. This perspective illuminates why many people complained about the impact of the tall, dark, Bank of America headquarters on an otherwise light-colored urban palette and shows the high visibility of Coit Tower and Telegraph Hill, to the left.

were the roots of the Roses' partnerships in 1950s–1960s urban revitalization projects. Their distinctive approach to development formulas was evident in their earliest projects, which evolved quickly from new residential construction to redesigning older structures such as a barn. *Sunset*'s 1946 headline for its coverage of the Roses' first home—"Done without Professional Aid"—echoed the do-it-yourself pride Caree Rose had conveyed to Terman (figs. 58 and 59). *Sunset* singled out space-saving innovations Stuart Rose had incorporated into the contemporary interior, admiring the "good tricks in mechanics and lighting." There were ingenious practical touches—from the ship anchors welded together to make andirons to the porthole niche for displaying sculpture, the built-in bookshelves, and the mahogany coffee table Stuart had designed and built. *Sunset* chose not to publish photographs of the house's quirkier elements—such as the den with built-in filing cabinets, gun storage, and a drafting table (fig. 60) or the bedroom that looked like a ship's cabin, with under-bed storage and two portholes. When the Roses refashioned an old Sausalito barn into a home in the early 1950s, they were part of a popular trend that "any big, bare, broken-down barn hits the average American"

58 Merchant builders Stuart and Caree Rose drew attention to the practical, creative, and space-saving features of their home in 1946. The notes appended to these photographs did not describe the views, volume, light, or flow of space, as architects did. The living room and dining area had large windows and views, although the furnishings faced the windowless interior and fireplace. On the left is a mahogany table designed and built by Stuart Rose, for which plans were available. The magazines on the table are *Californian*, *Sunset*, and *Log*. Compare this Rose home to the model-makers' AIA award–winning Marin home described in chapter 8.

with an immediate urge to remodel. The Roses, who lived in the home at the time, described some of their strategies. "This is the most enjoyable way of building," Stuart Rose reflected, "creating something out of what you have. But it's not the simplest and not the cheapest."[22]

By the time the Roses closed the door on speculative residential building, they had refined their design and marketing approach. With sophistication they worked the same contacts architects depended on in the allied design professions, whether the press, furniture retailers, realtors, or architectural photographers. Stuart Rose later claimed that four of their homes had appeared on the cover of *Sunset*, and as small builders they were unusually successful at getting in-depth press features.[23] One 1952 article, "He Has Fun and Profit Building the Unusual," featured a two-bedroom Sausalito house they had built into a steep slope with a spectacular view after bulldozing the site (fig. 61). In deciding whether to fit the house to the hill or the hill to the house, Stuart Rose chose the latter because he was able to sell the excavated land as fill. For their marketing strategy they had staged the house "with modern furniture from a Sausalito

59 This photograph featured several of the Roses' built-in efficiencies and original touches. The picture over the fireplace covers the opening to a heat circulator, with the picture backed by asbestos and hung away from the wall. The andirons are made from two welded anchors, and above the kitchen entrance (to the left of the fireplace) is storage space. Other details included exposed beams, slender steel tie rods, and built-in bookshelves with indirect lighting. The porthole window on the left was repeated in a small bedroom, which extended the nautical theme with a raised threshold and ship's cabin beds.

60 Stuart Rose's home office contrasts with the artists' studio built by Virginia Green and Leila Johnston in their Marin County home, described in chapter 8. When the office door closed, it hit a catch pin that locked and hid the file cabinets. The office had blueprint storage above the door and also a gun closet.

store, and hired a professional architectural photographer to supply dramatic prints of the house to local newspapers." Local and regional newspapers particularly "welcome the chance to use fine architectural photographs." The Roses upgraded to use a "photographer for *Sunset Magazine*," Ernest Braun. They also opened the house to the public for a week as a "community model home." The last house they built, Rose said, "sold to the first person who walked in the door." Stuart Rose discussed his unglamorous but innovative construction details. "We design for the view," he told the reporter, and "for easy living. And we have fun doing it." At $16,100 for the two-bedroom home, the Roses's homes were not inexpensive.[24]

The Roses' investment in Sausalito real estate placed them in direct competition with architects and landscape architects as Marin County began to bustle with the residential designs of up-and-coming and established architectural firms (such as George T. Rockrise, Campbell & Wong, Joe Esherick, and Wurster, Bernardi & Emmons) and designer-builders like themselves. When the AIA hosted its 1960 national meeting in San Francisco, the organizers arranged a tour introducing visiting professionals to sites of noteworthy design in the Bay Area. For the first time, the AIA published a guidebook to accompany its conference tour and provide other tourists with an itinerary. Researched and authored by Sally Woodbridge and John Woodbridge, *Buildings of the Bay Area* opened with Sausalito—not San Francisco. The Roses' homes were not included in the AIA guide. But the couple had long marketed their residences as "livable modern" to simultaneously benefit from popular design trends and distinguish their work from the alleged impractical qualities of architect-designed contemporary homes.[25]

Most U.S. architects and landscape architects in the 1950s, even those who had attended the world's exclusive professional design schools, ultimately worked the same

61 The Roses found a successful marketing niche in postwar Sausalito, building what they called "livable modern" homes like this one. Their houses were featured in the regional shelter magazines like *Sunset* alongside the designs of architects and landscape architects. By 1952, when this article appeared, the Roses had completed forty-two homes.

private home-building proving grounds as merchant-builders Caree and Stuart Rose. Lawrence Halprin recalled meeting Bill Wurster and Catherine Bauer Wurster in 1943 at the Harvard University Graduate School of Design at a moment when Bill was "switching from an emphasis on private residential work to wartime housing projects" and city planning.[26] Halprin admired Wurster's residential designs, especially their integration with landscape architect Thomas Church's gardens. Halprin's trajectory as a landscape architect provides a proximate comparison for the Roses. After wartime service in the Navy, Larry Halprin and his spouse and artistic collaborator, Anna Halprin, settled in the Bay Area as newcomers to the West Coast. Halprin took a position in Thomas Church's small office at $75 per week, over an offer from Bill Wurster. Halprin worked primarily on gardens and estates for an elite client base on the San Francisco peninsula south of the city, in northern Santa Clara County and San Mateo County. The Halprins bought a small bungalow in Marin County for $6,000. About the same time that *Sunset* covered the Roses' first home, the magazine gave Halprin a "small stipend" to see what he could craft in the modest yard of *his* first home. After a few years with Church's office, Halprin opened his own firm in 1948. Bill Wurster designed a home for the Halprins in Kentfield, another Marin community, where they moved in 1952. Unlike the Roses, the Halprins remained in the same home. Over the next decade, Halprin's office designed more than three hundred private gardens in the San Francisco Bay Area between 1949 and 1961.

Architects such as Halprin and Wurster, as well as merchant-builders Caree and Stuart Rose, made similar transitions in the 1950s from private residential design to urban civic-commercial development. In the 1960s Halprin welcomed the fresh challenges of large, complex sites with resonant social meaning—college campuses, shopping centers, parks, and housing developments. He noted that the most generative residential commissions allowed experimentation with details and environmental approaches he could use in public projects, such as pedestrian flow through outdoor spaces. Private homes, Halprin appreciated, had the additional advantage of relatively quick completion. Like Halprin, Stuart and Caree Rose took stock of which suburban residential design and marketing successes they could enlist in their next venture. With well-connected residential clients, designers also formed friendships with influential San Francisco civic leaders who wielded power in the downtown world of large-scale urban design commissions.[27] Overall, private home construction, through the designers, builders, clients, photographers, model-makers, and publicists, shared numerous ties with public sites and redevelopment leadership in San Francisco and other cities.[28]

As Bay Area architects and builders converged in San Francisco's dynamic and contested real estate environment, popular shelter magazines—especially *Sunset*—served as equalizing forces. The magazine was itself produced by a network of arts professionals, most notably the writers, editors, photographers, and graphic designers. Architecture and urban design writer Allan Temko, later honored as a leading critic with a Pulitzer prize, caught his break in popular architectural writing at *Sunset* in 1955. For a few years he contributed frequently, without a byline, to this staff-written magazine. His *Sunset* "copy was often transformed before it appeared in print," he remembered. Still,

Temko sent his *Sunset* tear sheets when Douglas Haskell, editor of *Architectural Forum*, approached him in 1957 about becoming the Western correspondent for that elite design journal. Temko enclosed three articles: "Life with the Auto," "The Broad-Source Light," and "There's a New Room in the Western House—the Family Room." The last resembled the articles about homes designed by the Roses, Wurster, and Halprin. Temko became the architectural critic for the *San Francisco Chronicle* in 1961.[29] *Sunset* also provided the Roses with a personal introduction for the Ghirardelli Square job; of the original 1962 development team, only editor Proctor Mellquist had met the Roses, because of the magazine stories featuring their homes.[30]

From Caree Rose's perspective, suburban home building allowed her to transition from corporate secretarial work to an independent real estate development partnership, but the nature of residential construction nonetheless constrained her role relative to her partner. In 1953 she summarized her career for the Terman researchers by saying she "works with husband in design and building of homes." Her day-to-day responsibilities included interior design, concept planning for their subdivisions, office and construction management, and publicity. But press coverage mostly mentioned Stuart Rose. Caree Rose did get some acknowledgment; in 1946 Stuart Rose had "fun building his own house," while "Mrs. Rose, who [was] her own interior decorator, [had] added to the spacious effect by the use of simple colors and uncluttered décor." For his part, Stuart Rose always said "we" and "our" to reporters when referring to his business. The Roses' decision in the mid-1950s to leave behind home-making in favor of downtown shopping center development propelled them both toward urban revitalization careers but affected Caree's and Stuart's trajectories differently.[31] When the couple turned to revitalizing old downtown buildings into retail centers, Caree Rose branched out into new niches of developer expertise such as tenant management and landscape design, while interior decorating and the orchestration of color schemes became less significant in her professional profile.

BIG IDEA, SMALL EXPERIMENT: THE VILLAGE FAIR

In the mid-1950s, in Sausalito, Stuart and Caree Rose turned to an eccentric new project of their own making that became the prototype for Ghirardelli Square and later provided the rationale for hiring them to plan the square. They redeveloped the obscure, "white elephant" 1920s Mason garage into a novel "art" shopping center named the Village Fair (fig. 62), which opened in early 1957. The Roses had by then completed several light industrial projects, such as small factories and a bowling alley.[32] The Village Fair idea hatched from their specific knowledge of Sausalito and the town's artist community, their general understanding of Bay Area consumer markets, and their familiarity with the garage and its owner. The Roses knew the structure inside and out. They had stored sails and related boat equipment there, in a room with a view of the Sausalito harbor.

When the Roses rented workshop space in the Mason building for their home design company in 1946, they joined a critical mass of other business-oriented artists who cohered to transform the garage. Ceramicist Edith Heath and her husband, Brian Heath, moved their pottery business, Heath Ceramics, into the garage's "immense" top floor, overlooking the harbor and Richardson Bay. This relocation expanded their cramped San Francisco basement studio into a factory. The Heaths kept more than a dozen employees busy meeting the demand for their California-identified stoneware. Heath Ceramics was one of many functional art pottery businesses in the state run by married partners. On the garage's second floor, Luther William (Bill) Conover had a wholesale operation where he produced his own unique wood, wrought iron, and canvas furniture.[33] The Roses' hobbies overlapped with the interests of the artist-entrepreneurs in their building; Caree Rose had recently taken up ceramics, while Stuart Rose pursued home carpentry. He designed and built furniture, like the unique mahogany table included in the 1946 *Sunset* story.[34]

Marin County was saturated with arts and crafts in the 1940s and 1950s, with a large population of ceramicists, architects, cartoonists, musicians, cinematographers, writers, jewelers, and sculptors in addition to a healthy distribution of San Francisco civic leaders such as Bill Roth and Justin Herman. Sausalito was growing, as evidenced by the AIA tour book, but it was a commercially sleepy town. Caree Rose later jested that in the early 1950s Sausalito had twenty-one bars and one Chinese restaurant with "a guy" standing outside trolling for customers. The marina and houseboat culture meant that

FACE LIFTING — Where once upon a time dripped grease from Maxwells and Model Ts, is now an art shopping center under one roof. Note open windows on Village Fair level. At left is new medical-dental building. (Les Walsh Photo)

62 In 1956 the Roses redeveloped a 1920s parking garage in Sausalito into an unusual indoor shopping center, the Village Fair. The project brought together artists and entrepreneurs who had already taken light industrial space in the building. The Trade Fair occupied the first floor, Heath Ceramics occupied the top level, and the Roses constructed an interior shopping street on the third floor, beginning with twelve stores. The Roses began as tenants in the building in 1946, when they rented space for their home design and construction business.

affluent visitors tied up their boats for a week at a time but had few places to spend money. The Mason building had colorful associations tied to Sausalito's past, although none of that history carried over literally into the Roses' redesign. Bootleggers had found the quiet waterfront location and parking ideal for stashing and transferring contraband, and at another point the building had housed an "elegant" Chinese gambling house. Bechtel Co. engineers had used the garage space in the early 1940s to lay out Marin County's nearby World War II shipyard, known as Marinship. The building itself was architecturally undistinguished.[35]

It was furniture designer Bill Conover who, in the late 1940s, began to capitalize on the local creative energy and turn the concrete garage into an unlikely tourist destination with international name recognition. On summer weekends in 1949, he and the Heaths set up tables in an adjacent vacant lot and sold "seconds" directly to the public. They invited other artists to join them, and an architect acquaintance designed a tent to shade the vendors. Conover gave the temporary open-air market a name—the Trade Fair.[36] A second successful summer motivated Conover to rent the garage's ground floor, at which point the Trade Fair migrated indoors. Soon it featured more than fifty vendors. When tourists treated the indoor space like a museum, Conover added imported gift items to encourage "impulse buying." Ten years later the Trade Fair had become "the largest gift store in the West" and "a worldwide enterprise," boosted by design awards garnered by Edith Heath and Conover. Whereas the Heaths continued in ceramic wares, Conover stopped making furniture to devote himself to the fair. He took yearly buying trips to "the Orient" and traded his woodworking tools for a suit and tie (fig. 63). [37]

About 1952, when the annual cycle of custom home building had begun to wear on the Roses, they saw potential for a retail village in the sturdy walls around their work-shop, the breathtaking views, and the humming Trade Fair downstairs. Ten years before Bill Roth bought the Ghirardelli factory, the Roses mobilized this potential to redevelop the Mason garage. They channeled the international recognition of Bill Conover's Trade Fair and added their own local merchant-builder expertise. The Bay Area location meant that their unusual project was in view of globe trotting architects and investors. The Roses talked over their idea for a retail village with the garage's owner, Fred Allensby, a friend and San Francisco "hotel man" for whom they had built two homes. Allensby liked their suggestions.

To carry out the retail village concept, the Roses reconstructed the garage's cavernous interior to create an unusual retail "neighborhood" on the third floor. They laid out interior streets, with street signs, potted trees, planter boxes, and benches (fig. 64). This new Village Fair shopping center encompassed twelve stores on the third floor, the Trade Fair on the first floor, Heath Ceramics on the top floor, and two existing ground-level shops (a beauty salon and men's-wear shop)—all tied together "as a unit" by the building's internal auto ramps. The twelve new interior shops had unique façades, each one "designed differently to give the feeling of a community whose residents have built their own homes." The Roses' choice of words bridged the couple's transition from home construction to retail. The individualized designs, which incorporated "old brick, adobe, pastel colors, filigree iron work and redwood," resisted the homogenizing trends

63 Bill Conover, pictured here, stopped making furniture once the Trade Fair became a large venture. He traded furniture design for a suit and tie. In the mid-1960s Conover became a consultant in the field of adaptive reuse, working for Ghirardelli Square's competitor The Cannery.

in shopping centers to regulate and standardize all aspects of storefronts. Floor-to-ceiling plate glass was housed within the old brick interior. The street names were historical (such as Water Street, the original garage's address) and cute (such as Binnacle Bight and Scupper Alley). They hoped for "browsing" rather than rushing crowds and from the first months in early 1957 staged "day-long entertainment." The new shops included an art gallery, record shop, and the Magpie (a bric-a-brac store selling Early Americana), as well as other stores selling wares from Mexico, Hawaii, and more far-flung places. Outside the building they planted a row of trees along the street. Reasonably sophisticated stores coexisted with a gimmicky garage entrance ramp reconfigured to look like a replica of Lombard Street, San Francisco's "crookedest" street. The center displayed some of the hand-built quirkiness and engineering ingenuity evident in the Roses' homes.[38]

The Village Fair, although tucked away in Sausalito, had the markings of a new "thing," as well as the promise of international tourist exposure because of its association with the Trade Fair.[39] The original twelve shops attracted more businesses and expanded

THIRD STORY STREET — This charming outdoor scene was shot at Village Fair which occupies the top floor of a one-time Sausalito garage. (See photo above). The 12 shops there are all completely new additions to the Southern Marin's city's commercial scene. (Les Walsh Photo)

64 Stuart and Caree Rose arranged potted trees on this interior street on the third floor of their unique Village Fair in Sausalito. When the photo was taken in 1957, there were twelve shops, each with an individual façade. Street signs (in this case Water Street) directed customers, and the windows at right (with window boxes full of flowers) opened to bay views.

through the building, growing eventually to a dense forty-eight outlets. More space became available in 1959 when Bill Conover moved the Trade Fair to a decommissioned Southern Pacific ferryboat he had rescued—the *Berkeley*—which he berthed at the Sausalito waterfront.[40] Heath Ceramics hired architectural firm Marquis & Stoller to design what *Architectural Forum* admired as "a handsome little factory" in Sausalito. Edith Heath worked so closely with Marquis & Stoller on the building that design critic Allan Temko listed her as an associated architect.[41] Shops, services, dining, and drinking establishments filled the newly available space in the Village Fair. The Roses selected tenants and opened three businesses themselves, including a coffeehouse and a beer garden.

For Caree Rose, the retail management experience at the Village Fair, unlike her role in the home-building partnership, gave her the leverage to fully evolve into a comanager and codeveloper. The Village Fair won her professional recognition for her contributions to the signature urban revitalization experiments of the 1950s and 1960s. One *San Francisco Chronicle* reporter wrote in 1970: "The Roses can take some credit as originators of the 'old building turned into chic shopping center' idea, having developed one of the first of the kind in an abandoned concrete garage in Sausalito in 1956—'The Village Fair.'"[42] Other reporters overlooked the Village Fair but still showcased the Roses on equal terms. Regarding the history of adaptive reuse, Mary Cooke observed in 1975 that "The couple credited with opening the eyes of America to this fact of business life is Stuart and Caree Rose who, twelve years ago, zeroed in on an old chocolate factory in San Francisco and created Ghirardelli Square."[43]

In January 1963, Stuart and Caree Rose were preparing for a vacation in the Caribbean when an unexpected phone call derailed their trip. Warren Lemmon wished to speak with them about Bill Roth's plans for the Ghirardelli factory buildings. The Roses were indeed "looking for new challenges." They were about to open another restaurant, the Cellars, in San Rafael; it would be well received, but it was more of what they had already accomplished in Marin. The Ghirardelli factory, on the other hand, was a major San Francisco landmark. Lemmon explained that the main development concept had already taken shape: a shopping and entertainment center emphasizing individual stores rather than chains and merchandise possessing a "foreign flavor." Lemmon had never met the Roses. He understood that the couple "managed a relatively small operation but somewhat similar in character in Sausalito called The Village Fair." Lemmon and Roth appreciated that "it was very difficult to obtain this sort of experience" due to the "uniqueness" of their concept and the wide-ranging talents they desired in a project manager.[44]

From their first meeting, Lemmon felt comfortable entrusting the Roses with preparing "a master plan for the entire development." He attributed to the Roses "a happy combination of sensitivity to design and quality and a healthy respect for costs" and believed that they combined the necessary contracting, tenanting, and management skills. Lemmon liked the Roses' business style. He wrote to Roth on the East Coast the next day, confirming that "Both Mr. and Mrs. Rose appear to be intelligent, enthusiastic, and personable." They "had excellent experience in developing the Village Fair and appear to have the

imagination, initiative and good taste to develop an interesting and attractive center."
Their current role encompassed "control of all phases of the operation, such as establishing
the general décor and specifying the type of signs which would be acceptable." They
had learned lessons from the Village Fair: "Mr. Rose commented that several of the
tenants were not of the quality he would prefer and that in a new project he would be
more discriminating." Privately, Roth speculated that by mixing in more organizations,
offices, and apartments Ghirardelli might "prevent the crowded jumpiness" of the
Village Fair. For Ghirardelli the Roses favored "small tenancies in the existing buildings
rather than trying to draw a major tenancy into the property." Lemmon walked through
the Village Fair with the Roses, and the following day they briskly toured the working
Ghirardelli factory. Arrangements for hiring the couple were settled quickly after a meeting
in Roth's San Francisco office.[45]

For the last time Caree Rose used secretarial work as a bridge to independent professional credentials in real estate development. Although Lemmon had consulted with
the Roses on an equal basis and recognized the Village Fair as their mutual accomplishment, he offered only Stuart Rose the initial two-month contract. If anything, Caree
Rose had been more eager than her partner to take on the San Francisco factory that
stood across the street from her high school.[46] It became apparent on the job that Stuart
Rose needed administrative help. Because the couple had "always worked together as a
team," Caree Rose stepped in as her husband's secretary. At the end of the trial period,
she "suddenly protested" that she was "doing Stuart's work" without pay. "It was a
costly project and we needed volunteers on it," they joked. "I wasn't on the payroll, like
a dummy," Caree said. After those two unpaid months, Caree and Stuart Rose became,
jointly, the comanagers of the Ghirardelli Square redevelopment project. A year later, in
anticipation of the tenants moving in, the Roses had so much office work that they had
to hire a stenographer. Caree Rose's transition to manager was complete.[47]

"HOLDING HANDS" IN THE BUSINESS SECTION

When Caree Rose mailed the Terman study psychologists articles about her career in
1973, she could not resist commenting on one of the newspaper photographs (fig. 65).
"I am quite sure we are two of the few people to have a full picture holding hands in the
green section," she wrote.[48] The "green section" carried business news. Sixty-year-olds
holding hands in the business pages was doubly unusual. Yet the photograph documented
a prevalent phenomenon in the urban redevelopment field: many professional collaborators
were holding hands. Bill Wurster and Catherine Bauer, Jean Kortum and Karl Kortum,
Ruth Asawa and Albert Lanier, Larry Halprin and Anna Halprin; the list goes on. This
was neither a secret, nor was it publicized. It was an unexamined fact shaping how the
design professions intersected with allied artistic fields.

The Roses provide insight into their era's married professional partnerships in urban
design and development fields while also differentiating the experiences of women from
men in the decades prior to feminist liberation. If the move from home-making to urban
commercial renewal had made a more dramatic impact on Caree Rose's career, the Roses'
years at the Village Fair and Ghirardelli Square nonetheless progressively equalized the

credit for their mutual accomplishments. The Roses had evolved together as codevelopers and comanagers. Their palpable energy for their work mingled with a shared sense of humor and irony about their respective careers. Caree and Stuart Rose finished each other's sentences. This reciprocal partnership showed in another newspaper photograph bearing the caption "Ghirardelli Square is a family project for them" (see fig. 56). In 1977, wrestling with presumptuous questions in a Terman survey about how she had supported her husband's career, and vice versa, Caree added an asterisk to insert her own terms: "We work as a team." This phrase was her refrain throughout the decades.[49]

In 1970, with Ghirardelli Square "virtually completed" and an international success, the Roses left behind the daily responsibilities of property management and opened their own real estate development consulting business. This life change provoked Caree Rose to reflect on the satisfactions she had found in her career. The square had become only "a question of management," she explained to the Terman researchers who had followed her life for fifty years. Now consultants, the Roses were courted once

Carrisma and Stuart Rose

65 Caree Rose sent this clipping to the Stanford University researchers who had followed her aspirations and life experiences since she was nine years old. She noted that not many people could say that they had appeared in the business section of the newspapers "holding hands." However, the urban redevelopment fields in the Bay Area were filled with spouses and partners working together or in parallel careers.

again for their ideas; "This we enjoy very much as it is purely a matter of telling them what to do but they have to do it, not us," she noted. Thanks to "very stimulating and diversified" work, they were both thriving. Over the next decade, the Roses advised dozens of clients: "Our work at Ghirardelli Square has given us a remarkable opportunity to showcase our thoughts and to give us an audience as wide as the entire world." Caree Rose's increased responsibilities since the early 1960s had come with an "increase in value to clients and consequent recognition therefrom." The challenges of consulting remained "exciting and rewarding," and she relished traveling "all over the country." She spent little time relaxing "because this work I'm involved in is so interesting to me it is recreation." At age seventy, Caree doubted that she could ever retire.[50]

In development consulting, however, the Roses lost the clear authorship credit inherent to their dedicated sites such as the Village Fair and Ghirardelli Square. In contrast, consulting architects and planners retained authorship and depended on the professional boost they usually received when their projects spread around the globe. The Roses claimed credit for helping to develop nearly fifty projects, including several internationally known sites such as Baltimore's Inner Harbor. Caree Rose's obituary emphasized their reach, "from Vancouver to Australia to the Netherlands."[51] Their Hawaii developments garnered coverage, including Eaton Square in Waikiki, King's Alley (now King's Village) in Honolulu, and several Maui shopping centers. But most of their sites were regional initiatives unknown outside their immediate area. The Roses' client list documents largely forgotten 1970s retail developments that emulated Ghirardelli Square, many of them in smaller cities and suburbs. If they were once distinctive, most of the place names became generic over the decades: the Marketplace in Glastonbury, Connecticut; Harbor Square in Vancouver; Mateo Square in San Mateo, California; Colony Bazaar in Columbus, Ohio; Keystone at the Crossing in Indianapolis; and the Maryland Plaza in St. Louis. In St. Louis the mayor gave Caree Rose the key to the city in 1973, in appreciation "for the couple's redevelopment work there." The contributions were unnamed.[52] With a few exceptions, the Roses received little press recognition for their work on these consulting projects, even at the time.

If stimulating consulting work did not accrue to their professional credit, the Roses were brilliantly compensated nonetheless. Real estate consulting nearly doubled their already high real estate management incomes. This financial success certainly enhanced Caree Rose's perception of consulting as fulfilling work. In 1976 she reported to the Terman researchers an impressive combined annual earned income of $58,000 for her husband and herself. Five years earlier, the salary potential of consulting work had already been evident. Between 1970 and 1971, she listed her own annual income as increasing from $10,000 to $15,000, and her husband's as moving from $16,300 to $18,000. The family income range of $27,000–$33,000 was approximately what the Roses earned during their years at Ghirardelli Square, according to Caree Rose's figures. In 1956, as designer-builders, they netted $10,000 together. During the war, Caree had taken home $250 a month, but for most of her time as a secretary she earned half that or less. Her trajectory relative to her cohort of Terman women is revealing as well. In 1940 Caree Rose's income from secretarial work was a quarter of the average Terman female's weekly salary. By the late 1970s, her income had outpaced the Terman median of $13,000 for career women, and the Roses' family income of $58,000 dwarfed the Terman mean for couples of $36,000.[53]

The *San Francisco Chronicle* predicted that the Terman researchers would be "fascinated" by Caree Rose's accomplishments; in 1964 she was "a partner in the development of a multi-million-dollar project that may well be the only part of the current San Francisco building boom that we will point to with pride to our grandchildren."[54] Had he lived until the 1960s, Lewis Terman would indeed have been surprised to find Carissima D'Orso Rose in this cohort of successful American career women. For one, despite being singled out as a gifted child, as an Italian American she was up against an ethnic and class bias in his study. That bias was already evident in 1922, when field researcher Helen Underhill took a dislike to Caree's mother, Mrs. Norma D'Orso. "[Caree's] mother treated me as if I were a peddler or agent where 'no peddlers or agents' were allowed! (I finally convinced her I had nothing to sell.) Unattractive in manner and personality," Underhill noted. She described the neighborhood as "once good" but "falling into decay." Caree D'Orso's home environment, in Dr. Terman's opinion, was not conducive to supporting the talents of gifted children. Her divorced parents, while fiercely proud of her, held a laissez-faire attitude toward her education. They did not especially encourage her academically, nor did they teach her to read before she began school in first grade. In another predictor of success, the number of books in the home, her family came up short. The average Termite home had 328 books. The D'Orsos' had 25. In the Terman cohort, by 1947 nearly 90 percent had attended college, and 70 percent graduated. By then Caree Rose had been made aware that she had fallen behind expectations. She left the survey pages about college blank, and she did not appear to have done much with her talents. Later she offered her Terman credential in the manner in which others mentioned their university degrees.[55]

In one respect—career fulfillment—Caree Rose's life experience placed her in the vanguard of the Terman women, a harbinger of women's liberation, independence, and the future broadening of career options. This vanguard was sociologically significant but numerically tiny. Caree Rose worked her entire life, whereas the majority of Terman women did not. Here it would have been difficult for Lewis Terman to draw conclusions. Most "gifted" women went to college, but few had careers. Caree did not attend college but found exceptional career success. Terman scholars later concluded that the women in Caree Rose's cohort who pursued careers and were childless found the most "joy in living." This description fit Caree Rose's profile.[56] The study's first "Information Blank for Women" was mailed in 1972, when the participants were sixty years old. The questions fished for hopes and regrets on the topic of "work patterns women follow." For Caree Rose, pursuing a career had been satisfying at all levels. She saw nothing she would want to change, in the past or the present. Everything had aligned: "As it was," "As I planned it," and "As I now would choose." In 1977 she checked off the most gratifying aspects of her work in recent years: financial gain; creativity, learning, stimulation, and personal growth; and recognition/competition.[57]

Finding it difficult to fit her less conventional accomplishments onto Terman's standardized forms (even the ones customized for women), Caree Rose sometimes added a personal letter or enclosures. In the 1970s, Caree Rose confided to the Terman researchers that "forms defeat me, and although I am very good at publicizing other people and things, I never quite know what to say about myself. Somehow, they always make me sound like Pollyanna or an idiot." Promoting "other people and things" was of course key to property management and real estate development. Efficiently, she enclosed "an article which appeared when we first went to Ghirardelli and one which appeared when we left." When asked to describe especially satisfying accomplishments, she answered, "Nothing stands out here. When I've done a good job of *anything*, it is a source of satisfaction to me."[58] The study director, Robert Sears, wrote back a few weeks later. Impressed by the articles, he was delighted to learn of her "connection" with Ghirardelli Square: "You did a wonderful job, if I may say so." Sears thanked her for "beautifying the world. We need it!"[59] In 1978 she invited Dr. Sears to dinner in Belvedere. Tired herself of returning forms "to inanimate objects" for all those years, she thought that Sears must have "a certain curiosity about the faceless beings who put crosses over everything."[60] As reflected in the Terman correspondence, her forthrightness and confidence ultimately overshadowed whatever insecurities she might have felt over the decades.

The partnerships of Caree Rose and Stuart Rose—as designers, merchant-builders, managers, real estate development consultants, and a married couple—offer new answers to key questions in the history of urban redevelopment. Their participation in the experimentation with new urban models of the 1940s–1960s illuminates a dynamic of creativity that tied together lay designers such as themselves with the professional architects, landscape architects, and planners whose contributions over these decades are better known. The couple's transition from home building in the 1940s suburban boom, to adaptive reuse and urban redevelopment, to the "master planning" of the Ghirardelli block shows their overlaps with professional architecture. Within that successful partnership, Caree Rose's distinct achievements mapped the trajectory of career women who were "holding hands in the green section." In the decades before feminism altered the language of career success and professional possibilities, women such as Caree Rose had found this professional success and matter-of-factly made their marks in the urban revitalization fields of the Bay Area.

Stuart Rose, for his part, was also energetic, experienced in small-scale urban commercial revitalization, and full of ideas in the winter of 1963. Warren Lemmon trusted Stuart Rose and Caree Rose immediately and looked forward with relief to turning over the master planning for Ghirardelli Square to them. He regarded the couple's deft first advisory letter to Bill Roth to be a turning point in Ghirardelli's redevelopment. In his dozens of carefully researched memos for Roth, Warren Lemmon made only one mistake of any significance. He thought that Stuart Rose was trained as an architect.[61]

Managing Property

An "Iffy" Collaboration

In 1964 the AIA awarded its first Medal for Collaborative Achievement to a modernist icon: New York City's Seagram Building, plaza, and Four Seasons restaurant. Two years later it awarded the second medal to a pioneering preservationist landmark: San Francisco's Ghirardelli Square. The juxtaposition is a striking illustration of how the era's awards as well as controversies often eroded the distinctions between renewal and preservation. But just as striking is the notion of an award for design "collaboration" at all.

The slippery concept of collaboration in urban design might seem timeless and generic, but locating it in 1960s redevelopment reveals that underneath collaboration's universalizing mantle stirred an array of experimental partnerships as well as purposeful exclusions. The AIA's recognition of Ghirardelli Square began with credit to the "foresight of a San Francisco civic leader, William M. Roth," and extended to the architectural firm of Wurster, Bernardi & Emmons, as well as Lawrence Halprin & Associates, as landscape architects. The recognition roster then broadened to include the engineers, general contractor, and "design consultants": architect John Matthias for the plaza shops, graphic artist Barbara Stauffacher, and sculptor Beniamino Bufano for his abstract bear. The Roses remained outside the circle of AIA honorees, marking exclusions within the medal's generous gesture. It did not occur to the award committee to acknowledge property managers as design collaborators, let alone the circle of retail and garden consultants those managers depended on. When the AIA communications officer sat down to draft the press release, he found that he needed to write to Wurster's office: "I discovered belatedly, however, that we have no information on the collaborators. . . . Since the award stresses collaboration, I feel that I must do more than list the engineers, landscape architect, contractor, consultants, and sculptor." The AIA did not even have handy information on Halprin's office.[1]

Property managers and architects subscribed to fundamentally contrasting views of so-called urban space. The architects' compelling "space" was the property manager's "rentable area." As Stuart Rose explained bluntly, "The one thing that architects do that I think is inexcusable: they use space because the space is there. They're not aware of the fact that every square foot or cubic inch of that space is worth money, and it should be earning its keep."[2] Compared with the primarily aesthetic, social, and often abstract language of architecture and urban design, property management focused on profit, expenses, land, ownership, pragmatic results, marketing—and property. The Roses' property-oriented development priorities coexisted with, informed, and occasionally contradicted the professional design considerations of urban space and architecture. At Ghirardelli Square and elsewhere, Halprin, the architects, and the design critics focused on urban landscape, flow and movement through spaces, the relationship of space to buildings, and the interactions of people within these spaces. The Roses understood those design considerations, but they saw rentable square footage as much as space, and land as much as landscape. The excavations, construction cranes, parking garages, economic projections, tenant management, landscaping, renovations—these elements often set property managers against the architects' commitment to "open space" and magnetic "character." At times this pitted land against landscape.[3]

On the job site in the 1960s, the Roses' 1940s pride as designers "without the benefit of architects" matured into a fraught and intense collaboration with numerous architects. Stuart Rose chose strong words to describe the outcome: "We succeeded not with the aid of the architects but in spite of the architects." Caree Rose fought her own battles, rearranging "all" of Lawrence Halprin's landscape designs after he completed the job. Over time, such disagreements were not forgotten but rather folded into a shared acknowledgment that the square's signature civic design achievements and economic vitality emerged from an adversarial style of collaboration involving many participants. Randy Delehanty, moving among his interviewees, solidified this redemptive retrospective view of the 1960s conflicts. By the early 1980s, conflict between architect and property manager served a consensus narrative about the square's participatory achievements.[4]

"Old-school" jealousies between architects and landscape architects over design roles at Ghirardelli paled next to the architects' differences with the Roses, Ruth Asawa, or Karl Kortum.[5] Viewed from outside the circle of those named by the AIA collaborative medal, the design solutions offered by architect Wurster and landscape architect Halprin were disturbingly similar to one another. The professional machinery that validated architecture and landscape architecture—such as the university degree programs and trade magazines—helped align their ideas. Yet the same university departments in which many of these practicing architects taught also intensified the competition among the professional design fields. The rise of urban design and urban renewal in the 1950s especially provoked architects, landscape architects, and planners to debate which field was best suited to lead the others in large-scale designs. Landscape architecture was caught in the middle. Despite hopeful rhetoric backing the field's potential for knitting together the urban built environment, urban design evolved quickly in the 1950s to favor architects and architectural approaches. The popularity of modernism and its focus on lines and geometric forms challenged the relevance of transient and decorative trees. In the balancing of fields within 1950s urban design, landscape architecture lost ground.[6] Doug Baylis titled his speech at the 1965 meeting of the American Society of Landscape Architects "Why Continue to Be the FORGOTTEN MAN, the Landscape Architect?"[7]

On site in Ghirardelli Square, however, the professional designers negotiated their differences smoothly, leaving the most significant disagreements to flare between the professional architects, on one side, and the allied fields, on the other—such as property managers Stuart and Caree Rose, retailing and garden design consultants Walter Doty and Maggie Baylis, artist Ruth Asawa, or preservation activists Karl and Jean Kortum.[8] The conflicts amplified by designers from outside the architectural professions, even outside the expanded network recognized by the AIA medal, defined the nature of collaboration. In 1966 Bill Wurster wrote to Stuart Rose about how to handle the ongoing arguments arising on site. "While we received an award for Ghirardelli Square for collaboration," Wurster noted in frustration, "it would hardly behoove me to attempt to settle Caree's, Doty's and Halprin's disagreement."[9]

This chapter considers the business of property management, tenant management, retail, and landscape design in producing large-scale 1960s collaborative civic-commercial projects. This perspective retrieves property-based critiques of the architect's spatial and aesthetic agendas, particularly on the project site as planned decisions were revised. Digging deeper into the business fields devoted to fostering novel retail models exposes more of the collaborative, hidden expertise that contributed to the era's fresh commercial designs. Ghirardelli Square's redevelopment gave urban design critics an effective example of collaboration (including the collaboration of the present with the past) as much as it became a model of preservation. Retail interior design and the pursuit of commercial vitality offered tools for modifying and "humanizing" urban redevelopment, whether in historic structures such as the Ghirardelli factory or in monolithic urban renewal complexes like Embarcadero Center. The new forms of large-scale property assemblage, sale, and development proliferating in the postwar years also generated new forms of property management.

"MANY MINDS AND NOT ONE"

Stories of top-down leadership prevailed in private redevelopment in the 1950s and 1960s. The *AIA Journal* citation for Seagram's 1964 Collaborative Medal quoted Philip Johnson in recognizing the "paramount" role of fellow architect Ludwig Mies van der Rohe in leading the "symphony" such that "everything" in the Seagram project bore his stamp. Similarly, investor Leonard Martin ran The Cannery as a "one-man show." Against such top-down standards, Ghirardelli participants would later conclude that their project's strengths derived from the large number of designers and from its spirit of disagreement.[10] When Stuart and Caree Rose were hired in the winter of 1963, however, the overwhelming research generated by Bill Roth and Warren Lemmon's consultations threatened to paralyze the project; the architects and developer were unable to settle the determinative land-use and design decisions.[11]

Hiring Caree and Stuart Rose became the catalyst for taming the unruly abundance of competing ideas into a master plan for the Ghirardelli site. By early May, the Roses had led the project out of its holding pattern by securing "certain basic decisions." Stuart Rose's imprint was especially obvious when Lemmon pressed Roth to take positions: "Are Stuart Rose's suggestions for tenancies acceptable?" "Is the 'European' theme for the shopping and entertainment center with emphasis on small shops carrying high quality merchandise, as suggested by Stuart Rose and Karl Kortum, appropriate?" What were Roth's views on Stuart Rose's proposed multistory garage? Had Halprin met the challenge of landscaping a garage roof? Lemmon asked Roth to review the "Stuart Rose economic projection for the project."[12] A few weeks later, Roth had made enough key decisions to move forward.[13]

Researching financial compensation for property managers, Warren Lemmon discovered that the options awkwardly blurred the roles of architect, owner, and salaried employee. Al Waller, the Town & Country manager, hoped "to obtain an actual interest in property rather than be limited to salary only" in his next contract, and he already earned $30,000 annually.[14] Lemmon told Roth that he would likely negotiate a percentage arrangement with the Roses that mirrored that of the architects, allowing the Roses a financial stake in the size of the project but stopping short of ownership. At the Village Fair, the Roses' responsibilities included "redesign of the original warehouse building so that it would be suitable for shops, supervision of all construction and alterations work (Mr. Rose is trained as an architect and has had experience as a contractor), securing of suitable tenants, and management of the property." Their compensation was set at 10 percent of "the cost of all work undertaken," including travel and incidentals. The Roses met frequently with the Village Fair's owner to review expenditures and keep costs down. They had requested the use of the same 10 percent formula at Ghirardelli. Lemmon reviewed the downsides: there would be little incentive to keep development costs down, and Ghirardelli's larger scale of work, relative to that at the Village Fair, would result in greater compensation. On the other hand, "normal architect fees" were 10 to 12 percent of the project cost, and "the Roses would be assuming appreciably more responsibility for the project than would the usual architect."[15]

Stuart Rose admitted that he had been "spoiled" by designing and building "his own things," but emphasized the architects' discomfort and jealousy, not his own, when describing their construction site conflicts. He described one memorable incident when Bill Wurster gave him "one of the greatest points of accolade I ever had." Stuart Rose and an architect "were arguing about something" in the square. Wurster "turned to his architect and said 'And why didn't you think of that?'" in reference to one of Rose's garage design ideas. Rose savored this compliment to his ingenuity although it further aggravated what Caree Rose called their "iffy" relationship with the architects. Stuart Rose elaborated:

At the outset they asked me if I can get along with architects, and I said yes, but I don't think that architects can get along with me. Because we have designed a great many things ourselves. And we have designed them and financed them and built them. Everything from homes to small factories to a bowling alley. And I'm not an architect. Don't pretend to be. But under the California law you can practice architecture even though you're not. . . . So there's always been a bit of friction and jealousy on the part of architects.

The "iffy" relationship was mutual. The architects also "resented" their dependence on Rose's expertise for meeting building codes, he said.[16]

Many of the Roses' criticisms fit into a refrain about architects' lack of business sense. Although Stuart Rose had corporate experience dating to his "fat" years with Western Pipe, he attributed the business skills in their partnership to his wife. Appraising Caree's secretarial work at Bank of America and Shell Oil, Stuart Rose explained, "Her business background was always good for us." At home, she managed the family finances. At the office, he counted on her to ask where the money was "coming from." That background, he believed, gave the couple rapport with developers and an edge over architects: "Developers sit next to financial people and they speak the same language."[17] Warren Lemmon, a businessman and administrator himself, appreciated the Roses' talent for watching the bottom line while understanding architecture.

Little that unfolded at Ghirardelli Square changed Lemmon's skepticism about architects' abilities to factor investors' profit into design. The Roses' economic projections satisfied Roth's concerns about the project's viability after delays in part due to the architects' struggle with the same projections. Toward the end of a long advisory board meeting in 1965, "Mr. Lemmon noted that one thing that has not been mentioned in the meeting is cost. He said that the return is not commensurate with the investment, and that on the second stage of the development the greatest possible economy in keeping with the first half, is necessary." Halprin, Stuart Rose complained, "has no consideration whatsover for the value of a dollar." Bill Roth himself curbed excess design spending, such as the cost of a kiosk architect, whose "work was absolutely first rate, but astoundingly expensive." This proposal Roth "cut . . . off at the heels."[18]

In addition to prodding architects for impracticality and inattention to expenses and profit margins, the Roses had a propensity to keep track of architects' occasional errors. The Roses mocked professional designers' overriding preoccupation with visual impact, to the detriment of basic function: "The most beautiful outhouse in the world is not worth a damn unless it has a hole in it." They described a miscalculation in which one of the square's buildings exceeded the 40-foot height limit. The Roses were not alone in these critiques. Reporting on a design conflict with a Ghirardelli restaurant tenant, Donn Emmons of Wurster, Bernardi & Emmons asserted that "architects have ruined more restaurants than any other single thing." The Roses' protective stance toward tenants tended to pit them against the architects. Most architects, the Roses said, leaned toward designing something "our tenant personally couldn't afford," and they generally ignored retail basics. One exception was another Wurster associate, Don Stover, who "understood what had to be done for the tenant."[19]

Looking back, Larry Halprin saw the square as an "early example" of the trend toward hiring multiple architects for single projects, especially in large-scale redevelopment. The 1981 Ghirardelli Square interviews helped Randy Delehanty understand why he "liked this more than so many other projects." Delehanty told Halprin that "one of the secrets is that it wasn't from one designer. It was Matthias, the office of Wurster, Bernardi, Emmons, yourself, there was Asawa. So that it's a conversation between many designers. . . . And although that's not consciously something that people are aware of, I think that subconsciously the fact that it is many minds and not one is why I like this project so much more than the totalitarian sense you often get when one designer, whoever it is, controls the whole space." Halprin agreed. John Matthias remembered "a fortunate combination of people" where "nobody was really searching for glory."[20] For Proctor Mellquist, "It was fascinating, the conflicts out of which things were resolved, because there was a difference of view at all times, often not just either-or, but maybe five ways to go." Stuart Rose said of the "original concept": "I wouldn't say it was ours—it was everybody's and Bill's."[21]

Delehanty's admiration professed a narrative in which strong-minded arguing among multiple designers, including many nonarchitects, defined a fraught democratic collaboration rather than the "totalitarian" control more common at the time. In 1981, basking in the model's success, the Roses and Lawrence Halprin could agree without irony that their hot 1960s disputes had benefited the project. The Roses credited "the infighting, even though it wasn't actually fighting," and "a combination of all the people and all of the confusion that made the Square what it is." Stuart Rose concluded that

"Ghirardelli was not built by any one or two people." Caree Rose added, "Not all of us got along very well either," to be followed by Stuart again, "Because we all had ideas and that is what really made it." A mellowed Lawrence Halprin said that an unusual team effort and multiple hands had given Ghirardelli its "humanity." They were "truly working together to the point that sometimes it's hard for me to even remember who did what to whom."[22]

The Roses remembered themselves as the lead advocates for conserving the factory's historic structures. "We wanted to save everything," Caree Rose said. This position, like so many others, they carved out defensively against the architects.[23] Stuart Rose constantly suspected the architects of disregard for the buildings' historical aspects. Choosing to build an underground garage rather than surface parking, for instance, was his effort to protect the pedestrian character of the block, retain buildings, and thereby solidify the preservationist legacy of the square. Rose explained that he "couldn't understand" others' willingness to demolish and build anew. There was "something about the charm of the old building." He singled out the impact of small irregularities, such as windows that didn't quite match, or uneven floors. "Otherwise between Larry and the architects . . . they would have torn it down."[24] Rose overstated the case; the architects did struggle to balance the pressures for preservation, financial returns, and design impact, and he acknowledged as much.[25] The Roses had to fight the prevalent development belief in the early 1960s that new structures maximized commercial density to produce higher returns on investment than existing structures. As codevelopers of a historic property, the Roses had a commitment to history and preservation that was site-dependent. In the 1950s they had turned a barn into a home and a 1920s-era parking garage into a shopping center, relishing the challenges and value of working with old properties. Yet in 1967 Caree Rose sat on a five-member urban renewal advisory panel for Redondo Beach, near Los Angeles. The redevelopment experts reviewing plans for the 50-acre Redondo Plaza included Justin Herman, director of the SFRA, and several others. Caree Rose advised the city to "tear down and disinfect the site."[26] For the Roses, preservation was not a fixed position inherently valued over urban renewal.

Architectural historian and Bay Area expert Sally Woodbridge, reflecting on this period of experimentation in which she participated, remembered: "Bill Wurster was *not* interested in the historical. *Not*. But no one was." Bill Roth wished to save the factory building, but she insisted that he was "not a preservationist."[27] The property managers' accounts restore the tension between the designers' social and aesthetic values of "urban space" and the managers' view of rentable square footage. That was not an absolute distinction, either, but it was a meaningful one. From Bill Roth's perspective, the most important way to protect his investment would come from neither the Roses nor the architects. He expected that the predicted rise in land values would offer the greatest return.

LANDSCAPE VERSUS LANDSCAPE ARCHITECT: "CAREE LOUSED IT UP"

The Ghirardelli factory buildings were situated in a lush garden, a relatively rare pleasure in downtown San Francisco. Here the factory employees (mostly Italian women) had taken their lunches. The garden's beauty and comfort served as a reprimand of sorts, because it was doomed. The block's interior would either be paved for surface parking or, as it happened, demolished for the underground garage excavation (fig. 66). Once Bill Roth accepted that the garden would have to go, he instructed Halprin and Wurster to cultivate that spirit in the new plaza. "In order to keep the old Ghirardelli feeling we want as much greenery, including trees, lawn, shrubs and espalier areas as possible."[28]

Surely the plantings, unlike sculpture or architecture, would fall clearly to landscape architect Larry Halprin's office. But that was not to be the case. Ghirardelli's greenery would prove especially susceptible to meddling. Many of the advisors felt qualified to express an opinion about "gardening." Furthermore, the integration of business and nature was a key element activating the civic-commercial plazas showcased in 1960s redevelopment. Caree Rose's responsibility for smoothly blending landscape design with the business formula brought her into regular conflict with Halprin. For most visitors, greenery pleased the senses. For management, decisions about greenery were as laden as the buildings with issues of preservation, urban design, and authorship.

The informal reviews of Halprin's first plans, submitted in August 1963, did not go well. Stuart Rose thought the proposed hard-topped modernist plaza spoiled the memory of "the natural, graceful lines of the present garden." All "natural grace" had been eliminated. "The present garden, which most were wont to preserve, meanders and wanders. Angles and straight lines were kept to a minimum. In the new concept, there is not a single curve. There is no element of surprise when you turn a corner." Instead Halprin's landscape had only "straight lines, square kiosks, a modern fountain with a modern metal sculpture." Halprin had made no effort to "maintain some of the fine old atmosphere and tradition." Proctor Mellquist wondered why the plaza had to be "hard."[29] Stuart Rose asked for Karl Kortum's reaction. Kortum wrote that Halprin "seems to be *advertising* the fact that the gardens are on the top of an underground garage."[30] Roth agreed with these critiques of Halprin's first design as sterile and overpaved.

The built plaza's sense of scale was elaborated and contested in terms of the garden plantings—particularly feelings of enclosure, intimacy, and warmth versus sterility,

66 Perspective of Ghirardelli factory grounds from the approximate vantage point of the future mermaid fountain, looking toward the bay, with the wood-frame box factory. Bill Roth razed this building to make way for the Wurster complex. The Ghirardelli factory's grass, gardens, and greenery—relatively rare in the downtown district—were enjoyed by employees.

expansiveness, and hard edges. Halprin revised the first plan quickly. He described his firm's new concept as "very gardeny" and "flowerful," with "vines climbing" and "plants dripping" from walls (figs. 67 and 68).[31] The advisory board found the next design to be a "great improvement."[32] While attentive to Roth's desire for greenery, it left other tensions over the character of the space unresolved. Halprin remembered "a real struggle, between those who wanted to make an almost kitschy garden space and myself and the architects who wanted to keep it more powerful as an idea and not fall into the trap of a kind of a fern bar, and over-Victorianize it." In Halprin's telling, the professional architects safeguarded the "more powerful" modern idea against the "kitschy" meddling of nonprofessional designers like the Roses.[33]

Halprin's early misstep set a tone of unease and made his designs vulnerable to scrutiny for years. Spring 1966 marked a low point for Halprin's control over the plaza landscape. That March, Roth and Lemmon hired Walter Doty, the retired editor of *Sunset* magazine, to serve as a consultant "on plant material" for the eastern half of the square. Doty would also advise the square's management regarding "promotional materials relating to plant material, working with the nurseries." Halprin's work was already subject to coordination with (and approval by) Wurster's office, Bill Roth, and the advisory board. Now Doty would "select the plant material and designate the types of soils" after Halprin had completed his landscape plans for the complex's second phase. No wonder Joe Bourg of Wurster, Bernardi & Emmons wrote to Lemmon, asking him "to clarify responsibilities and relationships as they relate to the planning and development of the garden areas." Lemmon replied, "Mr. Doty will be working with us on a continuing basis."[34]

Two months later, Doty's interventions in the eastern half had not pleased anyone. Doty had overcompensated for Halprin's stark sensibility. Halprin took issue at a May meeting with the now "cluttered aspect with too much color and too many pots." Walter Doty "countered that he understood the reason he had been employed was to provide attractive plant material and color which was missing when he commenced his work several months ago." After visiting the square, Roth sided with Halprin. The Roses asked for more precise instructions because Doty's approach, which resembled their own, had failed. In June, Mellquist reported to the advisory board that the "excess" of "improperly grouped," differently sized clay pots "had now been removed without return to the austerity of the earlier planting." By October, Halprin had regained the right to be consulted on color and plantings, but Roth provided strong guidance.[35]

The profitable garage building with a plaza garden on top showed the essence of the divide between property managers (land and investment) and architects (powerful urban space). In his Ghirardelli design, Halprin was caught between the barrage of opinions about the gardens, on one side, and the constraints of the garage structure, on the other. Halprin's creativity was beholden to the underground garage.[36] He thought plazas and fountains worked "very well on top of a roof," but gardens were a different matter. The fact that the plantings had to be placed "over the parking . . . produced a tremendous restriction on what I could do as far as 'gardens.'" In turn, "the ability to plant controlled to a certain degree what the design might be." Trees, for example, needed to be placed over garage columns. As Mellquist pointed out, after the excavation

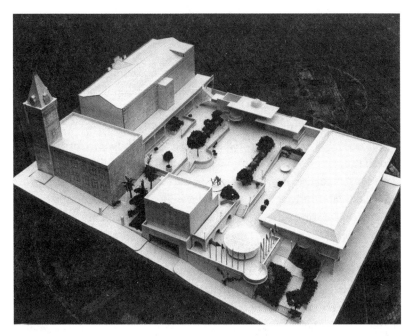

67 The landscape architects' in-house working model for the first phase of Ghirardelli Square shows the scarcity of greenery and plantings. For all the debate about the square's landscaping, the mundane rows of street trees added later around the sidewalk perimeter offered the most green. This early model still shows the carousel at the lower right and an abstract sculpture in the fountain. The innovative pedestrian ramps are in place.

68 This perspective foregrounds one of the modest rectangular planter-gardens in the square. Caree Rose objected to the lack of flowers and greenery and began to change Larry Halprin's plantings. Depending on the viewer's angle, the olive trees could provide a sense of greenery.

and removal of the box factory, "a 10-split level garage, meaning a 5-story building, was put in this hole. The roof of the building on the uphill side in three levels was the future plaza." This building was "completely concealed." Plaza visitors were unaware of standing above ten levels of parking.[37] The plaza's compelling "public place" emerged as one of Halprin's signature accomplishments, attracting international attention for his emphasis on pedestrian choreography and meaningful civic space. But the garage— the Roses's project, the economic driver—had come first (see fig. 40).

Even as the square's achievements boosted his landscape architecture practice, Halprin endured the surreptitious undermining of his designs in addition to the blunt challenges to his expertise. Property manager Caree Rose had unique access to the levers guiding landscape design. Taking advantage of her daily presence at the square, contrasted with Halprin's infrequent visits, she interfered with his layout and plantings behind his back. When Randy Delehanty asked the Roses about Halprin's Ghirardelli landscape plans, Stuart Rose blurted out, "Caree loused it up after he left." Caree Rose described how she had taken control: "You see I just managed to put myself in charge of the garden because I just happen to like gardens. And so nobody ever knew it, even Halprin." When "Halprin was all finished then I would go in and I would bit by bit get rid of all the stuff that he put in other than the trees and put in flowers for God's sake. People love to see flowers. People would go in that place and see all the flowers blooming and say 'It's incredible. . . . Look at all those flowers.'" After her interventions,

69 Caree Rose preferred colorful, bountiful, people-pleasing flowers for Ghirardelli Square. This wall fountain was in an area named Rose Court. On the ground in the square, the conflict between landscape architect and property manager had more consequences than tensions between landscape architect and architect.

70 Under Caree Rose's influence, Ghirardelli Square increased the number of plantings and flowers. Despite Lawrence Halprin's role as the square's landscape architect, Bill Roth hired former *Sunset* magazine editor Walter Doty to enhance the greenery and color. In turn, the proliferation of potted plants seemed to clutter the desired modern lines and were scaled back. This view of the planters also captures well-heeled clientele and Giovanni's restaurant sign at upper left.

"the only things left were . . . the structural things." In other words, she did not change the walls, paving, steps, ramps, built-in planters, or fountain structures. Caree Rose questioned Halprin's insistence on "dreary looking little old plants . . . in a place like that. And so we just changed it all, without saying anything" (fig. 69).[38]

Caree Rose's focus on whether the square was crowd-pleasing ("People love to see flowers") spoke to pedestrian life, retail and restaurant patronage, and, most importantly, her attention to economic vitality. In parallel to the mermaid sculpture controversy, Halprin defended his garden design on the basis of its powerful ideas and deemed the question of whether colorful flowers pleased visitors irrelevant. His position suggested to the Roses and Warren Lemmon that he had little concern for how design influenced the foot traffic and sales experienced by the property's tenants (fig. 70).

Halprin might not have realized how extensively his plantings were "loused up." The selection of plantings and their purchase from specific suppliers was delegated within Halprin's firm, often to longtime associate Jean Walton. Early in 1964 Walton, a landscape architect, toured nurseries near Los Angeles, reserving trees and shrubs to install later that year at the square. Halprin was less personally invested in the plant layout than one might assume. Furthermore, most landscape architects of Halprin's stature were dodging the label of "shrub planter." A professional landscape architect leaving behind private gardens for the thrill of shaping urban design and civic-commercial life hoped that the days of being called back to a job site when plants turned brown were past.[39]

In early 1969, the opening of the square's second, western half reignited old debates, this time focused on whether a sculpture or well-selected tree would better alleviate the alleged starkness of the new plaza. Lemmon and the Roses listened with dread as Roth discussed the prospect of a "sculptural unit" for the western plaza. Lemmon advised Roth accordingly, hoping to derail pressures for abstract sculpture. "You have commented on the natural charm of the East Half. With the starkness which now exists in the West Half, I believe some of the same natural charm and warmth is needed, rather than a modernistic element. Might not there be some appeal to a great old olive tree (not one of the smaller Halprin olive trees) with a built-in bench around it" and night lighting? "If the tree is well selected it could have great character and break the harshness of the Westerly Half." A "great" olive tree would do more to enliven and soften the plaza than a "modernistic" sculpture, but Lemmon and the Roses doubted whether Halprin could choose the right tree.[40]

Vine by vine, the correspondence between Caree Rose and Jean Walton traces the struggle over control and expertise between layperson and professional. Landscape architect Walton's influence over the designs seemed to cease the moment she selected plants. Caree Rose, as property manager, had the final say over planting outcomes. In one 1966 letter, Walton asked Caree Rose to take care of three landscaping matters. "Two of the vines on the east side of the Giovanni Restaurant are Virginia creeper rather than Boston ivy," Walton wrote. "They should be replaced." She instructed, "A piece of Acanthus is growing in with the camellias and azaleas," and should be "carefully removed." Finally, the cobblestones around the sycamore street trees needed resetting. Caree Rose pointed out that the two creepers "were originally specified by you. One of the vines was pulled out, and we replaced it with Boston ivy. We have found that Boston ivy adheres far better to the wall so we will change the two Virginia creepers." "After much looking I finally found a small piece of Acanthus," and she removed it. Yes, Caree Rose replied, it was a constant, expensive effort to maintain the cobblestones. She advised Walton to give "some thought to setting them in a different manner in the Westerly Half." In this mundane exchange, Walton conveyed both her investment in the outcome and her dependence on the property manager. Caree Rose judged and modified Walton's requests and derived authority and expertise from her hands-on management of the gardens.[41]

For years, the square's minor landscape design decisions arrayed management against professional expertise. Of the many individuals, from Karl Kortum and Proctor Mellquist to Walter Doty and Joe Bourg, who weighed in on the appropriate plaza landscape (including its larger symbolism), none were more invested than Caree Rose (fig. 71). She took satisfaction in her authorship of the Ghirardelli landscape, whereby the gardens spoke to history and preservation, theories of public enjoyment, economic vitality, and her role as a codeveloper. Her daily presence on the site ultimately gave her the advantage she sought over the landscape architects while leaving the "structural elements" to Larry Halprin. Caree argued that combining the janitorial and garden work would save money when she petitioned Lemmon to "be given responsibility for deciding what planting changes are needed." She subsumed design questions within

71 The integration of business and nature helped define the novelty of planned 1960s civic-commercial plazas such as the one at Ghirardelli Square. Caree Rose, Jean Walton, Walter Doty, Lawrence Halprin, Warren Lemmon, and others demonstrated that finding a satisfactory balance was a complicated negotiation over expertise; it was never a simple matter of choosing lemon trees. On the business side of this mix, Caree Rose was primarily responsible for tenant selection and management.

the profit margin and business of the square.[42] Doug Baylis, in his "forgotten man" conference address, put a fine point on the tensions between professional landscape architects and the millions of Americans who enjoyed gardening. He asked his colleagues, "Why do garden editors turn to, and quote, garden club ladies, even on design?" He pinned the problem on the insecurities of the landscape architecture profession and its undeniable overlap with the so-called garden club women. His toughest question was about submitting designs for critique: "Do you want—or could you even take— professional criticism, or do you really prefer the 'safe' comments of the garden club girls?" The crowd's response was not recorded.[43]

MARTINI MANAGEMENT:
TENANTS AS "THE STRONGEST PART OF THE ORGANIZATION"

Ghirardelli Square's civic-commercial magnetism, including its profitability, depended on the tenant roster. Architecture alone could not make the venture succeed. Caree Rose, aided by Stuart Rose and Warren Lemmon, took charge of tenant selection and management and proved to be good at it. Stuart Rose put it succinctly: "Without the tenants you don't have anything. They're the strongest part of the organization." The advisory board's plans emphasized unique, quality stores and restaurants, usually independent, artistic, international, and/or design-oriented. The Roses vetted prospective tenants and negotiated leases. They handled day-to-day issues on site. Caree Rose, in particular, fostered a sense of community among the first generation of tenants. Because Ghirardelli Square eschewed anchor stores and the neighborhood lacked existing retail foot traffic, the Roses' tasks differed from the formulaic leasing done at suburban shopping centers. Roth thought Ghirardelli was "more like a small village, and the manager is the mayor." The Roses would tackle "this problem of economics, design, design control, all the things that go into the mix."[44]

The Roses brought to Ghirardelli Square a concern for the tenants' financial success, in part because the concrete landscape of tenants shaped the shopping center's income as well. From a property management perspective, tenants and consumers, not just buildings and architects, "activated" the space of the complex and made it lively and distinctive. Steeped in the white-glove department-store history of San Francisco shopping, Caree believed she knew the changing local consumer market better than any retail specialist. She stood on equal social terms with the tenants. The Roses hosted events in a style that met the high standards of Bill Roth's upscale operation and the Roth family's elite status. The Roses' contacts overlapped with the Roths' but branched into fresh territory. Stuart Rose, from his Berkeley days, knew restauranteur "Trader Vic" Bergeron, as did Bill Roth. The Trader was the first tenant to sign. Caree Rose's cousin Sol Onorato operated the garage for the first few years. Henry J. Kaiser, the owner of Radio Station KFOG, was a friend of Stuart Rose's father. KFOG was the first tenant to open; its Clock Tower broadcasts proved to be a brilliant source of free publicity for the square. From running their own small businesses in the Village Fair and San Rafael, the Roses understood the risks faced by proprietors, especially in catering to untested comsumer trends.[45]

Under Caree Rose's leadership, the square's distinctive commercial vitality took shape. She learned the ropes of leasing because the city's realtors remained disinterested in the project. "They thought we were crazy," she said. On site every day, Caree worked with prospective tenants. The Roses scouted in the region for unique, creative tenants who had already proven themselves. Bay Area retailers often linked shopping districts with multiple branches across city and suburb and other divides. The Roses took chances with such untested businesses as a local architect selling his own mobile designs. With some concern, Caree Rose made his shop the Cocoa Building's first tenant and then monitored his sales closely ("What have I done to this nice man?" she worried). Although the square businesses met with enthusiastic reviews, Bill Roth remained preoccupied with maintaining merchandise quality against threats of tackiness and touristic schlock. One 1966 business publication was typical of the positive reception: "Two basic factors account for the rapid success of Ghirardelli Square—the historic character of the buildings themselves, and the quality of the tenants occupying the buildings."[46]

Stuart Rose described the environment at the square during the early years: "When we were there it was more of a family thing. We were all friends." The high percentage of mom-and-pop stores added personality and warmth but also made for more complex tenant needs. Caree Rose hoped to infuse the place with hospitality. Her management regime put a premium on settling differences, even difficult ones, pleasantly. Warren Lemmon told Roth he was pleased with the Roses' ability to organize special events, foreseeing good publicity and business for the tenants. Lemmon gave Caree Rose "the primary responsibility for leasing and public relations," in part because of her gracious character. He credited the Roses' "qualities of tact, persuasiveness and hard work" as important to the square's success. With the shops and restaurants open, Caree Rose turned more attention to promotional activities.[47]

Once the square was in full operation, one might use the term "martini management" to describe Caree Rose's approach to handling tenant interactions. At the end of the 9-to-5 workday, the tenants dropped by the property managers' office to settle any business. When they stopped in during this pause at the end of the day, Caree opened a well-used cabinet in the office and mixed cocktails to maximize the chances of a pleasant resolution. After "a little martini," she remembered with humor, "it's amazing how many problems were ironed out in just a few minutes and everybody had a lovely time. You were not bringing a tenant in to say 'Your merchandise is terrible and you have to do something about it.'" She preferred these tactics as a "much simpler way of doing business," in which the tenants knew what to expect.[48]

Caree Rose used the square's complex organizational structure to her advantage in tenant management. Speaking to tenants, she could blame the advisory board for rejecting their proposals of various sorts, when in truth the nitty-gritty of tenant negotiations rarely made it to the board. In this strategy and others, Warren Lemmon backed the Roses. Lemmon met daily with them for an hour, stopping by after his own workday at Matson Properties. Lemmon's appreciation of the Roses deepened after the couple moved on to international consulting; he returned from retirement to take over their position for a stint. Lemmon and Roth enjoyed the same martini management when meeting with the Roses at the square.

Reinforcing the family-like environment the Roses had cultivated among the tenants, in 1967 Warren Lemmon married Suzanne Carpenter, the owner of the bookstore on the main plaza at the square.[49]

In facilitating the sense of community among the square's tenants, Caree Rose drew on an optimistic, even-keeled personality and a long history of working with people. From childhood, she had been sociable and lively. From the Terman longitudinal study we know that she found herself sensitive to others' "feelings," yet could "ignore others when doing something important to her." She combined assertiveness and self-confidence with a thick skin and found that other people's praise or blame affected her little. Most slights bounced off her. She enjoyed a challenge and felt that she played her best "in a game against a greatly superior opponent." She liked people, "nearly everyone," but reserved dislike for "dictatorial or bossy people" and tended to "rebel inwardly at orders." If she came late to a meeting, she strode to the front of the room and took a seat instead of standing at the back. She enjoyed public speaking. These character traits and interpersonal skills suggest her promising fit with the leadership tasks of on-site property management and what the Roses and Roth regarded as community-building. Had she been able to glance back at her 1940 Terman questionnaire, she would have laughed. That year, on the eve of meeting Stuart Rose, she had expressed indifference to landscape gardening and said she disliked real estate salesmen.[50]

Tenant management was a responsibility within complex urban design projects that most architects readily ceded to others. Nonetheless, good tenant relations had the potential to lead architects to design commissions for retail projects. Usually this work involved a single interior store design, but the potential was grand, including, for example, securing a multistore commission for a department store chain. Tenant management, then, was primarily an unglamorous if important matter left to managers rather than architects, but it retained a glimmer of something bigger for professional designers. Lawrence Halprin recalled the distance he felt from the tenant world: "I didn't have any real influence on the mix of kinds of shops that were in there. The specific dealings with sales people and the specifics of who would move in, I enjoyed listening to it and I remember being concerned that there would be enough restaurants there . . . but nobody disagreed with that."[51]

Whereas Halprin maintained distance from tenants, a single architect in Wurster's firm—Joe Bourg—tried to wield more influence over the tenants, stirring up ill will. Warren Lemmon described for Bill Roth the negative economic repercussions of Bourg's gruff demeanor: "I think he has done a generally satisfactory job for his firm and us on the job from a strictly architectural standpoint, but he has frequently displayed a belligerence and lack of tact with those with whom he must deal. He doesn't get along well with the tenants." Tenants thought Bourg was "disgruntled" when they did not select his firm to do interior design work. His weak rapport at City Hall caused problems for tenants when permits did not come through as needed. Bourg locked horns regularly with the garage operator over the question of whether certain problems were design- or management-related. Because of Bourg, tenants believed the Wurster office had a "dictatorial attitude." Lemmon worried that these tensions were "significant factors which may discourage the prospect from becoming a tenant," but he reserved particular regret for Bourg's disrespectful treatment of Caree and Stuart Rose. Bourg "recurringly does battle as you know with the Roses." Lemmon described how "Joe had come into Stuart's office one day loaded and attacked both Roses viciously in the presence of others."[52]

The allegations against Bourg underscored the value of the Roses' daily work keeping tenants "happy," as Bill Roth put it, and also provide another glimpse of the disdain that sometimes traveled between architects and their collaborators in urban redevelopment.[53] The Roses themselves worked with collaborators whose contributions are even less well remembered.

MAGGIE BAYLIS, RETAIL SPY: "WRITING AS VISUAL TEACHING"

When they first sought tenants for Ghirardelli Square, the Roses conducted secret shopping missions to evaluate a retailer's atmosphere, inventory, and quality of customer. Soon, however, they lost their anonymity in the Bay Area retail community. Everybody knew them "after a while," so they could no longer go "incognito," Stuart Rose recalled of their scouting. They hired Maggie Baylis, "a delightful girl . . . with imagination" to be their "spy." Baylis browsed prospective shops and delivered insightful reports, embellished with her artwork. She had a "gift of seeing things and writing about [them]," Stuart Rose explained.[54]

Maggie Baylis was indeed a "talented girl," although at fifty she was about the same age as the Roses when they hired her. Building on her college studies in architecture, Maggie Hilbiber Baylis forged her own hybrid career as a best-selling writer and artist who exerted significant influence on grassroots landscape design in the mid-twentieth century. Her experience not only documents contributing "architects" whose work has been obscured but also illuminates how designer-outsiders created new professional paths and widened horizons on the transforming waterfront and skylines of the San Francisco Bay Area. Her time working at the square would mark the midpoint of a rewarding career combining graphic arts, garden writing, magazine production, and community activism. Whether investigating prospective tenants and merchandise, educating the public in landscape design, or campaigning for the Telegraph Hill Dwellers and San Francisco Tomorrow for responsible development, Maggie Baylis's articles, books, illustrations, and reports engaged the built and natural environments simultaneously. She expanded popular participation in designing, regulating, and preserving urban landscape and land one private garden or civic plaza at a time.

As a designer and writer, Maggie Baylis helped set the standards that made the square succeed, translating the purity of Bill Roth's merchandise concepts into a tenant roster that the Roses managed. Maggie Baylis and her husband, Doug Baylis, one of the top landscape architects in the Bay Area, were respected artists in the overlapping circles of the Roses, Mellquist, Halprin, Wurster, and Doty. The fact that the Roths and the Baylises hired the same architect—John Matthias—to design their respective homes reinforced those bonds. In her retail reports, Maggie Baylis extended these shared design sensibilities beyond the architects to the tenants and the merchandise. John Matthias, although an architect, believed that "merchandise forms décor" and proposed that in many regards the Ghirardelli buildings ranked "second place" in significance to the goods for sale. His light, glass-fronted shops brought this philosophy to life (see fig. 86).[55] Because Maggie Baylis's reports and contributions to tenant and merchandising negotiations were confidential, they were intended to be forgotten except by a very small leadership circle.

Maggie Baylis's credentials allayed Bill Roth's anxieties about design standards. In 1928 she (then as Maggie Hilbiber) had begun a career in architecture. At age sixteen she enrolled in the University of Pennsylvania School of Architecture, one of three women in her class of over 150. Given her young age at matriculation and her precocious choice of fields, she might have come to Lewis Terman's attention had she gone to the public schools in San Francisco with Carissima D'Orso instead of the schools in Tacoma, Washington, where she grew up. Her family struggled financially. In architecture school, according to family lore, she had only one dress, which she washed every night. With the Depression's worsening impact, she had to leave the architecture program after two years. At that time, her parents and two young siblings were living with her father's parents in Schwenksville, Pennsylvania. Her grandfather, a retired barber, owned a home there, which provided security to Maggie's immediate family. Her father Fred, an accountant, was unemployed. Fred and Erma Hilbiber returned to Washington State when Maggie left the university. There Maggie Hilbiber supported her family with income earned from an advertising position with the *Tacoma Times*.[56]

Mirroring the decisions of so many Bay Area colleagues who were professionally active at the juncture of the urban built and natural environments, Hilbiber both opened her own design practice and gained experience working for the shelter magazines. This career foundation would allow her to merge drawing, writing, publishing, and environmental activism. Initially, after leaving the *Tacoma Times,* she stayed in the fields of advertising and graphics, taking a contract position with Moore Dry Dock in Hawaii during the 1940s. Moving to the Bay Area in the mid-1940s, she opened a small graphics studio with a partner. Landscape architect Doug Baylis answered an ad from her studio offering "hands for hire," launching a lifelong personal and professional partnership. They married in 1948. He helped her get a job with *Sunset* magazine, where she spent four years as assistant art director until 1951.[57]

In this role at *Sunset,* Maggie Baylis wove together that magazine's support of lay and professional design in the late 1940s and early 1950s, to the benefit of Larry Halprin, Caree and Stuart Rose, Allan Temko, and others. She credited Walter Doty with teaching her how to write. The admiration was mutual. When she left the magazine, he thought *Sunset* would "never find another Maggie," a colleague with "so many talents."[58] At *Sunset* Doty, who shared Baylis's background in advertising, had initiated more active mentoring of young architects and landscape architects. Maggie Baylis felt "lucky to fall in with Doug's profession." Collaborating with her husband gave her a working knowledge and "awareness" of landscape architecture. He had completed his landscape architecture degree in 1941, a few years before they met.[59]

Maggie Baylis pioneered a widely emulated "how-to" publication niche in landscape design for home gardeners, working for shelter magazines and authoring several popular books. Joseph Howland, one of the magazine editors with whom she worked closely, said she "taught me to see writing as visual teaching." She also devoted time to urban environmental preservation. Howland, associate editor of *Better Homes and Gardens,* first met Maggie in 1946. Working with Howland, Doug and Maggie Baylis introduced innovative illustrated techniques for reaching the home gardener. When Howland moved two years later to become garden editor of *House Beautiful,* the Baylises switched magazines as well. Over the next eight years, the couple "created a memorable how-to series that in time all U.S. garden magazines adopted." Their contributions, particularly Maggie Baylis's "detailed explanatory drawings," helped make these the "golden years" of *House Beautiful.* By the mid-1950s they had "produced some of the best written and most superbly illustrated how-to garden stories ever created," according to Howland. In the early 1970s, after her husband's death, Maggie Baylis began to write and illustrate books, including *Plant Parenthood, The Punctured Thumb,* and the best-seller *House Plants for the Purple Thumb.* Her books and her work for urban environmental organizations exemplified how domestic scale complemented urban scale. She wrote more than most professional designers and drew more than most writers.[60]

An allied arts professional in urban design, Maggie Baylis had skills that fused writing and illustration to demonstrate grassroots power (hers and the public's) to shape the built environment. Her diverse design work was united by this focus on inventing, publicizing, and democratizing tools for ordinary people to use to take action, at small and large scales. Her working knowledge of architecture and landscape architecture informed her communications with professionals, but her grassroots approach derived from nonarchitectural perspectives. Baylis seeded the knowledge that helped people work the land. Like Jean and Karl Kortum, Maggie Baylis joined the community organizations (like the Telegraph Hill Dwellers) that fought freeways and large-scale commercial development. Unlike her confidential role at Ghirardelli Square, Maggie Baylis's larger career was under no obligation of secrecy. Because she had begun in architecture, both the roots and the branches of her design career shaped her trajectory. Yet, while admired and remembered by her close colleagues, Baylis's original and sustained contributions to popularizing landscape design—to "writing as visual teaching"—have not endured well. The style of the illustrated how-to guides she helped invent has become so commonplace that its origins would seem difficult to trace. Her larger impact as a writer, editor, and illustrator was better measured garden by garden.[61]

HUMANIZING THE EMBARCADERO "URBAN RENEWAL PROJECT"

In their careers as development consultants for distinctive retail and entertainment centers, Caree and Stuart Rose declined one important Bay Area client. The project managers for historic Ghirardelli Square were invited to "make a study of what the shortcomings were in the Embarcadero Center." The Roses decided that performing this study was "not for us" because the complex was basically "a concrete box."[62] Ghirardelli Square, and the Roses themselves, offered a successful civic-commercial model in 1970 that developers and managers saw as transferable to modernist renewal sites. Embarcadero Center, the third phase of San Francisco's Area E-1 redevelopment parcel, was far more complicated than single-tower projects like Crown Zellerbach or the Transamerica Pyramid. In 1967 the city unveiled Embarcadero Center's mixed-use design that included office space, a major hotel, retail, dining, and open space, but the complex of four towers and hotel was not completed until the early 1980s. Designed by Atlanta-based architect and developer John Portman, the center's axis flowed toward the Ferry Building and the waterfront. Embarcadero Center, while an emblem of large-scale, clearance-based downtown urban renewal, received recognition for its terraces and public art. Design professionals saw its elevated pedestrian plazas connected with bridges, pathways, retail, cafés, a stunning atrium, and gardens—punctuated throughout with sculpture—as a successful effort to establish a human-scale context for high-rise renewal. That formula earned recognition for the center and its architects, investors (including David Rockefeller), and the city's urban renewal administrator, Justin Herman.

Yet in the case of the towering Embarcadero Center, many additional contributors influenced its evolution by incrementally eroding its monolithic effects, sometimes years after the architects' plans were built. Modification over time was especially relevant for this complex because construction unfolded progressively over fifteen years and also because the public protested the original plan for creating a wall separating San Franciscans from their waterfront (see chapter 8). The complex's economic success would require more than the original vision and vital open-space amenities provided by the architects. The center soon faced numerous tenant vacancies. The owners called in a fresh roster of outside consultants to make suggestions for altering the "concrete box" and increasing rental income by attracting tenants.

Property managers needing to break down the large scale of urban renewal projects for better tenanting sought not only retail consultants like the Roses but also architects in the field of interior store design. This meant that through these small-scale, less prestigious commissions architects were tapped to improve upon their colleagues' redevelopment complexes. Such was the case at Embarcadero Center. Critic Allan Temko initially critiqued "the massive office slabs" as "a colossal blunder in civic design, cutting off sunlight and views across a wide swath of downtown." But by 1977, he conceded, "the great multi-level shopping esplanades at their base are one of the architect-developer John Portman's most successful ideas." Against the odds, a "true pedestrian's environment" had emerged and surged among the slabs. Whereas the center's retail, dining, and civic components had opened to a "rather dreary beginning, when the first building stood alone in 1971, it is now exploding with a rich mix of social energy," Temko reported. He invoked Jane Jacobs to explain its success, despite (or perhaps because of) her contempt for large-scale modernism: "This is one of the most vivid illustrations in the country of Jane Jacobs' theory that a large number of shops and eateries at sidewalk level is indispensable to the health of the city." Embarcadero Center's towers may have risen from urban renewal clearance, but Temko saw a welcome gesture to the "the impromptu variety and unpredictability of historic cityscapes." Most important, he noted, "the concept leaves room for individual architects to pit their own designs—in shops and bars and restaurants—against the overpowering towers which otherwise might simply crush them."[63]

Here was a recurrent theme for Embarcadero Center's commercial tenants and plazas: the efforts of retailers and their architects helped create a counterforce against the crushing monotony of the overpowering high-rises. Portman had provided a plausible framework at the base for ameliorating that monotony—interwoven levels layered with plazas, sculpture, and pedestrian bridges and a stimulating randomness in the placement of retail and dining. Yet without the artistry of the retail tenants and their own store designers, Embarcadero Center would have remained far more monolithic.

The interventions by the Cambridge-based company D/R are an instructive example of how retailers changed the experience and design of the monolithic Embarcadero Center. D/R, a modern home furnishings and clothing store, was founded in the mid-1950s by architect Ben Thompson. The company opened a two-story branch in Embarcadero's first tower, the Security Pacific Building, in October 1973. This followed the establishment of its first San Francisco store, which had been a plum tenant for Ghirardelli Square when it opened there in 1965. Thompson chaired the architecture program at Harvard's Graduate School of Design in the 1960s; in the 1970s he was the driving inspiration behind the reinvention of Boston's Faneuil Hall. As a modernist working with historical urban fabric, Thompson traveled in the same intellectual currents as Halprin and Wurster (although he did not know them well prior to opening his Ghirardelli store). The company carried imported goods, especially those exemplary of their country of origin, along with its own lines, and collaborated closely with Marimekko, the Finnish clothing and textile company. D/R illustrated how retail businesses linked disparate shopping centers through design consultants as well as loyal consumers.[64]

Ben Thompson, an adaptive reuse pioneer and admirer of Ghirardelli Square, had no inclination to fight high-rises. Instead he wanted to furnish them. Once D/R chose a space to lease in Embarcadero Center, the company hired Bay Area architect William Turnbull Jr. of the firm MLTW/Turnbull Associates to tackle the challenge—a selection *Interiors* magazine described as "provocative." This was Turnbull's first retail commission. He had begun architectural practice in 1960 with SOM's San Francisco office shortly after moving to the Bay Area from the East Coast. Turnbull's defining experience from his SOM years was working on the Monterey County Coast Master Plan, adopted in 1962, which established land-use guidelines to protect 100 miles of coast as development loomed. At the time he took on the Embarcadero Center store design, his projects included several acclaimed buildings and a master plan for The Sea Ranch development (a collaboration with his partners Charles Moore, Donlyn Lyndon, and Richard Whitaker [who had formed MLTW], and with Lawrence Halprin & Associates), Kresge College for the University of California, Santa Cruz, and many private homes. The Sea Ranch's success (see chapters 6 and 7) had recently propelled the MLTW partners in different directions to take up new opportunities; Turnbull had just established his own firm. He lived in Sausalito in a nineteenth-century home with his wife, Wendy Woods Turnbull, a freelance writer and editor working for *Time* and *San Francisco* magazines.[65]

With Turnbull's designation as architect, the D/R store in Embarcadero Center merged the stories of how a retail tenant and a retailer's architect together modified the complex. *Chronicle* critic Temko said of the finished store that Turnbull had best shown "how a skillful architect—far more fastidious in detail than Portman has time to be—can overcome the heavy frame of the skyscraper to create an ambiance that is residential in scale."[66] *Interiors* said that "Turnbull's vivid, irreverent solution" had carved out a unique environment (against the odds of Embarcadero's "powerful geometry") for client D/R.[67] Drafting his public statement about the D/R store, Turnbull referred to the center as the "Portman, Rockefeller Embarcadero Urban Renewal Project." The Embarcadero Center in 1973, even to the Bay Area architects intimately familiar with it, was still an urban renewal project (see fig. 114).[68]

Embarcadero Center's developers had imposed strict controls over the exterior and retained design approval over any internal changes. Within such master planning constraints, Turnbull attempted to create a unique D/R "place." He approached the store design challenge as a series of paradoxes. Rather than dwelling on the overwhelming crush of the slab towers, Turnbull exploited dynamic tensions. The concluding lines of his statement were excerpted widely: "The design game is foil and counterfoil, whimsy and recall; the delight of enjoying someone else's rather formal space." Turnbull identified the paradoxes. A store "known for its bright cheery personable materials" and its uniquely customized buildings, was opening in "a great grey impersonal concrete city within a city." The usually sunlit and plant-filled interiors of a typical D/R store would meet the "wide, low and dark" Embarcadero space (fig. 72).[69]

Turnbull's solutions included punching an 18-by-28-foot skylight into the concrete roof and building a staircase through a same-sized well in the floor to internally connect the two store levels. To defeat "the problem of monotony," his other interventions were less dramatic but equally influential. He described the strategies used:

Where the repetitive concrete structural grid dominated and rigidly organized all the spaces throughout Embarcadero Center, we mischievously ran surface mounted fluorescent light on a contradictory diagonal. Against the brutalist repetitive monotony of the exterior fin concrete walls we introduced new sheetrock walls in the skylight well filled with various sizes and shapes of openings recalling poetically all the idiosyncracies [sic] of residential Victorian San Francisco.

Turnbull enjoyed the subversiveness of incorporating "the light prefabricated wall studs used by cheap tract builders for low cost residential construction" and countered the plaza's brick paving with wood-block industrial flooring in a parquet pattern. He provided flexible display space, enhanced indoor-outdoor connections, and "an intermingling of the public and private spaces." D/R's flag, the key signage from the street, had detachable trailers so that "each day is different and the individual note is flying to be shared with every other person who collectively [makes] up 'the city.'"[70]

The Embarcadero Center managers looked to D/R and Bill Turnbull to loosen up the complex's overly controlling design policies, which they had come to realize constrained retail vitality and individual identity. Of course D/R also filled a good chunk of otherwise

72 By the 1960s, nature, plazas, art, and retail melded as part of the civic-commercial formula, regardless of architectural style. Embarcadero Center's management invited Stuart and Caree Rose to come over from Ghirardelli Square to help make the urban renewal project more human-scale. They declined. Another strategy for humanizing the monolithic complex was hiring the right store designers. With the results seen here, Embarcadero Center relied on a redesign by architect William Turnbull Jr. for tenant Design Research (D/R) to improve a low, dark location. Turnbull opened up the store's different levels and connected the interior to the outdoors and natural lighting. Modest alterations by store tenants (including a change in window glazing) helped as well: plants cascade down outside walls, boldly colored merchandise illuminates D/R's windows, and reflected sunlight improves the concrete structure. The shiny upper portion of Willi Gutmann's eight-story *Two Columns with Wedge* brightens the setting and demonstrates the value of public art. A small patch of blue sky indicates the environmental challenges created by downtown skyscrapers.

empty retail space in the first tower, providing what the Embarcadero executives described as "a major shot in the arm."[71] The minutes of a May 1973 meeting between Turnbull's firm and Jim Bronkema, the center's executive director, recorded: "E. C. *very* happy to have D/R, particularly because of D/R's Design Rep. Looking for D/R, Turnbull to force change in Portman design policies problematic to retail (graphics, bronze glass, etc.)." One pressing issue concerned Portman's choice of reflecting bronze solar glass. Turnbull argued that clear glass would open up the store interior to the outdoor pedestrian spaces and draw in shoppers. The developers agreed to pay for replacing the glass. This resolution acknowledged the needs of retail customers and individual stores in a way that the original architects had not.[72]

For Bill Turnbull, Ghirardelli Square offered the direct inspiration for his Embarcadero Center store design. In a draft of his Embarcadero D/R statement, he described how the Ghirardelli Square D/R provided a model by "celebrating the paradoxical conditions" of its own environment. The Ghirardelli store had created a "special 'place'" with a "geographic identity." Once again, the goal (and paradoxes) of downtown retail and pedestrian vitality stood irrespective of historic or modern context. Turnbull removed the reference to Ghirardelli Square in later drafts.[73]

At the time D/R opened late in 1973, Turnbull diplomatically observed that Embarcadero Center's plaza spaces had not yet achieved their intended dynamism. He saw signs of progress nearby: Portman's Hyatt Regency Hotel had a dramatic interior lobby, the adjacent Alcoa building was complete, and the second tower (the Levi Strauss block) was under construction. Turnbull hit an optimistic note: "Some day the plaza will be the people-filled promenade envisioned by Justin Herman and Wurster Bernardi and Emmons in the late 1950's. The problem, however, is now; the paradoxes need resolution."[74] Although one article told "How a Little Retail Chain from a Small University Town in the East Made Its Mark in a Great Gray San Francisco Megasystem," in many ways modernist Embarcadero's D/R had not come from Cambridge, Massachussets, but rather from preservationist Ghirardelli Square, a few blocks away.[75]

On one hand, "urban renewal projects" like Embarcadero Center were mind-numbingly monolithic and impersonal. On the other hand, they could be modified, and possibly even transformed, by retail. In the case of Embarcadero Center, the incremental changes given credit for "humanizing" the slabs were carried out by collaborating architects like Bill Turnbull, retailers such as D/R, and others. At the monolithic scale of urban renewal, later collaborators worked in dialogue with the original developers and architects. As D/R came to shape Embarcadero Center and ameliorate its design policies in the merging of planned retail and civic spaces, the store traveled from another place on the San Francisco waterfront—Ghirardelli Square. The similarities between Ghirardelli Square and Embarcadero Center in their efforts to create dynamic urban pedestrian spaces mixed with retail and dining, integrated into planned commercial developments, were as important as their obvious differences.

The accounts of the property managers and the accompanying retail and garden consultants in this chapter illuminate how the owners and developers faced a different set of motivations than the architects. They needed to recoup their investments and focused both on the short term (paying tenants) and the long term (increased land values). Achieving those goals required, if not partnerships, at least collaborations across a variety of fields not always recognized as urban design professions. In both Ghirardelli Square and Embarcadero Center, the attractive open-space amenities would not by themselves attract tenants and customers; that is where the property managers came in. In these expanded collaborative endeavors, even the landscape architect and retail interior architect were sometimes FORGOTTEN, as Doug Baylis said. For Baylis, and also for Turnbull, one solution was good publicity. D/R was possibly the best store remodel at Embarcadero Center, but it was definitely the best publicized. Baylis's solution for his landscape architect colleagues was to encourage better public relations. Landscape architects needed to create professional brochures, explain their projects, and undertake community service that conveyed their contributions. "Have you ever visited with the editors of House & Garden, House Beautiful, Architectural Record, Sunset, BH&G?" Doug Baylis asked the attendees of the American Society of Landscape Architects conference. "We will always be the low man on the totem," he argued, "unless we seek legitimate ways for a good public press."[76] Disruptive large-scale redevelopment, of course, had intensified the demand for such skills.

Movers and Shakers
Publicists and the Writing
of Real Estate

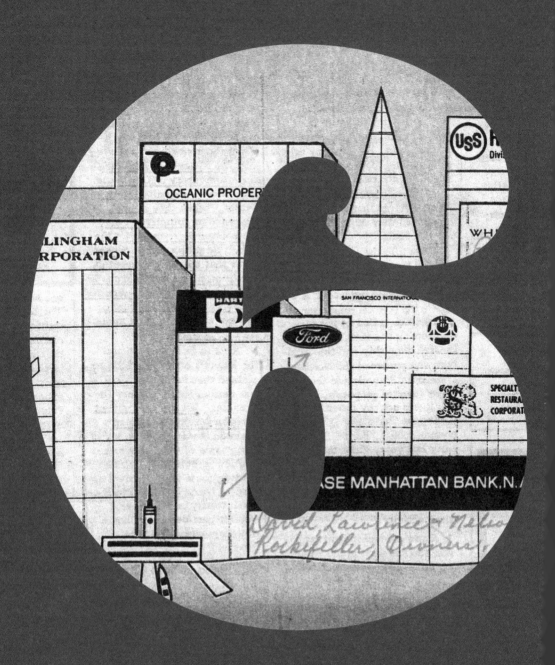

On the Sonoma coast three and a half hours north of San Francisco, the presence of investment machinery turning land into real estate contrasted starkly with the dramatic natural setting. In the summer of 1967, this machinery took the form of a giant rented purple sales tent pitched on the seaside meadows, its nylon flapping loudly in the wind. The occasion marked the official grand opening of The Sea Ranch. Marion Conrad, who coordinated the publicity and advertising for The Sea Ranch from its early planning stages, worked the tent's edges collecting feedback, and making sure that everyone had a brochure, a site map, and something to eat and drink.[1]

In 1963 Oceanic Properties had purchased 5,200 acres of coastal ranchland and meadows with the purpose of building a community of vacation and retirement homes. The price Oceanic paid for this 14-by-1-mile strip—$2.7 million—was about the same price that Bill Roth and his mother had paid for the 2.5-acre Ghirardelli property the previous year. Developer Al Boeke hired Larry Halprin to draw up a master plan for the site. Halprin, Boeke, and the other advisors set the goals of preserving meadows, clustering development, and blending the properties with the natural landscape. One of the original fifteen consultants told Boeke that, from a marketing perspective, Oceanic would need to construct a shopping mall and full-service resort to attract homebuyers. Boeke showed him the door, as he did other consultants who did not understand the "mindset" of coastal preservation and "living lightly on the land." But Boeke also knew that even if he had supported intense commercial development, his investors would not sink money into major commercial facilities at this unproven location— a barren, windswept coast hours from San Francisco (fig. 73).[2]

The Sea Ranch, like Ghirardelli Square, was "unusual real estate," to borrow Al Boeke's term. Within a few years, The Sea Ranch would be widely admired as a groundbreaking planning model embodying a landscape style that integrated built structures with their natural surroundings and minimized environmental destruction—all based on scientific environmental and wind studies, not guesswork. Architecturally, it became an iconic recreational type, credited with inspiring a generation of modern, wood-clad, weathered beach houses and ski resorts.[3] But in these early stages, the developer decided that the project would require unusually strong marketing. Targeted publicity would have to overcome reluctant investors' views of the project's long distance from population centers and difficult access along tortured roads. One "terribly, terribly conservative" San Francisco real estate marketing consultant bluntly told Boeke that the project would fail as envisioned.[4]

The site was at times desolate and unconvincing. The material conditions and climate of these coastal acres could be quite raw. On a two-day visit to the property in September 1963, Ray Menzel of the San Francisco public relations firm Foote, Cone & Belding scrutinized the land with preliminary plans in hand. He chatted with overnight guests at the Timber Cove Inn, the closest comparable destination, in order to understand the potential market. The inn offered sobering lessons. Menzel noted in his report, "The general landscape immediately surrounding the Inn is somewhat bleak—and even downright dirty." Unfortunately, "the greyish-brown dust typical of the area" aggravated travelers. Menzel understood why the Sea Ranch designers were tempted to maximize

73 By 1965, the first condominiums and general store opened on The Sea Ranch, a novel master-planned large-scale redevelopment on a remote stretch of the Sonoma coast. Resembling giant rock outcroppings, the new buildings are at the top center and right of the frame. The planners advocated for clustered development to preserve shared open space, and also for an integrated approach to blending buildings with the environment. Publicist Marion Conrad was instrumental in converting the sometimes stark coastal meadows into marketable residential real estate. Consultants like Conrad, Bobbie Stauffacher, and Larry Halprin worked together simultaneously on projects like Ghirardelli Square, The Sea Ranch, and the San Francisco International Market Center.

the ocean views using "great expanses of glass," but at the Inn, the windows were "constantly clouded with salt spray" that reached back hundreds of yards from the water. Menzel therefore recommended smaller, more intimate windows in public areas and guest rooms. These would encourage an "essence of snugness" and the "feeling of well-being that comes from seeming to be protected from the elements" so close to "a very active ocean." The inn, open only four months, had attracted a "quite cosmopolitan" clientele. Menzel picked up from travelers "a pretty strong negative reaction to the road—running from annoyance to fear." The trip from San Francisco was not only long; it was also potentially frightening.[5]

Oceanic assembled a complicated interlocking team of designers to make the most of this unusual setting. Besides hiring Halprin, Boeke gave Charles Moore and William Turnbull of MLTW the challenge of blending a ten-unit condominium into the edge of Black Point Cliff. Joseph Esherick designed The Sea Ranch's first single-family homes, as well as the combination general store/restaurant/sales building. Using low-lying buildings, wood shingling, sod roofs, and stone fireplaces, Esherick "mastered the laid-back Northern-California-reverse-snobbism-style-of-architecture," according to graphic artist Bobbie Stauffacher. Most of these architects were simultaneously employed on San Francisco waterfront projects. Joseph Esherick was at work on The Cannery for

Leonard Martin, down the street from Lawrence Halprin at Ghirardelli Square. These professional designers bought into the "unusual" real estate concepts behind The Sea Ranch, literally. Moore bought one of the condominium units he had designed. Halprin bought an isolated cliff-side lot at the southern edge of the property. Esherick purchased one of his own model homes. These sales were promising, but because Oceanic Properties was not building an architects' colony, it needed others to understand the lure as well.[6]

Boeke's designer-consultants who came together to plan the 5,200-acre Sea Ranch in late October 1963 brought West Coast environmentalist credentials that, although diverse, all emphasized protecting the public domain within the context of commercial private development. Bill Turnbull had just completed his work for SOM on the Monterey County Coast Master Plan. In addition to focusing on clustering development to conserve open space, Larry Halprin conducted studies on microclimates, salt spray inundation, forest management, and grasslands. This novel research was obviously possible only with the developer's support. In 1965 California led the nation in the "planning of cluster houses," Charles Moore was convinced. While working on The Sea Ranch, Moore wrote an essay on what California's recent architecture had contributed to "enlivening the public realm" through design. This research became the basis of the influential article "You Have to Pay for the Public Life." One of the many implications of Moore's provocative essay was that in the United States the urban public realm was a regionally defined construct. In California, he argued, architects should derive inspiration for enriching the public domain both from the new residential boom and from commercial developments like Disneyland or even the Nut Tree roadside attraction. Moore's argument matched the consultants' goals at The Sea Ranch—namely, using environmental planning and architecture to create a meaningful public realm through spectacular coastal preservation within the methods of large-scale private development. Experience on the ground at The Sea Ranch would test these ideals, and time would tell how well this private preservation vision for the public good would hold up. On the West Coast, Moore wrote, the absence of a long-standing "Establishment" to "shoulder the responsibility for or take a proprietary interest in the public realm" created an added burden and an opportunity for planners, architects, and the public.[7]

Oceanic Properties never assumed that it could rely on the promotional draw of inventive architects' associations with the property. Boeke assigned Marion Conrad Associates the task of coordinating publicity for the project. Later Boeke spoke in effusive terms of Conrad's contributions. When asked about the fifteen Sea Ranch planning and design consultants, Boeke mentioned Marion Conrad after Halprin and the two main architecture firms. Conrad, Boeke recalled, "was the most charming and toughest Master Sergeant I've ever met and I spent three years in the Army Infantry in World War II." Boeke continued, "I would credit her with putting The Sea Ranch on the map worldwide. She single-handedly, and with her office, did that job."[8]

It is clear why Al Boeke felt indebted to Marion Conrad. In May 1966, Conrad hit a publicist's home run for the risky Sea Ranch real estate venture when her efforts yielded a seventeen-page cover story in *Progressive Architecture*. The article "Ecological

Architecture" marked an unforgettable turning point for Boeke. Feature stories often capped years of effort by a dedicated publicist. During the summer of 1965, Conrad had visited New York City to meet in person with editors, distribute materials, and discuss the concepts behind The Sea Ranch (and her other clients' projects). If The Sea Ranch needed explanation to reach the San Francisco Bay Area and California regional markets, it was an exotic experiment to Manhattan editors—even to a design press open to following West Coast trends. Conrad kept Boeke apprised of her efforts. As he noted, "She just went at it and the seventeen pages in *Progressive Architecture* and the Japanese magazines and the two big French magazines in the first few years publicized The Sea Ranch. Those were all people that she dug out."[9] The editors, too, acknowledged Conrad's leadership. Will Mehlhorn, the architecture editor of *House and Garden*, wrote to "Miss Conrad" personally in July 1966 to express admiration for articles appearing in *Fortune*, *Venture*, the *Los Angeles Times*, *Progressive Architecture*, and *Look*. "I congratulate you on wonderful coverage in the national press," he said.[10]

The 1966 *Progressive Architecture* article asserted that The Sea Ranch had established a revolutionary planning philosophy; the larger goals of land stewardship for the public good, coastal preservation, shared ownership of "commons," and design restrictions offered alternatives to privatized suburban spread. The article expanded on the discrete contributions of the individual design firms but showcased the emerging concepts rather than the architects. Maude Dorr's introduction observed of the firms: "Between them, they have evolved a community that requires a readjustment of suburban living habits, of suburban real-estate techniques, and introduces a broader concept of land ownership, use, and stewardship. The story of Sea Ranch is one of a slow education between client, geologist, architect, real estate salesman, and the public."[11] Dozens of images related the Sea Ranch buildings to the coastal environment, documented interiors, and reproduced sketches, models, topographical charts, and wind studies. The only photograph of an architect was a small, informal head shot of Al Boeke, which underscored his coordinating role as the vice president of planning for Oceanic Properties. As a design *manager*, he had extracted this new development concept from a mix of architectural firms and consultants.

The 1967 grand opening drew San Francisco buyers through Marion Conrad's society and press contacts in the same way that the *Progressive Architecture* cover story stimulated architectural interest. Conrad presided over the opening as a younger "grand dame" of San Francisco society. More than a hundred people navigated the long drive from the city to see the project for themselves. Conrad's San Francisco restaurant client, "Trader Vic" Bergeron, who also owned Señor Pico's in Ghirardelli Square, catered the Sea Ranch opening party. The guests included the editor of the San Jose *Mercury*, who loved the property and later swore to Boeke that he had "talked to everybody about it. You should give me a fee for the sales I've made in San Francisco." The editor himself found the experience of getting there terrifying; he told Boeke that he had frozen at the steering wheel of his Rolls Royce until his hands were pried off by his terrified companion.[12] The editor might never again drive in the mountains, but Boeke could breathe easier. The risks for Oceanic Properties were beginning to diminish in the wake of a successful launch party.

The Sea Ranch was part of the regional network of large-scale planning projects that catalyzed real estate experimentation and unleashed a flow of ideas among rural, urban, and suburban places in the 1960s. Through allied design and development consultants like Conrad, these planning circuits connected urban renewal, new towns, and suburban shopping center development to the circuits of historical experimentation in the region of the Bay Area described in the previous chapters. In 1967 Marion Conrad was one of the most influential publicists in San Francisco. Her friend and colleague Bobbie Stauffacher ranked among the city's most talented and admired graphic artists. Their Sea Ranch years overlapped with their collaborations on Ghirardelli Square, the enormous (but never built) San Francisco International Market Center, the 8-acre Northpoint apartment and shopping complex, and many other newsworthy San Francisco water-front projects. The long drives between the Sonoma coast and the Bay Area, and the long hours spent at isolated Sea Ranch, intensified these city-based working relationships. Al Boeke remembered a strategic planning consultation with Marion Conrad in a Sea Ranch parking lot. She stood in the rain in her business attire and pearls while they conferred. On another occasion, after helping host a press visit and photo shoot, Bill Turnbull told Conrad how the extra time with Boeke had opened up productive conversations. She was glad for Turnbull, she said, but her experience was different: "I personally found those endless hours of waiting with him [Boeke], while Larry was out being photographed by *Look,* a little bit like a midsummer madness dream."[13] Although the long commute, the waiting around, and the scouting of Sonoma's coastal terrain gave the city consultants memorable times together, most Sea Ranch meetings, in fact, took place in downtown San Francisco.

The case of urban design in the Bay Area in the 1960s reveals the central creative role played by a publicist such as Conrad. Without public recognition, promotion, reviews, and press attention in some form, design careers and development projects alike were difficult to evaluate. This was particularly true of the new directions embodied in such planned postwar experiments as The Sea Ranch, Ghirardelli Square, and large-scale urban renewal. Of course publicists like Conrad remained at the margins of the design professions, and today her writing is hidden in the archived correspondence files of her clients. People hired Conrad because she could solidify a design career or real estate development by interjecting a fresh concept into a news story or trade journal. She was also known to save projects and careers by keeping news out of the city papers. Her words were always anonymous or attributed to others. The daily work of public relations firms was often dismissed as puffed-up promotion enlisted in amplifying others' ideas and agendas, and there was certainly plenty of puffery. Yet Conrad's career tells of a different kind of influence—one entangled with the design ideas that defined the era and the region.

Marion Conrad's story also demonstrates how public relations and journalism negotiated the evolving barriers between their fields in pursuit of urban criticism in the 1960s. Popular writing about the built environment—a world that was fundamentally imagined and experienced visually and through multiple senses—posed a distinctive challenge to genres of the written word. Working as a consultant-outsider, Conrad had a perspective on how politics and real estate coexisted in urban redevelopment that differed from architects' views and from City Hall's. Foregrounding her influence on the framing of design ideas and careers downplays the distinctions made in the contemporary architectural vocabulary between modernist and preservationist. A behind-the-scenes mover and shaker like Conrad worked with clients on both sides of such architectural divides.

The mid-1960s marked a deep convergence of Bay Area master planning projects with the region's designer-developer networks. In the space of a few years The Sea Ranch opened, Ghirardelli Square took off, and the Embarcadero Center and San Francisco International Market Center designs were unveiled, to list a few significant projects. These would become iconic models of environmentally aware, collaborative planning or, as in the SFIMC case, iconic failures of the same. In 1966 the Bay Area was proclaimed "The Designer's City" when the American Institute of Interior Designers met that September in San Francisco. A magazine story with that title began with Ghirardelli Square interiors and Jackson Square but quickly expanded to include an apartment in the Fontana Towers. Interior designers, architects, and artists found an amenable culture for their work in the Bay Area, the article reported. Their ranks included many one-person operations, as well as small and large firms, and were swelled by the region's distinctive design expertise in environmental planning, not to mention the related controversies.[14]

Striving to master "environmental complexes" was a California phenomenon that united small-scale urban historical "Cannery-style charm" with the large-scale "designed complex, whether urban, or rural, residential or commercial." Projects like Ghirardelli, the article said, were "microcosmic reflections of a larger concern—the planning of new 'environments.'" Other experiments, most notably The Sea Ranch but also Golden Gateway, similarly offered "a new community approach to the controversial 'complex.'" Bay Area designers sought to demonstrate that large-scale projects could also "provide individuality and grace" and "claim some consideration for the individual in a planned context."[15] These regional, planned environmental complexes—small and large, historical and modern, urban and rural—were precisely the concepts Marion Conrad promoted.

MARION CONRAD, MASTER BUILDER: "BETTER THAN ANY OTHER MAN IN THE FIELD"

During the 1960s, Marion Conrad Associates became one of the most powerful San Francisco public relations firms in the fields of architecture, planning, land development, the arts, and the hospitality industry. Conrad also had an influential record in political consulting. The fields of politics and architecture/planning/land development were naturally interrelated—a fact recognized and questioned by Conrad's critics and coveted by her clients. In San Francisco the new alternative newspaper the *Bay Guardian* provided the most vocal and sustained critiques of entrenched yet unexamined real estate investment practices in the late 1960s. Waterfront redevelopment and high-rise construction topped the list of divisive issues, and Marion Conrad's clients were embroiled in both (fig. 74). In February 1970 the *Bay Guardian* ran a cover story whose lead said it all: "San Francisco's waterfront has been put on the real estate market and is now being auctioned off to giant corporations by the City and Port of San Francisco." The city's leadership had "quietly," and without public debate, rushed to turn "this spectacular stretch of public land" over for massive developments like Embarcadero Center and the San Francisco International Market Center. Portions of that land, citizens' groups had long argued, should go toward affordable housing, an idea endorsed by Justin Herman and John S. Bolles. The article asked, "Should waterfront land go to people or to corporations?" A drawing of the city's skyline from the bay accompanied the story "$F Waterfront Co., Inc.: J. Alioto and C. Magnin, Proprietors since 1968." Specific banks, realtors, contractors, public relations firms, government agencies, investors, and foundations were implicated, with each one's name emblazoned at the top of a fictitious blocky skyscraper. Small crevices were reserved for the Ferry Building and the Bay Bridge. Marion Conrad Associates was among the fourteen spotlighted organizations.[16]

The *Bay Guardian* illustrator's purpose was to name some of the submerged, regular collaborations behind private redevelopment machinery, including developers

74 This February 1970 drawing critiqued the waterfront proprietors, not the city's actual skyline. The *Bay Guardian* suggested that cozy collaborations among these enterprises enabled high-rise crowding on the waterfront. Most of the businesses represented here did not have skyscrapers. Conrad's small basement office in her Pacific Heights home, for example, played an important role in bringing waterfront real estate development to fruition. The unbuilt San Francisco International Market Center was included as was Sea Ranch's Oceanic Properties (see chapter 10).

(Oceanic, Dillingham), architects (SOM), realtors (Milton Meyers), and publicists (Conrad, Whitaker & Baxter). The article was hardly an exposé revealing secret transactions since the organizations depicted in the drawing were followed in the mainstream news. To preserve the story's focus on selling off the public waterfront, the cartoon left out the names of corporations that had recently been in the news for building actual skyscrapers, such as Bank of America, Wells Fargo, and Alcoa. This exclusion kept the private skyscraper design controversies separate from the public stewardship questions raised by the article. The *Bay Guardian*'s real story was that transferring the San Francisco port from the state to the city had resulted in the auctioning off of the public's land; the drawing revealed the collaborations that facilitated that sale. Given the small size of Conrad's business compared with Chase Manhattan Bank or the Ford Foundation, Conrad Associates' appearance was testimony to the company's outsized influence. Marion Conrad's firm was in fact located in the basement of her Pacific Avenue home.

When Marion Conrad next appeared in the *Bay Guardian,* one year later, it was in a sympathetic story portraying her as the best in her business. This belated Valentine's Day issue probed the lives of married professional couples to assess the impact of women's liberation on the balance of work and family, and on women's careers particularly (fig. 75). The *Bay Guardian*'s readers may have found San Francisco's intensifying waterfront development alarming, but the Valentine's article gave readers reasons to admire Marion Conrad's professional accomplishments. The story sketched the texture of her busy office, her husband's support of her career, and her attitudes toward her own success and career women's obstacles generally.

75 Marion Conrad at her desk, in a Valentine's Day 1971 *Bay Guardian* issue that featured couples who juggled careers, families, civic work, and other activities. The alternative paper admired Conrad's achievements even as it exposed her role in promoting the high-rise waterfront. The interview gave her a chance to discuss frankly how she, as a successful midcareer professional, saw the impact of women's liberation on the young people in her office.

For twenty-five years, Conrad told the interviewer, she had worked in public relations and journalism. "For a long time, I had to be better than any other man in the field to gain acceptance. I think I still am. I'm aggressive and competitive and I think most women haven't allowed themselves to be that. They're told they should be homemaking." In between phone calls taken at her desk, she explained how she had watched "women's lib" affect the people in her office, who were mostly women. "I've had two women start to feel ready to assert themselves," only to find that their husbands resented that career success and their independent interests. Instead of supporting their wives, as her husband, Hunt Conrad, had, "they've been threatened, they've yanked their wives out of the job, and the city." Both women were now divorced. Marion and Hunt Conrad were raising three children. Hunt, who as a lobbyist spent stretches of time in Sacramento, could make breakfast and generally "keep the children alive when Marion is away."[17]

Conrad's career illuminates the feminism of her pre-1960s generation and its encounter with women's liberation. Conrad was a role model for younger women and men who worked with her in the 1960s, not to mention her peers. Born in 1925, she had come of age in the 1940s: "I think we're very old fashioned as far as women's lib is concerned. It's really after our time. I have sympathy with it in general, more than my husband. I can understand that women can do something jackassy like picketing a bar. Hunt would only see the jackassy side."[18] Her experiences explain how the woman in the expensive suit with pearls succeeded as an aggressive businesswoman, organized a peace movement, lamented the inability of younger men to accept women's independence, and yet maintained a sympathetic distance from the "jackassy" picketing of bars introduced by second-wave feminism. From Conrad's perspective, the younger generation's liberation had somewhat backfired compared to her own, a point she made to the reporter without any judgment.

Marion Kitchin and Hunt Conrad had known each other since childhood, and by the time they married in 1950, she had already laid the foundations of her future career. They grew up in Hillsborough, a suburban town on the peninsula just south of Burlingame and north of Redwood City. Her family had status but little money or entitlement. After attending the Katherine Burke School in San Francisco, she graduated from Sarah Lawrence College in Bronxville, New York, in 1946. Sarah Lawrence gave Conrad lifelong friends and professional contacts on the East Coast. She returned home and began working for the *San Francisco Chronicle*. As Kitchin jumped into organizing fund-raising galas and social club balls at the city's major hotels, she honed skills that would encourage her to gravitate toward public relations. Within a short time, she became the advertising and public relations director first of the Fairmont Hotel and then of the Palace Hotel. The same year she married Hunt, Marion went into partnership in a public relations firm with Dorothy Friend, an entertainment writer for the *News-Call Bulletin*. Conrad's time at the Palace Hotel introduced her to gourmet cooking, which became a passion and also a bridge to clients in the hospitality industry.[19]

From the start, Hunt Conrad supported his wife's unconventional choices. When for their wedding she "eschewed the more traditional white satin gown, and chose instead a becoming model of pale gray lace over silver gray taffeta," this was a small but symbolic indication of her independence. The newlyweds moved to Sacramento, where Hunt completed a graduate degree at the University of California, Davis, in agricultural science. Marion stepped from San Francisco's Palace Hotel into Sacramento's Hotel El Rancho, where she also directed advertising and public relations. She seized the opportunity to work in government as an aide to several state assemblymen. The Conrads next tried their hands as ranchers in the Central Valley near Fresno for four years, but soon returned to the Bay Area. At her customary pace, in 1958 Marion Conrad had twins and also founded Marion Conrad Associates. Leaving ranching behind, Hunt Conrad continued to work the land in a different capacity. He became a lobbyist for Kern County Land Company (later Tenneco), the Irvine Company, and Castle & Cook (the parent company behind Oceanic Properties).[20]

Marion Conrad would have appreciated the irony that one of the most influential public relations people in San Francisco would later find her own contributions unacknowledged. But she would not have been surprised. Few public relations professionals, no matter how accomplished, have attained a visible place in the historical record—in part because of the behind-the-scenes nature of their work.[21] Conrad also had experience with being undervalued by clients and had a forthright strategy for handling the situation. In the summer of 1967, Conrad canceled her contract with Lawrence Halprin & Associates, telling Halprin that he was incapable of understanding the scope and sophistication of her work to build his international profile. A typical aggravation was how Halprin's staff fumbled press inquiries Conrad had generated. "Too many cooks," she said. His attempt to lavish praise on her at the point of her resignation came too late. He took responsibility for appearing "unappropriately unappreciative," acknowledged the "intensity" of her work, and credited her "incredibly superb" job.[22]

Marian Conrad operated the hidden mechanisms of public relations that helped some projects shine and others fade, distributed funding and credit for new ideas, and saved the souls of other initiatives that might otherwise have failed. Conrad herself, however, was not hidden. According to the people who worked with her, she was a force. Columnist Herb Caen, a close friend and the godfather to one of the Conrads' children, was one of the powerful San Franciscans who knew her well. When she died suddenly in February 1974, he dedicated lines to her in the *Chronicle* that were remembered by her brother-in-law decades later as exemplary of Caen's ability "to capture the essence of a person's life in a few paragraphs."[23] Caen found it inconceivable that Conrad, "that incredible bundle of energy," had passed away.

Marion was different, a vital part of a city that is diminished by her departure: along with being a great wife, mother and three-star chef, she could organize a peace march, rally a protest, elect a Senator, promote a restaurant, and work—or play—all night and be ready for a couple of sets [of tennis] at dawn. . . . Literally and metaphorically, a mover and a shaker, and if life weren't in such bad taste, she would have lived to become a great gregarious old lady, running everybody and everything. Still, she did die at 48 the way she lived—running, running, running—and just maybe that's the way she wanted it.[24]

The *Chronicle* obituary described Marion Conrad as "one of the Bay Area's best-known and most respected public relations professionals." It listed a sampling of her clients (The Sea Ranch, Trader Vic's restaurants, Lawrence Halprin, the San Francisco Film Festival, the Actors' Workshop, the San Francisco Cancer Society), her civic work (the California Alliance for Peace, Big Sur Disaster, the NAACP Legal Defense Fund, Restore Fort Ross), and her advising of local and state elected officials. In 1959 Conrad already commanded attention as a mover and shaker. A reporter described her as "tall, stunning Marion, who 'stands her man' in the tough PR field masterfully." At this relatively early point in her career, Conrad was singled out for handling the accounts of "all kinds of 'male-reserve' business corporations."[25]

Marion Conrad and her office operated at the tightly integrated juncture of design, real estate, politics, and the hospitality industry. Understanding the strategies and methods by which Conrad boosted ideas, careers, and deals illuminates from an unfamiliar angle some of the leading experimental development projects of the 1960s.

COVER STORIES: "A PROFILE ON YOU, THE MAN"

Publicists knew that placing a single prominent, positive article on a client in a major publication could establish or transform the client's career. Dozens of years later, Al Boeke still marveled over Conrad's 1966 *Progressive Architecture* cover story on The Sea Ranch. The article staked out the ecological philosophy of the development, endorsed Boeke's leadership, and credited design innovation evenly among the architectural firms. Conrad similarly accelerated graphic designer Bobbie Stauffacher's career through publicity in architectural journals, as we shall see in the next chapter. She did far more than place stories and amplify her clients' news reach using press contacts. She often generated the core concepts that defined the careers of individuals such as Halprin, Stauffacher, and Boeke and of projects such as The Sea Ranch.

If Marion Conrad began to take her success with the design press for granted, the front-page *Wall Street Journal* (WSJ) profile she secured on Larry Halprin was another matter entirely. Ron Buel's thoughtful, balanced, "Shaping Cities: A Landscape Architect Generates New Ideas in Urban-Area Planning" appeared in the June 8, 1967, issue (fig. 76). The article placed Halprin at the leading edge of a profession undergoing radical change. The story was as gratifying to Conrad as it was to Halprin. Conrad wrote to Walter McQuade, the architectural editor of *Fortune* magazine, "I thought I'd make sure you got a chance to see this. I believe it is the first profile *WSJ* has ever done. Interesting to me and very possibly to you that they chose this field in general, and Lawrence Halprin in particular."[26] Only recently, Buel wrote, a landscape architect might have focused on private garden design, as Halprin had when he opened his firm in 1949. Now landscape architects had taken on responsibility for some of the era's most significant master planning. "The massive rebuilding going on in many of the nation's larger cities is giving designers like Mr. Halprin plenty of opportunity to test their ideas." As the article's subheading outlined, "Halprin Plans Mall, Novel Housing, Fights Freeway Expansion, Noise, Crowding and Ugliness."[27] One friend wrote Halprin from New York to mention the article he had just read about "a landscape architect who

76 The front-page June 8, 1967, *Wall Street Journal (WSJ)* story "Shaping Cities," about Lawrence Halprin, written by Ron Buel, set a new standard in public relations for the design professions—especially for landscape architects breaking into urban design. Watchers of the urban-environmental scene in San Francisco knew that publicist Marion Conrad had placed the story. The *WSJ* did not usually feature profiles; Conrad said Halprin's was a first for the paper.

generates new ideas."[28] This gratifying news angle describing him as a creative, cutting-edge master planner and artist certainly mitigated Halprin's aggravation at having his expertise challenged on projects like Ghirardelli Square.

Back in the Bay Area, design insiders recognized Marion Conrad's handiwork in the Halprin profile. Architect Bill Turnbull was working with Conrad on Sea Ranch publicity at the time. He congratulated her: "P.S. The piece on Larry in the *Wall Street Journal* was impressive, to say the least; nice work."[29] The article balanced praise for innovation with fair criticism. It described Halprin's focus on the internal, communal areas of projects, whether shopping malls or affordable housing. His 1950s Orchard Mall, while not the first of its kind, was more widely emulated than similar prototypes. The article also portrayed Halprin's humble side. He acknowledged mistakes, giving Buel an example of a project where his preoccupation with creative "design" had caused him to lose sight of the client's real needs. For a Navajo tribe, he and his partner had proposed updated hogans made from traditional mud materials. They were laughed out of their own presentation by the Navajo, who wanted ranch houses. Critics told Buel that Halprin cared more about politics than design and that when architects engaged in urban planning the results were "caricatures" of cities. Buel reported on Halprin's hopes to ameliorate racial tension with better design, and caught a glimmer of the self-importance of a man directing a forty-person staff. "Three-fourths of Mr. Halprin's total business, in fact, is planning big projects that will affect many people." Buel closed by noting Halprin's perception of himself as an artist and describing his environmental collaborations with his wife, dancer Anna Halprin.[30]

It had taken Marion Conrad two years to convince editors of general-interest news-papers or magazines to commission a "hard-hitting profile on Larry."[31] The long lead-up to "Shaping Cities" and the article's afterlife trace Conrad's behind-the-scenes efforts to craft the world's perception of her clients. Key to her strategy was an annual visit to New York City to meet with senior editors. During a January 1967 trip, she sat down with representatives of *Fortune, Venture, Architectural Forum, Newsweek, McCalls,* the *Saturday Evening Post, Look, Progressive Architecture, Family Circle,* and *Time.*[32] The meetings built on each other over time. In person, she focused attention on previous correspondence, highlighting ideas that otherwise languished in editors' in-boxes. The New York contacts complemented her West Coast base of regional editors for the major magazines. For several months prior to the appearance of the Buel article, for example, she checked with the San Francisco *Wall Street Journal* staff to find out whether Buel's story would run, and she spoke directly with the author, who lived in Los Angeles.[33] She leaned hard on Jay Iselin, at the time a senior *Newsweek* editor. In their January 1967 meeting, she encouraged Iselin to use Halprin's planning work in Washington, D.C., as "a possible peg for the larger piece on Lawrence Halprin." Iselin told Conrad that he lacked the "proper staff man to write the story" but hoped to find a freelancer. When the *Wall Street Journal* profile came out, Marion Conrad forwarded it to Iselin with the prod "Can *Newsweek* be far behind?"[34] A few months later, she followed up with her friend Jim Truitt, previously of the San Francisco *Newsweek* office but now in Washington, to see if he had been able to get Iselin's attention on her behalf. He had not.[35]

Conrad used "Shaping Cities" relentlessly to spur other stories. She sent a grateful telegram to Ron Buel immediately. Larry was temporarily unreachable, she said, "But all repeat all reaction garnered from LH&A, Associates, friends, and enemies spectacular and a great tribute to you. Congratulatory phone calls have kept all our lines busy all morning. Letters to you and editors will follow. Dumbfoundedly, Marion."[36] She coached Larry Halprin to do the same. When the weeks slipped by, she reminded him to thank John Lawrence, Pacific Coast Editor of the *Wall Street Journal,* and copy Buel. It was Lawrence who had written "the review of *Freeways* for the *Wall Street Journal* and without whom your profile could not have been." In his eventual letter thanking Buel, Halprin acknowledged the "favorable comments on it from everywhere in the country" and commented on "its sensitive and thoughtful quality."[37] Conrad, meanwhile, had already forwarded Buel's story to New York editors with whom she had met in January. She wrote to *Time:* "Has WSJ scooped the story, or started the story once again? Love, Marion." To Bill Emerson she said, "Could the enclosed rather extraordinary treatment of our client, Lawrence Halprin, rekindle or spur the Saturday Evening Post interest." She added Jack Fincher of *Life* magazine to her list, bantering: "How's Life? Love, Marion," and wrote John Poppy of *Look*.[38]

During her "short trip to New York to see the magazines," Conrad tested out editors' responses to specific projects in her clients' portfolios.[39] For example, in 1967 *Fortune* expressed interest in Ghirardelli Square on the basis of the AIA award and other recognition. Conrad gathered valuable feedback at this meeting. The editor explained that "their lack of good pictures" had prevented them from covering Ghirardelli earlier. They asked to keep photos Conrad had brought of the development and the new architectural model. *Fortune* did not wish to pursue the suburban thousand-unit Woodlake multi-family housing development in San Mateo but was open to a profile on its developer, Gerson Bakar. *Architectural Forum* was "remarkably" interested in Woodlake, Conrad reported to Halprin & Associates, but "rejected all Sturtevant's photographs, and liked only the new [ones]." She continued, "We then discussed the general trend in architectural photograph[y] which does indeed seem to be towards the more 'living' variety. We should discuss this general trend." Conrad pitched editors on thematic topics that would give writers a reason to mention her clients. Demand for street furniture, an area of strength for Halprin, had grown along with the proliferation of plazas; Halprin's Ghirardelli lamps were highly acclaimed. *Forum* thought street furniture was a potentially "major piece," as did its competitor *Progressive Architecture. Forum* had "already done too much" on Ghirardelli Square but would revisit it when the project was completed.[40]

Conrad's work with editors engaged, defined—and yes, promoted—the substance of design concepts. Conrad explained the ideas behind her clients' individual projects and shaped interpretations of the same. At *Look* Conrad "spent at least an hour discussing general concept, density, etc.," of Woodlake with Mary Simon and John Peter. Conrad had gotten to know Peter the previous spring during his research immersion at The Sea Ranch. *McCalls,* on the other hand, rejected Woodlake because the development did not allow children under fifteen, a serious drawback for this family magazine. Conrad reported to Al Boeke after the 1967 visit that *Time* and *Architectural Forum* were still considering Sea Ranch stories. This tour, she wrote, was generally "quite reminiscent of my trip a year-and-a-half ago when I saw them and introduced their thinking to The Sea Ranch concepts." *Forum* asked for complete information packets on Oceanic Properties' new towns.[41]

Conrad's exchange with *Fortune* magazine offers a particularly explicit example of how a publicist planted, defined, and amplified key concepts. At stake in this case was honing Halprin's identity as a "master planner" rather than as one among many design consultants or, worse, a "gardener." Conrad knew that Jeanne Krause at *Fortune* was planning a story on landscape architecture, so Conrad tailored her phone calls and correspondence prior to their January 1967 meeting in New York. Despite that meeting, in February Krause mailed a generic inquiry about Halprin's projects to his office. To compensate for Krause's apparent memory lapse, Conrad wrote an excruciatingly clear letter detailing how Halprin's projects epitomized environmental planning. Conrad validated Krause's own arguments: "Perhaps a new and total review for you of the Halprin office projects seen from the viewpoint or focus described by you as 'the increasing and perhaps historical role of the landscape architect as coordinating designer on projects which are a cooperative effort' will serve you best." Conrad nudged Krause's ideas along, writing: "As we discussed on the phone late last fall, landscape architecture in general, and Lawrence Halprin's firm in particular, has moved way beyond the delimitations of the past few decades and more into the role it once knew in Olmstead's day, with Larry Halprin well in the forefront of this movement." Conrad directed Krause's attention to the "describing term" environmental planning, as found on Halprin's letterhead. For five single-spaced pages, Conrad described Halprin & Associates as "master planners" who had, as in the case of The Sea Ranch, helped clients select appropriate architects and architecture. For the Kansas City Civic Center and downtown; for plazas in Portland, Oregon; for Riverbend in Atlanta; and for the Seattle Civic Center, Halprin had created master plans. For Akron, Ohio, and downtown Pontiac, Michigan, the Halprin firm had been retained "to conceptualize" the projects. Conrad's client led this revival, making the landscape architect responsible for bringing in architects, engineers, planners or other consultants. Not every scenario positioned landscape architects above the other fields; Conrad distinguished master planning from "joint ventures with architectural firms" and included Ghirardelli Square and Woodlake in the latter category.[42]

The individual projects Conrad described in her letter to *Fortune* receded behind her overall portrait of a field transformed. Rather than promotional bits on behalf of a designer or project, her pitch became a big story, one worthy of the front page of the *Wall Street Journal* or *Fortune*. Her themes asserted the landscape architect's shift toward coordinating the work of other design professions, conceptualizing projects, and leading the emergence of an influential field, environmental planning.[43] Conrad meticulously molded Halprin into the man of "new ideas," a master planner among designers who experimentally integrated the natural and built environments. This intense campaign of letter-writing and face-to-face exchanges with editors differed from the general copywriting of public relations, which she delegated to others in her firm. Conrad's focused pursuit of such design narratives showed a master builder at work.

Al Boeke's interviewer for *Progressive Architecture* listened to his account of how Marion Conrad "put The Sea Ranch on the map worldwide" and asked him whether Conrad had also helped secure the design awards. Boeke demurred. Publicists did put together awards nominations, although it appears that Marion Conrad did not. Arguably more important, however, were the career-defining articles substantively shaped by an engaged publicist, which contributed to professional consensus and recognition. Conrad's achievements rose to this level: clinching the front-page article on Halprin in the *Wall Street Journal* and promoting the appearance of Bobbie Stauffacher's graphics and The Sea Ranch in separate *Progressive Architecture* cover stories. These individuals and projects received recognition from the AIA and other organizations. Some of the awards preceded the articles, of course, but more of them followed. Conrad, as much as the project architects, ensured that the professional design world appreciated The Sea Ranch. Boeke wrote, "Thanks to dear Marion Conrad, the wonderful, wonderful, as I call her, sergeant/public relations lady, much of the professional world in the arts, architecture, planning, etc., and whatever spinoffs from there, knew there was a place in California called The Sea Ranch, which was different than any other place." Boeke acknowledged Conrad's role in explaining the northern California planned environmental complex.[44]

When Conrad resigned her account with Lawrence Halprin & Associates shortly after the *Wall Street Journal* profile ran, telling Halprin that he took her work for granted, the firm went back to handling its own publicity. An informed staff architect could answer inquiries and issue press releases. But even as they parted ways, Halprin asked for Conrad's assistance in influencing an upcoming article. *San Francisco* magazine had recently agreed to hire Ron Buel to write a story, another fruition of Conrad's years of dropping leads into editors' hands, but Halprin feared that too much attention to his own contributions might annoy his associates. Possibly he had taken grief for the *Wall Street Journal* profile's exclusive focus on him. He hoped to head off tensions: "I would like Ron on this to cover more of the office, less on me personally." Conrad reminded Halprin that this was a "story first conceived of . . . as a profile on you, the man, who has created the works that you have. However, slanting Ron more in the direction you would like should not be too hard for you to do on a personal basis. I am sure he is a clever enough journalist to make a greater inclusion of the office and its activities palatable" to the editor, Jack Vietor.[45] Conrad coached Halprin on "slanting" the writer, providing insight into her strategies for shaping and boosting careers.

"A MOVER AND A SHAKER"

Getting clients into the limelight made Marion Conrad's reputation, but equally impressive was how she remedied the inevitable bad press that erupted when real estate development and city politics mixed. Here Conrad's political contacts came into play. She knew how things got done in the city. She steered clients clear of icebergs and dove in to rescue them when needed. Volatile Lawrence Halprin, in particular, benefited from Conrad's ability to fix what he called "specific searing problems of Public Relations." When she resigned, he proposed that he could still call upon Conrad in emergencies: "I do not know how you would feel about this but I very much hope it's in the cards."[46] Landscape architect Richard Vignolo, a longtime associate in Halprin's firm, remembered that Halprin "could be a bulldog inside a china shop." Halprin's demand to remove Ruth Asawa's mermaid sculpture from the Ghirardelli Square fountain was but one example of many incidents. Vignolo chuckled when recalling Conrad's skills: "Anything where there was going to be a conflict, she helped smooth it down." Her sound advice and availability to the staff reassured the office. For Halprin's associates, if "you had a question about something or other you called Marion." Vignolo singled out Conrad's help in ironing out a public confrontation with Bay Area Rapid Transit (BART) that led to Halprin's resignation from his consultancy to the transit authority and to seemingly endless scrutiny of BART design decisions and Halprin's role. Former employee Peggy Knickerbocker described Conrad as someone who would fight for her clients and friends, reliably in good taste and with manners.[47]

A small but nasty outburst among members of the San Francisco Board of Supervisors in December 1965 revealed both Marion Conrad's political influence and the insecurities of Lawrence Halprin's profession. This episode, in which a supervisor flip-flopped his opinion of Halprin based on Conrad's input, illuminated the intertwining of Conrad's two main client areas: politics and urban design/development/the arts. The newspaper headline "Blake Has a Change of Heart" caught the bare story line. Returning from two weeks in Mexico, Conrad reviewed the newspaper clippings and mail she had missed while on vacation. One article leapt out. William Blake, on the San Francisco Board of Supervisors, had attacked Halprin's work for the Highway Commission regarding the options for a proposed Panhandle freeway that would have cut through Golden Gate Park. Blake had been a leading force in the city's antifreeway movement since 1959. Siding with the majority of the supervisors, who opposed the Panhandle plan, Blake took his objections to another level by lambasting Halprin personally. The president of the board vividly recalled Blake's opinion that Halprin "didn't know nothin'—he was only a gardener."[48]

Marion Conrad swung into action for Halprin. She wrote to Blake, explaining her delay in contacting him and enclosing the unfortunate article. "I don't think I've ever mentioned it to you Bill, but Lawrence Halprin & Associates is one of our clients. I herewith enclose a little background on the firm *and* the man, in the hope that you'll have a chance to look it over and correct at least some of your impressions of the scope of the Halprin activities." She continued: "And a point in fact, although I'm sure you are already probably quite aware of it and were merely misquoted: The Halprin office was asked by the Highway Commission to study various freeway routes, among which was the Panhandle . . . *not to design landscaping* for same." Conrad closed by cordially thanking Blake for his support of the Actor's Workshop, another of her clients. The Conrads, she wrote, hoped "to have another bottle of Sebastiani with you sometime soon in '66."[49]

Days later, the papers reported that Blake "today looks at landscape architect Lawrence Halprin in a new light." Blake now urged his colleagues to support Halprin's suggestion that the board send a delegation to Washington to secure more freeway planning time. The incredulous board president asked Blake whether Halprin was the same man he had dismissed two weeks earlier. Blake's reply: "Maybe he wasn't as bad as I thought he was." Still, Blake could not resist a potshot. Halprin had "done such a lousy job" designing the landscape for the proposed Panhandle Parkway that the board fortunately had rejected the project. Blake nevertheless concluded, "Maybe I misjudged him."[50] The backstory of Conrad's letter to Blake gives the news account a different spin. Conrad mailed Halprin a blind copy of her letter to Blake, along with the "Change of Heart" clipping. With this she concisely documented a publicist's hidden influence. Halprin's standing with the city's Board of Supervisors rested upon Conrad's networks and her systematic monitoring of the newspapers and numerous other sources.

Marion Conrad made a niche for herself in getting political careers established, a fact explaining her pull with the Board of Supervisors and at the state level. One of her protégés was Willie Brown in his first successful run for the state assembly in 1964. Brown biographer James Richardson credited the success of Brown's 1964 campaign following his failed 1962 run to an endorsement by the *San Francisco Chronicle*. Richardson wrote, "In Brown's view, the key to getting the *Chronicle* endorsement was Brown's budding friendship with Herb Caen, the newspaper's leading columnist. . . . Brown said he was introduced to Caen by a public relations woman who was helping Brown's campaign." Conrad, the unnamed publicist, set up a lunch with Brown and Caen so the men could meet. Brown recalled, "At lunch, we two no-nonsense guys who don't have a whole lot of sensitivity about people's feelings, started off playing, cutting each other. And he just started to laugh, and of course she was a little uptight because she couldn't figure out why I would be so direct, caustic, to Herb Caen. He finally told her we were having a good time and it's okay if you leave. She left. And we sat there and bullshitted the rest of the afternoon and then agreed that we better have lunch at least once or twice a week from that day on—and we did." For his part, Caen called Conrad "the demon publicist who invented Willie Brown." Brown's account of the lunch aside, others remembered that Conrad thrived in the predominantly male environment of politics. According to Stanford (Stan) Erickson, a key wordsmith in Conrad's firm, she was content being "one of the boys in dealing with these powerful men."[51]

Conrad counted enough members of the Board of Supervisors as her clients that she had a potential inside track with that decision-making body from the 1960s through the early 1970s: Roger Boas, Ron Pelosi, William Maillard, and George Moscone. Ron Pelosi was chair of the City Planning Commission when he enlisted Conrad in his run for supervisor. Other San Francisco politicians were not formally listed as clients by her firm but consulted with Conrad. Stan Erickson mentioned Conrad's strong working relationship with Mayor Joseph Alioto, as well as with John and Phil Burton, Democratic Party leaders. Erickson believed that "politicians liked Marion because she minced no words. She told them what they needed to hear whether they wanted to hear it or not." He added that, generally, "She was in a class all by her own."[52] Conrad's civic activities, including cofounding the California Alliance for Peace, added to her credibility and opened doors to meeting more progressive city leaders. Erickson thought her straight talk and trustworthiness gave her authority to influence her politician clients' positions.[53]

Three of Conrad's chosen specialties—publicity, real estate development, and politics—occupied ambiguous moral terrain in the public eye. These professions shared the shadow of seeming to be beholden to the highest bidder. Conrad "enjoyed working with architects and artistic people," Erickson confirmed, but not only because she appreciated the currency of optimistic renderings and civic pride. Conrad worked the tough side of redevelopment politics. She helped get projects built, "much of it backroom. But I can assure you if she chose to have something stopped she could do that. Everyone in development wanted to be on the good side of Marion. A word here, a piece of gossip there, and Marion could destroy. I think she did that very sparingly. She prided herself on being very moral. But she also was well aware of her failings." To Erickson, regarding politicians, Conrad "always gave the impression that she not only could help their career but be harmful to it." Erickson respected Conrad and from close exposure was confident in her moral compass. But he did not see her as innocent. This was a meaningful distinction. She managed the interface of her backroom deals with the "public" of public relations. Erickson followed Conrad's political skill, right up to the manipulative edges that made him uncomfortable.[54]

Conrad also had to bow to others' power to meddle with her clients' strategies. Erickson recounted negotiations between Conrad and Scott Newhall of the *Chronicle* over releasing the development plan for the SFIMC. Newhall phoned Conrad, wanting to know about the designs prior to their being presented to the City Planning Commission. Conrad "politely said he would have to wait until the presentation." A reporter working for Newhall then published a piece fomenting general "hostility" toward the unreleased plans, "quoting unknown sources." The story's inaccuracies, according to Conrad, forced her hand. She invited Newhall to "her house in Pacific Heights and over drinks discussed what the builders planned."[55] Newhall's tactic of publishing a provocative story leveraged from Conrad a premature preview of her client's proposal.

Conrad's business tactics merit attention because she was an assertive publicist maneuvering in heavily male professions during the 1950s and 1960s. Women were in fact thriving in public relations; according to the census, their national numbers grew from 2,000 in 1950 to 7,271 in 1960. By 1966 women accounted for about 25 percent of PR professionals. They reported high levels of job satisfaction and an average pay that was much higher than that of their sisters in related fields. The rough numbers in 1960 contrasted a woman's $11,358 average salary in publicity to a median of $3,479 for editors and journalists. Like Conrad, most women in public relations had first worked in journalism, with smaller numbers coming from editing, television, and radio. Fewer than a third specialized in the so-called "women's areas"; far more, like Conrad, had accounts in fields more easily classified as "men's areas." In the mid-1960s, the national trade magazine *Public Relations Journal* began to report new research on women in the field, focusing its inquiries in D.C., New York, and Chicago. One article zeroed in on the question of how "feminine" a woman needed to be in this assertive profession. Their recommendations cut straight down the middle: "Aggressiveness is necessary in public relations, but it should be tactfully restrained." A woman professional should not be too "girly-girly," nor should she "try to be one of the boys." Instead, "a plain feminine woman will be respected on her own merits." Although it was unusual to achieve Conrad's level of influence, women in public relations reported high degrees of comfort with their aggressive style, as well as optimism in facing the prevalent discrimination against women in their field.[56]

Conrad's professional demeanor, described as both tough and charming, went over well in architecture, politics, and real estate. These details of Conrad's management style had a political edge. Richard Vignolo said of her: "She was very decisive. She wasn't wishy-washy in any way at all. You listened to her." Halprin might not have always agreed with Conrad, "but in the end, Larry did what she said." Former employee Peggy Knickerbocker remembered Conrad as adventurous, fierce, and powerful. Conrad was a "ballsy businesswoman" who "got things done." With admiration, Vignolo described Marion Conrad as "a very brilliant woman. She was *unique*. First, in the PR aspects she was great, and also she was a political force in this town. She pretty much groomed all the young, progressive, liberal Supervisors who ultimately went on and became legislators and that sort of thing. She was really terrific. Wonderful woman. Relaxed, very warm, open. She was an excellent cook, great cook, was great at throwing parties, on the social scene."[57]

Marion Conrad's office, run out of the basement of her Pacific Avenue home, epitomized her successes as a power-broker publicist; it melded her legendary entertaining and coveted introductions, her social status and knowledge of the city's workings, her magnetic personality, and her staff's talents. Conrad was, as Herb Caen recalled, a gourmet cook, dynamic host, and master of arranging connections with food and drink. It was no coincidence that Scott Newhall came over for drinks along with the unveiling of the SFIMC redevelopment plans. For some ordinary meetings, Richard Vignolo recalled, Halprin's staff would go up to Pacific Avenue, "and she'd come out with pheasant and spread the tablecloth on this little lawn out in front, [and we'd] eat pheasant and drink champagne."[58] When Conrad invited journalist Stan Erickson to her house to discuss the prospect of working for her, he agreed to stop by because he had never been to a Pacific Heights home. He had also never seen a lobster. She cooked live lobsters and served Scotch. By doubling Erickson's salary, she convinced him to give up his newspaper job and work in PR for her firm.[59] Conrad's dinners built working relationships in part through impressing colleagues with her organizational abilities and high standards. One new contact, writing about publishing opportunities for Lawrence Halprin, had just met Conrad after hearing about her for years: "Enjoyed your friends and that dinner was out of this world. How do you manage to do everything to such perfection?"[60]

Marion Conrad made her office and its six employees central to the flow of insider information about redevelopment, local politics, and relevant San Francisco gossip. Conrad usually had several staff members who, Erickson recalled, were "attractive" young women "from socially prominent families." In 1966 and 1967 Peggy Knickerbocker and Linda Hale worked for Conrad. The firm counted among its clients some of the city's most popular restaurants and hotels, and Conrad used these connections system-atically. Many nights Knickerbocker and Hale went out on the town, visiting the Fairmont, L'Etoile, Ernie's, or one of Trader Vic's spots. The next morning, when newspapers called for gossip, Knickerbocker and Hale obliged with stories that put

Conrad's restaurant and hotel clients in the news. At least three times a week, Erickson called Herb Caen's assistant to provide "juicy" items about who was seen where. He could include a tidbit "about a person or company that Marion sought as a client" or "relay stories about politicians for whom Marion was working." When the stakes were high, Conrad phoned Caen directly. Erickson admired her "ear for such stories" and her "gift for making everything sound interesting." Conrad arranged complimentary meals at her clients' restaurants, as she did for Herb Caen several times a week.[61]

Her employees received much the same hospitality that she lavished on developers, architects, and civic benefactors. A tireless worker, she could be a "whirling dervish" in the office. When the atmosphere at 1948 Pacific Avenue became tense, Erickson described how Conrad would have a courier pick up Dungeness crabs, "and she would break out the good white wine from her wine cellar and we would all sit around eating crab and drinking on the floor seated on old newspapers. Marion, in her $1000 dress, would sit right down with us and out-eat everyone." Erickson added that her energy and style was such that "you wanted to be around her. She was her own circus with clowns, tigers, elephants and high-wire trapeze flyers in skimpy costumes."[62]

Those who worked with Conrad recalled absorbing an education in "how San Francisco worked," as Erickson phrased it. Others credited Conrad with introducing them to entrepreneurial business practices that shaped their subsequent careers. Peggy Knickerbocker worked for Marion Conrad Associates for a short while in the mid-1960s, soon after college. Knickerbocker, who became an influential food and travel writer, described her time with Conrad as instrumental to shaping her own sophistication in public relations and the hospitality industry.[63] Whereas Knickerbocker had been born into the city's establishment, Erickson had more to learn about San Francisco's power structure. Erickson was raised in San Bruno, about 25 miles south of San Francisco. His father was a mechanic, and his mother worked in the post office. A twenty-eight-year-old Army veteran and experienced reporter at the time he began working at Marion Conrad Associates, Erickson described himself as still "very naïve" in many ways, especially when navigating the "complex and shrewd individuals" who comprised the world of public relations, real estate development, and politics. When Erickson left the firm for McGraw-Hill, he found that "Marion was much admired by other professional women in the Bay Area," including his new boss.[64]

WRITING PR: "MORE BLUE SKY STANFORD, NOT SO MANY FACTS"
Good contacts opened doors, but the right kind of writing was the foundation of strong public relations. The task of identifying, hiring, and orchestrating writers drove Conrad's projects. Conrad, more an editor and impresario than a copywriter, relied on her staff members to produce the texts on which her clients' reputations depended. From the firm's founding, Mia Dixon was lead writer, while Conrad was "rainmaker," according to Stan Erickson. Dixon's departure from Conrad Associates was one reason Marion hired Erickson.[65] The firm needed to master clients' specialized languages, such as the vocabulary of urban design. Often that meant quietly hiring outside expertise. According to Erickson, the *Chronicle*'s City Hall reporter, Mel Wax, wrote speeches and press

releases for Marion Conrad Associates' politician clients. Wax worked for Conrad "unbeknownst to his editors," disclosed Erickson. "Mel was the most important political reporter in San Francisco and was, to a degree, on her payroll. I am certain that Mel did not slant any of his reporting to help Marion's clients. I am certain he was honorable that way. But he provided a lot of intelligence for Marion and he was a gifted writer."[66] Urban design criticism faced its own challenges, especially a dearth of journalists with adequate expertise—a complaint Conrad heard regularly from the general newspapers and magazines as she made inquiries.[67]

A misunderstanding that flared between Marion Conrad and Ron Buel, the author of the breakthrough *Wall Street Journal* profile on Halprin, illuminated the anxieties over maintaining a wall between journalism and publicity. A journalist's integrity could rise above the question of who paid for an article, but he or she nonetheless had to worry about the appearance of bias. A few weeks after Buel's *Wall Street Journal* article came out, Conrad approached him about writing a different profile for *San Francisco* magazine. Buel was interested, pending approval by his *Wall Street Journal* editors. He would willingly write the article for free, but he would certainly accept payment from the magazine if offered. Conrad wrote Buel to facilitate his meeting with *San Francisco*'s editor, Jack Vietor. She confirmed a $200 fee, half of which would be paid by the publisher and half by Lawrence Halprin & Associates.[68]

Ron Buel was deeply offended, replying to Conrad: "I cannot let the impression stand, even for a few days, that I would accept cash from Mr. Halprin's office for doing a story on him." Nor could he take gifts or favors from "anyone associated" with Halprin. "In the first place, it would appear as though there may have been some arrangement prior to my doing the piece on Mr. Halprin for the Wall Street Journal which would have compromised my independence in doing the article, which there was not." Similarly, he would not want his "independence as a journalist" questioned by *San Francisco*. He was sure editor Jack Vietor would agree. Conrad answered immediately, apologizing for any "insensitivity in the proceedings."[69]

Conrad provided the background, detailing the hard work done by editors and publicists to maintain sufficiently clear lines between independent journalism and public relations. The "offensive" offer had in fact originated with Jack Vietor, not Conrad. In 1965 Vietor had liked Conrad's idea of a profile on Halprin but had "had no staff writer who he thought 'right' to do the piece." At that time, Vietor suggested splitting the writer's fee between the magazine and Halprin's firm. The editor asked Conrad to find a qualified author. In the intervening two years, three Bay Area journalists had agreed to the arrangement but were refused the assignment by their own editors, who saw writing the story for *San Francisco* as competing with their regular beats. Conrad had mistakenly assumed, from Vietor's "matter-of-factness," that he often sought arrangements to split the writer's fee in order to run a high-quality local magazine on a tight budget. She was sorry that Buel had "misunderstood what was a completely above-board arrangement and that I have offended your sensibilities."[70]

Despite the aggravation, the Conrad-Buel flare-up indicated progress in the emergence of independent, informed urban design criticism, particularly its separation from the 1950s patterns of designers' self-promotion in architectural magazine writing (see chapter 9). To underscore her own integrity, Conrad had reviewed her labors to ensure that Buel's journalistic independence remained uncompromised. She reminded Buel that his "three fine and variegated pieces" were on her "EX-clients" (there had been two on Halprin and one on Gerson Bakar, Woodlake's developer). This removed her financial interest from the equation. "But this in no way changes my opinion that the articles are pertinent and that you would and should do a great job with them." Had Buel's letter arrived at another time, Conrad admitted, she might "feel some hurt feelings at your reaction." Instead, she smoothed things by inviting him to lunch at her place. That way, she said, "there can be no scrabble over whether it's 'Dutch.'"[71]

Conrad fared better when she hired Stanford Erickson to work full time for her firm. In Erickson she found a writer who mastered the complexities of new fields quickly, got along with the journalists her clients needed to impress, and could tell a story. Erickson was the person in Conrad's office who "wrote copy," Knickerbocker remembered, "sparkling copy." Erickson also had talent for minting a good marketing angle. At the time Conrad met him, Erickson was working at the *San Francisco Daily Commercial News,* fresh from military duty in Korea, where he had been the lead journalist for *Stars and Stripes* in 1965–66. The draft had plucked him from a likely Ph.D. at San Francisco State University, where he had completed a master's degree in English literature. For Erickson, journalism came before as well as after English literature. His first job after graduating in 1962 from the University of California, Berkeley, had been with the *San Francisco Examiner.* An editor had hired him as a summer replacement because of his blunt, perceptive critique of the paper during his interview. Erickson was soon fired, however, after writing a negative review of a movie that advertised heavily in the newspaper. He counted this as his first lesson in how money influenced journalism.[72]

At the *Daily Commercial News,* Stan Erickson's editor told him that Conrad, "an important friend, needed a story about the San Francisco International Market Center." He had not heard of the proposed project. In his brief career at the paper, Erickson had interviewed Governor Ronald Reagan, the city's mayor, "and just about anyone who was important in San Francisco." He agreed to write the piece. Conrad picked him up and drove him to 1620 Montgomery, where he interviewed the architects of Wurster, Bernardi & Emmons. He digested the materials Conrad handed him and finished the story for the next day's paper. Conrad liked the phrase—"a city within a city"—he had used to describe the massive center. That was the same day she invited Erickson for a drink at her house, fed him lobster, and convinced him to accept her job offer. For Erickson, who had become accustomed to writing "half of the newspaper each day," working in public relations, even for a driven employer like Conrad, would prove to be less demanding than journalism.[73]

Conrad sought out what she called "planning stories" for use in national publications. For her firm's "overwhelming media kit," they gathered biographical details from architects, write-ups by clients about their philosophy, photographs of architectural models and sites, and articles on designers' previous projects. They interviewed their clients. Among the list of things Conrad requested from the Sea Ranch consultants in

October 1964 were copies of "all unusual or interesting techniques or planning concepts used in this project." Erickson and Conrad would work the best bits from the designers and developers into the firm's statements and the media kit. For every project, Erickson customarily wrote five or ten "white papers," each one amplifying a different dimension to catch the press's interest.[74]

Erickson preferred journalism to the prose of publicity and was no fan of architectural writing, but he was good at all three. For architectural journals Erickson found that "the writing required was minimum facts and a lot of pretty words that signified nothing." He offered a not-quite-caricature: "When writing about The Sea Ranch it always was important to talk about the crashing waves that welcomed the surrounding cliffs as if beckoning the rough wood finishes of the Sea Ranch homes, encouraging the owners to sip their wine and not think about tomorrow and tomorrow." In this line of employment, he had little choice. "Most of that made me nauseous but I could out write everyone in 'blue sky' as she called it. 'More blue sky Stanford, not so many facts,'" Conrad would say. Architect-developer Al Boeke shared a dislike of design's insular language: "I am a person who avoids professional vocabularies. I don't use, if you'll pardon the expression, the cutsie-pie invented phrases and words that are invented in architectural and planning schools across the country. I just won't use them. I talk plain English."[75]

If Erickson and Boeke's positions at the outskirts of professional architecture informed their perspectives on the limitations of design language, architect clients resisted "blue sky" promotions at times. In January 1965, Joseph Esherick sent Marion Conrad detailed comments on the drafted "Fact Sheet" for The Sea Ranch. "Some of my questions relate to the sort of image that the sheet evokes and others to the correctness of the factual material," he explained. Esherick scrutinized the accuracy of fluffy publicity word choices. "Perhaps you should check out whether the four poster supports are in fact hewn," he suggested to Conrad.[76]

For every story Marion Conrad Associates pitched successfully, many more landed in the wastebasket. The dynamics of local press coverage differed from the workings of the design journals or national-interest magazines such as *Look*. In newspapers a "design" story might bounce among departments—city desk, financial pages, real estate, California Living. In May 1967, when the *New York Times* covered the year's twenty top AIA awards, the paper published a photograph of Sea Ranch Condominium One, designed by MLTW. That article prompted Turnbull to ask Conrad: "What happened with the San Francisco papers or Oakland: any coverage at all?" Conrad sent Turnbull a lone *Oakland Tribune* clipping, explaining that "we did service this in a very aggressive and extensive manner but, as you also no doubt know, the papers in San Francisco are not the *New York Times* when it comes to this kind of thing." Her office had "hand serviced" the story of the AIA award to the city desks of the *San Francisco Chronicle*, the *Examiner*, and the *Oakland Tribune*, and "it was rejected by all three." They brought it to "the financial pages of all three, again rejected." Finally, they had success with the *Chronicle/Examiner* real estate editors, who planned to fold the AIA award into a pending general story on The Sea Ranch. Conrad also raised fresh interest from the *Chronicle/Examiner* "California Living" section, which had been "the first publication to give The Sea Ranch notable space."[77]

The communications skills of a professional publicist included keeping stories out of the papers. Conrad told Erickson that "twenty-six old-time San Francisco families ran the city in a benign manner." One of her responsibilities was "to protect these families, primarily by keeping them out of the press." Conrad's connections to these families opened fund-raising avenues for her other clients and for the initiatives she supported, such as the peace movement.[78] According to Erickson, Conrad helped out Herb Caen by introducing his second wife to San Francisco society. That left Caen indebted, to a certain extent, but he retained the right to be unpredictable and occasionally vindictive. When he disagreed with one of Conrad's clients, her office considered it a "victory if he never said anything." Sometimes his comments stuck painfully to their mark, such as when he called the two hundred–ton black granite sculpture in front of the new 52-story Bank of America headquarters the "banker's heart." Conrad often represented the lead architects for the skyscraper and its plaza—Wurster Bernardi & Emmons.[79] Suppression could be as important as publicity.

On the Sonoma coast the conversion of land into real estate was more obvious than in the city, and the tensions between land and landscape more evident. Just as wind-blown meadows made its purple sales tent and marketing machinery more conspicuous, The Sea Ranch made the contributions of Marion Conrad to real estate development in the Bay Area more obvious as well. The lessons learned from planning The Sea Ranch circled back to the city, and popular writing about the built environment and architecture gained new audiences and urgency during the 1960s as large-scale master planning evolved. Conrad's experience reveals how "planning stories" were written and circulated, how public relations could make design careers, and how projects succeeded and failed in the political process. Publicity machinery honed a master plan's ideological clarity, won recognition for its designers, and earned profits for the investors. Such expertise played a critical role in launching "unusual" real estate developments such as The Sea Ranch and Ghirardelli Square, which were significant "environmental complexes" attentive to the perspective of the individual within an increasingly master-planned world. Without such promotion, the awareness (let alone the public meanings) of remote and unfamiliar projects would have been very different. They certainly would have been less cohesive and articulate.

Seemingly worlds apart for what they represented architecturally and where they sat on the urban–rural spectrum, The Sea Ranch and Ghirardelli Square were nonetheless similarly positioned by their designers, developers, and publicists as novel environmental planning models. Whether preservationist coastal development or repurposed historic waterfront, both claimed civic benefits for their land-use concepts and private open spaces. In these ways, The Sea Ranch and Ghirardelli Square presumed to limit negative environmental impact as well as to curb the profit premise of private development. The Sea Ranch, occupying land that under different political circumstances would have become a state park, experimented with shared private ownership of communal land. Ghirardelli Square's developer saved a local landmark from a high-rise fate and opened it to the consuming public. The fact that The Sea Ranch's "open space" was

77 The Sea Ranch store with its distinctive graphics by Bobbie Stauffacher embodied the development's real estate message: "General Store, Restaurant, Land Sales." Stauffacher's ram's-head logo for the development also cleverly doubled as two crashing waves or two seashells.

thousands of acres of windswept meadows and cliffs, while Ghirardelli's was a tiny urban plaza, makes the resonance more intriguing.

Delving into the work of Marion Conrad Associates raises explicit questions about the manipulative powers behind real estate development, whereas architectural journals rarely, if ever, addressed such issues. Conrad expertly navigated real estate development's moral complexities. Her exchanges with clients revealed her long-term strategies, her tough but winning persona, the backroom deals, the social contacts, the endless correspondence and meetings, the "blue sky" copy, and her intensity. These qualities made her small firm among the most powerful and respected in San Francisco. Her hidden work crafted the new concepts and profiles that defined professional architects and planners, as well as the newsworthy designs that made them famous. This, too, was shaping cities.

At the same moment developer Al Boeke admired the results of Conrad's publicity at The Sea Ranch opening, others began to wonder whether the project had betrayed its environmental ideals of responsible coastal stewardship. Graphic artist Bobbie Stauffacher was one such doubter. Of the opening, she wrote: "Hundreds of people were there. No shepherds. The only sheep were Vic's barbecued lambs, and potential buyers."[80] Sheep were on Stuaffacher's mind in part because she had designed the development's ram's-head logo. The graphic cleverly doubled as two crashing waves, or two seashells (fig. 77). Painted in white on the weathered boards of Esherick's Sea Ranch store and on a second, shedlike structure, her logo and the buildings together stood as roadside "markers" for the property. The graphics were very well received. One critic, however, captured the incomplete leap from a desolate coastal landscape into an effective visual vocabulary for real estate sales. He thought a cover photo from the *AIA Journal* made these buildings look like the "head structures of an abandoned coal mine."[81] The architects' efforts to relate their designs to the land and the environment were antithetical to mainstream 1960s modernism. Don Canty, managing editor at *Architectural Forum* during these years, recalled that one of the chief editors "dismissed" the demonstration projects at The Sea Ranch—Esherick's general store and Hedgerow Houses and MLTW's ten-unit condominium—as "stick architecture." Traditional modernists faulted the California development's "regionalism and naturalistic design" as chaining down the designers' creativitiy. The Bay Area's environmental complexes were not universally admired.[82]

As a graphic designer, Stauffacher's professional relationship to architecture and urban design differed significantly from Conrad's. For one thing, Stauffacher's visual arts career placed her work in direct competition with that of the architects. The practice of using landscape design to promote real estate development began to trouble Stauffacher, and her opinion of The Sea Ranch and her role in its success diverged from Conrad's. She came to focus on design's manipulative powers and questioned whether foregrounding design novelty had masked the land-grab on which the development of The Sea Ranch was premised. The temporary purple tent on the Ocean Terrace had left a permanent mark.

"Urban Renewal with Paint"
Graphic Design and the City

In the fall of 1963, at the same time she began working for Oceanic Properties on the coastal project that would become The Sea Ranch, graphic artist Bobbie Stauffacher's name was included on the construction board posted at the Ghirardelli factory excavation site (fig. 78). This was unusual. It was possibly unheard of. Architects, landscape architects, contractors, engineers, and city and state officials were listed on construction boards— not graphic designers. As in public relations, the graphic artist's role was downplayed and often anonymous.

Yet Stauffacher had recently begun to attract international accolades as an imaginative commercial artist. The American Institute of Graphic Arts (AIGA) in New York recognized her in 1962, 1963, and 1964 in the categories of promotional advertising, information design, and editorial design. The brochures, calendar, and greeting card singled out by the AIGA[1] were the typical small-scale canvases mastered by a budding graphics business (figs. 79 and 80). Several of the subjects depicted in these commissions, including a highway interchange and a new park, signaled Stauffacher's growing expertise in the built and natural environments. In 1962 her designs began to appear in galleries. The AIGA's New York City exhibition *Design and Printing for Commerce* including her artwork traveled to the Louvre.[2]

78 The spring 1964 construction notification board at Ghirardelli Square included Bobbie Stauffacher, the graphic design consultant, underneath the names of the architects, landscape architects, and engineers. This was a sign of the unusual collaboration behind the project as well as the central role played by allied design professionals.

By the mid-1960s, Stauffacher's graphics had leapt off the flat pages of calendars and brochures and onto the three-dimensional form of the city. Bobbie Stauffacher became a major player in a larger 1960s revolution in graphic design that ultimately transformed the language and legibility of architecture. The turning point came in 1966, when she painted The Sea Ranch's swim and tennis club interior with what would soon be called "supergraphics." More accurately, the true turning point occurred a year later. In March 1967 her friend and publicist Marion Conrad splashed Stauffacher's remote bathhouse interior onto the cover of *Progressive Architecture,* and thus onto the radar of the international design community (fig. 81).

Stauffacher's solo graphic artistry helped mark her clients' architecture as attention-worthy and successful. Soon her client base narrowed to favor prolific, influential architects and developers. She proved to be adept at translating inchoate or unfamiliar landscapes into appealing real estate imagery. *Harper's Bazaar* featured Stauffacher's trend-setting work in 1971, proclaiming: "Big, bold, colorful style—the cityscape as her found surface—marks her brochures, logos, periodicals, street signing program. Winner, second woman, AIA Industrial Design Medal. Designer of clarity for urban scene."[3] Her projects formed a versatile

79 Bobbie Stauffacher's early graphics for brochures, government reports, calendars, and holiday cards won awards. Her 1962 brochure for The Crossroads shopping center (11 × 11 inches), for the Harry Heifetz Company, garnered honors in the category of promotional design and advertising from the American Institute of Graphic Arts. Most of Stauffacher's clients were in real estate development, planning, architecture, and the arts.

80 Stauffacher's monthly San Francisco Museum of Art calendars earned her professional recognition and helped attract clients. This February 1964 calendar for the Museum (97 × 21 inches) was recognized by the American Institute of Graphic Arts in 1965 with an award for information design. One sees in her calendars the origins of ideas Stauffacher applied at The Sea Ranch, such as the bull's-eye in this example.

portfolio of new planning models, encompassing historic and modern, urban, suburban, and rural. But more often than not, commentators attributed to her work an "urban" sensibility.

The 1970 Industrial Arts Medal recognized Stauffacher's ability to reimagine scale, extend the possibilities of architectural form, and enrich the "vocabulary" of urban design. Nomination letters by noted architects and critics cited her experiments bringing two- and three-dimensional forms together through her painted "supergraphics." The Industrial Arts Medal represented one of the AIA's efforts to broaden what constituted architectural design. Donlyn Lyndon, a Sea Ranch collaborator who now headed MIT's architecture department, gave Stauffacher much credit for "the forming of a new consciousness in American architecture of the potential for elaboration of form through graphics and color." She had pioneered "an innovative approach to the overlapping of building form and graphic information." Most importantly, she had "added new dimension to the vocabulary of place definition with which architects are presently working."[4] Critic Allan Temko voiced the consensus that Stauffacher was "a superbly gifted graphic designer who has made significant contributions to architecture."[5] Her graphics included words, text, and typeface, as well as nontypographic shapes.

81 In March 1967 Marion Conrad's efforts placed Bobbie Stauffacher's supergraphics for the Sea Ranch bathhouse interior on the cover of *Progressive Architecture*. Stauffacher's environmental design work was instrumental in opening a closer integration between architecture and the graphic arts in the 1960s.

Working so closely in the 1960s with architects and planners honed and amplified Stauffacher's career but also erased it. Over time, Stauffacher became acutely aware of the mixed implications of her simultaneous achievements in urban design as a solo artist and as a collaborative commercial designer. Her 2006 memoir, "Duped by Design," offered an engrossing insider-outsider critique of the design field. Despite her professional stature and success in publishing *Green Architecture and the Agrarian Garden* and *Good Mourning California* with the international art and design press Rizzoli in 1988 and 1992, Stauffacher could not find a publisher for the memoir. The book, she was told, fell between the genres of autobiography and architecture.[6]

The story of how Stauffacher thrived professionally on the ambiguities between graphic design and architecture, and still felt disillusioned, placed another unpublished book (in this case, "Duped by Design") on the shelf of 1960s urban critiques. At the time she chose to study graphic design in the 1950s, she said, "commercial art was hucksterism and propaganda, low, vulgar, trivial, and done for money. Being a designer was acceptable, someone who builds, someone self-reliant, almost like being an architect."[7] Stauffacher's experience showed that graphic arts could be classified with both the "commercial" arts of real estate and the more elevated, "creative" urban design field. By the close of the 1960s, however, the environmental planning trends that had elevated her contributions to large-scale development had also left her high and dry. The anointing of her work as urban design would prove to be unsustainable in the field of architecture. Simultaneously, Stauffacher's successful promotion of The Sea Ranch provoked her to begin reclassifying design—whether graphic arts or architecture—as hucksterism and propaganda.

GRAPHIC DESIGN: "ARCHITECTURE THAT LITERALLY SPEAKS TO US ALL"

In the 1960s, graphic arts and typography broke through with new relevance for architecture and cities. Graphic designers such as Bobbie Stauffacher were called on not only to frame the conceptual underpinnings of real estate promotion through sales materials but also—albeit occasionally—to pronounce certain buildings as "architecture" through graphic markers. Architects, landscape architects, and planners had their own professional language to describe the built and natural environments, which did not always translate clearly to the general public. Logos, sales brochures, photographs, models and mock-ups, advertisements, and signs—such made up the middle ground of translation usually presided over by graphic artists. At the same time, this middle ground of promotion touched and partially defined the structures themselves and their environments. In some cases, designers applied graphics directly to the buildings.

For decades graphics had posed more of a threat than a boon to urban and rural environments. City planners had tried to control and dignify the disharmony of signs on urban streets since the early twentieth century, while roadside billboards provoked campaigns to protect the countryside.[8] To design professionals at midcentury, graphics in the cityscape for the most part represented disorder. The rise of architectural modernism further diminished designers' opinions of signs and lettering; graphics disrupted a building's clean lines and introduced unnecessary "decorative" elements. Stauffacher's colleagues attested to her leading role in reviving the possibilities for graphic arts to enhance the built environment. The president of the Northern California AIA chapter said her designs were "unique for an art so long neglected by architects and planners in their fight against visual chaos."[9] Allan Temko underscored the applicability of Stauffacher's strategies regardless of the location, scale, or age of a building and particularly admired how she "grappled with prototypical problems of the contemporary environment, including its degradation by ugly outdoor advertising, and solved those problems with dignity, grace, and wit, as well as boundless vitality." He cited her "less well known designs, done on modest budgets, such as the wonderfully optimistic 'supergraphics' for Boas Pontiac in San Francisco" (fig. 82).[10] For Boas Pontiac, Stauffacher had applied both words and graphic symbols to the building's exterior, combining concrete directional instructions (to the service department or used-car division) with evocative, relevant, generally promotional art.

As the horizons for graphic design broadened to include the built environment, a new generation of typefaces and symbols remade the substance of typography in the 1960s. The decade witnessed revolutions on multiple fronts in the world of graphic arts. A fresh range of artists melded graphics and environmental design, including Bobbie Stauffacher and Marget Larsen in the Bay Area and, in Southern California, Deborah Sussman, Corita Kent (Sister Corita), and Saul Bass.[11] A spare sans-serif typeface, Helvetica, took designers in the United States by storm, rising from nowhere to dominate typography for fifty years. Helvetica gave modernism new dimensions, a new vocabulary, and a new

82 Stauffacher's exterior signage for Boas Pontiac, underscoring the overall street-view effect of commercial supergraphics rather than the artfulness of individual applications. This dealership appeared in architectural magazines; photographers particularly appreciated the tire graphic and the impact of the broad stripes on the exterior architecture (especially in close-ups of the service entrance, which in this view is just beyond the frame on the right). Roger Boas served on the San Francisco Board of Supervisors.

reach. Stauffacher applied Helvetica typeface to not only her works in paper—the stationery, calendars, brochures, and reports—but also to buildings. Liberated from the fussiness of the popular typefaces in the United States, Helvetica had a spare and direct form that modernists appreciated, and some architects began to endorse its use. As the *Christian Science Monitor* noted in 1972, "The swirling patterns and camouflaged letters of the psychedelic artists in San Francisco are giving way to something they're calling 'Supergraphics.' Unlike psychedelic art, exotic and restless, Supergraphics are soothingly geometric and unfrenzied. The artists use entire buildings as their canvases."[12] By the late 1960s, painted supergraphics—bold, colorful, and outsized—were draped across buildings and invited new ways of thinking about graphics in the city. Whenever words were incorporated, they were usually in Helvetica (fig. 83).[13]

Of the various graphic arts revolutions in the 1960s, the phenomenon of supergraphics spoke loudest to the field of urban design; two-dimensional designs had the capacity to alter three-dimensional form through both graphics and color. From its first appearance, in *Progressive Architecture* in 1967, the term catapulted into popular usage. In 1969 it appeared in *Webster's Dictionary*.[14] Allan Temko underscored this breakthrough, naming

83 Stauffacher's supergraphics streetscape for the Kaiser building. Her most famous work at that time was for The Sea Ranch and Ghirardelli Square, but observers like Allan Temko, architectural critic for the *San Francisco Chronicle*, especially admired her local urban streetscape designs like those for Boas Pontiac and Kaiser, which mitigated the history of ugly outdoor advertising and gave modernist urban designers some new tools. Like the previous slide (see fig. 82), this one was used in Halprin & Associates' presentations to clients and colleagues to illustrate innovative landscape work and was not featured in a design magazine.

Stauffacher "one of those rare graphic artists who conceive of their work *architectonically*, in terms of multidimensional structure and space, rather than merely thin two-dimensional exercises on paper (although she is of course also a masterly designer of posters and brochures)." Temko elaborated: "Strong, lucid, rational, and elegantly disciplined, yet at the same time brimming with freshness and spontaneity, and fearless in color and scale, her compositions do not merely decorate the buildings they enhance, but are inseparable from their basic architectural meanings. For this alone, everyone who cares deeply for architecture must be grateful to her" (fig. 84).[15]

The alteration of scale inherent in the large lettering and graphics also had the effect of making the buildings and streetscape appear to be the playthings of some larger master planner or "superarchitect." In other words, designers recognized that outsized graphics, because "they cannot be contained within the frame of a single architectural plane," could make human beings feel like they were living in an architectural model. Design insiders speculated that supergraphics introduced ordinary people to the city planners' perspective: "For ages, architects have been looking down onto plans and into models, but the layman seldom shared this private, lofty view." Another article observed

84 Stauffacher's 1970 Industrial Arts Medal from the American Institute of Architects marked a peak of professional recognition. This photograph accompanied a March 1, 1970, *San Francisco Chronicle* feature on Stauffacher and shows the Sea Ranch building marker with Stauffacher's graphics in the background.

that the New York City street sweepers and garbage trucks with the word "sanitation" in Helvetica supergraphics "look like toy models."[16]

Stauffacher's recognition as a creative (rather than strictly for-hire commercial) artist rested primarily on the perception that supergraphics integrated modern art into architecture in stimulating new ways. Of course the relationship between art and architecture was a long-standing preoccupation among architects and critics alike. In the 1960s, along with large-scale urban renewal and the proliferation of plazas and skyscrapers, outdoor art enjoyed renewed popularity as developers and architects sought ways to humanize megaprojects. Architectural historian and critic Sibyl Moholy-Nagy said that Stauffacher's graphics contributed more artistic content than the current fad for abstract outdoor sculpture. The latter had some hefty financial backing; curated by public art consultants and redevelopment authorities, sculpture was increasingly funded through the new municipal set-aside programs, percent-for-art formulas, and corporate investors.[17] In contrast, "Supergraphics is a minor thing," architect Cesar Pelli wrote in 1970, but "it is a widening of the range of what architecture is. Paint used to be something outside the pale. And this is a breaking away from that—that colors in themselves can become architecture. It is one more tool."[18] To Gerald McCue, chair of Berkeley's Department of Architecture, "Barbara's 'super graphics' were among the first experiments in the use of bold pieces of graphic art as a part of the natural environment." She had been "instrumental in re-awaking architects to the potential use of modern art as an integral part rather than as a foil for the symbolism of modern architecture."[19]

Because later it became difficult to sort the origins of ideas and practices behind these artistic innovations, it is significant that so many colleagues and critics, in addition to the *Progressive Architecture* articles, credited Stauffacher with launching and defining supergraphics. The Milan magazine *Abitare* dedicated to the topic an entire issue titled "Where Graphics and Architecture Meet." The editors noted, "It has been said that art will only survive into the future if it is closely linked to architecture. We feel that if there is a way in which this marriage can be brought about, then it is the way pointed out by Barbara Stauffacher."[20] Al Boeke, who knew firsthand the competitive tensions The Sea Ranch's architects expressed about the graphic designer, maintained that Stauffacher "invented supergraphics at The Sea Ranch."[21] Her paint applied inside the locker rooms of the swim and tennis club garnered nearly as much splashy press as the architecture.[22] Her cooperation with architects defined the widespread appreciation for her designs while muddying questions of authorship. This problem would become more apparent over time.

Stauffacher put together a brochure explaining and illustrating her design practice in order to meet the increased press and client interest generated by the 1970 AIA Industrial Arts Award. She handed a copy to the *Examiner* photographer working on a story about her work. Her graphics sprang, she wrote, "from a typographic tradition sharing the same roots as much modern architecture. The basis of this tradition is the spare and disciplined organization of letter forms as blocks of positive and negative space intended to communicate information clearly in forms made naturally by modern typographic and reproduction techniques. This typography, like most modern architecture, is a function based and machine produced art form." Collaborating with different architects, she usually employed "paint or other flexible materials not constrained by the structural or spatial rhythms of the architecture." Her style was relevant "to a wide range of architectural problems, functional and otherwise, from the communication of directional information to the creation of visual effects." Among graphic artists and architects, Stauffacher was especially articulate in using words to explain designers' approaches to representing a visual and built world.[23]

One glimpsed in her writing, and in the 1960s language of art and architecture, just how Stauffacher's work wrought promising connections between the tiny artifact of typeface and the scale of the city. From the relationship of positive and negative space, experimentation with form, machine technology, and communications theory Stauffacher gave architects much to think about. She used the vocabulary of art as well as real estate. In the artistic traditions of typography were clues to her ability to communicate the intentions of mute architecture into concepts and experiences that the public could appreciate.[24] Marion Conrad's "blue sky" promotional copy applied words and symbols to architecture through the confines of print advertising or building signage. This was different.

Unlike the irreversible demolitions of urban renewal and the construction of monolithic superblock complexes favored during the 1960s, supergraphics (and graphic arts generally) could be reworked, revised, re-signed, and repainted. In the context of modifying the era's planned developments, the criticisms usually leveled against the graphic arts—impermanence, surface application, and superficiality—became strengths. Properly used, supergraphics invited incremental change, flexibility, spontaneity, multiple contributors, community involvement, and alternative perspectives.

Design trends in the 1960s were gravitating toward these goals of speedy environmental revitalization. In 1970 one reviewer called it "Urban Renewal with Paint." He explained, "There is a valid place for surface renewal as well as fundamental renewal. May we use paint wisely for urban revitalization." He gave an example of how surface could define architectural form. "If you can take a three-dimensional solid and dematerialize its corner, that is a pretty potent vocabulary." Surface applications could remake cities without the outrageous social and economic costs of bricks-and-mortar redevelopment. This type of environmental renewal could alter the meaning of single buildings as well as the urban scale.[25]

The revitalizing capacity of Stauffacher's supergraphics built upon other contemporary initiatives where urban rebuilding pressed paint into service. In addition to the growing popularity of grassroots community murals and graffiti, there were formal experiments such as the early 1960s paint program of the New York City Housing Authority (NYCHA). Based on NYCHA's first environmental arts achievements in East Harlem and Lower East Side housing projects, using support from its new Advisory Council on the Arts, in 1960 NYCHA hired Lilli Ann Killen, the art director of the Henry Street Settlement House. A Rockefeller Foundation grant-in-aid paid Killen's salary.[26]

The foundation reported that "Miss K's major effort has been to invent, design, and stimulate a whole new approach to painting under the NYCHA." This was no superficial accomplishment, since the housing authority reputedly spent $8 million annually on painting. Killen documented "how a tasteful use of color" could address the "extremely dreary and bleak" aesthetic and human challenges of existing NYCHA facilities. She critiqued an existing "classroom for Negro youngsters with uniformly colored walls and furniture exactly the color of the youngsters." Killen worked with painters and inspectors to raise expectations for the buildings' common spaces, using "murals, sculpture and decoration by good artists." NYCHA vice chair Ira Robbins saw a "'ripple' effect" of Killen's work on other public agencies and private developments. He next hoped "to engage a top-flight architect who would bring ideas and impetus to the relations of architecture and art."[27] Killen underscored what Bobbie Stauffacher learned five years later—that "art" was easier to alter than architecture in the equation of urban planning.[28]

Although Bobbie Stauffacher's supergraphics first flourished in a private locker room huddled on the windswept coastline of Northern California, within a few years her design mode was confirmed by the press as urban, her canvas the cityscape. Her work contributed directly to the rising trends of participatory public arts such as urban mural programs. Architects' interest in supergraphics as a design fad faded, while a broader interest in paint's potential social value and perceived relevance to solving urban problems grew. "Urban Renewal with Paint" probed this increasing public and grass-roots engagement: "As a fast and cheap means of enlivening our ghettos, our industrial areas and our too often drab city environments, paint can make an immediate contribution." Architect Hugh Hardy cautioned that calling supergraphics "cheap for the ghetto" risked sounding "condescending" or "second best." The strategy was low-cost, Hardy conceded, but its merits as a "good idea" stood apart from financial savings. Steadily, super-graphics had moved outdoors. The implications had grown accordingly: "Urbanistically (appropriately jumping up to a larger scale), paint is a quick, economical, and seldom used way of revitalizing 'blighted' areas."[29]

At many levels—artistic, conceptual, economic, and grassroots—Bobbie Stauffacher's graphics offered something fresh and hopeful to the world of 1960s urban design. Of course there were detractors. The long-term bias against graphic arts, no matter how they were valued as architectural, persisted. As Maude Dorr observed, "In spite of Michelangelo's four-year stint on the Sistine Chapel, and Stauffacher's three days at Sea Ranch, graphics still come hard to most modern architects."[30] But overall Stauffacher's work during the 1960s—in supergraphics but also in brochures, signs, murals, and publicity—epitomized for many architects why the graphic arts had found a new relevance to urban design. Developers like Al Boeke valued Stauffacher's skills in defining "place" in a decade when planned, large-scale real estate projects risked homogenizing the built environment. Graphic design joined with public relations and other allied commercial arts, including architectural rendering and model-making, to enhance the viability of novel projects, whether large-scale public or private urban renewal ventures, reinvented factories, or The Sea Ranch. Architects recognized how Stauffacher mediated between the professional and public worlds; this was the "architecture that literally speaks to us all."[31] The built landscape (designed or not) required translation, packaging, and marketing.

"THE ENEMY OF CUTE"

When Bobbie Stauffacher opened her firm in 1962, she discovered that "no one seemed to know what a graphic designer did." That did not slow her down; she soon found a demand for her skills. It was quite easy to set up her own shop. She did not need elaborate equipment, and her friend Larry Halprin rented her a small, congenial first-floor office at 1620 Montgomery Street. Proximity to Halprin's firm on the top floor and to Wurster, Bernardi & Emmons on the second floor helped her build a steady stream of clients. Without employees, she kept expenses down and enjoyed the flexibility and efficiencies of self-employment. A young, hip, widowed mother of one, Stauffacher also enjoyed the flirtations of the work world. As she recalled in her unpublished memoir, "Being a chick was good for business."[32]

Although she had been born in San Francisco, Barbara Levé Stauffacher's route to 1620 Montgomery Street and a career in design had spanned two continents and was anything but direct. Her circuitous trajectory illustrates 1960s transformations in the graphic arts at the intersection with urban design, from the inside. A phrase she began using in the 1960s to sum up her outlook—"the enemy of cute"—positioned her as a critic of the manipulative and superficial trends in her profession. That original phrase would vie with another one—"duped by design"—which embodied more profoundly her personal and professional commentary on the architectural and graphic arts fields. Tracing Stauffacher's career brings the origins of her critiques and disillusionment with the field into relief.

While enrolled in Galileo High School during the mid-1940s, Stauffacher had trained at the San Francisco Ballet School and took classes at the California School of Fine Arts (now the San Francisco Art Institute). At the age of sixteen, she and her mother had finagled permission for Bobbie to leave school under the ruse that her mother was going blind and needed her financial support. She met Frank Stauffacher at one of his "Art in Cinema" events at the San Francisco Museum of Art. She was seventeen; Frank was thirty. In the late 1940s, Stauffacher remembered, Frank filled the cinema audience with "Berkeley professors, with tweed jackets and frumpy wives, . . . architects and their dates, dressed in black, high-styled with expensive haircuts. Young lawyers in three-piece suits arrived with glamour girls choked with pearls. . . . Socialites, rich blondes devoted to the arts . . . artists on the GI Bill, Beat poets, and jazz musicians, in turtle-necks and Levi's, arrived late and slumped against the walls." Stauffacher added, "It was a pity to turn the lights off."[33]

Here, in San Francisco in the late 1940s, Stauffacher believed, the 1960s were born. Besides producing this venue for others' film-related arts and creating an appealing scene for San Franciscans, Frank was busy establishing himself in the world of experimental film. Bobbie fell in love. Her mother acted fast, whisking Bobbie off to New York City (their first trip out of state) to distract her daughter and in the hope that she might find success in a theater career. Bobbie and Frank married in November 1948 in Sausalito. The brief years of their marriage encompassed eventful lives. After a few years of college at the University of California, Berkeley for Bobbie; European travel; the birth of their daughter, Chloe, in London; schmoozing and partying in New York and San Francisco artistic circles; and Frank's continued success in filmmaking, Frank died tragically in 1955 of a brain tumor.[34]

Still very young, and now with a daughter and her mother, Lil, in tow, Bobbie Stauffacher returned to Europe and transformed herself into a Swiss-trained graphic designer. From 1956 to 1959 she studied graphic arts—specializing in letterforms and typography—with the leading modernist designer Armin Hofmann at Basel's Kunstgewerbeschule. During these years she learned a then-unknown typeface that would later be nicknamed "the typeface of the twentieth century." She became involved with engineer Heinz Hossdorf and found friends in the circles of artists, graphic designers, architects, and engineers.

After completing her training, Stauffacher spent several years jetting back and forth between Europe, New York, and San Francisco. She picked up work in commercial art and advertising. She got a job with the George Nelson design firm's team planning the 1959 American National Exhibition in Moscow. For that project she used the techniques Armin Hofmann had taught her to style "images of the Good-Life as intended by God and achieved by capitalism," particularly the "gadget-hypnotized message of the American Dream in red stripes, white stars, and blue skies." Throughout this period, her daughter remained primarily in a Rudolph Steiner school in the Alps, and Bobbie's professional and personal life was pulled back and forth across the Atlantic by her relationship with Hossdorf. Finally Hossdorf divorced his wife to marry another girlfriend. Bobbie returned to San Francisco, appraised the options in her hometown, and signed on to 1620 Montgomery.[35]

When Bobbie Stauffacher hung out her shingle as a graphic designer in 1962, local typesetters were unfamiliar with the sans-serif lettering she had mastered in Switzerland.[36] San Francisco typesetting fell into a few camps—the mainstream, business-ready Times Roman, Baskerville, or Garamond types; "Wild West" styles such as Gold Town, Old Town, or Playbill; and the emerging loose, hippie swirls and squiggles. According to Stauffacher, in 1962 Helvetica was "too clean and austere, too modern" for San Francisco. The name itself had been newly coined, using the Latin root for the English word "Switzerland," in order to help the typeface reach more global markets. Swiss-trained during the very years when the font was invented and spread by her teachers, Stauffacher was one of the first designers to introduce Helvetica to the United States. When it came time to order her company letterhead, she had to mail the specifications to Basel, where a typographer set her materials in Helvetica. Unless clients objected, she used Helvetica in her brochures, stationery, logos, calendars, and pedestrian signs—in everything. Her eye-catching monthly bulletins for the San Francisco Museum of Art—set in Helvetica, of course—found a wide circulation among people who could lead her to new commissions.[37]

Bobbie Stauffacher's work for Ghirardelli Square accelerated her transition from advertising, stationery, and ephemera to architecture and urban design. Even so, she ranked the artistic satisfaction of the project quite low in her overall career. For the square Stauffacher designed the wayfinding signs, tenant directory listing, garage signage, and other exterior graphics in the first phase of development. During construction in

1963–64, because Ghirardelli was off the beaten path for most San Franciscans, few people noted the novelty of a graphic designer listed on the site's construction sign. Her lack of enthusiasm for the project stemmed not from lack of professional recognition but rather from her assessment of her designs. Like all the site's furnishings and art, from the mermaid sculpture to the lampposts, Stauffacher's graphics balanced Ghirardelli Square's mix of historical and modern elements. Stauffacher surmised that the client preferred Clarendon (a typeface with serifs), not Helvetica. She took her design cue from the large, illuminated 1920s roof signs that spelled out "Ghirardelli" in Clarendon and dominated views of the factory. She worked with local sign-makers to customize the new illuminated lettering to echo the old (fig. 85). Years later Bobbie described Clarendon as "more corny, old San Francisco." But it was the "boldest face that had serifs." To Stauffacher, Clarendon typeface was "decorative," potentially a "derogatory, hypocritical, deceptive, manipulative, and excellent way to deceive through design."[38]

Clarendon typeface was a manifestation of what Stauffacher called "cute." She used cute with its less commonly intended meaning, suggesting something clever or deceptive. To Stauffacher, *cute* implied the use of graphics "to manipulate people and sell things," as differentiated from honestly presented intentions. This was not an incidental choice of words. She briefly considered retitling her memoir "The Enemy of Cute."[39]

85 Stauffacher used Clarendon type-face for Ghirardelli Square instead of the modernist Helvetica she was instrumental in bringing to San Francisco. She took her design cue from the large 1920s rooftop Ghirardelli sign. She worked closely with the sign-makers to customize the Clarendon lettering for this lit entrance arch. For her Ghirardelli retail client Hear Hear records, she used Helvetica and supergraphics.

Although Bobbie Stauffacher made these first contributions to Ghirardelli Square without fanfare or creative satisfaction, the square's advisory board decided early on that clear graphics and informational signs would make or break the development's economic success. The square was difficult to navigate. Many likened its character to a "medieval" maze of hidden plazas and narrow, twisting alleys. The complex defied most of the existing beliefs about retail development, which dictated simple layouts, one-story construction, anchor stores, and suburban locations. Charles Moore commended the "courageous" layout that "flies in the face of everything that shopping center proprietors hold dear." Standard retail wisdom hoped to lead consumers "inexorably past every shop in the place on the way to every other."[40] The management worried that shoppers and diners would have difficulty finding businesses located on upper stories, in basements, or around corners. Bill Roth's advisors saw the need to balance the site's "mystery" and "surprise" against possible "confusion." Following ideas recently articulated by Kevin Lynch in his 1960 book *The Image of the City,* the advisory board stressed the importance of "wayfinding" techniques. Lynch's research helped shift emphasis from the viewpoints of master planners and architects to the perceptions and mental maps of city residents. Stauffacher's other wayfinding work for such clients as the California State Expo and the Market Street redesign in San Francisco demonstrated the application of such abstract concepts to urban design.[41]

Wayfinding signs, along with lights and shop-fronts, had the potential to "activate" the edges of the plazas, not merely guide consumers to their destinations or solve circulation problems. For her retail clients at Ghirardelli Square, Stauffacher's interior designs allowed her more creative freedom while also contributing directly to these goals of activating the inert plazas with merchandise, dynamic graphics, and paying customers. She designed the interiors for Hear Hear record shop and PuddinTane boutique and painted a mural on the back outside wall of the bookstore (figs. 86 and 87). A few blocks down the waterfront at The Cannery, the Very Very Terry Jerry Mod Dress Shop hired her to design their interior, another project reviewed favorably.[42] When the square's second half opened in 1968, some of the advisors hoped that the vitality of bustling consumers directed by Stauffacher's signs, together with murals and storefronts such as that of Hear Hear, would displace the demand for a sculpture or fountain by serving the same purpose of enlivening—literally humanizing—the square.[43] The Hear Hear shop, photographed from the outside looking in, illustrates the impact of the bold supergraphics seen through floor-to-ceiling plate glass, which contrasted with the brick-wall frame of the old factory. The exterior abstract bookstore mural had a similar effect, although Stauffacher applied it to the concrete wall of one of the new retail buildings by John Matthias. This was yet another way Stauffacher's two-dimensional designs had sculptural and architectural implications, whether interior or exterior.

By the time Ghirardelli Square's western half opened in the midst of an economic slowdown in 1968, Stauffacher's international recognition as a solo designer had overshadowed her previously strong reputation in graphic arts. The square's management team hoped that a fresh round of Stauffacher commissions could lend designer-name cachet to the project. Just when Warren Lemmon was calculating how to get her

86 Stauffacher's interior for Hear Hear records appeared in multiple magazines. This view shows the effects of contrasting Ghirardelli's old brick exterior with the colorful store interior, transforming and activating the outdoor plazas. Loud graphics matched the store's record business.

87 Stauffacher's exterior mural behind the Ghirardelli Square bookstore. Ghirardelli's management hoped to capitalize on Stauffacher's rising fame by commissioning other custom designs and furnishings from her for the square. Her wayfinding work, such as creating retail directories and garage signage, was important to the square's economic viability. The labyrinthine qualities of the complex, when compared to modern shopping malls, required good instructions for locating businesses.

attention and the mermaid sculpture controversy was playing out in San Francisco, *Life* magazine published a story on supergraphics featuring Stauffacher. Her professional interest in the square had never been intense. Now she counted many other work demands, not to mention a new marriage to Daniel Solomon, a young architect in Halprin's office.[44]

The Ghirardelli complex, meanwhile, struggled with vacancies. The tenants were "frightened" and "nervous" about low revenue and foot traffic, especially in the newly opened section. The architects, owner, and property managers hoped Stauffacher would bring a magic touch, and mentions of her name peppered their correspondence about design problems. They brainstormed about "an additional Barbara Stauffacher mural" and concluded that "temporary banners designed by Barbara Stauffacher should also be hung from the easterly façade of the Information Center to draw customers to the second half." When Roth asked architect John Matthias for ideas to give the square "more life and character," Matthias suggested that Stauffacher "design all signs in the Square."[45] Unfortunately, Warren Lemmon noted, although she had previously taken that role, Stauffacher "in recent months has not had the time nor inclination to involve herself in details relating to the Square." The designers and managers appealed to her in February 1969 through Don Stover of WB&E. From supergraphics on the north wall of the Hallmark store to a "balloon man" selling Stauffacher-designed inflatables, they offered a list of suggestions. Their requests, Stover wrote to Stauffacher, "related to the program to increase activity and identity for the West Half. Due to tenant complaints, this has become an urgent matter. We hope you can give it your attention."[46] She did continue to help out, at a more modest scale, with the awnings, banners, trash receptacles, tables, and neon signs. The board's appeals to Stauffacher to boost customer circulation betokened their confidence in her work's ability to stimulate business.

"I ONLY WORKED WITH ARCHITECTS": PAINTING SEA RANCH

Like Ghirardelli Square's leadership, The Sea Ranch developers counted on Stauffacher to increase sales volume. The Sea Ranch work, however, classified Stauffacher more broadly as an environmental designer and planner and demonstrated the professional vulnerabilities she experienced by linking her graphic arts career to architecture and planning. From the moment she joined the Sea Ranch project, her identities as solo designer and commercial graphic artist intertwined. Al Boeke first encountered Stauffacher's work displayed at the San Francisco Museum of Art, and he sought her out on that basis. He hired her in 1963 to handle the graphics to be used in promoting the coastal real estate development. Oceanic Properties sought to create a commodity "that the real-estate men, bankers, and buyers can agree is profitable, photographic, and sexy," Stauffacher recalled. "My job, in addition to sitting in silent admiration at meetings, was to get Larry's sketches and master plans reduced in size and made camera-ready; to have the sales pitch and Larry's design criteria set in Helvetica, and to paste-up page after page of type and pretty pictures. Good Design was Good Business."[47]

Whereas her Ghirardelli work trafficked in leases and retail sales, at The Sea Ranch Stauffacher sold land (figs. 88 and 89). Her hand lent a simultaneously evocative and solid form to the real estate vision. Assembling brochures, renderings, and camera-ready images had a mechanistic ring to it. Yet Boeke regarded Stauffacher's sales documents as an artist's portfolio. Decades later he singled out one of her plans as it appeared in the November 1965 *Architectural Record*: "In my eyes that beautiful drawing that Barbara did is a sales material. This is telling a prospective buyer . . . this is a sketch of where we're going. It won't be exactly like this, but this is where our minds are—this is our mindset."[48]

As the artistic director responsible for visual materials, Stauffacher made "sketches" that were different from written sketches by publicist Marion Conrad or writer Stanford Erickson. The way that Stauffacher managed the photographic portraits of The Sea Ranch's coast offered a compelling example of how, composing with microdots of color, she related the tiny scale of topography to the large scales of marketing and public relations. The project's first photographer "made the barren land look like close-ups of the moon," Stauffacher remembered. She fired him. She turned next to "Sierra Club image-maker" Ernest Braun. He "photographed the land golden-glowing at dawn and sunset. Desire metamorphosed into small dots of four-color process printer's ink surrounded by the purity of white space. The wind didn't show."[49] Her description of managing the marketing impact of Braun's photographs at the ink-on-paper level (and firing his predecessor) exemplified the merging of her artistic and administrative skills. The need to do both was characteristic of work in the allied design fields.

Even though Stauffacher packaged Sea Ranch real estate in the anonymous traditions of commercial art, her greatest impact on the project's publicity was as an independent artist. Her solo achievements, in turn, elevated her relevance to the burgeoning field of environmental design. Her interior artwork at The Sea Ranch gained her the fame as an inventor of supergraphics. By most accounts, the three days Stauffacher spent during

88 Stauffacher's 1965 Sea Ranch brochure illustrated her work packaging the landscape with Helvetica typeface superimposed on the scenery. One unnamed professional photographer made the environment seem barren, rocky, and remote, like a moonscape. Stauffacher found an artist better suited to the development's promotional needs.

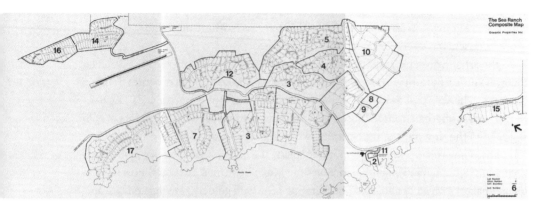

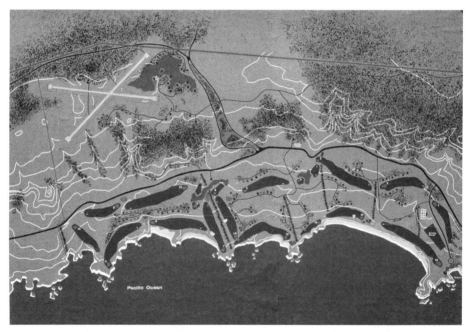

89 The top map is Stauffacher's 1965 depiction of sales lots at The Sea Ranch according to the environmentally sensitive master plans. The project gained renown for encouraging cluster development and open-space preservation, especially boosting Larry Halprin's career. These bald land plots, removed from the evocative photographs of cliffside meadows, still paled next to the bottom illustration. The lower plan, an earlier development concept showcasing a golf course, tennis courts, and small airport, revealed alternative directions not pursued.

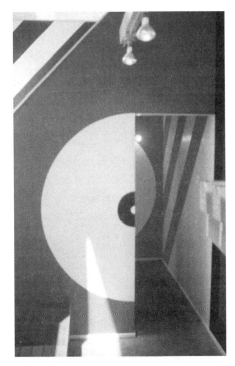

90 Interior, Swim and Tennis Club, The Sea Ranch. The image on the left echoes Stauffacher bull's-eye calendars from several years earlier (see fig. 80). The second view, of the toilet and sink, was rarely shown in magazines. It suggests the modesty of a design vision executed in a bathroom, even as the reflected half-heart is a creative and warming symbol. Larry Halprin used this image in lectures on exciting directions in transformative visual innovations.

the spring of 1966 painting designs on the walls of the swim and tennis club were freewheeling and contingent (figs. 90 and 91).[50] Only when Charles Moore and Bill Turnbull's club neared completion in February 1966 did Oceanic Properties conclude that the plywood interior walls, painted white, needed something else.[51] Al Boeke hired Stauffacher.[52] Unable to visualize the complicated space based on the plans, sections, and elevations sent to her by the architects, she loaded up on paint supplies and three helpers at the Mission Street sign-painting company Thomas-Swan & Sons. Once she got to The Sea Ranch, she would figure out what to paint. She described her paint selection as "anti-decorative," basic bull's-eye colors—black, white, yellow, blue, and red.[53]

Following the look of The Sea Ranch itself, with its shed-roofed forms hugging the cliffs, constructed in natural materials with natural finishes, Stauffacher turned to the surrounding environment for inspiration. This statement might at first seem contradictory, given that she approached the project with bull's-eye colors. But after she arrived at the women's locker room, entering an open door "like a trespasser sneaking in to spray-paint the sacred walls," she tuned into the environment. She described what happened next. "Outside, Pacific waves crashed into the cliff below so I decided to paint a giant wave." She combed the countryside for resonant textures. With the help especially of Ralph Quevas from the sign shop, they executed her idea, snapping strings saturated with charcoal against the wall, drawing circles, and painting alternating stripes of blue and white "until we had a twenty-five foot high Pacific wave crashing inside the architecture."[54]

In the cooperative nature of the work's execution and her ease admitting to seat-of-the-pants decisions, Stauffacher accepted contingency and collaboration in ways that were less familiar to architects. This was a cooperative endeavor. It progressed organically based on the architecture and the natural landscape. It was also indeed a bit like graffiti. Later Stauffacher described what she did next:

Now what? I turned around, sat on the floor, and stared at the space. There was a sauna on the second level, invisible, so I painted SAUNA (Helvetica, all caps) up the sauna door, and green strips following the architecture on the walls. Along the stairway wall leading up, I painted a wide red arrow pointing up, and on the opposite wall, a narrow black arrow pointing down. Half of a red heart, flush to the mirror, became a whole heart to someone looking in the mirror. The shapes were always simple, geometric, and hard-edged. The colors always pure, straight out of the can. Climbing up ladders, sitting down on the floor, stretching, bending, reaching; it was as much dancing as drawing.

Stauffacher's drawing depended upon the immediate space, and "dancing" through that space became part of her performance. Reviews commented on how her graphics increased the sense of movement through the interior rooms, imbuing them with motion and grace.[55]

Stauffacher worried about the commercializing implications of applying her graphics outdoors; initially, she had even resisted Boeke's request to paint interior walls. On their explorations of West Marin and Sonoma County, Stauffacher and Boeke took note of "old painted barns and weathered walls, painted with ads for seed, grains, soap, and tobacco." Faded paint was appropriate to the weather-beaten, rustic countryside. She feared that fresh paint would seem too commercial and would detract from the blending of built and natural environments. Stauffacher relented after seeing her Sea Ranch logo (along with some Helvetica type) on a board outside Joseph Esherick's general store. She compromised with commercialism by painting interiors. "Then only the people who've already bought into The Sea Ranch aesthetic have to see it," she remembered saying. Three days later, the deed was done. She had experimented several years earlier with some of the graphics, including the bull's-eye and heart, in her monthly calendars for the San Francisco Museum of Art, showing yet again how her work lifted from two-dimensional paper to three-dimensional architecture. "I combined the super-sized enthusiasm of California Abstract Expressionism with hard-edge Swiss graphics," she wrote, "and got, however superfluous and superficial, supergraphics" (fig. 92).[56]

The Sea Ranch's stated ideals of coastal preservation, environmental stewardship, and "the commons" conditioned Stauffacher's discomfort with commercializing coastal land in this way and made the development an easy target for skeptics. Her ram's-head design gave Reyner Banham, the British architectural writer, an angle for critiquing the development's marketing pitch. In an early review, Banham took aim: "Sea Ranch must be the first housing development with its own T-shirts," he scoffed. After noting the highway marker and its supergraphics, he drove up to the general store and began his

91 Interior, Swim and Tennis Club, The Sea Ranch. The lower photograph is of the crashing ocean wave Stauffacher described in detail; the second image is an especially dimension-bending application of paint to create a popped-out cube on a multiangled ceiling.

92 Stauffacher carefully controlled the application of supergraphics, such as this enamel sign, in outside settings at The Sea Ranch. As the trend gained in popularity she was disturbed to see others consume outdoor landscapes in the name of art and environmentally sensitive design.

tour there. Without naming Stauffacher as the artist, Banham observed that her logo design appeared on the shirts and, seemingly, on most of the store's merchandise. He called her logo the project's "trade mark." That Banham would become known in design circles for celebrating U.S. pop culture and for his sympathetic views of Los Angeles makes his comments about Sea Ranch's promotional goods particularly pointed. He continued, "And these T-shirts were not the only thing in the store that made us wonder what the hell the Sea Ranch was all about. If it sold any of the normal staples of life, the store kept quiet about them." In distinctive wording that announced the slippery scale of goods for sale, Stauffacher's graphics on the store building's exterior read: "The Sea Ranch: General Store, Restaurant, Land Sales" (see fig. 77). Banham then proceeded to mock the architects' acclaimed environmental "research" as mere "blue sky speculation" and sales talk. He described how he was "blown back out of the door" by a blast of "solar heat" from Charles Moore's apartment. He rolled the environmental and land sales pitches into one deceptive commercial enterprise.[57]

The Sea Ranch embellished Stauffacher's credentials as an environmental planner in part because she imposed restraints on commercialism. For design critics distressed by architecture's "increasing sell-out to blatant commercialism," Stauffacher's bold super-graphics potentially mediated a *better* outcome.[58] Without publicity and reviews, Stauffacher's interior Sea Ranch supergraphics would have remained virtually invisible. Marion Conrad ensured that these graphics were heralded as relevant to resolving the problems of environmental design, whether roadside rural, suburban, or urban. Endorsing the same theme, the Governor's Design Awards jury had unanimously singled Stauffacher out "for a special award of excellence in environmental design for the full scope of her work at Sea Ranch," said Allan Temko, who had served on the jury.[59]

Although Sea Ranch documents listed Stauffacher as a planner next to architects Joseph Esherick, Charles Moore, Al Boeke, and Lawrence Halprin, ultimately she was treated more as a commercial artist-for-hire.[60] That distinction had implications. Stauffacher's designs garnered AIA awards and national press, but they were executed in paint, signs, print, and paper. Her work was far more ephemeral and vulnerable than most buildings, sculpture, or even landscape architecture. Her athletic club interior at The Sea Ranch received enough publicity to lull her into expecting that its future was secure. Surely The Sea Ranch's owners and managers recognized the artistic merit and prestige of supergraphics, or at least the artwork's economic value to the complex. Yet the designs showcased on the cover of *Progressive Architecture* were painted over within ten years.

After 1967, Stauffacher did not visit the site for nearly forty years. When she returned, she learned that a 1970s remodeling by the Sea Ranch Association had long ago destroyed the artwork. Al Boeke took this fact as evidence of how difficult it was to find property managers who understood the development's values of environmental stewardship. "Some project manager came along and noted that the paint needed repainting and darned if he didn't have someone come and repaint the whole thing white." Boeke described Stauffacher's graphics as "an original public piece of art," despite its location in the private locker room. Accordingly, he reasoned, it should have been covered by California law requiring permission of the artist and owner for alterations. As a mere resident rather than developer, he later campaigned "hard" to have the interior "repainted exactly the way it was." He failed.[61]

Bobbie Stauffacher knew that her graphic design projects were inherently vulnerable to both destruction and copying, but additional kinds of erasure defined her 1960s design portfolio. Close collaboration with architects had undeniably launched her career but also obscured it. Stauffacher endured ambiguous and missing credits for her ideas and labors, as well as financial exploitation and the jealousies of architects. She never did hear directly from Charles Moore or Larry Halprin what they thought of her Sea Ranch designs (although Charles Moore told *Progressive Architecture* in 1967 that he was "delighted" with the graphics).[62] After Stauffacher told Halprin in 2007 that her Sea Ranch work had been defaced, he responded that it was "only a bathroom." Stauffacher did not regard his comment as humorous, even though Halprin was her friend and himself faced many crises regarding his work's survival. The truth was that Halprin did close studies of Stauffacher's interior swim club graphics when she first painted them, focusing on the details of her illusions and how paint and line transformed and distorted built form. In their study of detail, his office slides of her work were qualitatively

93 The tiny graphics work Stauffacher did for Wurster, Bernardi & Emmons's Bank of America architectural model was then used by the company as their corporate logo. However, the architects paid her on the basis of the model, and she did not bill Bank of America directly for having designed their logo. Here Stauffacher works on the model of the new San Francisco Bay Area Rapid Transit (BART) station for Powell Street. She inspects a mini "No Turns" sign in Helvetica typeface. The mediation by the architects between the graphic artists they subcontracted with and major clients like Bank of America or BART was a mixed arrangement for the consulting artists. Stauffacher had a steady stream of work but was usually paid according to the miniature scale and without credit.

different from the glossy impact photos in design magazines (see figs. 90 and 91). He included these slides in his lectures for colleagues and clients on inspirational ideas to shape the experience of the built environment. Nevertheless, the slights usually got back to Stauffacher, such as when she learned that architect Joe Esherick had asked Al Boeke why Boeke had hired Stauffacher instead of a "professional" for the Sea Ranch work.[63]

When Stauffacher designed a logo for Bank of America, an impressive corporate client, she was hired by the project's architects (Wurster, Bernardi & Emmons) rather than directly by Bank of America. "I only worked with architects," she remembered. But when architects mediated between a prestigious client and a graphic designer, the graphic artist's claim to authority, creativity, and pay became attenuated. The problem was that she handed her designs to architect Donn Emmons, who was also her landlord at 1620 Montgomery, so, as she wrote, "it was like any old job." That arrangement, Stauffacher underscored, "is why he felt free to have me do a logo, put it on his models of the building, and never pay me as if I were really doing a logo for BofA. He thought it amusing to let them use it without paying me."[64] The subcontracted and neighborly working relationship with architectural firms undermined Stauffacher's financial leverage and professional credit for her ideas. When the logo was applied to an architectural model, Stauffacher pointed out, architects were tempted to further diminish her creative contribution by treating it like a toy-scaled hobby rather than a major corporate account (fig. 93). And miniature payments followed.

"Collaboration" in the Sea Ranch and Bank of America cases could be a euphemism for shifting credit toward the architects and away from the graphic artist. The 1960s honors bestowed on Stauffacher for original contributions to environmental design faded into a standardized, vague acknowledgment that she had "collaborated" with architects such as Charles Moore, William Turnbull, and Hugh Hardy on novel projects. Typical of this style of credit would be the account in a text like *New York 1960:* "Working with the graphic designer Barbara Stauffacher, Moore had created a raucous new kind of architectural decoration consisting of superscaled elements painted onto and super-imposed over traditional architectural compositions."[65] Doling out specific credit for original ideas is elusive, and the tangled roots of supergraphics were already evident in the architectural magazines of the time that wrestled with the language of who invented what. Many articles simultaneously reviewed and blurred the lines of credit for con-temporary supergraphics work by Charles Moore, Robert Venturi, Donlyn Lyndon, Hugh Hardy, and Doug Michels (who worked for Charles Moore), as well as graphic designer Marget Larsen.[66]

In the commercial art of graphic design, good ideas were taken and copied by others without attribution. "Even I have begun copying myself now," Stauffacher told a reporter in 1970.[67] As an architectural photographer, Morley Baer regularly embroiled himself in negotiating credits for colleagues. While making arrangements to sell his photo-graphs of the Sea Ranch athletic club to Marion Conrad Associates in 1966, Baer noted, "Whenever, in your submissions, architecture is emphasized," credit should go to Moore/Turnbull. "Where interior colors and decoration are featured, credit should be requested for Barbara Stauffacher."[68] Although decorative work was a downgrade in the modernist design vocabulary, Baer tried to preserve Stauffacher's creative record. Attributions for graphic artists in ordinary commercial work were rarely explicit and were certainly more difficult to establish than for photographers, who often got a byline. The architectural profession, of course, habitually demanded attribution and credit for its practitioners.

Because graphic design was customarily defined as "commercial" art rather than, say, "urban design," it meant that Stauffacher's ideas would be picked up by many others, including the various elite architects with whom she worked.[69] Stauffacher did not make a concerted pitch to claim her design role at The Sea Ranch after the initial press coverage and professional recognition of her work waned. Many of the participating architects would publish their own accounts of the early planning and evolution of the development's environmental design ideals, particularly Larry Halprin and Donlyn Lyndon. The architects and planners documented, and disagreed about, their respective roles.[70] Instead, Stauffacher moved on. Eventually she became an architect. She wrote a lively, funny, bold (you could call it sans-serif) memoir with the honest title "Duped by Design." She was unable to publish it.

In the 1960s the design world recognized and honored Stauffacher's central role in forging a graphic arts movement with relevance to architecture and urban design. Her ability to think small (typography, dots of color, bathhouse interior) and big (oversized letterforms, cityscape, environmental planning) plus her application of paint to every surface and her interest in circulation and wayfinding—all of this offered a new vocabulary to urban design that situated architecture in a broader environmental context. Stauffacher's skills in defining "place," especially within large-scale projects, were appreciated by architects and by the growing field of environmental design. Stauffacher's 1970 Industrial Arts Medal cast her innovations as "supporting" only inasmuch as *all* allied arts were "supportive" of architecture from the perspective of professionally trained architects. Symbiotically, architecture had boosted her professional stature, as she had boosted the legibility and public appeal of architecture.

THE SEA RANCH'S "URBAN THING"

Stauffacher's contributions (as art director and planner) to the success of The Sea Ranch development, however, only deepened her concern that the project's underlying land grab had been masked by the promotion of coastal "preservation" through environmental design. Her critiques of commercialism in the late 1960s focused on the manipulations of using design to sell off land that otherwise would have been dedicated to a priceless public purpose. Stauffacher's analysis broke with the decades-old architectural and planning critiques of commercialism, which instead monitored the landscape to curtail the visual chaos of signs and graphics in urban and rural contexts. The Sea Ranch's inclusion in "The Designer's City" was only one indicator that the remote site was an integral part of San Francisco. Oceanic Properties originally paid about $500 per acre for the 5,200-acre parcel. In 1968 the most expensive homes sold for $40,000 an acre. Remote Sea Ranch had become part of San Francisco's real estate market, constituting what one commentator called "a far piece out of the high-rent district."

Despite the acclaimed marketing produced by Marion Conrad and Bobbie Stauffacher, it took the development a few years to find the right urban-oriented sales niche and the right property management team.[71]

By most measures, the coastal area that would become The Sea Ranch was rural. When Joseph Esherick contacted the Sonoma County clerk in December of 1963 for demographic statistics about the Del Mar site, he heard back that the voting population had dropped from 308 to 179 between 1954 and 1963 in the area between Fort Ross and Gualala. The clerk speculated that this was due to the closing of a sawmill. Because the numbers were so low, the clerk could survey the registrations. Housewives outnumbered ranchers seventy-five to twenty-two; the next largest occupational groups were nineteen mill workers and laborers and seventeen loggers and woodsmen.[72] During that exploratory phase of the project, Al Boeke cautioned his small army of San Francisco–based consultants that "the long-time residents along the Sonoma Coast are more rural than urban in their bias. We have already had evidence that they are quick to react to anything or anyone unusual in habit or appearance." The development's representatives would likely encounter what Boeke thought of as rural parochialism among the local population.[73]

Yet once the developers, designers, and publicists got to work on the coastal property, the real estate sales introduced both urban and antisuburban themes that increasingly aligned The Sea Ranch with San Francisco. Here the links among designers—whether within professional architecture and planning or less formally within allied fields such as graphic design and public relations—wove the histories of the Bay Area's diverse, experimental, large-scale 1960s real estate developments together. Such partnerships shaped how these places were defined and built and underscored the continuities among urban, rural, and suburban innovation, as well as between historical and modern. Bobbie Stauffacher and Marion Conrad stamped The Sea Ranch, Ghirardelli Square, and the San Francisco International Market Center with the same mid-1960s environmental planning vintage, akin to landscape architect Larry Halprin's imprint on these projects.

Because it was primarily a second-home development, The Sea Ranch inserted city people and an urban land-use concept into a rural area. The sales concepts, as a result, projected the property as simultaneously urban and self-consciously nonsuburban. The proposed handling of meadows and lawns spoke directly to this balance. From the earliest discussions, Sea Ranch planners assumed that "people desiring a suburban environment" would have no interest in the coastal properties and should be excluded from marketing projections. An internal 1964 review of proposed deed restrictions cautioned: "We don't particularly want or require highly trimmed 'lawns' in the suburban sense on the Sea Ranch." At the same time, management conceded that the resident sheep were not a viable trimming mechanism for the meadows.[74] Both The Sea Ranch and Ghirardelli specifically offered alternatives to the 1960s suburban residential and commercial markets, respectively.[75]

It turned out that closing real estate deals on the Sea Ranch parcels ultimately required an urban touch. Through trial and error, the developer learned that managers, like the design consultants, had to understand the project's environmental agenda, its urban target market, and its aesthetic ideals. Whereas The Sea Ranch's experience with marketing had exceeded expectations, its property management and sales were disappointing. The property manager position proved to be the weak link in the sales machinery. Boeke remembered the parade of a dozen managers over the first few years. He wondered whether he would ever locate "anybody with the experience to do this." As the failures accumulated, The Sea Ranch had to regretfully "sever the relationship with a whole bunch of people." The position, according to Boeke, "turned over rapidly because people just didn't get it. And they just couldn't do it." At last he found a "handsome, well-dressed, urban realtor" from the Bay Area named Bill Pouchelle. Pouchelle understood Conrad's and Stauffacher's marketing blueprint for The Sea Ranch and catered to city sensibilities.[76] Boeke tired of "people who are in the business of telling you whether or not something, whatever, urban thing, will survive in that location."[77] The most important urban thing to thrive at The Sea Ranch would be downtown San Francisco property values.

The developer banked on faith that the studied environmental sensitivity of the Sea Ranch master plan, in addition to homes designed to blend with the terrain, would sell real estate. The strategy of protecting coastal meadows and forests by clustering construction made it harder for critics to characterize Oceanic Properties as just another "beady-eyed developer waiting to gobble up your lovely coast." More positively, the project deservedly attracted attention for introducing "a broader concept of land ownership, use, and stewardship," as *Progressive Architecture* had noted. However, for preservationists there was one major flaw in this marketing appeal: the state of California had turned down the opportunity to purchase the entire 5,200 acres for a state park before Oceanic stepped in.[78] That fact cast a permanent shadow of lost possibility over the land and put an ironic twist on compliments to the developer regarding land stewardship. In early 1964, Oceanic still worried that the state might take the land if it could raise the money through a bond referendum. One internal report reviewing the risks facing investors and their options stated that "the greatest hazard is early condemnation of the whole parcel for park purposes where the value would be related primarily to our purchase price." Ultimately the owners donated 140 acres for a state park at the property's northern end. Any hoped-for appreciation for this generosity from regional preservationists evaporated quickly. Instead, environmentalists filed litigation to guarantee widespread public coastal access along the site's length rather than at the limited number of points preferred by the developers. In yet another parallel with San Francisco's north waterfront, the leading Sonoma preservationist championing access to the public tidelands at The Sea Ranch was Bill Kortum, Karl Kortum's brother.[79]

The Sea Ranch's designer-developer team endorsed the novel planning models of clustered housing, condominiums, and—more radically—communal private ownership of half of the land, but not all of the consultants were on board with this. Marketing advisor Ray Menzel thought the designers needed to glean hard lessons about urban design idealism from the failures in urban renewal planning. The Sea Ranch's clustering idea was admirable, and Menzel understood the purpose. However, he was concerned that "the cluster, if carried too far, might actually end up looking *over*planned." The ranchland that seemed so abundant was finite when divided among "greens, open space and clusters. It seems to me," Menzel wrote, that "we might find a little *less* community open space, and a little *more* individually-owned land might make it easier to sell. It's a terrible thing to question the 'ideal,' and I shudder to think how my 'compromising' might be received. But let's face it, some urban renewal projects have become famous for completely ignoring the habits and traditions of the human beings they were built for. Going too far with this cluster principle could lead to the same mistake."[80] Shaping human behavior through design idealism had limitations, as urban renewal had demonstrated. At The Sea Ranch, private ownership, not communal lands or "open space," ultimately would offer the foundations for sales and community-building.[81] Menzel, who worked in marketing rather than architecture or planning, was self-conscious about "questioning" a civic ideal held by the design professions. He expected pushback. However, speaking from the margins of the project's design team and preoccupied with the bottom line, Menzel critiqued the architects' ideals of including communally owned open space in a private real estate complex. He based his case on lessons learned from urban renewal—another type of environmental complex.

Larry Halprin was not surprised by the high price tags sprouting on Sea Ranch properties. He had anticipated this moment. When John Peter, the Modern Living editor of *Look* magazine, interviewed Halprin, Turnbull, and Boeke in March 1966, Halprin took issue with the presumption that it would be "tough" to sell Sea Ranch real estate. A transcription by Marion Conrad's office captured the conversation. Halprin asserted: "It's got nothing to do with selling land because that land has no value, in the sense that there is so little of it and it is so meaningful for not only people from this area, but for the whole goddamn United States." There would be "no tough battle" in terms of sales "from a development point of view." He conceded that "it's tough" that "people who have invested money in land can't go on indefinitely deferring" their returns. However, "in terms of real value, there is no toughness involved at all. The tough thing is to preserve the land well and let people live on it and enjoy it." It would be tough for investors to wait for cash returns. It would be tough to carry out conservationist goals. But it would not be difficult to sell the land. Halprin thought it was useless to apply market concepts of "demand" to Sea Ranch. "It's like saying, 'how much demand is there for a great and beautiful diamond?' There is no question of demand. It's a question of how many diamonds can you produce." Halprin got to his point. The land had "no value" because it was priceless.[82]

Look editor John Peter's questions uncovered a tension between the convergent architectural designs and unique landscape, on one hand, and disagreement about land and social values, on the other. Bill Turnbull agreed with Halprin that "the land is a marvelous magnet." Turnbull explained the challenge "to design against this landscape." Peter asked how architects of such distinctive styles could end up with convergent designs for the Sea Ranch buildings ("one can hardly tell one from another"). Turnbull responded, "The buildings though came out of a reaction to a piece of land, and to the climate problems on a piece of land. They also came out of exposure to a landscape, the business of driving once a week north along that coast." The designers shared the desire to relate closely to the landscape; barns and other "non-architectural structures" provided inspiration.[83]

How diverse would the community be, and whom did they envision as residents, Peter asked? "Do you have to create a kind of climate where it's kind of an intellectual/ egghead community where guys like Halprin live and architects live, and the kind of special houses . . . is this part of what's going to sell the thing?" No, Boeke and Halprin replied. They wanted The Sea Ranch to be a "real life vital type of place with people," Boeke said. Halprin explained that they had fought over whether the land would be "developed for rich people who are socially oriented," and they had rejected that "on principle." Peter asked, "Can a Negro build a cabin?" Yes. There were no restrictions on race, and "there are several Negroes who have already bought in." Still, Peter remained skeptical that the development would attract much economic, racial or ethnic diversity.[84]

By asking about the project's "economic level," Peter stumbled on the fundamental disagreement about the land's value. Halprin jumped in: "That's the point, the point is the goddamn land is selling too cheap anyway." Boeke interjected that the lots began at about $4,000 each, but Halprin continued. "In fact, my advice to management would be to increase the price of land—to double it." Peter was taken by surprise, having focused the interview on whether the developer would even be able to sell the land and whether the residents would be diverse. Peter asked Turnbull whether he felt the same way, namely, that the land was selling too "cheap." Turnbull again backed up Halprin. "Look, it's irreplaceable. There isn't any more in California." What architects Halprin and Turnbull saw in the coastal landscape—the priceless and sacred environmental concept of "the land"—was not universally perceived or valued. Peter appreciated the landscape but focused on how the development plan addressed pressures for afford-ability and racial and ethnic diversity. If sales prices increased to reflect the sacred land concepts Halprin described, affordability declined. Peter then asked one of the hardest questions for this group to handle, namely, couldn't they make this property a national park? The shadow cast by the fact that the land had been in the state parks pipeline but had not come to fruition as a park put any discussion of architectural design and devel-oper intent in a different, darker light. Only parkland could be simultaneously priceless and open to all. Once again, the conversation between design professionals, on one hand, and management and outside critics, on the other, pried open the debates about what was at stake in environmental design. This was Bobbie Stauffacher's worry: that honing ideals of environmental planning, site-sensitive architecture, and communal ownership was a cover for the fact that the 5,200 acres should not have been sold to private investors in the first place.[85]

"DUPED BY DESIGN"

The Sea Ranch represented Bobbie Stauffacher's best work on behalf of real estate development, but the project also turned her against those same publicity and design practices. Al Boeke praised Stauffacher's design program as honest, informative, com-pelling, original, and factual. This was "a new kind of advertising that really wiped out" the traditional ad agencies he usually hired. Most revealing, he said that the Conrad-Stauffacher real estate work was "not a con act." Stauffacher's artwork precisely captured the desired environmental planning message. However, the fact that her work was "not a con act" spoke volumes about the presumed standards of real estate promotion. The architects did not have to fend off that taint, even though they were part of the same environmental design and sales machinery.[86]

Stauffacher in fact felt sadly accountable for the success that had pushed the project away from its preservationist origins. Her reservations about the commercializing and manipulative implications of graphics came back to haunt her when "knock-off super-graphics took off, outside, on exterior walls." The "guaranteed-to be-preserved-forever" coastal meadows were plowed up. Caricatures of environmentally integrated architecture and "copycat condominiums" spread, sprouting "like poisoned wooden mushrooms from the earth." The Sea Ranch development (and its imitators) consumed land in the name of preservation.[87]

After Sea Ranch meetings, Stauffacher and Conrad "fled to any bar along the high-way not designed in good taste, not exclusive, not an enclave of the rich." Stauffacher worried about their naïveté as successful "career women" and how their talents had been used by others. Later Stauffacher wrote, "'It's all your fault,' Marion joked. Marion and I felt responsible for the press, the success, for our part in this project. Were we just naïve? Were all jobs like this? We looked like career women. We felt like road kill." The friends commiserated over gender politics that empowered and undermined them. Looking back after forty years, Stauffacher believed that, by the grand opening of The Sea Ranch in the summer of 1967, the original environmental concepts of living lightly on the land had already been sold out for real estate profit. The commercial machinery—and her role in establishing it—seemed repugnant to her. When Boeke fired Halprin around the time of the grand opening, Stauffacher read this as another sign that the environmental master-planning concept had lost out. Boeke himself left Oceanic Properties in 1969. He continued at The Sea Ranch as a homeowner, as did most of the other architects—whether or not they became cynical over the develop-ment's loss of civic and preservationist ideals.[88]

The "road kill" experience of marketing The Sea Ranch redirected Stauffacher's career, although her transition out of commercial graphic arts and into architecture was slow and incomplete. Besides the environmental planning credentials she pocketed from the project, Stauffacher gleaned an additional kind of "green" from The Sea Ranch. She turned her $40,000 compensation into a small cottage and property on Stinson Beach. Having collected a modest income as a graphic designer, this was a substantial boon. In the late 1970s she returned to the University of California at Berkeley for an architecture degree, graduating in 1981. Stauffacher's unpublished memoir addressed the impact on her carrer of the fact that her second husband, Daniel (Dan) Solomon, was an architect. When they married in 1968, Stauffacher's connections in the design world were "useful" to her husband, who was ten years her junior. She described how they worked together on jobs that she brought in during their first decade as a couple. Stauffacher expected that once she had a master's degree in architecture she would work in Dan's firm, but that did not go smoothly. She wrote that he criticized her "window details" and "let" her come in "only when he needed me to draw trees around his buildings." In 1988, when she published the prescient *Green Architecture*, "Dan used the book to attract landscape planning jobs into his office." Nevertheless, their marriage—in architectural terms, between a modernist and a postmodernist—lasted nearly twenty-five years (they divorced in the 1990s).[89]

With architecture degree in hand, Stauffacher had a career that continued to mix artistic genres; she published several books illustrated with her drawings and also won design competitions for public works. Applying to the American Academy in Rome for a fellowship, Stauffacher faced the question "What was I? Artist? Graphic designer? Architect? Landscape architect? Writer? Scholar?" She checked all the boxes, unsure whether that made her a "dilettante" or an "interdisciplinary artist." Awarded the prestigious fellowship, she spent 1983 in residence at the academy. An article she published in 1982, "Green Architecture," earned her a spot on the I. M. Pei team that won the competition to redesign the Tuileries Gardens in Paris. In the 1990s she was a partner in another winning proposal for a Battery Park City competition to design Vesey Green, and in the 2000s she codesigned the Ribbon of Light public art installation along the Embarcadero in San Francisco. Each professional success came with hard lessons and added insight into the limitations and disappointments in the design fields. During these years, Stauffacher refined her critical voice and found a broad platform by publishing *Green Architecture* and *Good Mourning California*. In the 2000s, the theme of her memoir "Duped by Design" encompassed both her older disillusionment dating to The Sea Ranch promotion and her entire career in graphic arts and architecture. She finally self-published a much-shortened version of the original memoir in 2012 under the more neutral title *Why? Why Not?*[90]

The Sea Ranch account was likewise the final straw that provoked Stanford Erickson, Marion Conrad Associates' top writer, to leave the field of public relations. Erickson returned to journalism. His reasons differed from Stauffacher's, yet their stories aligned. He respected Conrad but had been troubled by the "superficiality" of people with whom she often associated professionally. He remembered that many of the politicians she worked with "turned my stomach." He had never been drawn to public relations, but Conrad had recruited him with a higher salary and a lighter workload. Erickson had been in charge of the Sea Ranch account for about nine months when Conrad asked him to come upstairs and join her for a drink in her living room. As he recalled, "She rarely did this and only when there was a major problem. She said that she continued to want me to handle the writing and the PR for The Sea Ranch, but that I was not to go there and accompany any journalists there. She acknowledged that a great deal of the PR success was that journalists related to me and liked me." However, she said that the owner had "complained that I did not fit the image of The Sea Ranch. He specifically asked that Peggy Knickerbocker or Linda Hale handle the account because they were San Franciscan sophisticates." Erickson did not begrudge Oceanic's decision; unfortunately, it fit with his understanding of the public relations world. "Naturally, the owner was correct. I looked like a twenty-eight-year-old newspaper man. I probably had two suits at the time and rarely polished my shoes. I also was not cool, businesslike, and sophisticated." He was "upset" by this meeting but chose to not tell Marion Conrad. Within a few weeks, he had left for

McGraw-Hill. He stayed on good terms with Conrad and occasionally wrote articles for her but avoided her parties. The superficial element still rankled.[91]

Bobbie Stauffacher's and Stanford Erickson's respective departures from graphic arts and public relations marked personal, quiet critiques of real estate practices. Both Stauffacher and Erickson admired Marion Conrad and counted themselves among her friends. Erickson kept his feelings about the nature of the work to himself. The environmental and preservationist ideals their team had promoted so effectively exacerbated the contrasting reality of selling The Sea Ranch. In architecture, landscape architecture, and planning, The Sea Ranch became an iconic success story and an internationally recognized design model. But from the allied fields working closely with the architects to define and promote that enivironmental design model, Stauffacher and Erickson critiqued the project's premise and development process. Stauffacher particularly regretted the role design played in enabling the private consumption of coastal land. Design, as much as public relations, had facilitated the land grab. Stauffacher's and Erickson's involvement in packaging The Sea Ranch did not deeply invest them in that architectural story. Instead, in different ways, they critiqued the professed ideals of environmental design. They protested the exploitative process that converted land into landscape and then sold both. They each protested by changing career paths. At the time, they independently chose not to publish or similarly broadcast their disillusionment.

Marion Conrad's moral compass was more finely attuned to the channels of real estate promotion than Stauffacher's or Erickson's. Outside of commiserating with Stauffacher, Marion Conrad did not acknowledge any negative repercussions of her years working for The Sea Ranch. By most accounts, Conrad loved what she did. That did not prevent her friend Stauffacher from speculating that the Sea Ranch account took its toll on Conrad as well. Marion Conrad suffered a heart attack one Sunday morning in 1974 while playing tennis with friends. The night before, Stauffacher wrote, Conrad had stayed up late, "drinking and promoting The Sea Ranch."[92] This story, of course, reveals more about Stauffacher than Conrad. Stauffacher's analysis of real estate development, alongside Erickson's, ultimately distinguished their views from Conrad's. The critique laid out in "Duped by Design" was equally relevant to the era's large-scale public and private redevelopment projects in San Francisco. Real estate machinery might have been more obvious on coastal meadows than on downtown blocks, but in the 1960s other critics raised similar questions about the role of design in remaking urban land for sale.

Model Cities
"Think Big, Build Small"

In the early spring of 1960, the San Francisco press warmed up the city's anticipation of the competition for the Golden Gateway urban renewal site. Proposals were due March 8 and would be unveiled to the public ten days later. Despite insecurities among city leaders that no development team would step up, nine major players had already submitted preliminary plans for this prime waterfront land. It was the "largest number of bidders yet attracted to any redevelopment project in the Nation," said one editorial. The competition's apparent success flamboyantly declared that San Francisco's redevelopment program was finally on track. That most of the teams included San Francisco designers in some capacity pleased the local press. Rumors circulated that the developers had spared no expense in preparing architectural models and plans.[1]

In 1960 the guidelines for meting out land in federally supported urban renewal projects were still fluid, experimental, and under revision. Justin Herman, head of the San Francisco Redevelopment Agency, had decided to take his chances with a design competition. Herman recalled that people thought this was "irresponsible" and "politically dangerous."[2] The Golden Gateway competition, explained real estate editor Grady Clay, mixed "dollars and design" in novel ways by soliciting bids for the land and architectural plans simultaneously. Scanning the nation's urban renewal map, Clay noted that the few precedents for awarding projects based significantly on design had been deeply flawed. Futhermore, Herman's approach to the Golden Gateway competition broke with the template established by the nation's largest federal Title I redevelopment program at the time, run by Robert Moses in New York City. "Moses did not attach importance to urban and architectural design in his planning process," contends architectural historian Hilary Ballon. "He relinquished control of these fundamental aspects of renewal to the sponsor." Golden Gateway's competition, then, took on a high visibility that Justin Herman maximized. The models were on display for a month of public inspection. Then the AIA would descend on the city for their annual meeting. A blue-ribbon advisory panel of architects and development professionals selected by the SFRA would hear the competitors' presentations, deliberate over the models, and advise the city on selection. This judging would take place during the AIA convention, "before the eyes of the entire architectural profession, an awesome array of second-guessers."[3]

Besides amplifying the competition's international significance this schedule arranged around evaluating the urban design models altered the local conversation about redevelopment such that "the atmosphere of the city was supercharged with architecture talk and opinion," observed Clay. Further heightening the dramatic tension, the city's demolition of the renewal district—the wholesale produce market neighborhood—was timed to coincide with the AIA convention. Given Herman's staging of this sequence of events, Clay called the city's redevelopment chief an "impresario."[4]

Three hours after the submission deadline had passed on March 8, the competitors were still putting the final touches on their architectural models (figs. 94 and 95). *San Francisco Chronicle* columnist Art Hoppe described the scene. Inside a "huge room" overlooking the new Golden Gateway Avenue were "nine large booths, just like a country fair. In each booth, young men in Brooks Brothers shirtsleeves were feverishly assembling their wares." Reporters and architects "moseyed" about. "Stapler, said a young man bent

Golden Gateway

Advisory board members Morris Ketchum, Louis Kahn, Mario Ciampi (chairman), in foreground; extreme left, Donald Reay; center back, Karl Treffinger; right, Geoffrey Fairfax, architects, with WB & E-DeMars & Reay model

Joseph Eichler, Robert Anshen, Curtis Dinwiddie and Wm. Stephen Allen present their proposal to advisory board (seated, foreground, with Ketchum standing)

Edgardo Contini, Lawrence Halprin and John Carl Warnecke with model of design submitted by them with Gardner Dailey and Livingston & Blayney

Nathaniel Owings in last-minute consultation with sponsors Edward Keil and Lewis Kitchen

Architects Donald Reay and Vernon DeMars, advisers Lawrence Anderson and Minoru Yamasaki, Donn Emmons and adviser Henry Churchill with model of Wurster, Bernardi & Emmons—DeMars and Reay design

T. K. Kutay, Los Angeles, and San Francisco architect William Corlett (right) just before presentation of large-scale model for Daniel, Mann, Johnson & Mendenhall—Corlett & Spackman design; sponsors' group at left

94 This June 1960 photo essay in *Architectural Record* captured the teams of architects consulting and presenting, milling around the Golden Gateway competition models and renderings, steadying towers, and discussing each other's projects.

over the pieces of a display. Ruler. Scissors."[5] Hoppe followed their interactions closely. "Where's that screw? Shouted another young man in another booth, steadying 20 square blocks of towering apartment buildings with a forefinger." The reporters were awed by the "imaginative architecture." Hoppe knew the journalists were deeply interested in the designs but for the most part lacked expertise. The architects, on the other hand, could not resist judging each other's work. For example, one architect said that another's buildings were all right, "but I can't stand his open spaces."[6]

At the Eichler booth architect Robert Anshen "hovered about nervously" as his team corrected mistakes made by the second-choice model-making company he had hired. Hoppe found that "four men were on their knees with tiny little brushes, busily painting a cluster of twenty-two-story apartment buildings yellow." Anshen explained the origins of the problem: "'They got the wrong color on it,' he said. 'All the local model makers here were pre-empted, so we had to get a firm in Glendale for a rush job. Then the model was too big to get on the plane.'" Anshen had to call the director of

95 An audience view of the Golden Gateway competition presentations by architects and developers in March 1960. The winning team would be able to purchase this prime downtown site, assembled by the Redevelopment Agency, at a cut-rate price.

the Southern Pacific railroad to allow the model aboard an express passenger train from Los Angeles. "They finally let me bring it up here stamped 'Theatrical Baggage.'" Anshen returned his anxious attention to the young architects readying the model: "'Careful, men.'"[7]

The Golden Gateway architectural models, unveiled before the competitors' other documents and plans, made the first impressions on behalf of the entries (fig. 96). As artifacts, the models had inspirational, negative, and neutral impacts independent from the urban design visions they were intended to represent. Although this is usually the case for presentation models, it was especially true for the heterogeneous entries on display in this competition. Justin Herman realized too late that his agency had failed to include a uniform scale for the models in the competition's call for proposals. Better guidelines would have made the entries more comparable and contained costs. The submission by the Los Angeles firm Barrett-Diversified-Lesser-Braemar, described as "big as all outdoors," illustrated how a poorly conceived model could undercut a project's chances. The Redevelopment Agency staff nicknamed the entry "The Monster." The Monster emerged from the advisory panel discussions with yet another name: "The Angry Alligator." The model's large size, intended to impress, had backfired. Clay thought that it had "alienated the sophisticated jurymen."[8]

At the other end of the spectrum, another Golden Gateway model attracted so much admiration that the architect believed he had won (he had not). This "most startling entry" came from Jan Lubicz-Nycz, a young architect who had arrived in the United States from Poland in 1959. Lubicz-Nycz was a "haunted, hesitant, tense figure with long blond hair." His distinctive style helped his presentation stand out, but the model itself was provocative. In Clay's judgment, "The plastic model, starkly simple, had something breathtaking about it that made it one of the most stimulating entries of all" (see fig. 96, no. 5). Lubicz-Nycz's inanimate model, from its unveiling until after the competition's close, embodied for critics an imaginative way of thinking that they tied to his team's overall design proposals. "In retrospect," one newspaper columnist asserted, "it was Lubicz-Nycz who made the deepest impression."[9]

Another tension, not necessarily a competitive one, animated the expansive room of models; the "young men" running around with brushes and rulers contrasted with the two middle-aged women running the biggest model-making company in the Western United States and possibly the nation. Virginia Green and Leila Johnston owned San Francisco–based Architectural Models Inc. (AMI), which had built many of the models in the Golden Gateway competition (fig. 97). The partners had developed a system for handling the volume and confidentiality involved in competitions. Each urban renewal model took months and a large staff to complete. The model-makers rented separate space for each project to fend off prying eyes. A Stanford University campus planner remembered that Green "would have rooms locked and people sworn to secrecy. So if this room is working for Architect A, when the people left that room the door was locked and Architect B's people couldn't find out what Architect A was doing." Designs could leak out through countless channels, but an unauthorized glimpse of the model would give up secrets quickly.[10]

1. 2.

1. Skidmore, Owings & Merrill for Golden Gateway Center

2. Anshen & Allen for Eichler Homes, Inc., and Dinwiddie Construction Co.

3. 4.

3. Welton Becket & Associates and Lawrence Lackey for Kern County Land Company—Del Webb Construction Co.

4. Wurster, Bernardi & Emmons and DeMars & Reay for Perini-San Francisco Associates

5. 6.

5. Jan Lubicz-Nycz, John Collier and Philip Langley for Sidney Leiken Enterprises

6. John Carl Warnecke and Associates, Gardner Dailey, Victor Gruen Associates, Lawrence Halprin and Livingston & Blayney for Tishman Cahill Renewal Associates

7. 8.

7. Daniel, Mann, Johnson & Mendenhall and Corlett & Spackman for Barrett-Diversified-Lesser-Braemar

8. Angus McSweeney, Donald Beach Kirby and Loubet & Glynn for Utah Construction & Mining Co. and Henry C. Beck Co.

Who Will Do the Golden Gateway?

Last fall an advertisement appeared in newspapers all over the country which read: "Notice to developers: San Francisco is ready to go ahead with its fabulous Golden Gateway Project. Qualified developers are now invited to submit proposals for two portions of the Golden Gateway Project: (1) mall, garage and tower (suitable for apartments or offices); (2) a 2200-unit high rise residential development." To the surprise and gratification of San Francisco's Redevelopment Agency, which had run the ad, nine developers responded, each with strong financial capacity and each with a well-known architectural firm on its team as master-planner for the architectural side of the proposal and designer of the buildings in it.

The Golden Gateway project is the redevelopment of the city's present produce district, an area roughly north of the Ferry Building and east of the Appraiser's Building and Jackson Square. It is an area with a tremendous potential, especially in the role of tone-setter for the redevelopment—whether public or private, it is destined to come sometime—of the whole section of the city between Market Street and Telegraph Hill, along the waterfront and inland to the west. The location, the potential, and the initial push it got from a public spirited citizens' committee have made this the most glamorous of the West's redevelopment projects, and the public is as excited about it as the planning and architectural professions. Thousands of people have visited the Redevelopment Agency's offices to study the models and drawings of the nine designs; thousands more have seen the exhibition on the project at the San Francisco Museum of Art.

One reason for the glamor that attaches to Golden Gateway is that the Agency and its executive director, Justin Herman, have given it a unique set of conditions. Although the Agency will make the final decision as to which developer gets the chance to build the Golden Gateway, the procedures leading up to this point make inescapable the Agency's consideration of the architectural solutions along with the offerings of the financial proposals. To guide the five lay members of the Agency in their consideration of the environmental values and architectural amenities of the various designs, the Agency asked a panel* of six architects and a mortgage banker to evaluate for them each design on its own merits.

Each developer and his architects was asked to make a half-hour presentation of his design proposal to the advisory board, and then was questioned

continued on page 32-14

*Architects Mario Ciampi (chairman), Lawrence Anderson, Henry S. Churchill, Louis Kahn, Morris Ketchum, Minoru Yamasaki; and mortgage-banker-developer Ferd Kramer

32-4 ARCHITECTURAL RECORD *June 1960* WESTERN SECTION

96 The eight final Golden Gateway competition models. Jan Lubics-Nycz's unusual model is no. 5; no. 7 was dubbed first "The Monster" and then "The Angry Alligator"; no. 4 was the winning entry.

97 Leila Johnston and Virginia Green posed in 1967 with their patented contour machinery in their 11,000-square-foot factory. They made a provocative contrast with the men steadying towers in the anxious moments before the architects' deadline for submitting their Golden Gateway models. The model workshop met the same tight deadlines and also involved long hours, but the work was done behind the scenes. Green and Johnston's firm, Architectural Models Inc., had built many of the Golden Gateway entries.

Green and Johnston's business was admired as the "Cadillac of the model-making industry," said Calvin Imai, who worked for AMI starting in 1966.[11] Developers paid tens of thousands of dollars for the labor-intensive, imaginative models that they hoped would best express their design concepts. The low cost of Lubicz-Nycz's Golden Gateway model indicates that it was not one of AMI's. In fact, its perceived design "originality" may in part have reflected its fabrication by another firm, such that the Lubicz-Nycz model stood out better in a room dominated by Green and Johnston products. Ultimately, an AMI model backed the winning Golden Gateway proposal, that of the Wurster, Bernardi & Emmons architectural team partnered with Perini Land Development Company and DeMars & Reay, another San Francisco design firm (see. fig. 96, no. 4).[12]

What was at stake in the spectacle of an urban renewal competition? Architect Mario Ciampi, chair of the SFRA's architectural advisory panel, expressed the bold expectations for the site: "Here in the Golden Gateway can be created one of the brilliant achievements of Twentieth Century America."[13] Real estate editor Grady Clay was primarily interested in how the "design-plus-dollar proposals," particularly the architectural models, would determine the disposition of "19.7 acres of downtown land." When Clay called the intense five-day jury review "part side show, part corn," he intended this as a compliment. The competitors poured the same singular focus into their presentation showmanship that might have gone into a television "spectacular." Although the "theatrical baggage" label originated in the specific shipping problems of one Golden Gateway team, the term did resonate with the roles played by static architectural models in the competitors' presentation dramas. Golden Gateway had "produced one of the best-publicized competitions for a small piece of city land in the nation's history."[14] For Clay, the spectacle surrounding the models best opened up the design-and-dollars equation for public scrutiny.

What artists and planners called the "visualization" of proposed real estate developments relied on the skills of model-makers like Virginia Green and Leila Johnston and on the talents of photographers and renderers who similarly specialized in architecture, landscape, and the built environment. Since Karl Kortum and Scott Newhall had used watercolors to promote their historical concept for the north waterfront in 1949, the field of visualization within urban planning and design had deepened and spawned these specialized and intertwined professions. Model-making and its photographers, as well as architectural renderers, saw demand for their work grow with the increasing scale of urban redevelopment during the 1950s and 1960s. Public projects such as those sponsored by urban renewal began to rely on (and sometimes required) the fabrication of models in order to explain proposals to the average citizen.[15] So did the skyscrapers and ever-bulkier private commercial developments that depended on public approvals such as zoning variances and street closings.

Skeptics routinely dismissed architectural models as expensive, wasteful, and superficial sales tools intended to seduce and often mislead their audiences. The Golden Gateway models, together with the developers' bound proposals, were rumored to have cost the nine teams over $1 million—a terribly extravagant figure. More important, from the design professions' official standpoint, the models were derivative of and subservient to architects' real work. Gerald Ratto photographed Green and Johnston's products for decades and used a corner of their workshop to store his equipment. He tired of hearing model-making described as miniaturization. He insisted, "Model-making is not making a miniature of something. Model-making is more an interpretation or an expression of the building." The term miniaturization implied the use of precise technical skills and presumed that model-makers merely duplicated the vision of architects and planners. This reduced any creative role for model-makers, in part by associating the work with "toy cities" and therefore with children and hobbyists. Ratto argued otherwise. Most models preceded buildings, not the other way around. The three-dimensional models interpreted the architects' two-dimensional drawings. Photographing the models added yet "another layer" of artistic interpretation, "bringing it to another level."[16]

Scale was the minute terrain of architectural model-makers.[17] In the postwar large-scale redevelopment era, model-makers occupied a unique niche. The requirement of securing public support early in the planning stages for redevelopment placed pressure on the explanatory powers of architectural models and renderings. The unveiling of models, drawings, and the accompanying press releases usually unleashed public discussion and provoked agreement, anger, and modifications. Because of this, renderers, model-makers, and model-photographers forged relationships with the critics, press, design journal editors, and juries—direct relationships that were semi-independent of the architects or planners. In many ways, models were more useful than buildings—even to architects. By 1960, architectural models had the capacity to swing urban design decisions, structure competition for land, and generally set in motion the fate of neighborhoods, as Grady Clay noted.

AMI built the models for most of the major contested redevelopment sites on the north waterfront during the 1960s and early 1970s, from Golden Gateway to Embarcadero Center and the unbuilt San Francisco International Market Center. The obsessively "realistic" models, after all, described imagined places. And usually models, not the buildings themselves, were at the center of heated public debates. Although architectural model-makers are the focus of this chapter, including the affiliated visualization professions (especially renderers) helps clarify the precise dimensions of model-making within urban rebuilding. Small and large, technical and creative, men and women, representational and abstract, interpretive and descriptive, static and performative—there was much more in the models and their creators than first met the eye.

"BIG LITTLE BUILDERS"

If writers like Jane Jacobs and Grady Clay left the most explicit trail of ideas for understanding redevelopment, the model-makers hid their tracks. They were the least oriented around the written word. Unlike photographers or architectural renderers—equally visual communicators—the model-makers could not save copies of their projects. Design magazines rarely credited their work in publications. Model-making usually involved collaborative teamwork and authorship, unlike its sister fields of rendering and model-photography. In the Golden Gateway competition, model-makers such as Virginia Green and Leila Johnston were displaced and obscured by the knots of young men in Brooks Brothers shirts. The model-makers' invisibility in the design process was then replicated in the historical record of redevelopment, in part because of the lack of written records. Model-making companies, even those that had operated for fifty years, left behind little but empty warehouses when they closed. In architects' archives, a model-maker is most commonly represented by a cost estimate, a contract, and perhaps a few lines of correspondence registering appreciation or complaint.

"Virginia Green—you may have never heard of her," Henry Sanders told an interviewer in 1977 as he attempted to interject Green into the story of well-known landscape architect Thomas (Tom) Church. "She became known as the best model-maker in the United States," Sanders explained. AMI had designed and built Stanford University's campus model in the 1950s, and updated it over the years. Standing near the model, Sanders pointed out flaws in the recent work done on the Engineering Building by a "new person." In planning models, such mistakes undermined the architects' ability to envision their ideas. Virginia Green and the model were significant to retracing Church's creative process, Sanders said, because Church had done perhaps "a fourth of his thinking over that model." One could pull apart the sections and experiment with buildings of different heights and shapes. Green's design of the superior planning tool, the model, merited her inclusion in the historical record.[18]

Henry Sanders's unsolicited testimony opens a door onto a behind-the-scenes business, particularly addressing what made AMI thrive in the 1950s, 1960s, and 1970s. Virginia Green "did beautiful, beautiful work," he said. "I think it's one of the greatest stories of rags-to-riches I've ever heard. She's been written up, but nobody ever has really done a complete job on what she accomplished. She's remarkable. She trained a lot of people, and a lot of people are trying to emulate her work, but no one has taken her place." From nothing, Green had built "really a huge business," Sanders recalled. The story's details would vary in the telling, but certain elements remained steady. Green produced high-quality work. She struck out on her own and set standards for her profession. She built a large firm. And her shop became the training ground for the next generation of model-makers.[19]

Other colleagues singled out Green and Johnston's leadership in establishing sophisticated new standards for the expanding visualization professions. Photographer Ratto believed that "they probably were the first really innovative model-making people. Virginia Green was a very, very bright woman. Leila was a very good business person, and Virginia was more the creative end." Ratto speculated that they were "the first really professional model makers in the United States." Model-making arts had, of course, contributed to architectural practice for centuries, but the postwar large-scale development boom in the United States launched a new phase for the field. Green and Johnston's innovations "set the framework for a lot of work that followed." Ratto thought AMI had the business "pretty well locked up" in the 1950s and 1960s. One Bay Area architect, John Eliassen, never met Green but followed her career. He remembered her as a "nine-day wonder" who "consolidated a whole industry" only to be forgotten. Like many architects, he continued to make his own models in-house—partly out of financial necessity and perhaps also because he enjoyed the work.[20]

In the early years, AMI's most significant competitors were former employees who paid Green and Johnston's ingenuity the highest compliment by emulating their model-making machinery so closely that it became the subject of a lawsuit. Donald Nusbaum, fifty years later, remembered the impact of seeing Green's masterful presentation model of the Crown Zellerbach building in 1959 (fig. 98). At the time, he was finishing architecture school at the University of California, Berkeley, having transferred there from Green and Johnston's graduate school alma mater, the University of Oregon. The Crown Zellerbach model prompted him to research the company that built it. In AMI he found "a small-scale model shop that I had never seen the likes of before." By November 1961 he was working for Green and Johnston. There he met Nils C. Neklason, who had been with AMI since 1958. The two men hit it off. Within a year of Nusbaum's arrival they left AMI and established their own firm, Scale Models Unlimited (SMU). Despite the lawsuit sparked by this break, Nusbaum acknowledged that Green and Johnston "originally set the pace for architectural models in San Francisco" and noted their "artistic skills."[21] He particularly admired the topographic tool invented by Green and Johnston, which "saved a lot of time." The machine followed the contours of topographical maps to carve landforms and elevations into the base of a model. The time saved by this device was key to the efficiencies AMI offered master planning firms working with larger footprints (see fig. 96).[22] Seeing untapped potential in AMI's contour machine, which was awaiting a patent, Nusbaum and Neklason modified it for their own firm—thereby provoking AMI's lawsuit.[23]

The larger wave that lifted the model-making business to new professional relevance in the 1950s and 1960s was the rise of large-scale urban redevelopment and related controversies over the impact of such projects on U.S. cities. This encompassed more than urban renewal sites and downtown office buildings. Universities and hospitals expanded; suburban office parks, shopping centers, and residential developments took over orchards and meadows; vacation resorts and golf courses hired urban designers for the sculpting of vast rural parcels. The demands of redevelopment agencies, developers,

98 Virginia Green made her mark on urban design in 1955 with a model of the first steel-frame, curtain-wall sky-scraper in San Francisco—the Crown Zellerbach office building. This model toured widely, including out of state. It inspired architecture student Donald Nusbaum to consider the model-making business. After working for Green and Johnston he founded his own company, Scale Models Unlimited, and was representative of how Architectural Models Inc. trained entrepreneurs in the industry.

corporations, and institutions catalyzed the model-making industry, enlisting entrepreneurial artist-consultants such as AMI and SMU. The fundamental concept in the architectural model-making profession—scale—was embedded in the key redevelopment issues of the postwar decades.

Models were the leading edge for introducing new planning and architectural concepts to the public and for provoking reaction to design. The models were used to promote, of course, but they were also used to negotiate deals and compromises amid protests over the scale of redevelopment. The scale models sat, not always inertly, at the center of controversies over these issues. For city projects, models had to address the relationship between new construction and historical context. Should the model designer exclude adjacent blocks given that they were slated for clearance?[24] Or should the model demonstrate a sensitive relationship between a modern office building and the neighboring older downtown streets? Models engaged the debates over whether buildings would divide neighborhoods or block views and whether proposed projects were outsized, too tall, too dark, or too light.

The language of "building" slipped easily between descriptions of architectural models and the cities themselves. This resulted in a lot of puns that played off the premise that model-making enacted the real-life practice of city-building. One of the earliest articles on Green, from 1953, appeared in a "Stamps and Hobbies" newspaper column: "By profession Virginia Green is a sculptor and painter. However, for the past two years one of her major occupations has been building. She has built hotels in Hawaii and Havana, Cuba. She has built schools, houses, apartments, even restaurants. And she has quite a construction record. She completes her structures in about a week." At that point Green worked with cardboard, balsa wood, plastics, glues of different weights, a surgical knife, a salt shaker, a comb, copper wire, and masking tape; an assortment of screens, stains, paints, papers, and sand; and finally hairspray to keep materials from shedding.[25] Later the San Francisco Examiner's urban affairs writer Donald Canter covered AMI, recognizing the firm's expanded role. He called it "one of the nation's most thriving construction businesses. Skyscrapers go up in weeks and entire subdivisions in a matter of months." Reporters often noted the quick "construction" time for major projects in miniature. Model-making's economic fortunes depended on the actual construction industry's ups and downs, reinforcing the parallel, connected worlds of city modeling and city planning.[26]

Because their clients included most of the significant new projects in the San Francisco Bay Area, AMI identified closely with their home city's postwar redevelopment. Virginia Green had made her initial mark on urban design in 1955 with a model of the first steel-frame, curtain-wall skyscraper in San Francisco—the Crown Zellerbach office building—the model that inspired Don Nusbaum. Just two years earlier, her project list of hotels, restaurants, schools, apartments, and houses had captured a snapshot of San Francisco on the verge of transformation by skyscrapers and redevelopment. "We were here at the time San Francisco's building boom began, in the 1950s, and we've grown with it," Leila Johnston recalled in 1972. The model-makers' business escalated in part because skyscraper growth was contested. Many large-scale private projects required the closing and selling of streets or needed zoning exemptions. The city of San

Francisco's review of such proposals meant that developers hired model-makers to back their cases with tangible evidence. The multi-million-dollar skyscrapers that were "anathema to many," one reporter wrote, "all took three-dimensional shape first at Architectural Models, Inc." Although Green and Johnston "began in a small way," their San Francisco office towers included those for John Hancock, Alcoa, Bethlehem Steel, the Bank of America headquarters, Wells Fargo, and the International Building.[27]

When model-makers built entire neighborhoods and central business districts they experienced a bird's-eye sense of design and construction akin to that of city planning. One of SMU's lead model-makers, Kamran Kiani, singled out a 16-by-18-foot model of San Francisco as "one of the highlights of my life." The client, Bechtel Engineering Corporation, commissioned the model as a "gift" to San Francisco in 1978. Kiani began working for Don Nusbaum and SMU in 1970. He arrived in San Francisco with an architecture degree from the University of Florence when the Bay Area's large architecture firms were not hiring because of an industry recession. Kiani noticed SMU in the yellow pages, and his curiosity was piqued. He contacted the office, and SMU offered him a position after reviewing his portfolio. He found model-making more intellectually challenging than drafting for a large firm. Model work was more "diversified" and, ironically, three-dimensional. Plus he enjoyed working with his hands. The city model's display at public sites such as San Francisco International Airport, and his personal responsibility for updating it over decades all contributed to Kiani's attachment. His pride also derived from having led the completion of this large-scale project by fifty employees against a tight deadline. Kiani ordered T-shirts emblazoned with the words "We built San Francisco," marking the employees' investment in shaping "the city" (fig. 99).[28]

Their research into the larger urban context and civic setting for individual projects helped distinguish the "ingenuity" of model-makers from mere miniaturization.

99 Kamran Kiani of Scale Models Unlimited had these T-shirts printed in 1978 after a team of employees completed a major collaborative project making a model of San Francisco. The shirts captured the model-makers' pride and sense of having contributed to building at the urban scale.

Translating architects' blueprints into three-dimensional representations required that skilled model-makers extract relevant information about the city from varied sources. AMI produced a detailed brochure in 1967 explaining this work: "Research. Accuracy is born out of research. Often, Architectural Models must spend as much time in study as in construction." The firm had just completed its model for Embarcadero Center, the second major phase of the Golden Gateway urban renewal district. The AMI brochure explained that the five-block project's large size and complexity made it "necessary to research a large portion of downtown San Francisco." Because key neighboring buildings had not yet been constructed, the staff had "to consult many sources, sort reams of data, recalculate new scales, draft, study, plan, and produce."[29] This work also enacted the urban design decision-making process that shaped how the historical urban fabric of the city would meet new construction. Which adjacent buildings would still be there in five years? How would the old city meet the new one, literally?

Perhaps better than anyone other than the redevelopment authorities themselves, the model-makers and renderers understood how much the core character and climate of civic presentation had changed since the 1950s. One of the world's top architectural renderers, Helmut Jacoby, contributed five carefully framed illustrations to mediate San Francisco's public debates over the Embarcadero Center designs in 1967 (for three of them, see figs. 117–119). By then, Jacoby noted shortly afterwards, the transformed climate for redevelopment and its visualization was apparent: "In the early 1950's, every proposed project was received with optimistic anticipation, while today angry protest against announced new construction, even if the building concerned is of high architectural quality, grows more frequent." Accordingly, "Contrary public opinion and professional criticism alike have resulted in the formation of neighborhood building groups, landmark preservation committees, and architectural student protest groups." As concern for "rehabilitating" historical structures grew during the 1960s in the United States, interest in showcasing the architectural rendering of individual buildings declined in favor of showing more of the surrounding context.[30]

By the late 1960s, mobilization against needless demolition and skepticism over the sterility and anonymity of modern architecture had altered the rationales behind architectural models and changed the reception of models and renderings. An understanding of (and anxiety for) the wider context of future urban life rather than preoccupation with novel architecture seeped into design visualization fields. Model-makers and renderers calculated their designs to address an increasingly contentious redevelopment climate in which modernism and clearance had assumed more complicated and disturbing civic meaning.

TOOLS OF DESIGN

Models and renderings were tools for design as much as marketing tools in 1960s urban redevelopment. Sometimes the model's explicit role in design was obvious. The Golden Gateway competition deployed architectural models to provoke concrete dialogue about the city's future. Equally influential, but hidden from public view, were the back-and-forth exchanges visualization professionals had with architects over design questions. The creative identities assumed by model-makers, photographers, and renderers enriched how these artists used "layers of interpretation" to engage with architects' ideas, to borrow Gerald Ratto's phrase. Renderers and photographers, with their inter-related agendas, expanded the dimensions and complexity of visualization strategies while identifying what was nonetheless distinctive about the model-makers.

Despite the common presumptions about the purely technical work of architectural visualization, the accounts of their professions offered by model-makers, renderers, and photographers were suffused with stories of their direct participation in the design process. In part this was due to the feedback loops inherent to their trades. Model-makers were often the first to view an executed design after reading blueprints and converting them into three dimensions. Blueprints are notoriously mysterious and illegible to people without training in architecture, engineering, and construction. Their translation into three dimensions identified opportunities for revision and further experimentation, revealed mistakes, and opened a multidirectional conversation with the architects.

Kamran Kiani attributed his ongoing dialogue with architects to his own architecture degree. Kiani was likely right. Many of those who achieved leadership roles in the visualization fields during the 1960s and 1970s, including Kiani, Nusbaum, Jacoby, and Calvin Imai, who later took over AMI, had architecture degrees. Green and Johnston had MFAs in sculpture, but their program was in a School of Architecture and Allied Arts. "When I worked with architects in San Francisco," Kiani recalled, "very often I would call them and say if you let me do some changes it will [turn out] better. And they would look at it and say yes, you are right, go ahead and do the changes."[31] AMI detailed the firm's "hand-in-hand evolution" with architects "in their formulation of the design process." Master planning models exemplified what Green called "perpetual notion" in that architects reconfigured and studied them, and AMI also updated the models over the decades. Other model types provided tools for nuts-and-bolts problem-solving, such as analysis of projected wind-related impacts created by new skyscrapers or the placement of exposed buildings on The Sea Ranch. "In most cases a model is a solution to a specific problem," AMI explained. For the contested Bank of America headquarters, for example, "multiple problems required multiple models." But most models interpreted a dimension of time. They anticipated what unbuilt structures would look like and how neighborhoods would change in the future: "A model is more than duplication to scale. It shows a relationship to surrounding structures. Or topography. Or it fills in the gaps for anticipated expansion." Models articulated a client's "hopes" for the future, often framed through achieving better urban infrastructure: economically productive office towers, appealing recreation sites, and modern hospitals, universities, power plants, and highways. Only rarely did a client "hope" mainly to execute a stimu-lating architectral design.[32]

To promote their models' ability to communicate, Green and Johnston described the models as active participants—metaphorically "speaking," "translating," and making "clear" statements. Professional communication was their firm's artistry. Another urban design model, this one for the Capital Mall in Washington, D.C., extracted a considered reflection about the model's voice. "A model translates protracted time into contracted space," stated AMI's brochure. "It sifts through thousands of man-hours of study and planning, coordinates the results, and produces the statement. The statement then becomes its own tool for study. The model does not equivocate. It says what it has to say over the broadest possible range—to lay people and architects alike. It says it all in visual, tangible terms. Easily and without interruption." This was intellectually challenging work, translating time into space. The model-makers translated, sifted, coordinated, and produced; they did *not* duplicate. Because models spoke in "visual, tangible terms," they were potentially more direct, clear, long-lasting, and bold than verbal and even written communications. Although the model might appear to be inert, it had an active life attributable to the makers' skill. "It sells itself for pre-leasing or fund-raising. It shows itself inside out. It's taken apart, listened to, lit up, wind-swept, and photographed." The "visual, tangible" translations best captured the expressive manner in which Green and Johnston's models were tools of design embedded in that process.[33]

The architectural rendering business, also called architectural drawing, shared the same broad marketing imperatives as model-making. Yet rendering played roles in postwar urban design and architecture distinct from those of three-dimensional models. For starters, drawing held higher status within the arts. Drawing, of course, had intricate historical conventions. It meshed more explicitly with definitions of high art than did model-making and was trailed by a robust history of artistic criticism. Accordingly, renderers, whose careers also boomed alongside urban renewal and architectural modernism, have generated some scholarship—compared with scant attention to model-makers. Publications on renderers melded promotional portfolios of their projects with academic analysis, a commercial blend that mirrored the traditions of architectural criticism.

Illustrator Helmut Jacoby's career illuminates how architectural perspective drawing defined its place among the arts of urban design. Jacoby's career launched quickly in the mid-1950s because his first clients included such architectural stars as Philip Johnson, I. M. Pei, Marcel Breuer, and Kevin Roche. After training in mechanical engineering and architecture in Germany, Jacoby moved to the United States and worked for a few years. A 1953 bachelor's in architecture from Harvard, the related professional contacts, his traditional drawing skills—these elite characteristics elevated Jacoby's standing with architects. His commitment to accuracy, honed by his engineering background, suited him to the architectural trends of the 1950s—the boxes, angles, and structural experimentation of high modernism.[34]

Unlike architectural models, whose specific vantage points could not be controlled, architectural drawing required a "station point." Professional illustrators were often given the freedom to choose the perspective, which scripted the audience's view and largely determined a design's impression. Street-view, bird's-eye, or something else? Which side of the building would show to best effect? What features would be visible, which obstructed? The ensuing dialogue between renderer and architect over such decisions solidified an illustrator's contribution to design. Selecting the most effective station point and resolving dozens of other variables required talent and experience.

Throughout his career, Jacoby modestly and judiciously declined credit for shaping the designs of his prominent clients.[35] Yet he conceded that architects revised their designs based on his drawings, and reviewers zeroed in on this point.[36] One scholar in 1965 described how Jacoby's "exploratory talk about a commission" with a client could become "a heated debate about detail and even about architectural theories. Sometimes his drawings led to a reexamination and alteration of the design."[37] A striking example came from his collaboration with Philip Johnson. When Johnson began experimenting with postmodernism, Jacoby recalled that Johnson "needed my interpretation at this time more than ever, since it would take quite some time, til he could realize his conceptions." Johnson commissioned some renderings because he "simply wanted to see from my drawings how I viewed his architecture," Jacoby said. Other architects, such as Norman Foster, would drop by in person, describe their ideas, and tell "a story about their plans"—which Jacoby "then drew."[38]

Because architectural drawing could achieve an eye-level perspective of proposed buildings and future cityscapes, rendering seemed more capable than model-making of anticipating and shaping the human perspective of the built environment. The complex, subjective qualities critics admired in Jacoby's drawings help explain why architectural drawing was a lucrative niche for those who could deliver. Skillfully executed, an eye-level drawing cultivated the desired *attitude* toward a building for both layperson and design professional. This "station point corresponds to the actual view point of people passing or approaching the building," noted one expert, which is more "interesting" to city residents than other perspectives.[39] It was not enough to accurately capture a building's "conception" and "emphasize its unusual features." Rather the drawing should "generally create a feeling of pleasant anticipation."[40] Jacoby balanced his obsession with accuracy against this attention to feeling. One of his former drawing teachers said that Jacoby "successfully calculates the effect of a drawing on the viewer. He knows how to arouse interest and how to hold it, when to create tension and when to provide relaxation." Pleasant anticipation, tension, relaxation—this palette simulated "the subjective impressions of future viewers who will approach the building in varying moods," according to Jacoby.[41] These were not the evocative impressions sought by earlier generations of architectural illustrators using shaky lines, blurry watercolors, and what Jacoby called "soapy" effects.[42]

Renderers, then, were seen to have the edge over model-makers and most architects in exploring how people experienced built spaces. The resurgence of skilled, highly paid renderers in the 1950s and 1960s had reintroduced the atrophied art of drawing architecture into the design process. Talented artists like Jacoby met a growing demand from developers and the most respected architectural firms. This trend might be counterintuitive, one critic acknowledged: "It may seem curious but it is true that many architects cannot draw their creations in a form that might explain the project to a layman." From the viewpoint of his own field on this translation, photographer Ratto bluntly stated, "The architect is pretty much at the mercy of the photographer."[43]

How could a renderer, model-maker, or photographer understand a building and its environment better than an architect? From the model-maker's perspective, good marketing engaged the design choices that defined a project's vision, drew financial and political support, and won commissions and awards for architects. The model-makers' close knowledge of the project was thus instrumental to both the design process and many of the professional outcomes for the architect and investors. In San Francisco the Catholic Archdiocese used AMI's model of the proposed St. Mary's Cathedral to raise funds for an unusual modern design. AMI needed to convey the designer's "imagination," fresh architectural expression, and willingness to experiment (fig. 100). AMI's model of a proposed convention complex in Monterey, California, was intended to "stimulate interest in a municipal project," while a diminutive power station "toured the states of Oregon and Washington" to build public support. Coldwell, Banker & Co. used AMI's Embarcadero Center model to pre-lease the project's vast commercial space. The visual review judging most AIA and similar design awards depended not on site visits to completed projects but rather on representations of proposed work. Accordingly, Green and Johnston's firm "always shares the pride when such awards are won by our architect and designer friends."[44] Model-makers evaluated the quality of the architecture, not only the quality of models as artifacts.

Photographer Ratto offered a vivid story about the intimate, unique knowledge that visualization professionals often sustained with architectural designs because of their detail work with the models. Edward Durell Stone, an influential New York–based architect, had to fly to San Diego to appear on television and present his firm's designs for the Scripps Institute at La Jolla. As Ratto explained, the project had been designed

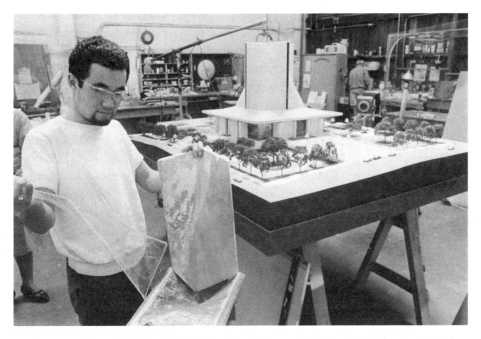

100 Dong Lim working on the St. Mary's Cathedral model at Architectural Models Inc. The *San Francisco Examiner* cropped a similar image for a 1967 article such that the tighter final frame featured only the model—not the makers.

by the firm's San Francisco office. Stone himself "didn't know a damn thing about it." Instead of consulting with "his own architects here who had designed it," Stone flew Ratto to San Diego from San Francisco. Over lunch, Ed Stone asked Ratto to "explain the project to him." Stone peppered Ratto with questions about the institute's design. Ratto recalled: "I was familiar with the model of course because I had worked on it." After lunch, he flew back to the Bay Area. Initially, the situation's novelty prevented Ratto from grasping Stone's approach. But upon reflection, Ratto understood that Stone had "wanted another viewpoint, an outsider's viewpoint." He "was also smart enough to know that I probably had a more intimate relationship with the model than any of his people did. And he was presenting the model." Architectural models—displayed in television studios and conference rooms—stood as distinct artifacts requiring interpretation for clients and other audiences.[45]

Whatever the pressures on allied commercial artists to duplicate a designer's vision, this was impossible. Gerald Ratto understood this with particular clarity, observing that "I cannot visualize and see the way someone else does. Nobody can." Speaking of a lead architect at the San Francisco office of SOM, Ratto said, "I can't be Chuck Bassett and Chuck Bassett can't be me." Each visualization professional inherently had a separate artistic identity, such that, as Ratto put it, "as a photographer I have to be honest and true to myself." That difference in "seeing" both defended the creative independence of photographers, model-makers, and renderers, and opened up space for conflict. In the perceptible distance between the architect and allied artists there was the potential for "locking horns."[46]

Of course visualization artists harbored their own opinions of architectural and urban designs (which sometimes were best kept to themselves). Just as Jacoby was drawn to the challenge of integrating modernist structures into the historical urban fabric, illustrators often meshed with certain architects and design schools. Architects with "pure and austere designs," for example, might turn to artists who depicted "strong blue skies and an abundance of greenery." For "architects who have the power and courage to display their radical designs in the preliminary stages," renderers could shape their reception and help ease the introduction of new concepts and directions that unsettled design culture. Renderers also faced decisions about "veiling" an architect's weaknesses. Most illustrators' conversations about foliage, light, shadow, angle, depth, color, and skies touched on judging the architect's talent and whether disguise and distraction were necessary. Debating when disguise shaded over into distortion and trickery occupied that creative ground between the architect and the visualization artist.[47] A backhanded compliment to the illustrator's artistry was the oft-expressed reservation "that a mediocre architect could derive professional advantages from attractive renderings done by someone else."[48]

As design tools, drawings and photographs traveled further than models and certainly further than buildings. However, models operated on an accelerated timeline because architects could use them immediately instead of waiting ten years for the building. For these reasons Ratto thought models were more "useful" and "interesting" than the buildings themselves; they made money for the architects by drawing new commissions and winning awards, even when the buildings were never constructed. Models also engaged the public.[49]

In the 1950s and 1960s arguably the most significant geographical and cultural leap made by renderings, photographs, and models was the trip from the United States to Europe. From an international perspective, the rising demand for renderings was inseparable from the proliferation of skyscrapers in the United States. An expanding architectural press, including *Architectural Forum, Architectural Record,* and *Progressive Architecture* boosted the reach of these images. Jacoby's illustrations "provided a European preview of the latest American buildings." His renderings sympathetically explained the skyscraper's radical disruption of the city to a resistant European audience.[50] Jacoby's reputation for accurate detail and honesty, together with his skill in interpreting the intensely vertical impact of high-rises on older urban neighborhoods, positioned him well for rendering contested skyscrapers and urban renewal projects.

Ultimately, a visualization artist's strong individual style ran into concrete as well as philosophical limitations. Helmut Jacoby, for example, took simultaneous pride in being the "extension to the architect's arm" while enjoying a reputation for design leadership and his own stylistic integrity.[51] One scholar captured a related contradiction binding the delineator's hand: "The stronger his personal style, the more consistent and the better the drawing may be. On the other hand, the quality of a good translation is, by definition, its anonymity."[52] A different reviewer admitted that Jacoby's technique was so dominant that all of the designs seemed to have been conceived by the same architect.[53] Partly for this reason, in design competitions Jacoby made a habit of accepting only one commission from each competitor pool. For the National Terminal competition at New York's Idlewild (now John F. Kennedy International) Airport, he remembered: "All at once I had four enquiries for drawings! Of course I didn't accept all four, but opted for one, as it turned out the wrong one!" Jacoby accepted Philip Johnson's commission, but Eero Saarinen's design won.[54] In contrast stood Virginia Green and Leila Johnston's system for accepting commissions from competitors and managing each client's design in secrecy. Although Jacoby had the same trust of architects, the distinctiveness of the drawing genre meant that he operated within a different set of limits than did model-makers.

The greatest limitation to the commercial artist's independent authorship, however, came in the realm of intellectual property law. By the mid-1960s, Jacoby had won the Birch-Burdette Prize, the top award in his field, three times—in 1962, 1963, and 1964. Critics regarded him as the best architectural illustrator of his generation in the United States. The first of several books publishing his portfolio was released in 1965. Jacoby hoped the book would establish his reputation in Europe, where he would soon reside for the remainder of his career. His rising professional stature and the elite caliber of his best-known clients, however, made an issue of Jacoby's artistic independence. He expressed the frustration concisely: "According to US copyright law, I am not the author of my drawings!" After Jacoby's first book with the German publisher Hatje came out in 1969, Philip Johnson told him: "We should not have let you do it." Johnson did not pursue the matter. But the infuriating legal principle of losing ownership of one's own designs stood.[55]

"MODEL BUSINESSWOMEN"

Shortly before picking up a surgical knife and committing to architectural model-making for the rest of her career, Virginia Green had dedicated herself to abstract sculpture. In 1947 she enrolled in the sculpture program at the School of Architecture and Allied Arts at the University of Oregon. Her 1950 MFA provided a way out of teaching art, which, after six years in the San Francisco schools, had become tiresome. Green had a promising future as a practicing artist. In 1950 she won a coveted fellowship to pursue independent study in sculpture. This recognition from the Albert M. Bender Grants-in-Aid in Art and Literature, administered by the San Francisco Art Association, placed her in good company; painter Richard Diebenkorn had been the art honoree three years earlier.[56] Following the plan laid out in her Bender application, Green left a civil service job in Eugene, Oregon, and moved back to San Francisco in 1950. She regarded San Francisco as having "a great deal to offer in the way of cultural and intellectual stimulation, which is necessary for the development of the fine arts in our present society."[57] It is likely that Green used part of the $1,200 stipend she received in 1951 to start what would become her internationally known architectural model-making company.

Virginia Green's background in abstract sculpture might suggest that she flip-flopped from one extreme to another, from the realm of modernist abstraction to the obsessive realism and precision of architectural models. Instead, her arts training helps unwind the clichés of model-making as technical duplication rather than creative design. In making the transition from abstract sculptor to model businesswoman, Green illuminated the creative life inherent to the allied visualization arts.

Virginia Green had been born in Oakland in 1920, a year after her father Eliot Green and mother Dorothy Taber were married. Virginia grew up in San Francisco. The federal census and military records trace her father's employment as an expert demonstrator in tractor and auto sales. A superintendent at Wells Manufacturing Company in 1942, Eliot Green was a hands-on mechanic as well as a salesman and supervisor. His passion was the crafting of precision scientific and medical instruments. Later Virginia Green's colleagues assumed that she had absorbed a love of machines, tools, and detail-oriented bench work from her father. After graduating from San Francisco State University in 1942 with a concentration in art education, Green taught elementary students in the San Francisco public schools before taking her chances on sculpture.[58]

Not coincidentally, Green's partner, Leila Johnston, followed a similar path. Johnston was born in 1916 in Spokane. By the time she attended Lewis and Clark High School, her father, Charley McMillen, was a retired farmer, while her mother taught in the public schools. Her older brother, Kenneth, worked as a blacksmith, while younger brothers Ralph and Don were in school. Leila attended Eastern Washington College of Education in Cheney. By 1940 she was teaching art in Ritzville, Washington, while lodging in the home of an elderly couple.[59] Soon thereafter, McMillen became Mrs. Leila Johnston. The details of this marriage are murky; perhaps the young man fought in the war and never came home. She remained Leila Johnston for the rest of her life. For Johnston, the perks of teaching never added up. In 1947 she enrolled in the MFA program at the University of Oregon. There she met Virginia Green, who became first her roommate, then her lifelong lover. In the spring of 1950 Johnston moved to San Francisco with Virginia. For a time, Johnston worked as a registrar in the San Francisco Museum of Art. When Green's business began to thrive such that she needed a full-time partner, Johnston joined the company in 1955 as secretary-treasurer. Although Johnston assumed responsibility for the business's financial side, she always remained a sculptor who loved working with her hands. Green continued as president.[60]

Green forged a bolder trail than Johnston through the Oregon sculpture program. Green's MFA thesis ("Cement—A Direct Building Material: Its Possibilities as a Sculptural Medium") and her two Bender grant applications show Green as a tireless researcher who explored the capacities of sculptural materials. Although she worked with wood, terra cotta, clay, stone, steel, cement, and volcanic tuff, the potential of building directly on an armature with cement (rather than casting or molding it) seemed especially promising. Using cement and various aggregates, Green experimented with shaping, color, curing, finish, texture, and weathering. She hoped to incorporate carving, too (fig. 101).[61] Most of her sculptures were designs abstracted from named subjects, such as Pelican, Torso, Fish, St. Francis, Rooster, Bird, and Prayer, suggesting influence from Bay Area artist Beniamino Bufano.[62]

Her professors commended Green for her experimental, entrepreneurial approach to sculpture in their letters on her behalf for the Bender application. The dean, Sidney Little, described her "superior ability." Green "excelled" in handling materials, her sculpture supervisor, Mark R. Sponenburgh, wrote. Professor Wallace Baldinger, an art historian, admired her clear, logical thinking and problem-solving skills. "Miss Green is alert to new ideas, cooperative in attitude, but independent in her thinking," Baldinger said. He saw "real vigor and directness of expression, and evidences of an enterprising

101 For her 1950 master's thesis capping an MFA in sculpture at the University of Oregon, Virginia Green worked with the possibilities of cement as a "building material" and "sculptural medium" and included this piece among many other examples. Her preference for abstract art confirms that she did not approach her model-making career as merely technical miniaturization.

and experimental spirit and untiring perseverance." She has "great possibilities" for "ultimate development into a creative sculptor."[63] Enterprising, alert to new ideas, experimental, tireless, direct, logical—these qualities served Green well when she launched her business in a short year or two.

Perhaps it was partly the influence of being enrolled in a sculpture program hosted in an architecture and allied arts school, but Virginia Green became interested in collaborating with architects long before she left Oregon. In her 1949 Bender application she had explained her plan to "gain practical experience, by working with architects, interior designers, and landscape gardeners, in designing and executing creative sculpture that is for a specific site and use." She would need to break into the field. Green anticipated having to network "to locate such men who are interested in this type of collaboration and offer my services." Her design aspirations already drew her to questions of setting and context, domestic or public, indoor or outdoor, and to the characteristics of space and the built environment. Green's agenda included making scale models and drawings "for discussion and re-designing" with architects.[64] Professor Wallace Hayden singled out Green's engagement with architecture and her commitment to site-specific, free-standing sculpture. "As an architect," he wrote, "I am interested in any advancement in the arts which is made by artists working in close collaboration with the materials and methods of the profession. Miss Green seems genuinely interested in doing something meaningful with cement and concrete in the 'round.'"[65]

Green was sensitive to the technical-creative divide the MFA program made explicit, given her primary passion for understanding materials. This divide permeated her fine arts education; she called sculpture, for example, "a field that demands both technical and creative ability."[66] Halfway through her program, Green believed that her design creativity had lagged. Materials knowledge came first for her and guided "the types of creative form and design" that followed. She was motivated "to develop more original and creative imagination in relation to sculptural ideas."[67] The Bender grant would allow her to do design projects for clients without depending financially on those commissions.[68] Of course she would still use the grant to experiment with materials. But she had learned in graduate school that in sculpture "one must try and achieve a balance between the creative aspects and the technical aspects if one is to succeed in the field."[69]

When she returned to San Francisco in the summer of 1950, Green's networking with architects and landscape architects first paid off in sculpture commissions and soon led her to the model-making industry. First she worked on a new Palo Alto park that became "an immediate sensation" when it opened in 1957. J. Pearce Mitchell Park was praised in the 1950s as a groundbreaking model for planned neighborhood recreation. Green designed two large, smooth, playful concrete bears for a playground in the park (fig. 102). She likely contributed more than this, given the prevalence of concrete and sculptural features in the park's overall design and the credit she was given by the local press as one of two "key planners" behind the project's "fresh thinking and new ideas."[70] However, the bears alone were a tribute to Green's materials expertise and creative ability. They survived changing safety standards, park vandalism, hard use, periodic renovations, and evolving tastes to entertain park users sixty years later.

By the time Mitchell Park opened in 1957, Virginia Green had moved on as an artist and sculptor to a fresh field of endeavor years earlier. Her model-making business had already proven its lucrative potential, and she had taken on major signature projects like the Crown Zellerbach building and Stanford University's campus. Such was the speed of architectural model-making compared with the slow pace of design and construction in the real world. Green had found a profession that would enable her to experiment with the sculptural possibilities of materials for the rest of her career. She began modestly in 1952 by building models on her coffee table with cardboard walls and "landscapes" of dried weeds from her garden. Several of the architects she met in San Francisco "suggested there was a promising field" in making presentation models; she charged $3 an hour. Green remembered "slim pickings" at first and several years of trying to convince others that she could produce precise and elegant scale models "to show clients how development projects would look." It was generally "hard to instill confidence in architects" that an outside firm could efficiently produce superior results and that it would be worth paying a high price for this service.[71] Yet soon she had forged connections to the most prestigious San Francisco firms, which would themselves soon secure the city's largest commissions. Two of her early architect-patrons were Chuck Bassett (SOM's chief designer) and William Wurster.[72] Once she established the value of her skills to architects, the model-making business took off and began to sell itself.[73]

102 Virginia Green's 1950s Mitchell Park bears were part of an admired regional park in Palo Alto designed by Robert Royston's landscape architecture firm. In addition to the playground sculpture, Green received credit for contributing to the larger park's planning. By the time Mitchell Park opened in 1957, Green's architectural model-making business had taken off, becoming the main vehicle for her professional interests in landscape, design, and public art.

Another Bay Area model-making company, Workshop Models, had helped pave the way for Green's business by proving the demand for this expertise in the late 1940s. Anne Luckhart had established the company in 1947 while an architecture student at the University of California at Berkeley, at the suggestion of another student. Luckhart had arrived in the United States from Canada with her husband in 1938 at the age of twenty-four, and by 1945 on one of her border crossings she called herself a draftswoman. When the model business grew, she brought in her husband, Chalmers Luckhart, who had tired of his job as a radio announcer. During busy stretches the Luckharts hired their artist-neighbors, a potter and a painter. Anne Luckhart was the "boss." Their company produced low-cost "sketch models" costing less than $100 for ordinary home builders, and they also worked for architects and institutional clients (fig. 103). Their larger projects included a $3,000 model of the Sunset Community Center for Wurster, Bernardi & Emmons in 1951 and a $6,000 model of the Stanford Medical Center, which took more than a thousand hours to construct. Because Wurster, Bernardi & Emmons and Stanford were both early clients for AMI, it is likely that the latter benefited when the Luckharts closed Workshop Models and opened a home and garden store in Berkeley in 1959.[74]

By 1961, AMI had become the largest model-making firm in the Western United States and was one of the two largest in the country. Their volume of work was doubling annually; Green and Johnston incorporated the business and applied for the patent for their topographical machine. Between 1961 and 1964, their staff grew from ten to seventeen and they moved from a smaller workshop in the South of Market neighborhood at 444 Clementina Street to an 11,000-square-foot plant at 363 Brannan Street, a mile away (fig. 104). One reporter described their "building business" as "one of the largest and most unusual in the country."[75] In 1961, recent work included models for the Golden Gateway competition, the Pacific Development plan at Sacramento, the "Spokane 1980" master plan, the University of Alaska, the University of California at Santa Cruz, Stanford University, Creighton University, and "numerous big business buildings."[76] Most models took between two and six weeks to complete, with clients paying up to $50,000. The largest projects required many months. By 1967 the staff produced hundreds of models annually. Oakland's Coliseum complex, the Capital Mall Master Plan in Washington, D.C., the Hawaii state capitol, "and a few thousand more architectural odds and ends" all first took shape at AMI. By 1972 the firm had grown again, to a staff of thirty.[77]

During the 1960s, Green and Johnston paced the industry with high-quality work, influential contacts among architects, patented and time-saving contour equipment, ingenuity with materials, and high-energy entrepreneurship (fig. 105}. They found that once AMI was established it did not need aggressive sales machinery or much of a front office. Their reputation within a tight industry, supplemented by their detailed brochures, kept the model-makers scrambling as one large-scale project after another transformed the city. International developers working in California helped spread AMI's reputation around the world. They conveyed this intensity to one reporter, who wrote: "The shop is their all-consuming interest, for neither Miss Green nor Miss Johnston is married and with business the way it is, about every waking hour is tied up on the job." Their attention to detail was legendary. To get the red-brown color right for the hills portrayed in their model of the Oroville Dam, planned for the Feather River in California's Sierra Nevada foothills, "the model-makers hiked up to the dam site, dug up soil, and put it through a meatgrinder" before applying it directly to the model. Demand for their firm's tiny trees and other fixtures spurred them to create a "Sears and Roebuck"–type catalogue to sell their line of supplies to architects, planners, and other model-makers.[78]

Green and Johnston led a dynamic workshop staffed by men and women who were "sculptors, artists and architects in their own right," said Johnston. They also came from theater, film, and writing fields. One newspaper feature described the owners as "former school teachers with an insatiable craving for creativity." Another saw Green in 1964 as "a small graying energetic woman who tripped around the huge room in sweater, slacks, and red sneakers."[79] Some of that playfulness came across in a group photo taken for the 1967 AMI brochure. Virginia Green knelt closest to the camera, and shop manager John Seaver stood above, surrounded by employees and at least one client (fig. 106). Johnston and Imai were out meeting with a client and missed the photo. The caption read, "The picture is of technique, ingenuity, art—the master craftsmen who make Architectural Models, Inc., work. And work better than any other concern of its kind."[80] Other AMI employees eventually founded their own model businesses, on more amicable terms than Nusbaum and Neklason. Noel Gregorian, who trained Imai,

103 A 1950 *Chronicle* feature story on Anne and Chalmers Luckhart's model-making business. Anne Luckhart, a "draftswoman" who had attended architecture school at the University of Califonia, Berkeley in the 1940s was "the boss." The Luckharts' company, Workshop Models, had several of the same clients as Green and Johnston, who picked up the Luckharts' momentum when Workshop Models closed in the late 1950s.

Model photos by Ernest Braun: Luckhart photo by Jim Morley
"THE BOSS" builds up a roof while her husband-apprentice uses a glue-gun to put finishing touches on a tract house to be used for sales purposes.

104 A photographer visiting Architectural Models Inc. for images to use with Donald Canter's May 22, 1967, *Examiner* article "Big Little Builders: Model Businesswomen" captured this overview of the workshop floor and the expansive, light industrial space.

went out on his own, as did Kathleen Seyfarth, who made her name in model trees (fig. 107).[81] At Johnston's initiative, in 1970 the firm shifted to a four-day, thirty-six-hour week. That provided breaks from "strenuous" work but also, as Canter reported, "allows her crews of artists and artisans time to pursue their own artistic careers over three-day weekends."[82]

One of Green and Johnston's favorite models was one they made of their own Mill Valley home in Marin County. The "Green-Johnston house" offers an illuminating residential counterpoint to the couple's San Francisco business designing models of skyscrapers, renewal projects, and university campuses (figs. 108 and 109).[83] Their AIA award–winning modern home, completed in July 1961, was designed by architects Claude Stoller and Robert Marquis and landscape architect Robert Royston (with whom Green had worked on Mitchell Park). Architectural photographer Ezra Stoller, Claude Stoller's brother, produced the AIA nomination photographs. The impressive home reflected their financial and professional success, embodying the fact that two women sculptors had focused their talents to create a lucrative new business with design

Masters of Miniature

They Think Big, Build Small

JUL 29 1964

By MILDRED SCHROEDER

Two refugees from school teaching, who paused to pick up master's degrees in sculpture, now operate their own building business that has become one of the largest and most unusual in the country.

It's Architectural Models, Inc., which expanded from a coffee table site in an Arguello St. apartment to a spacious 11,000 square foot plant on Brannan St.

Here Virginia Green, president, and Leila Johnston, s e c r e t ary-treasurer, head a staff of 17 who turn architects' blueprints into t h r e e-dimensional miniatures true in scale, color, texture, e v e n to the petunias in the window boxes.

Their models have been shipped off to job sites from Iraq to Australia and at any minute they will be constructing and landscaping replicas of projected apartment houses, subdivisions, college campuses, industrial plants, banks, hospitals, libraries.

Miss Green, a small graying energetic woman who tripped around the huge room in sweater, slacks and red s n e a k e r s, was reared h e r e, graduated from San Francisco State College and taught for six years.

"I had always been interested in sculpture and I was tired of teaching so I went to the University of O r e g o n for master of fine arts in sculpture," she explained. She did some abstract bears, the kind children climb on, for a Palo Alto playground and was between projects in 1952 when an architect

—Examiner photo by Bob Bryant

VIRGINIA GREEN, LEFT, LEILA JOHNSTON
With landscaping ready for Stanislaus College model

asked her to build some models for him.

She still shudders when she thinks about her first efforts "but that architect is still one of our clients."

Miss J o h n s t o n, from Spokane w h e r e she had taught art, had a non-teaching urge about the same time and also enrolled at Oregon for her master's. The two w o m e n met in graduate school and after receiving her degree, Miss Johnston took a museum job in San Francisco.

When the model business expanded off the coffee table and was big enough to support two people, she became a partner in 1955. Now neither one has time for sculpture.

Model - m a k i n g starts when the f i r m receives the architect's drawings and holds conferences with professional teams involved in the site, buildings, land-

scaping.

Land contours are reproduced in plastic foam, and nimble fingered employes skillfully construct buildings. An entire landscaping department creates all kinds of t r e e s, shrubs, flower gardens, plots of grass for the varied architectural demands.

In f r o m two to eight weeks a miniature of a multi-million dollar development is r e a d y. The Crown-Zellerbach, J o h n Hancock, Bethlehem Steel buildings all took three-dimensional shape first at Architectural Models, Inc.

One of t h e i r favorite models was the one they made of their own Mill Valley house, designed by architects M a r q u i s and Stoller and winner of a national American Institute of Architects award and a Homes and Better Living award.

---

105 Virginia Green and Leila Johnston leaned forward with the tools of their trade and a pleasant, businesslike demeanor (similar to their stance in fig. 97). Demand for their expert model furnishings such as trees, cars, and people inspired them to start a separate business supplying other model-makers and industries.

106 The employees of Architectural Models Inc. included artists and several architects, many of whom later founded their own model-making businesses. Green is kneeling, closest to the camera.

products commanding fees in the tens of thousands of dollars. Artists often craved a home built around their work space, the *Chronicle* noted. "Usually the financial status of most creative people prevents this desire from every [*sic*] reaching fruition, but when someone is fortunate enough to accomplish it, the result can be a joy to behold."[84] The house cost more than $50,000 to build.[85]

The home also interwove Green and Johnston's circles of architect friends with their personal and professional lives and elevated their identity as creative artists. Claude Stoller remembered his reaction to the commission: "When Va&L came to us to design their house we were delighted. What a chance to work with friends who were sophisticated and appreciative of good design!" Stoller knew the town and the site. He lived in Mill Valley, which had a population of about 12,000, and served on the Mill Valley Planning Commission for several years. The steep site offered stunning views, including of the bay. Carved from a former estate, the parcel had beautiful oaks and redwoods. Stoller had experience with the hazards and rewards of fitting designs to such a steep slope.[86] Royston also lived in Mill Valley, benefiting from Marin's concentration of artists and

107 "Tree Mentor" Alice Henderson, Architectural Models Inc. workshop, 1967.

108 Model of the Green-Johnston house, left, including a second "Little Green" house to the right, which Claude Stoller designed for a retired couple—Virginia Green's parents. Virginia Green's father, Eliot Green, required work space for making precision medical instruments, just as Virginia and Leila requested a workshop. The architects included this photograph (cropped closer to the buildings for greater realism) in publicity to promote the design during the year of planning and construction.

109 This close-up of the model appears even more realistic than the distance shots, demonstrating the talent involved in crafting the models, as well as Gerald Ratto's photographic choices in lighting and perspective.

architects. When Green and Johnston gave him the landscape commission it reinforced the continuity from Green's public sculpture days to her model-making business with Johnston and on to their status as patrons of cutting-edge modern architecture.

When their home received a prestigious Award of Merit in the 1963 AIA Honor Awards, it catapulted Green and Johnston into elite modernist design circles and thereby demonstrated the utility of residential suburban commissions to AMI's downtown renewal work (figs. 110 and 111). Selected out of 411 submissions, the Green-Johnston house shared the honor with Eero Saarinen and Associates' Trans World Airlines Terminal Building at Idlewild Airport. The jury stated that "The over-all standard of excellence was unusually high." This was not platitudinous, given the stinging reprimand issued by the previous year's jury against the state of the architecture field.[87] A year later in the custom-built category of the Homes for Better Living competition, Green and Johnston's home was among three chosen for top honors out of 211 submissions. All three winners in this national pool were from California, as were half of the entries. The jury singled out the home's "three levels of airy space tied strongly to a steep site" and admired how it was "split three ways" to take advantage of views. The spaces flowed smoothly, and the interior was "visually unified." The mid-level living room opened to the upper-level kitchen/dining area/entry and to the studio space below. Decks and bridges fit the building to the slope and helped "minimize disturbance" of the land.[88] Green and Johnston made use of the 1950s links between the residential and commercial design worlds, as had Caree and Stuart Rose and Larry Halprin.[89]

Claude Stoller attributed his award-winning "open" design for the Green-Johnston house to the clients. Because the house and studio were "designed for two lady artists" and were intended "for adults only, a plan with the three major spaces partially open to each other was possible."[90] Stoller explained: "Since there are no children, synonymous in my mind with major privacy problems, it was possible to dramatize this interlocking space by leaving the area between entry and dining floor and living room floor open so that this relationship is apparent." A reviewer noted that the dramatic siting on a steep slope benefited from ignoring "the safety of small children." The home's flowing interior and openness to the outdoors marked it as antithetical to the prevalent enclosing and enveloping suburban designs for growing families.[91] Green and Johnston had explicitly asked Stoller to prioritize a large living room, studio, and outdoor spaces; they enjoyed entertaining and disliked housework. The lower-level studio enabled them to pursue the "creative disorder" of sculpture, crafts, and model-making (figs. 112 and 113).[92] The lofty living room flowing onto the main outdoor deck also met these client priorities. The small kitchen and bedrooms were of little interest to the press (see figs. 110 and 111). *Progressive Architecture* complimented this example of the "very personal and intense exchange of ideas between architects and their house clients which often results in the most imaginative architectural solution."[93]

110 Virginia Green and Leila Johnston's 1960-61 Mill Valley home designed by Claude Stoller won a prestigious 1963 Award of Merit in the 1963 AIA Honor Awards, a distinction it shared with Eero Saarinen's Trans World Airlines terminal building at Idlewild (now JFK) International Airport. The open railings visible on the right were one example of why the house was considered unsafe for children. Photographed May 1, 1962.

111 Architect Claude Stoller said that the open levels of the Green-Johnston house were inspired by the fact that the two clients ("lady artists") had no children. Openness to the outdoors and the spacious living room were the requests of clients who enjoyed entertaining but not housekeeping. Accordingly, the compact kitchen and dining area behind the fireplace were of less interest. The concrete aggregate hearth was likely Green's contribution. Photographed May 1, 1962.

Considering that Green and Johnston were "refugees from school teaching" who had received sculpture MFAs in 1950, their fabulous AIA award–winning 1961 home in Mill Valley spoke to the speed with which the women professionally and socially established themselves in Bay Area design. Simultaneously they were successful business-women, artists, and patrons of significant modern architecture. Claude Stoller remembered: "We were together in a circle of friends allied in the design professions and arts in the Bay Area and met not infrequently at parties and gatherings of one sort or another. We tended to be more or less to the left of what was the political center at any particular moment. Modern Architecture, design, and modern art in general including painting, sculpture, weaving, pottery, dance, theater, photography, etc. was our passion."[94] For Stoller, the presence of several same-sex couples in this group was unremarkable. [95] Johnston's job as a registrar at the San Francisco Museum of Art beginning in 1950 accelerated their introductions to Bay Area artists. Johnston and Green also benefited from specific programs in early 1950s San Francisco that supported the collaboration of artists in civic design and city planning. Both participated in a July 1952 design workshop at the California School of Fine Arts, cosponsored by the AIA and Artists

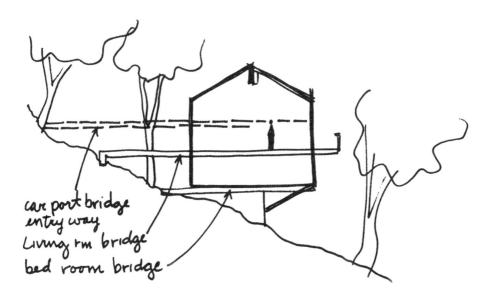

care port bridge
entry way
Living rm bridge
bed room bridge

112 Claude Stoller's elevation drawing of the Green-Johnston house shows the three levels of bridges and decks. The house left the hillside relatively undisturbed. Whereas the Roses fit the hill to the house, Stoller fit the house to the hill.

113 Contrary to the period's suburban emphasis on domestic life and children, Green and Johnston underscored their studio and entertainment spaces. The two women requested a large lower-level artists' studio. This perspective captures the openness to the home's middle level and the studio's high ceilings. Down the corridor are two small, low-ceilinged bedrooms, which went unnoticed compared to the work space and living room. Directly behind where the photographer was standing are floor-to-ceiling windows and a door leading to a patio shaded by the deck above. Photographed May 1, 1962.

Equity Association.[96] Their exhibition entry with architect Mario Gaidano and others—a "sumptuous, stylish restaurant and bar"—laid foundations for Gaidano's hiring of Green the following year to construct a model of a San Francisco apartment.[97] Once Green and Johnston established themselves in Mill Valley in 1961, they regularly entertained designer friends and colleagues and occasionally hosted gatherings for AMI staff.[98]

By 1970, Virginia Green and Leila Johnston had stepped back from making models and concentrated on running the business. In 1976 they turned the firm over to their hand-picked successor, Calvin Imai, who had worked for them for ten years. The couple retained ownership of their profitable, high-volume model supply business but left its day-to-day management to others. When Imai asked Johnston why they chose to approach him rather than the other employees about buying AMI, she told him it was because of his "love" for model-making.[99] Over the next decades, Imai guided the firm through the construction industry's ups and downs as the yellow pages listings of model-making companies cycled drastically. Individual firms like AMI persisted but periodically hired and fired staff. In 2014 Cal Imai reluctantly retired and closed the company after more than sixty years. Still, in the early twenty-first century, many of the leading architectural scale-model practitioners can trace their origins to Virginia Green and Leila Johnston's shop.[100]

VISUALIZING EMBARCADERO CENTER

On February 14, 1967, Embarcadero Center's designs were unveiled at the San Francisco Museum of Art and AMI's model of the waterfront urban renewal district occupied center stage (fig. 114). The model illustrated how residential Golden Gateway and commercial Embarcadero Center together cemented a new high-rise identity for the blocks west and north of the Ferry Building. Large black-and-white reproductions of Helmut Jacoby's perspective drawings, some 10 feet high, ringed the walls at the museum. Hundreds of glossy 8-by-10-inch photographs of the model and renderings were distributed. The developers' press release explained that the museum "setting was selected in view of the unprecedented attention that will be paid to the arts in the planned center."[101] Other promotional materials played this up: "Reflecting strong personal interest in art on the part of the developers, Embarcadero Center will become a home for sculpture and art to an extent never before accomplished in any one center anywhere. By agreement with San Francisco Redevelopment Agency, one percent of the total building investment is to be spent on art." The landscaped open spaces, plazas, sculpture, bridges, and pedestrian life would make the Center "a gracefully conceived, parklike addition to San Francisco's financial district."[102]

The "reveal" on February 14 concerned the center's design and its impact on the neighborhood, the skyline, and views within San Francisco; since Justin Herman and the SFRA had selected the investors for the $125 million project a year earlier, there was little mystery in the financial backing. The March 1966 SFRA announcement of the winning partners had named Texas developer Trammell Crow, Atlanta architect John Portman, and contractor Cloyce Box, director of the George A. Fuller Company. Shortly thereafter David Rockefeller joined the venture as lead investor in purchasing and

114 The architectural model of the proposed Embarcadero Center design by John Portman, unveiled on February 14, 1967. Cal Imai worked on this model with two other Architectural Models Inc. employees for nine months. Embarcadero Center included the four slim buildings centered in the photo and the unusually angled hotel to their left. The Golden Gateway complex and Alcoa building hold the front right sector of photograph, to the right of the highway entry ramps. The Ferry Building and ill-fated double-decked Embarcadero Freeway occupy the lower left. At the back right is the 52-story Bank of America headquarters, which was under construction and destined to be the city's tallest building (until the Transamerica Pyramid). The tallest proposed Embarcadero Center tower, on the left, would have risen 60 stories, disregarding the neighborhood's 25-story height limit. The model was photographed from many angles to make different points. According to Cal Imai, the model-makers had signed the bottom of the model and hidden tiny handmade sculptures inside the hollow buildings (see fig. 116).

developing the 8.5 acres of land.[103] A gauntlet of hearings and approvals loomed for Embarcadero Center, with variances required for height limits, zoning, setbacks, traffic, and street closings. Critics worried that San Francisco leaders would not give the design a meaningful review because of their outsized gratitude to the developers for the investment promise and their reverence for David Rockefeller. *Chronicle* writer Alan Temko said as much in his articles and at hearings, but he also sent scathing private letters to Rockefeller's architectural advisor (and cousin), Nelson Aldrich. Temko condemned San Francisco's city officials for their "provincial goggling." He wrote, "These pathetic little municipal politicians will not presume to be even mildly critical of a project with such powerful backing." San Francisco's new director of city planning, Allan Jacobs, had suggested judicious design modifications but was shut out by his own planning commission, Temko said.[104]

John Portman's Embarcadero Center plan in fact launched a tumultuous public debate about urban design that ebbed and flowed through the rest of the decade, critiquing the height and length of the project's buildings, its open spaces, architectural merit, public art, overall urban plan, and the elite walling off of San Francisco's waterfront from the people (fig. 115). Business and labor organizations supported the project and were happy to leave design questions to relevant municipal committees. After all, Embarcadero Center promised "9,000 man-years" of construction employment and advanced the city's aspiration to be the "Wall Street of the West."[105] The most aggressive disapproval came from San Francisco architects and planners and from organized citizens fighting Manhattanization. Two of the center's skyscrapers drastically exceeded the parcel's 25-story limit, and one would have become San Francisco's tallest building. The investors argued that 60-story and 46-story towers would make the project economically feasible and enable them to provide open space for the public. A third office building adhered precisely to the height limit but extended an unprecedented two blocks long, while the 16-story Hyatt would be the city's largest hotel. The slender slices of Embarcadero Center's towers contrasted favorably with the blocky rectangles recently sprouting in San Francisco. However, because the center's "old-fangled architecture" bore a resemblance to midtown Manhattan's 1930s Rockefeller Center, it seemed to simultaneously gesture back in time and kneel in deference to the outsider Rockefeller name.[106]

The February 1967 public unveiling of the Embarcadero Center model flushed hidden frictions with Golden Gateway into the open, despite Rockefeller's wishes and the SFRA's efforts "to resolve problems outside of the public arena" and "present a unified front" after meeting "quietly."[107] Indeed much of the resistance to Portman's designs originated from the developers of the adjacent Golden Gateway and from the local design community, which resented the "outsiders" involved in the project.[108] The press anticipated an impending "showdown" between Golden Gateway and Embarcadero Center. This design battle essentially pitted the same urban renewal project's first- and second-phase developers and architects against one another, with each party purchasing large parcels of urban renewal land from the city—although of course Golden Gateway had arrived first and negotiated its own deals.[109] Architect Donn Emmons of Golden Gateway's WB&E team exemplified the hard-edged "attack." Besides lamenting the "impenetrable barrier" of Embarcadero Center's two-block office building and the excessive 60-story tower, he said the hotel faced "the wrong way" and the design failed to effectively integrate the new renewal project with Golden Gateway.[110]

Several of the city's leading designers used the model and the renderings to assail Embarcadero Center as a planning "disaster," to quote architect Charles Bassett's testimony from a May 8, 1967, hearing. Bassett was a partner in SOM, which had hoped to be given Portman's job at this remarkable renewal site and still hoped Portman could be dislodged. SOM had designed the distinctive Alcoa tower on the intermediate renewal parcel that bridged the two major sites, Golden Gateway and Embarcadero Center. Bassett objected to "the almost indecent haste with which this thing has been jammed through." SOM's criticism was not architectural, he told the Board of Supervisors. Pointing to the model, Bassett said, "If you take these buildings and place them individually on a table, they look perfectly reasonable to us and are none of our business." Yet together, they disrupted the relationships among buildings and the entire downtown context. Bassett believed that the city should withhold approvals until planning director Jacobs could negotiate a better design solution with the developers. The Board of

This is the Golden Gateway viewed from the northern end of the Embarcadero Freeway. It presents a solid front of construction which offers its designers little cause for complaining about the rising of a "Chinese Wall" in other parts of the redeveloped area.

The Imaginative Embarcadero Center

115 Clippings saved in David Rockefeller's files tracked the Bay Area debates over the urban design implications of Embarcadero Center. This April 1967 photograph in the *San Francisco Chronicle* supported the recently unveiled Embarcadero Center designs by making the case that the Golden Gateway, the first phase of this urban renewal project, had already established an impenetrable wall. Thus the projected Embarcadero Center towers, although far exceeding existing height limits, would do little additional harm. Golden Gateway's architects thus had "little cause for complaining," although the design controversy received a great deal of press attention. While defending Embarcadero Center, the article still underscored that both upscale renewal projects cut the city off from its waterfront.

Supervisors upheld the project unanimously, but Bassett's comment that Portman "hasn't the slightest idea of what he is in for the next eight years" sounded to Rockefeller and Portman like a threat.[111] Rockefeller's advisor Aldrich knew that architectural criticism easily became personal and worried about the impact of Temko's tough front-page *Chronicle* reviews in early May of 1967. Temko won Aldrich over to endorsing some of his critiques. Aldrich balanced urban design as a "public good" against the designers' ego and the potential for their "private humiliation" if design changes ensued, but Temko responded: "These things can be done with tact, decency, and even psychological inventiveness that could persuade an admittedly proud man that it was his own idea to get some distinguished help in order to achieve a 'richer' or 'broader' design." Temko was more concerned about architect Portman's ongoing financial interest in the design as an investing partner.[112] The initially defensive developers did eventually make concessions by modifying the tower heights and "wall" effect (fig. 116).

The Embarcadero Center review process revealed that even leading architects depended on models and renderings to grasp the scope and impact of large-scale urban renewal. Architect Pietro Belluschi, who chaired the SFRA Advisory Committee, opened his February 14, 1967 commentary by explaining, "Unfortunately, we did not have the advantage of examining the excellent model and the brilliant renderings which are on display today. If we had, it would certainly have been easier for us to

116 Celebratory postcard of April 1970, "Topping-Off" Ceremony for the first Embarcadero Center tower, the Security Pacific National Bank (SPNB) building. Signing a 20-foot beam that will be hoisted to the top of the tower are, from left to right, Justin Herman, Carl Schieck of SPNB, Dianne Feinstein (president of the San Francisco Board of Supervisors), and Gar Davidson. Davidson was the investors' local representative, charged with easing the outsiders' entry into the Bay Area.

evaluate more accurately the architect's intentions." One could extrapolate to imagine how heavily citizens and politicians relied on visualization tools to interpret urban design if accomplished architects required them. The advisory committee acknowledged that "at first we were overwhelmed by the volume of buildings," but then accepted that towers made the project "financially viable." Ultimately, "the architects by their skillful renderings have given us an exciting vision" depicting "a shining example of the enormous opportunities which an intelligently administered Urban Renewal can offer." This large project could have "destroyed all human amenities." Instead, the committee concluded that the shops and "cascading" stairways between levels mitigated the center's "forbidding quality." Belluschi predicted that the mall's open-air pedestrian spaces and arts investment would be "the test and symbol of the project's success," much as public spaces had worked for Rockefeller Center.[113]

In giving Jacoby the Embarcadero Center commission, John Portman told him that "nothing would explain the impact of the new structures on their environment better than a realistic eye-level perspective." Tellingly, he left the selection of views and the perspectives within each view entirely to Jacoby.[114] Portman knew that words had limited power to convince San Franciscans that his designs had addressed the feared negative environmental effects imposed by the complex's height and bulk. He could testify in writing that the center preserved the city's east–west views because "the lines of sight for viewers high on the hills will tend to 'slide over' the Center's buildings, toward the Bay. North–south views within the Center will be preserved through sharply etched breaks in the structures."[115] But he wisely bet on effective visualizations to support such assertions. Portman visited Jacoby in New York and arranged an intensive immersion to prepare him for the assignment. Portman flew Jacoby to Atlanta to acquaint him with his previous work and review the Embarcadero Center plans. Then Jacoby traveled to San Francisco "so that the unique atmosphere of the city, and the site's unusual location, could be fully understood." There the renderer met with "participating agencies and individuals," studied the site and scale model, and took photographs. Jacoby settled upon five interrelated drawings that were "intended to be continuous" as one moved through the complex. Regarding the pedestrian terrace two stories above street level, he explained that the slender "towers are recessed and do not impose on pedestrians in the adjoining streets." Cutouts in the elevation provided "unhindered views" across the site, while openings in the terrace to the lower levels introduced sunlight as well as distant perspectives. The light-colored concrete "further contributed in the effort to avoid massiveness." Jacoby's renderings embellished Portman's strategies to minimize the center's environmental impact, relate new buildings to existing streets and the pedestrian experience, and preserve views. Jacoby had two months to complete the assignment (figs. 117–119).[116]

AMI's Embarcadero Center model—essentially a three-dimensional master plan—expressed the cumulative transformation of San Francisco by skyscrapers over the previous decade (see fig. 114). The AMI model, which took Cal Imai and three coworkers nine months to produce, represented a more collective and labor-intensive urban design undertaking than Jacoby's renderings. Researching planned demolitions

117 Helmut Jacoby's bird's-eye view of Embarcadero Center conveyed the "slender" towers, and packed in a great deal: the patterns of the raised terrace with shops and bridges, a close-up of the tower's ribs, the hotel and theaters, freeway, Ferry Building, the bay, and the Bay Bridge to Oakland. Jacoby explained that the architect had designed the high-rise towers so the Ferry Building tower would still be visible from the streets up the hill. Jacoby's station point needed to be close enough to convey the complex's detail. The Ferry Building's diminutive size in these plans made it the relic of San Francisco's past.

118 This third drawing in Helmut Jacoby's sequence of five Embarcadero Center renderings looked north from the heart of the complex toward its main entrance. According to Jacoby, it "features the pleasant, open quality of the space on the lower level" thanks to the cut-outs in the second-floor terrace. This rendering depicted the connection between towers and platform, as well as the signature floor tiling and the reflecting pool and fountain. One of the Golden Gateway apartment towers is visible in the background, through the "etched break" in the long office building. The diagonal direction of vision established two major vanishing points.

119 This street view of Embarcadero Center looks east along Sacramento Street toward the Bay Bridge. The drawing made the case that the 60-story tower would not negatively impact the pedestrian. In Jacoby's description, this rendering "impresses the relatively small scale of the two-story terrace upon the passerby. It clearly shows the setback of the office towers, which then appear distant over the landscaped edge of the platform." He gestured toward street vitality with three small stores and an entrance to the mall on the left. To the right, the back of an existing office building (100 California Street) shares the street with the proposed hotel further down the block.

and new construction, the model-makers knew as much as any San Francisco city planner how the old and new would coexist. Green and Johnston explained that their model illustrated how "the bygone focal point of San Francisco, its Ferry Building, will . . . stand as a diminutive testament to the magnitude of the Embarcadero Center." The model provided "insights into zoning and traffic issues" including height limits and street closures. The "slender, view-permitting" towers would contain nearly 3 million square feet of office space. "As in all models," Green and Johnston wrote, the Embarcadero Center model "puts a complex situation into one clear statement." The unveiled model instantly became a site for debating the city's past and future; its bird's-eye views allowed infinite perspectives of contested policy decisions.[117]

It is an intriguing fact that Embarcadero Center—a large-scale commercial renewal project whose planning was followed warily by critics for the center's impersonal character and inhuman scale—was also a favorite among architectural model-makers, who asserted their personal engagement with the model and its evolving role in the city's development. Although model-makers rarely signed their work, the designers signed this one—on the bottom, out of sight. Each time the center's plans were altered and the model went back to the shop for updating, the artists added their signatures. The individual makers also hid tiny handmade trinkets inside the model's hollow buildings. Cal Imai believed the small sculptures reflected the artists' love for their work and had the effect of transforming the model into a time capsule. For Imai, this was comparable to their leaving behind "individual parts of them." He could think of no other model that had elicited such idiosyncratic personalizing. Most models had a brief period of intense relevance and then disappeared. Embarcadero Center's large size, significance to the city, updating over decades, and continuous public display helped create camaraderie around the model among its makers.[118]

Cal Imai singled out the Embarcadero Center model as one of the most meaningful projects of his nearly six-decade career. It was his first, and it hooked him on the field. Imai had not intended to stay in the business when he joined AMI. With a bachelor's degree in architecture from Berkeley, in 1966 he had found the position with AMI by accident. He had just interviewed with the San Francisco office of SOM. One of AMI's owners, obviously at home in the SOM offices, plucked Imai's resume from the SOM application files. At least that was what Leila Johnston told Imai when she called him the next day to try to interest him in working for her. The challenges of model-making intrigued him. Imai accepted the offer, expecting to work for a while and then return to school for a master's degree in architecture. His first responsibility at AMI was converting construction blueprints into model drawings. Soon Johnston asked whether he wanted to begin hands-on model-making. The impact was immediate. "You couldn't drag me out of the shop," he remembered. He enjoyed the satisfaction of making something from scratch—cutting, scoring, assembling, and painting. He relished how the tiny pieces, hand-assembled, amounted to something much bigger and more beautiful than the sum of its parts. When the completed Embarcadero Center model was displayed in the developers' sales office in 1967, Imai invited his friends to come see it. His friends did not fully understand his pride; they had difficulty seeing that the model itself was a piece of sculpture and that the patient skill required for its crafting was remarkable. "This is it?" they asked.[119]

The Embarcadero Center urban renewal model in 1967, like the Golden Gateway competition models seven years earlier, embodied and channeled San Franciscans' debates and decisions over urban form and landscape. Theatricality in presentation and political decision-making over these models was the flip side of the collaborative, persuasive hidden business of model-making pioneered by Virginia Green and Leila Johnston. City planning director Allan Jacobs described his own frustrations in 1967 over John Portman's Embarcadero Center designs. Jacobs recalled, "We met at the San Francisco Museum of Art, around a model of the proposed project. Portman said that my opinion of his design was subjective and that he didn't see why he should have to be concerned with what I thought. My screaming reply—that as long as the project had to come before the planning department for my recommendation, he had goddamned well better be concerned with my opinion—was not considered friendly."[120]

The controversies over urban design became loud and public in the 1960s, and the shouting rose as the towers grew taller and more densely packed. When Bill Roth returned to San Francisco in 1969 after spending five years based in Washington, D.C., he found a "forest" of skyscrapers. Roth expressed concern that the expanding financial district threatened the environment and would "tip the peninsula and sink the city into the bay" unless curtailed and redirected by proactive municipal leadership and urban planning.[121] By the late 1960s waves of anti-high-rise mobilization met the announcement of certain skyscrapers and redevelopment proposals. Some projects, like Embarcadero Center and the Transamerica Pyramid, brokered modest design compromises and eventually found acceptance and even affection among San Franciscans. Other major plans were stopped by protests or lawsuits, such as North Waterfront Associates' San Francisco International Market Center and U.S. Steel's waterfront skyscraper located between the Ferry Building and the Bay Bridge.

When Embarcadero Center's developers signed a purchase agreement for 8.5 prime waterfront acres for $11.572 million in May 1966, the *Examiner* proclaimed it "the largest sale of unimproved land in San Francisco's history."[122] Silence greeted the news. Whereas design controversies plagued Embarcadero Center for years, the land sale provoked little discussion. The land from the first phase of Urban Renewal Project Area E-1, the 19.7 acres known as the residential Golden Gateway Center, were sold to Perini–San Francisco Associates for $8.45 per square foot based on their 1960 purchase option. The joint venture group behind the commercial Embarcadero Center phase paid $31 per square foot in 1966 for their 8.5 acres. In each case, when the city and the developer signed an Agreement for Disposition of Land for Private Development, it highlighted the core purpose of Title I policy—to sell government-assembled and -subsidized land to private investors.[123]

Investors such as the David Rockefeller/John Portman/Trammell Crow/Cloyce Box team understood precisely the likely windfall in land, despite the city's ongoing hand-wringing about downtown decline, population loss, and concerns about being able to lure private redevelopers for slum clearance. As they were finalizing the May 1966 purchase agreement, Trammell Crow told his Rockefeller partners that "Mutual

Benefit Life Insurance has bought one of the non-project parcels adjacent to the project property" to construct an office building. They "paid in excess of $100 a foot for the land." Two years later, Embarcadero Center's financial projections noted that "this property could conservatively be appraised *today* at a value of $125/sq. ft." The summary underscored that the price of $31 per square foot was "fixed with no escalation or price adjustment of any kind." For example, Embarcadero Center had until December 31, 1974, to buy the block for the final office tower at the price of $31 per square foot. Although these prices for urban renewal land in the 1960s raised little public interest, when their "bargain basement" terms continued to apply in the 1970s, they did become contested.[124]

Grady Clay, the close observer of San Francisco redevelopment, had predicted in 1960 that urban design concepts would increasingly influence city competitions for land, particularly urban renewal parcels. Because politicians, city bureaucrats, redevelopment officials, and the general public had scant basis for understanding design, architectural models would become more important in making these rebuilding decisions. Of course design had significance on its own terms, but from the perspective of postwar urban rebuilding, it mattered most to the mechanisms of land redistribution, Clay thought. It was also obvious to him, as a real estate writer familiar with land markets across the nation, that San Francisco's downtown redevelopment sites would be supremely desirable to investors. When in 1960 Clay emphasized how the visualization professions helped broker land descisions, however, he never imagined how completely the disagreements over landscape, space, and design would eclipse the sale of land in the public eye.

"The Competition for Urban Land"
Grady Clay's Lost 1962 Manuscript

THE GOLDEN GATEWAY

This chapter returns to the most familiar writing about redevelopment, namely, to the tradition of 1950s and 1960s urban criticism that produced Jane Jacobs's *Death and Life*, but it does so from an unfamiliar angle. Grady Clay began this journey on much the same page as Jacobs. But his 1962 manuscript about San Francisco, "The Competitors: A Study of the Competition for Urban Land," languished for reasons that will be explored here. Clay joined a contemporary wave of fresh urban criticism as philanthropic foundations, universities, and professional design journals sought writers who could critique large-scale redevelopment. Grady Clay's uneven experience with foundations and universities highlighted that the relative roles of newspaper journalists, academic scholars, and architectural critics in launching the new critiques were contested. His manuscript's disappearance also left a lasting gap in 1960s urban criticism; in particular, other viewpoints elevating responsible public land stewardship lost the amplification they might have gained by being aligned with a publication such as Clay's. His career as a writer and editor in landscape studies took off, but the manuscript on land vanished.

First and foremost, Clay saw urban renewal as a land problem. The federal Title I rebuilding programs of the Housing Acts of 1949 and 1954 had intervened in real estate markets with unknown consequences. Clay was especially concerned about the disposition of large redevelopment parcels assembled through eminent domain. By 1961, Clay had mapped out his challenge to the prevailing practice of selling (rather than leasing) renewal parcels. In 1964 he wrote succinctly: "The moment of climax is the sale of land. Here the fate of the new neighborhood is decided, the developer is chosen." But Clay also observed redevelopment's much broader impact on urban real estate beyond project boundaries. "Urban renewal has come to influence the amount, location and price of much land brought into the market in most large U.S. cities, and in many small towns," he argued. He zeroed in on the fact that cities increasingly "injected" subjective design factors into decisions about redistributing land. In place of long-standing practices of selling land to the highest bidder, Clay explained, now competitions "mixed dollars and design." Architect-developer teams submitted proposals in far-flung corners of the nation, with redevelopment authorities basing their selections at least as much on competitors' urban design visions as on their willingness to pay. These relatively new concerns about urban renewal, then, were manifestations of the defining issue in the history of cities—the competition for land.[1]

Rather than judge redevelopment, Clay chose the pragmatic goal of improving the urban renewal process to yield better projects, addressing the concrete options faced by districts that had already committed to clearance but still needed to formulate specific rebuilding plans. Clay offered steps that city administrators, business leaders, and citizens unschooled in architecture could take to integrate design choices into the economic competition for renewal land, with the goal of making renewal decisions more democratic and transparent. He tempered his optimism for better redevelopment results. "Competition cannot cure all the ailments of cities, nor can it remedy many of the built-in defects of present urban renewal practices," he wrote, "But it should enlarge the marketplace of ideas, expand the testing-ground for new ways of life, improve present methods of building cities, and improve the finished product." In the broadest sense, his book examined "a new technique for property development which couples art and economics, the public planner and private developer, the 'practical man' and the man of art. Out of these collisions recorded and projects examined should emerge a promising method for building a better urban environment." At the time, Clay wrote from two distinctly nonarchitectural perspectives—that of the real estate editor for the *Louisville Courier-Journal* and that of a new editor of *Landscape Architecture,* a magazine of the underdog design field. Clay also underscored two professions brought into the limelight and transformed by postwar renewal—public planning and private development.[2]

Clay believed that urban renewal competitions could give citizens more say over the changing form of their cities. He identified a lack of a "common understanding and language" about urban design. In a May 1960 address to the American Society of Planning Officials, Clay advised planners and journalists to use visualization strategies like models and renderings to explain urban design issues to the public. "These great hunks of physical environment hover around us," he noted, but urban form was hardly self-explanatory. Bureaucratic writing failed to "translate the planner's zoning envelopes, setback requirements and land-use regulations into the English language." Clay visited "planning offices around the United States, trying to understand what planners are doing to me and my environment. The ones with the clearest answers, it seems to me, had scale models." Rather than throw final designs at the public "as a fait accompli," planners and politicians should lay out the options and enlist citizen participation. "These choices, I think, ought in every instance to be illustrated graphically—with sketches, airviews, photomontages, scale models." The weakness of the written archive also favored visual approaches. "Even when policy shapes into action, there is an amazing lack of record-keeping," Clay told his audience.[3]

The goal of demystifying the redevelopment process motivated Clay to write a book, which in May 1960 he tentatively titled "Pressure Points in Urban Renewal Design" in a proposal for Ford Foundation funding. He had "in mind not so much a journalistic 'expose' as an exposure of the seldom-publicized pressure-points at which urban design is fixed," he wrote. "People keep asking me 'What can we do?,' as though they were helpless in the face of Great Forces totally beyond their control." Three case studies would show points where "both designer and interested citizen can exercise more influence." Clay's architect colleagues convinced him that they, too, learned about renewal projects when it was too late, only after redevelopment officials had committed to density, zoning, and other decisions that "poisoned" the outcome. Clay's list of possible cases was frankly vague: Louisville's Civic Center, San Francisco's Embarcadero Freeway, or perhaps Baltimore's Civic Center plan. Ford Foundation's Paul Ylvisaker wrote with the news that he would recommend the grant to his board, although he urged Clay to clarify his plans for specific cases.[4] Nonetheless, Clay's broad interests had taken shape. The Ford Foundation notified Clay over the summer that his grant had been approved, and that he would be hosted by the Joint Center for Urban Studies of MIT and Harvard University.[5]

As Clay settled into Cambridge, Massachusetts, for the Ford fellowship during the fall of 1960, news of an urban renewal competition gone awry in nearby Brookline provided the "aha" moment he had sought. His "reportorial instincts began twitching." Brookline's

Redevelopment Authority had designated "The Farm"—a former poor farm site now home to several hundred mostly Irish Catholic families—for clearance and redevelopment as affordable, mixed-income, higher-density apartment buildings. After digging into the complicated story, Clay came to see Brookline as the worst-case scenario in renewal competitions. At first the town's leadership was pleased with their surprising success in attracting nine proposals from substantial developer-architect teams. The dean of Harvard's Graduate School of Design, Josep Lluís Sert, agreed to chair the architectural advisory board. But soon the competition's promise was derailed by lawsuits and by complicated jurisdictional disputes between the City Council and elected redevelopment authority members.[6] "It was one of the most difficult competitions ever conducted," Clay told an Oklahoma City audience in 1963.[7] City officials, planners, and citizens lacked the skills and language to judge design. More to the point, how could cities weigh "nonmarket" design factors alongside economic projections? If one team bid millions of additional dollars for the land while a second offered a superior design, how should the city proceed?[8]

The Brookline story led Grady Clay to his manuscript's focus on San Francisco; more precisely, pursuing the impact of design competitions on the disposition of renewal land led him to Golden Gateway. If Brookline offered the worst-case scenario to Clay in 1960, San Francisco's Golden Gateway offered him the best.[9] In San Francisco, the Redevelopment Agency's new director, Justin Herman, used the competition to whip the city's lagging renewal machinery into shape. Herman orchestrated the influential design competition for the 19.7 waterfront acres cleared by relocating the city's wholesale produce market and removing a mix of waterfront commerce. The primarily residential Golden Gateway project comprised phase 1 of Urban Renewal Area E-1 in the city's redevelopment plans. Laying the groundwork for the competition, Herman traveled the country with Everett Griffin, chair of the Redevelopment Agency; they interviewed fifteen "creative" architects to gather ideas and seed interest. On the tour Herman heard "unsettling stories" about the Brookline competition and "was determined to avoid 'another Brookline,'" Clay wrote. Where Brookline's Architectural Advisory Committee had had to "commune" with the models and plans without guidance, San Francisco staged presentations by the investor-architect teams. Brookline's advisory committee had been unpaid. San Francisco's committee, comprised of eminent professionals (Mario Ciampi, Minoru Yamasaki, Lawrence B. Anderson, Louis I. Kahn, Henry S. Churchill, and Ferd Kramer) received daily compensation of $250 plus expenses.[10] Unlike in Brookline, San Francisco's deliberations were tape-recorded (and made available to Clay), and the Redevelopment Agency staff attended the proceedings. The "folklore" of the Golden Gateway competition was one of "spectacular success," which in turn attracted further investor interest.[11]

Clay homed in on a key issue regarding the "dollars" side of the redevelopment equation—a hardening bias in urban renewal policy toward cities selling rather than leasing land to private investors. He renamed his project "The Competitors: A Study of the Competition for Urban Land." Clay was impressed by Justin Herman's investigation of leasing options and other mechanisms for retaining city ownership of the Golden Gateway parcel or portions of it. Although Herman ultimately failed in these efforts, his attention to land stewardship helped rank Herman, in Clay's opinion, "as one of the first-rate men in the country on public purposes and policies for city development; potentially a good candidate to be Secretary of Urban Affairs if ever such a department is created." Unpacking the term "public planner," Clay examined what safeguarding the public's interest in redevelopment actually meant.[12]

The United Kingdom offered the counterpoint for Clay's analysis; there the government retained ownership of redevelopment sites. His research flagged a critical juncture in the United States when, at local, state, and federal policy levels, the door was still open to advocate for leasing urban renewal land to private investors. After Brookline and San Francisco, for his third and final case study Clay selected a recent competition to rebuild the Elephant and Castle commercial center in a still bomb-devastated central London neighborhood. State land ownership lowered entry barriers for developers to compete because they did not need the formidable cash required to purchase the land. As a result, Clay argued, the Elephant and Castle proposals (and British submissions generally) were more numerous, diverse, and creative than those in any U.S. competition. More than three hundred teams packed a September 1959 information session about the 3.2-acre London site. The planners received 35 bids, exceeding their "wildest dreams." The winning developer, the Willett Group, would own the buildings it constructed but lease the land from the London County Council. The winning architects, the Scottish firm of Paul Boussevain and Barbara Osmond (a married couple), combined an office block with a shopping center. They modeled the latter, one of Europe's first, partly on the new U.S. enclosed shopping malls such as Southdale Center near Minneapolis.[13]

Furthermore, a British planner could say what U.S. planners tiptoed around—namely, that selling urban renewal land to a private investor was "immoral." London County Council planning officer J. M. Hirsh told Clay, "We do not buy the land to hand it over to somebody else in small pieces, or to hand it over by competition in one big piece. It would be immoral for us to take land by compulsory purchase (condemnation) and hand it over [i.e. sell] to one man or one company." Leaseholds preserved the government's direct investment in projects and protected the public from deals that, over time, accrued excessive benefits to private buyers. Clay opened his London chapter by arguing: "This example suggests that the current prevailing practice in America of selling, rather than leasing, redeveloped land is open to question; and that the practice of leasing should be re-examined for greater use." And he closed with the same point: "It is high time for American cities to re-examine their present practice of selling off redeveloped land."[14] Clay could not have been more explicit about his agenda for revising the nation's urban renewal policy.

In identifying responsible land stewardship as the determinative factor in urban development, Grady Clay posed a fundamentally different moral question than Jane Jacobs had in her just-published book *The Death and Life of Great American Cities*. Like Jacobs, Clay feared the impact of top-down, clearance-based, monolithic, automobile-centered downtown renewal. He also worried about redevelopment's racial inequities. Because of the risks, he wrote in 1962, "I am sometimes tempted to join Jane Jacobs and say 'Damn the whole process,' the baby, the bath-water, and the municipal water system. But I have not done this."[15] Many cities had started down the path paved by eminent domain; as of December 1961, 25,000 acres were either cleared or in the clearance pipeline in the United States, overseen by 550 redevelopment agencies.[16] It was not too late to build better projects on those acres. "Whether urban renewal, as a technique for directing change is good or evil is a question to be debated elsewhere," Clay argued.[17] Debating the "good or evil" of the policy would not help cities already committed to it. City administrators needed concrete guidance in facing the damage and promise of redevelopment *now*, explaining Clay's sense of urgency. At stake were the largest parcels of urban land changing hands in modern memory.

Saying she rejected the premise of urban renewal, Jane Jacobs declined to serve on the Golden Gateway competition's Architectural Advisory Committee. Clay saw this as her missed opportunity to have a constructive, positive influence. The SFRA had "asked Mrs. Jane Jacobs, associate editor of *Architectural Forum*, then at home in Manhattan's Greenwich Village, writing a book. She refused, saying she didn't believe in that kind of redevelopment." Her subsequent 1961 book, Clay noted, indeed "made her point quite clearly." In contrast, Clay said, fearless critic Ferd Kramer, a Chicago real estate developer and the committee's "non-architect," used the advisory committee's platform to great effect. Golden Gateway's advisory committee influenced developer selection, weighed financial packages alongside the designs, and had a voice in setting policy priorities. Whatever Jacobs's beliefs, the land was already rubble. Even critics, *especially* critics, Clay thought, should have a role in the next round of decisions.[18]

Grady Clay shared Jane Jacobs's rare ability to navigate among architectural criticism, academic research, journalism, urban studies, foundations, and universities, such that reintroducing his lost 1962 manuscript captures a fuller portrait of urban criticism at this important juncture in the history of postwar redevelopment. In particular, it differentiates the impact of various writing genres during this ferment of new urban criticism. Clay, as a journalist and real estate editor, became entangled in and disadvantaged by others' debates over who should carry out the agenda of urban criticism—and what that agenda should be. Architectural criticism, mainstream newspaper columns, the alternative press, consulting reports, and publicity materials all shared the weight of printed texts, yet they lacked equal legitimacy. That is one reason that Clay's experience writing about renewal as a journalist working with scholars and philanthropic foundations, rather than as a scholar housed in a university or a writer of architectural criticism, is especially illuminating.

Clay focused on the limitations of words to interpret and shape a visual, material, built urban environment. Famously, Jane Jacobs did not offer visual evidence in *Death and Life:* "The scenes that illustrate this book are all about us," she wrote. "For illustrations, please look closely at real cities."[19] Clay made the case that understanding the visual materials portraying renewal—architectural models, renderings, and photographs— demanded analytical guidance, too. From his homes in Louisville, Kentucky, and Cambridge, Massachusetts, Grady Clay wrote about the interlocking of urban renewal and urban design in San Francisco, Brookline, and London. These were different touchstones from Greenwich Village and New York City and yielded different questions of morality, methods, and lines of analysis.

"NO LITTLE MUMFORDS": THE PLIGHT OF THE URBAN CRITIC

Clay was one of many writers, editors, scholars, and foundation leaders who lamented the absence of new ideas in urban development. Behind the scenes in the 1950s and 1960s, the field of urban criticism percolated with writers hoping to influence renewal strategies for the better. While pleased with Jane Jacobs's breakthrough in bringing vital commentary to a broad public, leadership from philanthropic foundations, universities, and professional journals continued to seed publications by other writers motivated to fill the voids in urban analysis. In 1961 no one could have anticipated the lasting power of Jacobs's framework or how it would crowd out other authors. Influential figures cultivating new talents in urban criticism included Chad Gilpatric and Paul Ylvisaker at the Rockefeller and Ford Foundations, respectively, and Douglas Haskell, editor of *Architectural Forum*. Grady Clay's foray into San Francisco renewal was honed in this international community soliciting fresh critiques that would transform the city.

Clay's experience as a real estate editor and journalist navigating foundation- and university-funded research threw into sharp relief the tensions between academic and popular writing, between publicity and critique, and between research and policy impact. Clay came to his work as a reporter with a distinct editorial voice and was a critic in his own right. "In the possible development of civic design critics," University of Pennsylvania planning professor William Wheaton said in 1958, "no better man is in sight than Grady Clay."[20] Yet many academics and foundations, to the extent that they were interested in journalists, expected Clay to merely report and disseminate their analyses. Design and planning practitioners, for their part, welcomed Clay's attention to their projects. But practitioners also tended to dismiss his writing as inadequately grounded in professional design concepts. When William Wurster circulated one of Clay's manuscript chapter drafts to WB&E's architects in 1961, one colleague responded, "Reads to me a bit like a superficial journalist. Is that what he is? Not impressed at all." Wurster, design school dean at the University of California, Berkeley, understood Clay's difficult position. After reviewing Clay's draft chapter, Wurster wrote, "I thought it a fascinating account; with some hesitation I would say that for *journalistic zing* you cartooned certain things and the stress was not so much on content as on process." Wurster was right; Clay was interested in process.[21]

The top-down demand for fresh analysis was enriched by enticements from major foundations, universities, and the architectural press, which in turn generated a series of conferences targeting writers during these years. Between 1958 and 1962, sandwiched between two conferences on urban design criticism where he had key roles, Grady Clay's San Francisco manuscript went from cradle to grave. During these years, Clay conceived, researched, and wrote the manuscript and then tried without success to find a publisher. For the 1958 event, the University of Pennsylvania Conference on Urban Design Criticism, Clay compiled the proceedings for the Rockefeller Foundation, the sponsor. The second gathering, The Press and the Building of Cities, was co-hosted by the journalism and architecture schools of Columbia University in October 1962. Clay gave the keynote address opening the Columbia conference. This workshop immersed thirty metropolitan daily "newspapermen" in multidisciplinary research and introduced them to leading figures in redevelopment fields. The contrast between the 1958 and 1962 meetings illuminates simultaneously the era's intense demand for critique and the conditions that constrained writers like Clay.

The 1958 University of Pennsylvania conference publicly affirmed the urbanists' private lament that American cities, despite their apparent dynamism, lacked adequate critique. The October 1958 meeting (at the Westchester Country Club in Rye, New York) immersed Clay in the issues plaguing urban design criticism in the 1950s, primarily from the architectural perspectives represented by journals such as *Architectural Forum,* where Jane Jacobs worked. The roughly twenty participants were mostly university-affiliated design practitioners, editors, and scholars. In addition to Clay, Lewis Mumford, Jane Jacobs, architectural magazine editors Doug Haskell and Tom Creighton, Gilpatric, and University of Pennsylvania planning and design faculty (such as Ian McHarg and David Crane), the attendees included I. M. Pei, Arthur Holden, J. B. Jackson, Louis Kahn, Eric Larrabee, Kevin Lynch, and Catherine Bauer. In a memo to the Rockefeller Foundation, Clay summarized the core challenge addressed at the conference: Why don't America's cities—their new suburbs, slums, and skyscrapers—get the kind of "close, local, systematic, and courageous criticism" they deserve? Why should movies, TV, plays, or paintings be lambasted by press critics while new buildings get little but routine praise from local newspapers? What can be done to improve critical analysis of city growth and design? The dearth of such criticism in the U.S. has been gnawing at a growing number of planners, architects, editors, and writers.[22] For city-watchers, the conference solidified an existing framework more than it advanced a new agenda. The consensus about the sorry state of urban criticism rested on consensus about the sorry state of cities themselves.

The conference participants' agreement in 1958 about the clichés paralyzing urban criticism itself helped Clay see the need for fresh critiques from nonarchitectural per-spectives. Although the conference consensus was not necessarily part of the problem, it gave Clay ideas for what he might do differently. Chad Gilpatric, whose concerns deeply shaped the meeting agenda, remained preoccupied with these issues, noting, for example, that even the commissioner of urban renewal, William Slayton, witnessed "a constant flow of clichés and stereotypes with very little analysis of city construction problems."[23] Gilpatric singled out Lewis Mumford as an exception, asking in 1958 "where there were to be found other Lewis Mumfords, who could bring his critical, philosophical and historical background to bear on problems of urban planning." Two years later, Gilpatric reported that architect William J. Conklin "knows of no little Mumfords in development."[24] The lockstep consensus was obvious to Clay at the con-ference's first session. All nineteen experts agreed on the problems of "sprawl and ugli-fication" and "were eager to seek further and deeper for causes and cures," to go beyond "catch phrases" to uncover "root metaphors."[25]

Despite all of this convergence, the 1958 conference launched one controversy. The attending editors from major architectural journals were welcomed as influential contributors but had to confront the message that they had failed at their jobs. Prior to the conference, planning scholar David Crane had circulated a thirty-six-page paper holding the magazines partly responsible for the field's collective inability to address the crisis that U.S. cities were "by common consent antiseptic, dull and meaningless at best, and at worst garish, pretentious and inhuman."[26] *Progressive Architecture*'s Tom Creighton penned a "very angry" response to Crane before the conference, and Douglas Haskell submitted a counter-report after the conference titled "*Architectural Forum*'s Adventure in Architectural Criticism: A Letter to Grady Clay of the Urban Design Criticism Conference."[27]

At the meeting, a lively discussion of obstacles preventing "courageous criticism" of the built environment tackled "the crippling journalistic myth that 'You can't criticize privately owned buildings' for fear of libel suits." Lewis Mumford had the first word on this subject. The myth was false, he said. Writers' fears of being sued by architects, he insisted, "persist only through misunderstanding." He did caution against saying "that *all* the works of a certain architect are bad." Jane Jacobs explained the inherent conflict discouraging journalists from criticizing their sources in design firms and provided examples of the types of requests architects made to reporters, such as "Don't rock the boat: we might lose that Federal grant."[28]

Haskell's conference counter-report deepened Clay's understanding of how architectural editors' efforts to bypass urban clichés and the celebratory traditions of architectural writing were being undermined from within the design professions. This was Haskell's perspective, of course, but he was an influential intellect in architectural criticism who had, since the 1920s, written for and edited such magazines as *The Nation* and *Architectural Record*. From 1949 to 1964—shadowing urban renewal's rise—he led *Architectural Forum* as editor. In his voluminous correspondence with hundreds of designers and writers over decades, he had worked to nudge along a paradigm shift in architectural writing. Since 1949 he had directed U.S. architects' attention to urban renewal and cities generally. To set his editorial record straight, Haskell described for Clay his long-standing agenda to teach "the ABC's" of architecture to a broad public and his recent initiatives at *Forum* to commission hard-hitting editorials (including those by Jane Jacobs and Frederick Gutheim).[29] Haskell saw his magazine as hampered by having architects as its primary audience and by the barriers between professions dedicated to urban renewal and cities. For years Haskell had aspired to draw planners to read *Architectural Forum* while stimulating architects' engagement with urban planning and with the unique challenges of design at the city scale. Planning expert Catherine Bauer relentlessly prodded Haskell on the fact that architectural journals had not addressed the reality that large-scale urban renewal now pulled architects and planners (let alone landscape architects) into closer collaboration.[30]

Doug Haskell acknowledged to Grady Clay that the genre of architectural criticism brought its own problems to the urban renewal table. Haskell explained why the trade magazines remained beholden to architects. True, newspaper journalists did not understand buildings, but "the incompetence of writers in the architectural field in meeting the public standard of knowledge (or ignorance) and concern (or unconcern) is prodigious." Most important, architectural criticism still relied on architects to furnish photos and materials for promotion rather than analysis. The impulse to gather design news "by the techniques of journalism" had not taken hold, according to Haskell (this was where Marion Conrad's efforts to seed general-interest features on designers entered the field's debates). Haskell exposed in valuable detail the "roots" of what plagued architectural criticism:

The most embarrassing question asked of *Forum* has been why certain buildings should be singled out to be dealt with in articles marked "criticism" while other buildings still get a "neutral" or "favorable" exposition which tells only about the constructive ideas in them. The answer is that this question goes to the roots of architectural journalism as practiced in America. The notion that the magazines are—and ought to be—"puff sheets" is widespread, and many architects want to bargain with these magazines as to where these architects will "place" their jobs for publication on the basis of which magazine will "give" *them* the most space, the best pictures, the most enthusiastic write-ups, etc. The magazine is quite brazenly viewed as a "publicity" outlet, and professional ethics are sometimes cited in favor of the proposition that architects, like the dead, deserve to have nothing but good spoken of them in "their" magazines. In the early days they used to pay for the photographs and sometimes for the plates, and sometimes when they want a special result today they still furnish a lot of material. One has to sympathize with the architects because the sincere majority are trying to carry forward an art in a civilization which gives the public virtually no visual training, and no comprehension of the deeper issues.

A sympathetic observer understood that architects saw their magazines as a "refuge" shielding the profession from a press and public unsophisticated about design. The techniques of journalism would help wean architectural critics from their promotional traditions, Haskell implied to Clay. *Forum*, he resolved, would "not retreat from its critical articles" and challenged others to raise the standard. Readers would have to be brought along.[31]

Regarding architects' inability to accept analytical critiques, Haskell spoke from bitter experience, which he did not tell Clay. Haskell had turned to Bill Wurster for advice in 1952 after a vitriolic reader reaction left him "shaken." Architect Pietro Belluschi wrote Haskell that *Forum*'s frank assessment of the United Nations Assembly building had "nauseated" him. "It is time indeed to take stock," Haskell admitted. "For some time I have been privately concluding that our critics are, generally speaking, propagandists and prophets rather than critics." Architectural critics delivered "important messages of their own," but they could not, in the tradition of literary criticism, take artists' intentions on their terms, seeing the world the artist hoped to create. Feeling beleaguered by the "sheer antagonism," Haskell second-guessed his own strategy: "The righteousness with which the best minds are knocking down my earnest effort and the genuine 'nausea' that it has produced in them give me some pause." Six years later he wrote a sanitized version of this for Clay.[32]

Clay's responsibility for the Urban Design Criticism conference proceedings also exposed him to fault lines over the role journalists specifically should play in jolting urban writing out of its moribund state. The issue on the table in 1958 was whether journalists would spark new ideas for cities or only "report" the findings of a new cohort of sophisticated, university-based, foundation-supported researchers. Clay and the

University of Pennsylvania sponsors expended significant energy compiling a summary report for the Rockefeller Foundation, but without satisfaction. William Wheaton summed up the frustrations for Gilpatric: "The major difficulty has been an unwillingness on the part of the professional planners and architects to accept popularized formulations of problems by Clay and perhaps an inability on his part to see nuances which are of great importance to the professional even though they might appear to be quite esoteric to the layman." Clay's eighty-page first draft prompted the faculty to generate a nearly forty-page outline for reworking the material. This conflict was not entirely unanticipated. Before the conference, David Crane and Frederick Gutheim separately had expressed reservations to Gilpatric that Wheaton and others at Penn had narrow notions of journalism's contributions. They seemed preoccupied with "giving special attention to more outlets for writers" rather than with transforming criticism in part by enlisting creative city journalists.[33]

Grady Clay was not ideally suited to merely report others' conclusions. The Penn conference's unified call for original, responsible criticism of large-scale renewal provided an expansive platform for Jacobs, Clay, and many others—yet simultaneously privileged architectural perspectives. Clay's background in the daily real estate pages propelled him in a different direction. By immersing Clay in this architectural perspective, the conference provoked him to look elsewhere to develop an independent critique of urban design and urban renewal. Clay also learned that despite the call for "courageous" urban criticism, most academics expected basic reporting and outreach from journalists rather than critical thinking. Gilpatric had hoped Clay would be the kind of cross-over journalist Gilpatric aggressively sought—someone with fresh ideas and street knowledge who could also engage with scholarly research. But Clay's "popularized formulations" proved too colloquial for the academic design professionals.[34]

Philanthropic foundations in this era (particularly Rockefeller and Ford) proved to be critically important in supporting conferences, providing grants, convening meetings, and shaping the future of urban criticism. Gilpatric left the 1958 meeting with his reservations about long-winded academic papers intact and with a renewed commitment to expand journalists' power to improve the urban environment. Gilpatric learned that his counterparts at the Ford Foundation did not share his faith in journalists. In March 1960 Gilpatric met with Paul Ylvisaker, the director of Ford's Public Affairs Program, and Robert Weaver, then associate director. Ylvisaker briefed Gilpatric on Ford's "massive" program in urban and regional affairs. He handed Gilpatric a list of Ford grantees, including university-based research initiatives such as the Joint Center for Urban Studies. Gilpatric noted that these programs used "large research sums to attract scholarly talents into urban studies, somewhat on the carrot-on-a-stick basis." Ylvisaker hoped that they would become "recruiting and training grounds for badly needed new talent." The research programs were complemented by other Ford initiatives, such as the "urban extension" project recently pioneered at Rutgers University and the University of Wisconsin, encouraging the development of urban studies programs. Ylvisaker did not anticipate sponsoring much in the humanities fields of history and philosophy. He was "all in favor of CG's [Chadbourne Gilpatric's] exploration of and findings of architectural critics who can write with competence and insight about city problems as a whole."[35]

Regarding journalists, however, Ylvisaker was blunt. He favored academic approaches to criticism. The Ford Foundation, Gilpatric noted, "at this time is not interested in the role that journalism and the press could play in urban problems." They went back and forth for a few minutes. Gilpatric staked out his own reasoning: "I said I thought this was important both because the press could spot problems" for research, "and also that good reporters and correspondents might have a use for reporting and critical functions regarding academic studies of urban problems. Y's [Ylvisaker's] view is that perhaps in a few years when we have more research would be the time to enlist the interest of the press."[36]

The Rockefeller–Ford Foundation divide over the role of journalists went to the heart of tensions over where new ideas in urban redevelopment originated. Although design and planning professionals, in the academy or in practice, *might* break through the intellectual stasis, outside critics, the press, and other laypeople perhaps had a better chance to shake things up. Gilpatric sought journalists who did more than bring others' research into public light. He expected reporters to foment creative thinking in urban redevelopment policy by expressing judgment and taking risks. Such journalists would have independent influence on existing projects and government agendas.

The final initiative Gilpatric supported in Rockefeller's Studies in Urban Design (SUD) program prepared the press to do just this. Although Gilpatric had prioritized this field for years, the formal granting program had been approved only in April 1962. With the consent of a newly appointed advisory board, Gilpatric planned to distribute $12,500 grants to ten adventurous journalists. He sought out new voices for his list of potential grantees, advised by architect Robert Geddes and Bay Area writer Allan Temko, who had received the first SUD grant.[37] Appointed urban design critic for the *San Francisco Chronicle* in October 1961, Temko offered influential commentary characterized by "full courage" that met Gilpatric's standards. Temko's front-page articles on the proposed San Mateo bridge "led to a public furor, a state investigation, and finally a radical revision of the project." His platform and impact had evolved since the *Sunset* magazine articles he gave as credentials when applying to be *Forum*'s West Coast correspondent a few years earlier. At the same time, Temko retained a foothold in architectural scholarship with a new book on Eero Saarinen.[38]

Clay sent Gilpatric the program for the October 1962 Columbia University conference, The Press and the Building of Cities, calling it a "direct outgrowth" of the Rockefeller-sponsored conference on urban design criticism.[39] Hosted by the schools of journalism and architecture and funded by the AIA, the Columbia conference invited thirty reporters from the nation's metropolitan daily newspapers. The three-day workshop was "designed to improve their skills in writing about urban revitalization and the design of buildings." The dean of Columbia's Graduate School of Journalism, Edward Barrett, said it was imperative that "American newspapers take a leading role in seeing that this building job is done right." Rather than the university-connected scholars, architects, writers, and editors who attended the 1958 Rye conference, journalists from metropolitan papers made up the main audience at Columbia.[40]

By styling itself as a concerted program to equip reporters to effectively tackle urban development, the Columbia conference came across as slightly patronizing to practicing journalists. Instead of networking through academia to find critics, as Gilpatric had, the Columbia conference organizers began with a list of thirty cities and their lead dailies. Barrett called executives at these papers and requested one "ideal candidate for the seminar." Barrett opened the conference with a talk titled "The Responsibility and Opportunity of Newspapers and Reporters," followed by Clay's keynote, "The Viewpoint of the Reporter." The first day's sessions were organized around "The Forces that Shape Cities" and "Standards for Evaluating Design." The workshops featured academics from disciplines such as economics, government, anthropology, political science, architecture, and city planning. That evening, the attendees listened to AIA president Henry L. Wright, and the commissioner of the Urban Renewal Administration, William Slayton. The second day, when the architecture school took charge, the condescending implications of inculcating reporters with architectural norms deepened. The journalists broke into smaller groups led by architecture faculty or architectural magazine editors, including Doug Haskell and Tom Creighton. That afternoon they visited New York City sites chosen to "exemplify good and bad approaches." The final day integrated the groups with a panel discussion titled "The Role of the Reporter and Critic." Chicago Mayor Richard J. Daley spoke at lunch.[41] George McCue, at that time urban design and arts critic for the *St. Louis Post-Dispatch,* told Gilpatric that the thirty journalists "showed sharp resistance to serving as press agents for architects or the AIA, which sponsored the conference."[42] The limitations architectural critics faced in 1958—being seen as boosters for the profession—seemed to be spreading into new channels rather than receding.

Shortly after the Columbia conference, Gilpatric retired the Rockefeller SUD program. The Ford perspective had prevailed: Gilpatric's own advisory board counseled that new urban knowledge would originate in university-based centers, and journalists would amplify those findings, check facts, and chase down answers provided by others. When Gilpatric's SUD board convened for the first and last time in September 1962 in Manhattan, it advised against his most recent proposal: an even smaller direct grant program (five grants of $3,000 each) to allow journalists to pursue innovative critical projects apart from their day jobs. The advisors concluded that the proposal "didn't provide for the effective guidance of newspaper writers on current issues and developments in urban design," although McCue's lukewarm response to the Columbia conference suggested that journalists bristled under too much guidance.[43]

Ultimately, Gilpatric's successes with the modest Rockefeller urban criticism program were more important than his failures, when explaining the decision to fold it. Gilpatric had backed Jane Jacobs's 1961 *Death and Life.* This book not only answered the call for fresh urban criticism; it also gave critics of urban renewal enough to talk about for five decades. Gilpatric conceded the battle and won the war. He continued to work with the handful of authors funded by the SUD initiative. Besides Jacobs, Gilpatric was proud of supporting Kevin Lynch in writing *The Image of the City* and Stephen Jacobs and Barclay Jones in penning *City Design through Conservation,* as well as Allan Temko and Edmund Bacon in writing their works.[44] He expanded his inquiries in the field, pressing elite university leadership several years later about how their schools engaged with local urban problems both as institutions and through faculty members.[45] A month after the Columbia conference, Gilpatric met with Harvard University urban design professor Martin Meyerson in Cambridge. Meyerson, the Joint Center's founding director, described the center's "episodic interest" in the power of the daily press. A grant to journalist Peter Braestrup resulted in an effective October 1960 *Harper*'s article, "What the Press Has Done to Boston and Vice Versa." Meyerson was less optimistic about the prospects for Grady Clay's manuscript. Clay's time at the Joint Center, he told Gilpatric, had produced "no interesting results."[46]

Between 1958 and 1962 Grady Clay traveled a significant intellectual distance as an urban critic, emerging with a land-centered critique of urban renewal. Despite Meyerson's assessment, Clay had a bright future and a long, productive career ahead of him as a writer and editor. In 1960 the Joint Center's commitment to land economics made it a logical host for Clay, considering his real estate background and research focus on how urban design was altering the competition for land within the renewal process. The Joint Center would soon foster a wave of scholarly urban criticism rooted in the fields of economics, politics, demography, and planning (and their ties to government policy) rather than in the discipline of architecture. The other grantee during Clay's tenure at Cambridge, Charles Abrams, is an important figure in mid-twentieth-century urban studies deserving of further research. A prolific author, original thinker, academic, and practitioner, Abrams's primary interests in land and housing underpinned a career that touched numerous universities and disciplines, from The New School to Columbia University. Abrams had a background in real estate law and, as the first general counsel for the New York City Housing Authority, he formulated its eminent domain policies. His first book, published in 1939, was *Revolution in Land,* and a 1953 article, "Urban Land Problems and Policies," offered a comparative analysis of how government policies were affecting land markets in nations around the globe. Given that Abrams also wrote about urban renewal in Louisville, Abrams and Clay obviously had a great deal in common. Despite Clay's fit with Abrams and the Joint Center's initiatives, the durable, traditional measurements of Clay's ideas about renewal land—publications—are scarce. It was difficult to debate Meyerson's point that Clay's research had few "results."[47]

By the time Clay went to New York in 1962 to give the Columbia keynote, he was worried about the future of his San Francisco manuscript. A series of publishing possibilities had failed to materialize. He met with Gilpatric, who captured a snapshot of Clay's thinking at that moment: "He is concerned . . . that some of the important issues emphasized will seem to be dated when the book comes out. The substance of the book deals with competitive pressures in the disposition of land in urban areas. One chapter is devoted to the views of Justin Herman, now heading the Redevelopment Authority in San Francisco."[48] The urban renewal practice of selling rather than leasing (or otherwise controlling) land had not ossified, yet the window for effecting change was narrowing. Clay's research into the redevelopment process could help open up decision making to citizen participation while fending off unhelpful anecdotes and rumors posing as facts. But every month redevelopment agencies moved forward, without the benefit of such research, to choose designs, sell land, imagine the future, and begin construction. Clay observed that some agencies strode purposefully and others stumbled, but all could learn from his findings. His instincts as a journalist told him to publish quickly to ensure the book's relevance.[49]

More than fifty years later, Clay's unpublished manuscript depicts the ferment in urban criticism just when Jane Jacobs's *Death and Life* appeared. The same top-down pressures and enticements from philanthropic foundations, universities, and professional journals that supported Jacobs fostered a generation's worth of important and fascinating ideas. Because Jacobs's book became so influential, it is tempting to label the other cohesive perspectives emerging at that time as alternative, or somehow marginal, critiques. From the historical moment of the late 1950s and early 1960s, however, Clay's ideas and others' had a fighting chance. Clay's distinction was that his critical journalistic perspective on urban renewal came to be grounded in the U.S. marketplace for land and the future of San Francisco.

SAN FRANCISCO: BEAUTY OVER GOLD, ART OVER MONEY

In his manuscript's introduction, Grady Clay explained that urban renewal marked a "sea change" in the long historical view of U.S. land markets. At the nation's origins, he noted, "Congress manipulated the price of land in many cities by selling land wholesale to speculating companies who laid out cities, sold lots, and established the basic pattern of land use and development." The government also carved "the wilderness into negotiable squares of land." After this initial government interference, the market had taken over. In Clay's view, the Housing Acts of 1949 and 1954 were the next "massive" marketplace interventions. These federal urban renewal acts had quickly "become as much a means of manipulating and re-distributing land values as one of creating new housing." Stabilizing central city land and building values had been the purpose of redevelopment from its origins, Clay argued; renewal would not have secured congressional support without that intent.[50] Novel urban design competitions had in just a few years begun allocating land in this newly configured market. Again from the long view, this time from the history of architectural competitions, this marked a "major" departure from past practices.[51]

In setting up his San Francisco case study of the Golden Gateway competition, Clay singled out the 1950s planning stories that previewed impending land stewardship conflicts. He detailed the sequence of civic committees, city and federal agencies, consultants, and reports that had guided urban renewal administrators toward the competition strategy they ultimately used for this downtown parcel. The 1957 "General Development Plan and Report" produced by SOM had been particularly influential. The city's business-backed Blythe Zellerbach Committee privately raised $35,000 to pay for the SOM study and scale model, which were contracted for the SFRA and the City Planning Commission (CPC). The 1957 report established that the city's power structure endorsed redevelopment. Far more detailed than a conceptual study produced the previous year by architect Lawrence Lackey for the CPC, the SOM plan operated on an expansive modernist scale, with a "vast" open mall, towers, and a landscaped plaza topping a parking garage. The SFRA incorporated elements from the SOM study, such as those governing site coverage by buildings, open space, and setbacks, into its competition guidelines for Golden Gateway two years later, in 1959.[52]

Because it revealed the vast privatization of public streets at the heart of the Golden Gateway, the SOM plan became significant to Clay's larger story.[53] It was impossible to overlook the substantial role of city streets in assembling this renewal parcel. SOM's report identified 77.7 acres potentially available for the site. Of these 77.7 acres, a staggering 46 acres consisted of existing streets. The proposed redevelopment parcel converted 21 acres of those former streets into buildable land for development by paring down 46 acres of former streets to 24.9 acres for new streets. Thus 21 of the plan's projected 52.8 net available acreage came from former streets. Second, Clay described how SOM's architectural model defined the public's reaction to the larger plan. The model was "handsome" but also "very dazzling, and very terrifying." It gave redevelopment what Clay and others called a "project appearance." As Clay wrote, "The scale models made it seem a repetition of clichés from a limited school of architecture: cubistic, glassy, ultra-formal, inhuman." This did not fit the Lackey report's sketchy vision and did not seem much like San Francisco. The model generated a strong negative response from the general public, but the Chamber of Commerce liked it. "To hell with gaslight and preservation," Clay paraphrased the chamber's views in 1957, a reference to the adjacent Jackson Square wholesale home furnishings district.[54]

For Clay and others, including David Rockefeller, Justin Herman was a key figure, an impressive administrator very much at home in his increasingly powerful "public planner" role. As San Francisco's redevelopment stalled in the late 1950s, the Blythe Zellerbach Committee and the San Francisco Planning and Housing Association hired another outside consultant, Aaron Levine, from Philadelphia's Citizens Council on City Planning. Levine visited San Francisco for two weeks in February 1959. He concluded that redevelopment needed more teamwork, political commitment, and coordination with federal agencies. Moreover, the CPC needed a bigger budget. After a national search for a new executive director of the SRFA, the city offered Justin Herman the position in May 1959, and he began officially on September 1. Since 1951 Herman had directed the regional office of the Housing and Home Finance Agency (HHFA). His previous role as the local federal administrator overseeing San Francisco's redevelopment meant that he knew how the SFRA could comply with federal terms quickly and push its programs forward. Within months of Herman's hiring, the SFRA was buying properties, clearing parcels, and selling land. Herman's leadership was credited, and blamed, for mobilizing the city's three redevelopment projects: the Western Addition, based on a controversial neighborhood clearance; Diamond Heights, a middle-income residential project on vacant land; and, of course, the Golden Gateway, which required demolishing the produce market and its surrounding low-density commercial district. Redevelopment supporters liked to say that the city went from being the national example of how not to do urban renewal to being held up as exemplary. After Herman's first week at SFRA he had written a compelling brief prospectus for Golden Gateway, which he packaged with the long redevelopment specifications; together these documents set the "powerful and prestigious bait" for developers—19.7 acres of choice downtown land.[55]

Herman was on the job a few months before "it began to dawn on him that the Golden Gateway might not be sold off like any other 'hot piece of dirt.'" The idea of combining design proposals and land bids, "I'll be frank to confess, didn't hit me at the federal level," he told Clay. Working for city government, however, he saw the potential of a process inviting design visions. Only after the competition guidelines were issued did Herman catch a glimmer of the inherent conflicts and lack of comparability between land bids and design proposals. To head this off, in February 1960 the SFRA asked the HHFA for authority to offer the land at a fixed price to equalize the playing field and allow focus on the designs. The HHFA denied the request, anticipating that "spirited" bidding would exceed SFRA's projections. Herman noted that "fixed-price sales for social objectives (in which I include urban design) are still new approaches." A change in the rules would have been unlikely so close to the competition deadline, but Herman's inquiry to the HHFA acknowledged the potential difficulties of evaluating entries that mixed dollars and design.[56]

After the proposals came in to the SFRA on March 8 and the models were assembled in large booths as at a county fair, Herman again tried to renegotiate the competition's most significant dimension—this time, to stop the land sale and retain city ownership of the redevelopment parcel. When one of the top three submissions (the entry by Tishman-Cahill Renewal Associates, which included Larry Halprin) proposed a leasehold, it handed Herman an opportunity to explore the viability of this option with the Urban Renewal Administration (URA) in Washington, D.C. At least one local real estate investor strongly favored SFRA leaseholds, emphasizing the long-term benefits to the public if the city could clear and redevelop the same sites in future decades without going through painful and expensive land acquisition again. With the SFRA chairman's support and some positive public sentiment, Herman proposed the idea to federal administrators. The URA turned down the leasehold, "since the record of redevelopment so far had been based almost wholly on land sales." The SFRA then concluded, "Leaseholds of publicly held land represent a substantial shift from previously held ground rules in the competition, and it is believed that this device should not be used without extensive public discussion and without being thrown open to all participants." The Tishman-Cahill proposal, previously ranked high, was rejected *because* it was based on leasehold rather than land purchase.[57]

A few months later, in August 1960, Herman made a last attempt to retain public land ownership using yet another planning mechanism. In the midst of negotiating with the two competition finalists, he proposed applying "reversion" to the binding agreement. Namely, after a fixed period in which a "handsome profit" was guaranteed the private developer, the land would revert to the city. The finalists, however, shut down that option. Their representatives responded that the developers were "unalterably opposed as a matter of political and economic philosophy to reversion of either the office building or any of the property rights it acquired." The URA, mooreover, continued to oppose the move. In November 1961 Herman told Clay: "Leasing was not prohibited by URA but it was and is highly discouraged." Herman was unwilling to pressure the URA or undertake a "tremendous" campaign to educate the public. "My personal convictions are that leasing or reversions would have been a fine idea. My agency did not think so," he said.[58]

For Clay, Herman's value to the national accounting of renewal rested on his advocacy for these public land stewardship issues of leasehold and reversion as much as on his authoritative scripting of the Golden Gateway competition or his reputation for leading the city's renewal initiative out of stagnation. Herman's actions acknowledged a critique of renewal policy that warranted broader discussion. Herman knew from the SFRA's projections that developers would make "fantastic" profits by renewal, even if the property reverted to the city. Open discussion of profits would improve negotiation, transparency on all sides, public acceptance, and the project outcome. Detailing the developer profit, for example, gave Herman more leverage to bargain for reversion and other mechanisms to boost the public interest and investment in land. In Clay's opinion, Herman should have put up a harder fight with the HHFA and URA for leasehold or reversion. But this did not diminish Clay's admiration for Herman's persistent efforts to roll back the scope of urban renewal land sales.[59]

Despite skepticism about their expense and effectiveness, design competitions were becoming popular in determining the selection of urban renewal developers and the disposition of redevelopment land in the early 1960s. Most journalists, businesspeople, city administrators, and citizens did not have the training or inclination to judge architecture, but it was less obvious to the general public that urban planners also lacked expertise in architecture. Clay helped break down those barriers by writing about the architectural models and their role in the selection process. He did not focus on the aesthetic qualities of the competition designs. Clay was not compelled to admire or judge design on terms separate from the land underneath. A real estate editor rather than an architectural critic, he did not believe that design had inherent, special values that rose above other characteristics of redevelopment. Clay demonstrated how nonarchitects and specifically city journalists could offer meaningful analyses of design and the built environment.

Yet the layers of disinterest slowly sedimenting around Clay's views underscored that his critique of selling renewal land to private investors and the risks of mixing dollars and design in redevelopment competitions were policy matters that did not see public debate. Golden Gateway's battle did attract followers. Justin Herman thanked *Architectural Forum* for dramatizing the competition so that readers could see clearly the juxtaposition of "art versus money." The spread of similar phrases sparked by the press coverage spoke to the resonance of that tension: art and money, dollars and design, beauty and gold, design and price. San Francisco's popular identification as an unusually beautiful *and* expensive city meant that the tension pitting landscape against land played out with particular intensity in the City by the Bay. The resonance, however, did not carry land sales or design competitions into the significant policy debates over redevelopment. Chad Gilpatric, for one, did not share Clay's "interest" in the competitions, and he could not agree that architectural models played a determinative part in decision making.[60] In 1958 Gilpatric spoke with Arthur Holden, an architect, New Dealer, and author of *Money and Motion*, who, like Clay, was researching land use, real estate, and economic controls. Holden found that "whenever he tries to raise this sort of question, his banker friends leave the room and academic friends urge him to talk in the language of some one discipline or other, or shut up." Many architects, Holden complained, "don't even try to understand the economic factors which largely predetermine their work." When the gap between dollars and design yawned too wide, disengagement resulted.[61]

Before federal and local land policies hardened against leaseholds and reversions and before design overwhelmed the judgment of dollars, Grady Clay and Justin Herman pointed to a brief window for addressing these critical questions deliberately. It helped Clay's case that Herman spoke openly about safeguarding public land as director of the SFRA. This underscored the legitimacy of positioning these potentially radical questions and options firmly within the mainstream U.S. urban renewal structure.

SIDEWALK SUPERINTENDENTS

As he revised his book manuscript, Grady Clay found an analogy that likened citizens' passive role in urban renewal to that of "sidewalk superintendents," a phrase that had gained popularity during the Depression. Manhattan's Rockefeller Center institutionalized the pedestrian's curiosity about its vast midtown construction site by including a viewer shelter and formally designating it for "sidewalk superintendents." Clay set the scene in a 1963 article: "One of the most familiar sights in America is the high board fence alongside a downtown street, with peepholes cut out for the 'sidewalk superintendent.' It's a great show." Sidewalk superintendents watched construction workers "wrestle a girder into place," becoming invested in the task. "Quickly enough, the onlooker begins to feel that he, himself, is a part of this great process, taking part in this drama of city-building." Clay let his readers down fast. "Nothing could be farther from the truth. The sidewalk superintendent is powerless, his name a mockery." Clay relentlessly described the "watcher" as impotent and remote. "Like the sidewalk superintendent, the average citizen of today's city may watch, but seldom intervene. The builders go their way, men in distant yellow hats, controlling aggressive and mysterious machinery. . . . The sidewalk superintendent goes his way to find another fence where he can stand, powerless" (fig. 120). The "feeling of having lost control over one's physical surroundings" had pervaded American society. This "alienation," evidence suggested, was "behind many of the current outbreaks of interracial violences, voter resistance to civic-improvement bond issues, vandalism, rowdyism and such disturbances." No wonder the average citizen distrusted "a great impersonal 'they' who are razing indiscriminately an entire neighborhood, the good buildings with the bad, for some devious purpose of their own."[62] The problem and opportunity Clay addressed in his book about urban renewal was part of a wider passivity troubling a participatory society.

Clay hoped that his book would help alter redevelopment terms so that real people, rather than invisible "machinations," could set more of the redevelopment agenda. Whereas ordinary citizens could shake off their passivity, business leadership adhered to "an outmoded process of city-building." They were unequipped to judge architecture, which they too often "dismissed as sissified, possibly un-American and certainly impractical and therefore unrelated to the 'real' needs of everyday life." Furthermore, after the Depression slump and wartime material shortages, business leaders were grateful for the construction cranes and did not feel compelled to scrutinize the appearance of new buildings. For most people, urban design was an artistic matter of personal opinion rather than business or law. Redevelopment merged the outmoded city-builders with design competitions, Clay wrote, "at a moment when the future form of our cities is being moulded and fixed, but before the final patterns are locked in."[63]

The peephole, while seductive at the street level, was not sufficient for engaging the public with the complexities of the renewal process or the built environment: "Most huge urban developments are thrust upon the public's gaze only after long private gestation," Clay said, confirming the worst suspicions of "closed-door" deals. In the face of this, Clay upheld the promise of design competitions like Golden Gateway. Developer presentations and models were expensive, but the costs were worth it, he argued. Competitions educated the citizenry about urban design, invited public opinion, and conceded possibilities of multiple outcomes. "Finally," Clay reasoned, competitions enabled "the flow of ideas." Well-run competitions "bring together new combinations of capital, entrepreneurs and designers, and in so doing, stimulate the interplay of ideas and innovations." Clay's "sidewalk superintendent" contrasted with Jane Jacobs's iconic sidewalk "ballet," in which the observed interactions of neighborhood street life provided an infrastructure combating urban isolation. Both models studied observation as a form of civic participation. But for Clay, empowering citizens to participate in citywide redevelopment eroded passive peeping and social alienation. Visual street clues said little about policy. Even skilled and dedicated observation, in this case of construction sites, would tell an incomplete and often misleading story.[64]

120 Grady Clay described "sidewalk superintendents" watching construction sites as symptomatic of citizens' passivity when it came to the enormous impact of urban renewal and urban design. The developers of Golden Gateway, the featured competition in Clay's unpublished 1962 manuscript "The Competitors: A Study of the Competition for Urban Land," built this viewing platform. Clay focused on the fact that redevelopment authorities were selling large tracts of land to private investors. He argued that matters of urban form and design were significant primarily for how they affected the city's decisions about land.

Clay's writings of the early 1960s reveal that he was closely attuned to the fluid "moment" in urban renewal policy when he could intervene "before the final patterns are locked in." He remained unperturbed by the spin and slickness of the promotion surrounding architectural design that repulsed Bobbie Stauffacher, Stan Erickson, and others. Clay rightly predicted that models and renderings would become increasingly significant in 1960s redevelopment—inextricably tied to the land questions beneath. As skyscrapers and large-scale projects (followed in the next chapter) proliferated, critics like Karl Kortum and Jean Kortum called out how the design promotion inherent to architectural competition intentionally obscured the more significant land stewardship decisions. Clay in 1960 championed the role of journalists, including himself, in unmasking the rebuilding process and highlighting the "pressure points" of redevelopment. By writing for the public, he intended to democratize the climate in which new ideas were vetted. City-builders, he wrote in 1963, were "no longer mysterious and distant manipulators, but ordinary men who sweat and stammer under the floodlights, and extraordinary men who convey, in words and sketches, an unforgettable vision of a better life in a new environment." Although the risk of being spellbound by developers' promises was ever present, Clay factored out the constant background noise of sales talk. PR served a purpose but was hardly worthy of comment. Clay trusted bystanders' abilities to cull out the phony. "The important thing here is that the public gets into the act in a significant way. . . . One gets a glimmer, in these competitions, of a possibility: that this obscure and often occult matter called urban design is not beyond the comprehension of the crowd." Clay's work demonstrated how the crowd could shape the urban environment at a time of drastic rebuilding, in terms distinct from (but relevant to) architectural practice.[65]

Western and Southern "root metaphors" informed Grady Clay's critical voice, particularly his thinking about citizen participation, urban open space, land, and the moral frameworks for these matters. By 1962, Jane Jacobs's Greenwich Village was already a foil for Clay's Western perspective. "In spite of what Jane Jacobs has written about urban open space in *The Death and Life of Great American Cities*, most of the American population west of West Greenwich Village believes in open space and is not afraid of it," he wrote. Urban open space was not a universalized zone of human interaction between planners and pedestrians but rather was historically grounded in specific regions and places where humans and nature had converged. These historical roots, Clay argued, originated in the U.S. West, not Greenwich Village: "The need for new open space in American Cities was not dreamed up by a Fancy Dan collection of European planners, as Mrs. Jacobs' book alleges. It is deep-seated, and springs from the historic experience in opening up the West, developing the countryside, and maintaining contact with the good rich soil. . . . It comes from a deep affinity for nature which cannot be dissipated by even the most brilliant of arguments." Clay's regional perspective was also evident in his recommendations to democratize the redevelopment process by inviting riskier new ideas from less conservative sources. He said that domination by deep-pocketed corporate developers stifled the opportunities to "po'-boy a development, to use a phrase common in Southern land-development work, and in Texas oil-drilling operations."

Inviting renewal proposals based on leasehold rather than land sale opened the door to scrappy entrepreneurs and nonelites who knew how to leverage "poor resources." Clay argued this case for including resourceful "shoestring" investors based on the London study, but he found support in Southern land development traditions as well. Jane Jacobs's book prodded Clay to be more explicit about the Western and Southern dimensions of his land-centered critique of urban renewal.[66]

CLOSING THE "PEEPHOLE"

Grady Clay gave voice to a conceptualization of urban renewal as land stewardship, one that the San Francisco example best helped him articulate but that all cities faced. Clay's San Francisco manuscript delivered a timely, constructive challenge to current redevelopment policy, rooted in the conviction that public land ownership underpinned responsible steward-ship. He demystified the design competition process to yield better results and advocated for citizen participation. Clay proposed guidelines for mixing the social values of good design with financial rewards to the city. Unlike most of his contemporaries, including Jane Jacobs, he refrained from judging the good or evil of urban renewal and addressed the fact that many cities had bought into clearance but did not clearly understand their options. Land had been purchased and assembled, but nothing dictated that it had to be sold. Renewal administrators and city leaders still had decisions to make about what they would actually build.

Grady Clay was fundamentally skeptical of the popular and policy assumptions in 1960 that the land markets in U.S. cities had collapsed. Indeed the premise behind Title I urban renewal was that cities—even San Francisco and New York City—needed deep subsidies in order to sell land to private developers. As a Louisvillian Clay understood that developers were biased against what one of the San Francisco competitors called "second- and third-class cities." That competitor cautioned that most "redevelopment will be in cities without any real investment potential." He went on to level a devastating assessment of Providence, Rhode Island: "Who's going to invest a Confederate dollar in that town? You'd be out of your ever-lovin' mind. The country is full of these towns that have lost their bargaining position in the American economy, and no out-of-town developer is going to put foot in one of them." Clay argued the opposite, citing Providence's "spectacular example of success rather than abandonment." Its College Hill renewal district had distributed investment widely and supported preservation "rather than the cataclysmic injection of a vast project into the historic fabric of the city."[67]

San Francisco offered one of the United States' most obvious cases where, despite desperate-sounding rhetoric from city officials that they could not attract developers to downtown land, in fact that land was supremely valuable. Writing to the president of the Royal Institute of British Architects, Clay said of Golden Gateway: "The site is so dramatic, hovering at the edge of a great city and its Bay," that the SFRA had to know "that a host of developers would give their souls to own a large (16 acre) piece of San Francisco land." Similarly, he noted, Philadelphia's Eastwick redevelopment site was "the first chance in 150 years to acquire more than 2000 acres of land next to a metropolis." The San Francisco parcel more effectively raised Clay's question of why it was necessary to sell the land. Despite Golden Gateway's obvious bargain at $8.45 per square foot and

Herman's frank accounting of fantastic developer profit, the city's civic leadership breathed a palpably giddy sigh of relief when the "unexpected array" of nine major investors stepped up. The *Chronicle* editors agreed that the investors had done "more than scatter skepticism and disbelief in the Golden Gateway Project. They restored, overnight, an atmosphere of excitement, a spirit of enterprise and intiative that have [*sic*] not been conspicuous on the local scene for some years." Clay appreciated the excitement of the "land rush" but thought it could be more democratic. Most important, because he thought developers would "give their souls" for the site, he refused to be surprised or impressed by the financial offers. [68]

Clay's manuscript emphasized fresh angles on urban renewal—the land sale hidden in plain sight and the importance of the urban design process over the buildings themselves. But Clay's San Francisco story fell into a narrative gap between the heart-wrenching drama of wrecking-ball clearance and the breathtaking drama of skyscraper construction. The public, already suspicious of what it regarded as aesthetic and even "sissified" choices, might not readily have seen the decision-making process of urban design as a page-turner.[69] Clay maximized the competition suspense and delivered a good story. He recounted the "plastic scale models standing like jeweled promises in the lobby of city hall" and the exhausted Architectural Advisory Board members turning off the tape recorder for the final time, its chair and business leader Everett Griffin acknowledging one of the most satisfying experiences of his career.[70] Golden Gateway gave Clay a nationally significant, richly documented example of a successful urban renewal competition, but his narrative emphasized process over final product. Instead of making headlines by protesting and stopping redevelopment projects, like his more famous contemporary Jane Jacobs, Clay intervened to improve outcomes.

Urban renewal was unfolding in a climate of hearsay, without benefit of research; Clay offered concrete, usable lessons for redevelopment authorities and planning commissions weighing the prospects for competitions that mixed "dollars and design." Had it been published, his book might have won a wider readership among those interested in cities and design, helped along by the facts that San Francisco was a well-loved city and the theme of competition made for good sport. This "spectacular" marked an urban frontier where private investment met public stewardship in new and contested ways. "The Competitors" also would have resonated with the sociological genre of Holly Whyte's *The Organization Man* and Vance Packard's *The Status Seekers*. Clay profiled a new generation of professionals remaking cities through urban renewal land—the private developer, public planner, and architect–urban designer.

Clay's colleagues at the Joint Center for Urban Studies, particulary Martin Meyerson, worked over a period of several years to help publish "The Competitors," but their efforts foundered because Clay's lively journalistic style did not meet a presumed scholarly bar. "Although the material it contained was interesting, original and informative, we did not consider it to have been prepared in a sufficiently scholarly fashion to merit publication under our auspices," concluded MIT's final grant report to the Ford Foundation.[71] The original intention had been that Grady Clay and Charles Abrams's Ford-funded "monographs" would be published in a scholarly Joint Center series on urban renewal. At the end of Clay's fellowship year, in the fall of 1961, he diligently sent out chapters for review, checked facts, corresponded with experts in England and Canada, and revised the draft. He slashed the Brookline chapter from fifty-five pages to nineteen in order to sustain focus on San Francisco. In late summer of 1962, Meyerson and William Wheaton deemed the manuscript ready to submit to the University of Pennsylvania Press. At the request of MIT lawyers, Clay had removed what they called "libelous passages," which indicated both the fear of lawsuits inherent to urban design criticism and Clay's at times irreverent writing. After the University of Pennsylvania Press rejected the manuscript in the fall of 1962 and Public Affairs Press turned it down the next April, Meyerson suggested extracting the core arguments for a Joint Center working paper, which Clay did. At the beginning of the grant, when Clay sent Paul Ylvisaker some of his speeches, Ylvisaker told Clay that he "enjoyed" them and wrote, "[I] wish you'd teach the academics how to write." That particular experiment did not turn out well for Clay. In 1964 a few speeches, articles, and the working paper were all that was left of "The Competitors." By the mid-1960s, too, the issues surrounding large-scale renewal had entered a new phase. In San Francisco that was most evident through intensified private redevelopment alongside urban renewal and through more organized battles over both.[72]

Clay's prediction that urban design would increasingly influence land decisions proved to be accurate. In "The Competitors" he admired the forces of private competition but advocated simultaneously for safeguarding the public domain and educating the public. Concluding the London chapter, Clay proposed, "With the land under municipal ownership, it will be easier to make certain it is developed properly . . . , maintained well, and contributes as much to the long life of the neighborhood as it does to its immediate rebirth. A nation [the United States] that prides itself on willingness to experiment would do well to adapt this long-tested technique to fit its own needs." For skeptics who thought that "only in San Francisco" could an urban design competition succeed, Clay had an answer: "Every town and city has thousands of unstudied but willing students, potential urban-design critics, or merely would-be good citizens of a visual world, eager to understand what they see."[73]

Grady Clay's direct assertion that the competition for land defined the urban renewal process in the mid-twentieth century and, more generally, has defined the history of cities, offers extraordinary clarity to other critiques. A prolific, influential writer with a seventy-year career, Clay created a deep archive, and ultimately it was not difficult to resurrect his 1962 book manuscript and the faint trail of his San Francisco writings. "The Competitors," however, gains immeasurably in significance by being placed next to the other books and writings that underscored similar themes, from Henry George's 1871 *Our Land and Land Policy, National and State* to the 1971 *Ultimate Highrise*, which I turn to in the conclusion. Clay's San Francisco manuscript is historically valuable for re-creating the land-based, participatory urban criticism gaining traction in the Bay Area in the early 1960s. His own first published book, *Close-Up: How to Read the American City*, which came out in 1973, became a foundational work in cultural landscape studies—a later history that makes more powerful the fact that Clay's land-centered critique was never published and went missing for so long.

Skyscrapers, Street Vacations, and the Seventies

On a spring day in 1968, Karl Kortum first encountered Ruth Asawa's mermaid sculpture by accident as he threaded through Ghirardelli Square from his Maritime Museum office on the way to Michaelis's grocery store. He enjoyed the "light-hearted" mermaids, Kortum wrote to Bill Roth in D.C. And he "wasn't the only one slowly circling the fountain to see what antics the frogs were up to on the other side." The next morning, Kortum read Larry Halprin's diatribe against the sculpture in the newspapers.[1] But Halprin's outburst wasn't the primary purpose of Kortum's letter. The sculpture controversy paled next to the new waterfront crisis Kortum thought a distant Roth should actually worry about. "On another subject," Kortum continued, architect Donn "Emmons and Halprin are using their participation in Ghirardelli Square as a platform to justify knocking down all those fine old buildings under Telegraph Hill and the erection of a 'megastructure' (Larry again)."[2] The proposed seventeen-acre, eight-block SFIMC would be, the papers confirmed, "the largest single private development in the city's history."[3] San Francisco's controversies over "enlightened" private renewal in the late 1960s and 1970s revealed how much had changed in north waterfront rebuilding battles since the previous decade, while so many of the actors remained the same.

The proposed SFIMC structure would have been the fourth-largest building in the United States. Poured into the narrow waterfront slice where hill met water, the massive, monolithic bulk devoted to wholesale home furnishings would spell disaster for this unique historic neighborhood born in the Gold Rush (fig. 121). The collision of March 1968 news stories threw into relief disturbing connections between Kortum's beloved Ghirardelli Square and the despised SFIMC. Since he had developed his 1940s plan for a historical maritime district, predating the deep imprint of modernist design firms, Kortum had monitored this place vigilantly for decades. Recently he had made a fresh survey of the waterfront. Kortum's tour began when the Washington Street ramp exiting the Embarcadero Freeway deposited his car "on a new street that I had never seen before." He was in the Golden Gateway. "The street passed through an artificial landscape, massy and cold. My memory of it is of cement slabs intellectually placed and cunningly colored, but which still made a wall. It is a landscape of isolation." He soon reached the "human scale" of San Francisco again. But "further along the waterfront is another project by the same architects." Northpoint was "slabby and massive and ugly and rudely crowds to the very sidewalk." It failed to relate to San Francisco and wasted its waterfront location. "In between, and linking these two projects, the same architects now propose to build a vulgar box around Telegraph Hill." The SFIMC would solidify the cumulative imprint on the waterfront by the same design teams—WB&E, often collaborating with Lawrence Halprin & Associates.[4]

When Kortum opened the December 1967 issue of *Designers West* magazine, he read a feature on Emmons accompanying a story about the SFIMC. The article promoted WB&E's cohesive influence. Of Emmons the magazine asserted, "The entire North Waterfront of the city is a credit to his imagination" (fig. 122). Emmons and his partners had "done more to change the face and texture of the City in the last two decades" than "any other man." Like Kortum, the article surveyed the terrain: "From the celebrated

121 The massive San Francisco International Market Center (SFIMC) fills the right half of this 1968 model, spilling over into the lower left corner. The North Waterfront Associates project would have leveled eight contiguous blocks of Gold Rush–era and early twentieth-century warehouses and manufacturing buildings in order to build this furniture trade mart. Halprin & Associates' rooftop gardens blended the complex into Telegraph Hill. Shared façade details help the eye distinguish the SFIMC, which is difficult to discern in part because the streets have disappeared under the mart. Critics accused a previous model of distorting the structure to minimize its impact.

restoration of Ghirardelli Square . . . ; to the eight acre apartment house and shopping development at Northpoint; on to the $100 million dollar International Market Center . . . ; and then to the $65 million Golden Gateway residential and shopping development at the eastern end; the magnitude of these composite projects staggers the imagination." The homogeneity so appealing to this design reviewer staggered Kortum.[5] The professional architectural view of the waterfront as an opportunity for large-scale private investment and design achievement had become mainstream, while Kortum's 1940s vision of the waterfront as a historically significant low-rise district under responsible public stewardship, had become the alternative, so-called activist (and obstructionist), perspective.

Such claims for architects' power over place endlessly aggravated Kortum. He publicized the SFIMC fight in a letter to the *San Francisco Chronicle* written a few days before he wrote to Roth: "Architects are called 'sensitive' and 'imaginative,' words that glibly roll off the tongues of politicians and are used as handy adjectives by journalists." Renderings and models backed up *Designers West*'s strategic architectural writing about the SFIMC. But "nobody really looks at the project." On what basis would the public and the Board of Supervisors judge the SFIMC case? The press "lauded"

WB&E's contributions to preservation while simultaneously reporting the firm's plan to level the eight-block site, including its nineteenth-century warehouses. Architectural language produced a "nightmarish thicket of words to conceal nightmare landscapes." Celebratory articles touting public access to the furniture mart would not change the fact that "this building is not for people, it is for chairs."[6] He would say that the renderings of kiosks, trees, flags, and awnings were "all designed to conceal a very large stupid building."[7] Words and visualizations might have appeared to be abstracted from the environments they represented, but their impact was real.

Kortum's critiques singled out how architects' influence cut across private preservation, private redevelopment, and public urban renewal projects. "If the other two wastelands these architects have created are joined by another in the middle," Kortum concluded of the SFIMC, "our celebrated waterfront will be dead."[8] The usual suspects—privatization and developer greed—only partly explained the threat. A single architectural firm hired by different clients throughout the decade's multiple private and government redevelopment efforts, both historical and modernist, had homogenized with its singular urban design vision what might otherwise have been a more diversely modernized and reimagined historical waterfront.

The SFIMC, a clearance-based renewal project, shared with historic Ghirardelli Square not only architects but also a publicist, Marion Conrad; a graphic designer, Bobbie Stauffacher; and a model-making company, Virginia Green and Leila Johnston's AMI.[9] A shared vocabulary of plazas, commerce and nature, breathtaking views, historical associations, cobblestones and olive trees, outdoor dining, international food and craft, and public art straddled the distinctions between renewal and preservation, low- and high-rise, and private and public that characterized 1960s development. The era's urban design language underscored that these crossover ideals blended commerce and open

donn emmons . . .
an architects
responsibility
. . . area planning

122 One design magazine said of architect Donn Emmons: "The entire North Waterfront of the city is a credit to his imagination." This was a grand claim, even by the standards of architectural publicity. Karl Kortum, who had shepherded a historical vision for the waterfront since the late 1940s, singled out that quote (accompanying this photograph) as emblematic of the threat urban designers posed. By 1968 Kortum regularly called out developers and architects for using design language to hide public land giveaways in the mounting controversies and lawsuits covering the waterfront.

space in a benign and appealing magnetism. The publicists, illustrators, model-makers, preservationists, and lawyers mobilized on all sides to create the written and visual vocabularies of redevelopment. Controversy and competitions exponentially increased the demand for their skills.

San Francisco's flashpoints of waterfront development—from the mermaid sculpture controversy to the SFIMC's contested bulk—demonstrated the charged values behind the implementation of these popular 1960s commercial landscape ideals and their open-space amenities. Karl Kortum expertly pinpointed some insidious implications of developers' benevolent urban designs. He told the *Chronicle* that the SFIMC "architects are using their participation in Ghirardelli Square as a hunting license to destroy these historic buildings." The public should know that the architects "had to be restrained from tearing down historic buildings at Ghirardelli Square too."[10] With fanfare the SFIMC developers renovated two early twentieth-century warehouses into the Ice House complex, an upscale interior design showcase akin to Jackson Square (fig. 123). That the investors planned to clear the rest of the 17-acre site was a contradiction most reviewers seemed to miss. "Heaven help us!," Kortum wrote Roth.[11] There was nonetheless promising news to report. In March 1968, an organization had formed to oppose the SFIMC. Kortum hoped Roth would support this new organization, called Protect Our Waterfront (POW). Karl Kortum knew POW intimately. Its chair was Jean Kortum, his wife.[12]

The SFIMC was first in a string of intensely contested private developments that transformed the city's waterfront battles between 1967 and 1972. From a primary focus on the landscape (building height, mass, location, view corridors, and architecture), controversies shifted to spotlight the city's stewardship of its land. The unbuilt SFIMC unleashed much the same frenzy of designs, publicity, and hearings as those projects that were built. The most infamous controversy surrounded Transamerica Corporation's announcement in January 1969 of plans for a new headquarters. The company proposed their 1,000-foot, pyramid-shaped skyscraper for the prominent intersection where low-rise Jackson Square and North Beach adjoined high-rise Embarcadero Center and the financial district. The Pyramid later took the title of San Francisco's tallest building from the just-opened Bank of America headquarters.[13] The high-rise's unusual shape, height, and "sensitive" location provoked a prolonged storm of debate over urban form and the skyline, with renegotiations and redesigns extending even after construction began (fig. 124).

Each of these private developments—Transamerica's pointy "dunce-cap" with its great height and SFIMC's massive box around Telegraph Hill—set off urban design controversies, but it was the land beneath the buildings that made them redevelopment landmarks. The battles over the SFIMC and the Transamerica Pyramid produced a series of lawsuits that challenged San Francisco's land disposition policies, particularly relating to selling city streets. In both projects investors' and architects' claims of civic benevolence and open-space "gifts" began to backfire. One lead SFIMC investor defensively assured the public: "It is wholly inconceivable that any of us would want to foist off something rotten on this city."[14] Increasingly, preservationists like Jean and Karl

Kortum critiqued developers' assertions that they prioritized the public's interests. Bill Roth's Ghirardelli model of the trusted private developer from five years earlier no longer applied. The Kortums scrutinized behind-the-scenes publicists and model-makers and lobbied to blunt the power of urban design language exercised by architects. Like-minded public-sector allies such as Supervisor Jack Morrison and Planning Director Allan Jacobs relentlessly raised similar challenges in public hearings, committee work, and negotiations.[15] The lawsuits were accompanied by broader public outrage over how easily and cheaply developers could buy city streets. A growing cohort of citizens' urban environmentalist groups articulated this concern for the streets and hired lawyers; the region's alternative press backed their publicity efforts. The experienced Telegraph Hill Dwellers (THD, veteran of the mid-1950s freeway fights) was joined by POW in 1968. Then, early in 1970, a new citywide umbrella organization, San Francisco Tomorrow (SFT), coordinated neighborhood groups to focus attention on waterfront

123 A street view in the brick warehouse and manufacturing district that the San Francisco International Market Center (SFIMC) would have cleared in 1968. This photo, taken near Green Street, looks west down Battery Street toward the Union Street intersection. At the end of the block on the left is the former National Ice & Cold Storage building, part of a complex that was the area's largest masonry structure. North Waterfront Associates (NWA) renovated this complex into the Ice House following Jackson Square's formula of remaking old buildings for the wholesale home furnishings trade. Critics pointed out that the SFIMC would nonetheless level 17 acres. The fact that public streets represented 22 percent of the private renewal project footprint became controversial. Although NWA resented the urban-environmentalists' street vacation lawsuit that stopped the SFIMC, NWA associate Ron Kaufman soon devoted himself to the adaptive reuse model instead of neighborhood clearance. Kaufman later renovated the 2-story warehouse just visible at the far right of the frame and many other structures over the decades, taking pride in the history of the district he and his partners had nearly demolished in 1968. Today this neighborhood shows the most significant impact of the 1960s–1970s street vacation lawsuits on San Francisco.

development issues such as proposed skyscrapers, the port's land disposition plans, and the bay's environmental conditions. Of the many urban environmental issues that mobilized the city's dynamic civic organizations, the recent 1966 defeats of the proposed Panhandle and Golden Gateway freeways particularly established Jean Kortum's leadership, connections, and political influence in San Francisco and the state.[16] The *Bay Guardian*, founded in 1966, provided fresh vectors for critiquing development, making the machinations of private redevelopment a bread-and-butter concern (fig. 125).

As the 1960s turned into the 1970s, nothing sharpened the crusade against large-scale private renewal projects more effectively than the lawsuits challenging the city's "street vacation" policies—the practice of closing public streets, increasingly with the purpose of selling the land to developers. The lawsuits originated in the SFIMC battle when routine municipal committee hearings in spring of 1968 confirmed that 22 percent of the privately owned site would consist of former public streets sold to the developer for a shockingly low price. The streets issue eclipsed some of the landscape critiques of the mart's height, mass, and open space that otherwise filled newspaper coverage. The SFIMC's opponents countered the developer's street grab with a potent vocabulary of responsible public land stewardship that provided a background narrative for the lawsuits. In the SFIMC case, the rhetoric against the principle of selling streets to developers

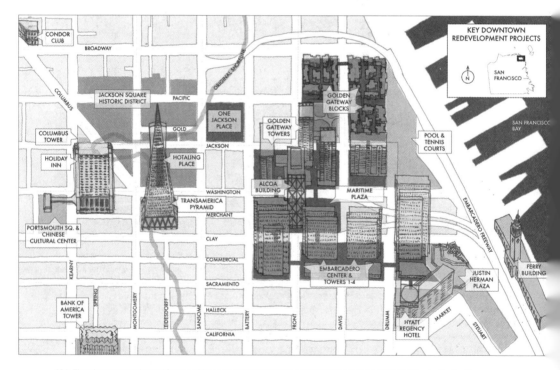

124 This drawing is adapted from a 1973 map appearing with a *Sunset* magazine article that took stock of how redevelopment had transformed the city's produce market district. The map situates the Transamerica Pyramid in relationship to the two major phases of Golden Gateway urban renewal and to Jackson Square. The San Francisco International Market Center site was immediately north of Broadway and the Golden Gateway.

125 A view of Coit Tower and Telegraph Hill that captured some of the distinct neighborhood qualities of the light-colored low- and mid-rise buildings; they matched the city's hills and then flowed into the warehouses and commercial buildings beneath. The city's 1960s urban-environmentalist groups such as Protect Our Water-front and Telegraph Hill Dwellers were identified with this district. They advocated for citywide issues of public land stewardship in redevelopment, especially pertaining to the waterfront. Their environmental planning expertise fought the stereotype reinforced by the daily newspapers that they were obstructionists who only cared about their own views and other superficial, aesthetic matters.

was powerful, but the attorneys found more legal traction in contesting the pricing policy that charged private investors half of the assessed market value. Building on the success of the SFIMC's street vacation lawsuit in slowing that project, the attorneys and community organizers refined their arguments in a lawsuit involving the Transamerica Pyramid site.[17] Other suits filed by this cohort of attorneys worked in tandem with the SFIMC and Transamerica cases during these years, winning land stewardship battles that had little to do with view corridors, architecture, and urban form.[18]

This chapter uses the street vacation lawsuits filed in the midst of these two pivotal urban design fights—those over the failed SFIMC and the successful Transamerica Pyramid—to trace the emerging campaign to hold the city and private developers to stricter standards of public interest in land disposition policies into the 1970s. THD, POW, their attorneys (Roger Kent, John Harman, and Hal Howard), preservationists Jean Kortum and Karl Kortum, and other organized citizens lobbied, testified tirelessly at hearings, and filed suits. They depicted urban design debates as distracting from (and sometimes concealing) the more important challenge of achieving equitable public land stewardship. By the early 1970s they began to win street vacation cases in lengthy appeals, with legal judgments often delivered long after the streets were gone and the new buildings completed. In the courtroom, the lawsuits displaced questions of design, height, open space, and location, although these issues persisted in municipal committee hearings and in the daily press. The preservationists, citizens' groups, and lawyers were neither simply antidevelopment nor selfishly preoccupied with preserving their personal city views. Instead they tapped long-standing traditions of making land-centered arguments about responsible public stewardship. Based on twenty years of their parallel roles leading plans for a historic waterfront and state maritime park, the Kortums especially were well prepared to engage development battles based on their expertise. For their purposes of a principled fight about public giveaways, the urban environmentalists contained, contextualized, and for the moment marginalized design questions.[19]

The street vacation cases reformulated "anti-Manhattanization" in the San Francisco Bay Area during the critical growth years when skyscrapers and urban renewal not only remade the skyline but remade the city's land disposition and urban design policies.[20] At the time preservationists seized on the street vacation lawsuits in the late 1960s, San Francisco's public controls over private development were in transition. The city's new planning director, Allan Jacobs, had recognized that San Francisco's public planning machinery, including a barebones master plan, was entirely inadequate to the current growth climate. A 1965 downtown zoning study had laid stronger foundations for controlling private redevelopment. However, when the Transamerica Pyramid tested these new zoning guidelines intended to protect the Portsmouth Corridor, the public controls simply collapsed.[21] During the late 1960s and early 1970s, Jacobs worked overtime with staff and consultants to draft a series of "pioneering" urban design controls that would be published in the 1971 *Urban Design Plan* and incorporated into a greatly expanded master plan.[22] San Francisco's first historic district, the adjacent Jackson Square, was passed in 1972. The SFIMC and Transamerica controversies educated Jacobs in the pressing need for (and challenges in) strengthening the public controls over private development. San Francisco's port land, having recently changed hands from state to city, tempted investors to propose controversial high-rise waterfront projects, as the rules were being renegotiated. The state played the most significant role in revising development regulations when it passed the 1970 California Environmental Quality Act (CEQA). CEQA applied tough new environmental impact reviews to public projects; in late 1972, a "bombshell" state supreme court decision expanded the required environmental reviews to private developments as well. In a brief five years, the public controls and guidelines relevant to urban redevelopment were dramatically transformed.[23]

In the 1967–72 gap before these multifaceted new public-sector regulations took hold over private and government renewal practices, San Francisco's urban environmental organizations and their attorneys staked out a policy strategy as private citizens on matters of responsible land disposition. On the ground, of all the street vacation lawsuits the forgotten SFIMC fight would prove to have the most significant long-term repercussions for the north waterfront. Grady Clay's observation that government urban renewal influenced neighboring land proved true; private developers in San Francisco soon emulated the large-scale land assemblage tactics of Title I renewal, including the allure of former street acreage. In 1968 private developers needed public approvals primarily if they wanted to buy streets or exceed newly zoned height limits—a fact that inherently intertwined land and landscape. Otherwise, in 1968 it seemed that developers could do pretty much as they pleased with their own land.

THE INTERNATIONAL MARKET CENTER: GARDEN GEM OR "GREEN HAIR-PIECES ON THE ROOF"

On July 15, 1968, San Francisco's Board of Supervisors met to consider an application from the ambitiously named North Waterfront Associates (NWA), developer of the SFIMC. The issue seemed narrow—NWA asked the city to close and sell two streets within the footprint of its proposed eight-block development. Ending designation as a street was a legal technique known as "street vacation"; selling the same land was a separate (but clearly related) municipal decision usually made at the same time as vacation. The board's Streets and Transportation Subcommittee had approved the request, 2 to 1, in late May. Between the time of the May vote and the July meeting, however, POW had filed a lawsuit with the Superior Court, obtaining a restraining order halting the project on behalf of taxpayer Jean Kortum. Leading up to the full Board of Supervisors hearing on July 15, the newspapers printed lengthy letters for and against the complex. POW's attorney, Roger Kent, prepared to face off against NWA's elaborate three-screen slide presentation with his own slide show and witnesses. The restraining order slowed the project for only a week, but it initiated the opponents' strategy of using the courts to fight the street policies.[24] The subsequent SFIMC street vacation lawsuit trained a spotlight on how public land stewardship practices subsidized private development. The fight inspired a cohort of San Francisco's citizen activists and public-interest lawyers to pursue the issue for a decade. But first, the public hearings stirred up general disbelief and protest—initially over the project's massive size. Soon, however, the protestors began to focus on the city's custom of selling streets at half price to developers.

Five days before the July board hearing on the street vacations, NWA presented a "drastic" redesign, inviting reporters and officials to view the new model (prepared by AMI) and new renderings (by Carlos Diniz) and collect a new press release (written by Marion Conrad Associates). The press release announced a turning point: NWA had reached an agreement with the City Planning Commission over the project's "design terms of reference," which were incorporated into City Planning Resolution 6215. City Planning Director Allan Jacobs had initially advised his commission to reject the massive project. But once the commission had approved the proposal in April and advanced the street vacation question to the supervisors, Jacobs negotiated the redesigned plan now on the table. Until he could implement a comprehensive citywide design plan, Jacobs experimented with brokering these case-specific design terms. The original SFIMC plan had a 23-story hotel that far exceeded the neighborhood's 84-foot height limit. The new design conformed to the height ceiling. Other improvements included the preservation of view corridors and the stepping down of building bulk to match the slope of Telegraph Hill (figs. 126 and 127). Jacobs now supported the project.[25]

Having settled with the city planning director, NWA hoped to defuse community opposition in anticipation of the full board hearing. The developer called in an engineer to testify about the dangerously dilapidated conditions of the neighborhood's Gold

Rush–era buildings in order to blunt calls for preservation. A surveyor certified the architectural model's accuracy against complaints that it distorted perspectives in NWA's favor. The complex design questions about height, mass, and views engaged public attention. Yet on the afternoon of July 15 everyone in the room knew that the project's future shape hung on the street vacation decision.[26]

The July 15 supervisors hearing, which adjourned after dawn the following morning, proved to be the longest and most heated in recent memory. At 2:45 a.m., the board voted 10 to 1 to approve the SFIMC street vacations. The dissenting vote came from Supervisor Jack Morrison, who had also voted against it at the May subcommittee meeting. Halprin & Associates' landscape architect, David Heldt, privately conceded that Morrison's closing arguments against street vacation were "very smoothly reasoned, though exaggerated." After twelve hours of presentations and debate, Telegraph Hill resident and THD's attorney, John Harman, gave an "emotional summation" asking the supervisors to vote against the project "or have it on your conscience."[27] On behalf of POW, Roger Kent appealed, "We don't want you to give up our streets for a wholesalers' graveyard." Supervisor William Blake, one of Marion Conrad's contacts, made the final argument supporting the SFIMC.[28]

126 Carlos Diniz's July 1968 rendering of the proposed San Francisco International Market Center emphasized the developer's claim that they had responded to design criticisms and would preserve views of Coit Tower and Telegraph Hill. This redesign underscored the newly compliant 8-story height compared with the original plans for a 23-story building that violated zoning limits. The buildings now followed the descending slopes of Telegraph Hill. The rendering's colors helped the buildings blend with the hill; Marion Conrad's July 10, 1968, press release described "a range of warm and earthy umber tones in the pigment" of the complex.

The subsequent votes throughout the early morning hours produced what the *Chronicle* called "the most restrictive contract ever approved between the city and a private developer." In exchange for the board's approving the street sale, NWA accepted seventeen covenants giving the city significant design controls over the project, along with several nondesign conditions, such as an enforceable plan to hire a certain number of "minority" workers. The negotiation traded design-based leverage over the developer for public land. Procedurally, the Planning Commission would approve construction plans, while the Art Commission and city engineer had to sign off on landscape designs. The contract emerging from the hearing required both a construction performance bond and a bond to guarantee landscape maintenance. Morrison's condition that two-thirds of the planned roof gardens remain open to the public passed. The contract's legal covenants would bind future owners. Morrison lost other demands—that 50 percent of the interior spaces welcome the public, that the developers retain part of the historic Seawall Warehouse, and that an independent architectural commission have jurisdiction.[29] THD's president, Gerald Cauthen, explained that although it might appear that government was meddling in private affairs, once NWA had decided they wanted streets, they

127 The first publicly displayed plans for the San Francisco International Market Center culminated in a 23-story hotel (visible here at the top center) that far exceeded the parcel's height limits. The colors of these earlier renderings were not naturalistic compared with those of Diniz and did not yet attempt to blend the market center with the surrounding historical environment. After reducing the height to conform to the 8-story limit, the developer still asked the city to close and sell the public streets for this bulky vision of a large-scale furniture mart topped by green space. The preservationists then claimed that the developer had never intended to build a 23-story hotel but had used design to manipulate and threaten the city into a false compromise. The citizens' groups began to move away from design-based critiques of height, bulk, and public amenity and instead questioned the land giveaways.

were "not in the legal driver's seat"; they had to negotiate with the city. THD respected the boundaries of private real estate but argued that the breathtaking northern waterfront "must be looked upon as belonging to all of San Francisco, just as Golden Gate Park does." In this case, preservationists surveilled the disposition of public streets and asserted the public's interest in the waterfront. Because California's Public Trust Doctrine specifically protected waterfront land for the benefit of the people, this was more than a symbolic claim.[30] Vigilant and deeply unsatisfied, Karl Kortum said the "compromise still hands over block after block of our city streets to the developers."[31]

When the meeting finally adjourned at 6:40 a.m., "cheers came from the cadre of professional men and women" who were employed to support the SFIMC project, according to one reporter.[32] In the run up to the SFIMC hearings, project director (and Dillingham Corporation executive) James O. Goldsmith kept NWA's unwieldy group of two dozen professionals in order, partly by demanding that they channel all inquiries through publicist Marion Conrad. Goldsmith circulated a "party line" memo to enforce convergence of concepts, approved phrases, and facts that conveyed the plan's elements. The last item advised the group to "always call Marion first if possible."[33] At their moment of victory in 1968, one could not distinguish the cheers of architects and landscape architects from those of publicists, photographers, engineers, managers, and lawyers. This constellation of professionals, on all sides of the projects, both enabled these disputes and depended on them.

POW's Jean Kortum questioned whether "design terms" were the appropriate tools for government to use to constrain private property. She admired the planning director's strategy, but design issues missed the "real question" of determining the best land use. In a letter to Supervisor Ron Pelosi, Kortum explained her shift away from design-based critiques, acknowledging their profound limitations. The negotiated design terms, she wrote, "are very general, give no sense of what the project might really look like." In frustration she observed that "the language is so 'soft.'" Because the commission could modify the guidelines, "the whole scheme breaks down." Planning Director Jacobs thought government "can legislate good taste." Without "binding power" over the developer, however, "all the good design clauses in the world (especially when they're billed as only 'purposes and intentions') will be meaningless." Kortum asked, "What is 'greater public benefit' and who decides? What is 'best architectural design' and who decides?" What would happen when Jacobs left the job? "This would appear to be planning-by-faith-in-Allan-Jacobs," she concluded. She still engaged with the SFIMC designs, as she had for months, complaining that "the public won't use these artificial and windswept rooftop gardens anyway. The 'gardens' on top of the Golden Gateway, by the same architect, are always conspicuously empty—and they're only one flight up!" But she primarily addressed land use. Supervisor Pelosi needed to consult the average "man in the street who cuts through an issue to the core." On the north waterfront, the man in the street understood that the SFIMC was the wrong choice for "that piece of land." San Francisco had too many pressing needs in addressing affordable housing, racial volatility, and recreation priorities to let this project go through.[34]

Underlying the SFIMC was a spectacular accomplishment in private urban land accumulation. The project's eight waterfront blocks stretched from Fisherman's Wharf to Golden Gateway. In 1962, when Bill Roth had "saved" the Ghirardelli factory buildings to public acclaim, Leonard Cahn quietly and systematically began buying land and purchase options on the north waterfront. Cahn lived in Mill Valley, near Virginia Green and Leila Johnston. Like the Roses, he built a design and construction business by riding Marin County's custom residential boom in the 1950s.[35] Like Karl Kortum, Cahn had a vision for San Francisco's waterfront that was rooted in his personal experience as a seaman in the late 1930s. But unlike Kortum, who worked toward city, state, and federal government stewardship, Cahn's dream was to own the land himself.

It took fewer than five years to buy the waterfront secretly. Cahn hired a young real estate salesman, Ron Kaufman, whose brief career had specialized in industrial properties with the firm Ritchie & Ritchie. Kaufman found a niche in convincing warehouse and manufacturing operations to move out of their historic multilevel north waterfront properties and into modern outlying facilities. While a student in Berkeley's new graduate program in real estate research and urban land economics, during the late 1950s Kaufman had worked three afternoons a week with Justin Herman at the Housing and Home Finance Agency's San Francisco regional office. In this "practical apprenticeship," Kaufman had learned the tools of assembling large development parcels by reviewing land appraisals for the Golden Gateway and Yerba Buena redevelopment sites. A few years later he applied those public-sector lessons in redevelopment land valuations to private acquisition of the adjacent waterfront north of Golden Gateway. Like other urban entrepreneurs in the early 1960s, Kaufman understood the investment wisdom of buying land across the street from renewal sites. He managed to keep the transactions quiet, which prevented real estate prices from rising. Although committed to Cahn's clearance and modernization plan, Kaufman had studied architectural history at Berkeley. He brought to the job an appreciation for the old warehouses he had systematically emptied out.[36]

Leonard Cahn achieved his "dream" by organizing twenty local investors, including the city's former planning director Roger D. Lapham Jr., to form North Waterfront Associates Inc. "We had achieved a unique and magnificent assemblage of land," Cahn wrote to the *Chronicle* editors in July 1968. Then came the investors' search for "a use worthy of the site." Late in 1964, NWA began consultations with a series of developers and designers. Several site plans became concrete enough to reach the press but all failed to gain traction until discussions with Henry Adams, a furniture industry leader, solidified the international trade mart concept.[37] In June 1967 the main partners—Cahn; Adams; contractor and developer Dillingham Corporation; architects WB&E; and landscape architects Halprin & Associates—had convened for only a few weeks. The venture blended two initiatives: modernizing the international wholesale furnishings trade and implementing a large-scale private urban design project. NWA anticipated that home furnishings would appeal to the design community and resonate with Jackson Square and other preservationist ventures, but the SFIMC was a clearance project.[38]

By January 1968, Leonard Cahn's ability to see a future city in this "hodgepodge of drafty, half-abandoned warehouses" had become part of the SFIMC publicity narrative.

One NWA statement said it "took a dreamer, . . . a man whose vision spans time and space," to achieve this level of master planning. "Where many of us at first saw the area as individual parcels of land, he conceived of it as an entity. It was he who quickened our imaginations." Yet the land ownership "vision" preceded any concrete plan for the waterfront imagined by the investors.[39] As Lapham recalled a year later, "We had to find a land use" in 1967 or "abandon the project."[40]

Marion Conrad Associates helped NWA extend its mission for the SFIMC beyond the vision of owning the historic waterfront. With the addition of WB&E and Lawrence Halprin & Associates, the publicists grafted design and landscape language onto the underlying feat of large-scale private acquisition. Before architects joined the team, the meeting minutes of the furniture trade and construction executives spoke plainly of "support facilities," interior halls, and parking spaces.[41] Conrad, relying on writer Stanford Erickson, scripted presentations, brochures, letters to editors, and press releases, then re-scripted them when the program changed. Her office collected "Statements of Purpose" and "Additional Quotable Material" from the participants and integrated the designers' ideas to articulate the project concepts in more public-minded terms discussing greenery and open space.[42] From Halprin's office, for example, Bob Buchanan and David Heldt sent Conrad some rough phrases to work with: "This project demonstrates a practical way to acquire landscape areas within the high density areas of our cities." It set "'a precedent for the urban land of the future city,' using large sections of the urban architecture as green parks, 'hanging gardens of Babylon in a contemporary context.'"[43]

Gearing up for the SFIMC's first public presentation of its plans at the San Francisco Museum of Art in late January 1968, Conrad's team emphasized the benevolence of the mart design in creating vibrant urban green spaces, showcasing a new rooftop park. This strategy for gaining public approval borrowed from the landscape architects' evocative terms more than the architects'. Heldt explained that the project would give San Francisco "a magnificent and unique six-block hillside garden-park overlooking the Bay, the waterfront, the bridges and downtown—a living tapestry of gardens and people in motion, interweaving on seven terrace levels." The designs so thoroughly integrated the "life-sustaining qualities of earth, rocks, water, grass, flowers and trees" into "this pace-setting business and commercial environment," Heldt claimed, that "we have turned the fabric of the business community from gray to green."[44] Maximizing the partnership of high-powered trade and world-class urban design, the landscape team explained that merging commerce, nature, and open spaces was a public-spirited innovation. These ideas about open space and commerce applied equally to old and new buildings and had the effect of minimizing such distinctions (fig. 128).

In contrast to the specific plans for the project's landscape architecture, the SFIMC's architectural details were extremely vague in the early brochure drafts. The buildings would "combine strength and grace to a remarkable degree." They were "muscular, vigorous—reflecting the busy hours of people at work and play—yet never stolid." Each mart structure was described by square footage, such as 2 million for home furnishings, 500,000 for clothing and accessories, and so forth. NWA promised a hotel, restaurants, theater, art galleries, shops, and 2,000 or 2,500 underground parking spaces. Early publicity materials described the hotel by its height and number of rooms (550–750), not its design. The project was a "city within a city, privately developed."[45]

The developers' progress depended on the city's cooperation. NWA's partners combed through pages of contacts in government, the press, and civic organizations in order to identify points of influence. The project managers consulted with Allan Jacobs and the Planning Department and initiated coordination with the port's waterfront studies undertaken by John Bolles's firm and Arthur D. Little. Beginning in July 1967, a stream of bureaucrats, elected officials, editors, and neighbors visited the architects' offices at 1620 Montgomery Street to view early presentations.[46] For the January 1968 museum presentation, the SFIMC team arranged an all-day rehearsal to work through the script and staging. Cahn, for example, would not sit at the "head table" but would remain in the audience as others recounted his visionary role.[47] Conrad made sure that the relevant city agencies saw the model and plans in advance. "Your 100 percent cooperation is appreciated," Goldsmith wrote to the numerous partners. "I am sure we all understand that we can afford no weak link."[48]

128 A second Carlos Diniz July 1968 rendering of the San Francisco International Market Center emphasized the new green spaces that the developer said would be accessible to the public in exchange for the city selling its streets. The watercolor rendering style was deliberately old-fashioned to evoke historical associations with the wharves, ships, bay, and hills, despite the planned clearance. Marion Conrad's office wrote, "Telegraph Hill actually flows right onto the roof deck in the central part of the project, and its overpowering presence will be felt from every outdoor vantage point." This rooftop park was the "green hairpiece" Karl Kortum described as a false public amenity masking a devastatingly destructive project.

For all the defensive planning leading up to the January 1968 unveiling of the plans, however, none of the diverse SFIMC partners anticipated resistance to selling public streets. Developers hoping to exceed height limits expected pushback from the city. Whereas Embarcadero Center flouted these limits by proposing a 60-story skyscraper in a 25-story zone, SFIMC's hotel placed a 20-story tower in an 8-story zone (see fig. 127). Because the SFIMC hotel loomed as "the only significant high mass in the entire area relative to Coit Tower," Halprin's office warned the developers that Allan Jacobs would reject the designs based on this fact alone. The closest Halprin's firm came to anticipating the street issue was noting the "absence of policy towards public oriented facilities." They found "very little effective pedestrian access through the site both E/W and N/S."[49] Other internal reservations about the central plaza and rooftop park surfaced as the project faced public scrutiny. Halprin's office jotted down opponent Karl Kortum's assertion that "even" Larry Halprin says the architecture "stinks."[50]

The controversy over city streets on the SFIMC site began with urban design decisions about view corridors, circulation arteries, height limits, and the destruction of historic properties—exactly the debates that were addressed through architectural models and renderings.[51] Accordingly, NWA's models and renderings drew sophisticated critiques from opponents even as they attempted to make the designs palatable. AMI's brochure explained that the SFIMC model "was designed to pass tough visual tests from every point of the compass. The tests came from those whose proprietary interests in San Francisco protect the city from real estate impulsiveness." View corridors were tied to streets, literally. "*View* is a key word to San Franciscans. It enhances real estate value, determines the city's personality." AMI's model situated the SFIMC within the surrounding site to allow analysis of views from all angles; it was displayed at eye level to "prove" to Telegraph Hill residents that there would be no obstruction and "counteract charges that no project looks very tall when viewed from above." Elsewhere THD noted that "the model doesn't show elevator shafts, ventilators, vents and other appurtenances which remain invisible in the promoters brochure and model."[52]

Between the January unveiling and the July 1968 hearing, the SFIMC's opponents successfully shifted the terms of debate from the mart's design and accessibility to the responsible stewardship of city land driven by the street vacation problem. The land ownership issues that would take down the project were little evident in models and watercolors. In July, Jacobs's endorsement of the now-conforming SFIMC design pushed opponents to dismiss the design framework entirely. THD's president, Gerald Cauthen, wrote to the *Chronicle*, "The developers could break up the façade, [p]ut in windows, take out vent stacks, plant trees on the roof, use bright colors or even provide 'a meaningful pedestrian experience.'—the problem would still be with us." Fixing the built form did not solve the larger issue that a massive wholesale furniture facility was ultimately a lousy use of the waterfront land.[53]

In response, the SFIMC doubled down on the idea that the public accessibility of its novel rooftop park offered a fair exchange for the city streets. To the critics, this missed the point. Streets were hardly generic land but rather represented transit, access, connections, and the potential for multiple uses. The SFIMC's July press release announced the developers' recalibration to emphasize public access, "magnificent" roof gardens, and other "sweeping changes" in design. Henry Adams stated that "approximately 1,889,000 square feet or 51 percent of the project (excluding the totally public parking area for over 2000 cars) will be open and accessible to public and visitor use." The center would offer "more retail space than Ghirardelli Square and the Cannery combined." The new plan, "with its contiguity and continuous access to the public," was "dependent on street vacations being asked of the City."[54]

Although the SFIMC's backers used a design-based definition of public stewardship to tout public access, citizen opposition moved on to the sale of the streets themselves. Karl Kortum's letters to the *Chronicle* tracked the intensification of the street vacation controversy. In March 1968 he attacked the project's accessibility, writing that "whole-saling is not a *public* activity, public relations fluff about open restaurants and plazas notwithstanding." He focused on the capacity of public relations language and architectural models to conceal. Most memorably, he wrote that even if the city wrangled a better design, "green hair-pieces on the roof still pass for parks and fool people in the four color brochure."[55] By July he had zeroed in on the city's land stewardship: "Green hair pieces attached to the cement roof are all that San Francisco gets in return for our streets."[56] Rooftop parks were a toupee coverup. Jean Kortum concluded a searing seven-page single-spaced memo to members of the Board of Supervisors with the single line: "Not a good enough reason to close public streets" (fig. 129).[57]

The SFIMC controversy drew unprecedented attention to the city's routine policy of closing streets and selling the land to developers. Suddenly, the key components that would comprise San Francisco's street vacation lawsuits for the next decade fell into place. The turning point came during the board's Streets and Transportation Subcommittee hearing when, under persistent questioning from Supervisor Morrison, the developer's representative confirmed that 22 percent of the private SFIMC site would consist of former streets.[58] This admission startled and energized the SFIMC's opponents; THD denounced this "tremendous and unjustified windfall for any developer!" The second piece of news disclosed at the hearing was the "bargain basement" price for the streets of $4.82 per square foot set by the city's assistant director for property.[59] Supervisor William Blake, who supported the SFIMC, said, "At that price, I know a lot of people who would buy land in that area." He added, "In fact, I might be interested myself."[60] The city's property office representative explained that the price was calculated at 50 percent of the streets' fair market value, on the rationale that adjacent property owners retained the other 50 percent of that value in easements. Opponents protested that this price defied both common sense and existing land appraisals. POW attorney Roger Kent presented a copy of a "fact sheet" from the developer's real estate broker that said as much: "Current market value of this land is conservatively estimated at $30 per square foot. Land for the nearby Rockefeller development was acquired at a cost of $31 per square foot." Kent claimed that the city's subsidy of $25 per square foot amounted to a gift of at least $5.5 million to NWA.[61] The next day Kent filed the first injunction, on behalf of Jean Kortum, alleging that the city had violated its own street vacation procedures in agreeing to the sale.[62] The "wholesale annexation of public streets for private benefit is

129 Jean Kortum as she appeared in the *San Francisco Chronicle* on July 13, 1968, with legislator John Burton
in the midst of the heated fight against the San Francisco International Market Center (SFIMC). Burton hoped
to lure the SFIMC to his district, away from the north waterfront. Besides speaking for the new group Protect
Our Waterfront (POW), Jean Kortum was claimant in a restraining order filed recently by POW's attorney, Roger
Kent, against the city's sale of public streets. The newspaper story cropped this image more closely, but Kortum and
Burton hoped the backdrop of another already cleared site would suggest other available locations for the SFIMC.
POW was not antidevelopment but offered strong input about where development should go. The urban-environ-
mentalist groups like POW aimed to spare the north waterfront warehouse district from demolition and instead
plan the area for appropriate public uses and much-needed affordable housing.

clearly contrary to public interest and therefore illegal," argued THD. The terms *public interest* and *private benefit* had legal meanings, but their colloquial usage was very resonant to San Franciscans as they scrutinized what looked like land giveaways (fig. 130).[63]

Over the next several weeks, the ramifications of San Francisco's street vacation policies unfolded on several fronts as the larger principles of enforcing responsible stewardship of the public domain on behalf of taxpayers came into focus. In one provocative reconceptualization, Jean Kortum argued that the city, rather than selling its land outright, should be recognized as a partner investor in this and other new developments based on the acreage of former streets.[64] In June, THD publicized how much the city typically *paid* to acquire streets. To widen Clay Street, San Francisco had paid abutting private owners $65.00 per square foot. It was "incredible," THD wrote to the supervisors, that the city sold for $4.80 and bought for $65.00. THD asked the board to investigate the situation, "which has ramifications beyond the Market Center case presently before you."[65] Although it still mattered that the mart would be monolithic and block views, the preservationists and lawyers began to let go of landscape issues to focus on land. Clinching this transition was THD and POW's conclusion in early July that the skyscraper

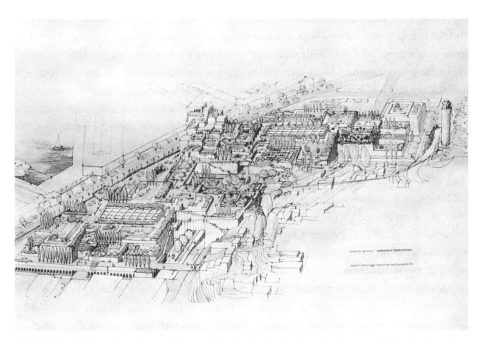

130 This Halprin & Associates drawing of the original urban design illuminated the large scale of the San Francisco International Market Center and the manner in which the private project erased public streets. Critics like Jean Kortum objected to the principle of selling the public domain to developers and fought the city's policy of selling the streets at half their appraised value. It became obvious to the preservationists early in the fight that the mart—a feat of secretive land acquisition—was first and foremost a "vision" of the private ownership of the waterfront. In San Francisco these urban-environmentalist experts made the erasure of public streets a policy issue in the courts—and won.

hotel had been a ploy. Gerald Cauthen told the director of SPUR, "It is now clear that the Northern Waterfront Associates never expected to build the hotel in the first place." The developers had manipulated the SFIMC's opponents by using an intentionally offending design to broker a fake compromise over height.[66] As Bobbie Stauffacher would say, the SFIMC's critics and the city's planners had been duped by design.

When Allan Jacobs came from Philadelphia to San Francisco in 1967 to take over as director of city planning, he recalled discovering that in San Francisco "the vacating and sale of streets was pretty normal" at that time compared with what happened in the cities he knew best: Cleveland, Pittsburgh, New York, Boston, and Philadelphia.[67] The Embarcadero Center urban renewal project introduced Jacobs to the role of streets in San Francisco development. When architect/developer John Portman unveiled his site designs in February 1967, the controversial two-block-long office building (the one Helmut Jacoby drew with a reassuring "etched break") necessitated the closure of Davis Street between Clay and Sacramento. Portman faced hostile reviews from resentful San Francisco architects, but Jacobs found the Planning Department virtually powerless when it came to preserving the streets. After the first tower was completed, in 1970, the Portman-Rockefeller team announced their willingness to divide the long building, provided they could increase its height from twenty-five to thirty-four stories. When Embarcadero Center's management eventually chose to keep Davis Street—now a 70-foot corridor separating the buildings—open, it was entirely their decision. Decades later Jacobs recalled, "We finally won on the one cross street." It was, he said, "the only damn thing that we won." Jacobs was left to express gratitude at the voluntary outcome, because the city had little leverage over former streets now owned by the developer.[68]

In fact, before Jacobs's time in San Francisco, a significant dispute between the SFRA and the state's port authority *had* flared in the early 1960s over the incorporation of streets and public trust land into the Area E/Golden Gateway/Embarcadero Center parcel. In 1960 Justin Herman and the SFRA had counted on buying the state's trust land within the project footprint for about $25, based on a nominal fee of $1 per street. However, the port authority took the position that "the streets should be entitled to full market value because they will be used as building sites." The numbers fluctuated over the several years of disagreement, but the two agencies remained "about $1 million apart" on the value of the state-owned streets in late 1961. This early 1960s dispute put the principle of public interest in waterfront land in the news and revealed that this transfer would constitute a sizable subsidy to the future private developer. At first glance it might seem that transferring the ownership of streets for Title I urban renewal land assembly would be a nonissue because it was subsumed within the sale of the entire renewal parcel to developers (which itself failed to foment significant public discussion). But that was not the case. On the other hand, the SFRA and the port authority ultimately resolved the issue by turning over public trust streets to waterfront developers, free of charge.[69]

The 1968 outcry over selling so many acres of public streets to enhance NWA's large holdings, backed by the SFIMC street vacation lawsuit, transformed San Francisco's status quo on these issues and invited closer scrutiny of city land stewardship. On

November 8, 1968, POW's Roger Kent filed a taxpayers' lawsuit in state Superior Court on behalf of Desmond and Valetta Heslet. The Heslets, who resided on Telegraph Hill, were respected for their community-building efforts and cultivation of public gardens. Desmond Heslet was a painter and artist with the *San Francisco Examiner*. Valetta Heslet danced in Hollywood musicals and had worked as a welder during World War II. The lawsuit asserted that the city's methods of vacating portions of Lombard and Montgomery Streets for the SFIMC violated its own charter, making the actions illegal. Specifically, the public land had not been advertised for sale and had not been sold to the highest bidder, as the charter required. The suit also claimed that the appraisal process had severely undervalued the land, which was worth much more than the $221,000 paid for it.[70] Given the city's ineffectual requests regarding Davis Street at Embarcadero Center during this same period, the radical potential of the SFIMC street vacation lawsuit stood out, as did the measured moral outrage.

Just as being adjacent to the Embarcadero Center and Golden Gateway urban renewal projects influenced the questions posed about the SFIMC land valuations, the waterfront location and intermingling with the port's public trust land also foregrounded land ownership patterns in the private SFIMC case. Jean Kortum learned in October 1968 that NWA had already applied to the port to acquire "surplus" property, anticipating the port's release of land for nonmaritime development. As the chair of POW, Kortum appealed to port authority chair Cyril Magnin to slow this transfer of trust lands. Just because NWA's project boundaries included port-owned streets and lots, she observed, that should not pressure the port to abandon its mandate to support maritime uses. The port should decide independently about "its own lands," disregarding the developer's demands and the city's street vacation votes. Kortum's economic case against NWA's proposal was equally strong. She found out that NWA expected a ninety-nine-year lease and full subordination in its terms of agreement with the port. Why would the port lease its land now? she asked Magnin. "It would pay the Port in the long run to let this land lie fallow under *its* jurisdiction rather than under that of a private developer, and wait out the inevitable escalation of the land value for a year or so." Given the prospects for financial gain, POW questioned "whether public properties should be leased 'under full subordination.'" Finally, the imminent transfer from state to city suggested that patience would benefit the public interest. Soon "leases would be limited to 66 years under a carefully worked out effort to protect public properties."[71]

The SFIMC's street vacation controversy, then, recast the resonant policy debates over the waterfront's public domain, and not merely among the project's opponents. During May, June, and July 1968, memoranda flew back and forth between Allan Jacobs and representatives of the port's two north waterfront consultant studies—Barry Wasserman of John Bolles's office and Claude Gruen of Arthur D. Little (ADL). The port had recently undertaken the first broad planning studies (by Bolles and ADL), while Jacobs had brought new leadership to the Planning Department. Jacobs, Wasserman, and Gruen corresponded about coordinating efforts, especially in the face of private development pressures. The all-night SFIMC Board of Supervisors meeting on July 15 inspired Gruen to strike a new approach. He interrupted a back-and-forth between Jacobs and Wasserman about the city's planning powers. Zoning restrictions, Gruen wrote his colleagues, were "strictly negative." Cities would always need eminent domain to discipline uncooperative owners. However, in the port's case they had an unusual opportunity: "the largest single chunk of the property is already owned by the public." Potentially, public land-owning agencies could finance and own projects undertaken on their property. Accordingly, "the land and its revenue generating improvements will remain forever in the public domain generating revenues to be used for other public goods and services." He continued: "Perhaps we should recommend a study of some arrangement that would permit this to be the case."[72] Jean Kortum would have seconded Gruen's suggestion, as would have Grady Clay.

Although NWA won all of the Planning Commission and Board of Supervisors votes, it lost the project. The Kent/Heslet street vacation lawsuit held a legal cloud over the site. That, combined with tight financing and the project's large size and complexity, ultimately spelled the SFIMC's demise.[73] Five months after NWA and the supervisors had endorsed the contract with seventeen covenants and a few weeks after Roger Kent had filed the lawsuit, the developers sought to back out of buying the streets. NWA returned to the supervisors to argue that without a street sale the contract was not binding.[74] The project's financier—Travelers Insurance Company in Hartford, Connecticut—objected to encumbering the project with such a restrictive contract. Travelers needed reassurance. If the developers merely wanted to build an international trade mart and had no need for public streets or roof gardens, they should be released from the design and other covenants. Without the streets, NWA's lawyers argued, "the owner can develop the land any way he sees fit as long as City codes and zoning regulations are met." According to the papers, the lender and NWA feared the suit "could delay the project long enough to kill it."[75]

The first week of January 1969, Lorraine Petty of the *Daily Commercial News* scooped the story that the SFIMC had committed to "another drastic design change—this time as a result of a court suit against sale of city streets for the project." A source at WB&E divulged that a new "block-by-block" plan would leave the streets intact. Although NWA's principals were "confident they could win the suit," Roger Lapham estimated that the delays could cost $2.5 million. The redesign eliminated the amenities and "garden effects." Allan Jacobs insisted to Petty that the new plan, which he had not seen yet, would still have to comply with the Planning Commission's design terms as established in the covenant.[76] The project never regained momentum and was declared dead in 1971. Travelers ended up with most of the land.[77]

The forgotten street vacation lawsuit and the SFIMC's failure together had the most measurable long-term impact on this substantial stretch of the north waterfront. The SFIMC's collapse initially devastated Ron Kaufman, who had devoted years to assembling the site for Cahn's clean-slate redevelopment plan. Kaufman later acknowledged that the lawsuit's success had allowed a preservationist approach to take root in the neighborhood. Within a few years, Kaufman had leveraged his incomparable knowledge of the area's properties into a career devoted to the historically sensitive adaptive reuse of the waterfront's warehouses and factories. A celebratory account of Kaufman's role on the north waterfront characterized this turn toward preservation as his own "enlightened private urban renewal." Against the clearance favored by Justin Herman, described in the book *The Old North Waterfront* as the "Robert Moses" of San Francisco, Kaufman "was almost alone in pursuing another, more novel way of redevelopment." With the neighborhood seemingly secure in the early twenty-first century because of historic district status, "it is important to also remember that most of the physical remains of the North Waterfront's colorful history came close to disappearing forever, but were saved by one of the early efforts at combining preservation and redevelopment." From Kaufman's perspective, the "grievously destructive lawsuit" had "indirectly" and unintentionally created the opportunity for Kaufman's "radical idea" of conservation to flourish.[78]

Contrary to Kaufman's harsh words for the "nuisance" street vacation lawsuit that he said represented only the "selfishness" of a retired lawyer and "several" hill residents, the neighborhood's preservation resulted directly from the organized citizens' campaigns of POW and THD against selling city streets in 1968. The street vacation lawsuits marked a novel public-interest tool in regulating urban land disposition, yet these new campaigns also built on the older 1940s adaptive reuse models established by Karl Kortum's vision of a historic waterfront district and the Maritime Museum. Both old and new waterfront campaigns by organized private citizens asserted the premise and power of responsible stewardship of public land, which was understood by its advocates to be a complex concept. Without detracting from Kaufman's later achievements in retaining the north waterfront's historic buildings, the crusade to "save" the neighborhood was in fact launched by the activists who challenged the then-common practice of selling city streets to developers and undermined NWA's clearance plan. In hearings and press coverage, the Kortums and other leaders and attorneys of THD and POW ridiculed design for its distracting controversies while simultaneously building evidence to prove that bargain street sales violated the public's interest in land.

In 1968 San Francisco's still-weak controls over private development and public interest were manifested in the restrictive SFIMC contract, dependent on design concessions, and in the Board of Supervisors' easy approvals selling city streets to developers. Although Allan Jacobs and the city's planning staff were working toward citywide design policy, toward an expanded master plan and the first historic district, and environmental impact reports were on the political horizon, none of this was yet in place. In that context, the victory against the monolithic SFIMC furniture mart on behalf of the public's interest in the low-rise, multiuse historic neighborhood interlaced with public streets, accrued to the citizen activists and the urban-environmentalist lawyers. That Kaufman came around to the preservationists' neighborhood plan without crediting them only makes the story of the street vacation fights more compelling and relevant.[79]

Because THD and POW asserted a *citywide* principle of public land stewardship, the SFIMC case made it harder to caricature preservationist "hill dwellers" for selfishly defending their own views against developers' greed. Gerald Cauthen's July 1968 letter to *Examiner* editor Charles Gould addressed how the newspaper covered the SFIMC. Cauthen wrote, "[I] ask that you end the news blackout of the controversy concerning the International Market Center." The mass media had not given the oversized proposal

131 This model promoted the original 1,000-foot-tall design of the Transamerica Pyramid as first presented to the Board of Supervisors and the public in January 1969. The shape, height, and location provoked an iconic urban design controversy. The photograph hazily gestured to the surrounding low-rise city; the skyscraper, San Francisco's tallest until 2017, would stand adjacent to the city's first historic district, Jackson Square. The final building design was shorter and squatter.

its due. "Neither have you made much effort to characterize those opposing the present plan as anything more than 'some people trying to save their views.'" While views were a legitimate concern, Cauthen said that most of the resisters "will gain nothing personally from their effort" and were motivated out of concern for the northern waterfront. Cauthen's THD was a "perfectly legitimate and responsible body of opposition." He reviewed the threats posed by the project. Although he thought Allan Jacobs had been duped by the high-rise hotel proposal into giving unwarranted concessions, Cauthen did not blame Jacobs. Rather, he thought, "If horse trading is to become part of the planning process, then our planners will have to learn horse trading." He invited the *Examiner* to investigate the project's alleged public benefits. "In asking that a sizeable portion of their facility be placed on public streets, the developers have elected to depart the domain of strictly private enterprise and thus subject their design plans to public scrutiny." Gould thanked Cauthen for his "logical" and "excellent" letter. THD pushed for press coverage of the SFIMC battle as a competition over land and the waterfront's future rather than depicting the project's opponents as seeking selfish preservation of their views.[80]

The same day the story broke that the lawsuit had pressured NWA to redesign its project without streets, Allan Jacobs was invited at the last minute to attend a meeting at Transamerica's offices. Jacobs and his staff, along with the city's public works director, engineer, and head of the Building Inspection Bureau, converged with others that afternoon at the four-story, lavishly restored Transamerica headquarters. There the assembled group was shown an architectural model of what would be the tallest skyscraper in San Francisco—a 55-story elongated pyramid.[81] When Transamerica publicized its plans later in January, the Pyramid became the next high-profile private development to galvanize the newly organized advocates for responsible stewardship of the public streets (fig. 131).

SKYSCRAPERS AND STREET VACATIONS: THE TRANSAMERICA PYRAMID

In 1970 one skyscraper in San Francisco was famously not a rectangle. The *Bay Guardian* editors featured the Transamerica Pyramid on the cover of its ambitious and groundbreaking 1971 critique *The Ultimate Highrise* (*UHR*; see fig. 6). Still under construction while the book was being researched, the Transamerica Pyramid's unusual shape, great height, and location at the edge of low-rise districts put it at the center of an iconic urban design controversy. Although today the Pyramid has become an object of affection, at the time it was proposed many loathed the building as an alien monstrosity inappropriate to San Francisco's unique skyline.[82] Yet Transamerica's most significant impact on San Francisco's landscape was through the street vacation lawsuits provoked when the corporation bought the street that bisected its site. For opponents hoping to stop, alter, or relocate the tower, it was famously a lost battle. For those who used the Transamerica case to challenge the city's practice of selling public land at a 50 percent discount to developers, the Pyramid was a triumphant victory. The Transamerica street vacation lawsuits were landmarks in defining and defending the public domain in San

Francisco amid large-scale rebuilding and developer initiative. The suits' significance rested not in arguments for preserving views, skyline, and streetscape but rather in its fight against the practice of giving up the city streets.

Between the Fontana Towers' 17-story wake-up call in 1961 and Transamerica's announcement in 1969, San Francisco's skyline had been transformed. Resisting Manhattan's symbolism in San Francisco had taken many forms over the decades, including concern about the concentration of poverty and the elevation of capitalist business values at the expense of all else. In 1969 skyscrapers became the locus of the city's anti-Manhattanization sentiment, and the national press began to report on the phenomenon: the Board of Supervisors' votes to override zoning laws, marches protesting the proposed U.S. Steel tower and Transamerica Pyramid, and the sheer volume of high-rise construction realizing the vision of San Francisco as the Wall Street of the West.[83] Whereas the Fontana Towers had violated "unwritten rules" about maintaining a low-rise waterfront and spurred passage of a 40-foot height limit, opponents now had to formulate strategies based on a litany of newly built and planned skyscrapers. Besides Embarcadero Center, the Alcoa building, and the Bank of America tower, the list of structures between 22 and 52 stories high included those housing Wells Fargo, the Wells Fargo Annex, Pacific Telephone, and Aetna Life, as well as the International Building. The Bank of America tower, as Allan Jacobs pointed out, violated another unwritten rule—namely, its massive black profile disrupted a light-colored, even white, city palette (see fig. 57). The national press repeated the cliché that organized opponents such as the Telegraph Hill Dwellers "are jealous of the views from their famous northeast look-out over the city," as the *Washington Post* reported. This mainstream coverage underscored the distinctiveness of the *Bay Guardian*'s attack on the economic rationale behind skyscraper development. Embarcadero Center, because of its associations with Rockefeller Center, and the Transamerica Pyramid, because of its attention-getting architecture and sheer height, were lightning rods for anti-Manhattanization in San Francisco. For their part, architects pointed to the new towers' redeeming feature of "opening land to the people through broad plazas." When a reporter asked architect Chuck Bassett of SOM why San Francisco had to keep getting taller, Bassett looked at him in amazement: "You can't put a layer of plexiglass around San Francisco and set it on your coffee table."[84]

Transamerica took pride in managing to build the tallest structure in San Francisco in this climate of increasing skepticism and organized activism. So much pride, in fact, that the company's public relations director, John Krizek, published an article titled "How To Build a Pyramid: A Kit of PR Tools Helps Win San Francisco's Approval for a New High-Rise Office Building," in the December 1970 issue of *Public Relations Journal*. Later reprinted in both *UHR* and the *Bay Guardian*, the article dramatized the company's strategies for maneuvering the difficult political climate. Because Transamerica declared its satisfaction in manipulating the system, the *UHR* and *Bay Guardian* editors had to add little (besides a few cartoons) to the reprints to make the same point (fig. 132). Krizek's article explained how "public relations played a major role in moving the project from plans toward reality." Although the "striking,"

THE BUILDING THAT IS BEING BUILT WITH A KIT OF PR TOOLS. TRANSAMERICA, A SAN FRANCISCO LANDMARK SINCE 1972, OVERCAME ALL OPPOSITION BY THE USE OF PRETTY CORPORATE SECRETARIES SERVING ICED TEA

132 The Transamerica Corporation was so pleased with how its publicity strategies overcame opposition to building the Pyramid that it did not anticipate backlash against the detailing of those methods in John Krizek's article "How to Build a Pyramid: A Kit of PR Tools Helps Win San Francisco's Approval for a New High-Rise Office Building," which appeared in the December 1970 issue of *Public Relations Journal.* This drawing, which appeared on the front page of the *Bay Guardian* on June 7, 1971, mocked Transamerica's pride in the power of promotional "tools." The Krizek article unwittingly confirmed the contention of critics that public relations was simultaneously powerful, manipulative, and ridiculous. The article itself also proved to be key evidence against Transamerica in the street vacation lawsuit over the city's sale of Merchant Street. The winning lawsuit demonstrated the power of land-based critiques amid the fallout of one of San Francisco's best-known urban design controversies.

"graceful," "soaring," "beautiful" design generated favorable international publicity, anti-high-rise sentiment in San Francisco required special handling. Krizek described the "complex community relations job."[85]

It was certainly illuminating for high-rise opponents to hear the public relations perspective recounted so elaborately. What earned Krizek a spot in the *Bay Guardian* and *UHR*, however, was his account of Transamerica's "surreptitious" dealings that were both absurdly small-minded and credited with great influence. Transamerica divulged that its representatives had infiltrated the opposition's meetings. At one rally of 125 protestors, there were "at least fifteen people, including wives, who were there representing the corporate staff, the architect's office, and other friends of the project— all incognito." At another rally, Transamerica's public relations manager met the opposition leaders as they approached the company headquarters. The manager "led a covey of attractive corporate secretaries out on the sidewalk to serve iced tea to the demonstrators, with news cameras as witnesses." In August, to draw attention to the upcoming Board of Supervisors vote on the vacation of Merchant Street, protestors planned another sidewalk demonstration declaring "Artists against the Pyramid." A pyramid of ice melted away, and demonstrators wore cardboard dunce caps. Again secretaries

133 Whereas the young designers and artists of Environment Workshop used street theater to protest the skyscraper, two equally young advertising executives disguised themselves to stage a counter-demonstration, lampooned by Mick Stevens. The artists' tools and construction crane were resonant motifs, and the crane's placement contributed to the drawing's message. Stevens's drawing "Artists *For* the Pyramid" appeared in the *Bay Guardian* on June 7, 1971, alongside the reprinted Krizek article detailing Transamerica's publicity strategies to overcome opposition.

carried out iced tea. Two "hippie-looking young men" joined in, as Krizek told it, "brandishing an 'Artists *For* the Pyramid' sign" and handing out leaflets (fig. 133). The counter-demonstrators were plants. They had their own ad agency and wanted to impress Transamerica with their creativity. Mick Stevens's drawing of the incident for the *Bay Guardian* showcased a construction crane and artists' tools. Bulldozers were old news because the site had been cleared a decade earlier, when the Montgomery Block was demolished. Krizek concluded with the story of how Transamerica rushed to construction by the end of 1969 by filing permit applications secretly, getting Christmas Eve approvals, and hiding a tractor behind the wall of a neighboring excavation—all in order to win a hefty state tax benefit. Krizek relished the opponents' discovery that they had been outmaneuvered (fig. 134).[86]

Despite the protestors' street theater, Krizek's pumped-up PR stagecraft, and heated confrontations at City Hall, the more important drama unfolded calmly and deliberately in the California courts over Transamerica's interest in buying Merchant Street. Amid the "hoopla," and despite losing all of the 1969 city hearings, several determined lawyers from the opposition quietly filed street vacation lawsuits in December 1969 and

134 The *Bay Guardian* offered a critical perspective of high-rise development and the city's steward-ship of the public domain not often seen in the mainstream media. Here Transamerica serves the building to the San Francisco press, who toast the Pyramid and "eat it up."

January 1970. They alleged that the city had wasted taxpayers' assets by selling streets cheaply in violation of the city charter. The lawyers and plaintiffs, compared with the young twenty-something architects and designers parading with dunce caps, were experienced advocates, generally of an older generation. In an unforeseen twist, the Krizek article would provide the opposition with precisely the evidence it needed to win the street vacation lawsuit against the Transamerica corporation. The piece of Merchant Street caught in the Transamerica footprint was small compared to the acreage of streets in the SFIMC proposal, but it engaged the same principle of fighting land give-aways to developers. [87]

When Allan Jacobs first viewed the Pyramid model on January 6, 1969, he explained to the Transamerica executives the role of the SFPD in approving the company's plans (see fig. 131). Preceding a CPC hearing, the SFPD would have to find that the vacation of Merchant Street or a transfer of its air rights complied with San Francisco's master plan. Second, the building site lay in a sensitive transitional neighborhood between high- and low-rise districts recently protected by a CPC resolution, and would thus require discretionary design review.[88] The 1,000-foot pyramid, exactly what planners had intended to prevent in this zone, would be the first test of this review power. Jacobs's staff prepared "urban design terms of reference" for the specific site. The terms guided an otherwise ad hoc process and gave the city a negotiating position, but they were not binding. The planners, developers, and architects quickly reached an impasse over the building's height. The planners' demands to better integrate the pyramid's base into existing city fabric and offer adequate public spaces had more traction with the developer's architect William Pereira.[89]

At a difficult June 1969, CPC meeting, the commissioners overrode their own Planning Department's negative recommendations and approved the Transamerica building, 5 to 2. By a closer vote of 4 to 3, the commission also found the street vacation in conformity with the master plan. Ten days earlier Transamerica had submitted a redesign that added public amenities to the base. Two levels of lobbies would be topped by a third-level plaza; now the base included terraces, landscaping, plazas, and shops, all of which would be accessible by stairs from the street. By purchasing more property on the block, the corporation explained, it lowered the Pyramid's height to 853 feet and reduced it from 55 to 45 floors while expanding the base from 133 to 150 feet across.[90] Transamerica hoped that buying additional lots abutting Merchant Street mitigated planners' concerns about neighbors' access. The building's shape, Transamerica argued, was chosen for "minimum interference with views." The site's zoning permitted more floor area than the Pyramid would use, which held the unspoken threat that the architect could revert to a bulkier design if the city disapproved the Pyramid.[91]

The two areas requiring approval, namely, the building designs and the street vacation, comprised a mixed agenda that forced the commissioners, planners, and public to grapple with how landscape and land interrelated. The Downtown Association found itself on the fence regarding the Pyramid's design but appreciated the building's anticipated $750,000 annual tax revenues to the city. The street vacation issue was simpler:

"Transamerica owns both sides of the street, so let them use it as they desire and request."[92] The young designers of the recently organized group Environmental Workshop pointed out that "all the architectural jargon such as light and air, preserving views, and landscaped plazas, are a smokescreen to cover up the fact that Transamerica is soon going to build itself the tallest monument west of Chicago."[93] Michael Doyle, a young landscape architect with Halprin & Associates, said the building belonged in a desert. Mrs. (Friedel) Hans Klussmann, a founder of the older advocacy group San Francisco Beautiful (and veteran leader of the 1940s fight to save the city's cable cars) thought the Pyramid had a certain elegance but fit better near Market Street. Much of the testimony appreciated the building's design but just not in that location.[94]

While architects and others protested the Pyramid's shape and location, the city's urban environmental organizations questioned whether the proposed sale met the legal (and popular) standards of public benefit. At the CPC hearing, a representative of watchdog group SPUR said: "Any vacation to private developers of a public street must be contingent upon major public benefits resulting from the development." Albert Meakin, president of the Citizens Planning Committee, and THD's Gerald Cauthen saw no demonstrable public interest represented in the project's amenities and therefore opposed selling the street. Architect Sherwood Stockwell agreed that this was "a matter of principle" and speculated that Transamerica could not build its Pyramid without Merchant Street. Commissioner Julia Porter reminded her colleagues that they "had repeatedly endorsed the closing of streets in San Francisco," pointing out how this case broke with precedent. Porter (who usually voted for development) asked Jacobs if he objected to this street closing because of the building's design. Jacobs replied no. Traffic, access, and fire risks compounded Transamerica's failure to comply with the design terms even in its improved plans; that failure meant "that no public benefit would be derived from the closing of the street area."[95]

Rather than being dismissed as irrelevant, minor streets like Merchant in fact provided the infrastructure that preserved the neighborhood's small-scale ownership patterns. Architect Stockwell reminded the CPC of the urban design benefits of small streets. The commission's own guidelines for the so-called Portsmouth Corridor (the key transitional area between the financial district to the south, Golden Gateway/Embarcadero Center to the east, and North Beach and the waterfront) assumed that "the street pattern in the area would work as a built-in control against the merger of a sufficient number of the small and narrow lots typical of the area to allow construction of really massive buildings." Jacobs added that small streets "would ordinarily protect against the accumulation of large parcels of property under single ownership on which high-rise buildings could be constructed.[96] Small streets had instrumentally spurred Jackson Square's development, especially given the district's lack of squares and plazas. From this perspective, Merchant Street made an illuminating comparison with nearby Hotaling Place. Both small streets shared the distinction, after 1972, of dead-ending into the Transamerica Pyramid. Yet in 1960 the city redesigned Hotaling Place with new paving, landscaping, and street furniture to enhance Jackson Square's intimate Gold Rush atmosphere. In contrast, the city accepted Transamerica's argument that Merchant Street was a useless alley and sold it to the developer (see fig. 16).

The Transamerica case now moved to San Francisco's Board of Supervisors, where the Merchant Street hearings strengthened the alliances forged previously in the SFIMC street battle but catalyzed new opposition leadership and new lawsuits. The supervisors had jurisdiction only over the street vacation proposals, which eased the transition from a design fight to a street fight. Fueled in part by the apparent injustice of the CPC's overruling its own planning director, public interest in the matter grew, and letters inundated the Board of Supervisors. Critics condemned the design as ugly, egotistical, overbearing, a monstrosity, Disneyesque, and so on. "Should corporate arrogance dictate San Francisco's urban form? Should a handful of appointed citizens with little, if any, knowledge of design override the recommendations of a professional urban design staff?" The street "is the property of all the people of San Francisco and should remain so," wrote Haruko Misumi to the board. As he had in the SFIMC street vacation case, Supervisor Jack Morrison registered the sole vote against the Merchant Street vacation in the Streets Committee hearing.[97]

The Environment Workshop encapsulated and fomented the urban design protests mounting on the eve of the board's August 1969 Transamerica hearings. The workshop represented the young generation of design professionals in the fields of architecture, landscape architecture, planning, environmentalism, and the arts. The cofounders were two landscape architects, Michael Doyle and Andy Butler, who both worked for Lawrence Halprin & Associates. Halprin allowed the group to use his offices for their weekly meetings, which drew ten or so regulars, supported by about twenty-five irregulars. The workshop had emerged late in 1968 at the height of the SFIMC controversy (when Halprin's office was part of the developer's team) and found its focus the next year in battling Transamerica. Another core member, Katherine (Kitsie) Carroll, worked for Allan Jacobs in the Planning Department. In a letter to the *Chronicle*, the group explained their goal of educating the public about how individual buildings influence the "general social and physical aspects of urban life" and how "architecture expresses cultural values." Susan Landor, at the time a Sierra Club photographer, recalled her interest in doing for the urban environment what the camera had done to promote wilderness awareness. Landor did not want her native San Francisco "to become another New York." The workshop mobilized against overdevelopment through urban design strategies; the street vacation hearings were the means to that end.[98]

The Environment Workshop members saw their youth and professional backgrounds as key to initiating urban environmental change. The attorneys and plaintiffs they stood with at the street vacation hearings, representing organizations such as THD or SFT, were often over sixty years old, and certainly over forty. The workshop criticized Pereira's "look-at-me" pyramid, explained how the tower violated planning codes, and asked the supervisors to vote against closing Merchant Street. As young people, they wrote in their *Chronicle* letter, "we will have to live longer with this gigantic urban eyesore longer than you—the over 30s—if it is built." They asked, "Please bridge the generation gap and join us in an appeal to the Board of Supervisors to stop the Building." Susan Landor recalled, "We were idealistic and fearless, imaginative and creative, and believed we could make a difference using our moxie."[99] Their counter-cultural protest tactics triggered backlash: "Have you seen this *group* of *long hairs* that disapprove the building?" one letter asked the supervisors. "Educated gentlemen" such as yourselves, the author implored, surely would not be "swayed by bare footed folks who for the most part look homeless."[100]

Environment Workshop's 1969 booklet *San Francisco and the Transamerica Pyramid* stirred the urban design opposition that carried people to City Hall in August. The straight-talking, heavily illustrated booklet explained how architecture and urban design integrated individual buildings into the character of a place and why the Transamerica Pyramid disrupted San Francisco's unique essence, scale, texture, hills, and views. Following environmentalist models, Michael Doyle's graphics captured how, thus far, San Francisco's building patterns had "accented" the city's distinctive hills and valleys. Accordingly, the financial district was a "man-made hill." Transamerica violated these patterns and threatened to pull the high-rise financial district northward, despite city planners' agreement that it should expand south (figs. 135–37). Doyle's drawings ("Some Thoughts on the Pyramid") offered ways of envisioning the building that were outside the box of promotional renderings. Landor's photographic composites patched the Pyramid into existing views, such as from Columbus and Broadway (the Condor Club's sidewalk) and from the 30th floor of the Wells Fargo building.

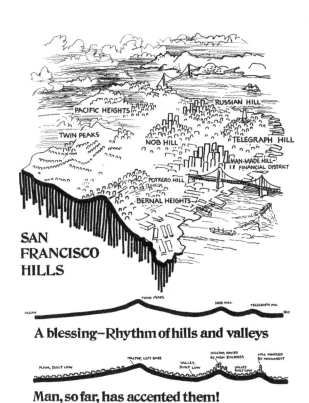

135 Michael Doyle, a landscape architect in Lawrence Halprin's firm, illustrated the planning concepts at stake in high-rise construction for a 1969 booklet produced by the Environment Workshop. The financial district, he explained, was a "man-made hill." The group rallied young designers who protested the Transamerica and U.S. Steel proposals and made many appeals to the general public. In San Francisco redevelopment, the urban built and natural environmental issues merged.

Rather than articulating a simplified antidevelopment position, Environmental Workshop's young designers expressed their professional opinion regarding the headquarters' location. The group spoke directly to Transamerica, hoping that the corporation would lead its peers in respecting the Portsmouth Corridor. The young architects, planners, and environmentalists admired the corporation's recent restoration of its current four-story building close to the Pyramid site. "Dear Transamerica," the twenty-somethings wrote. "We do want you in San Francisco. We think you are pretty groovy people. We do understand that you share with us a dream for San Francisco. We only want to point out that in its proposed location, your building would change the nature of the city that is yours, as much as ours." The workshop complimented the corporation's willingness to come down to street level to talk: "We couldn't have met you that way in Manhattan." San Francisco was unlike Manhattan in other ways: "New York is a city gone mad: anything built there is almost irrelevant, the city absorbs it." This urban design controversy represented neither a pro- versus anti-development divide nor mere personal aesthetic judgment, as Krizek's article and others alleged.[101]

Hundreds of people turned out for the August 25, 1969, Board of Supervisors meeting, which marked the peak of public mobilization against the Pyramid but also a decisive loss for its opponents. Measured by the protestors' demands, the August vote of 9 to 1 in favor of vacating 183.3 feet of Merchant Street was a complete defeat. The tallest building in San Francisco (up until 2017), in the shape of a pyramid, had been approved for the contested location, and another street had been sold at half price to a developer with-

136 With "Some Thoughts on the Pyramid," Michael Doyle provided alternative ways of thinking about the Transamerica proposal beyond promotional renderings.

I said, "Why should a pyramid
Stand always dully on its base?
I'll change it! Let the top be hid,
The bottom take the apex place!"

The New King's praises fill the land.
He clings to precept, simple, dull;
His pyramids on bases stand.
But—Lord, how usual!

"The Innovator"
by Stephen Vincent Benet

137 Michael Doyle's drawings managed to distill the Environment Workshop's frustrations with the Pyramid, but ultimately the group's critique was an articulate professional analysis of established planning concepts guiding high-rise development. They were not antidevelopment or merely obstructionist. When Doyle cofounded the Environment Workshop with Andrew Butler in late 1968, their employer (Halprin & Associates) was the landscape architect for the contested San Francisco International Market Center. In the Transamerica Pyramid case, the Environment Workshop protested the location and shape of the skyscraper, as well as Transamerica's decision to add plazas, terraces, and landscaping for the first City Planning Commission review and street vacation hearings but eliminate the public amenities two months later, once the project was approved.

out discernible public benefit. Jacobs walked away from the meeting more determined to improve the city's planning and zoning controls. He knew that the bar was too low in the Planning Commission's review of conformity with the city's master plan, especially concerning street vacations. Transamerica's attorney summed up the master plan's vague guidelines: "The streets must serve access and pedestrian and traffic flow needs where such needs exist." Jacobs committed to the complex undertaking of a new comprehensive plan. His staff had already begun drafting preliminary studies for the city's *Urban Design Plan*, adopted in August 1971, which sought to standardize how design fit within city planning policies. Crafting individual urban design terms of reference after each project had been announced came too late in the process, he said. The *Urban Design Plan* would take a strong stand against casually vacating streets for developers as part of Jacobs's efforts to create proactive, systematic policies. (fig. 138).[102]

As protest shifted that fall from urban design to the sale of city streets, the Transamerica case marked a turning point in holding San Francisco to stricter standards of public interest in negotiating large-scale redevelopment. For their part, the Transamerica representatives left the decisive August 1969 Board of Supervisors meeting feeling victorious. The volume of design protest faded in the face of this defeat. And yet many more hearings on the fate of Merchant Street were to come. A cohort of attorneys and plaintiffs stepped up to lead a new fight—first against Transamerica's purchase of

Merchant Street but soon to broadly challenge street vacation practices and the irresponsible stewardship of public assets that casual street vacations represented. Most of the lawyers and plaintiffs—such as John B. Harman and Albert Meakin—had emerged from the local urban environmental organizations THD, POW, and SFT and had attended public hearings since the SFIMC battles. They filed the first Transamerica-related lawsuits in December 1969, followed by another in January 1970. In April 1970, when the corporation requested a third portion of Merchant Street, the supervisors again approved the sale. Records of the supervisors' hearings reveal the protesting attorneys' increasing sophistication in challenging the city's land stewardship practices against the background of these losses. The courts were a different matter. Two years after filing their first lawsuit, the attorneys began to win the street vacation cases in November 1971.[103]

The event that provoked Harman, Meakin, and others to turn to the courts was a poorly attended November 1969 supervisors' meeting to review an additional 21.7 feet of Merchant Street requested by Transamerica. Two of the six people in the audience were Transamerica representatives, and the other four opposed the sale. In this intimate group, lawyer John B. Harman of THD and artist Albert Meakin of the Citizens Planning Committee bonded in their outrage over the proceedings. These two would form the backbone of the lawyer-plaintiff partnerships in the lawsuits. When Jacobs and the Planning Department reluctantly conceded this sale based on precedent, they cleared the way for the attorneys to take the lead against street vacations.[104] On December 9 John Harman with attorney Charles J. Quantz filed a lawsuit in California Superior Court on behalf of city resident and taxpayer Peder (Pat) A. Gunnufsen (a retired real estate broker and contractor), asking the judge to issue a restraining order against Transamerica. This first legal action challenged the results of the November meeting on procedural grounds, alleging that it had not met the legal requirements for a public hearing. It had been scheduled only two days in advance, and none of the 125 or so people on the supervisors' mailing list had received written notice.[105] These delay tactics put Transamerica on notice that their December 31 deadline for starting construction was in jeopardy.[106]

Defining the public-interest principles at stake in the street vacations was a pair of attorneys, John Harman and Hal Howard, whose legal work was affiliated with the city's urban environmental organizations, in part through such plaintiffs as Jean Kortum and Albert Meakin. Howard had just passed the California bar examination in 1969. Attending a THD talk about the Transamerica Pyramid had propelled Howard into partnership with the experienced Harman, who had begun formulating the legal arguments against street vacations. As a new attorney, Howard devoted hundreds of hours to researching the issues and writing briefs. Howard and Meakin became active in SFT, as did Jack Morrison and his wife, Jane Morrison. Jean Kortum's civic leadership included THD, the Bodega Bay fight, the Freeway Crisis Committee, and POW.[107] Meakin, an artist and printer, headed the Citizens Planning Committee. In 1964 he led a successful coalition protecting Golden Gateway Park from the proposed Panhandle Freeway. He was seventy when the Transamerica street vacation cases came under review. John Harman, representing THD, was about sixty years old and nearing retirement, having spent much of his career in public-sector regulatory fields and consumer

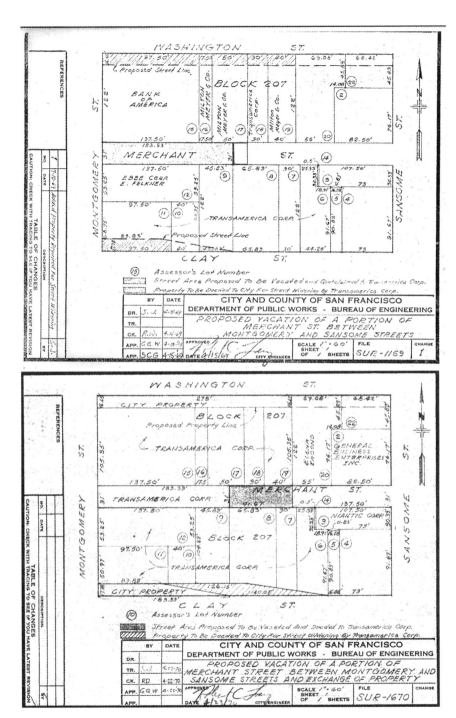

138 Merchant Street bisected the Transamerica headquarters' site, and a sequence of three surveys done between April 15, 1969, and April 22, 1971, documented the corporation's incremental purchase of the street and neighboring properties. The surveys depicted the land issues literally underneath the controversial Pyramid design. The street vacation hearings of the Board of Supervisors gave lawyers John Harman and Hal Howard a platform to challenge the practice of selling public streets to developers— a battle they soon took to the courts, and won. The first and third of the surveys are included here.

protection.[108] "You gentlemen are all attorneys," Harman told the supervisors and legal staff at one hearing, arguing why Transamerica's questionable machinations for more streets should be obvious to them.[109] The circle of legal expertise signaled a shift to the courts on this principle of equity and public interest in redevelopment.

John Harman became the spokesperson for the opposition at that November 1969 street vacation hearing, publicizing the worst part of Transamerica's redesign—the elimination of the public amenities it had added to secure CPC approval a few months earlier. He told reporters: "Whenever a big corporation wants public property, the supervisors just roll over play dead and give it to them." Only recently Harman had blended into hearings without distinction. At the November meeting Transamerica's attorney, Sam Roberts, argued that the company needed the additional 21.7 feet, to be purchased at the customary half-price fee, to "square" the site. Architecture remained outside the scope of street vacation hearings, but the withdrawal of negotiated public amenities at the tower's base directly contradicted the public-interest requirement of the city charter. The opponents "warned the supervisors to be wary of any architectural niceties outlined in plans for Transamerica." As Harman charged, "They used terraces and a plaza as bait the first time around. After they got what they wanted from the city, they pulled back the bait." The latest plans "eliminated a three-level terrace and landscaped plaza outlined earlier."[110] Still, the Streets and Transportation Committee voted 2 to 1 to advance the decision for a full board hearing, and the next day, the CPC approved the new building plans 4 to 3, again over Jacobs's objections. Mike Doyle said that the betrayal would "make young people more militant," and Harman called it a "travesty."[111] Harman continued to testify prominently at supervisors' hearings and administrative appeals but now switched his pursuit of the public-interest principle to the courts.[112]

As *San Francisco Progress* reported, "After all the hoopla of outraged protests over the Transamerica Pyramid proved futile, a group of persistent attorneys quietly took the issue to court." After the November procedural filing, on December 30 John Harman returned to court with new charges alleging that the city's director of property had undervalued Merchant Street by half. The suit asked the court to either make Transamerica pay the city the difference of $213,000 or stop the street vacation.[113] But Harman's first two Merchant Street lawsuits were the warm-ups for three Transamerica-inspired taxpayers' cases that would change the city's rules governing the closure and sale of public streets to developers: *Albert Meakin v. City and County of San Francisco et al.* (*Meakin* I); *June Harman v. City and County of San Francisco et al.* (*Harman*); and *Albert Meakin v. Steveland Inc. et al.* (*Meakin* II). The first two were filed in tandem early in 1970. *Meakin* I challenged only Transamerica's Merchant Street vacation on the basis of the city's undervaluation of the street, whereas *Harman* contested eight recent street vacations to achieve broader scrutiny of how the public's interest in land was safeguarded. The third case, *Meakin* II, came a year later and pushed the public-interest principle into new terrain. Taking up a developer's purchase of Ecker Street to build a bulkier tower, *Meakin* II sought to establish an alternative land valuation theory that better secured public benefits in the face of spreading large-scale and high-rise development.

Meakin I alleged that when the city sold Merchant Street to Transamerica for $62.50 a square foot and bought adjacent land from Transamerica for $125.00 a square foot, the sale violated the city charter. After two years, in November 1971, California's Superior Court ruled for the plaintiffs, finding that the value difference of $532,000 represented "a gift of public funds to Transamerica." The case, brought by John Harman and Hal Howard on behalf of plaintiff Albert Meakin and, once again, Peder Gunnufsen, built on arguments in the first Harman lawsuits regarding the city's valuation policies.[114] Howard called the victory "a landmark decision" that "would put an end to City Hall's 'giveaway' of public property for massive construction projects."[115] Judge Jay Pfotenhauer ruled that the 50 percent discount for streets sold to owners of abutting properties (to account for easements of access) was capricious and also violated the city charter's provision requiring the city to accept no less than 90 percent of the original appraised value. Hal Howard described his elation at discovering the Krizek article reprinted in the *Bay Guardian*. During Harman's questioning of the Transamerica executives, Krizek's article offered surprise evidence that cut through the men's "I don't remember" defense and established that the presidents of the three corporate entities within the Transamerica holding company had met regularly to review all the planning and protest details. The judge struck down San Francisco's 50 percent appraisal practice, and Transamerica paid the city an additional $532,000.[116] Design questions had dropped out. The Merchant Street lawsuits made responsible land stewardship a citywide public-interest concern separate from anti-high-rise sentiment.

The January 1970 *Harman* case built on the Transamerica-specific *Meakin* I but avoided contesting high-profile skyscraper cases so that the broader land principles at stake would take center stage.[117] Harman instead challenged eight private institutional developments that had quietly secured street vacations without controversy, including the Pacific Medical Center, the Shriners' Hospital, Pacific Gas & Electric, St. Mary's Hospital, and ITT Continental Baking Company. *Harman* posited that $800,000 worth of streets had been sold for half their value in these eight instances and asked the court to compel the city to collect the additional $400,000 from private interests. Alleging "the waste of municipal assets," John Harman filed the suit on behalf of his wife, taxpayer June Harman, a supervisor for the city's Parks and Recreation Department. *The Examiner* said that the suit accused the city of shortchanging "itself and its taxpayers." In October 1971 the state Court of Appeals dismissed the case. But when Harman and Howard won *Meakin* I a month later, Harman brought an appeal to the state Supreme Court and then won *Harman* in a unanimous decision issued May 15, 1972.[118] Following *Meakin* I, the judges found that the city charter "obviously sought to prevent the enrichment of individual private purchasers who in a noncompetitive sale would obtain city assets at less than fair value." The 50 percent policy had originated in the logic of an earlier era when small-scale abutting owners claimed continued access and thus easement value in the streets. By the 1960s, large-scale land acquisition for redevelopment by single owners had obliterated the neighbors, who found the highest value in selling their land to the developer who would "consolidate it with other properties." With this consolidation, the rights of access were "of no value" to the abutters. The city would have to assess the value of each street separately, not according to a 50 percent formula.[119]

With the *Meakin* I and *Harman* lawsuits moving through the courts, Merchant Street came back to the Board of Supervisors for a third and final review, and this time John Harman did most of the talking. During the spring of 1970, Transamerica requested vacation of an additional 91.67-foot portion of Merchant Street and proposed another redesign. Allan Jacobs and his staff, having shifted their energies to enacting the citywide *Urban Design Plan* and updated master plan, conceded approval.[120] The Department of Public Works had asked Transamerica to exchange land on Clay and Washington Streets that the city needed for street widening (at $125 per square foot) for another stretch of Merchant Street (at $62.50 per square foot) (see fig. 138). The new Merchant Street parcel included the 21.67-foot portion already vacated in November under a slippery assertion that the third vacation would resolve unclear property records from the chaotic early twentieth-century "earthquake days." Transamerica's attorney said that the company would buy the "useless stub-end street." At the first board hearing, Harman opened by stating that "all members of this Board are familiar with my participation in matters involving Transamerica and Merchant Street," particularly his litigation against the city and county and the company. This new street vacation, he said, was "an effort to affect a proceeding pending before the courts" by converting what had been a sale of street property (the basis of the lawsuit) into an exchange (governed by different laws). Harman protested against the atmosphere of inevitable approval and called the street-widening expense "madness." An SFT attorney asked if buying additional street enabled Transamerica to enlarge the building. Street vacation approval, he said, was the city's last power over Transamerica. Once it caved in, the city "will have completely lost control of the situation."[121] The supervisors again approved the vacation of Merchant Street at the 50 percent discount.

The attorneys representing THD, POW, and now SFT monitored the Streets and Transportation Committee docket of the Board of Supervisors for relevant cases involving city streets. In the spring of 1971, Harman, Howard, and Meakin joined again to bring a third significant lawsuit, this time over Ecker Street (here called *Meakin* II). A respected developer had asked to buy one block of Ecker Street adjacent to a Market Street site where plans included a 40-story tower. "The street will be resurfaced with brick, landscaped and remain open for pedestrians," said a city spokesman. The price was set at $290,625. "The proposed sale was moving smoothly along," a reporter noted, "when attorney John B. Harman of the Telegraph Hill dwellers asked why the developers want to buy the street if they aren't going to build on or over it." San Francisco's zoning administrator answered frankly: "Without the street, they could build about 865,000 square feet, or about 35 stories. With the street, they could build 1,041,000 square feet, or about 40 stories." The extra 176,000 square feet of rental space would generate $1.4 million in annual income for the company. Harman objected that "the sale of a public street simply to permit private interests to increase the height of their building . . . is not a proper basis for the sale of public property." At the full supervisors hearing a month later, the city explained that the additional space would generate $9,300 in annual property taxes. The developer pledged to keep Ecker open to the public as a walkway, connect it to a "sweeping pedestrian plaza" for the high-rise, and provide utility easements to the city. The supervisors, Planning Department, and director of property endorsed the sale.[122]

When *Meakin* II was finally won on appeal in 1977, the justices found that "the sale was not so much a sale of land, as a sale of developmental rights." Harman had brought in an expert witness offering an alternative theory for valuing the vacated land. Thus *Meakin* II not only followed the two previous lawsuits in alleging that violation of the city charter's bidding and appraisal requirements made the Ecker Street vacation illegal but also succeeded in getting the court to acknowledge the need for a new land valuation approach that safeguarded the public interest amid escalating development. The 1977 decision stated that when the plaintiff's first effort was stricken, he "came back with a new argument" defending the unconventional valuation. The singular purpose of the purchase, its highest and best use in appraisal terms, was as development rights for the large-scale developer. The trial court had denied this approach because it violated a principle in eminent domain cases that excluded evidence relating to a proposed specific use for a property. The appellate judges ruled that *Meakin* II was not condemnation but "more akin to any transaction negotiated between two private parties." The justices concluded that "the developmental rights were obviously the only thing of value that the city had to transfer to developers," which was precisely what the plaintiff's expert witness had argued. The 1977 decision reversed the previous judgment and validated the plaintiff's "method of computing value based upon reasonable certainty" regarding future land use. In the 1970s San Francisco's high-rise future was clear.[123]

The Transamerica-connected street vacation lawsuits—*Meakin* I, *Harman*, and *Meakin* II—together set higher land valuation standards for protecting the public interest as the city negotiated with the private sector over the growing demand for urban land. San Francisco's cohort of urban-environmentalist attorneys and plaintiffs (Kortum and Kortum, Harman and Harman, Meakin, Kent, and Howard), and the organizations behind them (THD, POW, SFT), moved on from their victory against the SFIMC to bring the Transamerica suits. The street vacation cases struck down the prevailing practice of selling city streets at half price to developers and introduced an alternative land value theory that supported *raising* the public land price based on the "reasonable certainty" of large-scale downtown redevelopment. During late 1960s and early 1970s—a period of intensified competition for urban land in San Francisco—the street vacation cases succeeded in distinguishing the enduring land question from the city's urban design and skyscraper controversies.

In the early twenty-first century, the city has many more tools for monitoring the equity of large-scale development, many of which date to the 1970s. Under Allan Jacobs's leadership, the city's Planning Department staff implemented the *Urban Design Plan*, a greatly expanded master plan, and its first historic district (Jackson Square). The most immediate effects of this changing regulatory balance were felt in San Francisco during September 1972. That month the city issued a moratorium on building permits for major construction projects until the implications of the recent state Supreme Court's CEQA ruling could be determined. If environmental impact reviews were going to be required for most private development projects, the administrative (and environmental) ramifications were staggering.[124] CEQA transformed the regulatory environment in which responsible stewardship of public land was defined and defended in urban development. In fact, the timing of the 1972 CEQA decision helps explain why the street vacation victories did not sustain the attention they earned. Street vacation lawsuits nonetheless have continued to play a role in San Francisco controversies over the public interest in land today, with references to *Harman* particularly increasing in recent years.[125]

When heated debate over the design of the overwhelming SFIMC project turned to a focus on street vacations in 1968, critics identified public stewardship of the waterfront as the real issue plaguing this private redevelopment. The SFIMC's opponents succeeded in blunting the power of design language, with Karl Kortum and Jean Kortum drawing attention to the "green hair-pieces" of the parks, singling out public relations phrases they said were "fluff" but also served to conceal and distort the land grabs at the heart of the deals. The Transamerica Pyramid became a flagrant urban design issue in January 1969 at the same moment that the SFIMC developers gave up their plans to buy city streets. The public review process transitioned the pyramid from a landscape "hoopla" over its shape, height, and location to a fight over the undervaluation of Merchant Street. Building on POW and THD's airing of the fact in the 1968 SFIMC case that the city habitually sold streets to developers at half price without bidding, the cohort of urban-environmentalist attorneys successfully restructured the city's handling of the public's interest in the streets by 1971 and 1972. These private citizens and their taxpayers' lawsuits were soon backed by the Planning Department's *Urban Design Plan*. The plan's 1970 *Preliminary Report* advised that in every case the city seek out "the least extensive and least permanent release of public rights in street areas." This improved on the Planning Department's current strategy of scrambling ad hoc to answer developers' demands in a time of loose, cheap street appraisals. Allan Jacobs's work on these plans represented the city's most vigorous effort to proactively use urban design to curb street vacations, thereby deploying the landscape-land dynamic in favor of the public interest.[126]

The 1967–72 fights over the streets elevated ever-present undercurrents about public land ownership, and questioned, as Grady Clay had, how architecture and urban design could possibly be adequate mechanisms for controlling the future of city land. Like privately redeveloped Ghirardelli Square a few blocks west and adjacent urban renewal sites Golden Gateway and Embarcadero Center just east, SFIMC and Transamerica exposed tensions between landscape and land, design and dollars, public and private, historic and modern. The taxpayer lawsuits leveraged the streets as useful and meaningful public land, not merely as redevelopment bargaining chips. The landscape battles continued to matter, but responsible public land stewardship and "giveaways" also became determinative factors in renewal decisions. In these controversies, preservationists and their lawyer allies experimented with fresh conceptualizations of the city's investment in private development. On the ground in San Francisco, today the greatest impact of these street vacation fights is evident in the eight-block stretch of the "old" north waterfront, where the SFIMC would have cleared the neighborhood's Gold Rush–era factories and historic warehouses. Instead, Karl Kortum's late 1940s citizen-activist vision of a historic maritime district backed by public ownership had prevailed, though amended to match the growing private-sector investment. Jean Kortum, Karl Kortum, John Harman, June Harman, Hal Howard, Albert Meakin, Roger Kent, THD, POW, and SFT stepped into a policy gap in the 1960s to launch more effective controls over private development and public stewardship.

On a bright fall day in October 1974, Mayor Joseph Alioto and Board of Supervisors president Dianne Feinstein dedicated Justin Herman Plaza with the help of Herman's widow and daughters. The "parklike area" stretched between John Portman's "glamorous" new Hyatt Hotel (part of Embarcadero Center's Area E urban renewal site) and the double-decked Embarcadero Freeway. The Ferry Building could be glimpsed on the other side of the freeway, a road Feinstein said she hoped would "come down soon" so the plaza could be expanded. Robert Caro's biography of Robert Moses, *The Power Broker,* had just come out, and Alioto could not resist comparing Justin Herman to Moses. Alioto "praised Herman as being in the same class as New York's Robert Moses, saying they were both men who 'could get things done, but Justin had more artistic insight.'" Then the mayor repeated some clichés about Herman's opponents: "Alioto contemptuously referred to environmentalists who successfully blocked the highrise development of the waterfront as 'dyspeptic obstructionists. . . . They don't want to do anything.'"[127]

Just as Justin Herman was not Robert Moses, the city's urban-environmentalist groups were not obstructionists. Over several decades they had injected their planning ideas, backed by broad-based expert analysis, into the city and state's political and legal processes in order to achieve their own development vision for the waterfront. Recognizing that the urban environmentalists were allied design professionals rather than cranky protestors foregrounds their expertise and their informed, proactive positions. They rooted their low-rise plans for the historical maritime properties in the responsible stewardship of an urban domain already known colloquially as public trust lands—distinguishing the waterfront's patchwork of public and private parcels. Their vision pre-dated the city's modernist plans, and at the 17-acre SFIMC site the preservationists pushed NWA developer Ron Kaufman to eventually accept and implement their renewal concept as his own. They were so successful that the developer they battled now takes credit for their ideas. In 1968 THD president Gerald Cauthen demanded that the mainstream press stop caricaturing preservationists as obstructionists selfishly protecting their precious views. But it took the city's alternative press to investigate seriously the preservationists' critiques of weak public land stewardship and developer land grabs in San Francisco. If Greenwich Village and Jane Jacobs had the *Village Voice,* San Francisco's urban environmentalists had the *Bay Guardian.* For those who saw urban renewal as a land grab from people of color and low-income citizens particularly, there were also the region's African American newspapers like the *San Francisco Sun-Reporter.*[128]

Conclusion
"Got Land Problems?"

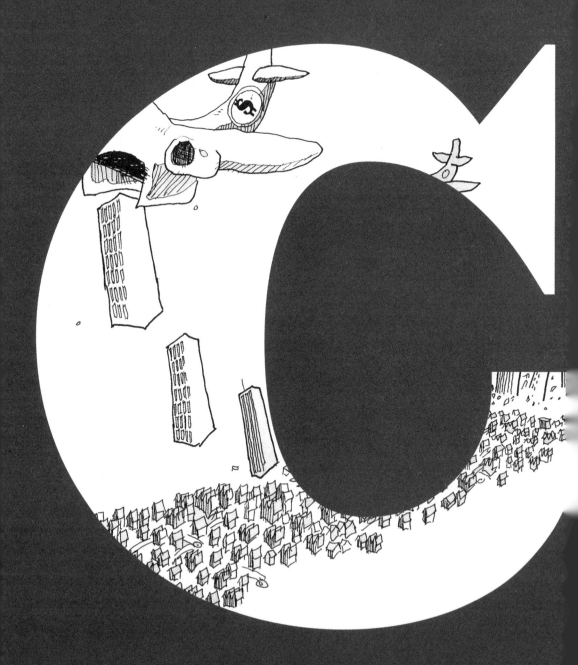

In 1974, Robert Caro's *The Power Broker: Robert Moses and the Fall of New York* heroically solidified the dominant framing of postwar U.S. urban redevelopment as a case of Jane Jacobs versus Robert Moses. We could say that *The Power Broker* was the bookend to *The Death and Life of Great American Cities.* Only after Caro's book was published, for example, did the mayor of San Francisco begin comparing SFRA director Justin Herman to Robert Moses.[1]

In the 1970s San Francisco produced a very different literature. One might imagine this conclusion by assembling a shelf of alternative books and writings on the nature of urban renewal. From Henry George's *Our Land and Land Policy* to *The Ultimate Highrise: San Francisco's Mad Rush toward the Sky,* this bookshelf would align the sequence of resonant yet forgotten Bay Area–based works into a new historiography. At times the shelf would create unfamiliar juxtapositions among known works, yielding new narratives. It could account for the character and impact of various writing genres, including public relations materials, Board of Supervisors minutes, street vacation lawsuits, and architectural criticism. The shelf would certainly hold unpublished works like Grady Clay's lost manuscript and Bobbie Stauffacher's memoir, "Duped by Design." We would have to make room for artifacts besides written works, such as Virginia Green's architectural models, the 1940s renderings of Karl Kortum's visions, or a yellowed news photograph of Caree and Stuart Rose holding hands in the business pages. The addition of such artifacts to a shelf holding texts would prompt us to notice the distinctive role words played in shaping a visual and material built environment. The published word is only the most conventionally articulate format for accessing the professions dedicated to city building.

UHR and like-minded 1970s publications, such as *The People's Guide to Urban Renewal,* chronicled a Bay Area–based critique that interlocked with that decade's street vacation lawsuits, alternative press, and urban-environmental groups with their arsenal of newsletters, booklets, cartoons, and street theater. This last story for the shelf, then, is one about *UHR* and San Francisco's anti-Manhattanization movement. This concluding chapter answers a question I posed in the book's introduction: how could it be that *UHR* was named in 1972 the most "important book on the urban question since Jane Jacobs's *The Death and Life of Great American Cities*" yet today is virtually unknown?[2]

The history of the anti-high-rise movement is more complex in San Francisco than in any other U.S. city.[3] Many sites discussed in this book—the Fontana Towers, Embarcadero Center, and Transamerica's Pyramid—played central roles in disputes over building heights. Height-limit proposals and studies (deploying various legal mechanisms) hung in various permutations over the city's skyline, either inspiring or infuriating, depending on one's perspective. Against this crowded backdrop, the 1971 publication of *UHR* by Bruce Brugmann, Greggar Sletteland, the *Bay Guardian* staff, and "52 other arch skyscraper foes" stood out. *UHR* set out to prove "that highrises cost the city more than they pay" (fig. 139).[4] The book challenged the presumed inevitability of skyscrapers, arguing that skyscraper advocates lacked proof for the alleged economic benefits they brought to cities. High-rise proponents had glossy brochures, public relations firms, and political contacts. What they did not have was hard evidence that towers created jobs or brought in more tax revenues than they consumed in city services. *UHR's* authors rested their case on exhaustive research into reams of government records. Height limits, no matter how complex and sensational their story, were only one quite narrow measure of anti-Manhattanization in 1970s San Francisco.

UHR was the brainchild of the *Bay Guardian*, the region's influential alternative newspaper. Founded late in 1966 by recent arrivals Bruce Brugmann and Jean Dibble, the newspaper staked a position outside the traditional power structure from which it pursued development and environmental stories relatively free from pressures endemic to the mainstream press. By then married a few years, the couple had surveyed U.S. metropolitan areas for a promising region in which to start an alternative paper. Brugmann became the editor, and Dibble used her business background as managing director.[5] Manhattanization was one of the *Bay Guardian*'s bread-and-butter topics, inspiring the editors to produce *UHR* because a book would attract wider and more sustained attention. *UHR* was colorful, collaborative, memorably illustrated, and bracingly opinionated. The book's conceptual originality, direct challenge to skyscraper advocates,

STOP THEM FROM BURYING OUR CITY UNDER A SKYLINE OF TOMBSTONES

Both the above pictures are of downtown San Francisco. Same spot. Same time of day. Same weather conditions. The top one was twelve years ago. The bottom one, last year. San Francisco was once light, hilly, pastel, open. Inviting. In only twelve years it has taken on the forbidding look of every other American city. Forty more skyscrapers are due in the next five years. They are as great a disaster for the city economically as they are esthetically. Ask a New York taxpayer.
What can you do to stop it?
Contact SAN FRANCISCO OPPOSITION, 520 Third Street (second floor) or telephone 397-9220.

139 Contrasting photographs of the San Francisco skyline in 1957 and 1969 made an effective advertisement for one of the city's antiskyscraper organizations. The ad, which appeared in the *San Francisco Chronicle* and the *Examiner* in October 1970, was reprinted in *The Ultimate Highrise* in 1971. This coincided with Alvin Duskin's 1971 campaign to limit building heights in the city to 72 feet.

and multipronged research earned it positive reviews. The *Washington Post* called it "a superbly documented book" by a "crusading newspaperman." In 1975 the *LA Times* said the book had "received favorable attention from university urban planning departments."[6] In Boston, where European-type restrictive height limits dated to the nineteenth century, Jane Holtz Kay of the *Boston Globe* described *UHR* as "a widely circulated quasi-underground study" that gave "statistical evidence that highrises burdened city services—fire, police, etc.—more than they re-paid."[7] Critics respected the book's frenetic, driven editorial style and its original research.

One East Coast review called out something else important about *UHR*'s San Francisco audience. The book won "awards all over the place," but in San Francisco it could not even buy advertising space in the *Chronicle* or the *Examiner*. It was a badge of pride for the book's editors that it was never reviewed in San Francisco or in the nation's two preeminent skyscraper cities—New York and Chicago. The book's art director heard that all copies in San Francisco's public libraries had been stolen. *UHR* could explain this too. The book documented how local media "underreported" and caricatured the anti-high-rise movement while actively promoting large-scale development. It tied that bias to the land and development investments made by the owners of the city's mainstream media, such as the publishers of the *Chronicle* and the *Examiner* and owners of television and radio stations.[8]

Whether admired, resented, or ignored, the book triggered a scramble among skyline-watchers for facts, usually in hopes of contradicting *UHR*'s findings. The San Francisco Planning and Urban Renewal Association commissioned a two-year, $300,000 study that found that skyscrapers more than paid for themselves. Brugmann shrugged it off, responding, "It's the same old businessmen making the same old report." A 1974 study by the Boston Municipal Research Bureau modeled itself on *UHR* but concluded that Boston's skyscrapers *did* pay their keep. The book and related *Bay Guardian* articles raised what critic Kay called the many "unstudied" questions surrounding high-rises.[9]

In the 1970s, the now forgotten *UHR* would have ranked with *The Death and Life of Great American Cities* because it critiqued decades of entrenched planning policies that promoted skyscrapers as a means of making San Francisco the Wall Street of the West. Puncturing the skyscraper mystique was a separate problem from unmasking urban renewal, despite their overlap in certain redevelopment projects. Reviewer Nicholas von Hoffman wrote in the *Washington Post* that "thirty souls in San Francisco—economists, architects, planners and desperate citizens"—had teamed up to produce this "surprising book." The researchers had assessed ten years of redevelopment policies nominally directed at tackling the "urban crisis" through rebuilding "the downtown with huge, flashy office buildings. Everywhere we're told that's how the city will save itself, will generate tax revenues, create jobs." Thorough research, however, pointed to the conclusion that San Francisco's skyscrapers were "destroying the economy." The authors were not in a position to offer solutions, von Hoffman acknowledged. But the book "can provide people with a blueprint, a way of looking at their towns and what's going on in them, a way of finding out, not what the urban crisis does, but what it is."[10]

The visual vocabulary the *Bay Guardian* artists developed to describe skyscrapers upended the conventions of high-rise renderings, which overwhelmingly were derived from promotional architectural materials (see chapter 8). As artists understood, people's visual perceptions of high-rises were intimately tied to their opinions of the towers, political or otherwise. The book's illustrations compared high-rises to filing cabinets, tombstones, or matchbooks, depending on the intended critique. According to *UHR*, all skyscrapers were rectangles and all architects were the same. Rectangles implicated the designers equally, obviating the need to even mention individual structures. This mirrored the editors' intent to move beyond contesting single buildings to challenge current development policies as a whole. The newspaper covered developers, but architects appeared in chapters only because of their influence in politics, bureaucracy, planning, or land investment rather than because of their role in design. The buildings were "bricks, and that's how Louis drew them," Brugmann remembered.[11]

"Louis" was Louis Dunn, who drew most of the *UHR* cartoons and was the book's art director. Like the delineators employed by architects, Dunn brought dead buildings to life, creating what architectural illustrators called "portraits." He did so here with a different argument, for a different client.

Dunn targeted what *UHR*'s authors saw as the unbalanced and disturbing values embodied in San Francisco's changing skyline and experimented with fresh "root metaphors" for framing high-rise development amid the frustration with existing clichés, in the spirit of Grady Clay.[12] Dunn's visual strategies engaged readers to critique the familiar, inherently static high-rise. He ignored stylistic differences among skyscrapers and lumped tall buildings together as indistinguishable slabs. Dunn "bent" or curved the rectangles to add dynamism and surrounded the structures with swarms of automobiles, which seemingly had eyes. He often added a jaunty fleck somewhere. This small bubble represented a click sound, like a cluck of the mouth or a snap of the fingers. Dunn intended the fleck to remind readers of the buildings' nonvisual dimensions. "It's like a little piece of electricity," he elaborated. "You don't really see it but it's there when people move, make a sudden movement." Most obviously, Dunn anthropomorphized skyscrapers. They had eyes, noses, mouths, arms, and legs. Occasionally they spoke. But they did not listen. They never had ears.[13] Dunn's themes included the complicity of business, media, and government in promoting high-rises; public giveaways to developers; and private-sector greed (figs. 140–146). And whereas architects' renderings isolated design from current events, a newspaper artist like Dunn probed such associations and found them to be a rich source of stimulating metaphors.

In a photograph at the back of *UHR* depicting its senior writers, artists, researchers, and editors, Louis Dunn stood at the far left (fig. 147). The photograph captured some of what energized the group—the shared mission to change people's minds, empower the citizenry, and radically improve San Francisco's future. "They were on fire. It was a very heady time," Dunn recalled.[14] For the photograph's setting they chose a partly cleared site in the controversial Yerba Buena urban renewal district, currently stalled by lawsuits against SFRA's relocation policies. The paper's editors occasionally reprinted this emblematic shot to rekindle its animating spirit. Bruce Brugmann stood at the center of the photograph on the top row, while Jean Dibble is the first woman on the left, on the lower tier. The *Bay Guardian* employed a small army of research interns for the book, which fed the newspaper for years with useful data. The photograph also spoke to the group's youthful informality and its gender balance. A contemporary cover from the magazine *San Francisco Business*—reproduced in another 1970s work, *Yerba Buena: Land Grab and Community Resistance in San Francisco*—serves as a useful contrast. "Four San Francisco Mayors" embodied the proximity of business and government in the city's older power structure—the proximity *UHR* hoped to subvert (fig. 148).[15]

The People's Guide to Urban Renewal, published in 1974, shared with *UHR* a collective grassroots approach to research that countered the prevalent fetishizing of consultants' expertise and reports. *The People's Guide,* a smaller collaboration by Leslie Shipnuck, Dennis Keating, and Mary Morgan, also relied on Louis Dunn's illustrations. Focusing on urban renewal rather than skyscrapers, the *Guide*'s authors similarly emphasized equipping citizens with tools to find information on their own. A drawing by Dunn ("Discover the Hidden Facts!") showed redevelopment data "hidden" in plain sight (fig. 149). Homeowners and residents could secure needed facts without difficult and intimidating digging. *UHR* also emphasized the power of ordinary people's finding out the real story. These books sought to put at people's fingertips the public information that corporations and government tended to hoard (fig. 150).[16]

The impact of *UHR*, *The People's Guide*, and the *Bay Guardian* extended beyond their effectiveness as circulating publications; they helped train a new generation of activists who spread out into the arts, journalism, and law with a focus on protecting the urban environment against overdevelopment.[17] Sue Hestor, wearing a floppy hat in the *UHR* photo, became one of San Francisco's most influential land-use lawyers and an advocate for slow growth, affordable housing, and equitable planning. For *UHR* Hestor compiled a chart of the 244 top donors to the city's victorious political campaigns; she identified how "persons connected with land/development/real estate" dominated the contributions. Hestor had arrived in San Francisco in 1969, transferred by a design firm led by architect Ezra Ehrenkrantz. Her job was editing planning documents, but soon she found herself immersed in waterfront development battles. She attended City Planning Commission hearings, followed Allan Jacobs's actions closely, and joined San Francisco Tomorrow. Her political organizing background swept her into helping to get an anti-high-rise proposition onto the November 1971 municipal ballot.[18] Hestor went to law school so that the "community side" would have an expert in land-use planning; she picked up where then-retired John Harman had left off. Looking back, she recalled that in San Francisco "planning issues and anti-war organizing seemed to overlap." Hestor began to leverage public-interest concessions from developers through filing lawsuits that challenged the accuracy of the environmental impact reviews now required by CEQA. She was the chief author of Proposition M that, when passed into law in 1986, limited office construction and preserved light industry in the South of Market neighborhood.[19] Proposition M and the city's 1985 Downtown Plan together marked a mid-1980s watershed of stricter growth controls in San Francisco.[20] Hestor's career traces a throughline of advocacy for higher standards of public land stewardship

Coit Tower Preserved

140 "U.S. Steal," by Louis Dunn, 1971. Land stewardship, corporate greed, the risks of accepting corporate benevolence, and giving away the waterfront were this illustration's themes. Issues not raised by Dunn in the drawing included architecture, landscape, and urban space. U.S. Steel proposed leasing port land to build its "10 mile high building" and out of "gratitude" built "this passenger terminal (which nobody needs)." In this manner, the city "loses a waterfront."

141 Louis Dunn's 1971 "Coit Tower Preserved" mocked development compromises. In the name of preservation, the city was lost in a forest of towers.

142 Louis Dunn, "Holding Hands," 1971. Dunn was especially pleased with his drawing of San Francisco's historic City Hall and an unnamed skyscraper, where he subsumed architectural style to the larger political point of business–government complicity. The tower took the lead in this stroll.

143 A television, radio, and newspaper joined hands and cavorted in a circle around a skyscraper, characterizing the mainstream media endorsement of high-rise construction.

in redevelopment, from the grassroots *UHR* and John Harman's taxpayers' street vacation cases to the policy pressures of CEQA reviews and Proposition M.

The Ultimate Highrise, Bay Guardian, and *People's Guide* succeeded because they aggressively focused on land and power, explicitly moving landscape and design to the margins. *UHR* in particular delivered a big idea to the redevelopment debate, questioning whether skyscrapers contributed to urban economies as claimed. *UHR* mapped the workings of power and identified the city's largest landowners and their political and economic influence. Systematically dismantling the framework supporting the city's rebuilding policies, this was indeed a fresh "way of looking" at the urban crisis. *UHR* offered a "blueprint" for moving forward with a renewed vision of the public interest and civic equity.

Placing *The Ultimate Highrise* (1971) on the shelf next to *The People's Guide to Urban Renewal* (1974) coaxes similar themes out of other adjacent titles. For example, San Francisco is the only U.S. city with a book that has "land grab" in the title: Chester Hartman's *Yerba Buena: Land Grab and Community Resistance in San Francisco* (1974). Hartman's book, later revised and republished with the title *City for Sale*, has offered a powerful analysis of the bias in San Francisco redevelopment toward selling the city, literally and metaphorically.[21] Together these 1970s publications built on the land stewardship and public-interest principles evident in the 1960s waterfront battles. They backed the like-minded efforts of those who filed the street vacation lawsuits, citizens' organizations like Telegraph Hill Dwellers and San Francisco Tomorrow, and the *Bay Guardian*. These books challenged skyscrapers and not only urban renewal policy. They gave citizens tools for identifying and proactively addressing redevelopment plans to control land by both the private and public sectors, whatever form those plans would take.

144 Louis Dunn, 1971. "In Our Studied Opinion" accompanied an analysis of three recent consultant reports favoring high-rises. *The Ultimate Highrise (UHR)* picked apart each study's reasoning, identifying examples of unquestioned assumptions and blind support. *UHR* called Claude Gruen a "professional your-conclusion-for-a-price consultant." *UHR* similarly dismissed the Willis Report as an "amateurish highrise glorification job." "Miss" Beverly Willis, an architect, had founded a thriving consulting practice in planning, design, and preservation. Architect Bobbie Sue Hood told the *Bay Guardian* it had published the best review of the McCue study, saying she had written that report for the firm. Bobbie Sue Hood to the Editor, *Bay Guardian*, April 12, 1972, 2.

145 Louis Dunn, 1971. In the Bay Area, where the anti-war movement permeated local politics, some of Dunn's towers arrived by airlift. His illustrations integrated high-rises with other contemporary concerns, such as the Vietnam War. This drawing depicted planes air-dropping skyscrapers, smashing up the residential areas below. It prompted this question: Where did high-rises come from? The first plane had a dollar sign, keeping financial motives in sight.

146 Louis Dunn, 1971. Agriculture—sowing, seeding, growing, and roots—gave people something fresh to ponder about high-rises as well. A man in business attire cracks a switch over two wrecking balls and a bulldozer, plowing furrows through low-rise neighborhoods. A second man with a seed sack plants towers in their wake. Dunn's choice of agricultural cultivation coaxing production from the land contrasted with the landscape architects' open spaces and rooftop gardens. Where urban design debates and competitions in this era usually occurred apart from site clearance, Dunn tied the two.

147 This photo of "writers, artists, and re-searchers" who contributed to *The Ultimate Highrise* appeared at the back of the book. The group, which posed on the Yerba Buena urban renewal clearance site, evoked the collective, gender-balanced approach that permeated the project. Louis Dunn stood at far left, lower tier, with Jean Dibble to his left. In the top row, at the center of the photo, is Bruce Brugmann. Sue Hestor wears the floppy hat.

148 The wood-paneled interior view of "Four San Francisco Mayors" contrasts with the staff photo for the *Bay Guardian*'s *Ultimate Highrise*. Chester Hartman chose this March 1973 cover from *San Francisco Business Magazine* to visually capture the city's political leaders in his book *Yerba Buena: Land Grab and Community Resistance in San Francisco*. From left to right: Mayors Elmer Robinson, George Christopher, John Shelley, and Joseph Alioto.

To portray these publications or the 1960s fights that preceded them merely as angry blasts from antidevelopment activists misses their context, long history, expertise, and relevance to the present. The language of "land grab" carries an aura of irate radical critique, but these 1970s publications matter-of-factly demonstrated the mundane threat within ordinary politics. They argued that land belonged transparently at the center of urban debates. Justin Herman thought the city should lease rather than sell its land to developers; this was one reason Grady Clay admired him. Clay framed redevelopment as competition for urban land and worried about the misunderstood impact of urban design on that distribution. Director of City Planning Allan Jacobs agreed that the city's street vacation policies were inequitable and discouraged the practice for individual cases and in the 1971 *Urban Design Plan*. The urban environmentalists proposed fresh conceptualizations for valuing urban land, outside the dominant business-government model, in the spirit of Henry George. In the Bay Area, those who advocated for improving the mechanisms safeguarding responsible public land stewardship were at the center, not the radical edges, of redevelopment.

When the specific redevelopment policy battles evolved in the 1970s, the ongoing inequities of access to urban land remained. *The People's Guide* asked: "How can people use a guide that is largely written about obsolete urban renewal programs and adopt it for dealing with community redevelopment programs that have not yet replaced them?" Unfortunately, the "basic realities" of urban life persisted beyond the lifespan of these programs: poverty, inadequate shelter, and the fact that "too often the poor have borne the brunt of the price for public improvements that have never benefitted them." Organized business, on the other hand, predictably managed to acquire from the public sector what

149 *The People's Guide to Urban Renewal* (1974), which also used Dunn's drawings, joined *The Ultimate Highrise* and the *Bay Guardian* in taking the approach that ordinary people could research relevant information regarding urban redevelopment and explained how citizens could get their questions answered and build their own expertise. The "hidden facts" were ultimately not very hidden.

it needed to "function efficiently and profitably." The mid-1970s represented a high-water mark for the publications (and also the street vacation lawsuits) that centered such issues. But whatever the status of civic debate, *The People's Guide* asserted, the "social struggles fought over the control and use of urban land grind onward."[22]

In the late 1960s and early 1970s, these Bay Area publications resonated with a rise in land-centered perspectives on redevelopment in other U.S. regions. Most notably, a land-grab critique united urban and rural civil rights organizers. Attorney Harold (Hap) R. Washington Jr. published two companion booklets, *Black Land Manual* and *Black Land Manual: Got Land Problems?*, in 1973. The first booklet surveyed South Carolina laws relating to the rights of heirs, partition, condemnation, and other legal devices "in order to help Black people retain more of their land." Washington, a civil rights activist who taught at Harvard University, Howard University, and North Carolina Central University, had moved as a child from New York City to South Carolina. He drew lessons from the black land ownership crisis on Hilton Head, where speculators backing resort development were using legal and illegal tactics to "separate Blacks from their land." Taking the long historical view of the problem, Washington dedicated *Black Land Manual* to "Aunt Sophie Daise and all of the freedmen who got the Forty Acres, but never got the mule." His practical manuals addressed the topics of "how land is gotten" and how it was lost. Whereas *Black Land Manual* instructed paraprofessionals and law students helping those whose rights were "in jeopardy," *Got Land Problems?* spoke directly to those who themselves were in jeopardy. Washington's publications joined the era's wave of "nascent organizations dedicated to stemming the tide of black land loss in the

150 Dunn's drawings of glassy automaton heads on bulldozers suggested that destruction and demolition were mindless. Or at least the minds were controlled from elsewhere.

South," as described by historian Andrew Kahrl.[23] Large-scale redevelopment pressures made the 1940s through the 1970s a prolific time for land-centered critiques across the nation, as westward settlement had done for Henry George's era a hundred years earlier.

During the same years that Washington was writing his *Black Land Manuals,* the Black Power movement initiated an urban land ownership strategy rooted in the crises wrought by Title I urban renewal. The Black Land organization, founded in the historically African American Shaw neighborhood of Washington, D.C., was part of this national trend. *Black Land News,* the Shaw group's newspaper, said that neighborhood residents had started the Black Land movement (BLM) because redevelopment had generated hope but not delivered. BLM's chairman was a young architect and planner, Bill Street, who had received his design degree from nearby Howard University. Street and his associates worked within mainstream organizations. For example, they got BLM representatives elected to Model Cities council seats, which gave them a role in the next generation of redevelopment programs following urban renewal. Street also founded the Black Land Design program to teach young people woodcraft, carpentry, design, and construction. Most important, the bustling BLM office had created its own professional master plan for the neighborhood, which included housing, parks, schools, a hospital, and a low-cost food cooperative that had already opened.[24]

In the late 1960s, BLM's leaders concluded that urban renewal had primarily benefited white "land grabbers." It was now time to aggressively build African American ownership of the neighborhood. "Private profiteers" had targeted redevelopment districts, "buying property and reselling it to the government at a higher price than they paid." This made true renewal harder to achieve "for poor black people." Why was black landownership the solution? "We have been pushed around from one urban renewal project to the other basically because we have never owned the land. . . . Power can only come to black people if they control land." Without BLM's intervention and vision, the federal government would "transfer this land (for very little money) to new 'owners.' Private developers (mainly white people) will be encouraged to buy the land in Shaw for rehabilitation and reconstruction."[25] Instead, "We feel that urban renewal gives us our first big opportunity to prove that black people can be landowners." Shaw residents would have to become "private developers," Street said. "It is obvious that whoever controls the land controls the development of that land." BLM's arguments meshed cleanly with Grady Clay's insistence that the competition for land drove urban redevelopment. BLM intended to fund its master plan without federal money. Staking out this independence for a *Washington Post* article on BLM, Street posed in front of a poster depicting John Carlos's famous Black Power salute at the 1968 Munich Olympics medals ceremony.[26]

Bill Street participated in a community "black-white dialogue" in February 1969 that was intended to reassure whites that the Black Power and Black Land movements were mainstream and nonthreatening. About sixty-five people, two-thirds of them white, met in a church basement in Cleveland Park, a D.C. neighborhood not far from Shaw. Wearing a suit and tie, architect Street explained to his discussion partner, Leslie Amouri, that African Americans had long campaigned for integration and the power of participation, but the nation's answer had always been "no" (fig. 151). Street tried to put

Amouri at ease: "I want to make sure you go home and sleep well. I just want you to say 'yes' to Black Power." Amouri did not understand how blacks were going to "get this power." Street replied, "Well, look, power has always been based on ownership of land, right?" Amouri persisted, saying, "Yes, but how are you going to get it? How are you going to get the land?" He worried that taking land likely involved violence. Street cited federal urban policy as his precedent, answering, "All the means are already there. Like Urban Renewal and things like that. It's all there." Although his white colleagues tended to associate Black Power with violence, Street noted, more prevalent was the systemic and legally sanctioned violence that the United States had inflicted on blacks for centuries.[27] BLM might seem radical through its connections to Black Power, but it was rooted in the all-American value of land ownership and in mainstream federal urban renewal policy.

Was owning land radical? In the early 1970s, the land-grab techniques associated with urban renewal were just what Black Power coveted. The Black Land movement, Golden Gateway's developers, and North Waterfront Associates pursued similar visions of private land ownership, enabled by the public sector and the techniques of urban renewal land assemblage, but only BLM was regarded as radical—even when the movement was led by an architect with a professional master plan. Nonethless, in 1970 it was plausible for a Black Power organization run by an architect-planner to claim that land was the basis of all power and to seek mainstream respect for that viewpoint. The constellation of resonant land-centered initiatives, particularly the pressures for urban renewal, made that position possible at that historical moment.

"THE RESTLESS PRESENT"

In recent years, advocates for equitable land stewardship in urban rebuilding have more often than not been pushed to the angry margins of civic dialogue rather than occupying the center and the mainstream. Once we leave the 1970s, the bookshelves on these topics thin out. The underlying advocacy for large-scale urban renewal that drove the public battles in the 1960s and 1970s was discredited, and although such policies have persisted, they no longer appear in the daily news. Without an effective framework that sees the competition for land as the systematic starting point for assessing urban policy, the topic of land stewardship more often arises when pushed into view by episodic crises and citizen protests. Channeling Grady Clay's 1962 manuscript, it is tempting to sketch out how today a land-centered critique might provide a sustained perspective for defining and analyzing gentrification, recent eminent domain litigation, municipal vacant building programs, the Occupy movement, or the local decision of a city like Asbury Park, New Jersey, to sell its waterfront to the highest bidder, to name a few examples. It is helpful to this prospective task of centering land in the urban narrative that many of the throughlines to the 1960s—such as Bill Street's prediction of a white land grab in the Shaw neighborhood of D.C.—hold steady today. Certain questions have gained in urgency, such as why so many U.S. cities have *no* competition for urban land. The land questions, like urban design controversies, are everywhere around us; the challenge is not in finding them but in prioritizing and organizing them, then arraying them together, as on a shelf.

This trend—to marginalize critiques of land competition in favor of landscape concerns—was especially evident in New Orleans and the Gulf region in the aftermath of Hurricane Katrina. In the news coverage of the rebuilding efforts, design and redevelopment stories proliferated, including those of modest "Katrina Cottages," New Urbanist neighborhood plans, and the proposed downtown National Jazz Center designed by starchitect Thom Mayne. These were stimulating ideas, to be sure, but they tended to overshadow the land issues underneath. For instance, the National Jazz Center was part of an extra-large-scale urban renewal proposal that would have demolished a million square feet of public buildings; City Hall, the Orleans Parish Civil District Court, the "old" State Supreme Court Building, and the Louisiana state office building would have had to be torn down. The massive project was not justified by direct storm damage, which had been relatively light in that area, but rather reflected a top-down clearance and redevelopment plan based on public ownership of the sites. Meanwhile, a month before the hurricane it had surfaced without much reaction in the press that a single California investor, Judah Hertz, had recently purchased 25 percent of New Orleans' Class A office space. The rebuilding debates flushed out the significance of his stake in the city when New Orleans leaders needed his cooperation for their downtown redevelopment plans.[28]

Land—more than the Jazz Center design, Katrina Cottages, or New Urbanist plans— was indeed the central issue at stake in New Orleans. Yet to the press and the general public the relevant land ownership patterns were secondary, and even accidental, discoveries rather than a starting point or part of a systematic, sustained perspective. The rebuilding "debate" labeled citizens who took land-centered positions as irate protestors. The January 2006 reaction to the controversial initial recommendations by Mayor Ray Nagin's Bring New Orleans Back Commission illustrates this point. Chaired by local developer and banker Joe Canizaro, the commission proposed replacing flood-prone residential neighborhoods with "wetlands" and "giving neighborhoods in low-lying parts of the city from four months to a year to prove they should not be bulldozed." The city would issue a four-month moratorium on building permits. This not only antagonized residents repairing their homes but gave neighbors too little time to come up with "acceptable" plans. Harvey Bender, a forty-four-year-old New Orleans East homeowner, said to Canizaro at an overflowing meeting at the Sheraton Hotel: "Mr. Joe Canizaro, I don't know you, but I hate you. I hate you, because you've been in the background scheming to get our land. I'm going to die on my land."[29]

The response to Mr. Bender should have been "Of course," surrounded as he was by news stories of huge government urban redevelopment projects, Hertz's private purchase of a quarter of New Orleans' prime office space, and the commission's Bring New Orleans Back proposal. Mr. Bender's perspective was strengthened by the longer history of post–World War II urban renewal, the 1960s BLM and the even longer twentieth-century history of eroding African American land ownership in the South underscored by Harold Washington Jr. The Gulf's unusual and tragic rebuilding circumstances put the ongoing, daily, "grinding" competition for urban land in the spotlight—with all of the accompanying economic, political, and legal machinations. If land ownership patterns had been centered

151 Bill Street, left, was an architect, planner, and chair of the Black Land movement in the Shaw neighborhood of Washington, D.C. He saw the promise of urban renewal techniques, as well as the risks posed by white "land grabbers." In this 1969 community "dialogue between black and white," Street said: "Well, look, power has always been based on ownership of land, right?" Black Power meant black land ownership, Street argued, which was a mainstream concept that should not threaten whites. Just as Ron Kaufman apprenticed with Justin Herman in the late 1950s to learn the land assemblage techniques of urban renewal and then applied that knowledge to assembling a 17-acre waterfront site for private redevelopment, Bill Street hoped to use the tools of urban renewal in favor of black land ownership. The early 1970s marked a high-water mark for land-centered redevelopment critiques.

and amplified in civic dialogue about rebuilding New Orleans, Mr. Bender would have appeared to be not an angry, emotional, conspiracy-prone "protestor" but rather a stakeholder in the transparent discussion of what to do with the land.

Mr. Bender's anger was a symptom of a larger problem. Most urbanites can recount recent urban design controversies but could not say who owns what land and with what consequences, as the 1970s literature implored and advised them to do. What kept the African American newspapers like the *Sun-Reporter* or *Black Land News* writing about urban renewal's land grab, separate from the street vacation lawsuits, the urban environmentalist crusades about land giveaways to developers, or Grady Clay's theory of the competition for urban land? The answer lies partly in perceiving the larger structural marginalization of such critiques—one race-centered, the other seemingly not—as one reason they have failed to find their commonalities.[30] What would it take today to consolidate land-based frameworks within urban policy debates? What if the shelf of works used in this study lined up neatly, and that line went back to Henry George and his *Our Land and Land Policy*—would that constitute an "alternative" critique? In 1869 Henry George made equitable urban land policy a national issue based on his San Francisco analysis, at a time when news of Western railroad grants and land grabs appeared daily in the headlines. In twenty-first-century urban redevelopment policies, how would it be possible to matter-of-factly center questions of land ownership and distribution as much as urban design and landscape? For that to happen, the land-grab critiques (labeled marginal protests) and business-government redevelopment plans (labeled professional and visionary) would have to be recognized as equally valid, expert frameworks in the competition for land.[31]

DESIGNS ON THE CITY

This book has explored how the San Francisco Bay Area, especially the city's north waterfront, served as a touchstone for the redevelopment experiments, conflicts, and stories of its time and place. In San Francisco critiques centered on public land stewardship gained momentum in the postwar decades as large-scale rebuilding and environmental planning models spread. Urban design decisions found a broad public following while simultaneously enduring high levels of skepticism and even ridicule. San Francisco incited louder, longer fights over the disposition of land than did most U.S. cities. In the 1960s, San Francisco generated a dynamic exchange over urban form (building height, mass, walls, views, plazas, and open space), on one hand, and land value, stewardship, and ownership, on the other. In illuminating how land vied with landscape, the San Francisco case also shows how land-centered critiques receded from core public debates. San Francisco's conflicts followed their own patterns, distinct from those of New York City and elsewhere. The Bay Area was not merely *against* development, despite the perceptions of New York investors like David Rockefeller. San Franciscans contested the foundations of large-scale redevelopment and high-rises based on long-standing ideals of responsible public land stewardship. The region's thriving allied arts and renewal professions, the "designer's city," applied their broad expertise, forged in a vibrant urban environmentalism and sharpened amid the resulting controversies.

The arc of contested developments in San Francisco makes the usual landscape terms "historicism" versus "modernism," "preservation" versus "renewal," as inscribed in architectural magazines of the day, read more narrowly as profession-based design language rather than as sweeping binary norms. The allied arts such as public relations, graphic design, model-making, and property management were not inherently more commercial than architecture, but they honed the public mix of dollars and design and thus often took the heat in 1960s redevelopment battles. Alongside architects, they worked on all sides of the region's contested urban environmental planning and development projects. However, architectural organizations had long used the term "allied arts" with the purpose of elevating architecture. This book's vantage point from outside professional design has instead shown these fields arrayed in a strong, decentered network or constellation—yet within this collaborative network, architecture still held a privileged place.

By now the Jane Jacobs versus Robert Moses framework has receded in this story as told on the ground in San Francisco. It glimmers here or there implicitly, such as when Karl Kortum asserted that modernist slabs ruined the human scale of San Francisco. Or explicitly, as when critic Allan Temko complimented John Portman's Embarcadero Center renewal complex for embodying Jane Jacobs's belief in the power of small business to enliven streets. Jacobs will always remain a deservedly revered figure in urban history, but her writings have also overshadowed other questions and obscured other starting points. Jane Jacobs's contact with the Bay Area was mostly long-distance. She declined the invitation to sit on the Golden Gateway competition advisory panel, saying she could not endorse urban renewal. The irony is that she would have fit right in. San Francisco overflowed with development projects awash in the debates and competitions that drove employment for writers, lawyers, publicists, artists, preservationists, photographers, and architectural model-makers.

It is also likely—in a city whose redevelopment news was made by the likes of Marion Conrad, Bobbie Stauffacher, Jean Kortum, Karl Kortum, Ruth Asawa, Caree Rose, Stuart Rose, Sue Hestor, Marion Conrad, Jean Dibble, Bruce Brugmann, Virginia Green, Leila Johnston, Beverly Willis, Kitsie Carroll, Anne Luckhart, John Harman, June Harman, Mike Doyle, Larry Halprin, Jean Walton, Marget Larsen, Grady Clay, and Louis Dunn—that Jane Jacobs's gender would have been unremarkable. Surrounded by these individuals, couples and partners, it would have been evident that the design, planning, and investment practices of large-scale urban redevelopment were already immersed in currents of gender upheaval. It was precisely the widely contested nature of the Bay Area's postwar redevelopment—its anti-Manhattanization, broadly defined—that caused so many women and men to be employed. The people in this account matured into their careers between the 1940s and the 1970s. By focusing on these years, this book has narrated stories of women's leadership in urban fields before second-wave feminism.[32]

Although the 1940s–60s era corresponds with a dip in the already dismal numbers of women in the architectural profession, *Designing San Francisco* suggests that when women increased their entry into architectural schools in the 1970s they did so based on the strength of that earlier participation in urban rebuilding as much as on combating their exclusion from architecture. Closer attention to this momentum in urban fields during the 1940s–70s would be as fruitful as zeroing in on the apparently lagging impact of second-wave feminism. This shift in emphasis speaks to the post-1970s lament that architecture stubbornly remains "male dominated" despite the aspirations and achievements of feminist liberation. As the historical narrative acknowledges the many forgotten participants in urban design and planning in the previous decades, it revises the expectations regarding the effects of 1970s women's liberation. Preliminary evidence suggests that San Francisco's experience did have a particular role in this post-1970s national story. Despina Stratigakos's indispensable *Where Are the Women Architects?* does not compare the experiences of specific cities, but it does recount an unusual number of significant events tied to San Francisco from the 1970s to the present. For example, the contentious resolution on the "Status of Women in the Architectural Profession" passed at the 1973 national AIA meeting in San Francisco; it called for increasing the numbers of women in the field and remedying the profession's discriminatory culture. "The Missing 32% Project," initiated to address the percentage of female architecture school graduates who leave the profession, was founded in 2013 by the San Francisco AIA chapter.[33] Although *Designing San Francisco* contributes to rethinking the "male domination" of architecture, ultimately the gender integration of the allied urban design and planning fields in the 1940s–70s stands on its own terms.[34]

San Francisco also witnessed the "power broker" spirit described by Robert Caro in his biography of Robert Moses. But whereas Caro sought to capture the centralized power wielded by Moses the individual, San Francisco's 1970s bookshelf told of a more diffuse brokering. Planning director Allan Jacobs wrote, "By 1972, I had come to appreciate San Francisco's no-power-to-anyone government." *UHR* revealed less acknowledged channels whereby land ownership and political influence converged to explain who benefited from the city's high-rise development vision—and it wasn't the ordinary citizen. *UHR*, as well as Grady Clay, identified pressure points in the redevelopment process open to public participation and helped entrench this "people's" approach in San Francisco. It was disagreement over the larger-scale urban future, not high-rises or urban renewal projects per se, that created so many opportunities for urban-engaged professionals. The history of the SFIMC exemplified that even when projects were not built, they employed a network of design professionals overtime in a city culture that fomented tensions between land and landscape.[35]

Despite its "no-power-to-anyone government," San Francisco's postwar renewal was marked by a sustained effort to curb the power of private developers' designs on the city. For all of the criticism heaped on Robert Moses for his "overreaching," as Hilary Ballon has argued, he turned land over to private investors without adequate controls, especially in the case of Title I urban renewal. San Francisco's north waterfront, a patchwork of public trust and private investment, brokered stronger controls due to the work of many allied experts in the private and public sectors.[36]

In Herb Caen's columns, San Francisco's redevelopment stories were inseparable from the formative political and generational experiences of the day. "Why don't 'they' do something about civil rights demonstrators, freeways, high-risers, Alcatraz and teen-agers?," he caricatured a grumbling San Franciscan as saying in 1964. In the 1960s Caen was preoccupied with the threats that both neighborhood clearance and "look-alike" skyscrapers posed to San Francisco. He conceded that the average citizen was likely more concerned with clearance projects than with protecting views: "Well, there are a thousand viewpoints in this viewtful city—and a view is sacred only to him who has one and is in danger of losing it."[37] Instead of emphasizing the class divisions over city views, architect Charles Moore imbued them with a landscape and design-based definition of the public good: "Indeed, in San Francisco as in few places, the view which gives a sense of the whole city is one of the most valuable parts of the public realm, one of the parts that is most frequently attacked and must be most zealously defended." But San Francisco's skyscrapers were "the West's largest filing cabinets," and it was "unfair, of course" to expect from them "any attributes of the public realm."[38] Moore inherently exempted skyscrapers, as "filing cabinets," from fundamental expectations of contributing to the public domain.

Yet many of the city's most iconic skyscrapers *did* incorporate the public realm, in the form of the land beneath them. Focusing on land and not views as a means of measuring the public domain reveals the shared concerns of neighborhood clearance and high-rise construction, of public and private redevelopment. The street vacation cases, for example, shared the fight against land grabs with San Francisco's well-known lawsuits against redevelopment clearance and resident relocation policies in the Western Addition and Yerba Buena districts. As redevelopment gained momentum, Herb Caen resented assertions that San Francisco was "dying" and needed skyscrapers to spark growth. He argued the opposite, that a city was dying when "real estate values" took precedence over "personal values."[39] Caen wrote in 1966 that San Francisco was a city "with a magnificent past, a restless present, and a future whose outlines—square and graceless—are already discernible."[40] The past unapologetically haunted Caen's columns. But the restless present obsessed him. In 1962 he warned that a "vertical earthquake" threatened the city with a square future of "blockbuster" towers. In 1976 he regretted that San Francisco had emulated New York's skyline: "It matters not how you feel about the new buildings, esthetically. They're not doing the job we were promised. As the high-rises went up, the taxes would come down, right? Ha."[41] Caen's point was straight from *UHR*. Views and aesthetics were not the real problems.

In the mid-1970s Caen and many others mourned that San Francisco's battle against high-rise domination was lost. *Bay Guardian* editor Bruce Brugmann disagreed. In his opinion, the fight was not measured by skyscrapers, plazas, or views. The battle was (and is) about whether the language of land, power, and responsible public stewardship claimed the center of the story or the margins.[42] In the twenty-first century Brugmann brushed off critics who said that the *Bay Guardian*'s anti-Manhattanization was an outdated, cranky antidevelopment voice from the radical 1970s. Such critics missed the paper's effort to center land and power rather than landscape, space, and design in the current U.S. narrative of redevelopment. Brugmann says that today we see the consequences of ignoring the *Bay Guardian*'s warnings against validating the business investors' and government urban renewal visions of land stewardship. Anti-Manhattanization arguments have been around even longer than Jane Jacobs or Robert Moses, but that does not make them outdated. In fact the longevity of these land-centered frameworks suggests that it is time that they received more attention rather than less.[43]

Because real estate has been such a significant subject in the United States, it needs to be explained why citizens know more about battles over the height and architecture of buildings and their open-space amenities than they know about land ownership patterns and their arguably more significant civic implications. This book has offered one answer to that question. In urban design, matters of form and civic space did not simply mask underlying moral questions of land stewardship like a green hairpiece, although no doubt some players sought that outcome. Instead, design-based and land-based frameworks were in dynamic tension with one another. The relationship between dollars and design has been historical and contingent. The case of San Francisco illuminates how land-centered critiques have receded to the margins of urban thinking about democratic civic life while urban space and form have taken the center. Yet by looking at the ferment of the 1940s through the 1970s, before the dichotomies of Jane Jacobs versus Robert Moses and preservation versus renewal locked in, we can see "alternative" frames that potentially give today's urban issues a different clarity.

Acknowledgments

Because this book evolved over ten years, I am deeply indebted to countless individuals and institutions who helped transform it—for their contributions, critiques, engagement, time, good will, and patience. Writing about the 1940s through the 1970s, and researching professions that often lacked concentrated archives and scholarship, I relied on interviews to provide context and details otherwise unavailable to a historian. It is gratifying to be able to thank these interviewees for their generosity in welcoming me into their living rooms and offices and for answering endless questions. Interviewees dug up documents and graciously answered follow-up inquiries, which sometimes arrived years after the interviews. Others took me on impromptu walks in San Francisco. Every interview was critical, but I must acknowledge the particularly timely or sustained contributions of the late Ruth Asawa, Bruce Brugmann, Stephen Canright, Jean Dibble, Louis Dunn, Stanford Erickson, the late Calvin Imai, Allan Jacobs, Aaron Peskin, Gerald Ratto, Nancy Shanahan, Bobbie Stauffacher Solomon, and Beverly Willis.

Many colleagues and friends read portions of the manuscript at various stages and offered detailed feedback after hearing my presentations. This commentary greatly improved the book, at every level, and for it I am grateful to Eric Avila, Tracy Bach, Robin Bachin, Michele Bogart, Nan Amarillo Boyd, Margot Canaday, Purcell Carson, Bruno Carvalho, Elsa Devienne, Mitch Duneier, Alice Echols, Phil Ethington, Ruth Flaxman, Julia Foulkes, Bill Gleason, Michael Gordin, Katya Gunther, Marta Gutman, Dirk Hartog, Joseph Heathcott, Anne Helmreich, Georgina Hickey, Bill Issel, David Jaffee, Temma Kaplan, Jerold Kayden, Melanie Kiechle, Lili Knorr, Seth Koven, Regina Kunzel, Bob Lake, Johana Londoño, Martha McNamara, Erika Milam, Allison Miller, Peter Miller, Mariana Mogilevich, Kathe Newman, Amy Ogata, Emily Prifogle, Nancy Rao, Gayle Rubin, Steven Rugare, Andrew Sandoval-Strausz, Sarah Schrank, Misha Semenov, Aaron Shkuda, Marc Stein, Sara Stevens, Mario Torres, Catherine Whalen, Carla Yanni, and Rebecca Zurier. Those who read the entire manuscript—Jacqueline Brandon, Ann Fabian, Julia Foulkes, Dan Horowitz, Mary Ryan, Damon Scott, Audra Wolf, and the anonymous readers for Princeton University Press—offered invaluable advice. For all of these contributions, I am indebted.

This book benefited from the insights of numerous audiences and works-in-progress discussion groups. In the Rutgers University Department of History, my home for nine years, the vibrant women's and gender history community was instrumental in launching and shaping this project. At Princeton University, I presented chapters in the Department of History; the American Studies seminar; the Women in Design and

Architecture group; the Princeton-Mellon Initiative in Architecture, Urbanism, and the Humanities; and the Architecture, Urban Space, and Democracy Workshop. My research has been sharpened by the comments from these remarkable colleagues. I am grateful for the opportunity to present early versions of the project at the New School; Baker-Nord Center for the Humanities at Case Western University; the Arts in Place Workshop at the Rockefeller Archive Center; the Harvard University Graduate School of Design; the Seminar on the City at Columbia University; Wellesley College; the University of Miami; the Bard Graduate Center in Decorative Arts, Design History, and Material Culture; and the Don Krueckeberg Doctoral conference at the Bloustein School of Rutgers University. An invitation to speak at San Francisco State University came at an ideal time, and participating in professional conferences including those of the Society for American City and Regional Planning History, the Urban History Association, and the Organization of American Historians opened up ongoing dialogue with colleagues.

I could not have written this book without the patient help, advice, and research finds of archivists, curators, and librarians: Bill Whitaker, Nancy Thorne, and Heather Schumacher, Architectural Archives, University of Pennsylvania; Janet Parks, Drawings and Archives, Avery Architectural and Fine Arts Library, Columbia University; Waverly Lowell, Environmental Design Archives, University of California, Berkeley; Michele Hiltzik Beckerman, Tom Rosenbaum, and the late Ken Rose, Rockefeller Archive Center; Lorna Kirwan, Susan Snyder, and Jack Von Euw, Bancroft Library, University of California, Berkeley; Christina Moretta and Wendy Kramer, San Francisco History Center, San Francisco Public Library; Gina Bardi, Diane Cooper, and Stephen Canright, San Francisco Maritime Research Center; Meredith Eliassen, Special Collections and Archives, San Francisco State University; Nancy Hadley, American Institute of Architects Archive; Layna White and Barbara Rominski, San Francisco Museum of Modern Art Archives; Mary Daniels and Ines Zalduendo, Loeb Library, Harvard Graduate School of Design. At Harvard University's Henry A. Murray Research Archive, Sonia Barbosa's persistence in securing permission for me to use the Terman Study records yielded extraordinary results. Individuals and organizations made available too many private collections to name, but the records kept by the Telegraph Hill Dwellers, Grady Clay, and Gerald Ratto Photography were especially indispensable. For their long-distance aid I thank John Russell and Kira Homo, University of Oregon Library and Special Collections; Jeff Gunderson, librarian, Anne Bremer Memorial Library, San Francisco Art Institute; Polly Armstrong, Special Collections, Stanford University; Heather Strelecki, American Institute of Graphic Arts; Steve Staiger, Palo Alto Historical Association; and Sharon Seymour, Sausalito Historical Society.

For research assistance in several of these archives and the Board of Supervisors records, George Mattson was incomparably creative in tracking down records. Justin Short gleaned relevant materials from Grady Clay's voluminous records. For taking time from their own work to tackle research and editorial tasks, I thank Brian Connolly, Patricia Hampson Eget, Pamela Epstein, Alix Genter, Melanie Kiechle, Alison Miller, Kara Schlichting, Katie Skeen, Kyla Sommers, Juliana Stern, Emmet von Stackelberg, and Nick Williams. Bob Geddes, Sue Hestor, Hal Howard, and Andrea Jepson generously shared their insights and recollections. The Princeton University Department of History staff—Brooke Fitzgerald, Judy Hanson, Pamela Long, Debbie Macy, Kristy Novak, Etta Recke, Max Siles, Jackie Wasneski, and Carla Zimkosk—helped manage the sometimes unwieldy stream of book illustrations, payments, scanning, computing needs, and mailings. At Rutgers University, I thank Candace Walcott-Shepherd and Dawn Ruskai for help with the business side of research support.

For direct financial support I am grateful to these institutions and foundations: Princeton University, Rutgers University, Stanford University's Center for Comparative Studies in Race and Ethnicity, the Beverly Willis Architecture Foundation, the James Marston Fitch Charitable Foundation, the Rockefeller Archive Center, the Graham Foundation, the Old Dominion Fellowship, Council of the Humanities, Princeton University, and the Barr Ferree Foundation Publication Fund, Department of Art and Archaeology, Princeton University. An earlier version of chapter 3 was published as "'Culture-A-Go-Go': The Ghirardelli Square Sculpture Controversy and the Liberation of Civic Design in the 1960s," *Journal of Social History* Vol. 44, No. 2 (2010), 379–412.

I count myself as incredibly fortunate to have had the opportunity to publish this book with Michelle Komie at Princeton University Press. Because wrapping up ten years of work neatly was not an easy production project, I am especially grateful for her commitment, patience, and editorial wisdom. The press's editorial and production professionals, especially Mark Bellis, Steve Sears, Ben Pokross, Hannah Zuckerman, and David Campbell, are a model publishing operation and an absolute pleasure to work with. I am uniquely indebted to copy-editor Marilyn Martin and her precise, painstaking reviews. In securing illustration scans and permissions, Bill Howze resolved administrative loose ends with resourcefulness and good cheer. For last-minute image reproductions, I thank photographer John Blaczewski and Peter Bae, director of circulation services at Firestone Library. Misha Semenov applied his remarkable talents to drawing the maps of his hometown.

A unique pleasure of writing this book has been spending time with my Bay Area family: Ruth Flaxman, Gary Flaxman, Laura Flaxman, Kenny Purser, Ava, Aziza, Mark Purser, and Jignasha Pandya. Although Caroline Hirasawa no longer lives in the East Bay, we did manage to meet there a few times. Finding the overlap of this book with each of their own passions has been a joy. To my immediate family—Keith Wailoo, Elliot, and Myla—words cannot express my appreciation for what we have built together. And I am fortunate to have a wonderful extended family, especially Bert, Lynette, Chris, Alisa, Andrew and Anthony, and the Wailoo-Singh-Lewis-Isenberg-Ellenbogens. For Keith—best friend, partner, and scholar extraordinaire—deepest thanks. Finally, dimensions of this project were implicitly shaped by my parents, although they are both long gone. I see echoes in chapter 6 of my father, Lee Isenberg, who worked in public relations. My mother's stories about being an architect must have sunk deeply into my young self. I often wonder what her response would have been to this book, but I know she would have enjoyed the journey of writing it. As a token of appreciation for her many gifts, I have dedicated the book to her.

Of course, responsibility for all errors remains my own.

Dedicated to my mother, Marian Ellenbogen Isenberg, in loving memory

"Street Widening Planned," *The Hartford Courant,* February 6, 1968

Abbreviations

AAUP	Architectural Archives, University of Pennsylvania
ADL	Arthur D. Little
AIA	American Institute of Architects
AIGA	American Institute of Graphic Arts
AMI	Architectural Models Inc.
BART	Bay Area Rapid Transit
BLM	Black Land movement
BOS	Board of Supervisors
CEQA	California Environmental Quality Act
CG	Chadbourne Gilpatric
COAAST	Californians Organized to Acquire Access to State Tidelands
CPC	City Planning Commission
CSM	*Christian Science Monitor*
DLMA	Downtown–Lower Manhattan Association
EDA	Environmental Design Archives
FFR	Ford Foundation Records
FHA	Federal Housing Administration
GGNRA	Golden Gate National Recreation Area
GSAR	Ghirardelli Square Architectural Records
HHFA	Housing and Home Finance Agency
HJMAD	*Helmut Jacoby, Master of Architectural Drawing*
KKC	Karl Kortum Collection
MLTW	Moore, Lyndon, Turnbull, and Whitaker
NAD	*Helmut Jacoby: New Architectural Drawings*
NPS	National Park Service
NWA	North Waterfront Associates
NYCHA	New York City Housing Authority
NYT	New York Times
RAC	Rockefeller Archive Center
POW	Protect Our Waterfront
RAPC	Ruth Asawa Private Collection
SFC	*San Francisco Chronicle*
SFE	*San Francisco Examiner*
SFE&C	*San Francisco Sunday Examiner & Chronicle*
SFHC	San Francisco History Center

SFIMC	San Francisco International Market Center
SFMM	San Francisco Maritime Museum
SFMRC	San Francisco Maritime Research Center
SFPD	San Francisco Planning Department
SFPL	San Francisco Public Library
SFRA	San Francisco Redevelopment Agency
SFT	San Francisco Tomorrow
SHS	Sausalito Historical Society
SMU	Scale Models Unlimited
SOM	Skidmore, Owings & Merrill
SPUR	San Francisco Planning and Urban Renewal Association
SUD	Studies in Urban Design (a Rockefeller Foundation program)
THD	Telegraph Hill Dwellers
UDJ	Urban Design Journalists (a Rockefeller Foundation program)
UHR	*The Ultimate Highrise*
URA	Urban Renewal Administration
WB&E	Wurster, Bernardi & Emmons
WSJ	*Wall Street Journal*

Notes

INTRODUCTION

1 "High Rises Favored by Mellon," *San Francisco Examiner (SFE)*, October 9, 1970, folder Real Estate—Embarcadero Center Clippings 1966, 1968, 1969, Box 412, RG 3, Rockefeller Family, Rockefeller Archive Center (RAC). Used with special authorization. For David Rockefeller's West Coast projects, the strength of the Sierra Club and environmentalism was an obstacle to negotiate, especially because environmentalists expected Rockefeller to be sympathetic to preservationist causes. One consultant told him that San Francisco was "the most 'alive' area for conservation exploitation in the entire United States." See Fred Smith, "Preliminary Report on San Francisco," July 11, 1969, folder Real Estate—Embarcadero Center 1966–72, Box 412, RG 3, Rockefeller Family, RAC. Used with special authorization.

2 I use the term *urban-environmentalist* in this book to describe the orientation of many individuals and groups toward analyzing, advocating for, and investing in their visions of how issues of the urban and natural built environments converged. This helps distinguish the San Francisco Bay Area from many other metropolitan areas in the United States during the 1940s–1970s period of urban renewal and large-scale rebuilding. The phrase is intended to evoke the professional orientation of those groups and individuals and the fact that, although many of them might have called themselves "activists" of some kind, my emphasis is on how their work in allied urban design and renewal fields underpinned their arguments and ideas. Finally, as artists, consultants, and professionals, even on different sides of development issues, they shared this focus on the urban environment—particularly on the public sector's role in urban land stewardship as well as urban design. In San Francisco the term *preservationist* was cast not only in the light of orientation toward the past and the relevance of history in the present but in this urban-environmentalism, a fact that the people studied in *Designing San Francisco* bring out.

3 Recent scholarship has fundamentally modified the fierce portrait of Robert Moses that has prevailed since Caro's biography and has vastly complicated the sympathetic admiration for Jane Jacobs. These revisions, however, still largely rest on the two figures and the polarized visions of cities they represent, always with New York as the model. See Alice Sparberg Alexiou, *Jane Jacobs: Urban Visionary* (New Brunswick, NJ: Rutgers University Press, 2006); *Robert Moses and the Modern City: The Transformation of New York*, ed. Hilary Ballon and Kenneth Jackson (New York: W. W. Norton, 2007); Anthony Flint, *Wrestling with Moses: How Jane Jacobs Took on New York's Master Builder and Transformed the American City* (New York: Random House, 2009); Roberta Gratz, *The Battle for Gotham: New York in the Shadow of Robert Moses and Jane Jacobs* (New York: Nation, 2010); Samuel Zipp, *Manhattan Projects: The Rise and Fall of Urban Renewal in Cold War New York* (New York: Oxford University Press, 2010); Max Page and Timothy Mennel, *Reconsidering Jane Jacobs* (Chicago: APA Planners, 2011); Peter L. Laurence, *Becoming Jane Jacobs* (Philadelphia: University of Pennsylvania Press, 2016). Glenna Lang, in her forthcoming book *Jane Jacobs's First City: Learning from Scranton, PA*, finds that Jacobs's hometown had a foundational impact on her conception of cities before she arrived in New York.

4 For an indispensable explanation of the waterfront's development, see Jasper Rubin, *A Negotiated Landscape: The Transformation of San Francisco's Waterfront since 1950* (Chicago: Center for American Places at Columbia College Chicago, 2011). For a helpful framing of how "public sphere" related to "public space," see Philip Ethington, *The Public City: The Political Construction of Urban Life in San Francisco, 1850–1900* (Cambridge, UK: Cambridge University Press, 1994).

5 For this book I am indebted to the following 1970s San Francisco studies, whose arguments, evidence, and selected cases gave me an understanding of both that decade and the previous ones: Chester Hartman et al., *Yerba Buena: Land Grab and Community Resistance in San Francisco* (San Francisco: National Housing and Economic Development Law Project, 1974); Frederick M. Wirt, *Power in the City: Decision Making in San Francisco* (Berkeley: University of California Press, 1974); Allan B. Jacobs, *Making City Planning Work* (Chicago: American Society of Planning Officials, 1978). See also Chester Hartman with Sara Carnochan, *City for Sale: The Transformation of San Francisco*, revised and updated edition (Berkeley: University of California Press, 2011).

This project has been especially fortunate to follow a wave of inspired, creative work on the San Francisco Bay Area: Paul Groth, *Living Downtown: The History of Residential Hotels in the United States* (Berkeley: University of California Press, 1994); Nan Alamilla Boyd, *Wide*

Open Town: A History of Queer San Francisco to 1965
(Berkeley: University of California Press, 2003); Richard A.
Walker, *The Country in the City: The Greening of the San
Francisco Bay Area* (Seattle: University of Washington
Press, 2007); Damon Scott, "The City Aroused: Sexual
Politics and the Transformation of San Francisco's Urban
Landscape, 1943–1964" (Ph.D. thesis, University of Texas,
Austin, 2008); Josh Sides, *Erotic City: Sexual Revolutions
and the Making of Modern San Francisco* (Oxford, UK:
Oxford University Press, 2009); Jessica Sewell, *Women
and the Everyday City: Public Space in San Francisco,
1890–1915* (Minneapolis: University of Minnesota Press,
2011); Marta Gutman, *A City for Children: Women, Architecture, and the Charitable Landscapes of Oakland, 1850–
1950* (Chicago: University of Chicago Press, 2014); Alison
Hirsch, *City Choreographer: Lawrence Halprin in Urban
Renewal America* (Minneapolis: University of Minnesota
Press, 2014); Amy Howard, *More than Shelter: Activism
and Community in San Francisco Public Housing* (Minneapolis: University of Minnesota Press, 2014); Ocean Howell, *Making the Mission: Planning and Ethnicity in San
Francisco* (Chicago: University of Chicago Press, 2015).

6 David Ross, "What Makes Beverly Run?," *San Francisco
Sunday Examiner & Chronicle (SFE&C)*, February 14,
1971, Beverly Willis Clippings file, San Francisco History
Center (SFHC), San Francisco Public Library (SFPL).
The premature passing of architect Zaha Hadid sparked
much commentary in 2016 on architecture as a "male-
dominated field." See Randy Kennedy and Robin Pogrebin,
"Architect's Reach Went Beyond Her Designs," *NYT*,
April 2, 2016, C1; Robin Pogrebin, "For Female Architects,
Many Hurdles in the Way," *NYT*, April 13, 2016, C1;
Despina Stratigakos, *Where Are the Women Architects?*
(Princeton, NJ: Princeton University Press, 2016).

7 Two key overview texts on gender and the professions
are Joan Acker, "Hierarchies, Jobs, Bodies: A Theory of
Gender Organizations," *Gender and Society*, Vol. 4, No. 2
(June 1990), 139–58, and Barbara Reskin, "Sex Segre-
gation in the Workplace," *Annual Review of Sociology*,
Vol. 19 (1993), 241–70. See also Ava Baron, *Work Engen-
dered: Toward a New History of American Labor* (Ithaca,
NY: Cornell University Press, 1991); Christine Williams,
*Gender Differences at Work for Men and Women in Non
Traditional Occupations* (Berkeley: University of Cali-
fornia Press, 1991); Claudia Goldin, *Understanding the
Gender Gap: An Economic History of American Women*
(Oxford, UK: Oxford University Press, 1992); Angel
Kwolek-Folland, *Engendering Business: Men and Women
of the Corporate Office* (Baltimore: Johns Hopkins Uni-
versity Press, 1998); Lisa Servon and Susan Fainstein,
Gender and Planning: A Reader (New Brunswick: Rutgers
University Press, 2005); Nancy MacLean, *Freedom Is Not
Enough: The Opening of the American Workplace* (Cam-
bridge, MA: Harvard University Press, 2008); Francine
Blau and Marianne Ferber, *The Economics of Women, Men,
and Work*, 6th edition (Boston: Prentice Hall, 2009); Alice
Kessler-Harris, *A Woman's Wage: Historical Meanings*,

updated edition (Lexington: University Press of
Kentucky, 2014).

8 The Wall Street of the West movement first took off in
San Francisco in the 1920s; at that time it was evidently a
real estate concept for the development of Montgomery
Street as much as it was a claim about the city's bank-
ing sector. See Dudley Westler, "Stable Realty Values
Create World Market," *San Francisco Chronicle (SFC)*,
January 4, 1928, M27. From David Rockefeller's New
York City perspective in 1969, San Francisco had a "reac-
tionary and hostile business climate" and was clearly
ambivalent about its ambition to remain the West Coast's
financial and business center. See Warren Lindquist to
Emmett Solomon, April 28, 1969, folder Real Estate—
Embarcadero Center 1966–72, Box 412, RG 3, Rockefeller
Family, RAC. Used with special authorization.

9 Suleiman Osman uses "Manhattanization" to describe
the development pressures experienced by Brooklynites
in the 1950s but explains that this phrase was not widely
used. He writes that the "contemporary use" originated
in 1960s San Francisco. It also represented anti-American
sentiment in 1920s London. See Osman, *The Invention
of Brownstone Brooklyn: Gentrification and the Search for
Authenticity in Postwar New York* (New York: Oxford
University Press, 2011), 293n4, 54–55.

10 "Brave New Year," January 4, 1976, reprinted in
Herb Caen, *Herb Caen's San Francisco, 1976–1991* (San
Francisco: Chronicle Books, 1992), 2.

11 For example, developers used the "tiresome theme" of
Los Angeles stealing San Francisco's "markets" to justify
the San Francisco International Market Center, discussed
in chapter 10. See Lynne Hoffman, "Manhattan West,"
Letter to the Editor, *SFC*, May 13, 1968. The competition
with Los Angeles is outside the scope of this book, but
Northern California did pride itself on historical authenticity, which it saw as lacking in the Southland. Sample
articles on the culture battles with L.A. include Herb
Caen, "San Franciscaena," *SFC*, April 29, 1965, and Neil
Morgan, "L.A.—Cultural Center," *SFC*, October 17, 1964.

12 Lewis Mumford, "Frozen Music or Solidified Static?
Reflections on Radio City," *New Yorker*, June 20, 1931,
reprinted in *Sidewalk Critic: Lewis Mumford's Writings
on New York*, ed. Robert Wojtowicz (New York: Princeton
Architectural Press, 1998), 57. See also Wirt, *Power in
the City: Decision Making in San Francisco* (Berkeley:
University of California Press, 1974), 193.

13 Both cities' regulatory environments had negotiated
such amenities from developers. Jerold Kayden, *Privately
Owned Public Space: The New York City Experience* (New
York: Wiley, 2000).

14 Henry James, *The American Scene* (Boston: Harper,
1907), 60–61.

15 Lewis Mumford, "Skyscrapers and Tenements," *New
Yorker*, June 3, 1933, reprinted in *Sidewalk Critic*, ed.
Wojtowicz, 100–101.

16 Jane Jacobs, *The Death and Life of Great American
Cities* (New York: Random House, 1961), 158. Her other

references to skyscrapers in *Death and Life* related to her disagreement with Le Corbusier's "Tower in the Park" ideal.

17 The same year that the Empire State Building was under construction, the *Chronicle* described a "towering nineteen story" building soon to open in San Francisco. See "Business Good in S.F. Section," *SFC*, August 16, 1930. The 30- and 31-story buildings were constructed in the 1920s. On San Francisco's tall buildings, see Bruce Brugmann and Greggar Sletteland, eds., *The Ultimate Highrise: San Francisco's Mad Rush toward the Sky* (San Francisco: San Francisco Bay Guardian Books, 1971) (*UHR*), 230.

18 Jasper Rubin, *A Negotiated Landscape: The Transformation of San Francisco's Waterfront since 1950* (Chicago: Center for American Places at Columbia College Chicago, in association with the University of Chicago Press, 2011). For the "privatism" of San Francisco's downtown growth coalition compared with D.C.'s, see Stephen J. McGovern, *The Politics of Downtown Development: Dynamic Political Cultures in San Francisco and Washington, D.C.* (Lexington: University Press of Kentucky, 1998). DeLeon's study of power through the lens of political science begins in the 1970s and focuses on progressive resistance to the pro-growth regime. Richard Edward DeLeon, *Left Coast City: Progressive Politics in San Francisco, 1975–1991* (Lawrence: University Press of Kansas, 1992). More about Title I appears later in this introduction.

19 Tourism industry studies are particularly relevant. One 1968 account noted that the city was holding its title as the financial and insurance capital of the West, with eighteen bank and twenty-eight insurance company headquarters. Its metropolitan population count of 3,040,800 (versus its city count of only 740,000) ranked it seventh largest in the nation; it was seventh in retail and fifth in dining and drink consumption. The population had grown 24 percent between 1950 and 1960 and was projected to grow at the same rate until 1970. Between 1965 and 1968, the number of convention attendees grew from 411,045 to 648,110, and hotel occupancy climbed from 79 percent to 88 percent, compared with national figures of 61 percent and 64 percent, respectively. See "Economic Evaluation of the City of San Francisco," ca. 1968, file Embarcadero Center—Hotels, Box 413, RG 3, Rockefeller Family, RAC. Used with special authorization.

20 Ada Louise Huxtable, "City for People: San Francisco Offers Its Inhabitants Much That New York Is Losing," *NYT*, May 8, 1960.

21 Nan Robertson, "G.O.P. Film Depicts 'Moral Decay,'" *NYT*, October 21, 1964, 35. See also Nan Robertson, "Goldwater Puts Off 'Moral Decay' Film," *NYT*, October 22, 1964, 1, 45.

22 Caen's column was interrupted only by his World War II military service and a hiatus spent at the *Examiner* in the 1950s. A special Pulitzer Prize in 1996 recognized Caen's civic leadership as "voice and conscience" for his city. See "Herb Caen Wins Pulitzer Prize," *SFGate*, April 10, 1996, http://www.sfgate.com/news/article/Herb-Caen-Wins-Pulitzer-Prize-Columnist-cited-2986663.php.

23 Jack Smith, "Torch Song for the Old S.F.," *Los Angeles Times*, August 30, 1972.

24 Chadbourne Gilpatric (CG), "California Trip, November 15, 1958, Folder 1958 July–December, Box 168, RG 12, Officers' Diaries, FA392, Rockefeller Foundation, RAC.

25 Herb Caen, "The Total City," August 30, 1964, and "Swim Dancer," July 30, 1964, reprinted in *The Best of Herb Caen, 1960–1975* (San Francisco: Chronicle Books, 1991), 78, 80.

26 See Caen, *The Best of Herb Caen, 1960–1975*.

27 MIT City Planning Study, Folders 3330.30–32, Box 375, RG 1.2, Series 200R, FA387, Rockefeller Foundation, RAC. For a more detailed analysis of the Rockefeller program, Gilpatric's cultivation of a cohort of urbanists, and Jane Jacobs's place in those efforts, see Peter L. Laurence, "The Death and Life of Urban Design: Jane Jacobs, The Rockefeller Foundation and the New Research in Urbanism, 1955–1965," *Journal of Urban Design*, Vol. 11, No. 2, 145–72.

28 On "the inchoate field," see CG, notes from phone conversation with Ada Louise Huxtable, October 16, 1958, Folder 1958 July–December, Box 168, RG 12, Officers' Diaries, FA392, Rockefeller Foundation, RAC.

29 CG, notes from meeting with William H. Whyte, March 8, 1960, Folder 1960, Pt. 1, Box 169, RG 12, Officers' Diaries, FA392, Rockefeller Foundation, RAC. See also Grady Clay, "What Makes a Good Square Good?," and Jane Jacobs, "Downtown Is for People," in *Exploding Metropolis*, ed. William H. Whyte (Garden City, NY: Doubleday, 1958). These essays first appeared in the April 1958 issue of *Fortune*. Peter Laurence describes how in 1958 the similarity between Clay's and Jacobs's urban analysis was apparent to contemporaries such as Ian McHarg; Jacobs and Clay sustained a lively correspondence during 1959. Whyte cut Clay's *Fortune* essay from 12,000 to 2,200 words. See Laurence, *Becoming Jane Jacobs*, 236, 269, 335fn3, 336fn7. Clay's substantial and admired published piece showing both his "townscape" critique and his parallel ideas to those of Jane Jacobs at the time is Grady Clay, "Metropolis Regained," *Horizon*, July 1959, 5–7, 10–15.

30 Jane Jacobs to CG, July 23, 1959, Folder 3381, Box 390, Series 200R, RG 1.2, FA387, Rockefeller Foundation, RAC.

31 On disarray, see ibid. See also Jane Jacobs to CG, July 17, 1959, Folder 3381; CG, notes from interview with Douglas Haskell, Folder 3380; and Comments on draft, CG to Jane Jacobs, May 19, 1960, Folder 3381, all in Box 390, Series 200R, RG 1.2, FA387, Rockefeller Foundation, RAC. For "elated," see CG, notes on Yoshinobu Ashihara dinner, March 18, 1961, Folder 1961, Pt. 1, Box 170, RG 12, Officers' Diaries, FA392, Rockefeller Foundation, RAC.

32 "Brilliantly conducted performance" from Grady Clay, "Competition for Urban Renewal Land," Working Paper, Joint Center for Urban Studies of MIT and

Harvard, Cambridge, MA, 1964, 10, Grady Clay archives, courtesy of Justin Clark.

33 The timeline for Clay's manuscript is documented in more detail in chapter 9.

34 The difference between the actual acquisition and clearance costs and the selling price of the land was subsidized by a two-thirds federal and one-third municipal formula. On Title I as a land program, see Hilary Ballon, "Robert Moses and Urban Renewal: The Title I Program," in *Robert Moses and the Modern City: The Transformation of New York*, ed. Hilary Ballon and Kenneth Jackson (New York: W. W. Norton, 2007), 97–105. Another contemporary study upholding San Francisco as an example of urban design influencing urban renewal is Thomas Kingsley, "The Design Process in Urban Renewal: An Analysis of the San Francisco Experience" (M.A. thesis, University of California, Berkeley, 1963), 32.

35 An additional nonremoval Title I project in San Francisco was the Diamond Heights residential project, which required little clearance. On the two types of renewal, see Richard Brandi, "San Francisco's Diamond Heights: Urban Renewal and the Modernist City," *Journal of Planning History*, Vol. 12, No. 2, 133–53.

36 "Saint Justin" is Hartman's term; Hartman says that in the "Mission barrio" Herman was known as the "white devil." See Thomas C. Fleming, "San Francisco's Land Development Program," *Sun-Reporter*, November 27, 1965, as cited in Hartman et al., *Yerba Buena*, 48–49.

37 "Justin Herman," editorial, *Sun-Reporter*, September 4, 1971, 7; Emory Curtis, "The Political Game," *Sun-Reporter*, September 18, 1971, 6. Historian Ocean Howell concluded in his study of the Mission District that, given his collaborative and even sensitive approach to working with community organizations on redevelopment, "Justin Herman did not exactly look like Goliath—or even like Robert Moses." See Ocean Howell, *Making the Mission: Planning and Ethnicity in San Francisco* (Chicago: University of Chicago Press, 2015), 259. Typical *Chronicle* coverage of Herman when he became redevelopment chief is James Benet, "S.F.'s Bouncy Redeveloper Meets Slum Problems Head-on," *SFC*, April 3, 1960, 7.

38 For an indispensable review of the relevant historiography, including an analysis of the limitations of Jane Jacobs's book in explaining manifestations of these divides, see Michael B. Katz, *Why Don't American Cities Burn?* (Philadelphia: University of Pennsylvania Press, 2012), 19–20, 40–41. See also Herb Caen, "Your City—And Mine," March 29, 1964, reprinted in *The Best of Herb Caen, 1960–1975*, 69–71.

39 Fleming founded the *Sun-Reporter* in 1944. See Max Millard, "Thomas Fleming, 'Good Soldier' of San Francisco's Black Press, Retires From Sun-Reporter At 89," July 28, 1997, www.sfmuseum.net/sunreporter/fleming .html, and Thomas Fleming, "Thomas C. Fleming's Weekly Report," *Sun-Reporter*, January 11, 1969, 9.

40 Quote from Sidney Wolinsky, "South of Market People Try to Stop Redevelopment," *Sun-Reporter*, November

15, 1969. South of Market's Yerba Buena project and the Western Addition were the two major San Francisco litigation battles with the San Francisco Redevelopment Agency (SFRA) over inadequate relocation in top-down clearance of affordable neighborhoods of nonwhite and low-income residents. In both cases community groups brought important lawsuits, with Yerba Buena's Tenants and Owners in Opposition to Redevelopment (formed summer of 1969) learning from the mid-1960s legal strategies of the Western Addition Community Organization. See Chester Hartman et al., *Yerba Buena: Land Grab and Community Resistance in San Francisco* (San Francisco: National Housing and Economic Development Law Project, 1974). Hartman was motivated to write the book upon seeing a PR blurb and photo of the architects' model of the Yerba Buena Center in the newsletter from a planning group that would be meeting in San Francisco in 1971. He did not want the "chamber-of-commerce rhetoric" to be the only view that visiting planners saw, when the "city's poor were being forced to pay for such 'progress.'" Hartman, *Yerba Buena*, 13.

41 Michael Cabanatuan, "Emory Curtis—S.F. Sun-Reporter columnist," *SFGate*, November 13, 2002, available at www.sfgate.com/bayarea/article/Emory-Curtis-S-F-Sun-Reporter-columnist-2754833.php, accessed October 6, 2016.

42 *UHR*, 114.

43 OED Online, s.v. "touchstone," Oxford University Press, September 2016, www.oed.com/view/Entry/203901?redirectedFrom=touchstone, accessed October 2, 2016.

44 Herb Caen, "The Vertical Earthquake," September 4, 1983, reprinted in *Herb Caen's San Francisco, 1976–1991*, 121.

45 Archaeologists seized on the discovery of more mundane artifacts of the frontier era, enriching a material archive that was understocked because of the 1906 earthquake and fire. In the 1960s, the 1906 earthquake, fire, and subsequent rebuilding boom were in fact relatively recent history.

46 Johann Rush, "Diggers Hunt San Francisco's Past: Gold Rush Relics Uncovered at Downtown Building Sites," *Christian Science Monitor*, September 17, 1974, 14.

47 Jacob Oser, *Henry George* (New York: Twayne, 1974), 28, 68.

48 Charles A. Barker, "Henry George and the California Background of *Progress and Poverty*," *California Historical Society Quarterly*, Vol. 24, No. 2 (June 1945), 97–115. Barker also traces the intellectual history of a regional, California school of economic thought to which George contributed. William Issel and Robert Cherney, *San Francisco, 1865–1932: Politics, Power, and Urban Development* (Berkeley: University of California Press, 1986).

49 Henry George Jr., *The Life of Henry George* (New York: Robert Shalkenbach Foundation, 1960), 210, as quoted in Oser, *Henry George*, 28.

50 Oser, *Henry George*, 17–28.; Henry George, *Our Land*

and Land Policy, National and State (San Francisco: White and Bauer, 1871).

51 Ibid., 23, 46.

52 Ibid., 4, 13, 17–18.

53 Ibid., 46. It is instructive to read George next to the contemporaneous 1868 fictional account by Horatio Alger, *Ragged Dick; or, Street Life in New York with the Boot Blacks* (Boston: Loring). Alger portrayed homeless children working in the streets as unproblematic; as junior capitalists they would rise or fall and sometimes attract the attention of wealthy benefactors. For George, the growing contrast in wealth pertained in manufacturing towns and countryside alike.

54 George, *Our Land and Land Policy*, 14, 17, 39. California, with its "subsoil resources," was also home in the 1860s to alternative land arrangements made to protect the "principle of the public interest" in land. See Barker, "Henry George and the California Background of *Progress and Poverty*," 113.

55 The Homestead Act required settlers to improve the property and pay a small registration fee. Land figured more explicitly in the environmental conservation movement, which at times intersected explicitly with urban environmental preservation during these decades. The role of women and men in Bay Area conservation is described in Richard A. Walker, *The Country in the City: The Greening of the San Francisco Bay Area* (Seattle: University of Washington Press, 2007). See also Gray Brechin, *Imperial San Francisco: Urban Power, Earthly Ruin* (Berkeley: University of California Press, 1999), for the integration of urban boom and environmental imperialism.

56 *UHR*, 95, 234–35.

57 *National Transportation Newsletter* (Washington, DC), 1972, quoted in "Findings of the *Guardian*'s Second Annual Investigative Project," *Bay Guardian Supplement*, November 1, 1972, 24.

CHAPTER 1
The Illustrated Pitch

1 In 1978, the SFMM became part of the Golden Gate National Recreation Area (GGNRA), becoming a separate national historic park only in 1989. Under GGNRA the SFMM was called National Maritime Museum, San Francisco, which did not match the museum's regional focus. Stephen Canright to Alison Isenberg, March 18, 2016.

2 Randy Delehanty interviews with Karl Kortum, June 12 and July 30, 1981, in Randolph Delehanty, "Interviews Concerning the Development of Ghirardelli Square, Conducted by Randolph Delehanty, 1981 February 18–November 4," BANC Phonotape 1419c, Bancroft Library. The establishment of the San Francisco Maritime State Historic Park, initially called a "State Historic Monument," took place on September 18, 1957.

3 Jacobs, *Making City Planning Work*, 177. See also "Tower Apartments by the Bay: Spaghetti Factory Will Go," *SFC*, November 29, 1960.

4 Although the plan for Gold Rush Plaza predated Disneyland, artist Hubert Buel had worked as an animator for Walt Disney and then done a short stint in set design for Twentieth Century Fox after serving in the Navy during the war. Stephen Canright, "Chapter 21: Museum Association Developments, 1964 through 1968," in "Draft Administrative History, San Francisco Maritime National Historical Park" (March 18, 2015), 319.

5 "Rejected High Rise Plan Proposal for Ghirardelli Center, San Francisco, CA, Circa 1964," A11.18453, Ghirardelli Center. San Francisco Maritime Research Center (SFMRC).

6 "Old Ghirardelli Plant May Be Sold," *SFC*, February 3, 1962, 3; "Ghirardelli Site for Apartments?" *SFE*, February 2, 1962, 3; and "Ghirardelli Chocolate Plant Sold," *SFC*, April 20, 1960, 1, all in folder Ghirardelli Square, *SFE* Clippings file, SFHC, SFPL.

7 Karl Kortum to William Matson Roth, April 25, 1962, Vol. 6: Development Ideas for Ghirardelli Block, BANC MSS 82/84 c, Ghirardelli Square Architectural Records, 1911–1979, Bancroft Library, University of California, Berkeley (GSAR); Delehanty interview with Kortum.

8 "Rejected High Rise Plan Proposal for Ghirardelli Center, San Francisco, CA, Circa 1964."

9 "The Ghirardelli Square Project," editorial, *SFC*, July 25, 1963, folder Wm Roth thru 1969, *SFE* Clippings file, SFHC, SFPL. See Carolyn Anspacher, "Ghirardelli Square," *SFC*, July 24, 1963, in File 014.I.A.6361, Lawrence Halprin Collection, Architectural Archives, University of Pennsylvania (Halprin Collection, AAUP).

10 "Ghirardelli Chocolate Plant Sold"; "The S.F. Victorian Mood," [publication title cut off], July 24, 1963, folder Wm Roth thru 1969, *SFE* Clippings file, SFHC, SFPL; Robert Anshen to Warren Lemmon, May 7, 1962; William Wurster to Warren Lemmon, June 11, 1962; Don Hatch, June 7, 1962; Kortum Memo, March 1, 1962, all in Vol. 6, GSAR.

11 "The Ghirardelli Square Project"; "Ghirardelli Square: The Focus of San Francisco's New North Waterfront Redevelopment" (1963), Bancroft Library f NA6216.S3 G4 1963. Lurline Roth's financial backing of the square appeared inconsistently in accounts.

12 "Montgomery Block Sold; Building May Be Torn Down for Parking Lot," *SFE*, December 28, 1947; "Famed Block Doomed; Old Montgomery Building Sold," *SFE*, May 25, 1951; Mary Crawford, "City Threatens Famed Building; Slum Clearing Program Hits S.F. Landmark, Long Resort of Artists," *San Francisco News*, July 1, 1952; John F. Allen, "Landmark Doomed; Office Building Planned on Site," *SFE*, July 10, 1953; "Old 'Monkey Block' Again Faces Doom," *SFC*, June 15, 1956; Tom Mathews, "'Monkey Block' Doom Near," *SFC*, January 25, 1959; "'Monkey Block' Half Torn Down,' *SFE*, June 24, 1959. All in folder San Francisco/Buildings/Montgomery Block, *SFE* Clippings file, SFHC, SFPL. On regrets, see Alison Isenberg interview with Bill and Joan Roth, New York City, April 27, 2011.

13 Isenberg interview with Bill and Joan Roth; Rubin, *A Negotiated Landscape*, 90.

14 Randy Delehanty interview with Stuart and Caree Rose, February 18, 1981, in Delehanty, "Interviews Concerning the Development of Ghirardelli Square."

15 I am indebted to Jasper Rubin for his masterful explanations of the port and planning in *A Negotiated Landscape*, esp. 39–42.

16 Ibid., 26, 101–5, 132–46.

17 Ibid., 26, 105, 132–46. Rubin illuminates the politics of the transfer from state to city and relates this to the details of the *Northern Waterfront Plan*.

18 Ibid., 23–25, 94–96, 123; T. J. Kent Jr., "Preface," in Jacobs, *Making City Planning Work*, ix–xvi; Jacobs, *Making City Planning Work*, 189.

19 San Francisco Department of City Planning, "Jackson Square," June 1971, included in National Register of Historic Places Inventory Nomination Form, "Jackson Square Historic District," PH0065935, November 18, 1971, available at http://npgallery.nps.gov/nrhp/AssetDetail?assetID=88623de1-6869-4e8f-84e0-bd8b966be34b; "Planning Analysis, Historical Site, Jackson Square," undated, courtesy of Beverly Willis; Maitland Zane, "Jackson Square Restrictions," *SFC*, June 21, 1972, 4; "The City's Only Historic District," *SFE*, March 4, 1973. The city passed a historic district ordinance for Jackson Square in 1972 after five years of disagreement. See Jackson Square folders, *SFE* Clippings files, SFHC, SFPL.

20 Stephen McGovern, *The Politics of Downtown Development* (Lexington: University Press of Kentucky, 1998), 63–64; Greg Donofrio, "'Food Slums': The Urban Renewal of San Francisco's Produce Market," paper delivered at the Society for American City and Regional Planning History Conference, 2009.

21 That clearance helped precipitate the mobilization of gay political organizing in San Francisco, as Damon Scott has documented in "The City Aroused."

22 Delehanty interview with Karl Kortum. The contestation over the proposed Ferry Building Park is described in Scott, "The City Aroused."

23 Yet another type of historically themed redevelopment was represented by resurgent destination retail streets like Union Street (included briefly in chapter 2); by the mid-1960s one could also visit lower Grant, Clement, and Post Streets.

24 Among the originators were E. M. (Ted) Griffith, Dorothy Lawenda, Howard Lawenda, John McGuire, and Clarence Slade. See Millie Robbins, "Echoes of History in Jackson Square," *SFC*, September 26, 1967, folder SF/Jackson Square 1960–1969, Clippings file, SFHC, SFPL. See also Polly Warfield, "Jackson Square Reclaimed: A New San Francisco Design Center," *SFC*, February 17, 1952, and "Jackson Square," clipping, September 21, 1952, both in folder SF/Jackson Square 1959 and previous, Clippings file, SFHC, SFPL.

25 San Francisco Planning Department (SFPD), "Jackson Square," 2; Maritime Museum Press Release, May 9,
1978; Jim Wood, "Bones of Gold Rush Ship Found in a Building Site," *SFE*, May 4, 1978, 3; and Hart Corbett to Karl Kortum, May 12, 1978, all in Box 34, Series 1, Sub 2, Vessels, Niantic, Karl Kortum Collection, HD1084, SFMRC (KKC). When Transamerica bought Merchant Street adjacent to Jackson Square to build its pyramid on Montgomery Street, the state quit-claimed the land to the city in order to declare it free of the "public trust" requirements preventing sale of port lands. Legislative Assembly Bill 1014, March 1969, Transamerica File 281–69, Board of Supervisors (BOS).

26 SFPD, "Jackson Square"; National Register of Historic Places Inventory Nomination Form, "Jackson Square Historic District"; "Hotaling Place Mall Okayed," *SFC*, August 19, 1960, 14; "City Renewal Bargain," *SFC*, August 23, 1960, 24. On the city's mix of oblivious, destructive approaches to the square with well-meaning investment, see "Shelve It," July 22, 1957. For typical compliments about private enterprise without "government subsidies" in Jackson Square and Union Street, see "Private Enterprise's Vigorous Spark," [publication name cut off], August 21, 1962. Both in folder San Francisco/Jackson Square Editorials, Clippings file, SFHC, SFPL.

27 Russ Cone, "A Quiet Miracle on Union Street," [publication name cut off], August 19, 1962, folder Dr. Rae Ashley, Clippings file, SFHC, SFPL.

28 Lynn Thomas, "Restored Commercial Buildings: How the City Saves Face," *San Francisco*, March 1968, cover story.

29 "At Fisherman's Wharf: 'Cannery' Plan—Not for the Fish," *SFE*, June 16, 1965; Rob Haeseler, "A Monumental Effort: The Cannery opens for Business," *SFC*, November 28, 1967; and Kevin Starr, "Cannery Row," [publication name cut off] November 10, 1977, all in folder Corp. Cannery, Clippings file, SFHC, SFPL.

30 Martin hired architect Joseph Esherick, giving him his first major commercial development project. Esherick had designed Martin's Marin home and some early Sea Ranch structures. Martin brought in Thomas Church, the alternate landscape architect Roth did not hire for Ghirardelli. Martin's team included graphic designer Marget Larsen (parallel to Ghirardelli Square's Barbara Stauffacher). When Martin hired William Conover, he matched the Village Fair roots of Ghirardelli's property managers, Stuart and Caree Rose.

31 Starr, "Cannery Row"; Herb Caen, "Eat, Drink, Be Merry," *SFC*, April 3, 1969, folder Corp. Cannery, Clippings file, SFPL.

32 Starr, "Cannery Row"; "At Fisherman's Wharf: 'Cannery' Plan—Not for the Fish"; Haeseler, "A Monumental Effort." See also Brian W. H. Taylor, "Wharf's Old Cannery Takes On a New Life," *SFE*, July 2, 1967; Eloise Dungan, "Getting Lost in the Cannery," [publication name cut off], May 5, 1968; and Margot Patterson Doss, "S.F. at Your Feet: The Fabulous Cannery," *SFC*, August 18, 1968; , all in folder Corp. Cannery, Clippings file, SFPL. Examples of Martin's waterfront collaboration included supporting a tourist trolley and paying the rent for Conrad Square to Southern Pacific Railroad, when Kortum miscalculated that they could get the land rent-free. See Kortum to Roth, August 18, 1967, Box 31, Series 2, Sub 5, Correspondence Binder regarding restoration/preservation Ghirardelli 1962–1970, KKC; Karl Kortum to Leonard Martin, February 12, 1964, Box 38, Series 1, Sub 2, file Joseph Conrad Square, KKC. On Conrad Square, see Stephen Canright, "Chapter 21," 337–48.

33 "The Changing North Face of San Francisco," *Sunset*, November 1967.

34 On Buel's style, see Gordon McClelland and Jay Last, *California Watercolors 1850–1970: An Illustrated History & Biographical Dictionary* (Santa Ana, CA: Hillcrest, 2002).

35 Karl Kortum, "The Founding of the San Francisco Maritime National Historical Park," unpublished typescript, SFMRC, PV 13 S315 K67 1990. Both Frederick Law Olmsted and Daniel Burnham had proposed waterfront parks for the site. See "National Register of Historic Places Register—Nomination Form, Aquatic Park Historic District," 1976, updated 1982, available at http://focus.nps.gov/pdfhost/docs/NHLS/Text/84001183.pdf.

36 Kortum and Spreckels had a friction-filled working relationship given their shared commitment to the city's shipping past and differing ideas for how a museum could best interpret that past. Nonetheless, Spreckels allowed Kortum to live rent-free in her garage apartment when he became curator and paid him a stipend of $150 a month until his city salary started. In 1949 and 1950, like Kortum, she pursued maritime museum campaigns. These sometimes reinforced, and sometimes interfered with, Kortum's work. See Clarence Lindner to Scott Newhall, September 19, 1949, and Alma Spreckels to Sidney Walton, January 11, 1954, both in Series 2, Sub 2, file Early SFMM Correspondence, 1949–1962. For Spreckels's ideas for the bathhouse and the museum, see Alma Spreckels to Edward Harms, June 1, 1949; Cecelia McCue to Edward Harms, May 31, 1949; and Spreckels to Harms, May 26, 1949, all in Box 4, Series 2, Sub 2, file 24, Museum History, 1948–1949. See also Pacific Steamship Association to Harms, April 23, 1951, in Box 4, Series 2, Sub 2, file Museum History, 1950–51; Isenberg interview with Stephen Canright, San Francisco, March 18, 2015.

37 Kortum, "The Founding of the San Francisco Maritime National Historical Park"; Kortum to Mr. Newhall, March 5, 1949, Binder SFMM, Vol. 1 (through 1950), SFMRC; Delehanty interview with Karl Kortum.

38 Kortum to Mr. Newhall, March 5, 1949. Kortum first proposed that the city's maritime scholars from the Marine Research Society lead the new institution. See Kortum, "The Founding of the San Francisco Maritime National Historical Park." Founded in 1929, Mystic Seaport collected vessels and artifacts in the 1930s and in the 1940s gathered old buildings from elsewhere to assemble an oceanside village.

39 Delehanty interview with Karl Kortum; Kortum, "The Founding of the San Francisco Maritime National Historical Park."

40 Kortum, "The Founding of the San Francisco Maritime National Historical Park."

41 Kortum addressed this second letter to Scott, the first to Mr. Newhall. See Kortum to Newhall, April 7, 1949, in Binder SFMM, Vol. 1 (through 1950), SFMRC.

42 Scott Newhall to Clarence Lindner, September 22, 1949, Series 2, Sub 2, Early San Francisco Maritime Museum Correspondence, 1949–1962, KKC, SFMRC.

43 Kortum, "The Founding of the San Francisco Maritime National Historical Park"; Delehanty interview with Kortum; Scott Newhall to Karl Kortum, June 6, 1949; and the Newhall-Lindner letters in Series 2, Sub 2, Early San Francisco Maritime Museum Correspondence, 1949–1962.

44 Kortum, "The Founding of the San Francisco Maritime National Historical Park."

45 Edward Harms to Mayor Robinson, April 25, 1950; Chairman to Coffman, March 6, 1950; and Walter Walsh to Dion Hom, March 3, 1950, all in Box 4, Series 2, Sub 2, file Museum History, 1950–51, KKC.

46 "Shrine on a Shoestring," *SFC*, February 22, 1953, in Box 4, Series 2, Sub 2, file Museum History, 1950–1951. Kortum could see the *Balclutha* on Sausalito's waterfront from his museum office. In 1988 the ship moved to Hyde Street Pier. Delehanty interview with Kortum. Canright to Isenberg, March 18, 2016.

47 Canright, "Chapter 21," 340–42; Delehanty interview with Kortum; Carl Nolte, "Jean Kortum: Key Figure in S.F. 'Freeway Revolt,'" *SFGate*, October 10, 2007, available at http://www.sfgate.com/bayarea/article/Jean-Kortum-Key-figure-in-S-F-freeway-revolt-2498516.php. Karl Kortum's strong pronouncements and forceful nature resulted in a pattern of fallings-out with colleagues.

48 Kortum said Lundburg swept aside Kortum's "beautiful" brochures, saying, "Get this shit off my desk." See Delehanty interview with Kortum. On his first realization of the oil money's potential, see Karl Kortum to Hugh Gallagher, September 15, 1954, Series 2, Sub 2, Early SFMM Correspondence, 1949–1962. The city's struggles to choose which park to put forward for the state's Tidelands Oil Funds were covered in the pro-SFMM *SFC*. Key coverage includes William Thomas, "City Will Consider Historical Center at Aquatic Park, *SFC*, December 16, 1956, 10; Richard Reinhardt, "$27 Million Civics Projects Under Study," *SFC*, December 20, 1956, 1, 14; Jack Burby, "Shift by Mayor: Project X Heads for Top Priority," *SFC*, September 11, 1957, 1–2; "What Project X Can Mean to S.F.," editorial, *SFC*, September 12, 1957, 24. Clear local coverage of complicated Tidelands Oil Fund implications is found in a series beginning with David Perlman, "How Should State Spend Large Tidelands Fund?," *SFC*, April 19, 1954, 1, 6. On federal jurisdiction as better protection than states against the "giveaway" of oil rights, see "Tidelands Hearing," *SFC*, March 9, 1948, 28.

49 "Shrine on a Shoestring." The Maritime Museum was never a true city museum, because the Museum Association operated it, leasing the Aquatic Park Building from the city for one dollar per year. San Francisco's Recreation and Parks Department paid Kortum's salary as a curator and provided janitorial service and a boiler mechanic until the building was transferred to the National Park Service (NPS) in January 1978. Canright to Isenberg, March 18, 2016, in author's possession.

50 Wallace Wortman to Board of Supervisors, November 14, 1969, and Enclosed Report, in Box 4, Series 2, Sub 2, File 23, Hyde Street Pier, 1968–1972, KKC.

51 Ibid. Jean Kortum wrangled attorney Hal Howard to sue the state and keep the Haslett Warehouse from being reassigned to nonmuseum purposes. See Harold Howard, "The Haslett Warehouse: The Tortuous Transition from Warehouse to Boutique Hotel," 2016, unpublished essay, courtesy of Hal Howard.

52 Scott Newhall suggested the title Project X for the SFMM's state park plans. See Cyril Magnin to Karl Kortum, April 7, 1961, and Trustees of the Maritime Museum Association, "Memorandum," April 7, 1961, both in file Fisherman's Wharf, 1961–1975, KKC.

53 Canright, "Chapter 21," 361–86; pencil quote on 372. See "Concern over a $10 Million Garage," *SFC*, 2.

54 Canright, "Chapter 21," 385–86.

55 Staci Steinberger, "Marget Larsen, 1922–1984," in Bobbye Tigerman, ed., *A Handbook of California Design, 1930–1965* (Cambridge: MIT Press, 2013), 158–59; Robert Brewster Freeman, "Marget Larsen," *Communication Arts*, Vol. 30, No. 1 (March–April 1988), 88–102.

56 Karl Kortum to Marget Larsen, January 18, 1965, in Box 5, Series 2, Sub 2, file 32, SF Real estate developments, 1959–1971, KKC.

57 Ibid. For an earlier Wharf scheme with Doug Baylis, see Karl Kortum to Dave Nelson, February 5, 1964, file Fisherman's Wharf, 1961–1975, KKC.

58 Kortum to Don Watson, July 19, 1962; Kortum to Thomas Bell, May 17, 1963; Kortum to Jess Chaffee, October 25, 1962; Kortum to Jack Dyson, March 19, 1962; and Kortum to George Maheras, January 15, 1962, all in Box 4, Series 2, Sub 2, File 2, Hyde Street Pier Furnishings, 1962–1966, KKC.

59 Kortum to Jack Hayward, July 14, 1970, and Kortum to Piero Patri, October 6, 1970, both in Box 4, Series 2, Sub 2, File 23, Hyde Street Pier Proposed Development, 1968–1972, KKC.

60 The key letter, including other attractions he visited, is Kortum to Piero Patri, October 27, 1970. See also Kortum to Al Gatov, December 30, 1970; Kortum to Piero Patri, November 9, 1970; ; Kortum to Piero Patri, October 6, 1970; Patri to file, Hyde Street Pier, November 9, 1970. The Haslett Warehouse ride would use technology like Disneyland's Pirates of the Caribbean and Haunted House. See also Larry Smith correspondence. All letters cited in this note are in Box 4, Series 2, Sub 2, File 23, Hyde Street Pier Proposed Development, 1968–1972, KKC. Negotiations for the city to take over from the state failed when the city required "an annual propitiatory tax, like a property tax, on the Haslett Building, on the pier surface area, and on the submerged land

under the pier. This made the proposition financially unfeasible, and Wrather dropped out in early 1972." Karl Kortum supported the proposal to move the SFMM under the NPS but did not originate the idea. See Canright to Isenberg, March 18, 2016, in author's possession.

61 The developer for the 1968 Hyde Street Pier plan was the Dillingham Corporation.

62 Karl Kortum, "Some Thoughts on Conversion of Ghirardelli Chocolate Factory into Offices/Apartments," March 1, 1962, Vol. 6: Development Ideas for Ghirardelli Block, GSAR.

63 Delehanty interview with Kortum.

64 Karl Kortum, "Some Thoughts on Conversion of Ghirardelli Chocolate Factory into Offices/Apartments," March 1, 1962, Vol. 6, GSAR.

65 "Ghirardelli Square: The Focus of San Francisco's New North Waterfront Redevelopment" (1963).

66 Roger Lapham Jr. was president of North Waterfront Associates. Karl Kortum, draft Letter to the Editor, *SFC*, March 25, 1968, 3, folder Protect Our Waterfront Committee, Box 5, Series 2, Sub 2, KKC, SFMRC.

CHAPTER 2
"Not Bound by an Instinct to Preserve"

1 Back matter, Photos AAB-8612 (September 25, 1958) and AAB-8590 (September 29, 1958), *San Francisco Call-Bulletin*, Folder S.F. Districts–Fisherman's Wharf–1950, San Francisco Historical Photograph Collection, SFHC, SFPL. Gurdon Woods was the sculptor.

2 B.W.N., "San Francisco: The Designer's City," *Interiors*, August 1966, 122–32. In contrast, in New York during the 1950s it was difficult to pinpoint artist-identified neighborhoods outside of Greenwich Village and SoHo. Pop artists lived in old sailmaking lofts condemned for the World Trade Center, and from the 1940s through the 1960s some lived in isolated pockets in Lower Manhattan and Brownstone Brooklyn. See Aaron Shkuda, *The Lofts of Soho: Gentrification, Art, and Industry in New York, 1950–1980* (Chicago: University of Chicago Press, 2016); Ann Fensterstock, *Art on the Block: Tracking the New York Art World from SoHo to the Bowery, Bushwick and Beyond* (New York: Palgrave MacMillan, 2013); Suleiman Osman, *The Invention of Brownstone Brooklyn: Gentrification and the Search for Authenticity in Postwar New York* (New York: Oxford University Press, 2011); Jed Perl, *New Art City: Manhattan at Mid-Century* (New York: Knopf, 2005).

3 Henrik Bull to Proctor Mellquist, May 22, 1962. Vol. 6, GSAR.

4 "Roth Named to U.S. Trade Post," *SFC*, July 31, 1963, 4. He immediate resigned as president of SPUR. A sampling of his many business commitments included serving as a director of Matson Navigation Company, and chairman of the board of Pacific National Life Assurance Company.

5 "Box with a View," ca. 1950s clipping in author's possession. Randy Delehanty interview with Proctor Mellquist, 1981, in Randolph Delehanty, "Interviews

Concerning the Development of Ghirardelli Square, Conducted by Randolph Delehanty, 1981 February 18–November 4," BANC Phonotape 1419c, Bancroft Library.

6 John Matthias, "Exterior Treatment of Ghirardelli Buildings," March 1, 1962, Vol. 6, GSAR.

7 Mellquist sketches accompanied June 19 and July 9, 1962, memos; Larry Halprin's sketch a June 27, 1962, cover letter to Bill Roth; and the Roth sketch a January 27, 1963, "Ghirardelli" memo, all in Binder 1, Box 1, GSAR.

8 Randy Delehanty interview with Warren Lemmon, August 4, 1981, in Delehanty, "Interviews Concerning the Development of Ghirardelli Square."

9 Randy Delehanty interview with William Roth, November 4, 1981, in Delehanty, "Interviews Concerning the Development of Ghirardelli Square." Bill Roth first met Delehanty when the latter took a course with him at the Kennedy School at Harvard University on the subject of nonprofit management. Isenberg interview with Bill and Joan Roth.

10 Roth eventually obtained a 6.5 percent loan in 1966 from Connecticut General Life Insurance Company. Randy Delehanty interview with Warren Lemmon.

11 Consulted experts included Anshen & Allen; Campbell & Wong; Thomas Church; Lloyd Flood; George Frizzell (an art appraiser); Paul Hammarberg, Albert-Lovett Corporation (Fontana Towers); Lawrence Halprin; Justin Herman; Ernest Kump; James Leefe; John Matthias; Proctor Mellquist; Patri, Patri, Patri; Rockrise and Watson; Skidmore, Owings & Merrill (John Wiese, Charles Bassett, and John Woodbridge); Bank of America; Gardner Dailey; Karl Kortum; Hatch, White, Hermann, and Steinau; Haas and Haynie (Robert Haynie); J. Francis Ward; Harry Rothrock (manager of shopping centers for Albert-Lovett Corp.); William Simpson; Al Waller (manager of Town & Country Shopping Centers, Palo Alto and San Jose); Robert Powers, Nut Tree; Fifth Avenue Shopping Center and Wax Museum, Scottsdale Arizona; Stuart and Caree Rose; and David Pesonen. See David Pesonen to Warren Lemmon, February 3, 1963, in Binder 1, Box 1, and Vol. 6, GSAR.

12 Delehanty interview with Lemmon. For an insightful article by a designer Roth consulted in 1962, see James M. Leefe, "Ghirardelli Square," *Interiors*, July 1965, 99.

13 Roth, "Ghirardelli," January 27, 1963.

14 David Pesonen to Warren Lemmon, February 3, 1963, Binder 1, Box 1, GSAR.

15 Campbell & Wong, May 31, 1962, Vol. 6, GSAR.

16 Ibid.; "Ghirardelli Property—Paul Hammarberg Development Suggestions," July 3, 1962, Vol. 6, GSAR.

17 Delehanty interview with Lemmon.

18 Delehanty interview with Roth.

19 Randy Delehanty interview with John Matthias, April 7, 1981, in Randolph Delehanty, "Interviews Concerning the Development of Ghirardelli Square." Warren Lemmon to William Roth, "Ghirardelli Property," July 9, 1962, Ghirardelli Memos file, Box 1, GSAR.

20 Halprin's firm had previously shared renovated loft space with Campbell & Wong. See Delehanty interviews with Lemmon and Roth. Mellquist compared Church and Halprin in depth in "Proctor Mellquist, Interview Conducted by Suzanne B. Reiss, 1978," 679–700, in *Thomas D. Church, Landscape Architect*, Vol. 2, Oral History Center, Bancroft Library, 1978.

21 Warren Lemmon to William Roth, "Ghirardelli Property—Justin Herman Suggestions," June 5, 1962; "Ghirardelli Block—Skidmore, Owings & Merrill suggestions," June 22, 1962; Warren Lemmon to William Roth, "Ghirardelli Block—Bank of America Suggestions for Development," June 29, 1962; and "Notes of Procter [sic] Mellquist, Editor of Sunset Magazine," June 19, 1962, all in Vol. 6, GSAR.

22 Thousands of African Americans, Japanese, Chinese, and Filipinos had been forced out of the Filmore Street neighborhood (Western Addition parcel A-1) and the older Victorian homes reduced to rubble. This was the site of the Japanese Cultural Center. Ten years later, the city's Chinese Cultural Center provoked Allan Temko's scathing 1971 review. Never before had the Chinese community "been screwed on so grand an architectural scale as in the new 'Chinese Cultural Center' towering above Portsmouth Square which—s' help me—is really a Holiday Inn." The land had "formerly belonged to the public." See "Dr. Fu Manchu's Plastic Pagoda: San Francisco's New 'Chinese Cultural Center' Has Given the 'Inscrutable East' the Worst Screwing It Has Had in a Century," *San Francisco*, May 1971, San Francisco Buildings—Chinese Cultural Center, VF Clippings, SFHC, SFPL.

23 Blanche Burnett, "Society Sketchbook: Neglected Art—Dining," March 30 1965, Vol. 1, Scrapbook of Clippings, 1964–67, GSAR.

24 Donn Emmons counted twenty-three restaurants in Tivoli Gardens. "Minutes of Meeting of Advisory Board—Ghirardelli Square, August 5, 1965," 1, in 014.I.A.946, Halprin Collection, AAUP.

25 Lawrence Halprin to Bill Roth, September 20, 1963, in Ghirardelli Memos—Warren Lemmon and Others, 1962–63, File 1 of 2, Box 1, GSAR. By 1967 some had tired of hearing Halprin sing the praises of Tivoli. See Ronald Buel, "Shaping Cities: A Landscape Architect Generates New Ideas in Urban-Area Planning," *Wall Street Journal*, June 8, 1967, 1. See also Wolf Von Eckardt, "Danish Pastry for Our Island Park," *Washington Post*, January 29, 1967, E3.

26 The dearth of U.S. examples in the early 1960s meant that other preservation-oriented urban experiments such as Gaslight Square in St. Louis, cited European models as well. See Alison Isenberg, *Downtown America* (Chicago: University of Chicago Press, 2004).

27 Warren Lemmon to W. M. Roth, "Ghirardelli Property—Al Waller Development," July 3, 1962, and Warren Lemmon to W. M. Roth, "Scottsdale Fifth Avenue Shopping Center," February 20, 1963, both in Binder 1, Box 1, GSAR.

28 "Notes of Procter [sic] Mellquist, Editor of Sunset Magazine," June 19, 1962, Vol. 6, GSAR.

29 Warren Lemmon to W. M. Roth, "Ghirardelli Property—Robert Powers (Nut Tree)," January 14, 1963, Binder 1, Box 1, GSAR; Alan Temko, West Coast Report, No. 7, December 23, 1960, Box 83, Folder 5, Douglas Putnam Haskell Papers, 1915–79, Avery Architectural and Fine Arts Library, Columbia University.

30 "Notes of Procter [*sic*] Melquist, Editor of Sunset Magazine."

31 Warren Lemmon to W. M. Roth, "Scottsdale Fifth Avenue Shopping Center"; Warren Lemmon to W. M. Roth, "American Heritage Wax Museum, Scottsdale, Arizona," February 20, 1963. By February 20, Lemmon copied Mellquist, Kortum, and Stuart Rose on these memos.

32 "The Changing North Face of San Francisco," *Sunset*, November 1967; John S. Bolles and Ernest Born, *A Plan for Fisherman's Wharf* (San Francisco: San Francisco Port Authority, 1961), 27.

33 Ibid.; "Notes of Procter [*sic*] Melquist, Editor of Sunset Magazine."

34 Ibid.; Lemmon to W. M. Roth, "Ghirardelli Property—Al Waller Development," July 3, 1962.

35 "Stanford Winery Facelift," *SFE*, December 14, 1960; "New Role Planned for Senator Stanford Winery: Old Structure to House Bank, Restaurant," *Palo Alto Times*, December 13, 1960; "Old Barn Gets Face Lifting," *Palo Alto Times*, November 24, 1961; "Happy Way of Preserving Old Landmark," *Palo Alto Times*, December 14, 1960; and George K. Thomson, "Bolles Takes Over Old Stanford Winery," *S.F. News Call Bulletin*, April 7, 1961, all in Stanford Lands Clippings and Ephemera, Box 2, Folder 1, Stanford Land and Clippings Collection (SC678), Stanford University Archives. On the original proposal, revisions, drawings, and seating plans, see Bolles Collection, Loeb Library, Harvard Graduate School of Design.

36 "New Role Planned for Senator Stanford Winery." Awareness of the "old California wineries" was growing in 1960; already eleven had been given landmark status. On wineries as deserving of a photo essay in *Architectural Forum*, see Temko, "West Coast Report, No. 7."

37 "'New Wine in Old Bottles'—Winery Begins Bright Metamorphosis Today," *San Francisco Daily Commercial News*, May 22, 1961.

38 "International Cuisine at a Winery," *SFC*, November 23, 1961; "Stanford Landmark: Winery to be Art Center," *Daily Review*, April 6, 1961. Wells Fargo and brokerage Irving Lundberg & Co. used "Old West" props. "New Role Planned for Senator Stanford Winery"; "Brokerage in a Barn," *SFC*, November 10, 1961. All articles cited in this note are in Stanford Lands Clippings and Ephemera.

39 "Old Barn A Novel Center," *Redwood City Tribune*, December 1, 1961.

40 "Old Orchard Is 15 Today," *Chicago Tribune*, October 10, 1971, T5.

41 "A Macy's Store for Palo Alto," *SFC*, October 13, 1961, 2.

42 Rubin, *A Negotiated Landscape*, 110, 125; Bolles and Born, *A Plan for Fisherman's Wharf*; John S. Bolles and Ernest Born, "Embarcadero City" (Plan for the San Francisco Port Authority, 1959); John S. Bolles Associates, *Northern Waterfront Plan: San Francisco* (San Francisco: Bolles Associates, 1968). Ernest and Esther Baum Born shared an architectural practice; they married in 1926 after meeting in architecture school at the University of California, Berkeley. Esther wrote the Fisherman's Wharf plan and contributed to "Embarcadero City." She also worked as an architectural photographer. Nicholas Olsberg, *Architects and Artists: The Work of Ernest and Esther Born* (San Francisco: Book Club of California, 2015), 230. On unveiling the Embarcadero City plans, see Michael Harris, "Waterfront 'City' Proposed by Port Authority," *SFC*, January 30, 1959, 1.

43 Bolles and Born, *A Plan for Fisherman's Wharf*, 26–31.

44 Temko, West Coast Report, No. 7. Temko described Bolles's "usual low level of design" in "West Coast Report, No. 1—September 30, 1959," 5, Box 83, Folder 6, Haskell Papers.

45 Campbell & Wong , May 31, 1962, Vol. 6, GSAR.

46 Temko, West Coast Report, No. 5, July 12, 1960, Box 81, Folder 2, Haskell Papers.

47 Local stories from Prudence Martin, "Mokelumne Hill: How a San Franciscan Rejuvenated a Decaying Town in the Mother Lode," *SFE*, September 4, 1960. The rest compiled from "To Present and Prospective Stockholders of Leger, Limited," June 12, 1961; Warren Lemmon, "To the Shareholders of Leger, Limited," August 7, 1962; "Leger Ltd., Interim Report, January 1961"; booklet "Leger, Ltd."; and Warren Lemmon to Shareholders of Leger, Ltd., December 30, 1963. For design coverage, see "In the Mother Lode Country: A Lesson in Restoration," *Pacific Architect and Builder*, March 1960. All items cited in this note are in folder Hotel Leger, Mokelumne Hill, 1960, Modernist landscape architect Robert Royston was one of the early investor-designer friends. See Robert Royston Collection, 1999–12, Environmental Design Archives (EDA), College of Environmental Design, University of California, Berkeley.

48 Compiled from "To Present and Prospective Stockholders of Leger, Limited," June 12, 1961; Warren Lemmon, "To the Shareholders of Leger, Limited," August 7, 1962; "Leger Ltd., Interim Report, January 1961"; booklet "Leger, Ltd." ; Warren Lemmon to Shareholders of Leger, Ltd., December 30, 1963. The two key articles on Mokelumne Hill were "In the Mother Lode Country: A Lesson in Restoration," *Pacific Architect and Builder*, March 1960, and Prudence Martin, "Mokelumne Hill: How a San Franciscan Rejuvenated a Decaying Town in the Mother Lode," *SFE*, September 4, 1960. All items cited in this note are in folder Hotel Leger, Mokelumne Hill, 1960, Robert Royston Collection, 1999–12.

49 Judith Anderson, "Gold Rush Country Hideaways," *SFC*, June 25, 1971, folder Beverly Willis, Clippings file, SFHC, SFPL.

50 Roth, "Ghirardelli," January 27, 1963.

51 For the perspective on this phenomenon of one key company, see Jane Thompson and Alexandra Lange, *Design Research: The Store That Brought Modern Living to American Homes* (San Francsico: Chronicle Books, 2010).

52 By 1960 there were many productive disagreements among architects over the theory and practice of the International Style, but nonarchitect preservationists such as Karl Kortum commented primarily on the universalizing, homogenizing design outcomes that ignored historical context and historical design styles. For insight into how the International Style had evolved between the early 1930s and the 1950s in relation to the modernist movement in architecture, with reference to Bay Area modernism, see Henry-Russell Hitchcock, "The International Style Twenty Years After," *Architectural Record*, Vol. 110, No. 2 (August 1951), 89–97; see also Henry-Russell Hitchcock, *Architecture: Nineteenth and Twentieth Centuries* (Baltimore: Penguin, 1958), 454 n1.

53 Warren Lemmon to W. M. Roth, "Ghirardelli Property—David Pesonen," January 10, 1963, and David Pesonen to Warren Lemmon, February 3, 1963, both in Binder 1, Box 1, GSAR. Soon after the Bodgea Bay victory, Pesonen started law school at Berkeley and built a distinguished career in law and environmental activism. See the David Pesonen papers, BANC MSS 98/133 c, Bancroft Library.

54 Kortum to Roth, August 22, 1963, Binder 1, Box 1, GSAR.

55 Kortum to Roth, February 13, 1963, Binder 1, Box 1, GSAR.

56 Pesonen to Lemmon, February 3, 1963.

57 Kortum to Roth, August 22, 1963.

58 Karl Kortum to Warren Lemmon, April 6, 1963, Binder 1, Box 1, GSAR.

59 Warren Lemmon to Donn Emmons, June 17, 1963, WB&E folder, Box 1, GSAR.

60 Pesonen to Lemmon, February 3, 1963.

61 Ibid.

62 Lemmon to W. M. Roth, "Ghirardelli Property—Al Waller Development," July 3, 1962.

63 Karl Kortum, "Some Thoughts on Conversion of Ghirardelli Chocolate Factory into Offices/Apartments," March 1, 1962, Vol. 6; Pesonen to Warren Lemmon, February 3, 1963; Kortum to Roth, February 13, 1963; Kortum to Lemmon, April 6, 1963.

64 Kortum to Roth, February 13, 1963. Positive reviews of Ghirardelli Square cut across architecture, business, the arts, and tourism.

65 Willis & Associates Inc., "Planning Analysis, Historical Site, Jackson Square, San Francisco"; Caroline Drewes, "The Magic of Union Street," *SFE*, Women Today, July 31, 1966; Kevin Keating, "The Horizontal Department Store," *SFE*, California Living, July 26, 1970, 18; and Oscar B. Teller, "Beverly Willis: Architect with Humanist Touch," *Philadelphia Inquirer*, December 21, 1975, all courtesy of Beverly Willis. See also R.L Revenaugh, "New Pride For an Old City Street," [publication name cut off], March 29, 1970, and other items in Beverly Willis Clippings file, SFHC, SFPL. The year 1966 was the first year for California's Governor's Design Awards; that year Bobbie Stauffacher also received recognition for her Sea Ranch supergraphics. See Michael Harris, "Northern Californians Win Top Design Honors," *SFC*, December 24, 1966, 2.

66 Lynn Thomas, "Restored Commercial Buildings: How the City Saves Face," *San Francisco*, March 1968, cover story. An example of the excellent recent case studies of late nineteenth- and early twentieth-century city-centered historic preservation movements, one that pays particular attention to women's roles, is Stephanie Yuhl, *A Golden Haze of Memory: The Making of Historic Charleston* (Chapel Hill: University of North Carolina Press, 2005). For an excellent overview, see *Giving Preservation a History: Histories of Historic Preservation in the United States*, ed. Max Page and Randall Mason (New York: Taylor and Francis Books, 2004).

67 Thomas, "Restored Commercial Buildings."

68 Quoted in Caroline Drewes, "Barbara Is Graphic about Her Success," *SFE&C*, Women Today, March 1, 1970, 5, in folder Solomon, B Clippings file, SFHC, SFPL. For Willis on the necessity of Manhattanization and the design challenges it brings, see David Ross, "What Makes Beverly Run?" *SFE&C*, February 14, 1971, Beverly Willis Clippings file, SFHC, SFPL.

CHAPTER 3
"Culture-a-Go-Go"

1 Frances Moffat, "The Fun of a Party That Moves," *SFC*, March 30, 1965, in Oversize Scrapbook No. 1: Clippings 1964–77, GSAR; Herb Caen, "The Power & The Glory," Herb Caen Columns 1964–65, Vol. 1, GSAR. Tour organizers published a catalog of advertisements (and a few essays) featuring the wealthy women of the city as models, identifying them by name. See "Tour of Dining Décor 1965: Catalogue," Box 14, File 7, Women's Board, 1934–1977, Administrative Records, San Francisco Museum of Modern Art Archives. The 1965 tour, organized around the art of dining, was the fourth and final of the "Tour de Decors" series that ran in 1955, 1957, 1960, and 1965. The museum added modern to its title in 1975.

2 Caen, "The Power & The Glory."

3 Herb Caen, "Fan Club," undated, Herb Caen columns 1964–65, Vol. 1, GSAR.

4 Elaine Reed, "Dining Décor on Tour," *San Francisco News-Call Bulletin*, Vol. 1, GSAR.

5 Undated column, Herb Caen columns 1964–65, Vol. 1, GSAR. Michael Kammen and others have explored the democratization of the arts in the 1960s and the alienation of artists from traditional museums. See Michael Kammen, *Visual Shock: A History of Art Controversies in American Culture* (New York: Knopf, 2006). See also the essays in *Reading California: Art, Image and Identity*,

1900–2000, ed. Stephanie Barron, Sheri Bernstein, and Ilene Susan Fort (Berkeley: University of California Press, 2000), and Sarah Schrank, *Art and the City: Civic Imagination and Cultural Authority in Los Angeles* (Philadelphia: University of Pennsylvania Press, 2009).

6 On sex and the shaping of San Francisco, see Josh Sides, *Erotic City: Sexual Revolutions and the Making of Modern San Francisco* (New York: Oxford University Press, 2009). Planning Director Allan Jacobs wrote about the city scene in 1968 in *Making City Planning Work* (Chicago: American Society of Planning Officials, 1978), 54.

7 "Notes of Procter [*sic*] Mellquist," June 19, 1962. On the emerging models for rooting American public life in commercial settings (especially planned ones), noting the leading role of California in this trend, see Charles Moore, "You Have to Pay for the Public Life," *Perspecta* Vols. 9–10 (1965), 57–97.

8 Delehanty interview with Roth.

9 Randy Delehanty interview with Lawrence Halprin, June 25, 1981, in Delehanty, "Interviews Concerning the Development of Ghirardelli Square." On the human scale, pedestrians, and orchestrated open spaces as preoccupations within urban design during the 1940s and 1950s, see Eric Mumford, "The Emergence of Urban Design in the Breakup of CIAM." On the persistence of these concerns, see Alex Krieger, "Where and How Does Urban Design Happen?" Both in *Harvard Design Review* (Spring/Summer 2006).

10 James M. Leefe, "Ghirardelli Square," *Interiors*, July 1965, 99. The Mandarin, founded by Cecilia Chiang, was a Ghirardelli Square restaurant of significant cultural impact; it was recently featured in Paul Freedman, *Ten Restaurants That Changed America* (New York: W. W. Norton, 2016).

11 Steven Roberts, "In San Francisco's North Beach, the Many Different Worlds and Generations Never Meet," *NYT*, November 4, 1969, 32. On urban renewal and the dislocation of queer residents and businesses, see Scott, "The City Aroused."

12 Isenberg interview with Ruth Asawa and Albert Lanier, San Francisco, March 31, 2005, transcript in author's possession. Ruth Asawa to Bill Roth, March 28, 1968, "Ruth Asawa's Sculpture and Controversy" file, GSAR. Asawa had prior warning of Halprin's disapproval; a year earlier he had voiced his objections to Roth and the square managers and, in an awkward conversation, to Asawa.

13 George Draper, "Scorn for a New Sculpture: Ghirardelli Square Controversy," *SFC*, March 26, 1968, 4, in Mermaid Sculpture file, Ruth Asawa Private Collection (RAPC). See also "Mermaid in Fountain Kicks Up Fuss," *San Francisco Examiner*, March 26, 1968, 16, in Sculpture Controversy file, 014.I.A.5910, Halprin Collection, AAUP.

14 Lawrence Halprin to Bill Roth, September 20, 1963, in Ghirardelli Memos—Warren Lemmon and Others,

1962–63, File 1 of 2, Box 1, GSAR. Halprin sought permission from Roth to commission the fountain sculpture, which Roth refused. See Warren Lemmon to Bill Roth, September 14, 1963, 4, in Tenant Reports, 1963–64 file, Box 1, GSAR. For the Fitzgerald sculpture, see also Lawrence Halprin, *Cities* (New York: Reinhold, 1963), 158. For Halprin's office drawings before the mermaid sculpture was installed, see 014.II.A.061 and 014.II.A061a, Halprin Collection, AAUP.

15 Lawrence Halprin, "Statement on the New Sculpture in the Fountain at Ghirardelli Square," March 22, 1968, 1, in Ruth Asawa's Sculpture and Controversy file, GSAR; Edmund N. Bacon, *Design of Cities* (New York: Viking, 1967). Bacon's principle is still applied today. See Kevin W. Sloan, "Second Man Missing: Lawrence Halprin and Associates' 1970s Heritage Plaza in Fort Worth Remains Uncomplemented and Undermaintained," *Landscape Architecture*, Vol. 93, No. 4 (April 2003), 82–89.

16 The glaring aspect of Halprin's statement is his repeated, nuanced description of Ruth Asawa as a man. Others pointed out that the "principle of the second man" made Halprin the second man to the "Victorian" era he disliked.

17 Duane A. Wakeham to the Editor, *SFC*, March 27, 1968, in P.R. Ghirardelli—Sculpture Controversy file, 014.I.A.6221, Halprin Collection, AAUP.

18 On "britches," see Allan Metz to Halprin, note written on top of "Scorn for a New Sculpture" article. Another message to Halprin read: "World Famous Landscape Architect Devotes Energies to the Burning Issues of American Cities Today." Both in 014.I.A.6221, Halprin Collection, AAUP. Some critics painted Halprin as primarily interested in monumental, sterile works, but these accusations were unfair given his unwavering dedication to creating lively, interactive public destinations. See Randy Delehanty interview with the Roses.

19 F. Blair Reeves to Charles Peterson, June 12, 1968; F. Blair Reeves to Halprin, June 7, 1968. Halprin's executive assistant wrote to his AIA counterpart, "We must get Larry on more panels, or otherwise more AIA contacts." Marvin Mayeux to Faynetta Nealis, June 13, 1968. All in 014.I.A.6361, Halprin Collection, AAUP.

20 "Architects Hear from Lady Bird," *SFC*, June 27, 1968, 11; "Lady Bird Loves the City," *SFE*, September 21 1966, in Vol. 1, GSAR.

21 Wolf Von Eckhardt, "Cityscape: What San Francisco Achieved, We Could Do with Powerhouse," *Washington Post*, June 13, 1965, File 014.I.A.6361, Halprin Collection, AAUP.

22 Elin Schoen, "Lawrence Halprin: Humanizing the City Environment," *American Way*, November 1972, 13, folder Lawrence Halprin, Box 1, GSAR. See also Theodore Osmundson to the Editor, *SFC*, March 29, 1968, in Sculpture Controversy file, 014.I.A.5910, Halprin Collection, AAUP.

23 Harriet Nathan interviews with Ruth Asawa in 1974 and 1976, in "Art, Competence, and Citywide Cooperation for San Francisco," 103–10, transcript, in Oral History Center, Bancroft Library.

24 A comprehensive review of Asawa's career is *The Sculpture of Ruth Asawa: Contours in the Air*, ed. Daniell Cornell (Berkeley: University of California Press, 2006).

25 For early reviews using these terms, see Martica Sawin, "Ruth Asawa," *Arts Digest* Vol 29, No. 6 (December 15, 1954), 22; "Eastern Yeast," *Time*, January 10, 1954, 54; Alfred Frankenstein, "Some Roses and Some Barbs for the Art Commission's Exhibit," *SFC*, April 11, 1954, 22; Miriam Dungan Cross, "Asawa Develops Art Form," *Oakland Tribune*, May 8, 1960, C-3; Gerald Nordland, "Ruth Asawa," *Art Forum*, Vol. 1 (June 1962), 1, 8.

26 On Asawa's ideas for the Art Commission, see Mildred Hamilton, "Ruth Asawa: Headlined Sculptress," *SFE*, March 31, 1968, Sunday Women section, 1, 10, in Mermaid Fountain file, RAPC. Yet another public art dispute from this period found Halprin and Asawa on opposing sides; Asawa protested Halprin's position in favor of the Vaillancourt fountain in the Embarcadero Plaza, see Mildred Hamilton, "The Careers That Grew Out of the Arts Project," *SFE&C*, January 27, 1980, in Clippings July 1979–June 1980 file, Box 1, GSAR. See also Andrea Jepson and Sharon Lipsky, *The Alvarado Experience: Ten Years of a School-Community Art Program* (San Francisco: Alvarado School Art Workshop, 1978); Andrea Jepson to Alison Isenberg, November 21, 2015, in author's possession.

27 Draper, "Scorn for a New Sculpture"; Ruth Asawa, "My Thoughts on the Ghirardelli Square Fountain Sculpture," March 1968, in Ruth Asawa's Sculpture and Controversy file, GSAR.

28 Warren Lemmon to W. M. Roth, "Ruth Lanier Sculpture," March 22, 1968, in Ruth Asawa's Sculpture and Controversy file, GSAR.

29 Asawa, "My Thoughts on the Ghirardelli Square Fountain Sculpture." For drafts of Halprin's statement, see 014.I.A.6221, Halprin Collection, AAUP.

30 "The Ghirardelli Square Mermaids," *SFC*, March 27, 1968, in 014.IA.5910, Halprin Collection, AAUP.

31 Lawrence Halprin, "Statement on the New Sculpture in the Fountain at Ghirardelli Square, March 22, 1968," 1.

32 Asawa, "My Thoughts on the Ghirardelli Square Fountain Sculpture." The fact that the ambiguity of abstract art often sparked controversy makes the ambiguity of "representational" mermaids noteworthy. Kammen, *Visual Shock*, xx–xxii.

33 Dr. and Mrs. Stephen A. Hunter to Mr. William Roth, March 26, 1968. For similar statements about abstract art, see Connie to Warren Lemmon, March 26, 1968; Mabel Harder to Mr. Roth, March 27, 1968; Duane Wakeham to *Chronicle* and John Gerling to Warren Lemmon, March 26, 1968. For more on "charming," see Kincaid letter, March 26, 1968, and Helen Farnsworth letter, June 19, 1968. All in Ruth Asawa's Sculpture and

Controversy file, GSAR. A *Chronicle* editorial also took a position against too much abstraction. See "The Ghirardelli Square Mermaids."

34 Mrs. Dandee Douglas to Mr. William Roth, March 29, 1968; Mrs. Ingram to President, Ghirardelli Square, March 27, 1968; Mrs. Gordon Grannis to San Francisco Art Commission, March 26, 1968, all in Ruth Asawa's Sculpture and Controversy file, GSAR.

35 The mayor found the sculpture, "particularly the mermaid with the baby, an arresting and imaginary concept." See "Art Row Spreads: Ghirardelli Mermaid Praised by Alioto," *SFE*, April 8, 1968, 16, in Mermaid Sculpture file, RAPC. One letter to Asawa related the fountain to Tivoli Gardens—"the same joie de vivre, the same festive fun, the same wonderful sense of play and imagination going off like fireworks! . . . Your wonderful mermaids in San Francisco acted like a magnet for every child who came to Ghirardelli Square." See Diana Merritt to Asawa, October 23, 1968, in Mermaid Sculpture file, RAPC. On "ecstatic" children, see Caree Rose to WMR, "Sculpture Caper," March 26, 1968, in Ruth Asawa's Sculpture and Controversy file, GSAR.

36 "Minutes of Advisory Board Meeting," November 6, 1963, in Advisory Board file, Box 1, GSAR.

37 In the 1950s, critics noted that cities were not hospitable to children. Josep Luis Sert, in a 1953 essay "Urban Design," described cities as places where "the children get run over." Quoted in Mumford, "The Emergence of Urban Design in the Breakup of CIAM," 11. Bufano's animals, scattered throughout San Francisco's open spaces, were known for their appeal to children. See Lynn Ludlow, "Bufano and the Little Ones," January 17, 1965, in "Bufano, B., 1965," *Examiner* Clipping Morgue, SFHC.

38 Fred Martin, of the San Francisco Art Institute, sympathized with Halprin about the fountain's cuteness and appeal to children but noted that Larry had lost this battle in public opinion. Fred Martin to Larry Halprin, March 26, 1968, in 014.IA.6221, Halprin Collection, AAUP.

39 Draft dated March 21, 1968, in 014.IA.6221, Halprin Collection, AAUP. Elsewhere Halprin distinguished between "Sculpture," and "Children's Sculpture." Halprin, *Cities*.

40 A Disney background artist taught Asawa "to draw in a very traditional way." See Terry Link, "The Art of Ruth Asawa," *San Francisco*, Vol. 15, No. 4 (April 1973). On Asawa's early years, see the essays by Jacqueline Hoefer and Karin Higa in *The Sculpture of Ruth Asawa*, ed. Cornell, 10–29, 30–41. Also Nathan interview with Asawa. Disney pioneered its audio animatronics at the 1964–65 World's Fair in New York City; the "It's a Small World" ride opened in Disneyland in 1966.

41 Draper, "Scorn for a New Sculpture," 4. On integrating art with home and children, see Bernice Stevens Decker, "Artist 'Crochets' Sculptural Forms," *Christian Science Monitor*, July 28, 1959, 12. Asawa framed the mermaids' tails using her wire technique.

42 Nathan interview with Asawa, 36–38.

43 Buel, "Shaping Cities," 1.

44 Jose Wilson, "Going Places, Finding Things in San Francisco," *House & Garden*, undated clipping, in Vol. 1, GSAR.

45 *Institutions* [a magazine of the service world], October 1967, in Vol. 1, GSAR.

46 There is a long history of the American public reacting to nudity in sculpture. See "Nudity, Decency, and Morality," in Kammen, *Visual Shock*, 47–87.

47 Warren Lemmon letter to Roth, July 19, 1967, in Ruth Asawa's Sculpture and Controversy file, GSAR. On the bathtub, see William Roth to Ruth Asawa, July 31, 1967, in Mermaid Sculpture file, RAPC. Roth approved casting "the lady" after inspecting the artist's progress on the mermaids during the summer of 1967. He respected both Halprin and Asawa and supported the latter's right to carry through her own concept for the commission. In 1952 Roth and his wife had been among the first to purchase Asawa's abstract wire sculptures.

48 Proctor Mellquist to Rupe, November 17, 1967, in Ruth Asawa's Sculpture and Controversy file, GSAR. See also Eloise Dungan, "'It's Always a Holiday Here,'" *SFE&C*, December 7, 1969, California Living, 18, in Mermaid Sculpture file, RAPC. Architect Bill Wurster used a double entendre: "I like it very much. Its robustness fits the fountain base; it has humor without being cutie pie." See William Wurster to Bill Roth, March 20, 1968, in Ruth Asawa's Sculpture and Controversy file, GSAR.

49 Halprin was not prudish about nudity. Lawrence Halprin and Jim Burns, *Taking Part: A Workshop Approach to Collective Creativity* (Cambridge, MA: MIT Press, 1974), 199–209.

50 "Office phone messages," March 26, 1968, in 014.IA. 6221, Halprin Collection, AAUP. Ruth Asawa to Bill Roth, March 28, 1968; Jeanne Fahey Crother to Ruth Asawa, March 26, 1968; Mrs. Samuel H. Coxe III to Bill Roth, April 4, 1968, all in Ruth Asawa's Sculpture and Controversy file, GSAR.

51 "Art Kutecture," in 014.IA.6221, Halprin Collection, AAUP.

52 Asawa to Roth, March 28, 1968. One admirer organized women to form a protective circle around the fountain to prevent the sculpture's removal. Nathan interview with Asawa, 85, 87.

53 One small article about Asawa's first exhibit of drawings did describe the artist as the sculptor "whose bronze nursing-mermaid fountain in Ghirardelli Square raised such a row when un-netted." January 9, 1969, clipping, Lanier, Albert and Mrs., 1972 and previous file, *Examiner* Clippings file, SFHC, SFPL.

54 Mrs. Coxe III to Roth, April 4, 1968. Herb Caen, "Loose as a Goose," April 5, 1968, in Vol. 1, GSAR. Poem, David Sawyer to Ruth Asawa, January 20, 1969, in Mermaid Sculpture file, RAPC.

55 Isenberg interview with Asawa and Lanier.

56 Andrea Jepson, "In Praise of Ruth Asawa," *SFE&C*, May 11, 1975, in Lanier, Albert & Mrs. Ruth Asawa Lanier, 1974–1975 file, *Examiner* Clippings file, SFHC, SFPL.

Asawa did not start her imaginative process with a statement about nursing. As of late 1966, Asawa envisioned four young mermaids (based on her daughter Aiko) on turtles. Water spurted from the tops of their heads. See Isenberg interview with Asawa and Lanier. Sketch in Ruth Asawa's Sculpture and Controversy file, GSAR. In a later newspaper account, Jepson described how "as a nursing mother I was the model for the mermaid in her fountain at Ghirardelli Square." See Hamilton, "The Careers That Grew Out of the Arts Project." Historically, people serving as models have become part of the story of the artworks and their sites in various ways. Kammen, *Visual Shock*.

57 Four months before the installation, Mellquist recommended that Roth proceed with the sculpture: "If it then seemed wrong, or disturbing to numbers of people, you could still take her home." Proctor Mellquist to Rupe, November 17, 1967, in Ruth Asawa's Sculpture and Controversy file, GSAR.

58 "Attitudes Inhibit Mothers," *New York Amsterdam News*, June 8, 1968; *Our Bodies, Ourselves: A Book by and for Women* (New York: Simon and Schuster, 1971), 219.

59 Sally Wendkos Olds and Marvin S. Eiger, M.D., *The Complete Book of Breastfeeding* (New York: Workman Publishing, Inc., 1972), xi. On babies seeing a breast by accident, see Lester Dessez Hazell, *Commonsense Childbirth* (New York: Putnam, 1969), 149. One authority noted that the percentage of women breastfeeding in the United States had declined to 21 percent by 1956. Alice Gerard, *Please Breast-Feed Your Baby* (New York: New American Library, 1970), 5–6.

60 Karen Pryor, *Nursing Your Baby* (New York: Harper & Row, 1963), 136, 92.

61 Gerard, *Please Breast-Feed Your Baby*, 9–10.

62 On "nonconformist," see Olds and Eiger, *The Complete Book of Breastfeeding*, 3. Many books described nursing as an "art"; *The Womanly Art of Breastfeeding* is the title of La Leche League International's guide, first published in 1958. Karen Pryor encouraged women to reconnect with their "truly feminine," accepting, cooperative, biological role, while *The Complete Book of Breastfeeding* asserted that giving in to "the feminine" through nursing did not conflict with a woman working or playing hard. Pryor, *Nursing Your Baby* 16; *The Complete Book of Breastfeeding*, 124–25. When privatized and circumscribed to the home and a few other places (car, park bench, or shopping mall), the "womanly art" of nursing required "generosity" and sacrifice that were incompatible with the "selfishness" of a career, or even a busy, about-town lifestyle. Feminists replied that breastfeeding mothers had more freedom of movement, not less, and argued that society would need to support working women who breast-fed. See also Benjamin Spock, *Baby and Child Care* (New York: Hawthorn Books, 1968), 74–77.

63 Marion Conrad to Temp, April 2, 1968, in 014.IA. 6221, Halprin Collection, AAUP.

64 "Best Public Orgy," *Bay Guardian*, July or August 2003, in Mermaid Sculpture file, RAPC.

65 "Ann Landers," *Washington Post*, June 12, 1969, L6. See also "Ann Landers," *Washington Post*, May 22, 1978, B6.

66 In the clubs, breasts also symbolized "mother," according to Berger. Arthur Asa Berger, "Varieties of Topless Experience," *Journal of Popular Culture*, Vol. 4 (Fall 1970), 421. The growing shelf of nursing books tried unsuccessfully to sort out what (if anything) sex had to do with nursing.

67 I use the term *sex district* advisedly. It conveys an important aspect of neighborhood reputation but can create the misimpression that such neighborhoods had little else. Most of these districts mixed many kinds of businesses, residences, institutions, and activities.

68 Nan Alamilla Boyd, *Wide Open Town: A History of Queer San Francisco to 1965* (Berkeley: University of California Press, 2003), 69, 87, 123, 133; Josh Sides, "Excavating the Postwar Sex District in San Francisco," *Journal of Urban History*, Vol. 32 (March 2006), 355–79.

69 Sides analyzes Doda's impact on the Broadway clubs, as well as the history of how the postwar sex district was distinguished from earlier commercial sex activities. See Sides, "Excavating the Postwar Sex District in San Francisco." See also "Topless Dancing," in Rachel Shteir, *Striptease: The Untold History of the Girlie Show* (New York: Oxford University Press, 2004).

70 The original 1970 sign had two "strategically placed" flashing red lights. See Café/Condor file; Doda, Carol, 1970–1973 file; Doda, Carol, 1974–1975 file; and Doda, Carol, 1976–1977 file, *Examiner* Clipping Morgue, SFHC.

71 Ben Thompson, "San Francisco Accessories," July 26, 1965, 5, in Design Research—Merchandising—Ben's Memos file, Box 1, D/R History, Design Research, Inc. Collection, 1953–1979; Ben Thompson to Armi, Henriette, and Nancy, August 19, 1965, 1, in Marimekko/Design Research, Inc. Early Correspondence, 1961–1963 file, Box 2, Marimekko/Design Research Correspondence 1961–1976, Marimekko Collection, 1951–1979, both collections in Cooper-Hewitt Design Archive, Smithsonian Design Museum, New York.

72 Kenneth Reich, "Atlanta's Underground Using Careful Supervision," *Los Angeles Times*, August 2, 1970, M10. Clip joints are adult entertainment venues that extort money from customers through various exploitations.

73 Neighboring Aquatic Park had developed as a gay cruising and sunbathing beach. See Scott, "The City Aroused," 266–67. On Aquatic Park as a site of radical sex and gay protests in 1965 and 1970, see Sides, *Erotic City*.

74 The Purple Onion took its name from a Parisian brothel. Seie Walter Blum, "'I'm Always One Step away from Disaster,'" March 6, 1966, clipping, Vol. 3, GSAR.

75 Randy Delehanty interview with Warren Lemmon, August 4, 1981, in Delehanty, "Interviews Concerning the Development of Ghirardelli Square." See also Donald Canter, "hungry i Turns to 'Art' Films," March 16, 1970, in San Francisco/Ghirardelli Square, 1970 file, Examiner Clipping Morgue, SFHC.

76 Frances Moffat, "The Pucci Party Was a Picnic," *SFC*, April 11, 1967, and Joan Chatfield-Taylor, "Bikinis and Coverups," *SFC*, April 7, 1966, both in Vol. 1. See also Merla Zellerbach, "Flash Panties for a New Freedom," *SFC*, July 24, 1968, in Vol. 3, GSAR.

77 Naomi Wolf, *Promiscuities: The Secret Struggle for Womanhood* (New York: Random House, 1997), 38–39.

78 Linda Nochlin's 1971 essay "Why Have There Been No Great Women Artists?" (*Art News*, Vol. 69 [January 1971], 22–39), often credited with launching feminist art history, was several years in the future. Feminists did not write much about breast-feeding in public in the 1960s and 1970s, as distinguished from breast-feeding in general. *Our Bodies, Ourselves* did not discuss nursing in public, although the book endorses "anything that increases your mobility," 225. For further readings, see Linda M. Blum, *At the Breast: Ideologies of Breastfeeding and Motherhood in the Contemporary United States* (Boston: Beacon Press, 1999). The mermaid fountain predates Judy Chicago's *The Dinner Party* (1974–79) by nearly ten years, suggesting the need to look more aggressively, and in unlikely places, for feminist art in the 1960s. Judy Chicago is a good starting point for understanding what kind of transition was marked by the year 1970. See Jane Gerhard, *The Dinner Party: Judy Chicago and the Power of Popular Feminism, 1970–2007* (Athens: University of Georgia Press, 2013). An insightful analysis of women, feminism, and access to public accommodations is Georgina Hickey, "Barred from the Barroom: Second Wave Feminists and Public Accommodations in U.S. Cities," *Feminist Studies*, Vol. 34 (Fall 2008), 382–408.

79 Michael Holleran, *Boston's "Changeful Times": Origins of Preservation and Planning in America* (Baltimore: Johns Hopkins University Press, 2001); J. Mark Souther, *New Orleans on Parade: Tourism and the Transformation of the Crescent City* (Baton Rouge: Louisiana State University Press, 2006); and Yuhl, *Golden Haze of Memory*.

80 Joan Woods, society editor, "A Plaza with a Legendary Past," *SFE*, May 3, 1964, in Vol. 3, GSAR.

81 Frances Moffat, "Is the Elite Stifling S.F.?," *SFC*, November 26, 1964, in Vol. 3, GSAR.

82 On this "relatively well-developed system of downtown open spaces, provided by a combination of private and public enterprise," see Garrett Eckbo, *Public Landscape: Six Essays on Government and Environmental Design in the San Francisco Bay Area* (Berkeley: Institute of Governmental Studies, University of California, 1978), 25.

83 Crown Zellerbach's plaza "has been first of all a magnificent gift of urban space, carved out of a rapidly declining waste, to the people of San Francisco." Allan Temko, *Two Buildings: San Francisco 1959* (San Francisco: San Francisco Museum of Art, 1959), 15. See also Alfred Frankenstein, "Ghirardelli Square: A SPUR 'Bright Spot' for San Francisco Week," September 4, 1966, 23, in Vol. 1, GSAR.

84 Lemmon to Roth, March 22, 1968. "Swinging," from undated Caen clipping, in Vol. 1, GSAR. Ronald A. Buel, "The Halprin Influence," *San Francisco*, March 1968, 40–43, in 014.I.B.2919, Halprin Collection, AAUP.

CHAPTER 4

Married Merchant-Buliders

1 Figure 53 was taken from a lower southeast angle in the square rather than from the upper southwest corner, as was figure 52.

2 Delehanty interview with the Roses. Theodore Bernardi to Warren Lemmon, October 1, 1962, WB&E folder; Stuart Rose to Warren Lemmon, May 3, 1963, Advisory Board folder; Stuart Rose to Warren Lemmon, June 3, 1963, Ghirardelli Square Memos—Stuart Rose folder; "Minutes of Advisory Board Meeting," August 27, 1964, Advisory Board folder. Caree's cousin Sol Onorato was a leading garage operator in the city and advised the developers. Joe Bourg to Warren Lemmon, October 9, 1963, Ghirardelli Square folder. All items cited in this note are in Box 1, GSAR. Onorato also consulted for the San Francisco International Market Center garage plans.

3 Frances Moffat, "Riding Herd on a Rich Heritage: Ghirardelli Square Is a Family Project for Them," *SFC*, October 7, 1964, 1s, in Vol. 3, GSAR. Richard Reinhardt, "Roth's Red Brick Rialto," *San Francisco*, March 1964, and Polly Ghirardelli Lawrence and Robbie Frederick, "Reflections on Things Past—and Present," *Spectator*, October 1964, both in Vol. 1, GSAR.

4 For a fascinating view of how focusing on construction machinery reorients postwar U.S. history, see Francesca Ammon, *Bulldozer: Demolition and Clearance of the Postwar Landscape* (New Haven, CT: Yale University Press, 2016). An influential history that uses the bulldozer to unite the story of environmentalism's rise in the suburbs as well as in the city and the rural American West is Adam Rome, *The Bulldozer in the Countryside: Suburban Sprawl and the Rise of American Environmentalism* (Cambridge, UK: Cambridge University Press, 2001).

5 For the purposes of *Designing San Francisco*, calling the Roses merchant-builders accurately reflects the language of their era, free from particular disrespect of their expertise. The term also captures the frank commercial element of their design careers; *designer-builders* is an ahistorical term that is also accurate in describing the Roses. There is, of course, a centuries-long history of builders working as designers, commanding increased attention in recent decades from scholars of vernacular architecture. Applied to the mid-twentieth century the term *merchant-builder* has most often referred to the suburban new town and large-volume residential developers, such as William Levitt and Levitt & Sons on the East Coast and Joseph Eichler and Eichler Homes on the West Coast. Architectural design awards in the 1960s often distinguished between architect and merchant-builder entry categories. The Roses, with fifty or so houses to their credit, were inconsequential to this larger story, but they and countless others were on a continuum with the famous builders. The overlapping construction, design, and financing approach also blurred the lines between builders and developers. Sara Stevens's research zeroes in on the real estate developers of this era, working closely with architects, and specifically working across suburbs and center cities. See her *Developing Expertise: Architecture and Real Estate in Metropolitan America* (New Haven, CT: Yale University Press, 2016). An older volume from within the business is Edward Eichler, *The Merchant Builders* (Cambridge, MA: MIT Press, 1982).

6 A sophisticated analysis of the intellectual crosscurrents shaping William Wurster and Catherine Bauer is Gwendolyn Wright, "A Partnership: Catherine Bauer and William Wurster," in *An Everyday Modernism: The Houses of William Wurster*, ed. Marc Treib (Berkeley: University of California Press, 1999), 184–203. Another model for studying such partnerships is Pat Kirkham, *Charles and Ray Eames: Designers of the Twentieth Century* (Cambridge, MA: MIT Press, 1998). Bauer died suddenly the same week that Ghirardelli Square opened. In the early 1970s, Ann Halprin began using the name Anna.

7 Delehanty interview with Roth.

8 Delehanty interview with Roth.

9 Louise Nelson Dyble, *Paying the Toll: Local Power, Regional Politics, and the Golden Gate Bridge* (Philadelphia: University of Pennsylvania Press, 2009).

10 "12-Shop Village Fair: Sausalito Shopping Center to Feature Building in Building," [publication name cut off], October 19, 1956, File 97.96; "Sausalito Story: Ghosts Astir as Onetime Garage Goes Sophisticate," *Marin Independent Journal*, March 16, 1957, M3, File 97.96; "Marin's International Market," *Marin This Month*, June 1959, 12–13, File 82.329, all at Sausalito Historical Society. Delehanty interview with the Roses.

11 Donna Horowitz, "Caree N. Rose, Developer," *Marin Independent Journal*, December 7, 1989; John Nickerson, "Stuart Rose, Landmark Developer, Dead at 89," *Marin Independent Journal*, March 26, 1999, C 1.

12 Carissima D'Orso Rose, Subject File 424, from Louis M. Terman et al., "Terman Life Cycle Study of Children with High Ability, 1922–1986," 2010, hdl:1902.1/00882, Harvard Dataverse, V3. The subject file was made available to the author by the Henry A. Murray Research Archive of the Institute for Quantitative Social Science at Harvard University, Cambridge, Massachusetts. It is hereafter cited as Terman Subject File 424.

13 "Never gone to business school" from Moffat, "Riding Herd on a Rich Heritage." Roberta Tasley's birth certificate gives Western Pipe as Stuart Rose's employer in 1935. Courtesy of Roberta Tasley. "Clairvoyancy" and "medium" from "Home Information Blank," December 18, 1922, Terman Subject File 424. The 1920 federal manuscript census lists Caree's father as a ceramic artist and her mother as a housewife; both sisters were bank stenographers in the 1930 federal manuscript census; the 1910 federal census enumerated a cousin and sister-in-law living with Caree's family as secretaries. The 1910 federal census listed Caree's father as an interpreter at a Medical Institute. He had arrived in the United States at twenty-two years of age from Naples, Italy, in 1893 and was naturalized in 1899. He had a few years of college.

Gennaro J. Dorso, page 19B, line 90, Enumeration District 0314, *Thirteenth Census of the United States*, 1910 (National Archives Microfilm Publication T624, roll 102); Records of the Bureau of the Census, Record Group 29, Washington, D.C.: National Archives and Records Administration. Carissima Dorsi, page 17A, line 65, Enumeration District 147, *Fourteenth Census of the United States*, 1920 (National Archives Microfilm Publication T625, roll 136), and Carissima Dorso, page 22B, line 53, Enumeration District 0344, *Fifteenth Census of the United States*, 1930 (National Archives Microfilm Publication T626, roll 207), both in Records of the Bureau of the Census, Record Group 29, Washington, D.C.: National Archives and Records Administration.

14 Pages of questions asked so-called Termites, from every angle, about their personality traits, preferences, activities, feelings, hopes, strengths, and weaknesses. Answers were then coded for quantitative analysis. When considered at the level of an individual such as Caree Rose, the file's narrative answers qualitatively measured subjects such as career and life satisfaction.

15 "Drift" covered in the 1939–40 survey; Caree Rose to Robert Sears and Lee Cronbach, May 4, 1973, enclosure, Terman Subject File 424.

16 1939–40 survey, Terman Subject File 424. Their first home in Sausalito was at 16 George Street.

17 On leaving cozy corporate life, see 1978 Survey, Terman Subject File 424; Delehanty interview with the Roses; folder Stuart Rose 1436–48, Phillip Fein Collection, 1964-1, Environmental Design Archives, University of California, Berkeley.

18 Horowitz, "Caree N. Rose, Developer"; "Roses to Leave Ghirardelli Square," *SFC*, October 3, 1970, 44. On their first and last homes, see Delehanty interview with the Roses.

19 1941, 1946, and 1956 surveys, Terman Subject File 424.

20 On flying, see Horowitz, "Caree N. Rose, Developer." Architect Beverly Willis was also a pilot.

21 Isenberg interview with Roberta Tasley, New York City, June 10, 2009.

22 "Western Interiors: Done without Professional Aid," *Sunset*, December 1946, 22; Kenneth Pratt, "A Sausalito Barn Becomes a Home," *SFC*, November 9, 1952, 1, 3L.

23 Regarding the claim about *Sunset* covers, see Horowitz, "Caree N. Rose, Developer."

24 "He Has Fun and Profit Building the Unusual," *Western Building*, October 1952, 18, 19, 53. On the first open-house day, the Roses counted 227 automobiles. The Roses had Bill Conover and the Trade Fair (discussed later in this chapter) furnish the home. See Kenneth Pratt, "A Builder Fits a Sausalito Hill to the House: The Result is 'Livable Modern,'" June 8, 1952, *SFC*, 3L; "Sausalito Creates," *SFC*, June 9, 1952, 34; Delehanty interview with the Roses. Modernist architects working in Marin, covered in chapter 8, were refining techniques to fit houses to hills in order to maximize the dramatic settings. A three-bedroom Rose custom home in Sausalito

was advertised for $31,000 in 1955. *SFC*, September 3, 1955, 24.

25 Sally Woodbridge and John Woodbridge, *Buildings of the Bay Area* (New York: Grove Press, 1960). Bookstores were unsure how to categorize the AIA guide; one store placed it on the engineering shelf. Isenberg interview with Sally Woodbridge, Berkeley, 2009. For "livable modern" in a Rose advertisement, see "Sausalito Creates"; Pratt, "A Builder Fits a Sausalito Hill to the House."

26 Lawrence Halprin, *A Life Spent Changing Places* (Philadelphia: University of Pennsylvania, 2011), 48.

27 Ibid., 33–50, 69–84, 104–8; Laurie Olin, foreword to ibid., ix. Raised in Brooklyn, Lawrence Halprin studied agriculture at Cornell University, had a research position at the University of Wisconsin (where he met Anna), and did his graduate work in landscape architecture at the Harvard Graduate School of Design. Time spent living in Palestine and shipping off from San Francisco to the Pacific theater while in the Navy were both formative experiences for Halprin before moving to the Bay Area at the end of World War II. The Halprins were introduced to Marin through Anna's aunt and uncle, not through architecture contacts in the city.

28 Architects' archived project files from this era reveal the complex web of their Marin County homes and who designed residences for whom.

29 Allan Temko to Douglas Haskell, October 28, 1957, in Box 83, Folder 5, Haskell Papers. Temko gave Proctor Mellquist, Lewis Mumford, and Bill Wurster as references. In 1957, Temko was the author of an award-winning 1955 Viking book on Notre Dame Cathedral, a recipient of a Guggenheim Fellowship, and a faculty member at the University of California.

30 Delehanty interview with the Roses.

31 "Western Interiors"; on the 1956 Terman form she called herself a "Decorator, Interior Colors." See 1953 and 1956 surveys, Terman Subject File 424.

32 Delehanty interview with the Roses; "Sausalito Story."

33 "12-Shop Village Fair"; "Sausalito Story"; Delehanty interview with the Roses. William Hendricks, "Big Pottery Business Started in Basement," September 12, 1948, in Heath, Edith, Clippings file, SFHC, SFPL. Examples of married partners or women running potteries during these years include Evelyn Ackerman and Jerome Ackerman, Laura Andreson, Otto Heino and Vivika Heino, Albert Henry King and Louisa Etcheverry King, Gertrudee Natzler and Otto Natzler, Marguerite Wildenhain, Jade Snow Wong, and the firm Architectural Pottery. See *A Handbook of California Design, 1930–1965*, ed. Bobbye Tigerman (Cambridge, MA: MIT Press, 2013), 20, 30, 32, 124, 126, 146, 196, 290, 300. Edith Heath describes in detail the many couples and teams in pottery production in the decades after World War II, including the waves of immigrant pottery workers from Mexico, Central America, and Vietnam. She describes the artist community in Sausalito, including the houseboats where the Heaths lived. See "Edith Heath: Tableware and Tile for the World, Heath Ceramics, 1944–1994," transcript, ed. Julie Gordon Shearer and Germaine LaBerge (Berkeley: Oral History Center, Bancroft Library, Regents of the University of California, 1995), 154–69.

34 1972 survey, Terman Subject File 424. Caree's father, a ceramicist, passed away just before the Roses opened their studio in 1946.

35 Renovations uncovered stenciled ceilings attributed to the gambling house and "Sausalito" in red letters on the roof, a beacon for propeller planes. See "Sausalito Story"; "12-Shop Village Fair." For a glimpse of Sausalito and Marin County in 1953, see Marjorie Salin, *The Talent around Tamalpais* (San Rafael, CA: Pacific Printers, 1953); "Sausalito Historic Districts," August 1, 1980, File 94.15, courtesy of Sausalito Historical Society (SHS).

36 "Edith Heath," 169. See also "Lichty Cartoons at Trade Fair," 1949 clipping, SHS 79.261B.

37 Betty Pepis, "Artisans on Coast Exhibit Products; 'Trade Fair' Shows Unusual Designs in Furniture and Also in Accessories," *NYT*, July 14, 1951, 16. Conover's co-investors included his mother, Julie Bell, Dick Wagner, and Bud Heibel. See "Marin's International Market," *Marin This Month*, June 1959, 12–13, File 82.329. In 1959 the Trade Fair occupied 7,000 square feet in the garage. All items cited in this note are courtesy of the SHS.

38 "12-Shop Village Fair"; "Sausalito Story"; Marjorie Trumbull, "The Illusion of Spring and a Bazaar in the Rain," *SFC*, March 19, 1957, 19. Based on these newspaper sources, the exact status of the building's original second floor at the time the Village Fair opened is unclear.

39 Precedents for adaptive reuse were scarce in the early 1950s, as discussed in chapter 2. Caree Rose remembered two possible examples, both regional—the Farmers' Market in Los Angeles and Sacramento's Town and Country Village shopping center (opened in 1946)—likely for having multiple unique, small tenants instead of anchor stores and for the inclusion of food, art, and rustic artifacts. Delehanty interview with the Roses.

40 It served as a "floating gift shop" from 1960 to 1973, when it was sold to the San Diego Maritime Museum for $100,000. See James Delgado, "Berkeley: Hard Worked in a Rough Service," *Sea Letter*, Vol. 42 (Spring/Summer 1990), 38–43; Louise Teather, "The Berkeley Takes New Orders," *Marin This Month*, March 1960; 10–11.

41 "Ceramics Factory in California," *Architectural Forum*, August 1961, 85; Allan Temko, "West Coast Report, No. 3—December 8, 1959," 9, Box 83, Folder 6, Haskell Papers.

42 "The Roses Leave Ghirardelli," Terman Subject File 424.

43 Mary Cooke, "Personalizing the Shopping Center," *Honolulu Advertiser People Report*, September 12, 1975, in file Ghirardelli Memos—Stuart Rose, 1963, 1970, 1975, Box 1, GSAR.

44 Delehanty interview with Lemmon; Warren Lemmon to W. M. Roth, "Ghirardelli Property—Stuart Rose Proposal," January 17, 1963, in Binder 1, Box 1, GSAR;

"The Cellars—Unique Dining," *SFC*, February 23, 1963, 9.

45 Lemmon to Roth, "Ghirardelli Property—Stuart Rose Proposal"; Delehanty interview with Lemmon; Delehanty interview with Roth. "Desperate" from Delehanty interview with the Roses. On "jumpiness," see "Addendum to [Roth's] Ghirardelli Memorandum of January 27, 1963," dated February 12, 1963.

46 Stuart's daughter recalled that, of the couple, "his wife was the entrepreneur, Caree. This part I know because I've heard the story a million times. They went to Caree and Stuart and said do you want to do it, and she says yes." Isenberg interview with Tasley.

47 Delehanty interviews with Lemmon and the Roses. On hiring a stenographer, see Warren Lemmon to Mildred Akins, May 15, 1968, File 014.I.A.6361, Halprin Collection, AAUP.

48 1973 survey, Terman Subject File 424.

49 1977 survey, Terman Subject File 424.

50 Caree Rose to Robert Sears and Lee Cronbach, May 4, 1973, enclosure in Terman Subject File 424; "Roses to Leave Ghirardelli Square"; 1962, 1973, and 1981 surveys, Terman Subject File 424. For employment offers while at Village Fair, see Moffat, "Riding Herd on a Rich Heritage," also enclosed in Terman files.

51 Horowitz, "Caree N. Rose, Developer"; "Roses to Leave Ghirardelli Square."

52 Cooke, "Personalizing the Shopping Center"; Horowitz, "Caree N. Rose, Developer"; "Roses to Leave Ghirardelli Square." King's Alley, with its irregular "Victorian" buildings illuminated in outline at night, superficially resembled Ghirardelli Square.

53 Joel N. Shurkin, *Terman Kids: The Groundbreaking Study of How the Gifted Grow Up* (Boston: Little, Brown, 1992), 228–29, 240–42.

54 Moffat, "Riding Herd on a Rich Heritage."

55 Shurkin, *Terman Kids*, 29, 42, 227–44.

56 Ibid., 29, 42, 232, 235, 243.

57 1973 and 1977 surveys, Terman Subject File 424. Most social scientists were ill equipped to evaluate or frame the distinctive career experiences of men and women in the mid-twentieth century, and those conducting the Terman study were no exception. There were signs of change in the 1970s when, after fifty years, the Terman researchers designed questions to ascertain patterns in women's lives relating to work, family, and personal satisfaction, which they compiled into 1972 and 1977 women-only surveys. Nonetheless, the study had collected an extraordinary base of data for understanding women's careers relative to men's.

58 1973 and 1981 surveys, Terman Subject File 424.

59 Robert Sears to Carissima D'Orso Rose, May 21, 1973, in Terman Subject File 424.

60 Carissima Rose to Robert Sears, January 30, 1978, in Terman Subject File 424.

61 Lemmon to Roth, January 17, 1963. The Rose advisory memo was "Ghirardelli Block Proposed Development," February 3, 1963. Delehanty interview with Lemmon.

CHAPTER 5
Managing Property

1 Ruth Asawa's sculpture was installed two years after the collaborative award. The press release noted Roth's mother's financial contribution. "News Release," April 1, 1966, AIA. Richard Stitt to Sherley Ashton, February 18, 1966. Record Group 806, Series 8, Collaborative Achievement in Architecture Award, 1966, Ghirardelli Square, American Institute of Architects Archives (AIA Archives), Washington, DC.

2 Delehanty interview with the Roses.

3 Critics and urban designers analyzed whether the new planned plazas indeed justified their expense. See, for example, Frank Fogarty, "The Earning Power of Plazas," *Architectural Forum*, January 1958, 106.

4 Ibid. Stuart Rose apologized to Delehanty for committing the strong words to a tape recording but did so nonetheless.

5 Old School from Allan Temko, "West Coast Report, No. 3—December 8, 1959," 4.

6 Alex Krieger, "Where and How Does Urban Design Happen?" 69; Eric Mumford, "The Emergence of Urban Design in the Breakup of CIAM," 17–18; Richard Marshall, "The Elusiveness of Urban Design: The Perpetual Problems of Definition and Role," in *Harvard Design Review* (Spring/Summer 2006), 30; Jill Pearlman, *Inventing American Modernism: Joseph Hudnut, Walter Gropius, and the Bauhaus Legacy at Harvard* (Charlottesville: University of Virginia Press, 2007).

Historian Cammie McAtee describes what happened in July 1954 when Reginald Isaacs, then chair of Harvard's short-lived Department of City Planning and Landscape Architecture, explained his "belief that landscape architecture students are the best equipped, from outlook and academic training, to become urban designers. I have found in my experience that landscape architects are the least afraid of space—the best able to handle the design of volume and space to create a satisfying environment." Walter Gropius dismissed Isaacs's assertion, countering that architects received the most relevant education to excel in urban design. Landscape students in combined design programs found themselves marginalized, and practitioners worried that they would be relegated to a more decorative role. Of course architects had their own insecurities regarding their profession. Cammie McAtee, "From the Ground Up: Hideo Sasaki's Contributions to Urban Design," in *Josep Lluís Sert: The Architect of Urban Design, 1953–1969*, ed. Eric Mumford and Hashim Sarkis (New Haven: Yale University Press, 2008), 179.

7 "Why Continue to Be the FORGOTTEN MAN, the Landscape Architect?," in folder ASLA (American Society of Landscape Architects) Presentation, Hartford 1965, Douglas & Maggie Baylis Collection, Environmental Design Archives, University of California, Berkeley. The status of landscape architecture had slipped since the decades when Frederick Law Olmsted and John Nolen had defined the early years of modern American city planning, offering solutions to integrating nature and urban life (such as Central Park) and creating urban civic centers.

8 Wurster's office made a failed bid to "take responsibility for Halprin's services" in the project's second phase, arguing that "the landscape work is so intricately interwoven with the architectural." See Albert Aronson to Warren Lemmon, September 28, 1964, WB&E folder, Box 1, GSAR.

9 William Wurster to Stuart Rose, August 17, 1966, 014.I.A.946, Halprin Collection, AAUP.

10 "Octagon Observer," *AIA Journal*, April 1964, 10. Courtesy of Nancy Hadley, AIA Archives. Phyllis Lambert's book on the Seagram building, documenting her central planning role in the project, provides an example of how gender can be written back into the center of 1950s and 1960s urban design in other skyscraper and urban renewal cities like New York or Chicago. See Phyllis Lambert, *Building Seagram* (New Haven, CT: Yale University Press, 2013). Collaborations on the original Four Seasons restaurant included tableware designed by Ada Louise Huxtable and her husband, industrial designer Garth Huxtable.

11 David Pesonen was the only other viable candidate besides the Roses. Pesonen's application letter was dense, insightful, and philosophical ("Ghirardelli Should Be Bach Not Bartok"); Pesonen's cogent layman's critiques of the Roses' approach, on one hand, and the architects' approaches, on the other, attracted Roth's attention. See Lemmon to W. M. Roth, "Ghirardelli Property—David Pesonen," January 10, 1963; Pesonen to Lemmon, February 3, 1963.

12 Warren Lemmon to William Roth, April 10, 1963, Binder 1, Box 1, GSAR.

13 Stuart Rose to Roth, May 3, 1963.

14 Warren Lemmon to W. M. Roth, "Ghirardelli Property—Al Waller Development," July 3, 1962, Binder 1, Box 1, GSAR.

15 Lemmon to Roth, "Ghirardelli Property—Stuart Rose Proposal," January 17, 1963. Lemmon later changed "architect" to "contractor" to describe Stuart Rose in the memo once he realized his mistake.

16 Delehanty interview with the Roses.

17 Ibid. "Family Finances," 1981 and 1973 surveys, Terman Subject File 424.

18 "Minutes of Meeting of the Advisory Board—Ghirardelli Square," August 5, 1965, 13; Delehanty interviews with the Roses and Roth.

19 Delehanty interviews with Donn Emmons and the Roses.

20 Delehanty interviews with Halprin and Matthias.

21 Suzanne B. Reiss, "Thomas D. Church Oral History Project," 685, Oral History Center, Bancroft Library; Delehanty interview with the Roses.

22 Delehanty interviews with the Roses and Halprin.

23 Mary Cooke, "Personalizing the Shopping Center."

24 Rose took credit for the engineering intervention that saved the factory's apartment building, which Halprin wanted to tear down for a new entrance. Delehanty interview with the Roses.

25 Proctor Mellquist to W. M. Roth, "Ghirardelli Meeting Today," September 28, 1964. Advisory Board folder, Box 1, GSAR.

26 Horowitz, "Caree N. Rose, Developer"; "Redondo Redevelopment Bids Expected within Six Months," *LA Times*, September 17, 1967; Delehanty interview with the Roses.

27 Isenberg interview with Woodbridge.

28 Bill Roth to Warren Lemmon, September 2, 1963. Binder 1, Box 1, GSAR.

29 Stuart Rose to Warren Lemmon, August 20, 1963. Halprin folder, Box 1, GSAR.

30 Kortum to Lemmon, August 22, 1963. A recent controversy had erupted over an underground garage for historic Portsmouth Plaza, which involved Douglas Baylis and Lawrence Halprin at different times. See Allan Temko, "West Coast Report, No. 7—December 23, 1960." See also the in-depth report on "Roof Gardens" in Allan Temko, "West Coast Report, No. 3—December 8, 1959."

31 On "flowerful" and "gardeny design," see Halprin to Roth, September 20, 1963.

32 Proctor Mellquist to W. M. Roth and Warren Lemmon, September 27, 1963, 014.I.A.952, Halprin Collection, AAUP.

33 On Kortum, see Rose to Lemmon, August 20, 1963; on factory employees, see Delehanty interview with the Roses; on plantings and "fern bar," Delehanty interview with Halprin.

34 Warren Lemmon to Joe Bourg, March 16, 1966, and "Minutes of Landscape and Design Meeting," May 21, 1966, both in 014.I.A.946, Halprin Collection, AAUP. From 1939 to 1954 Doty served as *Sunset*'s chief editor, after which he was the magazine's editorial research director until he retired in 1960.

35 "Minutes of Landscape and Design Meeting," May 21, 1966; "Minutes of Ghirardelli Advisory Board Meeting," June 16, 1966; and William Wurster to Stuart Rose, August 17, 1966, all in 014.I.A.946, Halprin Collection, AAUP.

36 John Matthias's plaza shops and the new pavilion buildings were also "designed as part of the garage structure." "Minutes of Advisory Board Meeting," November 6, 1963.

37 Delehanty interview with the Roses; "Proctor Mellquist, Interview Conducted by Suzanne B. Reiss, October 25, 1977," in *Thomas D. Church, Landscape Architect*, Vol. 2, 679–700; Roth memo, September 3, 1963.

38 Delehanty interview with the Roses.

39 For shrub planter, see Schoen, "Lawrence Halprin: Humanizing the City Environment." For a typical "dead plant" consult, see Dale Conrad to Lawrence Halprin, July 29, 1957, Barnaby Conrad file 014.I.A.521, Halprin Collection, AAUP. On Jean Walton and the nurseries,

see Ghirardelli Square Planting Correspondence & Notes, File 014.I.A.948, Halprin Collection, AAUP.

40 Lemmon to Roth, "Ghirardelli Square," January 20, 1969, File 014.I.A.947, Halprin Collection, AAUP.

41 Jean Walton to Mrs. Stuart Rose, August 18, 1966; Caree Rose to Miss Jean Walton, August 24, 1966. Both in File 014.I.A.948, Halprin Collection, AAUP. The Roses had many stories challenging Halprin's professional judgment about maintenance and what could grow where. Delehanty interview with the Roses.

42 Lemmon to Roth, "Ghirardelli Square Garden Service," January 25, 1965, in Ghirardelli Square Planting Correspondence & Notes, File 014.I.A.948, Halprin Collection, AAUP.

43 Doug Baylis, "Why Continue to Be the FORGOTTEN MAN, the Landscape Architect?"

44 Delehanty interviews with the Roses and Roth.

45 On KFOG and tenant problems, see Delehanty interview with the Roses. See also "Ghirardelli Square, San Francisco," *Western Market Highlights*, Winter 1966, in Vol. 1, GSAR.

46 Bill Roth's concern about tenants was well known among his advisors. See Delehanty interviews with Emmons and Roses; "Ghirardelli Square, San Francisco."

47 Lemmon to W. M. Roth, "Use of Joe Bourg," Dec. 17, 1964, WB&E file, Box 1, GSAR; Lemmon to Akins, May 15, 1968.

48 Delehanty interview with the Roses.

49 Delehanty interviews with the Roses and Lemmon; Frances Moffat, "Romance Bloomed on the Square," *SFC*, August 22, 1967, 14. The Lemmons settled in Kentfield.

50 Compiled from surveys, Terman Subject File 424.

51 Delehanty interview with Halprin. When Macy's department stores expanded in the Western United States, John S. Bolles, for example, won this multiple-store commission.

52 Lemmon chose to not share Bourg's worst behavior with Wurster, and he did not specify Bourg's accusations. Lemmon to Roth, "Use of Joe Bourg," December 17, 1964.

53 Isenberg interview with the Roths.

54 Delehanty interview with the Roses; Tenant Reports files, Box 1; Oversized Scrapbooks, GSAR.

55 "Minutes of Advisory Board Meeting," November 6, 1963.

56 Margaret (Maggie) Hilbiber was born in 1912 in Tacoma, Washington. Details of the family's life in Schwenksville come from the 1930 Manuscript Census, from Fred J. Hilbiber and family, page 3A, lines 34–40, Enumeration District 0134, *Fifteenth Census of the United States*, 1930 (National Archives Microfilm Publication T626, roll 2084); Records of the Bureau of the Census, Record Group 29, Washington, DC: National Archives and Records Administration; Margaret Hilbiber, Delaware Vital Records, microfilm, Dover: Delaware Public Archives, Ancestry.com, http://search.ancestrylibrary .com/search.db.aspx?dbid=1674; J. L. Pimsleur, "Obituaries: Maggie Baylis," *SFC*, December 24, 1997, A15;

"Biographical Note," Collection Guide, Douglas and Maggie Baylis Collection, 1999-4, EDA.

57 Ibid.

58 Doty quoted in Dr. Joseph E. Howland, "50 yrs of memories of Maggie, a dear friend," January 18, 1998, Baylis Collection, EDA.

59 "Maggie Baylis, Interview Conducted by Suzanne B. Reiss, June 27, 1977," in *Thomas D. Church, Landscape Architect*, Vol. 2, 521–50.

60 Howland, "50 yrs of memories of Maggie." Joan Mosslooper took over the "spy" work when Maggie Baylis left the square.

61 Doug Baylis has not received the attention of his fellow accomplished landscape architects.

62 Delehanty interview with the Roses.

63 Allan Temko, "A 'City of Tomorrow' Today," *SFC*, December 12, 1977, 4–5, Series IV, Box 9, File 28, in William Turnbull, Jr./MLTW Collection (2000–2009), Environmental Design Archives, College of Environmental Design, University of California, Berkeley.

64 Eloise Dungan, "Putting the Finnish Touch on an Opening," *SFE*, October 17, 1973, 26, in Series IV, Box 9, File 28, in William Turnbull, Jr./MLTW Collection. Marimekko was led by a woman (Armi Ratia) and shaped by its many female employees. It navigated uneven gender terrain in the international investment community. Designer Jane Thompson worked with her husband, Ben Thompson, during D/R's expansion to California and elsewhere, and also worked on Faneuil Hall. She had been the architecture editor at *Interiors* magazine and a founding editor of *Industrial Design*. See Jane Thompson and Alexandra Lange, *Design Research: The Store That Brought Modern Living to American Homes* (San Francisco: Chronicle Books, 2010).

65 L.W.G., "A Special Place for D/R," *Interiors*, March 1974, 111, Series IV, Box 22, File 383, in William Turnbull, Jr./MLTW Collection. Turnbull's marriage to Woods ended in divorce. He married architect Mary Griffin in 1985, and they worked together in the firm. See Paul Goldberger, "William L. Turnbull Jr., Architect, 62, Dies," *NYT*, June 30, 1997; Wendy W. Luers, "Soft Power of Art: Lifelong Cultural Commitment Pays Diplomatic Dividends," *Huffington Post*, November 18, 2010, http://www.huffingtonpost.com/wendy-w-luers/soft-power-of-art-lifelon_b_785711.html. Bill Turnbull's sister Margaret Turnbull Simon ran William Turnbull Associates' interior design division, working with Wendy Libby in the earlier years. Previously Margaret had worked eight years for the West Coast D/R. See "Scope and Contents Note," Inventory of the William Turnbull, Jr./MLTW Collection, 1959–1997, available at http://www.oac.cdlib.org/findaid/ark:/13030/kt5s20213j/

66 Temko, "A 'City of Tomorrow' Today," 5.

67 L.W.G., "A Special Place for D/R," 106. See also "D/R: A New San Francisco Store and Its Contents Are Complementary," *Architecture Plus*, January/February 1974, Series IV, Box 21, File 332, in William Turnbull, Jr./MLTW Collection.

68 For later drafts Turnbull changed it to "Embarcadero Center Project." Compare the typed publicity statement with the hand-written draft for the D/R store opening, October 7, 1973, both in Series IV, Box 9, File 28, in William Turnbull, Jr./MLTW Collection.

69 Typed publicity statement for Turnbull's D/R store, Series IV, Box 9, File 28, in William Turnbull, Jr./MLTW Collection.

70 Ibid. Clear published illustrations of the store are found in "D/R: A New San Francisco Store and Its Contents Are Complementary," and L.W.G., "A Special Place for D/R."

71 Donald Canter, "New Lease for the Center," *SFE&C*, August 12, 1973, in Series V, File 320, in William Turnbull, Jr./MLTW Collection.

72 D/R Meeting Notes, R. S./Jim Bonkema/Simon Snellgrove, 5/23/73, Series V, File 319, DR Store Embarcadero Center Meeting/Phone/and Field Notes and Contracts, 1973–1974, in William Turnbull, Jr./MLTW Collection.

73 Hand-written draft of publicity statement for D/R store opening, October 7, 1973.

74 Typed publicity statement for Turnbull's D/R store.

76 L.W.G., "A Special Place for D/R."

76 Baylis, "Why Continue to Be the FORGOTTEN MAN, the Landscape Architect?"

CHAPTER 6
Movers and Shakers

1 Barbara (Bobbie) Stauffacher, "Duped by Design" (unpublished memoir, 2006, in author's possession), 113.

2 Boeke's interest in New Towns was inspired by a trip to Sweden in the early 1960s. His major project prior to The Sea Ranch was the new community Miliani in Honolulu, Hawaii. Boeke scoped out the coastal Ohlson family ranch property and negotiated the purchase.

3 For a brief historical overview, see Donald Canty, "Origins, Evolutions, and Ironies," 2003, in Donlyn Lyndon and Jim Alinder, *The Sea Ranch: Fifty Years of Architecture, Landscape, Place, and Community on the Northern California Coast* (New York: Princeton Architectural Press, revised edition, 2014), 23–33. Two essays appreciative of the site's environmental conservation ideals are Sara Fingal, "Designing Conservation at The Sea Ranch," *Environmental History* 18 (January 2013), 185–90, and Sarah Williams Goldhagen, "In Praise of The Sea Ranch, a Sublimely Beautiful Example of Environmental Architecture," *New Republic*, November 2011.

4 "Al Boeke, Oceanic Properties, Vice President, The Sea Ranch, 1959–1969," 38. Interviews conducted by Kathryn Smith, 2008, Oral History Center, Bancroft Library, available at http://digitalassets.lib.berkeley.edu/roho/ucb/text/boeke_al.pdf.

5 Ray Menzel to Bill Matthews, "Inspection of the Sea Ranch at Pocket Bay," October 1, 1963, in Sea Ranch File 1, July 1963–February 1964, Job 6525, Joseph Esherick Collection, 1974-1, Environmental Design Archives, College of Environmental Design, University of

California, Berkeley. Braun also photographed Ghirardelli Square.

6 Stauffacher, "Duped by Design," 101. Moore's firm also designed the swim and tennis club. Charles Moore became the dean of the Yale School of Architecture in 1965.

7 Halprin's studies listed in "Management Meeting 3/ The Sea Ranch," November 18, 1963, Sea Ranch File 1, July 1963–February 1964, Job 6525, Joseph Esherick Collection; Charles Moore to Donald Canty, March 11, 1965, Series IV, Box 9, File 43, in William Turnbull, Jr./ MLTW Collection; Charles Moore, "You Have to Pay for the Public Life," *Perspecta*, Nos. 9–10 (1965), 57–97, reprinted in Charles Moore, *You Have to Pay for the Public Life: Selected Essays of Charles W. Moore*, ed. Kevin Keirn (Cambridge, MA: MIT Press, 2004), 123, 133–37.

8 Smith understood that Conrad "was actually quite important in this whole early period and she's been very little mentioned at all in any of the other publications." See "Al Boeke, 1959–1969," 30–31.

9 "Al Boeke, 1959–1969"; Conrad correspondence explaining The Sea Ranch to editors is discussed later in this chapter.

10 Will Mehlhorn to Miss Conrad, July 15, 1966, Series IV, Box 9, File 30, in William Turnbull, Jr./MLTW Collection.

11 "Ecological Architecture: Planning the Organic Environment," *Progressive Architecture*, May 1966, 121. Contrast this with the later struggles: Jim Burns, "Sea Ranch, Resisting Suburbia: After 20 Years, a Famed Development in Turmoil," *Architecture: The AIA Journal* 73, no. 12 (December 1984), 56–63.

12 "Al Boeke, 1959–1969," 89–90.

13 Ibid.; Marion Conrad to Bill Turnbull, April 8, 1966, Series IV, Box 9, File 30, in William Turnbull, Jr./MLTW Collection.

14 The article also said that the region's clients tended toward "super-conservative," but designers along this spectrum were enviably content professionally. See B.W.N., "San Francisco: The Designer's City," *Interiors*, August 1966, 122–32.

15 Ibid.

16 Dale Rosen, "$F Waterfront Co., Inc.: J. Alioto and C. Magnin, Proprietors since 1968," *Bay Guardian*, February 28, 1970, enclosed with Mr. and Mrs. Susselli et al. to Nelson Rockefeller, April 3, 1970, folder Real Estate–Embarcadero Center, N–Z, Box 412, RG 3 (unprocessed materials), Rockefeller Family, RAC. Used with special authorization.

17 "Marion & Hunt," *Bay Guardian*, February 26, 1971. By leaving out mention of Conrad's specific clients, the article dodged the contentious topics of real estate and politics.

18 Ibid.

19 Two organizations benefiting early from her energies were the San Francisco Peninsula Chapter of the Women's Action Committee for Lasting Peace and the Spinsters'

Club. See Zilfa Estcourt, "Peace Group Membership Drive Begins," *SFC*, November 19, 1947, 9; Mildred Brown Robbins, "From Where I Sit," *SFC*, January 11, 1947, 11; "Looks Like a Grand Party," *SFC*, March 3, 1946, 1S; and Karola Saekel, "Down on Plain Cooking," *SFC*, August 23, 1959, 10S, all in the Women's World section. See also J. L. Pimsleur, "Suzy West," *SFC*, July 24, 1997, A21.

20 Mildred Robbins, "Marion Kitchin Is Wed," *SFC*, January 30, 1950; "Marion Kitchin Betrothal to Hunt Conrad Revealed," *Call-Bulletin*, December 2, 1949; Jane Arnold, "Betrothal Tidings Revealed," *San Francisco News*, December 2, 1949; "Marion Kitchin Heralds Troth to Hunt Conrad," *SFE*, December 2, 1949; and Mildred Robbins, "From Where I Sit," *SFC*, December 2, 1949, all in Marion Kitchin Conrad files, courtesy of Alumni Records, Sarah Lawrence College Archives. Career information distilled from "Marion K. Conrad Biography," January 1967, and "Marion K. Conrad Biography," undated, circa 1973, in folder Marion Conrad, Vertical Files, SFHC, SFPL. "Marion Conrad Dies at 48," *SFC*, February 11, 1974, 37. Conrad's time as a rancher puts her subsequent years at Sea Ranch in a different light.

21 The 1960s advertising industry does have both academic scholarship and a popular boost from the 2007–15 television drama *Mad Men*, but there is far less on public relations firms. On the uneasy relationship between architects, the AIA, and advertising, see Andrew Shanken, "Breaking the Taboo: Architects and Advertising in Depression and War," *Journal of the Society of Architectural Historians*, Vol. 69, No. 3 (September 2010), 406–29.

22 Larry Halprin to Marion Conrad, July 4, 1967, in File 014.I.A.5913, Halprin Collection, AAUP. "Al Boeke, 1959–1969," 101.

23 Barnaby Conrad to Alison Isenberg, March 13, 2009; Barnaby Conrad, "In With the In Crowd Here and Abroad," *SFC*, July 10, 1988.

24 Herb Caen, "Marion," *SFC*, February 12, 1974, folder Marion Conrad, Vertical Files, SFHC, SFPL.

25 "Marion Conrad Dies at 48"; Saekel, "Down on Plain Cooking." Conrad's additional clients listed in press release biographies included SPUR, WB&E, Butterfield & Butterfield auction house, and the National Association of Bedding Manufacturers. Additional civic activities included working with the Northern California Multiple Sclerosis Society, the Bay Area Urban League, Northern California Americans for Democratic Action, and the San Francisco Children's Hospital. See "Marion K. Conrad Biography," January 1967, and "Marion K. Conrad Biography," ca. 1973.

26 Marion Conrad to Walter McQuade, June 16, 1967, in File 014.I.A.5915, Halprin Collection, AAUP.

27 Buel, "Shaping Cities," 1.

28 Elliot Glassberg to Larry Halprin, June 12, 1967, File 014.I.A.5915, Halprin Collection, AAUP.

29 Bill Turnbull to Marion Conrad, June 14, 1967, Series IV, Box 9, File 30, in William Turnbull, Jr./MLTW Collection; Buel, "Shaping Cities," 1.

30 Buel, "Shaping Cities."

31 Marion Conrad to Ron Buel, July 21, 1967, in File 014.I.A.5915, Halprin Collection, AAUP.

32 Marion Conrad to Lawrence Halprin & Associates, "New York Trip," January 31, 1967, 014.I.A.5913, Halprin Collection, AAUP.

33 Marion Conrad to Larry Halprin, May 24, 1967.

34 Conrad, "New York Trip," and Marion Conrad to Jay Iselin, June 16, 1967, both in 014.I.A.5913, Halprin Collection, AAUP.

35 Jim Truitt to Marion Conrad, August 22, 1967, in File 014.I.A.5915, Halprin Collection, AAUP.

36 Marion Conrad to Ron Buel, June 8, 1967, noon telegram, in File 014.I.A.5915, Halprin Collection, AAUP.

37 Marion Conrad to Lawrence Halprin, June 19, 1967, and Lawrence Halprin to John Lawrence, June 20, 1967, both in File 014.I.A.5915, Halprin Collection, AAUP.

38 Marion Conrad to Dick Saltonstall; Marion Conrad to Bill Emerson; Marion Conrad to Jack Fincher; and Marion Conrad to John Poppy, June 16, 1967, all in File 014.I.A.5915, Halprin Collection, AAUP.

39 Marion Conrad to Al Boeke, February 7, 1967, File 014.I.A.5913, Halprin Collection, AAUP.

40 Conrad, "New York Trip."

41 Ibid.; Conrad to Boeke, February 7, 1967.

42 Marion Conrad to Jeanne Krause, March 15, 1967, in File 014.I.A.5913, Halprin Collection, AAUP.

43 Ibid.

44 "Al Boeke, 1959–1969," 98, 128.

45 Marion Conrad to Larry Halprin, July 12, 1967, and Larry Halprin to Marion Conrad, July 4, 1967, both in File 014.I.A.5913, Halprin Collection, AAUP.

46 Larry Halprin to Marion Conrad, July 4, 1967.

47 Isenberg interview with Richard Vignolo, San Francisco, July 5, 2007; Isenberg interview with Peggy Knickerbocker, San Francisco, July 6, 2011.

48 Joseph E. Tinney was the board president. See Marion Conrad to Hon. William C. Blake, January 6, 1966, and "Blake Has a Change of Heart," enclosed clipping, both in File 014.I.A.5913, Halprin Collection, AAUP

49 Marion Conrad to Hon. William C. Blake.

50 "Blake Has a Change of Heart."

51 James Richardson, *Willie Brown: A Biography* (Berkeley: University of California Press, 1996). On "one of the boys," see Stan Erickson to Isenberg, October 11, 2011, in author's possession. Brown's sudden interest in defending Golden Gate Park against the threatened Panhandle freeway during the 1964 campaign was likely due to Conrad. See Herb Caen, "One of Those Things," *SFC*, December 2, 1986.

52 "Marion Conrad Dies at 48"; Erickson to Isenberg. According to Erickson, when Robert Kennedy's presidential campaign manager needed someone to handle his San Francisco campaign, he hired Conrad. See Erickson to Isenberg.

53 CAP organized one of the first peace marches in the Bay Area, and Erickson coordinated the publicity. CAP used Conrad's home address on the organization's stationary. See circa 1970 CAP letterhead and appeal notice, Folder 5, Box 73, J. B. Matthews Collection, David M. Rubenstein Rare Book & Manuscript Library, Duke University, Durham, NC.

54 Erickson to Isenberg.

55 Ibid.

56 Virginia Gibbs Weber and Walter Seifert, "National Survey Explores Role of Women in Public Relations," *Public Relations Journal*, July 1966, 33–34; Barbara Ireton, "The Female Practitioner Talks about Her Status," *Public Relations Journal*, September 1967, 14–15.

57 Isenberg interview with Vignolo; Isenberg interview with Knickerbocker.

58 Bill and Joan Roth admired a tripe dish Conrad prepared for special dinners. Isenberg interview with Bill and Joan Roth.

59 Erickson to Isenberg.

60 [Unclear] to Marion Conrad, April 1, 1967, File 014.I.A.5913, in Halprin Collection, AAUP. Bobbie Stauffacher emulated Conrad's use of hospitality to cement business deals and hosted a dinner party that ended with Marion "working as the PR woman for The Sea Ranch," Stauffacher recalled in "Duped by Design," 103. Marion Conrad was listed as a consultant to Boeke and Oceanic by November 1963.

61 Erickson to Isenberg. Other employees' names culled from Conrad Associates correspondence in 1966 and 1967 include Susan D'Amato, Connie Renner, Nancy Blaustein, and Jane O'Kane.

62 Erickson to Isenberg.

63 Isenberg interview with Knickerbocker. Photographs of Conrad and Knickerbocker appear with the story "Her First Show," *SFE&C*, Women Today, May 15, 1966, 8.

64 Erickson's new boss was McGraw-Hill's San Francisco bureau chief, Margaret Ralston Drossel. His mother came "from a very prominent and well-to-do family in North Dakota." See Erickson to Isenberg. See also "Margaret Ralston, 1919–2015," *Des Moines Register*, July 12, 2015.

65 Erickson's terms and perception of the division of responsibility. See Erickson to Isenberg. Dixon worked with Conrad on projects for many of the firm's major clients, including Willie Brown, George Moscone, Bill Roth (in his unsuccessful bid for governor), Ghirardelli Square, Victor Bergeron, and Cecilia Chiang (of the Mandarin Restaurant). Dixon later married Hunt Conrad after Marion Conrad passed away. Ms. Dixon's given name was Mary Elizabeth Hasson; her first marriage to "advertising man Daniel Dixon" ended in divorce in 1969, but she sustained a lifelong friendship with her mother-in-law, Dorothea Lange. See Gerald Adams, "Mia D. Conrad," *SFC*, April 29, 2001, A27.

66 Erickson to Isenberg. Wax served on the Sausalito City Council from 1964 to 1968 and spent two of those years as mayor. He maintained a reputation for integrity. See "Mel Wax—Journalist, Politician, Press Aide to Moscone," *SFC*, March 30, 2007.

67 Conrad, "New York Trip."

68 Marion Conrad to Ron and Jack, July 12, 1967; Ron Buel to Marion Conrad, July 18, 1967, in File 014.I.A.5915, Halprin Collection, AAUP.

69 Buel to Conrad, July 18, 1967; Conrad to Buel, July 21, 1967, both in File 014.I.A.5915, Halprin Collection, AAUP.

70 Conrad to Buel, July 21, 1967.

71 Ibid.

72 Erickson to Isenberg. Erickson had met his wife during his 1965–66 military tour in Korea.

73 Erickson to Isenberg. Erickson advised Halprin to "start referring to himself as a Master Builder." Erickson's letter says the article was on Embarcadero Center, but the details suggest it was SFIMC.

74 Erickson to Isenberg; planning stories in Donald J. O'Leary to All Consultants, "Sea Ranch—Publicity and Advertising," October 2, 1964, in Sea Ranch File 3, September 1964–January 1965, Job 6525, Joseph Esherick Collection.

75 Erickson to Isenberg; "Al Boeke, 1959–1969."

76 Joseph Esherick to Marion Conrad, January 20, 1965, in Sea Ranch File 3, September 1964–January 1965, Job 6525.

77 The unnamed *Oakland Tribune* clipping was dated May 18, 1967. See Bill Turnbull to Marion Conrad, May 22, 1967, and Marion Conrad to Bill Turnbull, May 23, 1967, both in Series IV, Box 9, File 30, in William Turnbull, Jr./MLTW Collection. See also John Leo, "Skidmore, Owings Is Presented with 5 of Architects' Awards," *NYT*, May 16, 1967, 47.

78 Erickson to Isenberg.

79 Ibid. See Herb Caen, "That's Me All Over," *SFC*, October 28, 1969. The sculpture's title is *Transcendence*, and it was created by Masayuki Nagare. Once he moved to McGraw-Hill, Erickson learned another lesson in communications and the city's old-time families. He attempted to interview Prentiss Cobb Hale (the father of Conrad's employee Linda Hale), chairman of Broadway-Hale, for a *Business Week* story. Hale let Erickson know (through his secretary) that Hale "was an owner. Managers took questions from the press."

80 Stauffacher, "Duped by Design," 113. The event was also describes in "Al Boeke, 1959–1969," 90.

81 "Coal mine" from Preston Geren, Letter to the Editor, *AIA Journal* Vol. 45, No. 6 (June 1966), 168, responding to the cover image of *AIA Journal* Vol. 45, No. 4 (April 1966).

82 Canty went on to a distinguished writing and editing career focused on architecture and cities. More than most New York City editors, Canty was predisposed to understand how California challenged the design establishment and traditional modernists. He had been born in Oakland, and his first position had been with *Western Architect and Engineer*. See Canty, "Origins, Evolutions, and Ironies," 25. Canty told WB&E early in 1965 that he "was captivated with Ghirardelli Square." See Donald

Canty to May Hipshman, January 28, 1965. This, along with a sampling of Canty correspondence with Moore, WB&E, and other Bay Area designers from 1965 can be found in Series IV, Box 9, File 43, in William Turnbull, Jr./MLTW Collection. See also Haskell Papers, Avery Architectural and Fine Arts Library, Columbia University.

CHAPTER 7
"Urban Renewal with Paint"

1 AIGA website, http://designarchives.aiga.org/.

2 The first exhibition listed on her resume was the 1962 "Trademarks USA" at the National Design Center, Chicago, Illinois. See Barbara Stauffacher, Graphic Designer, Resume, 1969, and Industrial Arts Medal, 1970, Barbara Stauffacher nomination, both in Record Group 806, Series 12, AIA Archives.

3 "100 Women in Touch with Our Times," *Harper's Bazaar*, January 1971.

4 Donlyn Lyndon to Committee on Institute Honors, AIA, October 3, 1969, Industrial Arts Medal, 1970, Barbara Stauffacher nomination.

5 Allan Temko to Committee on Institute Honors, AIA, October 13, 1969, Industrial Arts Medal, 1970, Barbara Stauffacher nomination.

6 Barbara Stauffacher Solomon, *Green Architecture and the Agrarian Garden* (New York: Rizzoli, 1988); Barbara Stauffacher Solomon, *Good Mourning California* (New York: Rizzoli, 1992). On her difficulties publishing the memoir, see Isenberg interview with Bobbie Stauffacher Solomon, San Francisco, July 2007.

7 Stauffacher, "Duped by Design," 16.

8 On the changing standards for Main Street's commercial signs, see Isenberg, *Downtown America*. On billboards, see Catherine Gudis, *Buyways: Billboards, Automobiles, and the American Landscape* (New York: Routledge, 2004).

9 George Agron to Committee on Institute Honors, AIA, October 7, 1969, Industrial Arts Medal, 1970, Barbara Stauffacher nomination.

10 Allan Temko to Committee on Institute Honors, AIA, October 13, 1969.

11 See Staci Steinberger, "Saul Bass, 1920–1996"; Jennifer Munro Miller, "Corita Kent, 1918"; Staci Steinberger, "Deborah Sussman." Other West Coast graphic artists of high repute included June Schwarcz, merry renk (Ruth Asawa's neighbor), Jack Stauffacher (Bobbie's brother-in-law), Don Smith, Gene Kavanaugh, Betty Brader, and John Follis. See Bobbye Tigerman, ed., *A Handbook of California Design, 1930–1965* (Cambridge, MA: MIT Press, 2013), 42–43, 142–43, 260–61. For a review of some of their relevant graphic and iconographic ideas during the 1960s, see Robert Venturi and Denise Scott Brown, *Architecture as Signs and Systems for a Mannerist Time* (Cambridge, MA: Harvard University Press, 2004).

12 John Arms, "'Entire Buildings Are Their Canvases,'" *Christian Science Monitor*, February 16, 1972, 15. See Gary Hustwit, *Helvetica: A Documentary Film*, 2007; Lars

Muller, *Helvetica: Homage to a Typeface* (Baden, Switzerland: Lars Muller, 2005); and Richard Hollis, *Swiss Graphic Design: The Origins and Growth of an International Style, 1920–1965* (New Haven, CT: Yale University Press, 2006).

13 Halprin, according to Stauffacher, disliked Helvetica at that time because of its German origins, calling it "Nazi graphics." See Barbara Stauffacher Solomon to Alison Isenberg, July 9, 2007.

14 Term coined by C. Ray Smith in *Progressive Architecture*, November 1967, according to Stauffacher, "Duped by Design," 109.

15 Allan Temko to Committee on Institute Honors, AIA, October 13, 1969.

16 "Supergraphics," *Progressive Architecture*, November 1967, 133; "Exterior Supergraphics," *Progressive Architecture*, December 1968, 120–27.

17 Sibyl Moholy-Nagy to AIA Jury on Institute Honors, September 26, 1969, Industrial Arts Medal, 1970, Barbara Stauffacher nomination.

18 Stauffacher, "Duped by Design," 112–33. See also Cesar Pelli, in C. Ray Smith, "Urban Renewal with Paint," *Progressive Architecture*, November 1970, 102.

19 Gerald McCue to Jury on Institute Honors, AIA, October 3, 1969, Industrial Arts Medal, 1970, Barbara Stauffacher nomination.

20 *Abitare*, October 1970, quoted in translation in Stauffacher, "Duped by Design," 111.

21 "Al Boeke, 1959–1969," 96.

22 In addition to the other articles cited here, a sampling of press coverage included: "California," *Look*, June 1966; "The Sea Ranch—Club d'Athleticisme," *L'Architecture d'aujourd'hui*, April–May 1967; "Pour 'Tromper' les Murs: Dix Pots de Peinture," *Elle*, July 1968; "En Californi un Village Neuf Construit comme un Paysage," *Elle*, April 1968. See Barbara Stauffacher, Graphic Designer, Resume, 1969, and the coverage described in Stauffacher, "Duped by Design," 109–13. Originally the athletic club was called Swim/Tennis Facility 1. Today it is known as the Moonraker Athletic Center, and it is owned by The Sea Ranch Association.

23 Stauffacher brochure included in February 13, 1970, *SFE* photo session records, BANC PIC 2006.029:041891.5— NEG, courtesy of Bancroft Library.

24 Gerald McCue to Jury on Institute Honors, AIA, October 3, 1969, and William Turnbull Jr. to Jury on Institute Honors, AIA, October 10, 1969, both in Industrial Arts Medal, 1970, Barbara Stauffacher nomination.

25 Smith, "Urban Renewal with Paint," 102, 106; "It's Supergraphics!" *Life*, May 1968, 79–82.

26 Killen began on July 1, 1960, at an annual salary of $8,500. CG interview with Ira S. Robbins, Roy R. Neuberger, and Charles Cook, May 26, 1960, in Folder 1960, Pt. I, Box 169, RG 12, Officers' Diaries, FA392, Rockefeller Foundation, RAC.

27 CG, notes on interview with Ira S. Robbins and Miss Lilli Ann Killen, October 19, 1960, in Folder 1960, Pt. 2, Box 170, RG 12 Officers' Diaries, FA392, Rockefeller Foundation, RAC.

28 Killen went on to a distinguished career as a mosaic muralist and sculptor, primarily in public spaces. See Gloria Negri, "Lilli Ann Rosenberg, 86," *Boston Globe*, August 12, 2011.

29 Smith, "Urban Renewal with Paint," and "Exterior Supergraphics," 120.

30 Maude Dorr, "Bathhouse Graphics: Make It Fun, Kid," *Progressive Architecture*, March 1967.

31 Frank Bouldin Hunt to Committee on Institute Honors, AIA, October 9, 1969, Industrial Arts Medal, 1970, Barbara Stauffacher nomination.

32 Stauffacher, "Duped by Design," 92, 95.

33 Ibid., 35, 42–44.

34 Ibid., 59–90.

35 Stauffacher, "Duped by Design," 1–34, 91; Barbara Stauffacher, Graphic Designer, Resume, 1969.

36 Stauffacher, "Duped by Design," 94.

37 Ibid.

38 Stauffacher to Isenberg, June 27, 2007.

39 Ibid. Her first use of the phrase dated to about 1967. Stauffacher recalled following Steve McQueen around her office at 1620 Montgomery during a scouting visit for the filming of the movie *Bullitt*. He "examined everything" on her walls, "a vermilion Helvetica 5 in a black square, a floor-to-ceiling *S*." No one since her mentor had studied her letterforms so intensely. She explained that she had learned these designs in Switzerland. "I guess it's the enemy of cute," she told McQueen. Jacqueline Bisset, as policeman McQueen's girlfriend, played a landscape architect working upstairs for Halprin & Associates. See Stauffacher, "Duped by Design," 92–93.

40 Charles Moore, draft of 1965 *Architectural Forum* review, Series IV, Box 9, File 43, in William Turnbull, Jr./ MLTW Collection.

41 "Minutes of Advisory Board Meeting," August 6, 1964, and August 5, 1965, in Advisory Board folder, Box 1, GSAR, Bancroft Library. On the California Exposition and Fair, Stauffacher worked with WB&E and Halprin & Associates; on the Market Street Project, she worked with Mario J. Ciampi and John Carl Warnecke, Joint Venture Architects. Similar Stauffacher projects included the John Hancock Tower, with I. M. Pei & Partners, Architects, Boston; the Southwest Urban Renewal Area, in Washington, D.C.; North Michigan Avenue, with Halprin & Associates, Chicago. See Barbara Stauffacher, Graphic Designer, Resume, 1969. On Lynch, see David Gibson, *The Wayfinding Handbook: Information Design for Public Places* (New York: Princeton Architectural Press, 2009), 14.

42 For activating edges, see Donald Carter to Don Stover, July 23, 1969, File 014.I.A.947, Halprin Collection, AAUP. Hear Hear was featured in "Kinetic Boutiques and Campopop Shops," *Progressive Architecture*, April 1969, 111. Stauffacher sat down at Ghirardelli Square with one of the magazine's senior editors, Jim Burns Jr., who offered some suggestions for the design. Burns soon left his *Progressive Architecture* job to move to San Francisco. See Halprin and Burns, *Taking Part*, xii–xiii.

Hear Hear and the Very Very Terry Jerry shop appeared in "Which Way?," *Architectural & Engineering News*, March 1969, 21–27.

43 Carter to Stover, July 23, 1969; Donn Emmons to Bill Roth, February 11, 1969, File 014.I.A.947, Halprin Collection, AAUP.

44 "It's Supergraphics!"

45 On the worried tenants and economic woes, see Warren Lemmon to William Roth, January 20, 1969. Other quotes are from Warren Lemmon, "Memo for File, Tour of Ghirardelli Square to Review Design Problems," February 24, 1969. On Stauffacher's reluctance to do more work for Ghirardelli, see Warren Lemmon to Barbara Stauffacher, November 13, 1968. Other references to Stauffacher's work are in Warren Lemmon, "Memo for File, Design and Construction Meeting," March 24, 1968; Warren Lemmon to Stuart Rose, "Design Considerations—Ghirardelli Square," October 23, 1968; and on Stauffacher's outdoor tables and umbrellas, see Joseph Bourg to Larry Halprin, March 4, 1968, File 014.I.A.947, Halprin Collection, AAUP.

46 Don Stover to Barbara Stauffacher, February 26, 1969, File 014.I.A.947, Halprin Collection, AAUP.

47 Stauffacher, "Duped by Design," 100–101; "Signs of Life," *Progressive Architecture*, June 1966, 207–8. Boeke told Foote, Cone, and Belding that they could work with Stauffacher or he would replace them with another firm. See "Al Boeke, 1959–1969."

48 "Al Boeke, 1959–1969"; "Subterranean Beautification," *Progressive Architecture*, May 1968, 168–70.

49 "Al Boeke, 1959–1969"; Stauffacher, "Duped by Design," 101. Boeke primarily sought out her visual talents, but Stauffacher also wrote exceptionally well.

50 Dorr, "Bathhouse Graphics," 156–61.

51 "Inspection Report MLTW," February 1, 1966, Series V, File 34, in William Turnbull, Jr./MLTW Collection. The Oceanic representative, disappointed by the white interior, requested "the design of a new and exciting color scheme" and maximum transformation at minimum expense. See Geoffrey Fairfax to William Turnbull, February 9, 1966, Series V, File 33, in William Turnbull, Jr./MLTW Collection.

52 Stauffacher believed that Moore and Turnbull submitted designs (involving "squiggles in magenta, turquoise, and chartreuse") to Boeke for the club interior, but Boeke rejected them and hired Stauffacher. Stauffacher to Isenberg, July 2007.

53 Stauffacher said these were colors used by "Constructivist revolutionaries, . . . De Stijl Neo-Plastic painters, and New York comic book artists." See Stauffacher, "Duped by Design," 105.

54 Ibid., 106. The other two assistants were Allen and Trevor Thomas. In the full trespassing quote, she said she was reminded of "the sacred walls of [architect Francesco] Borromini's San Carlo alle Quattro Fontane," a church in Rome with a light-colored interior.

55 Stauffacher, "Duped by Design," 106–7. See also Dorr, "Bathhouse Graphics," 156–61. For a comparison with roughly contemporary collaborative interior wall-painting technique, see Andrea Miller-Keller, "Excerpts from a Correspondence," cited in Sol LeWitt, *Sol LeWitt, Wall Drawings, 1968–1984* (Hartford, CT: Wadsworth Atheneum, 1984).

56 Stauffacher, "Duped by Design," 104, 108.

57 Reyner Banham, "Arts in Society: Architecture in Freedomland," *New Society*, January 6, 1966, Series IV, Box 9, File 30, in William Turnbull, Jr./MLTW Collection. Stauffacher later described the ram's-head logo as a "memorial." See Stauffacher, "Duped by Design," 104.

58 Sibyl Moholy-Nagy to AIA Jury on Institute Honors, September 26, 1969.

59 Allan Temko to Committee on Institute Honors, AIA, October 13, 1969.

60 "Oceanic Properties, Inc. Sea Ranch: Outline of Publicity Activity Possibilities, Oct. 1964," Sea Ranch File 3, September 1964–January 1965, Job 6525, Joseph Esherick Collection.

61 Stauffacher, "Duped by Design," 107; "Al Boeke, 1959–1969," 96.

62 Stauffacher, "Duped by Design." Moore's approval of Stauffacher's work is recorded in Dorr, "Bathhouse Graphics," 158.

63 On "bathroom," see Isenberg interview with Bobbie Stauffacher Solomon; Esherick's comment is in Stauffacher, "Duped by Design," 101. A contemporary essay is Denise Scott Brown, "Planning the Powder Room," *Journal of the American Institute of Architects*, April 1967, 81–83, reprinted in Denise Scott Brown, *Having Words* (London: Architectural Association, 2009).

64 Stauffacher to Isenberg, January 22, 2010. She designed other graphics for the Bank of America headquarters.

65 Robert A. M. Stern, Thomas Mellins, and David Fishman, *New York 1960: Architecture and Urbanism Between the Second World War and the Bicentennial* (New York: Monacelli, 1967), 544, 1208.

66 Articles crediting architects include "Supergraphics" and "Exterior Supergraphics." Contrast these with the *San Francisco Chronicle*'s feature calling Stauffacher "the originator of 'supergraphics.'" See Caroline Drewes, "Barbara Is Graphic about Her Success," *SFE&C*, Women Today, March 1, 1970, 5, in folder Solomon, B, SFHC, SFPL. Several of the AIA nominating letter-writers were the same individuals whose credited work later crowded out Stauffacher's. Marget Larsen's husband wrote that "Marget and Barbara Stauffacher were the earliest designers of supergraphics." See Robert Brewster Freeman, "Marget Larsen," *Communication Arts*, Vol. 30, No. 1 (March–April 1988), 93.

67 Drewes, "Barbara Is Graphic about Her Success."

68 Morley Baer to Marion Conrad, October 28, 1966, Series IV, Box 9, File 30, in William Turnbull, Jr./MLTW Collection.

69 On commercial artists, see Michele Bogart, *Artists, Advertising, and the Borders of Art* (Chicago: University of Chicago Press, 1997); Roland Marchand, *Advertising* the American Dream: Making Way for Modernity, 1920–1940 (Berkeley: University of California Press, 1985); on postcard artists, see Isenberg, *Downtown America*.

70 A sampling of publications by the architects and about the architects' legacies includes Donlyn Lyndon and Jim Alinder, *The Sea Ranch: Fifty Years of Architecture, Landscape, Place, and Community on the Northern California Coast* (New York: Princeton Architectural Press, Revised Edition, 2014); Lawrence Halprin, *Sea Ranch . . . Diary of an Idea* (Berkeley: Spacemaker Press, 2006); Lawrence Halprin, "Sea Ranch: Halprin's Recollections"; Donlyn Lyndon, "Sea Ranch: Lyndon's Assessment," *Progressive Architecture*, Vol. 74, No. 2 (1993), 92–93; A. Lange, "Why Charles Moore Still Matters: The Controversial Architect Continues to Inspire Former Colleagues and Collaborators," *Metropolis*, Vol. 33, No. 10, (2014), 85–97; K. Frampton, L. Lerup, and M. Wagner, *William Turnbull Jr.: Buildings in the Landscape* (Richmond, CA: William K. Stout, 2008); E. Ghenoiu, "Charles W. Moore and the Idea of Place," *Fabrications*, Vol. 18, No. 2 (2008), 90–119.

71 Art Seidenbaum, "Where the Upper-Middles Meet the Sea Idyllically," *LA Times*, July 17, 1968, A5.

72 Eugene Williams to Joseph Esherick, December 17, 1963, Sea Ranch File 1, July 1963–February 1964, Job 6525.

73 Al Boeke to William Mathews, July 12, 1963, Sea Ranch File 1, July 1963–February 1964, Job 6525.

74 "Del Mar Ranch Development," p. 2, Sea Ranch File 1, July 1963–February 1964; Al Boeke to Mr. H. W. Budge, "The Sea Ranch—Deeds, Covenants and Restrictions," June 5, 1964, p. 2, Sea Ranch File 2, March 1964–September 1964, Job 6525, Joseph Esherick Collection.

75 The two sites shared the recent history of mills and factories closing.

76 "Al Boeke, 1959–1969."

77 Boeke to Mathews, July 12, 1963.

78 Ross Lawler, "Developer Cites Need for Coast Planning," Speech delivered to the Fort Bragg Rotary Club, December 18, 1963, reprinted in a newspaper circa January 23, 1964, Sea Ranch File 1, July 1963–February 1964; Seidenbaum, "Where the Upper-Middles Meet the Sea Idyllically."

79 Frederick Simpich Jr. to Board of Directors, "Sea Ranch Development," February 20, 1964, 10, Sea Ranch File 2, March 1964–September 1964, Job 6525, Joseph Esherick Collection. Bill Kortum jumped into coastal preservation in the 1962 Bodega nuclear power plant fight organized by David Pesonen and Jean Kortum. Bill Kortum's Sea Ranch battles led him to cofound Californians Organized to Acquire Access to State Tidelands (COAAST), which in turn contributed to the passage of the 1972 Coastal Initiative and the formation of the Coastal Commission. The creation of Salt Point State Park, in which Kortum played a role, contrasted with the lost Sea Ranch parcel. Kortum was a veterinarian. See John Crevelli, *Bill Kortum, A Fifty Year History of Environmental Activism in Sonoma County* (CreateSpace Independent Publishing Platform, 2015). For an article placing The Sea Ranch in the legal contests over urban and suburban development and the Coastal Zone Act, see Daniel J. Curtin and K. L. Shirk Jr., "Land Use, Planning and Zoning," *Urban Lawyer*, Vol. 9, No. 4 (Fall 1977), 724–46. On the Coastal Commission as another example of California's unusual vigilance in regulating the waterfront public domain, see Sara Fingal, "Turning the Tide: The Politics of Land and Leisure on the California and Mexican Coastlines in the Age of Environmentalism" (Ph.D. thesis, Brown University, Providence, RI, 2012); Elsa Devienne, "Des Plages Dans la Ville: Une Histoire Sociale et Environnementale du Littoral de Los Angeles, 1920–1972" (Ph.D. thesis, Ecole des Hautes Etudes en Sciences Sociales, Paris, 2014).

80 Menzel to Matthews, "Inspection of the Sea Ranch at Pocket Bay," 6; Canty, "Origins, Evolutions, and Ironies." On the distinctiveness of condominiums in 1960s vacation communities, as well as the architecturally innovative model The Sea Ranch provided for condominiums, see Matthew Lasner, *High Life: Condo Living in the Suburban Century* (New Haven, CT: Yale University Press, 2012), 196.

81 The planning and real estate concept of cluster housing received attention in the general press at this time. See Tom Cameron, "Multi-Unit Project Has 'Single-Family' Look," *LA Times*, October 17, 1965.

82 "Conference at the Sea Ranch," Tape 2, March 30, 1966, William Turnbull Collection, IV 30, EDA.

83 Ibid.

84 Ibid.

85 Ibid. Boeke described in detail the persistence of the state park idea into the 1970s, and the moratorium effect of the Coastal Commission and related battles. See "Al Boeke, 1959–1969," 74–78, 111–24.

86 "Al Boeke, 1959–1969," 89.

87 Stauffacher, "Duped by Design," 113–15.

88 Ibid. Her ca. 1975 drawing "Lines, Lies, and Land(e)scapes" continued the gendered spin on the road-kill theme. The yellow lines of a highway threaten to split a woman's body in two—or emanate from between her legs, depending upon your reading. See Barbara Stauffacher Solomon, *Why? Why Not? 80 Years in 42,636 Words and 60 Pictures* (San Francisco: FunFogPress, 2013), 121.

89 Although Stauffacher's relationship with Dan Solomon had complex implications for her career that are beyond the scope of this book, I have included a few of her observations in this chapter. See Stauffacher, "Duped by Design," 129, 134, 154–55, 159. She removed most of the details of their relationship from the shorter, self-published version of her memoir, Solomon, *Why? Why Not?*

90 Barbara Stauffacher Solomon, "Green Architecture: Notes on the Common Ground," *Design Quarterly* No. 120 (1982), 3–31. The Tuileries competition involved the most blatant disappointment when she was told by her collaborators: "You cannot come into the meeting with us. The French Government has decided it doesn't want an American woman on the winning French team." The description of the competitions and the Rome Prize are from Solomon, *Why? Why Not?*, 122–43.

91 Erickson to Isenberg.

92 Stauffacher, "Duped by Design," 115. Stauffacher said that Conrad felt deeply ambivalent about public relations work and "hated" how good she was at it. Isenberg interview with Bobbie Stauffacher Solomon.

CHAPTER 8
Model Cities

1 "Nine Keys to Golden Gateway," editorial, *SFC*, March 10, 1960, 30. *SFC* Editorials in 1958 and 1959 signaled frustration with the city's anemic redevelopment program. See "A Mess Is Made of Redevelopment," editorial, *SFC*, October 15, 1958, 32; "A City Lagging behind the Rest," editorial, *SFC*, February 13, 1959, 28; "Open the Doors to Golden Gateway," editorial, *SFC*, May 18, 1959, 32.

2 Herman cited in Grady Clay, "The Competitors: A Study of Competition for Urban Land," August 10, 1962, chapter 3, 28, Grady Clay archives, courtesy of Justin Clark. Clark worked as a personal archivist to Clay. Soon after Clark completed his research on my behalf in Clay's records, the collection was divided and deposited by Clark and Clay in several research libraries.

3 On mixing "dollars and design," see Clay, "Competition for Urban Renewal Land,"14; on AIA timing, see Clay, "The Competitors," chapter 3, 34–35. The same month that Golden Gateway's proposals were due, March 1960, Moses was forced to resign as chairman of New York City's Mayor's Committee on Slum Clearance. Hilary Ballon explains that in leading Title I, Moses "conceived of design decisions as a matter of private choice, outside the sphere of government control." Although this was a common position at the time, "given Moses's conception of urban renewal as a building program, his lack of interest in design was a serious blind spot. For all his overreaching power, when it came to physical form and urban design, Moses did not go far enough." See Hilary Ballon, "Robert Moses and Urban Renewal: The Title I Program," in *Robert Moses and the Modern City: The Transformation of New York*, ed. Hilary Ballon and Kenneth Jackson (New York: W. W. Norton, 2007), 94, 108.

4 Clay, "The Competitors," chapter 3, 35–39.

5 Art Hoppe, "Money, the Root of All Projects," *SFC*, March 11, 1960, 28, quoted in Clay, "The Competitors," chapter 3, 38–39.

6 Ibid.

7 Anshen's San Francisco firm, Anshen & Allen, partnered with Eichler Homes Inc. of Palo Alto and Dinwiddle Construction Company of San Francisco. Ibid.

8 Clay, "The Competitors," chapter 3, 37–38.

9 For "startling" and "starkly simple," see ibid., 47. "Haunted" and "deepest impression" are from an undated column by Robert Krauskopf, *San Francisco Progress*, quoted by Clay in ibid. The Golden Gateway submission (for which Lubicz-Nycz teamed up with Sidney Leiken

Enterprises and contractor Theo. G. Meyer and Sons) was the first of his memorable design proposals in the United States.

10 For biggest company, see "Her World Is Lilliputian," *Las Cruces* (NM) *Sun-News*, January 25, 1961; "Harry L. Sanders Jr., interview conducted by Suzanne B. Reiss, May 24, 1977," in *Thomas D. Church, Landscape Architect*, Vol. 2 (1978), 652, Oral History Center, Bancroft Library. Photographer Gerald Ratto remembered shooting one of the Golden Gateway models in a sublet garage, a "funky old wooden building" where the model-makers "kept it pretty well under wraps." Isenberg interview with Gerald Ratto, San Francisco, July 8, 2011.

11 Isenberg interview with Calvin Imai, Oakland, June 23, 2009.

12 There is little focused scholarship on the Golden Gateway or Embarcadero Center urban renewal phases of San Francisco's downtown redevelopment. See Richard Brandi, "A Reevaluation of Urban Renewal in San Francisco," M.A. thesis, Historic Preservation, Goucher College, 2008, and Chandler McCoy, "San Francisco's Golden Gateway Redevelopment Project," paper presented at the Society for American City and Regional Planning History Conference, September 2009.

13 Mario Ciampi, "An Outline of Procedure for Architectural Advisory Panel Evaluation of Nine Proposals by Developers and their Architects," March 29, 1960, quoted by Clay in "The Competitors," chapter 3, 41, and reproduced in Appendix C to that manuscript.

14 Clay compared the presentations to Dave Brubeck's all-out performance at the 1956 Newport Jazz Festival, where Brubeck recalled that the band had decided to "throw our whole life into one tune." Quoted in Clay, "The Competitors," chapter 3, 1.

15 In 1967 AMI's brochure read: "It has become almost mandatory" for large-scale federal projects to "require a model." A model ensured the final approval necessary before awarding a government contract. "Another example of civic planning" came from Minnesota, where the client was a mayor's committee and community planning board. A planning model of a Minnesota town was "supported through HUD [the U.S. Department of Housing and Urban Development] and [the] Housing Act of 1954." See Virginia Green and Leila Johnston, AMI brochure, circa 1967, courtesy of Gerald Ratto, private collection. Green's signature appears in the brochure; to attribute authorship of ideas, I assume that Johnston worked with Green on the brochure.

16 Ibid. Isenberg interview with Ratto. City Planning Director Allan Jacobs said that if one model-maker could not "do the job" for a designer, another would step in. Isenberg interview with Allan Jacobs, San Francisco, October 17, 2011.

17 Andrew Hamilton notes that architectural historians have only recently begun to probe the theoretical frameworks for understanding scale historically and contextually, and his forthcoming scholarship makes a foundational contribution to this effort. See Andrew Hamilton, "On Scale," in *Scale and the Incas* (Princeton, NJ: Princeton University Press, forthcoming). See also Albena Yaneva, "Scaling Up and Down: Extraction Trials in Architectural Design," *Social Studies of Science*, Vol. 35, No. 6 (December, 2005), 867–94; Rem Koolhaus, "Bigness," in Rem Koolhaus and Bruce Mau, *S, M, L, XL*, ed. Jennifer Sigler, 2nd edition (New York: Monacelli, 1998) 495–516.

18 Reiss interview with Sanders, 651.

19 Ibid., 651–52. The contrast between aggressively documenting landscape architect Church and accidentally finding model-maker Virginia Green is worth underscoring. Sanders's arrival at Stanford in 1956 as the university's first full-time planner followed his time at positions in San Francisco's Department of City Planning and the Redevelopment Agency, which he left about 1954. See Barbara Palmer, "Harry Sanders, Former Director of Campus Planning, Dead at 89," *Stanford News Service*, April 28, 2004.

20 Isenberg interview with Ratto; Meredith Eliassen to Alison Isenberg, e-mail, October 21, 2011.

21 Isenberg phone interview with Don Nusbaum, September 6, 2011.

22 Ibid. See also Virginia Green and Leila M. Johnston, Apparatus for Making Topographical Models, US Patent No. 3,137,209, filed July 27, 1961, and issued June 16, 1964. For the lawsuits, see *Architectural Models Inc. v. Nils Neklason and Donald Nusbaum*, 264 F. Supp. 312 (N.D. California 1967), and *Architectural Models Inc. v. Nils Neklason and Donald Nusbaum*, 397 F.2d 405 (9th Cir. 1968). See also *Architectural Models Inc. v. Nils Neklason and Donald Nusbaum*, decision dated February 24, 1967. A second decision dated July 11, 1968, confirmed the first decision on appeal (397 F.2d 405). AMI's first machine was delivered about June 1960. On Nusbaum and Neklason's last day at AMI, September 28, 1962, Green and Johnston warned them against trying to replicate their machine, which had had a patent application pending since July 1961. Contour machinery described in Canter, "Big Little Builders."

23 Nusbaum and Neklason claimed that they had been forced out of urban renewal bidding by Johnston and Green's influence in SFRA competitions. SMU's modifications to the invention were sufficiently significant that they successfully defended themselves against AMI's lawsuit. See *Architectural Models Inc. v. Nils Neklason and Donald Nusbaum*, decision.

24 Regarding Helmut Jacoby's rendering of Boston's Government Center in 1964, one scholar wrote: "Since the building is located in a redevelopment area, its immediate surroundings, i.e., its neighboring buildings, could be neglected." See Helmut Jacoby, *Helmut Jacoby: Architectural Drawings* (New York: Praeger, 1965), 100.

25 "Architect's Models Are Fascinating," [publication name cut off], June 14, 1953, Stamps and Hobbies Section, Virginia Green Clippings file, SFHC, SFPL, courtesy of Meredith Eliassen, Archives and Special Collections Department, J. Paul Leonard Library, San Francisco State University. Typically AMI received coverage in the business or hobby pages, and sometimes under urban affairs, but not in design columns or publications.

26 Canter, "Big Little Builders." AMI's "landscape department" mirrored the administrative divisions within city government. On the construction industry impact, see Isenberg interview with Imai.

27 "A Model Look at the City," *SFE*, May 29, 1972; Schroeder, "Masters of Miniature," both in AMI Clippings file, SFHC, SFPL, courtesy of Meredith Eliassen.

28 Kiani bought the company from Nusbaum and reestablished it in Memphis in 2000. Nusbaum thought the city model project was doomed to be an expensive overtime fiasco, and the staff dreaded all-nighters. In the end, SMU paid only forty-five minutes of overtime. Kiani built many of the skyscrapers and landmarks. As of 2011, people still called to ask where this model of San Francisco was (he has lost track). Isenberg telephone interview with Kamran Kiani, October 8, 2011.

29 AMI brochure. Other projects in the brochure described the importance of models to depicting the "civic setting" for public buildings, "today's urban architecture," and "civic planning." AMI's "Spokane 1980" model rested on different fieldwork—250 photographs of buildings in the city's central district taken by Johnston's brother Donald McMillen. Spokane was Johnston's hometown, spurring the *Spokane Daily Chronicle* to publish a story on Johnston and the model when it was displayed widely during August 1961. See Hazel Barnes, "Model Builder Notes," *Spokane Daily Chronicle*, August 24, 1961, 8.

30 Helmut Jacoby, *Helmut Jacoby: New Architectural Drawings* (*NAD*) (New York: Praeger, 1969), 5.

31 Isenberg interview with Kiani.

32 AMI brochure.

33 Ibid. The brochure contrasted models with renderings and photographs: "If one picture is worth a thousand words, one model's worth becomes millions."

34 On Jacoby's links to high modernism, see Greg Castillo, "Triumph and Transformation: American Modernism, 1952–1968"; on his career, see Thomas Mellins, "Helmut Jacoby's Architectural Renderings: The Drawing as Analogue," both in *Helmut Jacoby, Master of Architectural Drawing* (*HJMAD*), ed. Helge Bofinger and Wolfgang Voigt (Tubingen, Germany: Wasmuth, 2001), 27–28, 35–45. Most of the essays in this volume expand upon Jacoby's career.

35 Bofinger, "Helmut Jacoby—Master of Architectural Drawing," in *HJMAD*, 13. The variables affecting the renderer's stunning number of interpretive choices are described in *NAD*, 5–8, and Claudius Coulin, "Introduction," in *Helmut Jacoby: Architectural Drawings*, 5–8. For an explanation of how specific audiences for drawings (fine arts commissions, banks, college boards, government agencies, businesses and industries, builders, and the architects) influenced Jacoby's interpretive choices, see *NAD*, 5–8.

36 Gerwin Zohlen, "'In a Drawing, What I Want to See Is What Is Coming': An Interview with Helmut Jacoby," in *HJMAD*, 50–53.

37 Coulin, "Introduction," in *Helmut Jacoby: Architectural Drawings*, 8.

38 Zohlen, "'In a Drawing," 50–5.

39 Coulin, "Introduction," in *Helmut Jacoby: Architectural Drawings*, 7.

40 "Introduction," in *NAD*, 7.

41 Coulin, "Introduction," in *Helmut Jacoby: Architectural Drawings*, 5, 7.

42 Zohlen, "'In a Drawing,'" 49–51. On the history of architectural drawing, with some detail on Hugh Ferris and Jules Guerin, two of the evocative twentieth-century masters, see Wolfgang Voigt, "'Portrait Painters of Buildings': The Fate of Architectural Illustration and Professional Renderings from 1800 until Today," in *HJMAD*, 15–21.

43 Frederick A. Usher, "Introduction," in *Building Illusion: The Work of Carlos Diniz* (Tokyo: Process Architecture, 1992), 8–10; Isenberg interview with Ratto.

44 AMI brochure.

45 Isenberg interview with Ratto.

46 Ibid.

47 *NAD*, 7–8; Zohlen, "'In a Drawing,'" 55–56. Jacoby said that he "often could not draw Pei's work well, but Johnson's I could always draw well." Some architects, he said, "I cannot relate to whatsoever." See Zohlen, "'In a Drawing,'" 56.

48 Coulin, "Introduction," in *Helmut Jacoby: Architectural Drawings*, 5.

49 Ratto added that if the architect waited to "use" a project until after it was built, he would be behind the times. From a photographer's point of view, buildings were also more limited than models in how one could control light. Isenberg interview with Ratto.

50 Bofinger, "Helmut Jacoby—Master of Architectural Drawing," 9–10; Derek Walker, "Introduction," in Helmut Jacoby, *Architectural Drawings, 1968–1976* (London: Thames and Hudson, 1977); Derek Walker, "Helmut Jacoby: An Appreciation," in *HJM AD*, 60. On how Jacoby's career fit between the United States and Europe, see Werner Durth, "Broken Mirrors: Reflections on a Visit to Helmut Jacoby's Studio," *Daedalus*, September 1987, 92–105.

51 Zohlen, "'In a Drawing,'" 53.

52 "Introduction," in *NAD*, 7.

53 "The Obsessive Eye," *Architects' Journal*, Vol. 166, No. 31–35 (1977), 374–75.

54 Zohlen, "'In a Drawing,'" 51. When Jacoby opened his studio in 1956, "a guy" named Schwartz produced presentation drawings for many New York architects. If Pei used Schwartz, then Johnson would not. Ibid., 49.

55 Zohlen, "'In a Drawing," 53. On his hopes for the book, see Voigt, "'Portrait Painters of Buildings,'" 20.

56 In 1950 the Bender trustees expressed concern that the art awards "all [seemed] to be on the extremely modern side." That year Ansel Adams was appointed chair of the Bender jury. See "Albert M. Bender Memorial Trust, Board of Trustees Minutes from October 16, 1950"; "Albert M. Bender Grants-in-Aid in Art and Literature 1942–1951," Albert Bender Grants-In-Aid, 1941, San Francisco Art Institute Archives; "Two Here Win Art Awards," June 16, 1950, in Virginia Green Clippings file, SFHC. See also "Two Graduates Receive Awards," *Oregon Daily Emerald*, September 27, 1950, 5. Although successful, the program concluded with the 1951–52 competition.

57 Virginia Green, "Program for Albert M. Bender Grant-in-Aid," January 1950, Virginia Green Bender Applications (unprocessed materials), Albert Bender Grants-In-Aid, 1941, San Francisco Art Institute Archives.

58 *Franciscan*, Vol. 16 (San Francisco State College, 1941), 84, and Vol. 17 (1942), 78–79, courtesy of Special Collections/Archives, J. Paul Leonard Library, San Francisco State University.

59 Leila M. McMillen, page 3B, line 69, Enumeration District 0171, *Fifteenth Census of the United States*, 1930 (National Archives Microfilm Publication T626, roll 2518), and Leila J. M. McMillen, page 61B, line 54, Enumeration District 1-17, *Sixteenth Census of the United States*, 1940 (National Archives Microfilm Publication T627, roll 4331), both in Records of the Bureau of the Census, Record Group 29, Washington, D.C., National Archives and Records Administration; *Kinnikinick* (Cheney: Eastern Washington College of Education, 1936), 25, 26, 29. Leila's grandfather, a homesteader in 1877, laid out the town of Endicott as paymaster for the Oregon-Washington Railroad and Navigation Company. See Barnes, "Model Builder Notes"; 1940 Spokane City Directory.

60 Barnes, "Model Builder Notes"; Schroeder, "Masters of Miniature."

61 Virginia Green, "Cement—A Direct Building Material: Its Possibilities as a Sculptural Medium," M.F.A. thesis, School of Architecture and Allied Arts, University of Oregon, Eugene, April 1950.

62 Virginia Green, "A Program of Study and Work for the Albert M. Bender Grant-in-Aid," February 1949; Green, "Program for Albert M. Bender Grant-in-Aid," January 1950, both in Virginia Green Bender Applications (unprocessed materials), Albert Bender Grants-In-Aid, 1941, San Francisco Art Institute Archives.

63 Sidney W. Little to Bender Grants-in-Aid, February 23, 1949; W. S. Hayden to Bender Grants-in-Aid, February 22, 1949; M. R. Sponenburgh to Bender Grants-in-Aid, February 22, 1949; and Wallace S. Baldinger to Bender Grants-in-Aid, January 29, 1950, all in Virginia Green Bender Applications (unprocessed materials), San Francisco Art Institute Archives.

64 Virginia Green, "A Program of Study and Work for the Albert M. Bender Grant-in-Aid," February 1949, and Virginia Green, "M.F.A. Thesis Program: An Investigation of Plastic Materials," February 1949, both in Virginia Green Bender Applications (unprocessed materials).

65 Wallace S. Hayden to Bender Grants-in-Aid.

66 Virginia Green to Bender Grants-in-Aid, February 20, 1949, Virginia Green Bender Applications (unprocessed materials).

67 Virginia Green, "Program for Albert M. Bender Grant-in-Aid," January 1950.

68 Virginia Green, "A Program of Study and Work for the Albert M. Bender Grant-in-Aid"; M. R. Sponenburgh to Bender Grants-in-Aid, February 22, 1949.

69 Virginia Green, "A Program of Study and Work for the Albert M. Bender Grant-in-Aid."

70 Royston said that mid-1950s parks followed two models: the "outdoor gymnasium" formula or that of Boy Scouts distributing "seeds." See Jocelyn Dong and Thea Lamkin-Carughi, " 'Radical' Mitchell Park Turns 50," *Palo Alto Weekly*, April 11, 2007, 19. See also Reuben M. Rainey and J. C. Miller, *Modern Public Gardens: Robert Royston and the Suburban Park* (San Francisco: William Stout, 2006), 94–110; "Palo Alto's Mitchell Park, A West Coast Design Leader," *American City*, Vol. 72, November 1957, 29; R. Burton Litton Jr., ed., *Landscape Architecture 1958* (San Francisco Museum of Art), 11, 32; and *Palo Alto Times*, April 12, 1957, all in Mitchell Park folder, Clippings file, Palo Alto Historical Association. See further Schroeder, "Masters of Miniature."

71 "Her Toy Cities Make Dreams Come True," *Toledo Blade*, April 2, 1961, 6; "Architect's Models Are Fascinating." "Precise and elegant" from Claude Stoller to Alison Isenberg, November 8, 2011.

72 Stoller and Imai thought SOM gave Green the first model assignments (Stoller specified Bassett). See Schroeder, "Masters of Miniature"; Isenberg interview with Claude Stoller, Berkeley, October 21, 2011; Isenberg interview with Imai. Sanders said that Green began as a draftsman and in-house model-maker for WB&E. See Sanders interview with Reiss.

73 Barnes, "Model Builder Notes."

74 The founding year for Workshop Models was 1947 or 1948, when architect Mario Corbett was one of their associates. Lois Cronk was listed as a partner in 1951. Despite their ranking among "the best in the country," Anne Luckhart did not relish the business side of model-making. Their daughter, Dean Luckhart, became a landscape architect. "We wish people wouldn't call our work 'miniatures,' " Luckhart said. See Ogden Tanner, "These Models Show the Client What Architecture Means," *SFC*, July 9, 1950, 3L; Jackson Doyle, "$3000 Model of Sunset Project Will Be Displayed at Art Festival," *SFC*, October 14, 1951, 17; Marjorie Trumbull, "Exclusively Yours," *SFC*, August 19, 1959, 43; "Giant Model On Display," *SFC*, August 11, 1957, Peninsula Section, 1. See also Annie E. Gourley, page 17, "Census Returns for 1916 Census of Prairie Provinces" (LAC microfilm roll T-21948), Statistics of Canada, Record Group 31-C-1, Ottawa, Library and Archives Canada; Anne Evelyn Luckhart, *Manifests of Alien Arrivals at Blaine, Washington, 1924–1956* (National Archives Microfilm Publication 2675039), Records of the Immigration and Naturalization Service, Record Group 85, Washington, D.C., National Archives and Records Administration; *San Francisco City Directory* (San Francisco: R. L. Polk, 1948), 1159.

75 "Her World Is Lilliputian"; Barnes, "Model Builder Notes"; Schroeder, "Masters of Miniature." Imai said there were few competitors besides SMU during the first decade. On industry's growth, see "Models Catch Eye of Builders: Maker Turns Hobby to Vocation," *NYT*, October 9, 1960, R1. Harry Sanders said Green's first location was in a little store on Clement Street, "way out on the avenues." Clementina Street was in San Francisco's Mission district. See Sanders interview with Reiss.

76 "Her World Is Lilliputian"; "Her Toy Cities Make Dreams Come True," 6; "Women Have Lucrative Jobs in Making Scale Models," *Gettysburg Times*, October 28, 1961, 8.

77 The staff was still about seventeen full-timers. See Canter, "Big Little Builders."

78 "Her World Is Lilliputian"; Canter, "New Lease for the Center." Gerald Ratto photographed the model supply catalogue. See Isenberg interview with Ratto.

79 Canter, "Big Little Builders"; Schroeder, "Masters of Miniature."

80 Employees in the photo included Noel Gregorian, Dong K. Lim, Alice Henderson, Susan Beard, Gary Groves, Ralph McMillen, Bill Hartman, Oyars, Steve, David, and Bernice. Other names were John Buckle, Herb Coffman, Steve Coty, Jay Blaze, and Kathleen Seyforth. Compiled from *Examiner* photo-shoot documents, Isenberg interview with Imai, newspaper stories, and the AMI brochure.

81 Imai said that AMI's training to become a model-maker lasted two years. See Isenberg interview with Imai. Seyfarth described AMI's Alice Henderson as her "tree mentor." Seyfarth married a landscape architect and came to AMI with model-making experience in 1972. See Marcia Tanner, "The Forest of Seyfarth," *Garden Design*, Vol. 12, No. 4 (September–October 1993), 25.

82 Canter, "Big Little Builders." Imai remembered Green and Johnston as excellent bosses; Ratto thought "they were good to work for." Nusbaum hoped to make SMU less top-down than AMI. See Stoller to Isenberg; Isenberg interviews with Ratto, Imai, and Nusbaum.

83 On their favorite model, see Schroeder, "Masters of Miniature."

84 "Women Have Lucrative Jobs in Making Scale Models." The AIA *Chronicle* competition named the home its Bonanza section's March 1962 House of the Month. See Theodore Bredt, "An Artist's Dream House," *SFE&C*, March 4, 1962, Bonanza, 24–25, in folder Green-Johnston Project, Robert B. Marquis Collection, 2009-04, Environmental Design Archives, College of Environmental Design, University of California, Berkeley.

85 Green-Johnston project bids and design costs, Folder 219, Box 9, Robert B. Marquis Collection, 2009-04. The Green-Johnston house street address was 370 Summit Avenue, Mill Valley.

86 Stoller told of a homesite where a bulldozer slipped down the slope. See Claude Stoller to Alison Isenberg, November 8, 2011, and December 12, 2011.

87 *AIA Journal*, May 1963, 48–49; "A.I.A. Award Program for 1963 Honors 13 Buildings," *Architectural Record*, March 1963, 14.

88 Five of 605 submissions won first honors in the merchant-built category. The houses were between 1,500 and 2,500 square feet. See "1964's Best Merchant-Built and Custom Houses," *House & Home*, Vol. 16, No. 1 (July 1964), 67, 77, 80–81. The Homes for Better Living Awards were sponsored by the AIA, *House & Home*, and other magazines. The program began in 1956 as the culmination of a regional contest for Western houses, and soon expanded to become a national award. See Nancy Hadley to Alison Isenberg, e-mail, November 1, 2011.

89 Other recognition followed for the Green-Johnston house. See "The Good Life in the Tree Tops," *Sunset* (March 1963), 234–36; "Local Prize Winner," *Mill Valley Record*, February 27, 1963; "Residential Design Awards Presented by National Landscape Association," *Pacific Coast Nurseryman and Garden Supply Dealer*, April 1975, 14; and untitled clipping, *Arts and Architecture*, May 1961, 24, all in Robert Royston Collection, 1999–12. See also "Award-Winning Mill Valley Home," *San Rafael Independent Journal*, February 21, 1963, folder Green-Johnston Project, Robert B. Marquis Collection, 2009-04.

90 Marquis and Stoller, "Descriptive Data, 1963 AIA Honor Awards Program," Honor Awards, 1963, Green-Johnston House nomination, Record Group 806, Series 6, AIA Archives. The submission included fourteen Ezra Stoller photographs. See Claude Stoller to Alison Isenberg, November 8, 2011.

91 "Green-Johnston House," Box 1, Folder 9, Robert B. Marquis Collection, 2009-04; Bredt, "An Artist's Dream House," and "Exploitation of Rational Structure," *Progressive Architecture* (May 1964), 171–77, Box 3, Folder 40, Robert B. Marquis Collection, 2009-04; "Award-Winning Buildings Avoid Architectural Cliches," *NYT*, June 2, 1963. A California Redwood Association magazine advertisement underscored how the house ran against the established grain. The photographer staged the Green-Johnston house with two young children playing on the unsafe deck. Undated California Redwood Association advertisement clipping, p. 110, in Box 3, Folder 41, Robert B. Marquis Collection, 2009-04.

92 "Green-Johnston House." Sadly, Mr. Green did not live long in the new Mill Valley home; he passed away in 1961. The architects took the unusual step of sketching two alternatives—Marquis offered a Bay Region scheme, but Green and Johnston preferred Stoller's "more Harvard Bauhaus" design. See Claude Stoller to Alison Isenberg, November 8, 2011, and December 12, 2011. "Creative disorder" from Bredt, "An Artist's Dream House."

93 "Exploitation of Rational Structure."

94 Claude Stoller to Alison Isenberg, November 8, 2011. "Refugees" from Schroeder, "Masters of Miniature."

95 Stoller wrote, "So Va.&L. were a couple of same sex lovers, one of several such in our circle. I can't remember that we made much of it. . . . 'Gay,' 'Lesbian,' "out of the closet," were not in our vocabulary. Of course in la vie academe it was quite different." Claude Stoller to Alison Isenberg, November 8, 2011.

96 Alfred Frankenstein, "There's Nothing Gazoonish about the Gazebo at the Art Festival," *SFC*, October 12, 1952, This World, 29; Alfred Frankenstein, "An Answer from the Art Commission on Civic Support for Visual Arts," *SFC*, March 20, 1955, This World, 11. A photo of Johnston at a SFMA event accompanies "S.F. Socialites See 'Wild Beasts,' " *SFC*, March 22, 1953.

97 "Architect's Models Are Fascinating."

98 Stoller named a few in his circle, where architectural commissions often reinforced these networks, as in the case of the Green-Johnston house and Heath Ceramics' new factory: "Jack Campbell and Worley Wong architects, Bill Gilbert structural engineer, Larry Halprin landscape architect, Anna Halprin dancer, Joe Esherick architect, Anne Folsom writer and photographer, Gene Tepper designer, Freda Koblick sculptor, Lucia Bogatay architect, Bobby Stauffacher graphic designer/landscape architect, Keith Monroe sculptor, Art Carpenter cabinet maker, Edith Heath potter." Ruth Asawa and Al Lanier were Stoller's friends as well. See Claude Stoller to Alison Isenberg, December 12, 2011. Inevitably, not everyone in these circles got along with each other. Isenberg interview with Bobbie Stauffacher Solomon. On networks in California arts, see *Reading California*, ed. Barron, Bernstein, and Fort.

99 When Green and Johnston sold their model supplies company, AMSI Miniatures, in 1982, an article described it as "the nation's largest producer of landscaping materials for architectural models." See Lloyd Watson, "People in Business: Small Is Beautiful," *SFC*, November 4, 1982, 29. Imai relocated AMI from San Francisco to Oakland. See Isenberg interview with Imai; "A Model Look at the City."

100 In addition to noting the industry impact of the former AMI employees mentioned previously, see also a story on Lisa Gemmiti by Virginia Gardiner, "Working in a Model World," *SFC*, January 28, 2004.

101 Alan Bell, Bell & Stanton Press Release, February 14, 1967, 2, and SFRA, "Technical Support Data for Embarcadero Center Proposal in Golden Gateway Renewal Area," February 14, 1967, folder Real Estate—Embarcadero Center, N–Z, Box 412, RG 3, Rockefeller Family, RAC. Used with special authorization. Portman's position as both architect and developer was unusual. John Portman and Jonathan Barnett, *The Architect as Developer* (New York: McGraw-Hill, 1976). On the display and hand-outs at the museum, see *NAD*, 58–59.

102 "Embarcadero Center" brochure, San Francisco, February 1967, folder Real Estate—Embarcadero Center, N–Z, Box 412, RG 3, Rockefeller Family, RAC. Used with special authorization.

103 Technically the developers won exclusive 90-day negotiating rights to purchase the property. During the negotiation window, David Rockefeller signed on publicly. Box, who was also the president of Oklahoma Cement Company, named Fuller as "the largest building contractor in America." The SFRA specifications were issued February 18, 1966, proposals were due March 24, 1966, and the selection meeting was held March 29, 1966. Four developer teams submitted proposals, but not all planned to purchase the entire parcel. The SFRA press release said the four teams "requested anonymity." Herman strongly preferred that the site go to a single developer. In other renewal projects he would favor selling smaller urban renewal parcels to diverse investors. $125 million figure taken from the February 14, 1967, Bell & Stanton press release, although projects, of course, varied. An accompanying SFRA fact sheet listed David Rockefeller as owning 50 percent of the venture (through Westway Bay Inc.), with Crow, Portman, and Box owning 16.67 percent each. See "Developers Vying for Final Golden Gateway Projects," *San Francisco Daily Commercial News*, March 28, 1966; William Thomas, "Golden Gateway: $100 Million Within 5 Blocks," *SFC*, March 30, 1966, 1, 18; and Elmont Waite, "$100 Million Man: Big Spender of Golden Gateway," *SFC*, March 31, 1966, 1, 17, all in folder Real Estate—Embarcadero Center Clippings, 1966, 1968, 1969, Box 412, RG 3, Rockefeller Family, RAC. Used with special authorization. See also "Golden Gateway Commercial Parcels," SFRA Press Release, March 29, 1966, and SFRA, "Statement of Conditions," February 18, 1966, folder Real Estate—Embarcadero Center 1966–72, Box 412, RG 3, Rockefeller Family, RAC. Used with special authorization. After the developers were announced, some members of the Board of Supervisors loudly objected to outside investors, particularly those with Texas "oil money."

104 Alan Temko to Nelson Aldrich, July 27, 1967, folder Embarcadero Center Design/Construction—Controversy, Box 412, RG 3, Rockefeller Family, RAC. Used with special authorization.

105 Bell & Stanton Press Release.

106 Ibid. See also SFRA, "Technical Support Data for Embarcadero Proposal." Quote from Hearings Transcript, Board of Supervisors, April 3 and 5, 1968, 83–85, enclosure, Gerald Noble to Warren Lindquist, [April 1968], folder Embarcadero Center Design/Construction—Controversy, Box 412, RG 3, Rockefeller Family, RAC. Used with special authorization. See also Mel Wax, "Temko vs. Herman: Angry Debate on Embarcadero," *SFC* April 28, 1967, 6.

107 Justin Herman to Allan Carpenter, March 14, 1967; David Rockefeller to John Harper (president, Alcoa), March 8, 1967, both in folder Embarcadero Center Design/Construction—Controversy, Box 412, RG 3, Rockefeller Family, RAC. Used with special authorization.

108 By November 1966 Golden Gateway's executive director, Allan Carpenter, had already objected to the two-block office building and the tallest tower. The investors then suspected that Herman had downplayed the Golden Gateway disagreements. See Robin Hood to John Portman, November 21, 1966, and additional 1966 correspondence in folder Embarcadero Center Design/Construction—Controversy, Box 412, RG 3, Rockefeller Family, RAC. Used with special authorization.

109 "Rockefeller Sends Realty Aide Here For 'Showdown,'" *SFE*, March 6, 1967, 3. For the behind-the-scenes efforts to negotiate agreement among parties, see February–May 1967 correspondence, including letters between Herman and Carpenter and from Fred Smith to Warren Lindquist, May 23, 1967, in folder Embarcadero Center, Design/Construction—Controversy, Box 412, RG 3, Rockefeller Family, RAC. Used with special authorization.

110 Emmons quoted in Mel Wax, "Embarcadero Center Showdown," *SFC*, March 6, 1967, 1. The first changes SFRA negotiated did not silence critics. See SFRA, "Golden Gateway Plan Changes," April 4, 1967; Mel Wax, "A Blast at Embarcadero Center Plan," March 22, 1967, 1, 7; Russ Cone, "'Rockefeller West' Plans Blasted by Designers," *SFE*, March 22, 1967; and Gar Davidson to Warren Lindquist, March 22, 1967, all in folder Embarcadero Center Design/Construction—Controversy, Box 412, RG 3, Rockefeller Family, RAC. Used with special authorization. For additional early reviews, see "The City's Growth to a New Larger Scale," editorial, *SFE*, April 14, 1967, 30; "A Magnificent Urban Concept," editorial, *SFC*, March 2, 1967; and "Sparring Begins on Embarcadero Center Plan," *SFC*, February 16, 1967, all in RG3, Box 412, folder Real Estate—Embarcadero Center 1967, Box 412, RG 3, Rockefeller Family, RAC. Used with special authorization. See also Wallace Tucker, "60-Story Coast Building Planned, Hotel also Proposed for Complex in SF," *NYT*, February 15, 1967.

111 "Remarks by Mr. Charles Bassett," San Francisco Board of Supervisors Meeting, May 8, 1967, transcribed by Arnold & Palmer Associates, and Rockefeller to Portman, May 11, 1967, both in folder Embarcadero Center Design/Construction—Controversy, Box 412, RG 3, Rockefeller Family, RAC. Used with special authorization. After Portman's designation as project architect in 1966, SOM's Nat Owings called Warren Lindquist to say Owings's opinion of Portman was "not very high." Warren Lindquist to David Rockefeller, April 18, 1966, in folder Real Estate—Embarcadero Center 1966–72, Box 412, RG 3, Rockefeller Family, RAC. Used with special authorization. On Alcoa's objections to Portman's designs, see Warren Lindquist to David Rockefeller, February 22, 1967, and Fred Whitman to David Rockefeller, February 17, 1967, both in folder Embarcadero Center Design/Construction—Controversy, Box 412, RG 3, Rockefeller Family, RAC. Used with special authorization. When they began working together, Portman did not have a publicity brochure to send to Rockefeller, who was unfamiliar with his work. See Portman to Leslie Larsen, March 2, 1966, in folder Embarcadero Center Design/Construction—

Controversy, Box 412, RG 3, Rockefeller Family, RAC. Used with special authorization. See Lindquist correspondence over a January 1969 letter from Stanley Sinton, president of SPUR, on how the developers fielded ongoing design complaints, in folder Real Estate—Embarcadero Center N–Z, Box 412, RG 3, Rockefeller Family, RAC. Used with special authorization.

112 Temko, "A Chance for Greatness," *SFC*, May 6, 1967; Temko, "Shadow of Folly for S.F.," *SFC*, May 8, 1967. Temko credited Scott Newhall with the page-one placement. See Temko to Aldrich, June 28, 1967; Aldrich to Temko, July 18, 1967; and Temko to Aldrich, July 27, 1967, all in folder Embarcadero Center Design/Construction—Controversy, Box 412, RG 3, Rockefeller Family, RAC. Used with special authorization. The investment team did evolve; Cloyce Box pulled out on April 2, 1968, when his construction firm did not get the contract. He sold his share to Warren Lindquist and James Caswell. See "Embarcadero: Land Deeded for New Center," *SFC*, June 12, 1968, folder Embarcadero Center Clippings 1966, 1968, 1969, Box 412, RG 3, Rockefeller Family, RAC. Used with special authorization.

113 "Remarks by Pietro Belluschi on Report of the Advisory Committee to the Urban Redevelopment Authority," February 14, 1967. Belluschi's panel included Gerald McCue, Thomas Church, and Jesse Reichek. See folder Embarcadero Center Design/Construction—Controversy, Box 412, RG 3, Rockefeller Family, RAC. Used with special authorization. In addition to Church's Stanford campus work with AMI, Belluschi knew AMI's models firsthand; St. Mary's Cathedral was his design.

114 *NAD*, 58–59.

115 Bell & Stanton Press Release.

116 Jacoby singled out his Embarcadero Center drawings as offering insight into a typical project. See *NAD*, 58–59.

117 AMI brochure. Based on AMI's Embarcadero Center model, Portman declared them "the best" in the business and commissioned them for projects around the United States. See Isenberg interview with Imai.

118 Imai estimated that there were about twenty signatures. Sometimes only a distinctive base—a unique notch or a particular wood—identified the model-making company. As of 2016 the Embarcadero Center model is still displayed in the owner's (Boston Properties') sales office. See Isenberg interview with Imai. Kamran Kiani described a similar attachment at SMU for their San Francisco city model. Isenberg telephone interview with Kamran Kiani.

119 Isenberg interview with Imai.

120 Jacobs, *Making City Planning Work*, 1.

121 Scott Blakey, "SPUR Chief Hits the Skyscrapers," *SFC*, September 17, 1969, 1.

122 Donald Canter, "100 Million Gateway Complex: Rockefellers in 5-Block Deal," *SFE*, May 27, 1966, in folder Real Estate—Embarcadero Center Clippings, Box 412, RG 3, Rockefeller Family, RAC. Used with special

authorization. The sales price was capped at this. The 1966 proposal guidelines explained that the parcels would be sold for between $10 million and $11.572 million, depending on the current appraisals being made for the SFRA. "Golden Gateway Commercial Parcels," SFRA Press Release, March 29, 1966.

123 Donald Canter, "Center Chief Is Ousted in Gateway Rift," *SFE*, August 10, 1970, in folder Real Estate—Embarcadero Center 1967, Box 412, RG 3, Rockefeller Family, RAC. Used with special authorization.

124 JRHB to WTL, March 11, 1966, in folder Real Estate—Embarcadero Center 1966–72, and James M. Caswell Jr. to Eugene R. Black Jr., December 23, 1969, enclosure "Embarcadero Center—San Francisco, California," in folder Real Estate—Embarcadero Center A–M, both in Box 412, RG 3, Rockefeller Family, RAC. Used with special authorization. "Bargain" from Canter, "Center Chief Is Ousted in Gateway Rift"; see also Keith Power, "Mendelsohn's Plea On Gateway Land," *SFC*, June 24, 1974, 4.

CHAPTER 9
"The Competition for Urban Land"

1 Clay, "Competition for Urban Renewal Land," 3, 1, and Grady Clay, "Competition for Land in Urban Renewal: Innovations of the 1960s," speech given at Salzburg Seminars in American Studies, January 1968, Grady Clay archives, courtesy of Justin Clark.

2 On mixing dollars and design, see Clay, "Competition for Urban Renewal Land," 14. See also Clay, "The Competitors," preface, 1–3. Clay laid out his intentions to make the Boston-based magazine a "major force" in urban criticism in a long memo detailing his view as a journalist of the problems in the field and the solutions. Not trained in design, Clay brought an expansive definition of landscape to this task. See Grady Clay CG, "A Program of Urban Criticism," June 8, 1958, Grady Clay archives, courtesy of Justin Clark. The interrelationships between Grady Clay and John Brinckerhoff Jackson's writings and editorial roles on the landscape-land dynamic remain to be explored. On Jackson, see scholarship by Paul Groth and Helen Lefkowitz Horowitz. For recent urban renewal frameworks in addition to previously cited works, Elihu Rubin, *Insuring the City: The Prudential Center and the Postwar Urban Landscape* (New Haven, CT: Yale University Press, 2012); Christopher Klemek, *The Transatlantic Collapse of Urban Renewal: Postwar Urbanism from New York to Berlin* (Chicago: University of Chicago Press, 2012).

3 Grady Clay, "The Planner and His Critics," speech given at the American Society of Planning Officials meeting in Miami Beach, May 25, 1960, in University of Pennsylvania Community Planning Conference, Folder 3905, Box 457, RG 1.2, Series 200R, FA387, Rockefeller Foundation, RAC.

4 Grady Clay, "Pressure Points in Urban Renewal Design," May 18, 1960; Grady Clay to Paul Ylvisaker,

June 19, 1960; Paul Ylvisaker to Grady Clay, June 30, 1960; and Grady Clay to Paul Ylvisaker, November 16, 1960, all in MIT, Studies to Appraise Current Programs in Urban Renewal (August 4, 1960–December 31, 1963), Grant No. 60-394, mcf reel 0393, Ford Foundation Records (FFR), RAC. Clay took leave from the *Courier-Journal* in July and was on the grant payroll in October.

5 On the rise of urban studies during these years and the Joint Center's place in that, see Eugenie Birch, "Making Urban Research Intellectually Respectable: Martin Meyerson and the Joint Center for Urban Studies of Massachusetts Institute of Technology and Harvard University, 1959–1964," *Journal of Planning History*, Vol. 10 (August 2011), 219–38.

6 Grady Clay, "Open Competition vs. the Closed Deal," *The Sou'easter: American Institute of Planners Southeast Chapter*, March 1963, Grady Clay archives, courtesy of Justin Clark. For his description and analysis of the Brookline competition, see Clay, "The Competitors," chapter 2, 1–19. The long draft of his Brookline chapter, before Clay chopped it down to primarily introduce San Francisco, is still extant (in the author's possession).

7 Grady Clay, "Urban Design as an Instrument of Public Policy," Oklahoma City speech, July 9, 1963, Grady Clay archives, courtesy of Justin Clark.

8 Grady Clay, "Open Competition vs. the Closed Deal." Clay simplified the Golden Gateway dollars and design problem to state that "a man" offered $8 million for the parcel but the city "turned around" and sold it to another "man" offering only $6 million, plus a better design and other "extras" that the market could not price. See Grady Clay, "The Cityscape," 1962, National Trust for Historic Preservation reprint, Grady Clay archives, courtesy of Justin Clark.

9 Twenty-five years later, Golden Gateway was still "at the top of the list" among hundreds. Society Hill ranked "perhaps second." Grady Clay, "Design Competitions: Lessons from the Past," Wallenberg Memorial Lecture, University of Michigan, Ann Arbor, October 8, 1985, Grady Clay archives, courtesy of Justin Clark.

10 Anderson, Professor of Architecture at MIT, also served on Sert's Brookline architectural advisory committee. Architect Nelson W. Aldrich, director of the Boston Arts Festival and architectural sounding board to his cousin David Rockefeller (particularly on Embarcadero Center), was the third member of the ill-fated Brookline committee. See Clay, "The Competitors," chapter 2, 8–9.

11 Clay, "The Competitors," chapter 3, 33–35, 44, 78–79.

12 CG, notes on interview with Grady Clay, October 1, 1962, Folder 1962, Pt. 2, Box 171, RG 12, Officers' Diaries, FA392, Rockefeller Foundation, RAC.

13 Clay bypassed notable U.S. urban renewal projects he had already researched, including Philadelphia's Society Hill and Southwest D.C., to focus on the London case. See Clay, "The Competitors," chapter 4, 1, 6–8, 12.

14 Ibid. Bracketed material "[i.e. sell]" added by Clay.

Golden Gateway advisory board member Ferd Kramer similarly challenged his colleagues by asserting that it was a "perversion of the national housing act to use the power of eminent domain" to build luxury apartments on renewal land (chapter 3, 55). Historians have just begun to analyze the Elephant and Castle center; a recent dissertation includes it when tracing property management and design strategies for shopping malls and how standardization encouraged international commercial property speculators. See Sam Wetherell, "Pilot Zones: The New Urban Environment of Twentieth Century Britain" (Ph.D. thesis, University of California, Berkeley, 2016), 103–8.

15 Grady Clay, "Let's Bring Urban Renewal Back into the City; or, Competition Is the Planner's Best Friend," speech given at the ASPO Conference, Atlantic City, May 2, 1962, revised and printed as "The Cityscape," National Trust for Historic Preservation, both in Grady Clay archives, courtesy of Justin Clark. See also Grady Clay, "The Cityscape," *Historic Preservation*, Vol. 15, No. 1 (1963).

16 *NAHRO* (National Association of Housing and Redevelopment Officials) *Newsletter*, cited in Clay, "The Competitors," chapter 1, 1.

17 Clay, "Competition for Urban Renewal Land," 2.

18 Clay, "The Competitors," 34. Ferd Kramer was later credited with advancing racial integration in Chicago. Jacobs very selectively included San Francisco in her book. She discussed North Beach and Telegraph Hill as examples of the capacity of cities to "unslum," reinforcing her arguments about the Village. Of San Francisco's urban renewal, she mentioned only the Western Addition. As of December 1958, Jacobs had never been to San Francisco or Los Angeles but told Gilpatric that she planned to visit soon because she had "indulged in opinions and critical comments." See Jacobs, *Death and Life*; CG, notes from telephone call to Jane Jacobs, December 2, 1958, Folder 1958 July–December, Box 168, RG 12, Officers' Diaries, FA392, Rockefeller Foundation, RAC. Peter Laurence cites early 1959 correspondence between Jacobs and Clay and between Jacobs and Bauer about planning Jacobs's trip to California. See Laurence, *Becoming Jane Jacobs*, 262–69.

19 Jacobs, *Death and Life*. Clay's manuscript had a detailed list of illustrations; however, the extant draft did not retain copies of the actual images. Appendixes were included. See Clay, "The Competitors."

20 CG, notes from telephone call to William Wheaton, May 13, 1958. See also CG, notes from meeting with William Wheaton, May 7, 1958. Both in Folder 1958 May–June, Box 168, RG 12, Officers' Diaries, FA392, Rockefeller Foundation, RAC.

21 Wurster to Clay, October 26, 1961. See also Clay to Wurster, October 12, 1961, and Clay to Wurster, October 31, 1961, in Correspondence File C, 1961–62, Box 12, William W. Wurster Administrative Files, EDA.

22 Other participants were Leslie Cheek Jr., Frederick Gutheim, Gordon Stephenson, and Edward Weeks.

See Grady Clay, "Urban Design Criticism: A Report on the University of Pennsylvania Conference on Urban Design Criticism," circa November 1958, University of Pennsylvania Community Planning Conference, Folder 3905, Box 457, RG 1.2, Series 200R, FA387, Rockefeller Foundation, RAC. Rockefeller Foundation's Humanities Division had funded related faculty projects at the University of Pennsylvania.

23 CG, notes from interview with William L. Slayton and Frederick O'Reilly Haves, March 19, 1962, Folder 1962, Pt. 1, Box 171, RG 12, Officers' Diaries, FA392, Rockefeller Foundation, RAC. After a meeting with architect Josep Lluís Sert, Gilpatric recorded, "Sert agrees that although there is widespread and growing interest in what he calls urban design, discussion of problems is loaded with clichés." See CG, notes from interview with Jose Sert, December 9, 1960, Folder 1960, Pt. 2, Box 170, RG 12, Officers' Diaries, FA392, Rockefeller Foundation, RAC.

24 CG, "Critical Viewpoints in Urban Design," notes from meeting with Ian McHarg and William Wheaton, May 7, 1958, Folder 1958 April–June, Box 168, RG 12, Officers' Diaries, FA392, Rockefeller Foundation, RAC.; CG, notes from meeting with William J. Conklin, May 15, 1960, Folder 1960, Pt. 1, Box 169, RG 12, Officers' Diaries, FA392, Rockefeller Foundation, RAC. Clay ranked Mumford's *New Yorker* "Sky Line" pieces as the most influential of urban criticism. A selection of these 1930s columns has been reprinted in *Sidewalk Critic*. For a more detailed account of the 1958 conference, see Laurence, "The Death and Life of Urban Design," and *Becoming Jane Jacobs*.

25 Clay reported a "sense of crisis" in "Urban Design Criticism." For Clay's detailed list of his own recommendations, see Clay to CG, "A Program of Urban Criticism."

26 David Crane, quoted in Clay, "Urban Design Criticism"; CG, notes from telephone call to David Crane, September 29, 1958, Folder 1958 July–December, Box 168, RG 12, Officers' Diaries, FA392, Rockefeller Foundation, RAC.

27 Douglas Haskell, "*Architectural Forum*'s Adventure in Architectural Criticism: A Letter to Grady Clay of the Urban Design Criticism Conference," circa January 1959, in Grady Clay Correspondence, RG2, GC Series 200/1959 (mcf reel 12), FA400, Rockefeller Foundation, RAC.

28 "More writing done from outside journalistic staffs" might help, Jacobs said. See Clay, "Urban Design Criticism." On the long-term impact of the 1928 libel suit threats, see Haskell to William Wurster, January 14, 1954, Box 24, Folder 6, Haskell Papers.

29 Haskell, "*Architectural Forum*'s Adventure in Architectural Criticism." Documenting his long-standing editorial efforts, see Douglas Haskell to Messieurs Paine, Frey, and Beard, "Architectural Record's Sales Letter," November 2, 1960, and Mr. Paine to Mr. Luce, April 13, 1960, both in Box 81, File 2, Haskell Papers. See also Douglas Haskell to Sigfried Giedion, March 24, 1955, in Box 8, File 2, Haskell Papers.

30 See especially correspondence with Catherine Bauer about Haskell's efforts to expand *Forum*'s reach to planners. Compared to traditional architects, urban designers served a municipality rather than a private client, Bauer wrote, and had to resolve conflicts among even collaborators. Urban designers usually had to "contribute important ideas," discern "what the city really needs and wants," and prepare to dig in for long-term implementation. Bauer also criticized *Forum* for failing to cover major San Francisco issues. See "Memo to D. Haskell from C. Bauer: Next Step for Arch Forum?"and Douglas Haskell to Mrs. William Wurster, March 28, 1961, both in Box 24, File 5, Haskell Papers; "Memo to D. Haskell from C. Bauer: Next Step for Arch Forum? How Urban and Metropolitan Plans Are (or Could Be) Carried Out," September 29, 1956, in Box 24, File 6, Haskell Papers. Haskell sponsored a 1956 round table, Rental Housing in Urban Renewal, which brought together fifteen developers, architects, planners, and federal and city administrators in Washington, D.C. See "Master Copy, Architectural Forum Round Table on Rental Housing in Urban Renewal," January 24–25, 1956, Box 73, File 1, Haskell Papers. See other round tables in Box 73, File 6, Haskell Papers.

31 One reader first thought a review was "unfair to so nice a building, but by the time he had come to the end of the article he could see the critic's point, and he realized the fairness of the criticism." See Haskell, "*Architectural Forum*'s Adventure in Architectural Criticism."

32 Douglas Haskell to William Wurster, November 4, 1952, Box 14, File 6, Haskell Papers.

33 William Wheaton to CG, July 17, 1959, and David Crane to CG, April 13, 1961, both in University of Pennsylvania Community Planning Conference, Folder 3905, Box 457, Series 200R, RG 1.2, FA387, Rockefeller Foundation, RAC. See also CG, notes from meeting with David Crane, August 22, 1958, and CG, notes from meeting with Frederick Gutheim, July 21, 1958, both in Folder 1958 July–December, Box 168, RG 12, Officers' Diaries, FA392, Rockefeller Foundation, RAC.

34 It is likely that drafts of Clay's long report to Rockefeller on the 1958 conference, along with his correspondence with Penn faculty about revisions, are held in one of the relevant archives. Apparently the report was never revised to the satisfaction of the parties involved. The University of Pennsylvania's Institute for Urban Studies continued working with Clay, despite these problems. See the records of a June 1962 convening under Wheaton's leadership of the Ford-funded urban renewal grantees, UPenn, Studies to Appraise Current Programs in Urban Renewal, Grant No. 60-344, mcf reel 0393, FFR, RAC.

35 CG, interview notes from meeting with Paul Ylvisaker and Robert Weaver, March 15, 1960, Folder 1960, Pt. 1, Box 169, RG 12, Officers' Diaries, FA392, Rockefeller Foundation, RAC. For an account of how Ford expanded the urban extension program to other land-grant and state universities, see "Urban Extension: A Report on the Experimental Programs Assisted by the Ford Foundation," October 1966, FFR, RAC.

36 CG, interview notes from meeting with Paul Ylvisaker and Robert Weaver, March 15, 1960. Six years later Weaver became the first U.S. secretary of Housing and Urban Development. Wendell Pritchett, *Robert Clifton Weaver and the American City: The Life and Times of an Urban Reformer* (Chicago: University of Chicago Press, 2008).

37 CG, notes from interview with Allan Temko, August 22, 1962, Urban Design Journalists (UDJ), RG2, GC Series 200R/1962 (mcf reel 29), FA400, Rockefeller Foundation, RAC, and CG, notes from interview with George McCue, April 2, 1962, Folder 1962, Pt. 1, Box 171, both in RG 12, Officers' Diaries, FA392, Rockefeller Foundation, RAC.

38 CG, notes on conversation with Allan Temko, November 30, 1961, Folder 1961, Pt. 2, Box 170, RG 12, Officers' Diaries, FA392, Rockefeller Foundation, RAC; Allan Temko, *Eero Saarinen* (New York: G. Braziller, 1962). See also Allan Temko, "How Not to Build a Ball Park," *Harper's Magazine*, August 1961.

39 On keynoting, see CG, notes on interview with Grady Clay, October 1, 1962, Folder 1962, Pt. 2, Box 171, RG 12, Officers' Diaries, FA392, Rockefeller Foundation, RAC. For "direct outgrowth," see Grady Clay to CG, September 28, 1962, UDJ, RG2, GC Series 200R/1962 (mcf reel 29), FA400, Rockefeller Foundation, RAC.

40 "For September Issues of Architecture Journals," Columbia University press release, August 3, 1962, UDJ, RG2, GC Series 200R/1962 (mcf reel 29), FA400, Rockefeller Foundation, RAC.

41 Ibid.; Schedule of Events, The Press and the Building of Cities, September 12, 1962; Robert Hewes, "Participant Selection," June 27, 1962. For a list of participants, see Doris Radford to CG, enclosure, October 15, 1962. All items cited in this note are in UDJ, RG2, GC Series 200R/1962 (mcf reel 29), FA400, Rockefeller Foundation, RAC.

42 CG, notes from interview with George McCue, October 4, 1962, in Folder 1962, Pt. 2, Box 171, RG 12, Officers' Diaries, FA392, Rockefeller Foundation, RAC. There were no women among the thirty journalists. No women presented, although Aline Saarinen was invited. McCue had expected that the Columbia program would be "a promotional venture in defense of architecture." See CG, notes from interview with George McCue, April 2, 1962, in Folder 1962, Pt. 1, Box 171, RG 12, Officers' Diaries, FA392, Rockefeller Foundation, RAC.

43 The modest grant would provide a travel stipend, and the results would be published in their respective newspapers. See CG, "Possible Small Grants to Newspaper Critics," October 10, 1962, and RXC comment to file, 1962, both in UDJ, RG2, GC Series 200R/1962 (mcf reel 29), FA400, Rockefeller Foundation, RAC. Robert Geddes helped Gilpatric conclude that it was time to shut down. For Geddes's increasing consultant role, see CG,

notes on telephone calls to Robert Geddes, October 5, 1962, and October 17, 1962, Folder 1962, Pt. 2, Box 171, RG 12, Officers' Diaries, FA392, Rockefeller Foundation, RAC.

44 Situating the work of Jones and Jacobs in the San Francisco context of growing attention to older buildings and the absence of publications about incorporating new structures into old cities, see CG, notes from meeting with Barclay Jones and Stephen Jacobs, June 24, 1958, Folder 1958 May–June, Box 168, RG 12, Officers' Diaries, FA392, Rockefeller Foundation, RAC.

45 For examples see CG, notes from interview with Kingman Brewster Jr., Yale University, November 1962; CG, notes from interview with Charles Whitlock, Harvard University, October 30, 1963; and CG, notes from visit to the University of Chicago, May 21, 1963, in Folder 1962, Pt. 2, and Folder 1963 January–1964 September, Box 171, RG 12, Officers' Diaries, FA392, Rockefeller Foundation, RAC.

46 CG, excerpt from CG visit to Cambridge-Boston, talk with Martin Meyerson, November 16, 1961, UDJ, RG2, GC Series 200R/1962 (mcf reel 29), FA400, Rockefeller Foundation, RAC.

47 Charles Abrams, "Urban Land Problems and Policies," *Housing and Town and Country Planning* (1953), 3–57. Abrams lived in Greenwich Village. His career would shed more light on why the land economics perspective supported by the Joint Center did not influence urban studies historiography as forcefully as the urban renewal critiques of Jane Jacobs. I am indebted to Julia Foulkes for sharing her research on Abrams.

48 CG, notes on interview with Clay, October 1, 1962.

49 A check of internal Urban Renewal Administration (URA) records confirms Clay's "instincts" to publish quickly because the policy issue of "disposing" of redevelopment land through leasehold was a topic prioritized for closer scrutiny during the spring of 1960. The URA central administration also began to analyze its own data regarding disposition methods and marketing. See S. Leigh Curry to Charles Oswald, "Suggested Subjects for Consideration by Federal Urban Renewal Council," June 20, 1960, in folder Deputy Commissioner 1960 (Oswald). See also David Walker, Urban Renewal Commissioner to Regional Directors of Urban Renewal, "Land Disposition: Bi-monthly Land Disposition Summary," January 20, 1960, and Acting Urban Renewal Commissioner Oswald to Regional Administrators, "Land Disposition Analysis, October 10, 1960, both in folder All Regions 1960. All in Box 359, RG 207, Chronological Files, 1958–1960. For additional correspondence on URA and Federal Housing Administration (FHA) strategizing around leaseholds in 1960, see folder Leases: FHA, Box 4 of 9, Finance Branch Subject Files, 1948–68, and folder Project Financing 1960, Box 338, General Subject Files, Personnel to Publications. All items cited in this note are found in the General Records of the Department of Housing and Urban Development, URA, National Archives and Records Administration, College Park, MD.

50 Clay, "The Competitors," chapter 1, 45.

51 Clay tracked the rising number of conservative attacks on renewal and planning as un-American invasions of property rights, as articulated by Jo Hindman in a January 1959 *American Mercury* article, "Terrible 1313." See Clay, "The Competitors," chapter 1, 46.

52 The rough order of events follows. In 1955 the Board of Supervisors approved the Embarcadero–Lower Market Redevelopment Area E. In 1956 architect Lawrence Lackey wrote a concise, conceptual report for the City Planning Commission, "The Elements of Replanning Area E." The Real Estate Research Corporation issued another study. In August 1956 the Housing and Home Finance Agency (HHFA) approved the Capital Grant Reservation for Area E. Land appraisals took place in late 1957 and early 1958. The Blythe Zellerbach Committee spent $35,000 to hire Nat Owings of SOM, who contracted with SFRA and CPC. SOM produced the May 31, 1957, "General Development Plan and Report" and an architectural model. On July 9, 1958, SFRA submitted to HHFA an eligibility and relocation report. The freeway revolt intervened. Aaron Levine, from the Citizens' Council on City Planning of Philadelphia, was then brought in during February 1959. Levine advised building more aggressive support behind renewal. That led to the hiring of the new SFRA executive director, Justin Herman. See Clay, "The Competitors," chapter 3, 1–27.

53 The 1957 SOM plan revealed another important aspect of "the competitors" Clay studied. Architectural firms like SOM, developers like William Zeckendorf, and investor–civic leaders like David Rockefeller moved in the same circles, competing for the same projects around the nation. A San Francisco competition did not occur in isolation, despite the perceived differences of the West Coast. SOM, for example, was hired in 1949 to orchestrate planning for Robert Moses's Title I slum clearance work in New York City. This job helped the firm grow and earned it credit and blame for the related urban design decisions. Through the Downtown–Lower Manhattan Association (DLMA), Rockefeller was instrumental in planning the World Trade Center and worked with Robert Moses on this and other initiatives. See Ballon, "Robert Moses and Urban Renewal," 108–9. DLMA, which also hired SOM, has records at RAC.

54 Clay, "The Competitors," chapter 3, 21–24.

55 From his HHFA position, Herman had counseled the SFRA for years on how to speed up its redevelopment machinery. Annabelle Heath assumed the directorship of the regional HHFA office when Herman resigned. The previous SFRA director, Eugene Riordan, who had been in the job since 1954, stepped down amicably. Quote from ibid., chapter 3, 25–28. See Jack Burby, "U.S. Agency Backs S.F. Building Limit," *SFC*, November 12, 1958, 2; "U.S. Names New Housing Chief Here," SFC, February 12, 1959, 8; Jack Burby, "M. J. Herman Named City Slum Chief," *SFC*, May 22, 1959, 1–2; Big Building Plan: Western Addition Slum Lands on Sale in February," *SFC*, Octo-ber 14, 1959, 1; "Slum Agency Is Running Out of Cash," *SFC*, November 18, 1959, 2; "2 Big Properties Acquired for Golden Gateway," *SFC*, February 10, 1960, 31; and especially James Benet, "S.F.'s Bouncy Redeveloper Meets Slum Problems Head-On," *SFC*, April 3, 1960, 7.

56 Clay, "The Competitors," chapter 3, 28, 33. SFRA's request went to the HHFA on February 18 and was denied on March 1.

57 In addition to Halprin, Tishman-Cahill Renewal Associates included developer James Scheuer, Tishman Realty, Cahill Construction, architects John Carl Warnecke and Associates, architects Gardner Daily and Associates, Victor Gruen, and Livingston and Blayney. See ibid., 36, 66. On developer support, see "An Eye to the Future: Leases Proposed to Avoid Future Redevelopment Problems," *SFC*, January 13, 1960, 2.

58 Herman's August 11, 1960, request for reversion was recorded in meeting minutes; developer rejection was recorded in an August 30, 1960, letter; see also Justin Herman to Grady Clay, November 8, 1961, all quoted in Clay, "The Competitors," chapter 3, 66–67, 73. Besides the winning team, Perini-San Francisco Associates, the other finalist was Kern-Webb, comprising Kern County Land Company, Del E. Webb Construction, Welton Becket and Associates, and Lawrence Lackey. Clay offered a close analysis of the dollar-design trade-offs in these final negotiations.

59 Ibid.

60 Clay, "The Competitors," chapter 3, 33–35, 44, 78–79. CG noted on Clay's May 1960 speech "The Planner and His Critics," "I regard the attached as being of only slight interest." See CG, memo, September 7, 1960, Grady Clay Correspondence, RG2, GC Series 200/1960 (mcf reel 13), FA400, Rockefeller Foundation, RAC. In 1963 Clay heard "the flat statements that 'competitions are dead from now on.'" See Clay, "Open Competition vs. The Closed Deal."

61 CG, notes on interview with Arthur Holden, December 3, 1958, in Folder 1958 July–December, Box 168, RG 12, Officers' Diaries, FA392, Rockefeller Foundation, RAC.

62 Clay, "Open Competition vs. The Closed Deal."

63 Ibid.

64 Ibid.

65 Ibid.

66 Clay, "The Cityscape," 5. The po'-boy in redevelopment was more likely an architect, Clay said, as in the case of Jan Lubicz-Nycz in Golden Gateway. See Clay, "The Competitors," chapter 1, 32–34.

67 Clay, "The Competitors," chapter 3, 86. Recently Philadelphia's late 1950s decision to sell the Eastwick acreage, and also the terms of sale, were back in the news as the original redevelopment agreement neared expiration. See Samantha Melamed, "City Seeks End to Troubled, 60-Year Eastwick Urban Renewal Effort," philly.com, October 17, 2015, http://articles.philly.com/2015-10-17/entertainment/67591639_1_darby-creek-city-hall-residents.

68 Grady Clay to Sir William Holford, October 23, 1961, in "The Competitors" correspondence file, Grady Clay archives, courtesy of Justin Clark. See also "Nine Keys to Golden Gateway," editorial, *SFC*, March 10, 1960, 30. On Title I as hoping for a land rush, see Ballon, "Robert Moses and Urban Renewal," 103.

69 Clay's focus on competition, process, and decision making should be compared to Robert Caro's *The Power Broker* a decade later and to the latter's dramatic story of destruction, rebuilding, and power, told through biography.

70 Clay, "The Competitors," preface, 2, introduction, 56.

71 MIT, "Report on Urban Renewal Grant," September 8, 1964; MIT, "Fiscal Report, Appraisal of Current Programs in Urban Renewal," September 1, 1964. Both in MIT, "Studies to Appraise Current Programs in Urban Renewal" (August 4, 1960–December 31, 1963), Grant No. 60-394, mcf reel 0393, FFR, RAC.

72 On "libelous," see Martin Meyerson to William Wheaton, August 20, 1962; William Wheaton to Paul Ylvisaker, August 17, 1962; and June 1962 convening of the Ford urban renewal grantees, all in UPenn, Studies to Appraise Current Programs in Urban Renewal, Grant No. 60-344, mcf reel 0393, FFR, RAC. Meyerson anticipated a thousand copies in series by "scholars," Clay explained to literary agent Lurton Blassingame at a time when Clay hoped a trade book would complement the scholarly print run. See Grady Clay to Lurton Blassingame, December 17, 1961; Grady Clay to Lurton Blassingame, December 6, 1961; Lurton Blassingame to Grady Clay, December 4, 1961, all in "The Competitors" correspondence file, Grady Clay archive. The file correspondence over the draft is extensive. See Grady Clay to Miss Jane E. Hinchcliffe, May 2, 1963, and Paul Ylvisaker to Grady Clay, November 16, 1960, both in MIT, Studies to Appraise Current Programs in Urban Renewal (August 4, 1960–December 31, 1963), Grant No. 60-394, mcf reel 0393, FFR, RAC.

73 Clay, "The Competitors," chapter 4, 12; chapter 5, 14–15.

CHAPTER 10
Skyscrapers, Street Vacations, and the Seventies

1 Given Ghirardelli Square's achievement as "the most acclaimed use of a square block in the Western United States," Halprin's outburst reflected his "egomania" and seemed "silly." See Karl Kortum to Bill Roth, March 28, 1968, Box 31, Series 2, Sub 5, correspondence binder regarding the restoration/preservation of Ghirardelli, 1962–1970, KKC, SFMRC. On the square's success, see Karl Kortum, draft Letter to the Editor, *SFC*, March 25, 1968, 3, folder Protect Our Waterfront Committee, Box 5, Series 2, Sub 2, KKC, SFMRC. Part of Kortum's letter was published as Karl Kortum, "A Box around the Hill," Letter to the Editor, *SFC*, April 22, 1968.

2 Kortum to Roth, March 28, 1968.

3 Ron Moskowitz, "Market Center Is Set to Go," *SFC*, July 17, 1968, 1, SFIMC Clippings file, SFHC, SFPL.

4 Kortum, draft Letter to the Editor, *SFC*, March 25, 1968.

5 SFIMC article, *Designers West*, December 1967, 28, SFIMC Files, Project numbers 68003, 67033, William W. Wurster/WB&E Collection, EDA, University of California, Berkeley.

6 Kortum, draft Letter to the Editor, *SFC*, March 25, 1968.

7 Ron Moskowitz, "A Heated Hearing on Market Center," *SFC*, July 16, 1968, 1, and Russ Cone, "10 to 1 Vote for Huge Market: Board Talks Past Dawn," *SFE*, July 16, 1968, 1, both in SFIMC Clippings file, SFHC, SFPL.

8 Kortum, draft Letter to the Editor, *SFC*, March 25, 1968.

9 The earliest SFIMC minutes listed Helen Faibush as graphic artist.

10 Kortum, draft Letter to the Editor, *SFC*, March 25, 1968.

11 Kortum to Roth, March 28, 1968.

12 Ibid. The developer's demolition of the Seawall Warehouse was another call to arms for preservationists.

13 Bank of America and Transamerica shared the same corporate origins, but by the 1960s the two companies had separated. Transamerica sought a public identity.

14 "The Hill and the IMC," undated April 1968 clipping, SFIMC file, Telegraph Hill Dwellers (THD) Collection. Planning Director Allan Jacobs recalled losing his temper after Donn Emmons told him that SFIMC would be "great" for the city. Jacobs said to Emmons, "As long as you have a client in tow don't you ever dare tell me what's good for San Francisco." See Isenberg interview with Jacobs.

15 Jack Morrison was a supervisor from 1961 to 1969. Morrison and his wife, Jane Morrison, were liberal state Democratic Party leaders. After earning a master's degree in creative writing, he worked for ten years as a reporter covering politics for the *SFC*. He served in many civic bodies and became closely identified with the city's neighborhood organizations such as SFT (which Jane chaired at one point) and environmental campaigns to control development, especially on the waterfront. Jane Morrison was an editorial director at KNBR-NBC Radio. Jack brought a rare critical perspective on development to the Board of Supervisors and later served on the port commission. See Biography, Finding Aid, Jack Morrison Papers (SFH 24), San Francisco History Center, SFPL.

16 Scott Blakey, "Environment Gadflies: A New Group 'To Save the City,'" *SFC*, March 19, 1970, 4. For an understanding of the freeway revolts and San Francisco's role in starting this national trend, see William Issel, "Land Values, Human Values, and the Preservation of the City's Treasured Appearance: Environmentalism, Politics, and the San Francisco Freeway Revolt," *Pacific Historical Review*, Vol. 68, No. 4 (November 1999), 611–46; Raymond Mohl, "Stop the Road: Freeway Revolts in American Cities," *Journal of Urban History*, Vol. 30, No. 5 (July 2004), 674–706; and Eric Avila, *Folklore of the Freeway* (Minneapolis: University of Minnesota Press, 2014), 28–32. Avila points out that San Francisco provided the "template by which white affluent communities successfully challenged downtown and suburban interests to stop the freeway."

17 "S.F. Sale of Land for 'Pyramid' Ruled Illegal," *SFC*, November 23, 1971, 2.

18 The untold story of the street vacations (alongside San Francisco's longer history centering the competition for urban land) contrasts with the extensive scholarship on urban public land as "space" in many genres from political philosophy to environmental design. For historiography on the study of the design and use of urban plazas since William Whyte's work in the late 1970s and the place of San Francisco in that field, see Anastasia Loukaitou-Sideris and Tridib Banerjee, "The Negotiated Plaza: Design and Development of Corporate Open Space in Downtown," *Journal of Planning Education and Research*, Vol. 13 (1993), 1–12. On San Francisco's unusually strict regulations governing privately owned plazas, see John Zacharias, Ted Stathopoulos, and Hanqing Wu, "Spatial Behavior in San Francisco's Plazas: The Effects of Microclimate, Other People, and Environmental Design," *Environment and Behavior*, Vol. 36, No. 5 (September 2004), 638–58.

19 Many factors in the story reinforce the argument that the lawyers and environmental organizations were motivated by the principle of revealing and curbing the land giveaways to developers, although the stereotype of opposition groups using any legal tactic to stop development dies hard. Here the outpouring of private letters to the Board of Supervisors and organizations like the THD endorsed the moral outrage Harman, Howard, and the Kortums expressed publicly. The lawsuits discussed in this chapter, with the exception of the SFIMC suit, could not hope to "stop development"; the likely outcome was recouping for the city the sale proceeds at 100 percent of appraised value rather than the 50 percent discount. These fees would do little harm to the Transamerica Corporation, and the judgments would not stop construction. That the slow lawsuits won mostly on appeals filed long after construction ended underscores this reality. Finally, the sequence of cases and the fact that the last lawsuit discussed in this chapter proposed an alternative theory of land valuation helps confirm that the lawyers and their backing organizations were seeking to establish principles for safeguarding public land, not just experimenting with delay tactics. Of course the Kortums had also thrown their life-work on the side of responsible stewardship of public land.

20 A speculative note is warranted on the prevalence of street vacation fights in other U.S. cities and on their meanings outside the context of land-based narratives centered in *Designing San Francisco*. These protests in San Francisco against the cut-rate sale of downtown public streets, which manifested themselves in hearings, public response, and lawsuits, do not appear to have been prevalent in the 1960s in other skyscraper cities such as New York City, Chicago, or Boston. The lawsuits fit with San Francisco's longer history of land-centered critiques, but comparative research into how other cities treated the sale of city streets remains to be done. It is unclear whether San Francisco's distinctive pattern can be explained by different city appraisal practices for vacating streets, different overall street vacation policies, different real estate cultures (views on Manhattanization or environmentalism, for example), or something else. It is likely that the street vacation acts do not vary much from state to state; in San Francisco the lawsuits were based not on these acts but on charter provisions that regulated bidding for city property and on appraisals to safeguard public assets. There are thousands of street vacation cases going back to the late nineteenth century, when they were tied to the assemblage of industrial sites and locations for railroad depots, for example. In the post–World War II era, the implementation of street vacation lawsuits related to a wide range of development and land questions associated with shopping malls, eminent domain, and so on. Regionally, the cases were indeed more concentrated in California and New Jersey, but only a fraction of those were related to downtown development pressures. These preliminary regional comparisons are based on a Westlaw search. For an example of how varying U.S. city business cultures yielded different real estate patterns, see Mona Domosh, *Invented Cities: The Creation of Landscape in Nineteenth-Century New York and Boston* (New Haven, CT: Yale University Press, 1996).

21 The city's planners had fought for floor area ratios (FARs, as distinct from height limits) to control buildings' bulk in the 1950s but had settled for watered-down versions from a reluctant Board of Supervisors, which conceded only after Justin Herman and other federal officials said they would not support renewal such as Area E Golden Gateway Redevelopment without FARs. James R. McCarthy to Members of City Planning Commission, "The Floor Area Ratio: Reconsideration of this Method of Controlling Building Bulk in Central Urban Areas." FARs were still novel, having been implemented in New York City and Chicago. Bogner files, Loeb Library, Harvard Graduate School of Design.

22 Released in nine installments of preliminary studies beginning March 1969, the design element was published as *The Urban Design Plan for the Comprehensive Plan of San Francisco* (San Francisco: Department of City Planning, May 1971), adopted by the City Planning Commission on August 26, 1971. Jacobs had difficulty getting even a modest financial commitment for this planning study. See "The Urban Design Plan," in his *Making City Planning Work*, 189–223. On the national significance of San Francisco's *Urban Design Plan* and 1985 *Downtown Plan* and their "pioneering roles in urban design history," see Richard Hu, "Urban Design Plans for Downtown San Francisco: A Paradigm Shift?" *Journal of Urban Design*, Vol. 18, No. 4 (2013), 517–33; City of San Francisco, *Downtown Plan 1985*, Ordinance No. 414-85, San Francisco, CA.

23 "Landmark Case," September 26, 1972; Donald Canter, " 'Bombshell' Stalls Big S.F. Buildings," *SFC*, September 28, 1972; and other clippings, all in folders Courts: Calif. Supreme Court 1972—April & May, and Courts: California Supreme Court, 1972, October, *SFE* Clippings files, SFHC, SFPL. A remarkable contemporary overview of how the era's laws interwove around the *Urban Design Plan* to establish San Francisco's urban environmentalism is Patrick J. O'Hern, "Reclaiming the Urban Environment: The San Francisco Urban Design Plan," *Ecology Law Quarterly*, Vol. 3 (1973), 535–95.

24 In obtaining the restraining order, POW alleged the use of illegal procedures in the board's street vacation process, including the developer's failure to deposit the required $220,872 cash security. See Mike Mahoney, "Market Center Hung Up—On a Point of Law," *SFC*, June 4, 1968, 1.

25 Donald Canter, "New Mart Center Wins First Test," *SFC*, April 12, 1968, SFIMC Clippings file, SFHC, SFPL. See also SFIMC files, THD Collection.

26 Moskowitz, "A Heated Hearing on Market Center," 1; Cone, "10 to 1 Vote for Huge Market," 1; and "Revised Design for New Market Center," [publication name cut off], July 11, 1968, all in SFIMC Clippings file, SFHC, SFPL. See also "International Market Center's Plans and Modifications," *Marion Conrad Associates NEWS*, July 10, 1968, SFIMC File 014.I.A.4626, Halprin Collection, AAUP.

27 David Heldt, "SFIMC Hearing Before Full Bd Supervisors," July 15, 1968, SFIMC File 014.I.A.4622, Halprin Collection, AAUP.

28 Moskowitz, "A Heated Hearing on Market Center"; Cone, "10 to 1 Vote for Huge Market." Kent spent his legal career until 1965 with major San Francisco firms. He was known foremost for his leadership roles on the Democratic State Central Committee and many political campaigns from 1954 to 1965. See Finding Aid, Roger Kent Papers, BANC MSS 74/160 c, The Bancroft Library, University of California, Berkeley.

29 Ron Moskowitz, "Market Center Is Set to Go," *SFC*, July 17, 1968, 1; "Revised Design for New Market Center"; Moskowitz, "A Heated Hearing on Market Center." All in SFIMC Clippings file, SFHC, SFPL.

30 Gerald Cauthen, "Dear Sir," June 25, 1968, SFIMC file, THD Collection. "Statement of Robert B. Morrill to the Streets and Transportation Committee of the San Francisco Board of Supervisors," May 29, 1968, BOS file 218 68/A. Jasper Rubin argues that the doctrine's application to waterways made this "the particular geography associated with the public trust." See Rubin, *A Negotiated Landscape*, 26.

31 Kortum, draft Letter to the Editor, *SFC*, March 25, 1968.

32 Russ Cone, "10 to 1 Vote for Huge Market."

33 Weekly Meeting, July 1967/ NW Proj, SFIMC File 014.I.A.4623, Halprin Collection, AAUP. Karl Kortum emphasized that WB&E "hires a public relations expert." Kortum, draft Letter to the Editor.

34 Jean Kortum to Ron Pelosi, April 28, 1968, Box 1, Folder 19, Jack Morrison Papers (SFH 24), SFHC, SFPL.

35 Nes Young, "A Belvedere Home," *SFC*, July 5, 1959, Bonanza, 8.

36 Robert Courland, *The Old North Waterfront: The History and Rebirth of a San Francisco Neighborhood* (San Francisco: Ron Kaufman Companies, 2004), 129–34. Kaufman's mentor at Berkeley, Paul Wendt, was an influential scholar in establishing real estate studies in the university. See Paul Wendt, *Real Estate Appraisal: A Critical Analysis of Theory and Practice* (New York: Henry Holt, 1956).

37 Leonard Cahn, "The North Waterfront Project," *SFC*, July 15, 1968, SFIMC Clippings file, SFHC, SFPL; Paul Avery, "Bold New Plan for S.F. Waterfront," *SFC*, December 4, 1964, 1.

38 Robert H. Goldsmith to Distribution Code 10, June 29, 1967, and "List of Interested Parties Who Have Seen the Project Presentation," ca. December 7, 1968, both in SFIMC File 014.I.A.4633, Halprin Collection, AAUP.

39 Statement of Purpose, North Waterfront Associates Inc., January 22, 1968, File 014.I.A.4623, Halprin Collection, AAUP.

40 Tom Caylor, "Controversy on the Waterfront," *San Francisco Business*, May 1968, SFIMC file, THD Collection.

41 Organizing memos, June 8 and June 15, 1967, SFIMC File 014.I.A.4622, Halprin Collection, AAUP.

42 David Heldt to Marion Conrad, January 18, 1968, "Additional Quotable Material," File 014.I.A.4623, Halprin Collection, AAUP. See Conrad correspondence with Gerald Nordland, SFMA Archives.

43 "Introduction and Urban Landscape Philosophy," from Bob (Buchanan) January 24, 1968, edited by Dave Heldt, January 25, 1968, File 014.I.A.4623, SFIMC, Halprin Collection, AAUP.

44 David Heldt, SFIMC Memorandum, January 18, 1968, File 014.I.A.4623, Halprin Collection, AAUP. See also Heldt to Conrad, SFIMC Statement of Design Purpose, Landscape Architects, January 15, 1968; Robert Buchanan, SFIMC Statement, January 17, 1968; Donn Emmons, "Statement for Architectural Policy and Purpose for SFIMC Project," January 12, 1968. All in File 014.I.A.4623, Halprin Collection, AAUP.

45 Marion Conrad Associates, "First Draft Copy for Presentation Brochure—SFIMC," undated, SFIMC File 014.I.A.4623, Halprin Collection, AAUP.

46 "List of Interested Parties Who Have Seen the Project Presentation," ca. December 7, 1968, SFIMC File 014.I.A.4623, Halprin Collection, AAUP.

47 Henry A. Adams, Statement of Purpose, January 22, 1968, File 014.I.A.4623, Halprin Collection, AAUP.

48 Jim Goldsmith, "Summary of January 8 Meeting, Course of Action for Future," January 9, 1968, SFIMC File 014.I.A.4623, Halprin Collection, AAUP. An October 17, 1967, presentation at SFMA was not open to the public.

49 Although Halprin then served on President Lyndon Johnson's national Advisory Council on Historic

Preservation, Halprin's firm offered only a weak caution against "ignoring the potential" of using existing façades from the district's Gold Rush–era buildings. See LH, DRC, DH, RB to Donn Emmons, et al., "North Waterfront Project Re-Design," December 13, 1967, File 014.I.A.4623, Halprin Collection, AAUP. Dealing with contradictions as to whether Halprin could weigh in on the Seawall Warehouse, Heldt to Emmons et al., "SF North Waterfront Re-Study, Seawall Warehouse Preservation," November 2, 1967, SFIMC File 014.I.A.4623, Halprin Collection, AAUP.

50 Notes, File 014.I.A.4626, Halprin Collection, AAUP.

51 THD's first comprehensive critique enumerated these complaints. See George Raad, THD, "The Impact of the Proposed International Market Center on San Francisco's Waterfront and Telegraph Hill" (undated, circa January 1968), Box 1, Folder 19, Jack Morrison Papers (SFH 24), SFHC, SFPL.

52 AMI brochure; Ron Moskowitz, "The 'Final' Market Center Plan," *SFC*, July 12, 1968, 1, SFIMC Clippings file, SFHC, SFPL. See also Raad, THD, "The Impact of the Proposed International Market Center on San Francisco's Waterfront and Telegraph Hill."

53 The CPC rejected THD's proposal to drop the height limit on the SFIMC site from 84 to 40 feet. See Donald Canter, "New Mart Center Wins First Test."

54 "International Market Center's Plans and Modifications."

55 Karl Kortum, draft Letter to the Editor, *SFC*, March 25, 1968.

56 Karl Kortum, Letter to Editor, "A Disaster to San Francisco," *SFC*, July 8, 1968; Karl Kortum, Letter to Editor, "An Eight Story 'Chinese Wall,'" *SFC*, July 9, 1968, SFIMC Clippings file, SFHC, SFPL.

57 Jean Kortum to Terry Francois (and Jack Morrison), "Questions on North Waterfront Associates Project," June 6, 1968, Box 1, Folder 19, Jack Morrison Papers (SFH 24), SFHC, SFPL.

58 Ibid.; Jerry Burns, "Market Center: Debate on Street Closing," *SFC*, May 24, 1968, SFIMC Clippings file, SFHC, SFPL.

59 THD to Board of Supervisors, "For Immediate Release," June 3, 1968, SFIMC file, THD Collection.

60 Burns, "Market Center: Debate on Street Closing."

61 "Statement of Roger Kent before the Streets and Transportation Committee of the San Francisco Board of Supervisors, May 29, 1968, Box 1, Folder 19, Jack Morrison Papers (SFH 24), SFHC, SFPL. See also Jean Kortum to Francois (and Morrison), "Questions on North Waterfront Associates Project." As was discussed in chapter 8, the value of $31 per square foot in the Embarcadero Center land sale was a capped figure set by the SFRA; the Embarcadero Center buyers estimated the market value conservatively at $100 (not $31) per square foot at the time they signed the land disposition agreement.

62 Mahoney, "Market Center Hung Up—On a Point of Law." See Street Vacation Files 218-68/A, International Market Center, San Francisco Board of Supervisors.

63 THD to Board of Supervisors, "For Immediate Release," June 3, 1968.

64 Jean Kortum to Francois (and Morrison), "Questions on North Waterfront Associates Project"; Jerry Burns, "Market Center: Debate on Street Closing."

65 THD to Board of Supervisors, "New Facts Concerning Street Vacation," June 10, 1968. SFIMC file, THD Collection.

66 Gerald Cauthen to John Jacobs, SPUR, July 5, 1968, SFIMC file, THD Collection.

67 T. J. Kent Jr., Preface to Jacobs, *Making City Planning Work*, xi. Vacating streets was commonplace in large-scale urban renewal. San Francisco's practice of vacating streets at the request of private investors was different. First impressions convinced Jacobs that "giving up public land" was "a terrible idea" and "inequitable." Isenberg interview with Jacobs.

68 Donald Canter, "Rockefeller Will Divide His Waterfront 'Wall,'" *SFC*, October 18, 1970; Donald Canter, "Twin Buildings to Rise 34 Stories," *SFC*, June 22, 1971. Both in EC Clippings file, SFHC, SFPL. Isenberg interview with Jacobs. Roth knew David Rockefeller from Roth's days in D.C. Isenberg interview with Bill and Joan Roth.

69 "Port to Sell Gateway Area Land," *SFC*, March 18, 1959, 2; "Gateway Dispute to Be Aired in Sacramento," *SFC*, December 27, 1961, 24; "Gateway Street Fight Flares Again," *SFC*, May 29, 1962, 2; "Port Streets—More Talk, No Decision," *SFC*, June 5, 1962, 36.

70 "Waterfront Center Hit By New Suit," *SFC*, November 8, 1968, SFIMC Clippings file, SFHC, SFPL; Kathleen Sullivan, "Memorial Will Honor Heslets," *SFGate*, July 17, 1998.

71 Jean Kortum to Cyril Magnin, October 7, 1968, SFIMC file, THD Collection; Cyril Magnin, "The Future of the Embarcadero," address to SPUR, December 17, 1963, Box 1, Folder 19, Jack Morrison Papers (SFH 24), SFHC, SFPL. NWA was emulating the Embarcadero Center and Golden Gateway developers' achievements in buying public trust land; the city had secured that land for the Title I projects. On how NWA fit with the port's wooing of nonmaritime urban developers, see Richard Reinhardt, "On the Waterfront: The Great Wall of Magnin," in *UHR*, 108.

72 Claude Gruen to Barry Wasserman, "Comments on Implementation," July 15, 1968, Box 1, Folder 19, Jack Morrison Papers (SFH 24), SFHC, SFPL. For the background of this dialogue among the City Planning Office and consultants over SFIMC, see Allan Jacobs to William Brinton, Memorandum, May 16, 1968, and Allan Jacobs to Claude Gruen, Arthur D. Little Inc., and Barry Wasserman, John Bolles Associates, Memorandum, May 17, 1968. Claude Gruen to Allan Jacobs, Barry Wasserman, "The Northern Waterfront," June 13, 1968. All items cited in this note are in Box 1, Folder 19, Jack Morrison Papers (SFH 24), SFHC, SFPL.

73 Jerry Burns, "Sale of Streets," and Donald Cantor, "Waterfront Market Plan Dies," *SFE*, January 14, 1971, both in SFIMC Clippings file, SFHC, SFPL.

74 See Roger Kent to Board of Supervisors, December 9, 1968, and Marion Conrad Associates, December 1968, "Statement," both in Box 1, Folder 19, Jack Morrison Papers (SFH 24), SFHC, SFPL.

75 "Taxpayer's Suit Could Halt Waterfront Development," undated December 1968 clipping, and Gerald Cauthen to Board of Supervisors, December 5, 1968, both in SFIMC folder, THD Collection.

76 Lorraine Petty, "Project Gives Up Street Closing Bid," *Daily Commercial News* (*DCN*), January 6, 1969, and Lorraine Petty, "$2 Million Sting Seen at Mart Center," *DCN*, January 9, 1969, 1, both in SFIMC folder, THD Collection.

77 The project concluded with a bizarre open call for ideas for the "land." See Donald Cantor, "Waterfront Market Plan Dies," *SFE*, January 14, 1971; "Waterfront Land Open to Ideas," *SFE*, January 15, 1971. The SFIMC Clippings file traces its last years, SFHC, SFPL. The Ice House was the only concrete outcome of the investment.

78 Courland, *The Old North Waterfront*, 36–46.

79 The THD and POW lawyers remained the key advocates against street vacations for several years. Jacobs noted that in late 1970 several planning commission members "took a strong stand against street vacations and supported restrictive legislation" but took a "go slow, wait and see" approach. Jacobs, *Making City Planning Work*, 208–9. He incorporated the position against street vacations into the 1971 *Urban Design Plan*.

80 Gerald Cauthen to Charles Gould, July 2, 1968, and Mr. Gould to Mr. Cauthen, July 10, 1968, both in SFIMC folder, THD Collection.

81 Jacobs, *Making City Planning Work*, 159–62; brochure "A Colorful History Preserved in the Renovation of the Transamerica Building," ca. 1967, Transamerica files, THD Collection.

82 For letters for and against the Pyramid and Merchant Street Vacation, see Street Vacation Files 281-69, Merchant Street/Transamerica Corporation, San Francisco Board of Supervisors (Transamerica File 281-69, BOS), and for letters about Transamerica to CPC, see Allan Jacobs Collection, THD Collection.

83 The U.S. Steel controversy came just after the major Transamerica approvals but overlapped the unfolding Merchant Street drama. U.S. Steel was a significant test for the new urban-environmentalist coalition, particularly over the use of public trust lands, and complements the street vacation cases covered in this chapter. In late 1969 the company and its local partners proposed an ultimately unbuilt 40-story tower that would have topped a commercial complex just south of the ferry terminal building. The high-rise would have stood on a platform over public property leased from the city under its new direct responsibility for port lands. See "Building a Tower at the Waterfront," editorial, *SFE*, July 8, 1970, San Francisco Embarcadero Center file, *SFE* Clippings Collection, SFPL. Herb Caen's position against the U.S. Steel tower helped turn the political tide to defeat the proposal. See *UHR*, 112–24.

84 "Skyscrapers Soaring in San Francisco," *Washington Post*, June 29, 1969; Stanford Sesser, "Manhattanization in San Francisco," *Wall Street Journal*, November 6, 1970; "Bay Waterfront High-Rises Draw San Franciscans' Ire," *Washington Post*, November 11, 1970; "Save Vistas, San Franciscans Ask," *Christian Science Monitor* (*CSM*), December 3, 1970; David Holmstrom, "Citizens Say No! 'Manhattanization' for San Francisco?" *CSM*, December 30, 1970.

85 John Krizek, "How To Build a Pyramid: A Kit of PR Tools Helps Win San Francisco's Approval for a New High-Rise Office Building," *Public Relations Journal* (December 1970), 17–21, reprinted in *Bay Guardian*, June 7, 1971.

86 The December 31, 1969, deadline qualified the company headquarters for a state tax benefit that allowed insurance companies to deduct real property taxes from the premiums tax they paid California on policies written in the state. See Krizek, "How to Build a Pyramid."

87 Harold L. Howard, "The Street Vacation Cases," unpublished article, 2016, in author's possession. Roughly 10 percent of the Transamerica site consisted of former streets, compared with the SFIMC's 22 percent. A first-person account of the role of lawyers in the housing and welfare lawsuits against the SFRA, 1966–70, is Jerome Carlin, "Store Front Lawyers in San Francisco," in *Culture and Civility in San Francisco*, ed. Howard S. Becker (Piscataway, NJ: Transaction, 1971), 125–51.

88 City Planning Commission Resolution No. 6112, June 29, 1967, Transamerica files, THD Collection.

89 Pereira to ABJ, April 16, 1969, and CPC minutes of June 26, 1969, both in Transamerica files, THD Collection.

90 Pete Kirby facilitated the basic information flow between Pereira's office and Jacobs's staff. See "TA Notes from ABJ Conf. about 5-20-69"; PS to ABJ, on an informal meeting with Pete Kirby, February 24, 1969; BP to ABJ, "Re: Columbus Avenue," December 1, 1970; and 2-14-69 TA meeting notes, TA asking for UDTR, all in Transamerica files, THD Collection.

91 Core Planning Department documents were Allan Jacobs, "Memorandum, R69.24 Vacation of a Portion of Merchant Street between Sansome and Montgomery Streets," June 23, 1969; ABJ to CPC, "Transamerica Building: Discretionary Review of Building Application No. 367584," June 26, 1969. The record of the hearing is "Minutes of the Regular Meeting Held Thursday, June 26, 1969, San Francisco City Planning Commission," 1–33, submitted by Lynn Pio, secretary. See also hand-written CPC notes, "Transamerica Hearing, 6-26-69," R.69.24 and 6396. Transamerica commissioned a traffic study by Wilbur Smith Associates. The revised June 16 plans required vacating the street rather than air rights. All in Transamerica files, THD Collection.

92 Lloyd Pfleuger, Downtown Association, prepared statement, June 26, 1969, entered in CPC minutes and mailed to the BOS Streets and Transportation Committee, July 25, 1969, Transamerica File 281-69-1, BOS.

93 Environment Workshop to Dear Sir, June 26, 1969. Transamerica Letters to CPC folder, THD Collection.

94 To Jacobs's chagrin, the discussion opened with a letter from the mayor supporting Transamerica. Joseph Alioto to San Francisco City Planning Commissioners, June 26, 1969, and Peter Swirsky notes, "Transamerica hearing," June 26, 1969, Transamerica files, THD Collection; Damon Scott, "When the Motorman Mayor Met the Cable Car Ladies: Engendering Transit in the City That Knows How," *Journal of Urban History*, Vol. 40, No. 1 (2014), 65–96.

95 For Jacobs, "design," defined narrowly to mean aesthetics, was the least significant of his objections to the Pyramid. Dissenting commissioners William Brinton and Morton Fleishhacker criticized Transamerica's "total lack of cooperation" with the Planning Department and their "token" changes. Provoked by Transamerica's lawyer, Brinton said that "the Commission had an obligation to protect private as well as public interests." See "Minutes of the Regular Meeting Held Thursday, June 26, 1969." Julia Porter represented the earlier generation of environmental urbanism in the Bay Area. The scale of Manhattanization and urban renewal clearance had broken ties with Porter's era; her support of the high-rise vision for the city alienated the new generation of "activists" who did not see how Porter's earlier "reform" work was a forerunner to their own more confrontational approach. See William Issel, "A Different Era: Julia Gorman Porter's San Francisco Liberalism," *The Argonaut*, Vol. 19, No. 2 (Winter 2008), 76–85. On Porter voting with the development "bloc," see *UHR*, 71.

96 "Minutes of the Regular Meeting Held Thursday, June 26, 1969."

97 For "corporate arrogance" see The Environment Workshop to Supervisors, July 14, 1969, and Haruko Misumi to Chairman of the Supervisors, August 20, 1969, both in Letters of opposition July–August 1969 folder, Transamerica File 281–69, BOS. Many opposing letters to the supervisors critiqued the June 26, 1969, CPC approval; designers were heavily represented, and there were form letters, as well as petitions organized by groups such as the Jackson Square Association.

98 Moffat said Halprin approved of their activism. See Frances Moffat, "They Want to Save the City," *SFC*, August 17, 1969; "Don't Build It," *SFC*, July 29, 1969, 36; and Susan Landor Keegin to Alison Isenberg, December 18 and 19, 2015, latter two in the author's possession. Carroll pursued a graduate degree in journalism, another tie among the young allied professionals in this larger story. "Katherine Carroll Craven," obituary, http://www.legacy.com/obituaries/sfgate/obituary.aspx?pid=175661196.

99 "More than one marriage resulted from connections made in that group," Landor said, including her own to lawyer Stafford Keegin. Moffat said Halprin approved of their activism. See Frances Moffat, "They Want to Save the City"; "Don't Build It"; Susan Landor Keegin to Alison Isenberg, e-mails, December 18 and 19, 2015; and "Katherine Carroll Craven."

100 "An Old Bay Area Liver" to BOS, August 13, 1969, and Robert Cranmer to Board of Supervisors, July 11, 1969, both in Letters of support folder, Transamerica File 281–69, BOS. Many letters supporting the Pyramid named the Environment Workshop.

101 *San Francisco and the Transamerica Pyramid* (San Francisco: Environment Workshop, 1969, Transamerica files, THD Collection.

102 Merchant Street was 31 feet wide. "Minutes of the Regular Meeting Held Thursday, June 26, 1969"; Jacobs, *Making City Planning Work*. Transamerica executive John Beckett said of Jacobs's book: "It almost made me vomit." See "The Pyramid Turns 10," *SFE*, September 8, 1982. For a close study of the *Urban Design Plan*'s distinctiveness, see Steven L. Vettel, "San Francisco's Downtown Plan: Environmental and Urban Design Values in Central Business District Regulation," *Ecology Law Quarterly*, Vol. 12 (1985), 511–66.

103 The Merchant Street hearings and lawsuits together followed the attorneys' growing outrage over the larger principle of selling the public streets to developers.

104 When conceding, Jacobs did cite his previous objections. See Jacobs to CPC, "R69.56—Vacation of an Additional 21.7 Foot Portion of Merchant Street between Sansome and Montgomery Streets," November 6, 1969, Transamerica files, Allan Jacobs Collection, THD Collection. The company's modified designs submitted in October required a second CPC review as well as the November Streets Committee hearing.

105 The clerk made six phone calls to notify interested parties four hours before the meeting began. Transamerica File 281–69, BOS. See "Suit over Vacated Street: Court Asked to Stop the Pyramid," *SFC*, December 10, 1969, 4.

106 Although Judge Edward O'Day declined to stop construction, the case remained under review. See "Suit over Vacated Street: Court Asked to Stop the Pyramid," 4; Howard, "The Street Vacation Cases."

107 Quantz provided office space and other indirect support. Roger Kent, a major player in the state Democratic Party, was about sixty at the time of the SFIMC cases. See Howard, "The Street Vacation Cases."

108 After receiving a B.A. in 1933 from the University of Santa Clara and a law degree in 1936 from Hastings, Harman worked in private practice from 1936 to 1942 at Fort Bragg, CA. He served in Tokyo with the army's Price and Distribution Division. He worked in the Office of Price Administration in the late 1940s and the Office of Price Stabilization in the early 1950s. More recently he held senior positions in a range of consumer and taxpayer protection and corporate regulatory fields. See "Regional Counsel, John B. Harman," note to file, August 8, 1951, and John B. Harman, "Transamerica," June 12, 1970, both in John B. Harman folder, Clippings file, SFPL.

109 Transcript, "Meeting of the Streets and Transportation Committee of the Board of Supervisors of the City and County of San Francisco, May 28, 1970, City

Hall, San Francisco," 1–23, Merchant Street Vacation/Transamerica File 281-69-6, BOS.

110 Jerry Burns, "Transamerica Asks for More of Merchant Street," *SFC*, November 13, 1969, 4; George Agron to Board of Supervisors, November 26, 1969, Transamerica File 281-69-3, BOS; Swirsky, "Transamerica Full Board, 8-25-69," Transamerica files, THD Collection.

111 Notes, "TA Bldg-CPC," November 13, 1969, and Allan B. Jacobs to CPC, "Transamerica Building: Discretionary Review of Revised Plans under Building Application No. 367584," November 13, 1969, both in Transamerica files, THD Collection.

112 Transamerica later had to refile at least two building permits to fix flaws created in its frantic December filing. In a "final, final" unsuccessful administrative appeal, Harman also appeared before the city's Board of Permit Appeals on January 19. See "Pyramid Foes Lose 'Final' Appeal," *SFC*, January 20, 1970, 2.

113 The December lawsuit was again filed on behalf of taxpayer Gunnufsen. Harman argued that, contrary to the city's charter, the street had not been advertised for the highest bid, and notification of the vacation was not conspicuously posted. See "Pyramid Foes in Court Again," *SFC*, December 31, 1969, 4; "Transamerica—City Deal for Merchant St. 'Violated' Charter," *San Francisco Progress*, November 26, 1971, Merchant Street Vacation/Transamerica File 281-69, BOS.

114 They added Meakin in order to have a plaintiff with title to property qualifying for the provision under which they filed the lawsuit. See Howard, "The Street Vacation Cases."

115 The judge denied the allegations of improper notification procedures. See "S.F. Sale of Land for 'Pyramid' Ruled Illegal."

116 "Transamerica—City Deal for Merchant St. 'Violated' Charter." Howard relished winning the public-interest case against lawyers from the defense's prestigious firm. See Howard, "The Street Vacation Cases."

117 *Harman v. City and County of San Francisco*, 7 Cal.3d 150, available at http://scocal.stanford.edu/opinion/harman-v-city-and-county-san-francisco-30223. See Architect Henrick Henrick Bull to Editor, *SFC*, July 25, 1969, 42.

118 "Abandoning of Streets Challenged," *SFE*, January 16, 1970, John B. Harman folder, and "Blocked Streets: City Land Sale Ruling," *SFC*, May 16, 1972, folder Courts: Calif. Supreme Court 1972—April & May, both in *Examiner* Clippings file, SFHC, SFPL; *Harman v. City and County of San Francisco*, 20 Cal.App.3d 736 (1971); 97 Cal.Rptr. 906 Court of Appeal, First District, Division 4, California. See also *June Harman, Plaintiff and Appellant, v. City and County of San Francisco et al., Defendants and Respondents*, Civ. 29197, October 21, 1971. For opinion on hearing, see 101 Cal.Rptr. 880, 496 P.2d 1248.

119 The judges agreed with the plaintiff that the legislature had "reposed the regulation of the sale of such streets exclusively with the municipalities." They implied a missed opportunity by specifying that *Harman* did

not ask them to determine whether "the vacation was required by public interest or necessity and was not effected merely for the benefit of adjoining private owners." See *Harman v. City and County of San Francisco* [7 Cal. 3d 150] [S.F. No. 22859, Supreme Court of California, May 15, 1972.]; *June Harman, Plaintiff and Appellant, v. City and County of San Francisco et al., Defendants and Respondents*, Counsel John B. Harman for Plaintiff and Appellant, opinion by J. Tobriner.

120 Allan Jacobs to CPC, "Statement Concerning Transamerica Building Revisions," April 16, 1970, Transamerica Files, THD Collection.

121 Transcript, "Meeting of the Streets and Transportation Committee of the Board of Supervisors of the City and County of San Francisco," and Transcript, [Board] Hearing, June 29, 1970, City Hall, Chambers of the Board, 1–17, both in Transamerica file 281-69, BOS.

122 "A Small Street vs. Big Building," *SFC*, May 5, 1971; William O'Brien, "A High-Rise Battle Brewing in Alleyway," May 5, 1971; and Russ Cone, "Skyscraper Is Given OK by Supervisors," June 8, 1971, all in John B. Harman folder, Clippings file, SFPL.

123 Civ. No. 38673, Court of Appeals of California, First Appellate District, Division One, March 29, 1977; *Albert E. Meakin, Plaintiff and Appellant, v. Steveland Inc. et al., Defendants and Respondents* (opinion by Lazarus, J., with Molinari, P. J., and Sims, J., concurring); and Counsel Harold L. Howard and John B. Harman for Plaintiff and Appellant. See 68 Cal. App. 3d 490, 502, 137 Cal.Rptr. 359 (1977). See also "Suit to Void Street Sale as a 'Gift,'" *SFC*, May 26, 1972.

124 "Landmark Case"; Canter, "'Bombshell' Stalls Big S.F. Buildings"; and other clippings in folders Courts: California Supreme Court 1972—April & May, and Courts: California Supreme Court, 1972, October, *SFE* Clippings files, SFHC, SFPL.

125 Aaron Peskin borrowed Allan Jacobs's Transamerica file to fight a planned condominium complex next to the Transamerica site in 2010. Jacobs's Transamerica file is now in the THD Collection. See Isenberg interview with Peskin and Nancy Shanahan, Telegraph Hill Dwellers, San Francisco, October 19, 2011; Rachel Gordon, "S.F. Supes Knock Down Plan for New Condo Tower," *SFC*, April 21, 2010.

126 The street guidelines are found in San Francisco Department of City Planning, *Citywide Urban Design Plans, Preliminary Report No. 8* (October 1970), chapter 3, 1–15, and *Urban Design Plan*, 50–52, 70–71.

127 "Justin Herman Plaza," *SFC*, October 23, 1974, 4.

128 *San Francisco Progress*, for example, reported on the street vacation lawsuits more often, quoted lawyers Harman and Howard's views, and scooped the story about NWA giving up their streets deal. On the role of the *Voice* in creating "*intellectual* opposition to Moses," see Robert Fishman, "Revolt of the Urbs: Robert Moses and His Critics," in *Robert Moses and the Modern City: The Transformation of New York*, ed. Hilary Ballon and Kenneth Jackson (New York: W. W. Norton, 2007), 125–26.

CONCLUSION

1 Moses was a builder and planner, not a widely published author; thus his place in urban history has depended primarily on how others, especially Caro, represent him and his archive of written and other administrative work—in addition to his material imprint on the New York metropolitan area. Robert Caro, *The Power Broker: Robert Moses and the Fall of New York* (New York: Knopf, 1974). Alioto's perspective on Herman and SFRA was unique; he chaired the Redevelopment Agency from spring 1955 to winter 1959, the period of delay and frustration that preceded Justin Herman's leadership of the agency. Alioto's relationship with the current mayor, George Christopher, was rocky. There is evidence that he supported the "artistic" interest in urban design that he praised in Herman. See Michael Harris, "Slum Agency Picks Alioto; Mayor Upset," *SFC*, December 19, 1956, 1; "Slum Redevelopment: South of Market Plan 'Dead,'" *SFC* August 27, 1958, 3.

2 *National Transportation Newsletter* (Washington, DC), 1972, quoted in "Findings of the *Guardian*'s Second Annual Investigative Project," *Bay Guardian Supplement*, November 1, 1972, 24.

3 For detailed overviews of the city's height limit campaigns, see Frederick Wirt, *Power in the City* (Berkeley: University of California Press, 1974), chapter 8, and Hartman with Carnochan, *City for Sale*, chapter 12. On height limits in the nineteenth and early twentieth centuries, see Sarah Landau and Carl Condit, *Rise of the New York Skyscraper: 1865–1913* (New Haven, CT: Yale University Press, 1996); Carol Willis, *Form Follows Finance: Skyscrapters and Skylines in New York and Chicago* (New York: Princeton Architectural Press, 1995).

4 *UHR*, 36.

5 Bill Roth was the first investor in the *Bay Guardian* (outside family), purchasing $5,000 worth of stock in 1966. See Isenberg interview with Bruce Brugmann and Jean Dibble, San Francisco, March 20, 2015.

6 Michael Kernan, "Look What They've Done to My Town," *Washington Post*, April 16, 1972, E1; Daryl Lembke, "Study Endorses SF High-Rise Trend," *LA Times*, March 26, 1975.

7 Jane Holtz Kay, "Skyscrapers No Longer Seen as an Unmitigated Good," *Boston Globe*, August 13, 1972.

8 Kernan, "Look What They've Done to My Town"; Isenberg interview with Dunn, October 17, 2011; *UHR*, 82–84, 114; "Suppressed," *Bay Guardian*, April 12, 1972, 24.

9 Daryl Lembke, "Study Endorses SF High-Rise Trend," *LA Times*, March 26, 1975; Kenneth Campbell, "High-Rises Said to Bring High Revenue," *Boston Globe*, May 15, 1974, 7; Kay, "Skyscrapers No Longer Seen as an Unmitigated Good." *UHR*'s authors scrupulously noted their sources and methods, describing in detail, for example, how they modeled their economic analysis on the work of Raymond J. Green of the Urban Land Institute. See *UHR*, 36.

10 Nicholas von Hoffman, "Finding Out the Urban Doctor Was a Quack," *Washington Post*, February 7, 1972, B1. See also Judy Hillman, "Towering Costs," *Bay Guardian*, November 23, 1971, 17. On the interlock of land ownership patterns with the "economic/political concentration of power" and on the conclusion that the "nine largest private landowners own 7.3% of the city's total acreage, about 35% of the city's choice acreage," see *UHR*, 85–86.

11 Isenberg interview with Brugmann and Dibble. On shifting from fighting single buildings to a regional strategy and how that merged the "environmentalists and urban conservationists," see Alvin Duskin, Foreword, *UHR*, 12. The book's sole essay on architecture is "'Damned Monoliths': An Architectural Critique of Highrise," by John Kenyon, which argues that high-rises are "barely" architecture. "Technically superb" but "utterly dead," they are closer to "gigantic machines." See *UHR*, 177–87.

12 A study of the vast cartooning of postwar urban redevelopment remains to be written.

13 Isenberg interview with Dunn, October 17, 2011.

14 Dunn grew up in Wichita and attended the University of Kansas. He majored in journalism, minored in art, and picked up carpentry. He spent several years in St. Louis, living in the bohemian Gaslight Square neighborhood and working as an advertising agency artist. When he arrived in San Francisco about 1962, Dunn drove trucks and tested out life as an abstract expressionist painter. His wife was a dancer. Dunn came to the high-rise topic from a general interest in buildings and cities. He loved model-making and designed and built his own writing "shack." Personally, with his family, he enjoyed some of the city's new plazas, such as Maritime Plaza at the Alcoa building, and the Vaillancourt fountain. He described his ten years with the *Guardian* as the "best time of my life." Isenberg interviews with Dunn, October 17, 2011, and March 17, 2015.

15 For more on the context of the photo, see Marsha Berzon, "Redevelopment: Bulldozers for the Poor, Welfare for the Rich," *Bay Guardian*, April 17, 1970; reprinted in *UHR*, 202–12.

16 Leslie Shipnuck and Dennis Keating with Mary Morgan, *The People's Guide to Urban Renewal and Community Development Programs* (Oakland: Maud Gonne, 1974). Keating became an influential planning scholar. Shipnuck, an activist, was a registered architect in the East Bay.

17 John Kenyon, an architect, pursued a career that wound through design, planning, and visualization. See Kenyon, "Allan Temko: Reflections on a Long Friendship," *Berkeley Daily Planet*, March 17, 2006.

18 *UHR*, 72–79. The Duskin Initiative (Proposition T) put a citywide 6-story (72-foot) limit on the ballot during a mayoral election. Ehrenkrantz's firm was Building Systems Development. See Sue Hestor to Alison Isenberg, e-mail, July 12, 2016.

19 Prior to joining the architecture firm, Hestor had worked six years organizing students against the Vietnam War. She passed the bar in 1976 after graduating from

Golden Gate University School of Law. She noted the anti-poverty organizations and the lawsuits against the SFRA, but did not see land-use lawyers representing the public interest against developers with their "huge line" of attorneys. About 1979 she founded San Franciscans for Responsible Growth, an outgrowth of SFT's downtown committee. As of 2016 she was still working for development mitigation in San Francisco. See Hestor to Alison Isenberg; "Three Questions for Sue Hestor," *SFC*, October 24, 2010, C3; Isenberg interview with Peskin and Shanahan. On the Duskin initiatives and growth control in 1970–72, see McGovern, *The Politics of Downtown Development*, 69–77. The overlap of the peace movement and planning was evident in other examples. For instance, Marion Conrad was an officer in the California Alliance for Peace, along with Roger Kent, and Joan Roth was on the executive committee. See California Alliance for Peace solicitation, October 10, 1970, Folder 5, "California Alliance for Peace," Box 73, J. B. Matthews Collection, David M. Rubenstein Rare Book & Manuscript Library, Duke University.

20 The story of the *Bay Guardian*, late 1960s street vacations, and the deeper land stewardship currents they tapped complicates the understanding that (as Richard Hu notes) "The progrowth culture dominated San Francisco's planning without any challenge until the early 1970s." The street vacations illuminate how framing this history as debates "for and against growth" oversimplifies that past, even as it recognizes the watershed of "the mid-1980s when the Downtown Plan and Proposition M were passed to restrict unfettered urban growth." See Richard Hu, "To Grow or Control, That Is the Question: San Francisco's Planning Transformation in the 1980s and 1990s," *Journal of Planning History*, Vol. 11, No. 2 (2012), 141–60. On the impact of the 1985 plan combining growth controls and a "beauty contest," see Katherine Crocker and Dawn Haeckel, "Commercial Growth Management Techniques in San Francisco," *Journal of Urban Planning and Development*, Vol. 119 (1993), 137–49.

21 Hartman with Carnochan, *City for Sale*.

22 Shipnuck and Keating with Morgan, *The People's Guide to Urban Renewal*, iii–iv.

23 Washington's history of black land ownership erosion was shaped by the Great Migration of African Americans from South to North. Harold R. Washington Jr., *Black Land Manual* (booklet, 1973), 1–25; Washington, with P. Andrew Patterson and Charles W. Brown, *Black Land Manual: Got Land Problems?* (Frogmore, SC: Penn Community Services and Black Land Services, 1973), 1–16; Andrew W. Kahrl, *The Land Was Ours: African American Beaches from Jim Crow to the Sunbelt South* (Cambridge, MA: Harvard University Press, 2012), 253–54. Another path-breaking book on black land ownership is N.D.B. Connolly, *A World More Concrete: Real Estate and the Remaking of Jim Crow South Florida* (Chicago: University of Chicago Press, 2014). See also Gil Bliss,

"Harold R. Washington Jr., Activist, Ground-Breaking Harvard Professor, *Boston Globe*, September 11, 2011.

24 Street, only in his mid-twenties, relied on his experience directing neighborhood planning for the United Planning Organization. He worked part-time at Yale University as an architectural critic "for black students." See Bill Street, "The Land Grabbers"; Marlowe Key, "Black Land Victory!!"; "Why Land?"; "Why Black Land Movement?"; Otis Daniels, "Urbanization in Shaw"; and "Black Land Design," all in *Black Land News*, No. 9 (May 1, 1971). The group also started a low-cost food cooperative and planned cooperative health-care projects. See Joseph Whitaker, "Group Seeks Shaw Land Control," *Washington Post*, October 29, 1969, C1.

25 Ibid. *Black Land News* asserted that in D.C. the Redevelopment Land Agency was prevented by legislation from "freezing" adjacent land to protect it from privateers.

26 When he spoke with the *Washington Post*, Street did not use the term "land grab," but otherwise the concepts were identical to those expressed in *Black Land News*. See Whitaker, "Group Seeks Shaw Land Control."

27 The dialogue took place at Cleveland Park Congregational United Church of Christ. See Mary Wiegers, "Dialogue between Black and White: A Dialogue about Black Power," *Washington Post*, February 11, 1969, B1. D.C. and the Shaw neighborhood particularly were still in the shadow of the April 1968 unrest after the assassination of the Reverend Martin Luther King Jr.

28 Over the past few years several articles had quietly tracked Hertz's purchases. The Chicago-based owner of the Hyatt Regency New Orleans Hotel, Laurence Geller, CEO of Strategic Hotels, also had a strong hand to play in New Orleans' downtown rebuilding plans. See Greg Thomas, "Towering Investor," *Times-Picayune*, August 7, 2005; Rebecca Mowbray, Michelle Krupa, and Greg Thomas, "New City Hall, Jazz Park Planned Near Superdome," *Times-Picayune*, May 31, 2006; Kate Moran, "Sold on the City," *Times-Picayune*, March 8, 2009. On Morphosis designs, see Nicolai Ouroussoff, "Designing New Orleans," *NYT*, August 28, 2007. "Katrina Cottages" had a lasting influence as flexible and long-lasting shelter alternatives to FEMA trailers. See "Market for Katrina Cottages Expands," *St. Petersburg Times*, May 17, 2008, 2F; Doug MacCash, "New Urbanism Dominates Rebuilding Chatter," *Times-Picayune*, November 14, 2005.

29 Mr. Bender's comments were widely reported in the national press, and the "angry" meeting (including his participation) was documented by photographer Ben Margot. Mr. Bender was described as a "laid off city worker." His quote from the meeting is a composite of the slight variations found in news coverage. See Gary Rivlin, "Anger Meets New Orleans Renewal Plan," *NYT*, January 12, 2006, A18; Gordon Russell and Frank Donze, "Rebuilding Proposal Gets Mixed Reception," *Times-Picayune*, January 12, 2006; Brian Thevenot, "Canizaro Takes the Heat in Plan for City's Future," *Times-Picayune*, March 19, 2006.

30 To better answer these questions for the 1950s and 1960s, it would be useful to pursue what historian Jennifer Hock has called "Jane Jacobs's Silence on the Issue of Race." See Jennifer Hock, "Jane Jacobs's Silence on the Issue of Race," conference paper, Society of American City and Regional Planning History, Baltimore, 2011, in author's possession.

31 The twenty-first century could learn about the normalization of "land-grab" frameworks from Henry George's day, when the *Chicago Tribune* reported the plight of the Northern Pacific railroad: "Wholesale Grabbing of Its Great Land-Grab by Trusted Agents." See "The Northern Pacific Claims to Be the Victim of Immense Frauds," *Chicago Tribune*, April 10, 1881, 6.

32 For an especially insightful analysis of recent scholarship by feminist art historians and cultural geographers regarding gender and the city, see Scott, "When the Motorman Mayor Met the Cable Car Ladies." Scott observes the potential for not only seeing "women as agents of historical change" but also understanding how gender acts as a "system of meaning." Adding "knowledge about space, place, and landscape" to urban histories complicates the gender implications for analyzing historical change. Adding knowledge about land complicates it further.

33 Stratigakos traces the cyclical laments about the scarcity of women in architecture. For mentions of San Francisco, see Despina Stratigakos, *Where Are the Women Architects?* (Princeton, NJ: Princeton University Press, 2016), 12, 33, 28, 16–18; Randy Kennedy and Robin Pogrebin, "Architect's Reach Went Beyond Her Designs," *NYT*, April 2, 2016, C1; Robin Pogrebin, "For Female Architects, Many Hurdles in the Way," *NYT*, April 13, 2016, C1.

34 As women fanned out into most corners of urban redevelopment work in the 1950s or 1960s, these were not female-identified fields. When architects disdained graphic design, public relations, or property management at this time, it was due to their place in design hierarchy, not to their associating the work with women. The generation occupying the core of this book (Marion Conrad and Bev Willis most explicitly) commented with perspective on the coming of second-wave feminism. An excellent piece describing Beverly Willis's support for equal pay for equal work, child-care centers, and revamping corporate policies to acknowledge women while simultaneously acknowledging that "she is not one of your Women's Lib females" is David Ross, "What Makes Beverly Run?," *SFE&C*, February 14, 1971, Beverly Willis Clippings files, SFHC, SFPL.

35 Joel Schwartz's research placed Moses firmly within a broader policy machinery. See Schwartz, *The New York Approach: Robert Moses, Urban Liberals, and Redevelopment of the Inner City* (Columbus: Ohio State University, 1993). Jacobs's comment hints at one reason that San Francisco has fascinated a generation of political scientists, including Frederick Wirt and Stephen McGovern. Jacobs titled his chapter on the 1972–74 period "Power Brokers" to capture the impact of federal programs concentrating more power in the mayor's office and meddling more with the planning department's agenda. See Jacobs, *Making City Planning Work*, 266.

36 Ballon, "Robert Moses and Urban Renewal," 113.

37 Caen, "Your City—And Mine."

38 Charles Moore, "You Have to Pay for the Public Life," *Perspectiva*, Nos. 9–10 (1965), 57–97, reprinted in Charles Moore, *You Have to Pay for the Public Life: Selected Essays of Charles W. Moore*, ed. Kevin Keirn (Cambridge, MA: MIT Press, 2004), 115, 138.

39 Caen cited the liberal Christian journal *Christianity and Crisis*. He referenced T. S. Eliot, in "The Rock," for a similar point about the meaning of a city—whether seeing urban density as a way for people to achieve love and community or "to make money from each other." See Caen, "The Vertical Earthquake."

40 Herb Caen, "Remembrance of Things Future," November 13, 1966, reprinted in *The Best of Herb Caen, 1960–1975*, 122.

41 "When we were all young and dumb, it was an article of faith that there were only two Real Cities in the land—New York and San Francisco." See Caen, "Brave New Year," 2.

42 Isenberg interview with Brugmann and Dibble.

43 In 2012 Brugmann and Dibble sold the *Bay Guardian* to San Francisco Media Co., which folded the paper in October 2014. Brugmann, Dibble, and Tim Redmond have sought ways to continue some of the *Guardian*'s reporting traditions. On Shaw today, see Eugene Meyer, "Washington's Shaw Neighborhood Is Remade for Young Urbanites," *NYT*, December 1, 2015.

The language of land grab is applied far more often to other parts of the globe, making its relative absence in the U.S. general urban historiography more striking. See, for example, Fred Pearce, *The Land Grabbers: The New Fight Over Who Owns the Earth* (Boston: Beacon Press, 2012); John C. Weaver, *The Great Land Rush and the Making of the Modern World, 1650–1900* (Montreal: McGill-Queen's University Press, 2003); Carl Nightingale, *Segregation: A Global History of Divided Cities* (Chicago, 2012); Alexander Reid Ross, ed., *Grabbing Back: Essays against the Global Land Grab* (Oakland: AK Press, 2014). While the history of indigenous peoples has long focused on land battles and land loss, recent scholarship has intensified that analysis. Here, I would like to acknowledge a debt to William Cronon's foundational scholarship, particularly *Changes in the Land* (New York: Hill & Wang, 1983) and *Nature's Metropolis* (New York: W.W. Norton & Company, 1992). The long-ago undergraduate thesis I wrote on nineteenth-century San Francisco, advised by Bill (and originally inspired by Ann Fabian), was my first introduction to the terrain of *Designing San Francisco*.

Archives Consulted

The collections consulted in each archive are indented below the archive names.

The American Institute of Architects Archives, Washington, D.C.
  AIA Awards files, Record Group 806

American Institute of Graphic Arts, New York

The Architectural Archives, University of Pennsylvania, Philadelphia
  Lawrence Halprin Collection

Avery Architectural and Fine Arts Library, Drawings and Archives Department, Columbia University, New York
  Douglas Putnam Haskell Papers, 1915–79

The Bancroft Library, University of California, Berkeley
  BANC MSS 82/84 c, Ghirardelli Square Architectural Records, 1911–79
  BANC PIC 2006.029—NEG, Fang family *San Francisco Examiner* archive negative files
  BANC PIC 1982.114—PIC, Ghirardelli Square Construction Photographs
  BANC Phonotape 1419c, "Interviews Concerning the Development of Ghirardelli Square, Conducted by Randolph Delehanty, 1981 February 18–November 4."
  Oral History Center

Beverly Willis private collection, New York

Cooper-Hewitt Design Archive, Smithsonian Design Museum, New York
  Design Research Inc. Collection
  Marimekko Collection, 1951–79

Duke University, David M. Rubenstein Rare Book & Manuscript Library, Durham, NC
  J. B. Matthews Collection

Environmental Design Archives, College of Environmental Design, University of California, Berkeley
  Douglas and Maggie Baylis Collection, 1999-4
  Joseph Esherick Collection, 1974-1
  William Turnbull Jr./MLTW Collection, 2000-9
  Phillip Fein Collection, 1964-1
  Robert B. Marquis Collection, 2009-04
  Robert Royston Collection, 1999-12
  William W. Wurster/Wurster, Bernardi & Emmons Collection, 1976-2
  William W. Wurster Administrative Files

Frances Loeb Library, Graduate School of Design, Harvard University, Cambridge, MA
  John S. Bolles Collection
  Walter Bogner Collection

Henry A. Murray Research Archive, the Institute for Quantitative Social Science at Harvard University, Cambridge, MA
  Louis M. Terman, Robert R. Sears, Lee Cronbach, Pauline S. Sears, and Albert Hastorf, "Terman Life Cycle Study of Children with High Ability, 1922–1986," 2010, hdl:1902.1/00882, Harvard Dataverse, V3

Gerald Ratto Photography, private collection, San Francisco

Grady Clay Archives, private collection

Palo Alto Historical Association, Palo Alto, CA

The Rockefeller Archive Center, Sleepy Hollow, NY
  Ford Foundation Records
  Rockefeller Family Records
  Rockefeller Foundation Records

Ruth Asawa private collection, San Francisco

San Francisco Art Institute Archives,
Anne Bremer Memorial Library
    Albert Bender Grants-in-Aid, San Francisco
    Art Association Records

San Francisco Board of Supervisors
    Street Vacation Files 218-68/A
    International Market Center
    Street Vacation Files 281-69
    Merchant Street/Transamerica
    Corporation

San Francisco History Center, San Francisco
Public Library
    Jack Morrison Papers (SFH 24)
    San Francisco Ephemera, Biography,
    Vertical File, and Clippings Collections
    San Francisco Historical Photograph
    Collection

San Francisco Maritime Research Center,
San Francisco Maritime National Historic Park
    Karl Kortum Collection, HD1084
    Object Collections
    San Francisco Maritime Museum Records

San Francisco Museum of Modern Art,
Library and Archives
    Administrative Records, San Francisco
    Museum of Art

San Francisco State University,
Archives and Special Collections Department,
J. Paul Leonard Library, San Francisco

Sarah Lawrence College Archives,
Bronxville, NY

Sausalito Historical Society, Sausalito, CA

Stanford University, Special Collections and
University Archives, Stanford, CA
    Stanford Land and Clippings Collection
    (SC678)

Telegraph Hill Dwellers private collection,
San Francisco

University of Oregon, Special Collections
and University Archives, Eugene

Interviews by the Author

The following are in chronological order.
The interviews not cited in the book have
provided background material.

Ruth Asawa and Albert Lanier
    (San Francisco, March 31, 2005)
Beverly Willis
    (New York City, June 19, 2006)
Denise Scott Brown
    (Philadelphia, July 17, 2006)
Bobbie Stauffacher Solomon
    (San Francisco, July 2007 and July 6, 2011)
Richard Vignolo
    (San Francisco, July 5, 2007)
Roberta Tasley
    (New York City, June 10, 2009)
Sally Woodbridge
    (Berkeley, 2009)
Calvin Imai
    (Oakland, June 23, 2009)
Bill and Joan Roth
    (New York City, April 27, 2011)
Peggy Knickerbocker
    (San Francisco, July 6, 2011)
Gabriel Metcalf, assisted by Jennifer Warburg
    (San Francisco, July 7, 2011)
Gerald Ratto
    (San Francisco, July 8, 2011)
Don Nusbaum
    (telephone interview, September 6, 2011)
Kamran Kiani
    (telephone interview, October 8, 2011)
Stanford Erickson
    (telephone interview, October 15, 2011)
Allan Jacobs
    (San Francisco, October 17, 2011)
Louis Dunn
    (San Francisco, October 17, 2011, and March 17, 2015)
Aaron Peskin and Nancy Shanahan
    (San Francisco, October 19, 2011)
Claude Stoller
    (Berkeley, October 21, 2011)
Stephen Canright
    (San Francisco, March 18, 2015)
Bruce Brugmann and Jean Dibble
    (San Francisco, March 20, 2015)

Index

Image Credits

1 From Bruce Brugmann and Greggar Sletteland, eds., *The Ultimate Highrise: San Francisco's Mad Rush toward the Sky* (San Francisco: San Francisco Bay Guardian Books, 1971). Illustration © Louis Dunn, all rights reserved. The titles given to Louis Dunn's illustrations are my own, based on a drawing's main concept or borrowed from Dunn's words.

2 From Brugmann and Sletteland, *The Ultimate Highrise.* © Louis Dunn.

3 HI326, The Architectural Archives, University of Pennsylvania, by the gift of Lawrence Halprin.

4 *Bay Guardian,* February 28, 1970, 2, folder Real Estate-Embarcadero Center, N–Z, Box 412, RG 3 (unprocessed materials), Rockefeller Family, Rockefeller Archive Center. Courtesy of Rockefeller Archive Center; used with special authorization. Used with the permission of Mick Stevens.

5 "Map of Railroad Land Grants," WHS-HD 197 G46, 1871, Wisconsin Historical Society.

6 © Louis Dunn.

7 BANC PIC 1982.114—PIC, Ghirardelli Square Construction Photographs, Box 2:2, The Bancroft Library, University of California, Berkeley.

8 AAA-6818, folder S.F. Parks–Aquatic–Plans & Proposals, San Francisco History Center, San Francisco Public Library. From *San Francisco News,* May 8, 1950, 1.

9 A11.18453, Ghirardelli Center, San Francisco Maritime Research Center.

10 AAA-6739, San Francisco History Center, San Francisco Public Library. Reproduced in Dick Chase, "'View from the Hills' Battle Rages," *S.F. News-Call Bulletin,* March 7, 1962, 37.

11 CB612, The Architectural Archives, University of Pennsylvania, by the gift of Lawrence Halprin.

12 *Daily Commercial News,* November 13, 1963, Vol. 3, BANC MSS 82/84 c, Ghirardelli Square Architectural Records, 1911–79, The Bancroft Library, University of California, Berkeley.

13 Drawn by Misha Semenov, in collaboration with Louis Dunn.

14 *San Francisco News-Call Bulletin,* May 20, 1963, 11, Telegraph Hill Dwellers Collection.

15 AAB-9118, San Francisco History Center, San Francisco Public Library. Reproduced in Polly Warfield, "Jackson Square Reclaimed: A New San Francisco Design Center," *San Francisco Chronicle,* February 17, 1952.

16 AAB-9171, San Francisco History Center, San Francisco Public Library.

17 BANC PIC 2006.029:139568.02.15—NEG, Fang family *San Francisco Examiner* photograph archive negative files, The Bancroft Library, University of California, Berkeley.

18 SAFR4463, San Francisco Maritime Research Center.

19 SAFR19870, San Francisco Maritime Research Center.

20 SAFR 19846, San Francisco Maritime Research Center.

21 SAFR 14665, San Francisco Maritime Research Center.

22 SAFR 22911, San Francisco Maritime Research Center.

23 AAB-5843, San Francisco History Center, San Francisco Public Library. Photo by Karl Kortum and used with the permission of John Kortum.

24 AP wire photo, MOR-0809, San Francisco History Center, San Francisco Public Library.

25 SAFR 22912, San Francisco Maritime Research Center.

26 SAFR 19843, San Francisco Maritime Research Center.

27 "Hyde Street Pier" (San Francisco, CA), ca. 1968, William W. Wurster/Wurster, Bernardi & Emmons Collection, Environmental Design Archives, University of California, Berkeley.

28 AAB-8612, San Francisco History Center, San Francisco Public Library.

29 John S. Bolles Collection, Graduate School of Design, Harvard University.

30–31 "New Role Planned for Senator Stanford Winery: Old Structure to House Bank, Restaurant," *Palo Alto Times,* December 13, 1960. Courtesy of Steve Staiger, Palo Alto Historical Association.

32 BANC PIC 080105.02.05—NEG, Box 2986, Examiner Collection, The Bancroft Library, University of California, Berkeley. Reproduced in Prudence Martin, "Mokelumne Hill: How a San Franciscan Rejuvenated a Decaying Town in the Mother Lode," *San Francisco Examiner,* September 4, 1960, folder Hotel Leger, Mokelumne Hill, 1960, Robert Royston Collection, 1999–12, Environmental Design Archives, Berkeley.

33 BANC PIC 080105.01.02 and .01—NEG Box 2986, *Examiner* Collection, The Bancroft Library, University of California, Berkeley. Photograph by Ted Streshinsky. Found in Prudence Martin, "Mokelumne Hill: How a San Franciscan Rejuvenated a Decaying Town in the Mother Lode," *San Francisco Examiner,* September 4, 1960, folder Hotel Leger, Mokelumne Hill, 1960, Robert Royston Collection, 1999-12, Environmental Design Archives, Berkeley.

34 HI418, The Architectural Archives, University of Pennsylvania, by the gift of Lawrence Halprin.

35 014.IV.A.17, The Architectural Archives, University of Pennsylvania, by the gift of Lawrence Halprin, 2010 accession. Photo by Roger Sturtevant.

36 014.IV.A.17, The Architectural Archives, University of Pennsylvania, by the gift of Lawrence Halprin, 2010 accession. Photo ca. 1965 by Ernest Braun.

37 Courtesy of the estate of Warner Jepson, all rights reserved.

38 CC134, The Architectural Archives, University of Pennsylvania, by the gift of Lawrence Halprin.

39 FI405, The Architectural Archives, University of Pennsylvania, by the gift of Lawrence Halprin.

40 014.II.A.061 and 014.II.A061a, The Architectural Archives, University of Pennsylvania, by the gift of Lawrence Halprin.

41 *"Ruth Asawa and Her Children—at Work."* Courtesy of George Eastman House International Museum of Photography and Film and the Imogen Cunningham Trust. © 1958, 2016, Imogen Cunningham Trust, www.ImogenCunningham.com.

42 014.I.A.6221, The Architectural Archives, University of Pennsylvania, by the gift of Lawrence Halprin.

43 BANC PIC 1982.114—PIC, Ghirardelli Square Construction Photographs, The Bancroft Library, University of California, Berkeley.

44 Courtesy of the estate of Warner Jepson, all rights reserved.

45 Courtesy of the estate of Warner Jepson, all rights reserved.

46–47 Photos by the author, 2007.

48 AAB-2968, San Francisco History Center, San Francisco Public Library.

49 CC127, The Architectural Archives, University of Pennsylvania, by the gift of Lawrence Halprin. Photograph by Fred Lyon. Used with the permission of Fred Lyon Studio.

50 AAA-7302, San Francisco History Center, San Francisco Public Library.

51 BANC PIC 1982.114—PIC, Ghirardelli Square Construction Photographs, Box 1, folder Sept. 1964, The Bancroft Library, University of California, Berkeley.

52–53 BANC PIC 1982.114—PIC, Ghirardelli Square Construction Photographs, Box 2:2, The Bancroft Library, University of California, Berkeley.

54 BANC PIC 1982.114—PIC, Ghirardelli Square Construction Photographs, Box 1, folder Demolition and Construction Photos by Stuart Rose (first manager), 1963–64, The Bancroft Library, University of California, Berkeley.

55 CB608, The Architectural Archives, University of Pennsylvania, by the gift of Lawrence Halprin.

56 *San Francisco Chronicle*, October 7, 1964, 1s, Vol. 3, BANC MSS 82/84 c, Ghirardelli Square Architectural Records, 1911–79, The Bancroft Library, University of California, Berkeley.

57 HI533, The Architectural Archives, University of Pennsylvania, by the gift of Lawrence Halprin.

58–59 Folder Stuart Rose 1436–48, Phillip Fein 1964-1 Collection, Environmental Design Archives, University of California, Berkeley. Reproduced in "Western Interiors: Done without Professional Aid," *Sunset,* December 1946, 22.

60 Folder Stuart Rose 1436–48, Phillip Fein 1964-1 Collection, Environmental Design Archives, University of California, Berkeley.

61 "He Has Fun and Profit Building the Unusual," *Western Building,* October 1952, 18–19, 53.

62 From "Sausalito Story: Ghosts Astir as Onetime Garage Goes Sophisticate," *Independent Journal,* March 16, 1957, M3. Accession 97.96. Courtesy of Sausalito Historical Society. Photograph attributed to Les Walsh.

63 From a photo shoot for *Marin This Month,* June 1959, 12–13, montage by Marge Salin. Accession 82.329. Courtesy of Sausalito Historical Society. Photograph used with the permission of Fred Lyon Studio.

64 From "Sausalito Story: Ghosts Astir as Onetime Garage Goes Sophisticate," *Independent Journal,* March 16, 1957, M3. Courtesy of Sausalito Historical Society. Photograph attributed to Les Walsh.

65 From "Roses to Leave Ghirardelli Square," *San Francisco Chronicle,* October 3, 1970, 44, Box 1, folder Ghirardelli Memos: Stuart Rose, BANC MSS 82/84 c, Ghirardelli Square Architectural Records, 1911–79, The Bancroft Library, University of California, Berkeley.

66 CB605, The Architectural Archives, University of Pennsylvania, by the gift of Lawrence Halprin.

67 014.IV.A.135, The Architectural Archives, University of Pennsylvania, by the gift of Lawrence Halprin.

68 014.IV.A.239, The Architectural Archives, University of Pennsylvania, by the gift of Lawrence Halprin.

69 47G310, The Architectural Archives, University of Pennsylvania, by the gift of Lawrence Halprin.

70 CC225, The Architectural Archives, University of Pennsylvania, by the gift of Lawrence Halprin. Photograph by Fred Lyon. Used with the permission of Fred Lyon Studio.

71 014.IV.A.239, The Architectural Archives, University of Pennsylvania, by the gift of Lawrence Halprin.

72 II710, The Architectural Archives, University of Pennsylvania, by the gift of Lawrence Halprin.

73 FI108, The Architectural Archives, University of Pennsylvania, by the gift of Lawrence Halprin.

74 From Dale Rosen, "$F Waterfront Co., Inc.: J. Alioto and C. Magnin, Proprietors since 1968," *Bay Guardian,* February 28, 1970, enclosed with Mr. and Mrs. Susselli to Nelson Rockefeller, April 3, 1970, folder Real Estate–Embarcadero Center, N–Z, Box 412, RG 3 (unprocessed materials), Rockefeller Family, Courtesy of Rockefeller Archive Center; used with special authorization. Used with the permission of Tim Redmond, Bruce Brugmann, and Jean Dibble.

75 "Marion & Hunt," *Bay Guardian,* February 26, 1971. Used with the permission of Tim Redmond, Bruce Brugmann, and Jean Dibble.

76 "Shaping Cities: A Landscape Architect Generates New Ideas in Urban-Area Planning," *Wall Street Journal,* June 8, 1967, 1.

77 FH711, The Architectural Archives, University of Pennsylvania, by the gift of Lawrence Halprin.

78 BANC PIC 1982.114—PIC, Ghirardelli Square Construction Photographs, Box 1, folder June 1964, The Bancroft Library, University of California, Berkeley.

79 Barbara Stauffacher, *The Crossroads,* brochure, Peter Bradford and Associates, 1962. Courtesy of AIGA Design Archives. Used with the permission of Barbara Stauffacher Solomon: http://bit.ly/1OVkdN5.

80 Barbara Stauffacher Solomon, *San Francisco Museum of Art,* program guide, February 1964. Courtesy of the San Francisco Museum of Modern Art Archives.

81 *Progressive Architecture,* March 1967. Photograph by James.

82 JA208, The Architectural Archives, University of Pennsylvania, by the gift of Lawrence Halprin.

83 JA205, The Architectural Archives, University of Pennsylvania, by the gift of Lawrence Halprin.

84 BANC PIC 2006.029:041891.05.01—NEG, Fang family *San Francisco Examiner* photograph archive negative files, The Bancroft Library, University of California, Berkeley. Photograph by Matt Southard.

85 CC302, The Architectural Archives, University of Pennsylvania, by the gift of Lawrence Halprin.

86 From "Kinetic Boutiques & Campopop Shops," *Progressive Architecture,* April 1969. Photograph by Jeremiah O. Bragstad.

87 CB716, The Architectural Archives, University of Pennsylvania, by the gift of Lawrence Halprin.

88 Barbara Stauffacher Solomon, Sea Ranch printed material, ca. 1965, offset lithograph, 9 × 9 in (22.86 × 22.86 cm), San Francisco Museum of Modern Art, gift of The Sea Ranch Archives. © Barbara Stauffacher Solomon. Photograph by Katherine Du Tiel.

89 Barbara Stauffacher Solomon, *The Sea Ranch,* design brochure, ca. 1965, offset lithograph, 9 × 9 in. (22.86 × 22.86 cm), San Francisco Museum of Modern Art, gift of the artist. © Barbara Stauffacher Solomon. Photograph by Don Ross. FF432, The Architectural Archives, University of Pennsylvania, by the gift of Lawrence Halprin.

90 FH320 and FH319, The Architectural Archives, University of Pennsylvania, by the gift of Lawrence Halprin.

91 FH318 and FH328, The Architectural Archives, University of Pennsylvania, by the gift of Lawrence Halprin.

92 IC212, The Architectural Archives, University of Pennsylvania, by the gift of Lawrence Halprin.

93 BANC PIC 2006.029:041891.05.02—NEG 19A, Fang family *San Francisco Examiner* photograph archive negative files, The Bancroft Library, University of California, Berkeley.

94 Clipping of Golden Gateway Competition, *Architectural Record,* June 1960, Western Section, 32–34. 014.I.A.905, The Architectural Archives, University of Pennsylvania, by the gift of Lawrence Halprin.

95 SFH 371, Redevelopment, folder Golden Gateway Competition, 1960, San Francisco History Center, San Francisco Public Library.

96 Clipping of Golden Gateway Competition, *Architectural Record,* June 1960, Western Section, 32–34. 014.I.A.905, The Architectural Archives, University of Pennsylvania, by the gift of Lawrence Halprin.

97 BANC PIC 2006.029:140346.01.24—NEG, Fang family *San Francisco Examiner* photograph archive negative files, The Bancroft Library, University of California, Berkeley.

98 AAZ-0365, San Francisco History Center, San Francisco Public Library.

99 Photograph courtesy of Kamran Kiani.

100 BANC PIC 2006.029:140346.01.18—NEG, Fang family *San Francisco Examiner* photograph archive negative files, The Bancroft Library, University of California, Berkeley.

101 Virginia Green, "Cement—A Direct Building Material: Its Possibilities as a Sculptural Medium," MFA thesis, School of Architecture and Allied Arts, University of Oregon, April 1950.

102 Mitchell Park, 1958, Environmental Design Archives, University of California, Berkeley. Photograph by Robert Tetlow.

103 Ogden Tanner, "These Models Show the Client What Architecture Means," *San Francisco Chronicle,* July 9, 1950, 3L.

104 BANC PIC 2006.029:140346.01.27—NEG, Fang family *San Francisco Examiner* photograph archive negative files, The Bancroft Library, University of California, Berkeley.

105 From Mildred Schroeder, "Masters of Miniature: They Think Big, Build Small," *San Francisco Examiner,* July 29, 1964, Architectural Models Inc. Clippings file, San Francisco History Center, San Francisco Public Library. Photograph by Bob Bryant.

106 From an Architectural Models Inc. brochure, ca. 1968, Gerald Ratto private collection. Photograph by Gerald Ratto.

107 BANC PIC 2006.029:140346.01.14—NEG, Fang family *San Francisco Examiner* photograph archive negative files, The Bancroft Library, University of California, Berkeley.

108 Robert B. Marquis Collection, Environmental Design Archives, University of California, Berkeley.

109 Robert B. Marquis Collection, Environmental Design Archives, University of California, Berkeley.

Reproduced in "Twin Houses by Marquis and Stoller, Architects," *Arts and Architecture*, May 1961, 24.

110–111 © Ezra Stoller/Esto.

112 Robert B. Marquis Collection, Environmental Design Archives, University of California, Berkeley.

113 © Ezra Stoller/Esto.

114 Press release photograph, folder Real Estate—Embarcadero Center, N–Z, Box 412, RG 3, Rockefeller Family, Rockefeller Archive Center. Courtesy of Rockefeller Archive Center; used with special authorization.

115 "The Imaginative Embarcadero Center," *San Francisco Chronicle*, April 13, 1967, 38. Courtesy of Rockefeller Archive Center.

116 Postcard, folder Real Estate—Embarcadero Center 1966–72, Box 412, RG 3, Rockefeller Family, Rockefeller Archive Center. Courtesy of Rockefeller Archive Center; used with special authorization.

117–119 Press release print of a Helmut Jacoby drawing, folder Real Estate—Embarcadero Center, N–Z, Box 412, RG 3, Rockefeller Family, Rockefeller Archive Center. Courtesy of Rockefeller Archive Center; used with special authorization.

120 AAB-8828, San Francisco History Center, San Francisco Public Library.

121 From Architectural Models Inc. brochure, ca. 1968, Gerald Ratto private collection. Photograph by Gerald Ratto.

122 Photograph of Donn Emmons in a *Designers West* clipping, December 1967, William W. Wurster/ Wurster, Bernardi & Emmons Collection, Environmental Design Archives, University of California, Berkeley.

123 CG432, The Architectural Archives, University of Pennsylvania, by the gift of Lawrence Halprin.

124 Drawing by Misha Semenov, adapted from "Changing San Francisco: You'd Never Know the Old Produce Market," *Sunset*, March 1973, reprint in folder Real Estate—Embarcadero Center, N–Z, Box 412, RG 3, Rockefeller Family, Rockefeller Archive Center.

125 HI333, The Architectural Archives, University of Pennsylvania, by the gift of Lawrence Halprin.

126 Box 1, Folder 19, Jack Morrison Papers (SFH 24), San Francisco History Center, San Francisco Public Library. Courtesy of the Family of Carlos Diniz/Carlos Diniz Archive.

127 FC633, The Architectural Archives, University of Pennsylvania, by the gift of Lawrence Halprin.

128 Box 1, Folder 19, Jack Morrison Papers (SFH 24), San Francisco History Center, San Francisco Public Library. Courtesy of the Family of Carlos Diniz/Carlos Diniz Archive. Quotation from "San Francisco International Market Center Statement of Purpose—Lawrence Halprin," January 19, 1968, File 014.I.A.4623. The Architectural Archives, University of Pennsylvania, by the gift of Lawrence Halprin.

129 BANC PIC 2006.029:140669.03.03—NEG, Fang family *San Francisco Examiner* photograph archive negative files, The Bancroft Library, University of California, Berkeley. Photograph in "Butchertown Proposal: Market Center Shift Rejected," *San Francisco Chronicle*, July 13, 1968, San Francisco International Market Center Clippings file, San Francisco History Center, San Francisco Public Library. Used with the permission of John Kortum.

130 FC628, The Architectural Archives, University of Pennsylvania, by the gift of Lawrence Halprin.

131 AAZ-0364, San Francisco History Center, San Francisco Public Library.

132 *Bay Guardian*, June 7, 1971, front page. Used with the permission of the *Bay Guardian*. Courtesy of Louis Dunn, Bruce Brugmann, and Jean Dibble.

133 From Brugmann and Sletteland, *The Ultimate Highrise*. Used with the permission of Mick Stevens.

134 From Brugmann and Sletteland, *The Ultimate Highrise*. Used with the permission of Mick Stevens.

135–137 Illustration by Michael Doyle, from "San Francisco and the Transamerica Pyramid," Environment Workshop, 1969, Telegraph Hill Dwellers Collection. Used with the permission of Susan Landor Keegin.

138 Transamerica/Merchant Street Vacation File 281-69, San Francisco Board of Supervisors.

139 From Brugmann and Sletteland, *The Ultimate Highrise*. Used with the permission of the *Bay Guardian*. Courtesy of Louis Dunn, Bruce Brugmann, and Jean Dibble.

140–146 From Brugmann and Sletteland, *The Ultimate Highrise*. © Louis Dunn.

147 From Brugmann and Sletteland, *The Ultimate Highrise*. Courtesy of Louis Dunn, Bruce Brugmann, and Jean Dibble.

148 Cover, *San Francisco Business*, March 1973, reproduced in Chester Harman et al., *Yerba Buena: Land Grab and Community Resistance in San Francisco* (San Francisco: Glide, 1974), 44. Courtesy of San Francisco History Center, San Francisco Public Library.

149 From Leslie Shipnuck and Dennis Keating with Mary Morgan, *The People's Guide to Urban Renewal* (Oakland, CA: Maud Gonne Press, 1974), 20. Courtesy of Louis Dunn.

150 *The People's Guide to Urban Renewal*, frontispiece. Courtesy of Louis Dunn.

151 From Mary Wiegers, "Dialogue between Black and White: A Dialogue about Black Power," *Washington Post*, February 11, 1969, B1. Photograph by Harry Naltchayan/Getty Images.

Acknowledgments image From "Street Widening Planned," *Hartford Courant*, February 6, 1968, 4. Photo by Robert B. Ficks. Copyright © 1968, Los Angeles Times. Reprinted with permission.